ISBN 978-0-243-24830-8
PIBN 10790401

1 MONTH OF
FREE
READING

at
www.ForgottenBooks.com

---◇---

By purchasing this book you are
eligible for one month membership to
ForgottenBooks.com, giving you
unlimited access to our entire
collection of over 700,000 titles via
our web site and mobile apps.

To claim your free month visit:
www.forgottenbooks.com/free790401

English
Français
Deutsche
Italiano
Español
Português

www.forgottenbooks.com

Mythology Photography **Fiction**
Fishing Christianity **Art** Cooking
Essays Buddhism Freemasonry
Medicine **Biology** Music **Ancient
Egypt** Evolution Carpentry Physics
Dance Geology **Mathematics** Fitness
Shakespeare **Folklore** Yoga Marketing
Confidence Immortality Biographies
Poetry **Psychology** Witchcraft
Electronics Chemistry History **Law**
Accounting **Philosophy** Anthropology
Alchemy Drama Quantum Mechanics
Atheism Sexual Health **Ancient History**
Entrepreneurship Languages Sport
Paleontology Needlework Islam
Metaphysics Investment Archaeology
Parenting Statistics Criminology
Motivational

MANUAL OF THE GOSPELS:

BEING AN ABRIDGMENT OF THE AUTHOR'S

"Harmony and Exposition of the Gospels;"

FOR THE USE OF

SUNDAY SCHOOLS, BIBLE CLASSES, AND FAMILIES.

By JAMES STRONG, A. M.

EDITED BY DANIEL P. KIDDER.

New-York:

PUBLISHED BY CARLTON & PHILLIPS,

200 MULBERRY-STREET.

1853.

EDITOR'S PREFACE.

THIS little volume, as intimated in the title-page, is de-. signed to furnish, in a cheap form, the most essential portions of the Author's larger work, " A NEW HARMONY AND EXPOSITION OF THE GOSPELS," and is published in accordance with a notice appended to the Preface of that work. It accordingly consists of two somewhat distinct parts, namely, an abridgment of the Harmony, and a condensation of the Exposition ; and these have been arranged, for the sake of convenience, in such a manner that they may be printed and used either separately or in one book, containing the *text* on the left-hand page, and the *explanation* on the right.

What is here called the *text*, is simply the "leading text" of the larger work, or that column which is there printed in larger type, including the "inserted clauses" in smaller type from the parallel columns ; these latter are here distinguished also by the number of the chapter and verse from which they are taken, prefixed in still smaller type, within brackets [ ]. For instance, in the following passage on page 39 :—

13 And he went forth again by the sea-side ; **Mark II.** and all the multitude resorted unto him, and he taught them. 14 And as he passed by [MATT. IX, 9] from thence, he saw [LUKE V, 27] a publican, Levi, [MATT. IX, 9] named Matthew, the son of Alpheus, sitting at the receipt of custom, and said unto him, Follow me : and he [LUKE V, 28] left all, arose and followed him.

The words **Mark II.**, in the right corner, show that the
general account of the event in question, as given in
the larger type, is taken from the 2d chapter of Mark,
—the beginning of the several verses being indicated
by the figures ^{13} and ^{14}; and the words from thence and
named Matthew, in the smaller type, are taken from the
9th chapter and 9th verse of Matthew; also the words
a publican and left all are from the 5th chapter and 27th
and 28th verses of Luke.   These marks of chapter and
verse the scholar need not observe when reading, but only
when studying or reciting.

This part of the work, therefore, is adapted to the
capacity of the youngest children, who can read; and in
Sunday schools it is recommended to use it even in the
lowest or "Testament classes," in the manner indicated
under "*Directions for using this work*," at the close of
this Preface.   More advanced scholars may use it in a
similar way, but after a more thorough study,—especially
Bible-classes, in connection with the Question-book.
Families also will find it a convenient and complete ab-
stract of the Gospels, for all ordinary purposes of history.

No changes have been made in the language of the
common text, except occasionally a *euphemism*, where the
meaning is not affected.   The references at the foot of
the page, are only to passages quoted or directly alluded
to.   The reasons for the arrangement of the events, as
well as for the notation of time and place, as given at
the titles of the sections, must be sought in the larger
work, where the passages are exhibited in full in parallel
columns, and every requisite explanation is subjoined.

The other portion of this little work is merely a re-
print of the *Exposition*, as contained in the larger work,
—which has been carefully revised with a view to its
special adaptation for this use.   It has been thought best

to add it here, simply because in no other form could the explanations requisite to accompany the text be given with sufficient brevity.

To prevent all misconception of its design, therefore, we wish here to state distinctly, that it is intended merely as a concise COMMENTARY, and in no sense as a rival *translation* for popular or any other use. On this account, different terms and phrases from those employed in the common version, have generally been purposely used, for the sake of more accurate explanation or greater vividness by the variety,—just as the definitions in a *dictionary* avoid the use of the word to be defined, and employ others instead, as nearly synonymous as possible. Neither must this be supposed to be a *paraphrase* of the text; on the contrary, it is meant to keep closely to the tenor of the original language, and to copy its very phraseology,—with merely such a latitude in terms as is necessary to convey its meaning to the modern reader. Wherever the explanation requires an expansion or illustration, it is distinguished as such, by the use of brackets [ ], both for the sake of brevity and to avoid the inconvenience of notes at the foot of the page.

Some may think that a popular commentary, in the usual form of annotations, would have been more satisfactory; the task would certainly have been easier in many respects. To have adopted such a form, however, would have been to destroy the two chief features of this work, upon which the usefulness of its plan must mainly depend, namely, its *compact form* and its *continuous arrangement*: regular "notes" would not only have occupied much greater space, and have presented the ideas in a more diluted and far less terse and picturesque manner; but they would also have broken up the train of thought into detached paragraphs of explanation, and compelled the reader to refer continually to the text, in order to keep to the thread of the discourse. A commentary in such a form can never be made an interesting *reading-book*, at least for youth; and even for purposes of consultation, it is apt to enlarge unduly upon one part of the text, and leave other points untouched.

For these reasons, as the Author in substance states in the Preface to his larger work, he has pursued a different method in this Exposition; and it is for these reasons that we have adopted it for the present purpose. Yet no one who has tried his hand at such an effort will suppose that the labor of elucidating the meaning of the sacred text has thereby been lightened; on the contrary, it has been much increased. On the present plan, how to convey the requisite explanation in the prescribed compass, and yet have the whole read smoothly, must have been continually a matter of the greatest difficulty, and one that required the most careful management. It was impossible to exhibit the process by which conclusions were reached, and yet the results were to be so stated that the reasons should spontaneously occur to the reader. Superadded to this was the necessity of adhering to the turn of thought, and even to the style of language, as found in the original of the text; and at the same time, of so elucidating both these as to show, in one sentence, what the text *says*, and what it *means*, as well as the connection between the phraseology and the sense. All these steps might easily have been drawn out in notes, while they were present to the mind; but on the contrary, a single expression only could be given, to embody and vindicate the results of tedious study and consideration. And even this expression had to be so worded as to distinguish, on its very face, the explanatory from the original matter. Nor was any allusion to the Greek words of the text admissible, in order to develop the meaning silently assigned to them; nor any discussion of conflicting opinions allowable : but one sense could be given, and that must be promptly and unequivocally stated, and then be left to the candor of the reader, to accept or reject as the general bearing of the context might warrant. These were some of the embarrassments of the present undertaking; and they are here only referred to for the purpose of explaining certain peculiarities in its execution, that might not otherwise be understood. The version of the poetical parts of the text was particularly beset with difficulties, not so much arising from the restraints imposed by the laws of metre, as from the peculiar manner in which the New Testament writers quote passages from the Old Testament—these being also generally passages of great scope of meaning and highly rhetorical structure.

The *Notes* in the larger work have been dispensed with here, both because they are mostly incidental and subsidiary, and especially because there was no room for them in the present arrangement. No serious disadvantage will result from their absence to the most of those for whom this work is designed ; and a question now and then in the Question-book, bearing upon them, being on a minor and collateral point, may either be wholly passed over or the answer elicited from the context. Those who wish a full elucidation of all the minutiæ, of course will procure the larger volume itself.

The main passages explained in this part of the volume are the same as those given on the opposite pages, and are indicated in the same manner. The minor additions from the parallel passages—which are often more minutely noted here than in the "inserted clauses" of the *text*—are denoted by a small italic letter at their beginning, referring to the chapter and verse as given at the foot of the page, and by a small upright stroke (|) at their close.

The mode of using this part of the volume as a text-book is particularly treated of in the Preface to the QUESTIONS, which it is specially designed to accompany, and more at length in the "*Directions*" at the close of this Preface. Aside from this use, however, it will be found to answer the purposes of many who cannot afford a more expensive commentary, and its continuous form will peculiarly adapt and recommend it to families and general readers. The portable shape of the entire book affords a hope that it may indeed become a "*Manual,*" especially with Christian youth.

DIRECTIONS FOR USING THIS WORK IN SUNDAY SCHOOLS.

THE great object of the series, to which this, as a text-book, belongs,—namely, in connection with the full "Harmony and Exposition," and the "Questions on the Gospel History,"—is two-fold: first, a more THOROUGH study of the contents of the four Gospels, as a *connected history;* and, secondly, the introduction of greater SYSTEM into the instruction of the different grades of scholars in Sunday schools. In order to effect these results the most perfectly, it is recommended that teachers and pupils pursue the following plan in studying these volumes.

1. *Let the entire school study the same lesson.* Each Sunday, after having recited the lesson in the several classes, let the scholars be examined upon it, in concert, from the desk, at the close of the exercises; and let the lesson be then assigned them for the next Sunday. This will produce uniformity, regularity, and progress in the studies.

2. *Let the teachers meet at some stated time during each week, and recite together the lesson for the following Sunday.* They will thus be prepared to explain it properly to their classes. For this purpose they ought to provide themselves with the full "Harmony and Exposition," to be used in connection with the "Questions." Let this be a *thorough* exercise, and let every matter of interest, connected with the lesson, be sifted to the bottom.

3. Let the senior scholars recite, in class, suitable answers to all the questions in the Question-book, in the

manner prescribed at the close of the Preface to that volume. These will need the full form of the "Manual," (*i. e.* both its parts.)

4. Let the scholars who are not sufficiently advanced to do this, recite answers to the questions in the larger type; and let the teacher explain those in the smaller type to them. For the most of these scholars, the *text part* of the Manual (*i. e.* the "Compendium") will be sufficient.

5. Let all the scholars who are too young to learn answers to any of the questions, but who can read, be furnished, during recitation, with the text part of the Manual; and after reading the appointed lesson from it, by verses (or, better, by sentences or paragraphs), in turn, let the teacher ask them simple questions upon it, according to their capacity, as they pass through it or at its close.

6. If there are any children in the same school who cannot read, let their teacher slowly and carefully read the lesson to them, from the text part of the Manual, stopping at any striking incident or expression, to ask them what it was, or to see if they understood it. In this way, if the exercise be made spirited and brief, their attention can be better kept up than by a continuous recitation; and they will retain many valuable facts and explanations in their memory.

7. In each of these exercises *let the teacher show a lively interest in the improvement of the class,* and they will seldom be backward in returning it with diligence and success. Above all, let the teacher illustrate, apply, and enforce the *practical* parts of the lesson, as opportunity may serve, with a view to direct religious impression; for in this personal mode of communication only will the truths of the gospel take effect upon the hearts of the scholars.

TABLE OF CONTENTS.

THE LIFE OF CHRIST.

Time, about *thirty-five years.*

CHAPTER I.

INTRODUCTORY EVENTS.

Time, about *thirteen months.*

CHAPTER II.

CHRIST'S INFANCY, CHILDHOOD AND PRIVATE LIFE.

Time, about *twelve years and five months.*

CHAPTER III.

THE INTRODUCTION OF OUR SAVIOUR'S MINISTRY.

Time, about *one year.*

CHAPTER IV.

THE FIRST YEAR OF OUR SAVIOUR'S MORE PUBLIC MINISTRY.

---◆---

CHAPTER V.

THE SECOND YEAR OF OUR SAVIOUR'S MORE PUBLIC MINISTRY.

B

CHAPTER VI.

THE THIRD YEAR OF OUR SAVIOUR'S MORE PUBLIC MINISTRY.

PORTION I.

CHRIST'S SUBSEQUENT STAY IN GALILEE.

Time, *six months.*

--------◆--------

CHAPTER VI.—PORTION II.

CHRIST'S SUBSEQUENT ITINERANCY THROUGH JUDEA AND PEREA.

Time, *six months less one week.*

CHAPTER VI.—PORTION III.

ĊHRIST'S LAST SOJOURN AT JERUSALEM, UP TO HIS FOURTH PASS-
OVER.

Time, *three days.*

——————◆——————

CHAPTER VI.—PORTION IV.

THE INCIDENTS OF CHRIST'S PASSION.

Time, three days.

------------◆------------

CHAPTER VII.

CHRIST'S SUBSEQUENT STAY ON EARTH.

Time, *forty days.*

TEXTUAL INDEX.

(FOR FINDING ANY PASSAGE.)

————◆————

N. B.—The figures in the *smaller type*, in this Table, represent tho▲
passages which, being parallel with the "leading text," are n▲
exhibited in full in this work.

MATTHEW.

CHAP.	VERSE.	SECT.	CHAP.	VERSE.	SECT.	CHAP.	VERSE.	SECT.
i.	1–17	9	**vii.**	7– 11	86	**x.**	29– 31	52
	18–25	7		12	45		32, 33	72
ii.	1–12	13		13, 14	95		34–36	123
	13–15	14		15–18	45		37	98
	16–18	15		19	18		38, 39	72
	19–23	16		20, 21	45		40–42	61
iii.	1– 3	18		22, 23	95	**xi.**	1	61
	4	6		24–27	45		2– 19	48
	5– 12	18		28, 29	34		20–24	48
	13–17	19	**viii.**	1	45		25– 27	83
iv.	1–11	20		2– 4	37		28–30	80
	12	29		5– 10	46	**xii.**	1– 8	41
	13–16	32		11, 12	95		9– 14	42
	17	30		13	46		15, 16	43
	18	33		14– 16	35		17–21	43
	19–22	33		17	35		22–32	51
	23–25	36		18–27	55		33	45
v.	1–12	45		28– 34	56		34–50	51
	13	77	**ix.**	1	56	**xiii.**	1– 9	53
	14–16	54		2– 8	38		10–23	54
	17–24	45		9	39		24–36	53
	25, 26	70		10–17	57		36–53	54
	27–30	45		13	41		54– 58	60
	31, 32	104		18– 26	58	**xiv.**	1, 2	62
	33–48	45		27–34	59		3– 5	28
vi.	1– 8	45		35–38	61		6– 12	62
	9– 15	86	**x.**	1	61		13– 21	63
	16–18	45		2– 4	44		22–36	64
	19– 21	52		5–14	61	**xv.**	1– 11	67
	22, 23	54		15	48		15–20	67
	24	100		16	78		21–28	68
	25– 34	52		17–20	123		29	69
vii.	1– 5	45		21, 22	123		30–39	69
	6	78		23–26	78		39	70
				26, 27	54			
				28	123	**xvi.**	1–12	70

MATTHEW.

CHAP.	VERSE.	SECT.	CHAP.	VERSE.	SECT.	CHAP.	VERSE.	SECT.
xvi.	13–28	72	xxii.	34–40	118	xxvi.	64–68	129
xvii.	1–13	73		41–46	119		69–75	128
	14–21	74	xxiii.	1–12	120	xxvii.	1, 2	130
	22, 23	75		13	51		3–10	133
	24–27	76		14–21	120		11	130
xviii.	1–7	77		22	45		12–14	130
	8, 9	45		23–28	51		15–30	132
	10	77		29–39	120		31, 32	134
	11–14	99	xxiv.	1–10	123		33–35	134
	15–35	77		11, 12	123		36	134
xix.	1	79		13–51	123		37, 38	134
	1, 2	93	xxv.	1–13	123		39–43	134
	3–12	104		14–30	110		38	134
	13–15	105		31–46	123		45–47	134
	16–26	106	xxvi.	1, 2	123		48	134
	27–29	106		3–5	124		49	134
	30	106		6–13	111		50	134
xx.	1–16	106		14–16	124		51–53	134
	17–19	107		17–19	125		54–56	134
	20–28	108		20, 21	126		57–61	135
	29–34	109		22–29	126		62–66	136
xxi.	1–9	112		30	126	xxviii.	1	137
	10–17	113		31–33	126		2–4	138
	18–22	114		34, 35	126		5, 6	139
	23–46	115		36–56	127		7–10	139
xxii.	1–14	97		57	129		11–15	140
	15–22	116		58	128		16	146
	23–33	117		59–63	129		16–20	147

MARK.

CHAP.	VERSE.	SECT.	CHAP.	VERSE.	SECT.	CHAP.	VERSE.	SECT.
i.	1	3	iii.	19–21	51	vi.	30–44	63
	2	48		22–35	51		45–56	64
	3–5	18	iv.	1–9	53	vii.	1–16	67
	6	6		10–22	54		17–23	67
	9–11	19		23	53		24–30	68
	12, 13	20		24	54		31–37	69
	14	29		24	45	viii.	1–9	69
	14, 15	30		25	54		10–21	70
	16–20	33		26–29	53		22–26	71
	21–28	34		30–34	53		27–38	72
	29–34	35		34	54	ix.	1	72
	35–38	36		25–41	55		2–13	73
	39	36	v.	1–21	56		14–29	74
	40–45	37		22–43	58		30–32	75
ii.	1–12	38	vi.	1–6	60		33	76
	13, 14	39		6–11	61		33–40	77
	15–22	57		11	48		41	61
	23–28	41		12, 13	61		42	77
iii.	1–6	42		14–16	62		43–48	45
	7–12	43		17–20	28		49, 50	77
	13–19	44		21–29	62	x.	1	93

MARK.

CHAP.	VERSE.	SECT.	CHAP.	VERSE.	SECT.	CHAP.	VERSE.	SECT.
x.	2-12	104	xiii.	1-33	123	xv.	24	134
	13-16	105		34	123		25	134
	17-29	106		35, 36	123		26	134
	30, 31	106		37	123		27, 28	134
	32-34	107	xiv.	1	123		29-41	134
	35-45	108		1, 2	124		42-44	135
	46-52	109		3-9	111		45-47	125
xi.	1-10	112		10, 11	124	xvi.	1	137
	11	113		12-16	125		2-4	139
	12-15	114		17-31	126		5-8	139
	15-17	113		32-50	127		9	138
	18-24	114		51, 52	127		9, 10	142
	25, 26	86		53	129		11	142
	27-33	115		54	128		12, 13	143
xii.	1-12	115		55-65	129		14	144
	13-17	116		66-72	128		15-18	144
	18-27	117	xv.	1-5	130		19	148
	28-34	118		6-19	132		20	148
	34-37	119		20, 21	134			
	38-40	120		22, 23	134			
	41-44	121						

LUKE.

CHAP.	VERSE.	SECT.	CHAP.	VERSE.	SECT.	CHAP.	VERSE.	SECT.
i.	1-4	1	v.	39	57	ix.	61, 62	55
	5-25	3	vi.	1-5	41	x.	1-3	78
	26-38	4		6-11	42		2	61
	39-56	5		12-19	44		4-11	61
	57-80	6		20-23	45		12-15	48
ii.	1-7	8		24-26	45		16	61
	8-20	10		27-38	45		17, 18	83
	21	11		39	67		19	144
	22-39	12		40	78		20-22	83
	40-52	17		41-44	45		23, 24	54
iii.	1-18	18		45	51		25-37	84
	19, 20	28		46-49	45		38-42	85
	21, 22	19	vii.	1-10	46	xi.	1-13	86
	23 .	19		11-17	47		14-26	51
	23-38	9		18-35	48		27, 28	51
iv.	1-13	20		36-50	49		29-32	51
	14	29	viii.	1-3	50		33-36	54
	14, 15	30		4-8	53		37-42	51
	16-30	32		9-18	54		43	120
	31	32		19-21	51		44-46	51
	31-37	34		22-25	55		47-51	120
	38-41	35		26-40	56		52-54	51
	42-44	36		41-56	58	xii.	1	52
v.	1-10	33	ix.	1-6	61		1	70
	11	33		7-9	62		2, 3	54
	12-16	37		10-17	63		4, 5	123
	17-26	38		18-27	72		6, 7	52
	27, 28	39		28-36	73		8, 9	72
	29-38	57		37-43	74		10	51
				43-45	75		11, 12	123
				46-50	77		13-31	52
				51-56	79			
				57-60	55			

LUKE.

CHAP.	VERSE.	SECT.	CHAP.	VERSE.	SECT.	CHAP.	VERSE.	SECT.
xii.	32	123	xvii.	11–19	79	xxii.	18–23	126
	33, 34	52		20, 21	102		24–38	126
	35–38	123		22–24	123		39	126
	39, 40	123		25	72		40–48	127
	41, 42	123		26–32	123		49	127
	43–46	123		33	72		50–54	127
	47, 48	123		34–37	123		54–60	128
	49	123	xviii.	1–14	103		61, 62	128
	50	127		15–17	105		63–71	129
	51–53	123		18–30	106	xxiii.	1–3	130
	54–59	70		31–33	107		4–7	130
xiii.	1–9	52		34	107		8–12	131
	10–17	94		35–43	109		13–16	132
	18–21	53	xix.	1	109		17–25	132
	22–30	95		2–9	110		26	134
	31–33	96		10	99		27–31	134
	34, 35	120		11–28	110		32–33	134
xiv.	1–15	97		29–38	112		34	134
	16–24	97		39–44	112		35	134
	25, 26	98		45, 46	113		36, 37	134
	27	72		47, 48	114		38	134
	28–33	98	xx.	1–19	115		39–43	134
	34, 35	77		20–26	116		44, 45	134
	35	98		27–38	117		46–48	134
xv.	1–32	99		39	117		49	134
xvi.	1–13	100		40–44	119		50–54	135
	14, 15	101		45–47	120		55, 56	135
	16	48	xxi.	1–4	121	xxiv.	1, 2	139
	17	45		5–17	123		3–11	139
	18	104		18	52		10	142
	19–31	101		19–33	132		13–35	143
xvii.	1–4	77		34–36	132		36–49	144
	5, 6	74		37, 38	114		50–52	148
	7–10	106	xxii.	1	123		53	148
				2–6	124			
				7–13	125			
				14–17	126			

JOHN.

CHAP.	VERSE.	SECT.	CHAP.	VERSE.	SECT.	CHAP.	VERSE.	SECT.
i.	1–18	2	v.	1–47	40	viii.	12–59	82
	19–36	21	vi.	1–3	63	ix.	1–12	87
	37–51	22		4	63		13	88
ii.	1–11	23		5–13	63		14	87
	12	24		14	63		15–41	88
	13–22	25		15–21	64	x.	1–21	88
	23–25	26		22–24	64		22–39	89
iii.	1–21	26		25–71	65		40–42	90
	22–36	27	vii.	1	66	xi.	1	91
iv.	1–42	29		2–10	79		2	111
	43–45	30		11–53	80		3–46	91
	46–54	31	viii.	1	80		47–53	92
				2–11	81			

JOHN.

CHAP.	VERSE.	SECT.	CHAP.	VERSE.	SECT.	CHAP.	VERSE.	SECT.
xi.	54	93	xiii.	21–38	126	xix.	16–18	134
	55–57	111	xiv.	1–31	126		19–30	134
xii.	1–11	111	xv.	1–27	126		31–42	135
	12–15	112	xvi.	1–33	126	xx.	1	139
	16	112	xvii.	1–26	126		2	139
	17, 18	112	xviii.	1	126		2–10	141
	19	112		2, 3	127		11–18	142
	20–50	122		4–9	127		19, 20	144
xiii.	1	126		10–12	127		21–25	144
	2–15	126		13–27	128		26–29	145
	2	124		28–38	130		30, 31	149
	16	78		39, 40	132		1–23	146
	17–19	126	xix.	1–3	132	xxi.	24, 25	149
	20	61		4–16	132			

ACTS.

i.	1	149	i.	13	44	i.	18, 19	133
	2–12	148						

1 CORINTHIANS.

xi.	23–25	126	xv.	5	144	xv.	7	148
xv.	5	143		6	147			

TABLES

OF MEASURES, WEIGHTS, MONEY, TIME AND WINDS,

MENTIONED IN THE NEW TESTAMENT.

I. MEASURES OF LENGTH.

NAME.	NATION.	USE.	PROPER COMPUTATION. feet. inches.	CURRENT VALUE. feet. inches.
[Foot].............	General.	All dimensions.	1 0·1	1 0
[Cubit]...........	Roman.	"	1 5·47	1 6·2
Ell.............	Greek.	"	1 6·2	1 6·2
["Cubit"]........	Jewish.	"	1 9·8	1 6·2
Pace............	General.	Land.	2 6·3	2 6·3
Fathom.........	Greek.	Depth.	6 0·8	6 0·8
Reed...........	Jewish.	Extent.	10 1·35	10 1
Stone's-throw...	General.	Distance.		
Stadium, Furlong.....	Greek.	"	606 9 or	0·10536 mile.
Sabbath-day's Journey.	Jewish.	"	2000 Jewish cubits.	6 stadia.

II. MEASURES OF CAPACITY.

NAME.	NATION.	USE.	PROPER COMPUTATION. bush. pks. gals. qts. pints.	CURRENT VALUE. bush. pks. gals. qts. pints.
[Xestês,] Cup....	Greek.	Dry things.	. . . . 0·95	. . . . 0·95
Chœnix, Bowl	"	"	. . . . 1·98	. . . . 1·98
Modius, "Bushel."	Roman.	"	. . . 1 1·85	. . . 1 1·85
Metrétês, Firkin..	Greek.	Liquids.	. 8 2 . 1·7?	. 8 2 . 1·8?
Seah............	Jewish.	Dry things.	. 11 3 . 1?	. 8 3 . 1
Bath...........	"	Liquids.	. 11 3? .	. 8 3 .
Cor...........	"	Dry things.	14 3 . .	12 2 . . .

C

III. Weights.

NAME.	NATION.	VALUE.
Libra, Pound.	Roman.	lbs. oz. drs. (Avoirdupois.) 0 11 8·67

IV. Moneys.

NAME.	NATION.	METAL.	PROPER VALUATION. $ cents. mills.	CURRENT WORTH. $ cents. mills.
Lepton, "Mite"..........	Greek.	Bronze.	...	...
Quadrans, Farthing.....	Roman.	"	... ... 0·5	... ... 1·2
Assa'rius, Penny.......	"	"	... ... 2·4	... ... 2·4
Dena'rius, Shilling.....	"	Silver.	... 15 9·7	... 15 9·7
Drachma.........	Greek.	"	... 17 4·7	... 15 4·7
Didrachma.....	"	"	... 35 5·9	... 30 4·7
Stater......	"	"	... 70 1·9	... 61 9·4
[*Shekel*] or	Jewish.	" }	... ... 3·7	... ... 8·9
Silverling......	Greek.			... ... 8·9
Mina, "Pound"......	"	"	17 59 3·2	15 47 3·8
Talent......	"	"	1058 59	928 43

V. Festivals.

NAME.	TIME OF BEGINNING.	DURATION.	EVENT COMMEMORATED.
Passover..........	14th even'g of March moon.	8 days.	Deliverance from Egypt.
Pentecost........	42 days after Passover.....	1 "	Promulgation of the Law.
Feast of Tabernacles.	15th even'g of Sept. moon.	8 "	Thanksgiving for Harvest.
" *Dedication.*	25th " Nov. "	8 "	Consecration of 2d Temple.

VI. HOURS.

NIGHT.

WATCHES.	NAME.	DURATION (about).
1st or "Evening" Watch,	1st hour,	from 6 P. M. to 7 P. M.
	2d "	" 7 " 8
	3d "	" 8 " 9
2d or "Midnight" Watch,	4th "	" 9 " 10
	5th "	" 10 " 11
	6th "	" 11 " 12
3d or "Cockcrowing" Watch,	7th "	" 12 " 1 A. M.
	8th "	1 A. M. to 2
	9th "	" 2 " 3
4th or "Dawn" Watch,	10th "	" 3 " 4
	11th "	" 4 " 5
	12th "	" 5 "

DAY.

NAME.	DURATION (about).
1st hour,	from 6 A. M. to 7 A. M.
2d "	" 7 " 8
3d "	" 8 " 9
4th "	" 9 " 10
5th "	" 10 " 11
6th "	" 11 " 12
7th "	" 12 " 1 P. M.
8th "	1 P. M. to 2
9th "	" 2 " 3
10th "	" 3 " 4
11th "	" 4 " 5
12th "	" 5 " 6

VII. WINDS.

NAME.	LANGUAGE.	SOURCE.	CHARACTER.
Notus......	Latin.	S. W. }	The sultry "Sirocco."
Lips........	Greek.	N. W. }	Rough and raw.
Caurus.....	Latin.	N. N. E.	Clear and fresh.
Bo'reas	Greek.	E. N. E.	
Euroc'lydon	Greek.		The furious "Levanter."

Note.—The chief cause of the uncertainty and discrepancy in the preceding values, arises from the mixed character of the currency and measurements of Judea in the time of Christ, in consequence of which quantities were often estimated at a foreign rate. The Roman has been assumed below as the standard in *coins*, on account of the prevalence of their mintage among their provincial subjects; while the Greek has the preference in other matters, because of the general adoption of their terms.

THE LIFE OF CHRIST.

(Embracing a Period of about *thirty-five years.*)

CHAPTER I.

INTRODUCTORY EVENTS.

(Time, about *thirteen months.*)

§ 1.—*Preface to Luke's Narrative.*

[1] FORASMUCH as many have taken in band   **Luke I.**
to set forth in order a declaration of those
things, which are most surely believed among us,
[2] even as they delivered them unto us, which from the
beginning were eye-witnesses, and ministers of the
word; [3] it seemed good to *me* also, having had perfect understanding of all things from the very first,
to write unto thee in order, most excellent Theophilus:
[4] that thou mightest know the certainty of those things
wherein thou hast been instructed.

§ 2.—*Introduction to John's Memoir.*

[1] In the beginning* was the WORD, and   **John I.**
the Word was *with* God, and the Word *was*
God: [2] the same was in the beginning with God: [3] all
things were made by him, and without him was not
anything made that was made. [4] In him was life,
and the life was the light of men; [5] and the light
shineth in darkness,—and the darkness comprehended
it not. [6] There was a man sent from God, whose
name was John; [7] the same came for a witness, to
bear witness of the Light, that all men through him

---

* Compare Gen. i, 1.

2

THE LIFE OF CHRIST.

(Embracing a Period of about *thirty-five years.*)

CHAPTER I.

INTRODUCTORY EVENTS.

(Time, about *thirteen months.*)

§ 1.—*Preface to Luke's Narrative.*

VARIOUS persons have already compiled accounts **Luke I.** of those remarkable events which, [2] handed down orally by the original eye-witnesses of the facts and laborers in the gospel, [1] have become the settled basis of our Christian faith. [3] But having myself carefully investigated the whole history from its beginning, I have deemed it proper for me also to write it out in a clear and connected manner for your perusal, noble Theophilus, [and thus to publish it to the world in a more authentic form.] [4] This will serve to establish you fully in the truth of what you have learned on the subject.

§ 2.—*Introduction to John's Memoir.*

[1] At "the beginning" of time existed the LOG'OS, **John I.** [or supreme "*Manifestation*" of the divine charac- ter.] He abode in equal and intimate union with the eternal Father, and was himself *actual Deity.* [2] This Person, I repeat, was peculiarly in society with God at the very origin of all creation. [3] All existences were brought into being by his efficient agency, nor has any object ever existed independently of him. [4] For in him lies the grand source of universal *life,* [spiritual as well as physical,] and by this self-inherent "Life" it was that he constituted likewise the "*Light*" of the human race;—[5] as a torch gleams forth upon surrounding darkness, although [as in this case] the dense gloom refuse the genial ray. [6] There was a messenger of divine appoint- ment, by the name of *John,* [7] who came expressly as a prophetic *witness* concerning THE LIGHT, in order that all, through his

2*

might believe : [8] he was not that Light, but   JOHN I.
was sent to bear witness of that Light;
[9] *that* was the true Light, which lighteth every man,
that cometh into the world. [10] He was in the world,
and the world was made by him, and the world knew
him not ; [11] he came unto his own, and his own received
him not : [12] but as many as received him, to them gave
he power to become the sons of God, even to them
that believe on his name ; [13] which were born, not of
blood nor of the will of the flesh nor of the will of
man, but of God.

[14] And the Word was made flesh and dwelt among
us, (and we beheld his glory, the glory as of the only-
begotten of the Father,[*]) full of grace and truth.
[16] And of his fullness have all *we* received, and grace
for grace ; [17] for the *Law* was given by Moses, but
grace and *truth* came by Jesus Christ : [18] no *man* hath
seen God at any time ; the only-begotten Son which
is in the bosom of the Father, he hath declared him.
[15] *John* bare witness of him and cried saying, This
was he of whom I spake, He that cometh *after* me,
is preferred *before* me ; for he *was* before me.[†]

§ 3.—*The Birth of John the Baptist predicted.*
(Jerusalem, the Temple, Holy Place; [middle of *May ?*] B. C. 7.)

[1] The beginning of the gospel of Jesus   **Mark I.**
Christ the Son of God :

[5] There was in the days of Herod the king   **Luke I.**
of Judea, a certain priest named Zacharias,
of the course of Abia ;[‡] and his wife was of the
daughters of Aaron, and her name was Elisabeth :
[6] and they were both righteous before God, walking
in all the commandments and ordinances of the Lord
blameless. [7] And they had no child ; and they both
were now well stricken in years.

---

[*] See Matt. xvii, 1–9. [†] See verse 30, § 21. [‡] See 1 Chron. xxiv, 10

3

persuasion, might confide in the coming Messiah. **JOHN I.**
⁸ This John, however, was far from being himself
" The Light ;" his office was simply thus to testify respecting
that illustrious personage. ⁹ *He* was the *true Light*, who, appearing in the world [as a public religious teacher], now en-
lightens all men, without distinction, in saving truths. ¹⁰ He
continued for a time in this world personally, and although the
world—with all its inhabitants—was the product of his power,
yet did it not acknowledge him. ¹¹ He even came to the land
peculiarly his own, and his own people refused to welcome him !
¹² Some, nevertheless, did receive him, and on these he conferred the princely privilege of being constituted *children of
God*, upon their trusting in him for salvation; ¹³ and they
were born such, not by virtue of descent from pious ancestors,
nor as a result of natural inclination, nor in consequence of
human contrivance, but purely by the regenerating grace of
God.
    ¹⁴ The eternal *Log'os* accordingly became incarnate, and
dwelt awhile among us in a human "tabernacle," *full* of
grace and reality.—We ourselves witnessed an exhibition
of his celestial glory, which was truly befitting a Father's
" dear and only Son."—¹⁶ Yes, from that " FULLNESS " of his, all
of *us* have derived grace, and in large supplies. ¹⁷ Now Moses
introduced a dispensation of inexorable *law;* but *grace*, and
the *reality* of what that ritual typified, came by the mediation
of Jesus Christ. ¹⁸ [Nor could these have come through any
other channel;] for a mortal has never ocularly seen, nor
adequately comprehended, the Deity. It remained for the
only Son, the partner of His nature and society, to portray
Him [in all His relations of mercy and love, which he did by
thus entering the world in human form].
    ¹⁵ To this effect was the above testimony of John the Baptist,
when he publicly declared, " This is the person whom I meant,
when I lately said, 'A certain individual (the long-expected
" Comer ") among my disciples, ranks nevertheless, even now,
as my Teacher,' for he has been from eternity my Principal."

§ 3.—*The Birth of John the Baptist predicted.*

(Jerusalem, the Temple, Holy Place ; [middle of *May ?*] B. C. 7.)

¹ The following is properly the first event in the   **Mark I.**
history of the gospel.—⁵ Under the reign of Herod   **Luke I.**
" the Great," there lived in Palestine a certain priest,
Zechariah by name, belonging to the sacerdotal " Class of
Abijah." His wife Elizabeth was also a lineal descendant of
Aaron. ⁶ Both were noted for their piety, being irreproach-
able observers of all the moral and ceremonial precepts of the
Jewish law. They had no children however, Elizabeth having
never been blessed with offspring; and both were now considerably past the prime of life.

3.*

⁸ And it came to pass, that while he exe-   LUKE I.
cuted the priest's office before God in the or-
der of his course, ⁹ according to the custom of the
priest's office his lot was to burn incense when he went
into the temple of the Lord : ¹⁰ and the whole multitude of the people were praying without, at the time of
incense.   ¹¹ And there appeared unto him an angel of
the Lord, standing on the right side of the altar of incense ; ¹² and when Zacharias saw him, he was troubled,
and fear fell upon him.   ¹³ But the angel said unto him,
Fear not, Zacharias : for thy prayer is heard ; and
thy wife Elisabeth shall bear thee a son, and thou shalt
call his name JOHN : ¹⁴ and thou shalt have joy and
gladness, and many shall rejoice at his birth ; ¹⁵ for he
shall be great in the sight of the Lord,—and shall
drink neither wine nor strong drink ;[*] and he shall be
filled with the Holy Ghost even from his birth.   ¹⁶ And
many of the children of Israel shall he turn to the
Lord their God : ¹⁷ and he shall go before him in the
spirit and power of Elias, to turn the hearts of the
fathers to the children,† and the disobedient to the wisdom of the just ; to make ready a people prepared for
the Lord.   ¹⁸ And Zacharias said unto the angel,
Whereby shall I know this ? for I am an old man,
and my wife well stricken in years.   ¹⁹ And the
angel answering said unto him, *I am Gabriel*, that stand
in the presence of God ; and am sent to speak unto thee
and to show thee these glad tidings : ²⁰ and behold,
thou shalt be *dumb*, and not able to speak until the day
that these things shall be performed ; because thou
believest not my words,—which shall be fulfilled in
their season.   ²¹ And the people waited for Zacharias, and marveled that he tarried so long in the temple : ²² and when he came out, he could not speak unto

---

* Compare Num. vi, 2–12.   † See Mal. iv, 5, 6.

4

⁸ Now it happened on one occasion, when the turn   LUKE I.
came for Zechariah's " class " to officiate as priests
in the Temple, ⁹ that it devolved upon him by lot, according
to the usual mode of distributing the priests' parts, to burn incense within the sanctuary.   ¹⁰ During this ceremony, the
whole congregation—then unusually large—was silently offering up prayer in the court [of Israel] outside the Temple.   ¹¹ At
this moment an angel appeared to him, standing by the right-
hand side of the altar of incense.   ¹² Zechariah being very much
agitated and alarmed at the sight, ¹³ the angel said to him,
" Calm your fears, Zechariah : your prayer [for the redemption
of Israel] is about to be answered; and [as an event introductory to this,] your wife Elizabeth will ere long bear you a son,
whom you must name JOHN [i. e. *Jehovah-given*].   ¹⁴ His birth
will fill you with joy, and prove a blessing to many besides;
¹⁵ for he will become an eminent servant of the Lord.   He must
abstain [like a Nazarite] from all intoxicating drinks, and the
consecrating influence of the Holy Spirit will rest upon him
from his very birth.   ¹⁶ By his instrumentality many of the
Israelites will be converted to the true and spiritual service
of their divine Messiah, ¹⁷ whose *harbinger* he will be, coming
with the temper and energy of another Elijah, to—

——————— ' restore the sacred sentiments·
Of your forefathers in their fallen sons,'—

and by reforming the perverse Jewish people to the religious
views and expectations of the holy men of old, prepare them
to receive and obey Him readily when He comes."   ¹⁸ " But
by what token," said Zechariah, " am I to be assured that this
will happen to an old man like myself, my wife too being
now far advanced in years ?"   ¹⁹ The angel replied, " I am
GABRIEL, [i. e. *Man-of-God*,] an attendant in the immediate
presence of God, and have been sent to communicate to you
this good news.   ²⁰ But since you are inclined to doubt what
I say, (which is nevertheless sure to be performed in due
time,) and to require proof, mark this :—you will be struck
dumb, and not recover the power of speech until the accomplishment of this event."

²¹ The congregation meanwhile were anxiously waiting for
Zechariah, and wondering at his long stay in the sanctuary.
²² When he came out, however, he found himself unable to

4*

them; and they perceived that he had seen   LUKE I.
a vision in the temple, for he beckoned unto
them and remained speechless. ²³ And it came to
pass, that as soon as the days of his ministration were
accomplished, he departed to his own house.

²⁴ And after those days his wife Elisabeth hid herself five months, saying, ²⁵ Thus hath the Lord dealt
with me in the days wherein he looked on me, to take
away my reproach among men.

§ 4.—*The Annunciation to Mary, that she is to be
the Mother of the Messiah.*

(Nazareth; [early in *November?*] B. C. 7.)

²⁶ And in the sixth month the angel Gabriel was
sent from God unto a city of Galilee named Nazareth,
²⁷ to a virgin (espoused to a man whose name was
Joseph) of the house of David, and the virgin's name
was Mary: ²⁸ and the angel came in unto her and said,
Hail, thou that art highly favored, the Lord is with
thee; blessed art thou among women. ²⁹ And when
she saw him, she was troubled at his saying, and cast
in her mind what manner of salutation this should be.
³⁰ And the angel said unto her, Fear not, Mary: for
thou hast found favor with God. ³¹ And behold,
thou shalt bring forth a son, and shalt call his name
JESUS: ³² he shall be great and shall be called the Son
of the Highest; and the Lord God shall give unto him
the throne of his father David, ³³ and he shall reign
over the house of Jacob forever, and of his kingdom
there shall be no end.° ³⁴ Then said Mary unto the
angel, How shall this be, seeing I know not a man?
³⁵ And the angel answered and said unto her, The Holy
Ghost shall come upon thee, and the power of the
Highest shall overshadow thee; therefore also that

° See Dan. ii, 44; vii, 27.

5

utter a word to them. They soon understood that LUKE I.
he had witnessed some supernatural occurrence
within the "Holy Place," for he could only intimate to them
what had taken place by gestures. In this speechless condition he continued; [23] and at the expiration of his regular
week of public ministration he returned home.

[24] Soon afterward the angel's prediction began to be realized,
and Elizabeth secluded herself for the present from the ostentation and distraction of society; yet cherishing the pious
thought, [25] "How graciously has the Lord dealt with me, in
condescending to remove my stigma among my acquaintances
of being childless!"

§ 4—*The Annunciation to Mary, that she is to be the Mother of
the Messiah.*

(Nazareth; [early in *November ?*] B. C. 7.)

[26] Five months passed thus quietly with Elizabeth. Some
time in the sixth, however, the same divine messenger was
dispatched to a town called Nazareth, in Galilee, [27] with a
message to a young woman of that place, named Mary, of the
lineage of king David, at this time engaged to be married to a
person of the name of Joseph. [28] Upon entering the house,
the angel saluted her, "Hail, highly favoured! The Lord's
blessing rest upon you, happiest of women!" [29] She, however, was completely disconcerted at such a visit and address,
endeavoring in vain to divine the meaning of the salutation;
[30] but the angel said to her, "Be not amazed, Mary; the Lord
has deigned to show you a peculiar favor: [31] you will shortly
become the mother of a son (you are to call him JESUS
[i. e. *Saviour*]), [32] who will be divinely great, so as to be justly
entitled SON OF THE MOST HIGH. On him will Jehovah confer
the promised throne of his ancestor David; and he will thenceforth hold sovereign rule over the [true] descendants of Jacob,
establishing a spiritual kingdom that has been predicted as
never to terminate." [34] "How," inquired Mary, "will this
occur? I am not married." [35] The angel replied, "The *Holy
Spirit* will descend upon you with His creative energy, and at
the same time you will be environed with the influence of the
Supreme Jehovah, uniting Himself with the immaculate off-

5*

holy thing which shall be born of thee, shall   Luke I.
be called the *Son of God.*   ³⁶ And behold,
thy cousin Elisabeth, she also shall have a son in her
old age; ³⁷ for with God nothing shall be impossible.
³⁸ And Mary said, Behold the handmaid of the Lord;
be it unto me according to thy word. And the angel
departed from her.

§ 5.—*Mary's Visit with Elisabeth.*
(Juttah; [*November ?*] B. C. 7.)

³⁹ And Mary arose in those days and went into the
hill country with haste, into a city of Juda, ⁴⁰ and
entered into the house of Zacharias, and saluted Elisabeth. ⁴¹ And it came to pass, that when Elisabeth
heard the salutation of Mary, she was filled with the
Holy Ghost, ⁴² and she spake out with a loud voice
and said, Blessed art thou among women, and blessed
is thy offspring; ⁴³ and whence is this to me, that the
mother of my Lord should come to me? ⁴⁴ For lo,
the voice of thy salutation sounded in mine ears with
joy. ⁴⁵ And blessed is she that believed; for there
shall be a performance of those things which were told
her from the Lord.

⁴⁶ And Mary said, My soul doth magnify the Lord,
⁴⁷ and my spirit hath rejoiced in God my Saviour.
⁴⁸ For he hath regarded the low estate of his hand-
maiden; for behold, from henceforth all generations
shall call me blessed: ⁴⁹ for he that is mighty hath
done to me great things; (and holy is his name;) ⁵⁰ and
his mercy is on them that fear him, from generation
to generation. ⁵¹ He hath showed strength with his
arm, he hath scattered the proud in the imagination of
their hearts; ⁵² he hath put down the mighty from
their seats, and exalted them of low degree; ⁵³ he hath
filled the hungry with good things, and the rich he hath
sent empty away: ⁵⁴ he hath holpen his servant Israel,

spring thus created, which on that account will LUKE I.
likewise be styled SON OF GOD.—[36] Even your relative Elizabeth, old and hitherto childless as she is, will in a
few months become the mother of a son; [37] so that nothing
which God has declared, is too difficult for Him to accomplish." [38] With this explanation, Mary expressed her acqui-
escence in the divine will.—The messenger then departed.

§ 5.—Mary's Visit with Elizabeth.
(Juttah ; [November ?] B. C. 7.)

[39] In a few days Mary started for the hilly region of Judea,
eager to witness the good fortune of her relative. Upon
reaching Juttah, the town where Zechariah resided, [40] she went
directly into his house and affectionately greeted Elizabeth,
[41] who was so agreeably taken by surprise as to affect her with
physical sympathy. She was instantly inspired with the Holy
Spirit, [42] and exclaimed aloud, "Happiest of women! favoured
with a most blessed Offspring !—[43] But why am I thus honoured
with a visit from my Redeemer's mother? [44] Joy thrilled my
very frame the moment I heard your salutation, [that greeted
me with such glad news.] [45] Happy, indeed, is she who [un-
like some] doubted not the Lord would accomplish what He
promised her !"

[46] Mary also [catching the inspiration of the occasion,] broke
forth in the following

RHAPSODY OF PRAISE.

"My inmost soul extols the Lord most high,
[47] Exulting in my promised Saviour-God,
[48] Who thus disdains not my obscurity.
His humblest vassal I, yet after this
My fame, the wide world o'er, shall ever be,
'How happy she, [49] by Heaven distinguished thus !'—
Yes ! highest praise and reverence are His due,
[50] Who tenderly regards His worshipers
Sincere, down to their latest lineage.
[51] He, by His sovereign arm of providence,
Confounds and dissipates pride's cherished schemes ;
[52] Deposes potentates and lordly ones,
But raises humble merit from the dust.
[53] He satisfies the hungry poor that ask,
With earthly comforts and heaven's richer store ;
But from his bounty spurns the pampered rich.—
[54] His chosen people Israel He upholds

6*

in remembrance of his mercy; ⁵⁵as he   LUKE I.
spake to our fathers, to Abraham and to his
seed, forever.°
⁵⁶And Mary abode with her about three months, and
returned to her own house.

§ 6.—*The Birth and Naming of John the Baptist.*
(Juttah; [latter part of *February ?*] B. C. 6.)

⁵⁷Now Elisabeth's full time came ; and she brought
forth a son. ⁵⁸And her neighbours and her cousins
heard how the Lord had showed great mercy upon
her ; and they rejoiced with her. ⁵⁹And it came to
pass, that on the eighth day they came to circumcise
the child ; and they called him *Zacharias*, after the
name of his father. ⁶⁰And his mother answered and
said, Not so ; but he shall be called JOHN. ⁶¹And they
said unto her, There is none of thy kindred that is
called by this name. ⁶²And they made signs to his
father, how *he* would have him called. ⁶³And he
asked for a writing-table, and wrote saying, His name
is JOHN. And they marvelled all. ⁶⁴And his mouth
was opened immediately and his tongue loosed, and
he spake and praised God. ⁶⁵And fear came on all
that dwelt round about them : and all these sayings
were noised abroad throughout all the hill-country of
Judea. ⁶⁶And all they that heard them, laid them up
in their hearts, saying, What manner of child shall this
be ! And the hand of the Lord was with him.

⁶⁷And his father Zacharias was filled with the Holy
Ghost, and prophesied saying, ⁶⁸Blessed be the Lord
God of Israel, for he hath visited and redeemed his
people, ⁶⁹and hath raised up a horn of salvation for us
in the house of his servant David ; ⁷⁰as he spake by
the mouth of his holy prophets, which have been since

° Gen. xii, 2, 3, &c.

7

By succor nigh, still mindful [55] (so He vowed,   LUKE I.
And such declared Himself, in times of old,)
Perpetually of kindness ofttimes pledged
To Abraham and his whole posterity."
[56] After staying with Elizabeth about three months, Mary
returned to her home.

§ 6.—The Birth and Naming of John the Baptist.
(Juttah; [latter part of *February* ?] B. C. 6.)

[57] The period of Elizabeth's confinement now drew near.
After the birth of her son, [58] her neighbours and relatives,
hearing of the peculiar blessing which the Lord had conferred
upon her, came together to rejoice with her.   [59] On the eighth
day, those assembled at the circumcision and naming of the
child were for calling him "*Zechariah*," after his father.
[60] But his mother objected, saying, "No, no; he is to be called
John."   [61] "Why?" replied they, "there is none in your family
of that name."   [62] So they appealed to his father, and asked
him by signs, "by what name he would have him called?"
[63] Zechariah, beckoning them to hand him a tablet, wrote upon
it this answer: "JOHN is to be his name." This made all
present wonder still the more.

[64] No sooner had Zechariah done this, than he spoke out,
having recovered the use of his tongue, and praised God, as in
the subjoined hymn.—[65] These occurrences produced a great
sensation among the neighbours, and even became the common
topic of conversation throughout the entire "Highlands" of
Judea.   [66] All who heard them recounted, regarded them as
no ordinary events; and every one spontaneously exclaimed,
"Well! what sort of a man will this child make?" These expectations were heightened by witnessing the divine blessing,
that continued to attend him.

[67] Zechariah, on this occasion, was filled with divine inspiration, and under its influence uttered the following

PROPHETIC RHAPSODY.

[68] "Praised be Jehovah, Israel's faithful God;
For lo! He comes to cheer and ransom us
[69] By a Redeemer clothed with kingly power,—
A Scion from His chosen David's stock,
[70] (As oft He promised, in the words He bade
His sainted prophets speak in days of yore,)—

7*

the world began :* [71] that we should be saved   .LUKE I.
from our enemies and from the hand of all
that hate us ; [72] to perform the mercy promised to our
fathers, and to remember his holy covenant, [73] the oath
which he sware to our father Abraham,† [74] that he
would grant unto us, that we being delivered out of
the hand of our enemies, might serve him without fear
[75] in holiness and righteousness before him, all the
days of our life. [76] And thou, child, shalt be called the
prophet of the Highest; for thou shalt go before the
face of the Lord to prepare his ways, [77] to give knowledge of salvation unto his people by the remission of
their sins [78] through the tender mercy of our God,
whereby the *day-spring* from on high hath visited us,
[79] to give light to them that sit in darkness and in the
shadow of death, to guide our feet into the way of
peace.

[80] And the child grew and waxed strong in spirit, and
was in the deserts till the day of his showing
unto Israel.   [4] And the same John had his   **Matt. III.**
raiment of camel's hair, and a leathern girdle
about his loins ; and his meat was locusts and wild honey.

§ 7.—*Joseph's Vision of an Angel in a Dream.*

(Nazareth; [*April?*] B. C. 6.)

[18] Now the birth of Jesus Christ was on   **Matt. I.**
this wise : When as his mother Mary was
espoused to Joseph, before they came together, she was
found with child of the Holy Ghost : [19] then Joseph her
husband, being a just man, and not willing to make her a
public example, was minded to put her away privily.
[20] But while he thought on these things, behold, the
angel of the Lord appeared unto him in a dream saying,

---

* Especially Isa. iv, 2 ; xi, 1 ; Jer. xxiii, 5, 6 ; xxxiii, 15 ; Zech.
iii, 8 ; vi, 12.

† Gen. xii, 2, 3, &c.

8 .

[71] A Saviour from our spiritual foes,   LUKE I.
From all of men's or fiends' malignant power.
[72] Thus He effects His pristine kind intent,
And ne'er His righteous '*covenant*' forgets,—
[73] Established by His pledge to Abraham,—
[74] Vouchsafing us the high prerogative
To freely worship Him [75] throughout our lives,.
Unawed by human thrall or inward guile
To mar our dues entire to God and man.
[76] And as to you, my son, your rank will be,.
'Supreme Messiah's Herald ;' an envoy
Dispatched to usher in the Heavenly King,
His entrance to His subjects you'll prepare,
[77] By teaching them *salvation's science true*.
Henceforth 't is found in PARDON FREE for sin,
[78] Atoned through the compassion of our God.
Lo! ere this full-orbed ' Sun ' of mercy shines,
The dawning beams in you are shed from heaven,
[79] To glance upon the pathway of our Tribes,
Who grope benighted in the 'deadly shade'
Of sinful wandering far from truth, and thus
To point our footsteps to the safer track."

[80] The boy [as above intimated] displayed, as he grew up, great vigor of mind as well as moral energy and virtue. [Upon arriving at manhood,] he secluded himself in the lonely retreats of the "Deserts" of Judea, until the time of his entrance upon his public ministry. [4] In this   Matt. III. retirement he [practiced the austere mode of life of the ancient prophets and Nazarites ; being] dressed merely in a coarse shirt made of camel's hair, which was gathered by a belt of undressed skin at the waist, and subsisting on the locusts [with which that region swarmed], together with the honey that the wild bees stored [in hollow trees and fissures of the rocks].

§ 7.—*Joseph's Vision of an Angel in a Dream.*
(Nazareth ; [*April ?*] B. C. 6.)

[18] The birth of Jesus Christ occurred under the fol-   Matt. I. lowing circumstances.—His mother Mary was engaged to be married to Joseph ; but before the marriage was consummated, it became apparent that she was about to become a mother (from the preternatural agency of the Holy Spirit, [as it afterward appeared]). [19] Upon this discovery, her intended husband Joseph, who was a conscientious observer of the Jewish law, and yet felt reluctant to subject her to its full penalty of public ignominy, was inclined to adopt the milder course of divorcing her privately.

[20] One night, as he lay pondering this subject, he had a dream, in which he saw an angel, who thus addressed him :—

D   8*

Joseph, thou son of David, fear not to take   MATT. I.
unto thee Mary thy wife : for that which shall
be born of her is of the Holy Ghost ; [21] and she shall
bring forth a son, and thou shalt call his name JESUS,
for he shall save his people from their sins.   [24] Then
Joseph, being raised from sleep, did as the angel of the
Lord had bidden him and took unto him his wife :
[25] and when she had brought forth her first-born son,
he called his name JESUS.

[22] Now all this was done, that it might be fulfilled
which was spoken of the Lord by the prophet saying,[*]
[23] Behold, a virgin shall bring forth a son, and they
shall call his name *Emmanuel*, (which being interpreted is, *God with us*.)

CHAPTER II.

CHRIST'S INFANCY, CHILDHOOD AND PRIVATE LIFE.

(Time, about *twelve years and five months*.)

§ 8.—*The Nativity of Christ.*

(Bethlehem ; [about the first of *August?*] B. C. 6.)

[1] And it came to pass in those days, that   **Luke II.**
there went out a decree from Cesar Augustus,
that all the world should be taxed ; [2] (and this taxing was
first *made* when Cyrenius was governor of Syria :) [3] and
all went to be taxed, every one into his own city.   [4] And
Joseph also went up from Galilee out of the city of
Nazareth, into Judea unto the city of David, which is
called Bethlehem,[†] (because he was of the house and
lineage of David,) [5] to be taxed, with Mary his espoused wife.   [6] And so it was, that while they were
there,[7] she brought forth her first-born son, and wrapped
him in swaddling-clothes and laid him in a manger ;
because there was no room for them in the *inn*.

---

[*] Isa. vii, 14.   [†] See 1 Sam. xvi, 1.

9

"Joseph, you need not hesitate, although David's   MATT. I.
descendant, to receive Mary, your affianced bride,   ————
for her future offspring is the miraculous progeny of the Holy
Spirit. ²¹ She will give birth to a son, whom you must name
JESUS, [i. e. *Saviour*,] because he will deliver his [spiritual]
people from their sins."
   ²⁴ Joseph, on rising next morning after this prophetic dream,
obeyed the angel's injunction. He at once brought his bride
home ; ²⁵ but awaited the developments of providence, till
after the birth of this her first child, which, as it was a boy,
he named JESUS, as directed.
   ²² The circumstances of this birth were thus an exact accomplishment of [the higher sense of] that divine declaration
through Isaiah,—

> ²³ "Mark you the youthful daughter still unversed
> In married life ? that very maid will yet
> The early mother of a son become,
> Whom you may know as styled IMMANUEL,"—

a Hebrew term, signifying *God-incarnate.*

———◆———

CHAPTER II.

CHRIST'S INFANCY, CHILDHOOD AND PRIVATE LIFE.

(Time, about *twelve years and five months.*)

§ 8.—*The Nativity of Christ.*

(Bethlehem; [about the first of *August ?*] B. C. 6.)

   ¹ Not long after John's birth, an edict was issued   Luke II.
by the Roman emperor Augustus, requiring a census   ————
to be taken of the whole population of Palestine. ² (This
register was the basis of the tax subsequently levied by
Quiri'nus, when pro-consul [i. e. lord-lieutenant] of Syria.)
³ All the inhabitants accordingly repaired to the several towns
where their families originated, to be registered [at the same
place with their other connexions, and where their entailed
estates lay]. ⁴ Among the rest, Joseph went from his residence at Nazareth, in Galilee, to the town of Bethlehem, the
birth-place of his ancestor David, ⁵ for the purpose of being
enrolled there, accompanied by his wife Mary, now near the
time of her confinement.
   ⁶ While they were there, [waiting for their turn,] the expected event occurred. ⁷ Mary accordingly gave birth to her
first child, a son ; and after swathing the infant with the
usual bandages, she cradled him on the platform projecting
into one of the stalls surrounding the *khan* [i. e. public house],
where they were obliged to lodge, the interior building itself
being preoccupied by other travelers.

9*

§ 9.—*Christ's Ancestry, both Natural and Legal.*

1 The book of the generation of Jesus Christ, the **Matthew I.** son of David, the son of Abraham: 23 being (as was supposed) **Luke III.** the son of Joseph, which was the son of Heli, 24 which was the son of Matthat, which was the son of Levi, which was the son of Melchi, which was the son of Janna, which was the son of Joseph, 25 which was the son of Mattathias, which was the son of Amos, which was the son of Naum, which was the son of Esli, which was the son of Nagge, 26 which was the son of Maath, which was the son of Mattathias, which was the son of Semei, which was the son of Joseph, which was the son of Juda, 27 which was the son of Joanna, which was the son of Rhesa, which was the son of Zorobabel, which was the son of Salathiel, which was the son of Neri, 28 which was the son of Melchi, which was the son of Addi, which was the son of Cosam, which was the son of Elmodam, which was the son of Er, 29 which was the son of Jose, which was the son of Eliezer, which was the son of Jorim, which was the son of Matthat, which was the son of Levi, 30 which was the son of Simeon, which was the son of Juda, which was the son of Joseph, which was the son of Jonan, which was the son of Eliakim, 31 which was the son of Melea, which was the son of Menan, which was the son of Mattatha, which was the son of Nathan, which was the son of David, 32 which was the son of Jesse, which was the son of Obed, which was the son of Booz, which was the son of Naasson, 33 which was the son of Aminadab, which was the son of Aram, which was the son of Esrom, which was the son of Phares, which was the son of Juda, 34 which was the son of Jacob, which was the son of Isaac, which was the son of Abraham, which was the son of Thara, which was

2 Abraham begat **Matt. I.** Isaac, and Isaac begat Jacob, and Jacob begat Judas and his brethren, 3 and Judas begat Pharez and Zara of Thamar, and Pharez begat Esrom, and Esrom begat Aram, 4 and Aram begat Aminadab, and Aminadab begat Naasson, and Naasson begat Salmon, 5 and Salmon begat Booz of Rachab, and Booz begat Obed of Ruth, and Obed begat Jesse, 6 and Jesse begat David the king, and David the king begat Solomon of her that had been the wife of Urias, 7 and Solomon begat Roboam, and Roboam begat Abia, and Abia begat Asa, 8 and Asa begat Josaphat, and Josaphat begat Joram, and Joram begat Ozias, 9 and Ozias begat Joatham, and Joatham begat Achaz, and Achaz begat Ezekias, 10 and Ezekias begat Manasses, and Manasses begat Amon, and Amon begat Josias, 11 and Josias begat Jechonias and his brethren about the time they were carried away to Babylon; 12 and after they were brought to Babylon Jechonias begat Salathiel, and Salathiel begat Zorobabel, 13 and Zorobabel begat Abiud, and Abiud begat Eliakim, and Eliakim begat Azor, 14 and Azor begat Sadoc, and Sadoc begat Achim, and Achim begat Eliud, 15 and Eliud begat Eleazar, and Eleazar begat Matthan, and Matthan begat Jacob, 16 and Jacob begat Joseph the husband of Mary, of whom was born Jesus, who is called Christ: 17 so all the generations from Abraham to David are fourteen generations, and from David until the carrying away into Babylon are fourteen generations, and from the carrying away into Babylon unto Christ are fourteen generations.

the son of Nachor, 35 which was the son of Saruch, which was the son of Ragau, which was the son of Phalec, which was the son of Heber, which was the son of Sala, 36 which was the son of Cainan, which was the son of Arphaxad, which was the son of Sem, which was the son of Noe, which was the son of Lamech, 37 which was the son of Mathusala, which was the son of Enoch, which was the son of Jared, which was the son of Maleleel, which was the son of Cainan, 38 which was the son of Enos, which was the son of Seth, which was the son of Adam, which was the son of God.

10

§ 9.—Christ's Ancestry, both Natural and Legal.

(Compiled from the Old Testament,* and Public Family Records of the Jews.)

GENEALOGICAL TABLE:

Showing Christ's Descent from the Patriarch Abraham, and that He was the Heir of the Direct Line of King David, [both by His Mother Mary and Reputed Father Joseph].

Lu. III.	No.	MATERNAL Name	No.	PATERNAL Name	Mat. I.
38	1	Adam	1		
	2	Seth	2		
	3	Enos	3		
37	4	Cainan	4		
	5	Mahal'aleel	5		
	6	Jared	6		
	7	Enoch	7		
	8	Methuselah	8		
36	9	Lamech	9	[As in Luke.]	
	10	Noah	10		
	11	Shem	11		
	12	Arphaxad	12		
35	13	Salah	13		
	14	Eber	14		
	15	Peleg	15		
	16	Reü	16		
	17	Serug	17		
34	18	Nahor	18		
	19	Terah	19		
	20	Abram	1	Abraham	2
	21	Isaac	2	Isaac	
	22	Jacob	3	Jacob	
33	23	Judah	4	Judah	
	24	Pharez	5	Pharez	3
	25	Hezron	6	Hezron	
	26	Ram	7	Ram	
	27	Ammin'adab	8	Ammin'adab	4
32	28	Nahshon	9	Nahshon	
	29	Salmon	10	Salmon	
	30	Boaz	11	Boaz	5
	31	Obed	12	Obed	
	32	Jesse	13	Jesse	
31	33	David	14	David	6
	34	Nathan	1	Solomon	
	35	Mat'tathah	2	Rehobo'am	7
		Mainan			
		Me'leah			
30	36	Eli'akim	3	Abijah	
	37	Jonan	4	Asa	

Lu. III.	No.	MATERNAL Name	No.	PATERNAL Name	Mat. I.
	38	Joseph	5	Jehosh'aphat	8
30	39	Adai'ah	6	Jeho'ram	
	40	Maasei'ah	..	Ahaziah	
29	41	Levi	..	Joash	
	42	Matthat	..	Amaziah	
	43	Jorim	7	Uzziah	
	44	Eleazar	8	Jotham	9
	45	Joseh	9	Ahaz	
28	46	Er	10	Hezekiah	
	47	Elmo'dam	11	Manasseh	10
	48	Cosam	12	Amon	
	49	Addi	13	Josiah	
	50	Maasei'ah	14	Jehoi'akim	11
27	51	Neriah, g'nd-father of	1	Jeconiah	
			..	(Captivity.)	
	52	Salathiel	2	Salathiel	12
	53	Zerub'babel, g'ndfather of,	3	Zerub'babel	
	54	Rephai'ah	..	Hananiah	
	55	Arnan	..	Rephai'ah	
26	56	Obadiah	..	Arnan	
	57	Shechaniah	4	Obadiah	13
	58	Shemai'ah	5	Shechaniah	
		Mattathiah	..	Shemai'ah	
		Maath			
25	59	Neariah	..	Neariah	
	60	Elio'enai	6	Az'rikam	
	61	Joha'nan	..	[Unknown.]	
	62	Amoz	..	[Unknown.]	
	63	Mattathiah	7	Sadok	14
24	64	Joseph	8	Achim	
	65	Jannah	9	Eli'ud	
	66	Melchi	10	Eleazar	15
	67	Levi	11	Matthan	
	68	Matthat	12	Jacob	
23	69	Eli	13	Joseph, repu-ted father of	16
	70	Mary			
	71	JESUS	14	JESUS	17
	71				17

* Gen. v, 3–32; x, 22, 24, 25; xi, 10–27; 1 Chron. i, 1–4, 17–19, 24–28, 34; ii, 1, 4, 5, 9–12, 15; iii, 5, 10–24; Ruth iv, 19–22.

10*

§ 10.—*The Appearance of an Angel to certain Shepherds, who thereupon Visit the Infant Saviour.*

(Pastures near Bethlehem; [first of *August ?*] B. C. 6.)

⁸ And there were in the same country shep-   **Luke II.**
herds abiding in the field, keeping watch over
their flock by night.   ⁹ And lo, the angel of the Lord
came upon them, and the glory of the Lord shone round
about them; and they were sore afraid.   ¹⁰ And the
angel said unto them, Fear not; for behold, I bring
you good tidings of great joy, which shall be to all
people : ¹¹ for unto you is born this day in the city of
David a Saviour, which is Christ the Lord.; ¹² and this
shall be a sign unto you, Ye shall find the babe wrapped
in swaddling-clothes, lying in a manger.   ¹³ And suddenly there was with the angel a multitude of the heavenly host, praising God and saying, ¹⁴ Glory to God
in the highest, and on earth peace, good will toward
men.

¹⁵ And it came to pass, as the angels were gone
away from them into heaven, the shepherds said one
to another, Let us now go even unto Bethlehem and
see this thing which is come to pass, which the Lord
hath made known unto us.   ¹⁶ And they came with
haste and found Mary and Joseph, and the babe lying
in a manger.   ¹⁷ And when they had seen it, they
made known abroad the saying which was told them
concerning this child.   ¹⁸ And all they that heard it
wondered at those things which were told them by the
shepherds : ¹⁹ but Mary kept all these things and pon-
dered them in her heart.   ²⁰ And the shepherds returned, glorifying and praising God for all the things
that they had heard and seen, as it was told unto
them.

11

§ 10.—*The Appearance of an Angel to certain Shepherds, who thereupon Visit the Infant Saviour.*

- (Pastures near Bethlehem; [first of *August ?*] B. C. 6.)

⁸ At the time of Christ's birth, a party of shepherds   **Luke II.**
were grazing their flocks near Bethlehem, having
strolled thither in quest of pasturage.   One night, as they
were out in the open meadow, patrolling by turns near them,
⁹ suddenly an angel appeared, casting a celestial radiance all
around them.   Terror seized them at the sight; ¹⁰ but the
angel bade them, " Be not frightened ; I have good news for
you, and for your whole nation.   ¹¹ There is just born, in
David's native town, your [spiritual] Deliverer, the divine
Messiah.   ¹² You may recognize Him thus : you will find an
Infant in swathing bands reposing in a manger adjoining the
inn."—¹³ Immediately a vast chorus of celestials joined the
angel in thus celebrating the event :—

> ¹⁴ " Let heaven with praise to God resound!
> We welcome sacred bliss o'er earth ;
> Propitious pledge with mortals found,
> [In their divine Redeemer's birth !]"

¹⁵ No sooner had the heavenly choir reascended, than the
shepherds proposed among themselves to " go at once over to
Bethlehem, and witness the interesting fact thus divinely revealed to them."   ¹⁶ Eagerly hasting thither, they soon discovered Joseph and Mary's lodging-place, with her Infant
cradled in the designated spot.   ¹⁷ Upon this identification,
they related what the angel had declared to them would be
the character of the child.   ¹⁸ The account astonished all their
hearers, ¹⁹ except Mary, who treasured up this new incident
with a mother's fond reflections.   ²⁰ The shepherds returned
to their flocks, with joyful adoration to God, who had thus
favored them with a celestial announcement and its verification.

11*

§ 11.—*The Circumcision and Naming of Christ.*

(Bethlehem; [early in *August?*] B. C. 6.)

²¹ And when eight days were accom-   LUKE II.
plished for the circumcising of the child,
his name was called JESUS, which was so named of
the angel before he was born.

§ 12.—*The Infant presented at the Temple, to be Legally Redeemed.*

(Jerusalem, the Temple, Gate of Nicanor; [middle of *September?*]
B. C. 6.)

²² And when the days of her purification according
to the law of Moses* were accomplished, they brought
him to Jerusalem, to present him to the Lord, ²³ (as it
is written in the law of the Lord,† Every first-born
male shall be called holy to the Lord;) ²⁴ and to offer
a sacrifice according to that which is said in the law
of the Lord,‡ A pair of turtle-doves or two young
pigeons.

²⁵ And behold, there was a man in Jerusalem whose
name was Simeon; and the same man was just and
devout, waiting for the Consolation of Israel: and the
Holy Ghost was upon him. ²⁶ And it was revealed
unto him by the Holy Ghost, that he should not see
death, before he had seen the Lord's Christ. ₂₇ And
he came by the Spirit into the temple; and when the
parents brought in the child Jesus, to do for him after
the custom of the law, ²⁸ then took he him up in his
arms, and blessed God and said, ²⁹ Lord, now lettest
thou thy servant depart in peace, according to thy
word: ³⁰ for mine eyes have seen thy Salvation,
³¹ which thou hast prepared before the face of all people; ³² a light to lighten the Gentiles, and the glory of
thy people Israel. ³³ And Joseph and his mother

---

* Lev. xii, 2, 4.   † Num. xviii, 15, 16.   ‡ Lev. xii, 8.

12

§ 11.—*The Circumcision and Naming of Christ.*
(Bethlehem; [early in *August?*] B. C. 6.)

²¹ Upon the eighth day the child was duly cir- LUKE II.
cumcised, and named JESUS, as the angel had prescribed.

§ 12.—*The Infant presented at the Temple, to be Legally
Redeemed.*
(Jerusalem, the Temple, Gate of Nicanor; [middle of *September?*] B. C. 6.)

²² At the end of the forty days required by the Mosaic Law,
before male infants and their mothers become ceremonially
" clean," the parents took the babe to Jerusalem; ²³ in accordance with the divine statute, directing " every first-born
male [human as well as of cattle] to be set apart as sacred to
the Lord, [but allowing children to be redeemed from exclusive devotion to religious pursuits by the payment of a certain
sum of money (5 *shekels*, i. e. about $3)],"—²⁴ and for the pur-
pose of offering the associated sacrifice, " either a brace of turtle-doves or of common young pigeons."

²⁵ There resided in Jerusalem, at this time, an individual
by the name of Simeon, well known for his upright and pious
character, who was daily expecting the coming of the " Con-
soler of Israel." In one of his frequent seasons of prophetic
influence, ²⁶ he was divinely assured that he should not die
before beholding the Messiah whom Jehovah had promised.
²⁷ By the prompting of the Holy Spirit he had repaired to the
Temple, and when Jesus's parents brought in their child,—
to perform the legal ceremonies respecting him,—²⁸ he at once
[recognized in him the long-looked-for Redeemer, and] taking
him from their arms, embraced him with delight, praising God
and exclaiming,—

²⁹ " Welcome Thy servant, Heavenly Master, hails
This designated token of release
From earthly toil; I now can die in peace,
³⁰ Content that these expectant eyes have gazed
Upon the promised Saviour, ³¹ now sent forth
By Thee among mankind with generous care,
³² To illuminate dark souls in Gentile lands,
And doubly thus exalt Thy chosen race."

³³ Then turning to the parents, who were much surprised at

12*

marveled at those things which were spoken   LUKE II.
of him. ³⁴ And Simeon blessed them, and
said unto Mary his mother, Behold, this child is set for
the fall and rising again of many in Israel, and for a
sign which shall be spoken against ; ³⁵ (yea, a sword
shall pierce through thy own soul also ;) that. the
thoughts of many hearts may be revealed.

³⁶ And there was one Anna, a prophetess, the daughter of Phanuel of the tribe of Aser : she was of a great
age, and had lived with a husband seven years from
her virginity ; ³⁷ and she was a widow of about fourscore and four years, which departed not from the
temple, but served God with fastings and prayers night
and day. ³⁸ And she, coming in that instant, gave
thanks likewise unto the Lord, and spake of him to all
them that looked for Redemption in Jerusalem.

³⁹ And when they had performed all things according to the law of the Lord, they returned into Galilee
to their own city Nazareth.

§ 13.—*The Visit of the Magi.*
(Jerusalem and Bethlehem ; [*July ?*] B. C. 5.)

¹ Now when Jesus was born in Bethlehem   **Matt. II.**
of Judea, in the days of Herod the king, behold, there came wise-men from the east to Jerusalem,
² saying, Where is he that is born King of the Jews ?
for we have seen his star in the east, and are come to
worship him.

³ When Herod the king had heard these things, he
was troubled and all Jerusalem with him.   ⁴ And when
he had gathered all the chief-priests and scribes of the
people together, he demanded of them where Christ
should be born.   ⁵ And they said unto him, In Bethlehem of Judea : for thus it is written by the prophet,*

---

* Mic. v, 2–4.

this language concerning their child, [34] he con-   LUKE II.
gratulated them with a benediction. To Mary he
made this prophetic remark : "This infant will prove
the means of spiritual *elevation* to those of the Jews who receive him, and an occasion of *stumbling* [still deeper into sin
and misery] to many others, who will make him a mark for
their calumny. [35] By their treatment of him, men's real
characters will thus be tested ; [those who admit his claims,
showing thereby the soundness of their religious principles,
and their openness to conviction ; while those who refuse and
oppose him, will but expose their carnal-mindedness and inveterate hatred of truth and goodness.] And the shafts aimed
at him will transfix your heart also with sympathetic grief!"

[36] There was at the same time in the city an inspired female,
Anna by name, (daughter of one Phanu'el, a descendant of the
tribe of Asher,) who had been permitted to enjoy but for seven
years the society of the husband whom she had married in early
womanhood, and who had now reached the advanced age [37] of
eighty-four years. This venerable widow spent her whole time
at the Temple, devoted to frequent fastings and continual
prayer. [38] She, therefore, joining the company as Simeon was
expressing his rapturous emotions, united in adoring the child
as her divine Redeemer, and hastened to impart the joyful tidings to all those in Jerusalem who were awaiting the predicted
Deliverer.

[39] After fulfilling the legal ceremonies which called them to
the capital, the parents returned to Bethlehem, [where, however, they were soon compelled to leave Palestine for a considerable time ;] and subsequently they removed to Galilee, and
settled in Nazareth, their former place of residence.

§ 13.—*The Visit of the Magi.*

(Jerusalem and Bethlehem ; [*July ?*] B. C. 5.)

[1] In the course of the year ensuing after the birth   **Matt. II.**
of Christ, (occurring, as above, at Bethlehem, in
Judea proper, toward the close of the reign of Herod the
Great,) there arrived at Jerusalem a deputation of Magian
philosophers, from [that part of Arabia which borders upon
Palestine on] the East, [2] who were inquiring, "Where may we
find the *King of the Jews*, that is recently born? We saw
from the distant East what we took to be his birth-star, and
have come to do him homage."

[3] King Herod becoming apprised of this occurrence, his jealous disposition at once took the alarm, for the whole city
was also thrown into commotion by the news. [4] He accordingly convened the entire San'hedrim, and proposed to them
the question, "What, according to their Scriptures, was the
destined place of the Messiah's birth?" [5] They promptly
answered, "*Bethlehem*, in Judea-proper;" on the authority of
that passage in Micah's prophecy to this effect :—

13*

⁶ And thou Bethlehem, in the land of Juda,   MATT. II.
art not the least among the princes of Juda ;
for out of thee shall come a Governor, that shall rule
my people Israel.

⁷ Then Herod, when he had privily called the wise-
men, inquired of them diligently what time the star
appeared.   ⁸ And he sent them to Bethlehem and said,
Go and search diligently for the young child ; and
when ye have found him, bring me word again, that I
may come and worship him also.

⁹ When they had heard the king they departed ; and
lo, the star which they saw in the east went before
them, till it came and stood over where the young
child was.   ¹⁰ When they saw the star, they rejoiced
with exceeding great joy.   ¹¹ And when they were
come into the house, they saw the young child with
Mary his mother, and fell down and worshiped him ;
and when they had opened their treasures, they presented unto him gifts, gold and frankincense and
myrrh.

¹² And being warned of God in a dream that they
should not return to Herod, they departed into their
own country another way.

§ 14.—*The Flight into Egypt.*
(From Bethlehem ; [*July ?*] B. C. 5.)

¹³ And when they were departed, behold, the angel
of the Lord appeareth to Joseph in a dream, saying,
Arise and take the young child and his mother, and
flee into Egypt, and be thou there until I bring thee
word ; for Herod will seek the young child to destroy
him.

¹⁴ When he arose he took the young child and his
mother by night, and departed into Egypt ; ¹⁵ and
was there until the death of Herod : that it might
be fulfilled which was spoken of the Lord by
14

6 "[Dark is the cloud impending o'er the land;   MATT. II.
Butgleams of happier times break through the gloom.]————
Jehovah singles thee, O Bethlehem,—
Ephra'thah once; though small thy borders seem,
Compared with many towns of Judah's tribe,
Yet large the honor destined thee among
Its Principalities-of-'thousands' all.
For out of thee will rise the Heaven-sent Prince,
A pastoral sway to bear o'er Israel's fold."

7 Having obtained this information, Herod immediately invited the Magians to a private interview with him, in which he carefully inquired the precise time when they first saw the so-called Star. 8 He then dismissed them, with instructions to "hasten to Bethlehem, and there ascertain with exactness every fact relating to any such infant; and if they succeeded in discovering him, to return to him with the information," pretending that he "was himself equally desirous of visiting this royal personage, and of showing him suitable deference." 9 In pursuance of the king's directions they set out, guided in their nocturnal journey by a [preternatural] meteor, which seemed a sudden reappearance of the star, and moved in advance of them until they reached the village of Bethlehem, when it remained stationary immediately over the house where the babe's parents were lodging. 10 Reanimated at the sight of the "star," 11 they entered, and at once beheld the child in his mother's arms. [Satisfied that they now had found the object of their search,] they threw themselves in reverential homage before him; then unlocking their caskets, they made him presents of gold, frankincense and myrrh. 12 During that night, a preternatural dream occurred to [one of] them; which induced them, instead of returning to Herod, to take another route homeward.

§ 14.—*The Flight into Egypt.*

(From Bethlehem; [*July ?*] B. C. 5.)

13 The night after the departure of the Magians, Joseph dreamed that he saw an angel, who said to him, "Get up quickly! make ready the babe with his mother, and escape with them into Egypt; there remain, until I give you notice to return : king Herod is trying to find the infant, in order to kill him." 14 Joseph, awaking with terror at the divine warning, immediately roused his wife with the intelligence, and although it was still night, started with her and the babe with all haste for Egypt. 15 There they continued out of Herod's reach,

14.*

the prophet,* saying, Out of Egypt have I   MATT. II.
called my Son.

§ 15.—*The Massacre of the Bethlehemite Infants.*

(Bethlehem; [*August?*] B. C. 5.)

16 Then Herod, when he saw that he was mocked
of the wise-men, was exceeding wroth, and sent
forth and slew all the children that were in Bethlehem and in all the coasts thereof, from two years
old and under, according to the time which he had
diligently inquired of the wise-men.   17 Then was
fulfilled that which was spoken by Jeremy the prophet saying,† 18 In Rama was there a voice heard,
lamentation and weeping and great mourning, Rachel
weeping for her children and would not be comforted,
because they are not.

§ 16.—*The Return from Egypt.*

(To Nazareth; [*April?*] B. C. 4.)

19 But when Herod was dead, behold, an angel of
the Lord appeareth in a dream to Joseph in Egypt,
20 saying, Arise and take the young child and his
mother, and go into the land of Israel; for they are
dead which sought the young child's life.   21 And he
arose and took the young child and his mother, and
came into the land of Israel.   22 But when he heard
that Archelaus did reign in Judea in the room of his
father Herod, he was afraid to go thither: notwithstanding, being warned of God in a dream, he turned
aside into the parts of Galilee; 23 and he came and
dwelt in a city called Nazareth: that it might be fulfilled which was spoken by the prophets,‡ He shall be
called a Nazarene.

---

* Hosea xi, 1.   † Jer. xxxi, 15.   ‡ Compare Isa. liii, 1-3.

15

until that tyrant's death freed them from all ap- **MATT. II.**
prehensions of danger in returning. Thus the
divine declaration in the mouth of the prophet
Hose'a became literally applicable in the present case,—

"I kindly led my son from Egypt's thrall."

§ 15.—*The Massacre of the Bethlehemite Infants.*

(Bethlehem; [*August ?*] B. C. 5.)

[16] Herod, soon suspecting that he had been duped by the
Magians, in his rage dispatched a party of men to murder
every male infant in the town of Bethlehem and its environs,
of two years of age or less; hoping to make sure of every one
born since the utmost time of the "star's" appearance, as he
had carefully ascertained it from the Magians. [17] Then ensued
a scene of wo among the bereaved mothers of Bethlehem, to
which might fitly be applied the language of the prophet
Jeremiah,—

[18] " Heard you that doleful sound, that late arose
In Ramah's hamlet,—shrieks and bitter moans?
'T was Rachel starting from her tomb hard by,
Her offspring to bewail! Her anguished heart
Rejects all solace, for they are no more,"—

[being snatched from her then by captivity, but now by
death.]

§ 16.—*The Return from Egypt.*

(To Nazareth; [*April ?*] B. C. 4.)

[19] Upon the death of Herod, Joseph, still in Egypt, dreamed
that he saw an angel, [20] who said to him, "You may now return with the child and his mother to Palestine: the tyrant
that plotted the infant's destruction is lately dead." [21] Accordingly, the next morning he made ready his wife and her
child, and journeyed back with them to his native country.
[22] But upon reaching its confines, he learned that Archela'us
had succeeded his father Herod the Great in the capacity of
ethnarch of Judea proper; which so alarmed him, [on account
of that prince's well-known resemblance in disposition to his
father,] that he hesitated to return to Bethlehem, within his
territories. From this uncertainty he was relieved by a divine
communication in a dream, in pursuance of which he continued his journey as far as the territory of Galilee. [23] Here
he crossed over, and fixed his residence once more at Nazareth.—This circumstance led to the fulfillment of many prophetical intimations [of the obloquy which the Messiah would
experience,] as Jesus thus became confounded with the " des-
picable *Nazarenes.*"

15*

§ 17.—*The Boyhood of Jesus.*

(Nazareth and Jerusalem; [*April* 9–19?] A. D. 8.)

[40] And the child grew and waxed strong in spirit, filled with wisdom; and the grace of God was upon him.

Luke II.

[41] Now his parents went to Jerusalem every year at the feast of the passover : [42] and when he was twelve years old, they went up to Jerusalem after the custom of the feast. [43] And when they had fulfilled the days; as they returned, the child Jesus tarried behind in Jerusalem ; and Joseph and his mother knew not of it. [44] But they, supposing him to have been in the company, went a day's journey ; and they sought him among their kinsfolk and acquaintance : [45] and when they found him not, they turned back again to Jerusalem, seeking him. [46] And it came to pass that after three days they found him in the temple, sitting in the midst of the doctors, both hearing them and asking them questions. [47] And all that heard him were astonished at his understanding and answers. [48] And when they saw him, they were amazed ; and his mother said unto him, Son, why hast thou thus dealt with us? behold, thy father and I have sought thee sorrowing. [49] And he said unto them, How is it that ye sought me? wist ye not that I must be about my Father's business? [50] And they understood not the saying which he spake unto them. [51] And he went down with them and came to Nazareth, and was subject unto them : but his mother kept all these sayings in her heart.

[52] And Jesus increased in wisdom and stature; and in favor with God and man.

16.

§ 17.—*The Boyhood of Jesus.*

(Nazareth and Jerusalem; [*April* 9-19?] A. D. 8.)

40 The child, as he grew up, expanded also in men-   **Luke II.**
tal powers, especially evincing uncommon *discre-*
tion; insomuch that it was evident that the special influences
of Heaven were over him.

41 Both his parents were in the habit of attending the Passover
festival every spring at Jerusalem. **42** Accordingly, when he
had reached twelve years of age, he accompanied them in one of
these yearly visits to the capital. **43** After they had accomplished the ceremonies of the paschal week, the family took up
their homeward journey; but the boy stayed behind in the city,
without either his father or mother being aware of it. **44** Supposing that he was somewhere among the party with whom
they were traveling, they did not notice his absence until [each
family assembled for refreshment and repose at] the close of
the first day's journey. They then searched anxiously for him
among all the tents of their relatives and acquaintances; **45** but
not finding him there, they returned the next morning to Jerusalem, to look for him. **46** It was not until the day after their
return, that they discovered him in [an ante-room of] the Temple, sitting in the middle space assigned to the pupils of the
public religious teachers, listening to their instructions, and
eliciting information from them by inquiries. **47** All who
heard him were amazed at the sagacity displayed in his answers to the teachers' questions. **48** Upon seeing him in this
situation, his parents were quite astounded; and his mother
asked him reprovingly, "My child, why have you treated us so
thoughtlessly? We have both been looking for you with the
greatest anxiety." **49** Jesus merely replied, "Why, mother,
did you give yourselves so much distress in searching for me?
You did not reflect that I would most likely be found in the
mansion of my [*Heavenly*] Father." **50** They, however, did not
comprehend the meaning of his expression. **51** He accompanied them, nevertheless, back to Nazareth, where he continued to maintain his filial relations toward them.—The
incidents of this visit to Jerusalem made a deep impression
upon his mother's memory.

52 The youthful Jesus rapidly matured in mind and body,
developing a moral character that won the approbation of
Heaven and the esteem of men.

E   16*

CHAPTER III.

THE INTRODUCTION OF OUR SAVIOUR'S MINISTRY.

(Time, about *one year*.)

§ 18.—*The Mission of John the Baptist.*

(Desert of Judea, along the Jordan; [*March ?*] A. D. 25.)

[1] Now in the fifteenth year of the reign of **Luke III.**
Tiberius Cesar, Pontius Pilate being gov-
ernor of Judea, and Herod being tetrarch of Galilee,
and his brother Philip tetrarch of Iturea and of the
region of Trachonitis, and Lysanias the tetrarch of
Abilene, [2] Annas and Caiaphas being the high-priests ;
the word of God came unto John the son of Zacharias
in the wilderness : [3] and he came into all the country
about Jordan, preaching the baptism of repentance for
the remission of sins, [MATT. III, 2] and saying, Repent ye ;
for the kingdom of heaven is at hand : [3] for this is [4] as it is
written in the book of the words of Esaias the prophet saying,* The voice of one crying, In the wilderness prepare ye the way of the Lord, make his paths
straight ; [5] every valley shall be filled, and every
mountain and hill shall be brought low, and the
crooked shall be made straight, and the rough ways
shall be made smooth : [6] and all flesh shall see the
salvation of God.

[7] Then said he to the multitude [MATT. III, 5] from Jerusalem and all Judea and all the region round about Jordan,
that came forth to be baptized of him, [MATT. III, 6] in Jordan, confessing their sins, O [MATT. III, 7] Pharisees and Sadducees, generation of vipers, who hath warned *you* to flee
from the wrath to come ? [8] Bring forth therefore
fruits worthy of repentance : and begin not to say
within yourselves, We have Abraham to our father ;

---

* Isa. xl, 3–5.

17

CHAPTER III.

THE INTRODUCTION OF OUR SAVIOUR'S MINISTRY.

(Time, about *one year*.)

§ 18.—*The Mission of John the Baptist.*

(Desert of Judea, along the Jordan ; [*March ?*] A. D. 25.)

[Luke III.]

¹ In the fifteenth year from the date of the [associate] reign of the Roman emperor Tiberius, while Pontius Pilate was proc'urator of Judea, Herod An'-tipas tetrarch of Galilee, his brother Philip of Iture'a, Trachoni'tis, and the adjacent territory, and Lysanias of the district around Ab'ila, ² [Joseph surnamed] Caiaphas being at that time the Jewish high-priest, and Hananiah [a former incumbent] his deputy; John, the son of Zechariah, received a divine mandate, while yet in the " Desert " of Judea, directing him to proceed to his destined mission. ³ Accordingly, he passed through the whole neighboring region that borders upon the river Jordan, zealously proclaiming to all, the necessity of immediate penitence and reformation, in order to obtain the divine pardon for their prevalent sins; at the same time instituting the ceremony of *baptism* in token of their sincere repentance, *a* to which duty he exhorted them by declaring that " the predicted ' Reign of the divine Messiah ' was close at hand !"l—⁴ John, *b* as he himself professed,l was the person ultimately intended by that passage of Isaiah,—

" Hark ! in the van of the returning host,
Proclaims the *pioneer*, ' Clear ye the way
Amid the deserts for Jehovah's march !
Straighten the highway for his retinue !'
⁵ Soon to its margin each ravine shall rise,
Each hill and knoll be graded to a plain ;
The tortuous path become an avenue,
And rugged passes smooth for easy ways.
⁶ Then [will Jehovah's glory stand confess'd,
When] all mankind shall see this rescue wrought."

⁷ While he was thus preaching, very many *c* of the inhabitants of Jerusalem, besides the general mass of the people of Judea Proper, especially those living at the mouth of the Jordan,l flocked to hear him. *d* The most of them became penitent under his exhortations,l and submitted to the prescribed *baptism*, *d* which was performed with the water of the river at hand.l *e* Perceiving, among the rest that came to receive the ceremony, several of the Pharisees and also of the Sadducees,l he thus boldly addressed them : " You brood of crafty vipers ! think you to make me believe that anything can have roused *you* to escape the divine vengeance for your iniquity ? ⁸ If you would really avert that doom, you must exhibit the genuine effects of repentance, [in a hearty reformation of your lives ;] instead of flattering yourselves with the boast, ' We are Abraham's descendants, [and therefore heirs to the divine blessing, promised

a Matt. iii, 2.   *b* Matt. iii, 3.   *c* Matt. iii, 5.   *d* Matt. iii, 6.   *e* Matt. iii, 7.

17*

for I say unto you, That God is able of these . LUKE III.
stones to raise up children unto Abraham.

⁹ And now also the ax is laid unto the root of the trees ; every tree therefore which bringeth not forth good fruit, is hewn down and cast into the fire.   ¹⁰ And the people asked him saying, What shall we do then ? ¹¹ He answereth and saith unto them, He that hath two coats, let him impart to him that hath none ; and he that hath meat, let him do likewise.   ¹² Then came also publicans to be baptized, and said unto him, Master, what shall *we* do ?   ¹³ And he said unto them, Exact no more than that which is appointed you. ¹⁴ And the soldiers likewise demanded of him saying, And what shall *we* do ?   And he said unto them, Do violence to no man, neither accuse any falsely ; and be content with your wages.

¹⁵ And as the people were in expectation, and all men mused in their hearts of John, whether he were the Christ or not ; ¹⁶ John answered saying unto them all, I indeed baptize you with *water* [MATT. III, 11] unto repentance : but one mightier than I cometh [MATT. III, 11] after me, the latchet of whose shoes I am not worthy to [MARK I, 7] stoop down and unloose [MATT. III, 11] and bear ; he shall baptize you with the *Holy Ghost* and with *fire :* ¹⁷ whose fan is in his hand, and he will thoroughly purge his floor, and will gather the wheat into his garner ; but the chaff he will burn with fire unquench-able.—¹⁸ And many other things in his exhortation preached he unto the people.

18

in the covenant with him.] I tell you, God could   LUKE III.
supply a posterity to Abraham out of the very stones
that lie strewed about here, [if worthy human successors should fail]! [9] Ah! at this very hour the ax of exter-
mination lies ready at the foot of the trees [in the orchard of
the Jewish nation]; and, ere long, every tree that fails to
yield the required fruit of holiness will be felled to the earth,
and consumed as fuel by the judgments of God."

[10] Upon hearing these denunciations, the populace inquired
of him, "What course, then, must we pursue?" [11] He simply
replied [by instancing benevolence as a specimen of their religious duty], "Let every one of you that possesses two *tunics*
[i. e. shirts], share his abundance with some one who has none
at all; and if any of you has more provisions than he has
special need of, let him act in a similar manner." [12] Certain
publicans [i. e. Jewish sub-collectors of the Roman tribute]
also, who came to receive baptism at his hands, asked him,
"Teacher, what line of conduct must we follow in our repentance?" [13] To these he likewise merely answered, "You
must not extort from the peasantry a larger tax than that imposed by the legal assessment farmed out to you for collection." [14] A third class also, the soldiers [i. e. Jews who had
enlisted as privates in the provincial Roman army], put the
same question to him—"What must we, too, do in the matter
of reformation?" To them he returned answer in like manner—"Deprive no inhabitant of his property by pillage or in-
forming against him, but be satisfied with your allowance of
stipend and rations."

[15] As the people were in a state of suspense in view of John's
procedure, debating in their minds whether or not he was the
expected Messiah, [16] John himself undeceived them in their
surmises by declaring in public, "*I* merely baptize you with
water, [a] to betoken the purifying character of your repentance; but the expected 'Comer' is soon to be [a] among my
disciples, who is so far my superior, that I am unworthy to
perform for him even the [b] menial office of untying [a] and
carrying his sandals. *He* will baptize you in a more momentous sense, enduing some [who cordially embrace him,]
with the miraculous influences of the Holy Spirit, but overwhelming others [who reject him,] with the consuming vengeance of the Almighty; [17] for the winnowing-shovel [of his
testing doctrines] is soon to be grasped by his hand, with
which he will morally winnow the contents of the threshing-
floor of this his ancient heritage, and then he will collect his
true followers, like the precious grain, into the storehouse of
security; but the impenitent, as refuse straw, he will irretrievably consign to the flames of divine retribution."

[18] By many illustrations such as these, John continued for
several months to warn the concourse of approaching events
[under the Messiah].

a Matt. iii, 11.   b Mark i, 7.   18*

§ 19.—*The Baptism of Christ.*

(The Jordan, near its mouth; [*August?*] A. D. 25.)

¹³ Then cometh Jesus from [MARK I, 9] Naza-   **Matt. III.**
reth of Galilee to Jordan unto John, to be
baptized of him. ¼ But John forbade him, saying, I have need to be baptized of *thee,* and comest
thou to *me?* ¹⁵ And Jesus answering said unto
him, Suffer it to be so now; for thus it becometh us to fulfill all righteousness. Then he
suffered him. ¹⁶ And Jesus, when he was baptized,
went up straightway out of the water : and lo, [LUKE III, 21]
as he was praying, the heavens were opened unto him,
and he saw the Spirit of God descending [LUKE III, 22] in
a bodily shape like a dove and lighting upon him ; ¹⁷ and
lo, a voice from heaven saying, This is my beloved Son,
in whom I am well pleased.—²³ And Jesus   **Luke III.**
himself began to be about thirty years of age.

§ 20.—*The Temptation of Christ.*

(The Desert of Judea, and Jerusalem ; [*September* and *October?*]
A. D. 25.)

¹ Then was Jesus [LUKE IV, 1] (being full of   **Matt. IV.**
the Holy Ghost, as he returned from Jordan) led
up of the Spirit into the wilderness, to be tempted of
the devil : [MARK I, 13] and he was with the wild beasts.
² And when he had fasted forty days and forty nights
[MARK I, 13] (tempted of Satan), he was afterward a hungered. ³ And when the tempter came to him, he said,
If thou be the Son of God, command that these stones
be made bread. ⁴ But he answered and said, It is
written,* Man shall not live by bread alone, but by
every word that proceedeth out of the mouth of God.
⁵ Then the devil taketh him up into the holy city, and

---

* Deut. viii, 3.

§ 19.—*The Baptism of Christ.*

(The Jordan, near its mouth ; [*August ?*] A. D. 25.)

¹³ While John was thus preaching and baptiz-   **Matt. III.**
ing, Jesus also journeyed from his residence in
Galilee to the scene of John's operations at the Jordan, for
the purpose of receiving at his hands the same rite, [in
consecration to his public office.] ¹⁴ John [having always
known his relative to be eminent in religious attainments,
and destined to some distinguished sphere of action,] at first
objected—" It were more suitable that I should be baptized by
you, than that you should come to *me* for that purpose."
¹⁵ Jesus, however, replied, " Wave this deference for the present,
and baptize me ; for it is proper that we should both of us thus
fulfill every ceremony pertaining to our respective offices." To
this persuasion John yielded, and administered the rite. ¹⁶ As
soon as Jesus ascended the banks of the stream, after being
baptized, *a* while uttering a brief prayer,¹ suddenly the sky appeared to be parted above him, forming a passage, through
which the divine Spirit, *b* under the physical form I of a *dove*,
was seen to descend and alight upon him. ¹⁷ At the same
time, a voice was heard issuing from the sky, which declared,
" This is My dear and only Son, in whom My highest wishes
meet !"
²³ At the time of this induction into his public   **Luke III.**
office, Jesus (as was nearly true of John also) was
thirty years old, or slightly over.

§ 20.—*The Temptation of Christ.*

(The Desert of Judea, and Jerusalem ; [*September* and *October ?*] A. D. 25.)

¹ Immediately after the baptism of Jesus, *c* as he   **Matt. IV.**
was returning home with his mind deeply imbued
with the spiritual influences there received,I he felt
himself urged by a divine impulse to withdraw into the most
lonesome part of the Desert of Judea, *d* inhabited only by wild
beasts,I and there undergo an ordeal of diabolical temptation,
[as an additional preparation for his work.] ² Accordingly,
having continued there for forty days without having eaten or
drank anything during the whole time, at last, when hunger began to press severely upon him, ³ the Arch-fiend, *d* having failed
in his other modes of attack,I now appeared to him in a visible form, and thus artfully addressed him : " If you are actually the ' Son of God,' why do you not at once order the
stones lying here to become loaves of bread, [to relieve your
wants] ?" ⁴ Jesus quietly replied, " Because the sacred word
declares, ' Human beings are not sustained simply by their
ordinary aliment, but can subsist by other means which the
power of God may provide.' " ⁵ Foiled in this attempt, the
Evil Spirit next invited him to accompany him to Jerusalem,

a Luke iii, 21·   *b* Luke iii, 22.   *c* Luke iv, 1.   *d* Mark i, 13.

19*

setteth him on a pinnacle of the temple, ⁶and   MATT. IV.
saith unto him, If thou be the Son of God,
cast thyself down : for it is written,* He shall give his
angels charge concerning thee, [LUKE IV, 10] to keep thee ;
and in their hands they shall bear thee up, lest at any
time thou dash thy foot against a stone.   ⁷ Jesus said
unto him, It is written again,† Thou shalt not tempt
the Lord thy God.   ⁸ Again, the devil taketh him up
into an exceeding high mountain, and showeth him
all the kingdoms of the world [LUKE IV, 5] in a moment of
time, and the glory of them ; ⁹ and saith unto him, All
these things will I give thee, [LUKE IV, 6] (for that is delivered unto me, and to whomsoever I will, I give it,) if thou
wilt fall down and worship me.   ¹⁰ Then saith Jesus
unto him, Get thee hence, Satan ; for it is written,‡
Thou shalt worship the Lord thy God, and him
only shalt thou serve.   ¹¹ Then the devil, [LUKE IV, 13]
when he had ended all the temptation, leaveth him [LUKE IV, 13]
for a season ; and behold, angels came and ministered
unto him.

§ 21.—John's Testimony to Jesus.

(Bethany-beyond-Jordan ; [early in *March ?*] A. D. 26.)

¹⁹ And this is the record of John, when the   John I.
Jews sent priests and Levites from Jerusalem, to ask him, Who art thou ? ²⁰ And he confessed and denied not, but confessed, I am not the
Christ. ²¹ And they asked him, What then ? art thou
Elias ?§ And he saith, I am not. Art thou that prophet ?‖ And he answered, No. ²² Then said they unto
him, Who art thou ? that we may give an answer to

---

* Psa. xci, 11, 12.   † Deut. vi, 16.   ‡ Deut. vi, 13.   § See Mal. iv, 5.
‖ See Deut. xviii, 15.

and there take his station upon the roof of the MATT. IV.
["Royal Portico" of the] Temple, [on the south-
east corner, overhanging the deep precipice of the
valley of Jehoshaphat,] [6] and then urged him to this display
of his power : "Now, if you are the 'Son of God,' show your
confidence in Him by precipitating yourself off here ;" at the
same time [availing himself of Christ's own method of argument, by] appealing to that promise of the Scriptures,—

> " [For] He will screen you as with able care
> Of chosen angels, whose should be the trust
> a Of guarding you [whatever path you tread
> In life's rough course] ;[1] their active hands, unseen,
> Will stay you, as the gentle nurse supports
> The tottering babe, nor suffers it to trip
> Its tender foot against a wounding stone."

[7] To this suggestion Jesus promptly retorted, "The inspired
volume also warns us, 'Never provoke Jehovah your God, [by
impatiently requiring of Him a special exhibition of His
power].'" [8] [Baffled still in his artifices,] the Genius of evil
makes one more bold effort, by prevailing upon Christ to return to the Desert, and there conducts him to the commanding summit of a mountain [afterward called Quarantania[,
from which he points out to his view, [b] in rapid succession,[1] all
the principalities of the surrounding region, expatiating upon
their grandeur, [9] and ending with this proposal : "I will
pledge you the possession of all these dominions—[c] for they
come peculiarly within my province, and I can enable any one
that I choose to acquire them,[—on condition that you will for
this once prostrate yourself in homage before me." [10] At this
suggestion, Jesus indignantly exclaimed, "Begone, Satan !
The Scriptures command, Bow in homage [or] ' [religious ador-
ation] before Jehovah your God' alone, 'and serve Him' only,
as a superior Being." [11] Having been thus entirely repulsed,
the Enemy of good abandoned the design of tempting Jesus
for the present, and retired. After this, angels came and supplied the physical wants of the Son of man.

§ 21.—John's Testimony to Jesus.

(Bethany-beyond-Jordan ; [early in March ?] A. D. 26.)

[19] The San'hedrim at Jerusalem [hearing of John's JOHN I.
proceedings] sent a deputation from the ecclesiastical orders to inquire of him, "In what character are you
acting?" In reply, [20] the Baptist frankly acknowledged, "I
am by no means the Messiah [as you seem to suppose]."
[21] "What office, then, do you bear?" rejoined they ; " are you
the returning Elijah?" John answered, "I am not he."
Again they asked him, "Are you the 'Prophet' predicted by
Moses?" John still responded, "No." [22] [Discouraged at
length in guessing,] they said to him, "Tell us plainly what
position you do sustain. We wish to return a distinct answer

a Luke iv, 10.   b Luke iv, 5.   c Luke iv, 6.

20*

them that sent us: what sayest thou of thy-   JOHN I.
self? [23] He said, I am the voice of one crying, In the wilderness make straight the way of the
Lord, as said the prophet Esaias.* [24] And they which
were sent were of the Pharisees: [25] and they asked him
and said unto him, Why baptizest thou then, if thou be
not that Christ nor Elias neither that prophet? [26] John
answered them saying, I baptize with water; but there
standeth one among you, whom ye know not: [27] he it
is, who coming after me, is preferred before me, whose
shoe's latchet I am not worthy to unloose. [28] (These
things were done in Bethabara beyond Jordan, where
John was baptizing.)

[29] The next day John seeth Jesus coming unto him,
and saith, Behold the Lamb of God, which taketh away
the sin of the world! [30] This is he òf whom I said,†
After me cometh a man which is preferred before me;
for he was before me. [31] And I knew him not; but
that he should be made manifest to Israel, therefore
am I come baptizing with water, [32] And John bare
record saying, I saw the Spirit descending from heaven
like a dove, and it abode upon him. [33] And I knew
him not; but he that sent me to baptize with water,
the same said unto me, Upon whom thou shalt see the
Spirit descending and remaining on him, the same is
he which baptizeth with the Holy Ghost: [34] and I
saw and bare record, that this is the Son of God.

[35] Again the next day after, John stood and two of
his disciples; [36] and looking upon Jesus as he walked,
he saith, Behold the Lamb of God!

---

* Isa. xl, 3.   † See verse 27.

21

to the body that sent us on this errand; whom do JOHN I.
you profess to be?" ²³ John replied, "I am the person ultimately referred to by the prophet Isaiah,
where he says,—

> 'Hark! in the van of the returning host,
> Proclaims the *pioneer*, "[Clear ye the way]
> Amid the deserts for Jehovah's march!
> Straighten the highway [for His retinue !]"'"

²⁴ The greater part of the deputation belonged to the sect of
the Pharisees; ²⁵ in their jealousy, therefore, [for the mainten-
ance of existing religious arrangements and prerogatives,] they
demanded of him, "Why, then, do you take upon you to baptize, if you are neither the Messiah, nor Elijah, nor yet the
promised 'Prophet'?" ²⁶ To this John returned, "*I* merely
baptize with water; but yonder, in your midst, stands One, of
whose character you are little aware. ²⁷ He, (the expected
'Comer,') although among my disciples, ranks even now as my
Master; [for He was from eternity my Principal,] insomuch
that I am not worthy to perform for Him even the office of
untying his sandal-thongs."—²⁸ These occurrences took place
in the Bethany on the eastern shore of the Jordan, where John
was then baptizing.

²⁹ On the day following, John observed Jesus at a distance
walking toward him, and immediately pointed him out to the
bystanders, by saying, "Yonder comes the divinely-appointed
Sacrifice, who will atone for the sins of the human race! ³⁰ He
is the One of whom I yesterday and before declared, A certain
person ' (the expected "Comer") among my disciples, ranks
even now as my Master, for He was from eternity my Principal.'
^{31, 33} I did not indeed [when I first used that expression] my-
self recognize yonder person in that character, [although well
acquainted with him personally;] but the same Being who
commissioned me thus to baptize with simple *water*, also gave
me this token: 'When you meet a person upon whom you see
the Divine Spirit physically descend and rest, that is He who
is to baptize with the *Holy Spirit*.' ³² Accordingly," continued
John in his testimony, "at yonder person's baptism I saw the
Divine Spirit descend, under the form of a dove, and rest upon
him. ³¹ I was then apprized that this was He, whose public
introduction [as the Messiah] to the Jewish people was the
object of my mission to baptize with *water*, [as a type of the
spiritual baptism which he would impart]. ³⁴ Having personally witnessed the above fact, I confidently assert that He is
the ' Son of God,' [as then announced]."

³⁵ Again on the ensuing day, John was standing in the exe-
cution of his public duties, while two of those who had attached
themselves to him as disciples happened to be near him. ³⁶ Just
then casting his eyes toward Jesus, who was walking within
sight, he repeated the declaration, "Yonder is the divinely-
appointed Sacrifice for sin!"

§ 22.—*Christ gains his first Disciples.*

(Bethany-beyond-Jordan ; [early in *March?*] A. D. 26.)

³⁷ And the two disciples heard him speak,   JOHN I.
and they followed Jesus.   ³⁸ Then Jesus
turned and saw them following, and saith unto them,
What seek ye ?   They said unto him, Rabbi,
(which is to say, being interpreted, Master,) where
dwellest thou ?   ³⁹ He saith unto them, Come and
see.   They came and saw where he dwelt, and
abode with him that day ; (for it was about the tenth
hour.)   ⁴⁰ One of the two which heard John speak,
and followed him, was Andrew, Simon Peter's brother.
⁴¹ He first findeth his own brother Simon, and saith
unto him, We have found the Messias, (which is,
being interpreted, the Christ.)   ⁴² And he brought
him to Jesus.   And when Jesus beheld him, he said,
Thou art Simon the son of Jona ; thou shalt be called
Cephas, (which is by interpretation, A stone.)

⁴³ The day following Jesus would go forth into Galilee, and findeth Philip and saith unto him, Follow me.
⁴⁴ (Now Philip was of Bethsaida, the city of Andrew
and Peter.)   ⁴⁵ Philip findeth Nathanael and saith
unto him, We have found him of whom Moses in the
law and the prophets did write,* Jesus of Nazareth,
the son of Joseph.   ⁴⁶ And Nathanael said unto him,
Can there any good thing come out of Nazareth ?
Philip saith unto him, Come and see.   ⁴⁷ Jesus saw
Nathanael coming to him, and saith of him, Behold an
Israelite indeed, in whom is no guile !   ⁴⁸ Nathanael
saith unto him, Whence knowest thou me ? Jesus
answered and said unto him, Before that Philip called
thee, when thou wast under the fig-tree, I saw thee.

---

* See Gen. iii, 15 ; xlix, 10 ; Deut. xviii, 18 ; Psa. ii, 6–9 ; Isa. ix, 6 ;
xi, 1–5, 10 ; liii, 2–12 ; Jer. xxiii, 5, 6 ; xxxiii, 15 ; Ezek. xxxiv, 23 ;
Dan. ix, 25 ; Mic. v. 2 ; Hag. ii, 7 ; Zech. iii, 8 ; ix, 9 ; xiii, 7 ; Mal.
iii, 1 ; iv, 2.

22

§ 22.—*Christ gains his first Disciples.*

(Bethany-beyond-Jordan; [early in *March ?*] A. D. 26.)

[37] The two disciples above referred to, on hear-   JOHN I.
ing John's remark, immediately attached themselves to Jesus, [38] who thereupon turning round and noticing them following him, inquired, "Do you wish to ask
me anything?" They replied, "Rabbi," (a Hebrew term,
importing *Teacher*,) "where is your home? [We are anxious
to receive private religious instruction from you.]" [39] Jesus
rejoined, "Come, and I will show you." At this invitation
they accompanied him to his lodgings, and spent the rest of
the day with him, it being then about the tenth hour
[i. e. about 4 o'clock, P. M.]. [40] One of these two was Andrew, [41] who, on leaving Jesus, first sought his own brother
Simon (afterward surnamed Peter), and eagerly told him,
'We [whom the Baptist has incited to be on the look-
out] have just discovered the MESSIAH!" (the Hebrew form
of the title *Christ*, [i. e. *Anointed*.]) [42] With ready zeal, his
brother at once returned with him to Jesus, who, as soon as
he saw him, said to him, "You are now called '*Simon*, the
son of Jonah;' but your name [as my disciple] shall henceforth
be CEPHAS," (the Syro-Chaldee equivalent of *Peter* [i. e. *Rock*,
in Greek]).

[43] The next day, as Jesus was setting out for his home in
Galilee, he met Philip, and briefly bade him "become his disciple." [44] Philip, who was a citizen of Bethsaida (in Galilee),
the native town also of Andrew and Peter, [45] went and found
Nathanael [surnamed also Bartholomew], and told him, "We
have just now discovered the One predicted by Moses and the
[later] prophets, in the person of *Jesus* the Nazarene, the son
of Joseph!" [46] Nathanael incredulously replied, "Can any
eminent person be expected to arise from that miserable village of Nazareth?" "Still," said Philip, "Come with me, and
see for yourself." [47] To this proposal the other acceded; and
as Jesus observed Nathanael approaching, he remarked of him
to the rest, "Yonder comes a genuine Israelite, a model of sincerity!" [48] Nathanael, overhearing it, asked him with surprise, "How [being a stranger] have you learned anything
of my character?" Jesus replied, "Before Philip spoke
to you I [mentally] saw you sitting under the fig-tree!"

22*

⁴⁹ Nathanael answered and saith unto him,   JOHN I.
Rabbi, thou art the Son of God ; thou art the
King of Israel.   ⁵⁰ Jesus answered and said unto him,
Because I said unto thee, I saw thee under the fig-tree,
believest thou ? thou shalt see greater things than these.
⁵¹ And he saith unto him, Verily, verily, I say unto you,
Hereafter ye shall see heaven open, and the angels of
God ascending and descending upon the Son of man.

§ 23.—*Water changed to Wine at a Wedding.*

(Cana ; [former part of *March ?*] A. D. 26.)

¹ And the third day there was a marriage   **John II.**
in Cana of Galilee ; and the mother of Jesus
was there : ² and both Jesus was called and his disciples, to the marriage.   ³ And when they wanted
wine, the mother of Jesus saith unto him, They have
no wine.   ⁴ Jesus saith unto her, Woman, what have
I to do with thee ? mine hour is not yet come.   ⁵ His
mother saith unto the servants, Whatsoever he saith
unto you, do it.   ⁶ And there were set there six waterpots of stone, after the manner of the purifying of the
Jews, containing two or three firkins apiece : ⁷ Jesus
saith unto them, Fill the waterpots with water ; and
they filled them up to the brim.   ⁸ And he saith unto
them, Draw out now, and bear unto the governor-of-
the-feast ; and they bare it.   ⁹ When the ruler-of-the-
feast had tasted the water that was made wine, and
knew not whence it was, (but the servants which drew
the water knew,) the governor-of-the-feast called the
bridegroom, ¹⁰ and saith unto him, Every man at the
beginning doth set forth good wine ; and when men
have well drunk, then that which is worse : but *thou*
hast kept the good wine until now.   ¹¹ This beginning
of miracles did Jesus in Cana of Galilee, and manifested
forth his glory ; and his disciples believed on him.

23

⁴⁹ [Convinced by this exhibition of superhuman   JOHN I.
knowledge,] Nathanael exclaimed, "Teacher, you
are indeed the Messianic ' Son of God,' and promised
King of the Jewish people!"   ⁵⁰ "Ah!" rejoined Jesus, "you
do well to believe in my Messiahship, because I told you that
I saw you under the fig-tree ; but [let your faith reach still
further, for] you will yet meet with much greater wonders.
⁵¹ Yes," continued he, addressing the disciples collectively, "I
assure you that you will soon witness miracles wrought by me
stupendous and successive, as if the very sky were parted (as
in Jacob's dream), and the celestials were passing up and down
on me, the ' Son of man,' [who will form the mystic ladder
along which will thus be conveyed the rich spiritual blessings
then prefigured to mankind] !"

§ 23.— Water changed to Wine at a Wedding.

(Cana; [former part of *March ?*] A. D. 26.)

¹ On the day after Jesus's departure from the Jor-   **John II.**
dan, there was a marriage-festival in the village of
Cana in Galilee, at which his mother was present, ² and to
which Jesus and his disciples were also invited.   ³ [Toward
the close of the wedding-week,] the wine provided for the occasion began to fail ; and his mother [in confidence of his
supernatural resources] informed Jesus, " The wine is falling
short."   ⁴ He, however, replied, " Do not interfere with me just
now, mother ; the right time for the exertion of my power is
not quite arrived."   ⁵ His mother, accordingly, simply gave
orders to the domestics to "follow his directions strictly."
⁶ Now there happened to be at hand six stone jars, containing
the water used by the family for their ceremonial purifications,
after the Jewish custom, that might hold two or three *metre'tœ*
apiece [i. e. from 16 to 24 gallons].   ⁷ Jesus, therefore, ordered
the servants, " Fill up these jars with water ;" and they did so
to the very brim.   ⁸ He then directed them, " Now dip out
some, and carry it to the *architricli'nus* " [i. e. president of the
entertainment, chosen from among the guests].   They did so ;
⁹ and as soon as he had tasted the water thus converted into
wine,—not being himself aware of its origin, although the domestics who had dipped it up knew,—he [privately] summoned
the bridegroom, ¹⁰ and pleasantly reminded him, "The rule in
such feasts is, first to set on the best wine, and afterward,
when the guests have satisfied their thirst, wine of an inferior
quality ; but *you* have reserved the choice wine till now."
¹¹ This first instance of his public miracles Jesus wrought
[as above stated] at Cana in Galilee ; and by thus manifesting
his exalted character, confirmed his disciples' confidence in
him.

23*

§ 24.—*Christus makes a short Visit to Capernaum.*

([Middle of] *March*, A. D. 26.)

[12] After this he went down to Capernaum,   JOHN II.
he and his mother and his brethren and his disciples ; and they continued there not many days.

CHAPTER IV.

THE FIRST YEAR OF OUR SAVIOUR'S MORE PUBLIC MINISTRY.

§ 25.—*At his First Passover, Christ expels the Traders from the Temple.*

(Jerusalem, the Temple, Court of the Gentiles; [*Friday, March 22 ?*] A. D. 26.)

[13] And the Jews' passover was at hand ; and Jesus
went up to Jerusalem, [14] and found in the temple those
that sold oxen and sheep and doves, and the changers of
money sitting : [15] and when he had made a scourge of
small cords, he drove them all out of the temple, and
the sheep and the oxen ; and poured out the changers'
money, and overthrew the tables ; [16] and said unto them
that sold doves, Take these things hence : make not my
Father's house a house of merchandise. [17] (And his
disciples remembered that it was written,* The zeal of
thy house hath eaten me up.) [18] Then answered the
Jews and said unto him, What *sign* showest thou unto
us, seeing that thou doest these things ? [19] Jesus answered and said unto them, Destroy this *temple*, and in
three days I will raise it up. [20] Then said the Jews,
Forty-and-six years was this temple in building, and
wilt thou rear it up in three days? [21] (But he spake of
the temple of his *body*. [22] When therefore he was
risen from the dead, his disciples remembered that he
had said this unto them ; and they believed the Scripture, and the word which Jesus had said.)

---

* Psa. lxix, 9.

§ 24.—*Christ makes a short Visit to Capernaum.*

([Middle of] *March*, A. D. 26.)

[12] After this wedding, Jesus made a journey to **JOHN II.**
Capernaum, in company with his mother and her
other children, attended by his disciples also, where
they remained for a few days.

CHAPTER IV.

THE FIRST YEAR OF OUR SAVIOUR'S MORE PUBLIC MINISTRY.

§ 25.—*At his First Passover, Christ expels the Traders from the Temple.*

(Jerusalem, the Temple, Court of the Gentiles; [*Friday, March* 22 ?] A. D. 26.)

[13] The approaching Passover Jesus attended at the capital.
[14] On entering the Temple area, he found numerous persons in
the "Gentiles' Court," selling cattle, sheep and pigeons for the
sacrifices; and near by sat brokers, changing money for the
temple offerings. [15] Hastily twisting some rush ropes [used
for leading the animals to slaughter] into a whip, he plied it
so vigorously that he soon cleared the court of the cattle-dealers
and their stock. [16] The traders in pigeons he sternly commanded, "Carry these chattels instantly away from this place!"
[15] Then overturning the brokers' benches, he spilled their bags
of coin upon the floor. [16] [The only explanation for these authoritative measures that he deigned meanwhile to make to
the awe-struck venders was this:] "I shall not suffer you,"
said he, "thus to turn my Father's sacred Mansion into a sales-
room!" [17] (This remark of Jesus brought to his disciples'
mind the complaint of the Psalmist:—

> "The blood indignant boils within my veins,
> That sinners desecrate Thy hallowed Shrine,
> [Who tread with impious feet its much-loved courts]!")

[18] The Jewish authorities who stood by, [taken by surprise at
Christ's procedure,] asked him, "What miraculous token have
you to exhibit to us, of [divine] authority to act in this high-
handed manner?" [19] "Demolish this *temple* if you will," returned Jesus, (pointing to his own person,) "yet before three
days elapse, I will rear it afresh! [That is the only attestation
of my mission which you need look for.]" [20] "Indeed!" said
they sneeringly; "this magnificent Temple has been already
forty-six years undergoing repairs, and do you talk of rebuilding it at once in *three days?*"—[21] In this remark [they totally
misconstrued Christ's language; for] he referred simply to
his own body, the "temple" of the incarnate Deity. [22] Long
afterward, therefore, when he had risen from the tomb on the
third day after his death, this ominous expression recurred to
his disciples' memory; and the striking coincidence of this
fact with the predictions of the Old Testament, as well as with
this his own declaration, greatly strengthened their faith in
him as the promised Messiah.

F   24*

§ 26.—*The Interview with Nicodemus.*

(Jerusalem; [between *March* 22 and 28?] A. D. 26.)

²³ Now when he was in Jerusalem at the   JOHN II.
passover in the feast-day, many believed in
his name, when they saw the miracles which he did.
²⁴ But Jesus did not commit himself unto them, because
he knew all men, ²⁵ and needed not that any should
testify of man ; for he knew what was in man.

¹ There was a man of the Pharisees   John III.
named Nicodemus, a ruler of the Jews :
² the same came to Jesus by night, and said unto him,
Rabbi, we know that thou art a teacher come from
God ; for no man can do these miracles that thou doest,
except God be with him.   ³ Jesus answered and said
unto him, Verily, verily, I say unto thee, Except a
man be *born again*, he cannot see the kingdom of God.
⁴ Nicodemus saith unto him, How can a man be born
the second time when he is old ?   ⁵ Jesus answered,
Verily, verily, I say unto thee, Except a man be born
of water and of the Spirit, he cannot enter into the
kingdom of God : ⁶ that which is born of the flesh, is
flesh ; and that which is born of the Spirit, is spirit.
⁷ Marvel not that I said unto thee, Ye must be born
again : ⁸ the *wind* bloweth where it listeth, and thou
hearest the sound thereof, but canst not tell whence
it cometh and whither it goeth ; so is every one that
is born of the Spirit.   ⁹ Nicodemus answered and said
unto him, How can these things be ?   ¹⁰ Jesus answered and said unto him, Art thou a master of Israel,
and knowest not these things ?   ¹¹ Verily, verily, I say
unto thee, We speak that we do know, and testify that
we have seen ; and ye receive not our witness : ¹² if
I have told you *earthly* things, and ye believe not, how
shall ye believe if I tell you of *heavenly* things ?—
25

§ 26.—*The Interview with Nicodemus.*

(Jerusalem; [between *March* 22 and 28?] A. D. 26.)

²³ During Christ's continuance at Jerusalem, through   **JOHN II.**
the rest of the week of the paschal festival, numbers of
the citizens and visitors became convinced of his prophetical character, by witnessing the miracles which he publicly
wrought during that time.   ²⁴ He was cautious, however, of divulging his full claims to the Messiahship in public, being well aware of
the real state of their minds, [that their religious views and feelings
were still too imperfect to warrant it.   ²⁵ No person, it is true, had
informed him on these points,] nor did he need such information
concerning any one; for [by his divine omniscience] he was able to
read perfectly the human heart.

¹ Among these half-converts was an individual by the   **John III.**
name of Nicodemus, a Pharisee and member of the Jew-
ish San'hedrim.   ² [Pressed by his convictions, and yet
fearful of risking a public espousal of Jesus's cause,] he at last sought
a private interview with him one evening, and thus introduced his
errand: "Respected Teacher, myself and many others are satisfied
that you are indeed a divinely-appointed religious instructor, for no
person could possibly effect such signal miracles as you are daily
working in our sight, unless he was proceeding under the sanction
of God;—." ³ Jesus cut short this preamble by solemnly declaring
at once, "I assure and warn you, that *unless a person becomes* RE-
GENERATE [by a thorough change of his moral affections through
celestial influences], *he need never hope to share in the ' Reign of the
divine Messiah!'*" ⁴ "How," inquired Nicodemus, [still misconceiv-
ing the nature of that reign,] "can such a total revolution be expected to occur in [the mental habits and relations of] a person of
my age? It seems to me as impossible as that one should be born
over again in a physical sense." ⁵ Jesus still responded, "I solemnly
reiterate to you, that *unless a person becomes regenerate by the influence of the Holy Spirit,* at the same time that he adopts a new religious system upon baptism, he can never come under the 'Reign
of the divine Messiah!' ⁶ As [to your reference to physical birth,]
the offspring of human parents is of course a mere human being;
so [that no repetition of the process, were that possible, could effect
any improvement. But on the other hand,] the product of the
Holy Spirit's operation is [a heart] conformed to His own spiritual
nature. ⁷ You need not be surprised, therefore, at my assertion,
that 'it is indispensable for every one of you to become regenerate
[in moral affections].' ⁸ Let me refer you to the *wind*, [as an illustration of such secret operations in nature,] which blows this way
or that, apparently at its caprice, and you can only hear its murmur
as it rushes along, without at all learning where it first set out, or
to what spot it is hurrying;—equally mysterious is the regenerating
agency of the divine Spirit upon any human heart." ⁹ "Still,"
urged Nicodemus in an inquiring tone, "I do not clearly understand
this." ¹⁰ "What!" exclaimed Jesus, "are you a professed expounder
of religion to the chosen people, and yet ignorant upon this fundamental subject? ¹¹ I solemnly assure you, that I tell you [in my
public discourses, as well as now,] nothing but what I personally
know as an eye-witness [in the divine councils]; and yet you all
seem inclined to reject my declarations. ¹² [You seek explanation
from me; but] if you thus discredit what I tell you of mere *earthly*
requisites, what prospect is there of your concurrence on my
proceeding to disclose truths relating to the *heavenly* world?

25*

¹³ and no man hath ascended up to heaven, JOHN III.
but he that came down from heaven, even
the Son of man which is in heaven.

¹⁴ And as Moses lifted up the serpent in the wilderness, even so must the Son of man be lifted up ; ¹⁵ that
whosoever believeth in him should not perish, but have
eternal life : ¹⁶ for God so loved the world, that he
gave his only-begotten Son, that whosoever believeth
in him should not perish, but have everlasting life.
¹⁷ For God sent not his Son into the world to condemn
the world, but that the world through him might be
saved : ¹⁸ he that believeth on him, is not condemned ;
but he that believeth not, is condemned already, because he hath not believed in the name of the only-
begotten Son of God.   ¹⁹ And this is the condemnation,
that light is come into the world, and men loved darkness rather than light, because their deeds were evil :
²⁰ for every one that doeth evil hateth the light, neither
cometh to the light, lest his deeds should be reproved ;
²¹ but he that doeth truth, cometh to the light, that
his deeds may be made manifest, that they are wrought
in God.

§ 27.—*Christ's Public Labors elicit Further Testi-mony from John.*

(Along the western side of the Jordan, [at the shore opposite East
Bethany?] in Judea, and Enon in Samaria; *Summer* of A. D. 26.)

²² After these things came Jesus and his disciples
into the land of Judea ; and there he tarried with them
and baptized. ²³ And John also was baptizing in
Ænon near to Salim, because there was much water
there ; and they came and were baptized: ²⁴ (For
John was not yet cast into prison.)

²⁵ Then there arose a question between some of
John's disciples and the Jews, about purifying ;

13 And yet [no one else can impart this knowledge ; for] **JOHN III.**
no human being certainly has ever visited the celestial
abode, [so as to obtain this information,] except Him
who is now arrived from thence, namely, the 'Son of Man,' whose
proper residence is in heaven. 14 "[But as you have come in pursuit of religious instruction," continued Jesus, "I will declare to you some important truths.] You
remember that on one occasion Moses reared a '*brazen serpent*'
upon a pole within the gaze of the Israelites wandering in the desert,
[that they might turn their eyes toward it in confidence of being
thereby cured of the venomous bites with which they were afflicted ;
—now, as to His exaltation in dignity and power that you are anticipating,] it is in a similar manner that the 'Son of Man' is destined
to be suspended on high [by crucifixion ; and for a like but higher
object, 15 namely], that whoever relies upon Him under this relation
may be rescued from spiritual death, and gain the immortal blessedness which His 'Reign' affords. 16 Yes, God has so compassionated
the fallen human race as to yield up His dear and only Son, to ransom
the soul of every true believer in him from endless misery, and purchase for him that bliss eternal! 17 Think not that He has dispatched His Son hither to avenge the cause of His peculiar people
upon the other nations of the earth ; his, on the contrary, is the
mission of *redeeming* the souls of all mankind. 18 Every person, therefore, that heartily confides in him, is secure from all vengeance of
the Almighty ; but every one that refuses to do so, is already exposed to Jehovah's sentence, for the very reason that he has withheld his confidence from God's dear and only Son. 19 Their sentence
is based upon this just ground, that the great Illuminator of mankind
has now appeared in their midst ; but they seem to prefer their spiritual darkness to the enlightenment which He offers them, thus hoping
to screen their corrupt principles and actions. 20 For those whose
conduct is reprehensible, naturally dislike such religious light [as
they might derive from candidly consulting such a Teacher], and
therefore they avoid it, lest their iniquity should be exposed ;
21 whereas every one whose course is based in moral rectitude, rather
invites the most searching rays of doctrine, being conscious that his
actions would thereby be portrayed as honestly conformed to the
divine will."

§ 27.—*Christ's Public Labors elicit Further Testimony from John.*

(Along the western side of the Jordan, [at the shore opposite East Bethany?] in
Judea, and Enon in Samaria ; *Summer* of A. D. 26.)

22 Shortly after the close of the paschal week, Jesus went out with
his disciples into the open country along the Jordan, where he continued for several months, [preaching and] employing them to baptize those who received his doctrines. 23 John, too, was now preaching and baptizing great numbers, who resorted to him at a place
called Enon, [i. e. the *Fountain*,] near the village of Salim, which
offered the advantage of numerous springs of water [that did not
fail during the dry season, and was at the same time a little withdrawn from the sultry valley of the Jordan, to which he was usually
obliged to have recourse]. 24 (This was previous to John's imprisonment, [as will presently be related].)

25 In consequence of this simultaneous baptism by Jesus and John,
a discussion arose on one occasion between some of their respective
followers, [brought on by a certain Jewish attendant upon Christ's
public services questioning, in a supercilious tone, a group of John's
Samaritan converts,] as to the comparative efficacy of their master's

[26] and they came unto John and said unto him,   JOHN III.
Rabbi, he that was with thee beyond Jordan,
to whom thou barest witness,* behold, the same baptizeth, and all men come to him.   [27] John answered and
said, A man can receive nothing, except it be given
him from heaven.   [28] Ye yourselves bear me witness†
that I said,‡ I am not the Christ, but that I am sent before him.   [29] He that hath the bride, is the bridegroom ;
but the friend of the bridegroom, which standeth and
heareth him, rejoiceth greatly because of the bridegroom's voice : this my joy therefore is fulfilled.
[30] He must increase, but I must decrease.   [31] He that
cometh from above is above all ; he that is of the earth
is earthly, and speaketh of the earth ; he that cometh
from heaven is above all : [32] and what he hath seen and
heard, that he testifieth ; and no man receiveth his
testimony.   [33] He that hath received his testimony,
hath set to his seal that God is true : [34] for he whom God
hath sent, speaketh the words of God ; for God giveth
not the Spirit by measure unto him.   [35] The Father
loveth the Son and hath given all things into his hand :
[36] he that believeth on the Son, hath everlasting life ;
and he that believeth not the Son, shall not see life,
but the wrath of God abideth on him.

§ 28.—*The Imprisonment of John the Baptist.*

(Castle of Mache'rus, a little east of the Dead Sea, in Pere'a ; [*October ?*] A. D. 26.)

[17] For Herod himself had [LUKE III, 20] added   **Mark VI.**
yet this above all, that he sent forth and laid
hold upon John and bound him in prison for Herodias'
sake, his brother Philip's wife ; for he had married
her : [18] for John had said unto Herod, It is not lawful

---

* Chap. i, 26-34, § 21.   † Verse 26.   ‡ See chap. i, 21, § 21.

27

reformatory baptism. [26][Unable to settle the de-　JOHN III.
bate satisfactorily,] the latter applied to John himself with the anxious question, "Teacher, that individual whom we noticed among your followers on the other
side of the Jordan, and on whom you bestowed such deferential
eulogies, is now actually making proselytes himself, baptizing
crowds from all directions!—[What does he mean by thus
usurping your province?]" [27]John checked their invidious
remarks by replying, "No one can really enjoy such distinction,
except in the order of divine providence; [so that, if he is indeed
exercising the influential ministry that you say, it must be by
divine sanction.] [28]As to myself, you have yourselves just admitted that I publicly declared, 'I am not the Messiah,' but that
I am only commissioned to precede Him on an errand of preparation. [29]As in nuptial ceremonies, the *bridegroom* himself
is the principal person, while his *par'anymph*, [i. e. "groom's-
man," negotiating the match on his part,] who stands at the door
of [the apartment where he is first introduced to] the bride,
merely has the pleasure of hearing him express his satisfaction
at the sight of her features; so my delightful task is now consummated, [when I have thus presented the multitudes to him
of whom you speak.] [30]It must, therefore, be expected that he
should gain in celebrity, while I decline in public importance.
[31]"The ground of this superiority," continued John, [in
reference to Christ,] "lies in His superior origin. A mere man,
like myself, of earthly extraction, can only discourse intimately
of what relates to this world; while He, as coming from heaven, so far transcends any mortal nature, [32]that he reveals the
divine counsels as an ear and eye-witness. Yet how few of his
hearers cordially admit his statements! [33]although this would
only be acknowledging the veracity of God; [34]for in this divine commission he really utters the mandates of the Deity,
whose full inspiration he enjoys, [unlike the limited influence
under which the ancient prophets spoke.] [35]This plenary endowment is from his Heavenly Father's ineffable delight in
His Son; [36]and hence, whoever embraces these promulgations
of the latter, is thereby admitted to the immortal blessings of
the 'Messiah's Reign,' while over all others the vengeance of a
slighted God already impends!"

§ 28.—*The Imprisonment of John the Baptist.*

(Castle of Mache'rus, a little east of the Dead Sea, in Pere'a; [*October ?*] A. D. 26.)
[17]The occasion of the seizure and confinement of　**Mark VI.**
John the Baptist, was as follows. Herod An'tipas
[while on a visit to Rome] had seduced Herodias, the wife of
his half-brother Philip, [at whose house he lodged, to accompany him home. Determined to make her his wife, yet wishing to obtain some sanction in the popular eye for such a flagrant step, he sent for John for that purpose.] [18]But John
promptly told him, "The laws of God and man forbid you to

for thee to have thy brother's wife, [Luke III, 19] MARK VI.
and reproved him for all the evils which he had
done. ¹⁹ Therefore Herodias had a quarrel against
him, and would have killed him; but she could
not: [Matt. XIV 5,] and when *he* would have put him to
death, he feared the multitude; because they counted him as
a prophet. ²⁰ For Herod feared John, knowing that he
was a just man and a holy, and observed him; and
when he heard him, he did many things, and heard
him gladly.

§ 29.—*On his way to Galilee, Christ converts a Samaritan Woman.*

(Shechem; [*December?*] A. D. 26.)

¹ When therefore the Lord knew how the **John IV.**
Pharisees had heard that Jesus made and
baptized more disciples than John, ² (though Jesus
himself baptized not, but his disciples,) [Matt. IV, 12] and
when he had heard that John was cast into prison, ³ he left
Judea and departed again [Luke IV, 14] in the power of the
Spirit into Galilee. ⁴ And he must needs go through
Samaria: ⁵ then cometh he to a city of Samaria which
is called Sychar, near to the parcel of ground that
Jacob gave to his son Joseph.* ⁶ Now Jacob's well
was there: Jesus therefore being wearied with his
journey, sat thus on the well; and it was about the
sixth hour. ⁷ There cometh a woman of Samaria to
draw water; Jesus saith unto her, Give me to drink;
⁸ (for his disciples were gone away unto the city to buy
meat.) ⁹ Then saith the woman of Samaria unto him,
How is it that thou, being a *Jew,* asketh drink of me,
which am a woman of *Samaria?* (for the Jews have
no dealings with the Samaritans.) ¹⁰ Jesus answered
and said unto her, If thou knewest the gift of God, and

* Gen. xlviii, 22.

marry your brother's wife during his lifetime." MARK VI.
[19] Enraged at this interdict, [a] [which was also
coupled with a rebuke for his wicked conduct in
general,] [and instigated by Herodias, who conceived a deadly
grudge against John for this advice, [b] he would have had him
executed on the spot; [but was forced to content himself with
putting him in close custody, [c] (a frequent specimen of his
tyrannical government,) [being apprehensive lest his death
might cause an outbreak among the common people, who revered him as a prophet. [20] Indeed [Herod's own respect for
John's character soon returned to check him from such a violent measure ; for] he had been accustomed to regard him as
a person of eminent integrity and sanctity, and [on account of
his honesty and popular influence, had, to some extent,] made
him his adviser, doing many things at his suggestion, and
listening to his admonitions with a degree of pleasure.

§ 29.— *On his way to Galilee, Christ converts a Samaritan Woman.*
(Shechem ; [*December ?*] A. D. 26.)
[3] [d] Shortly after John's imprisonment, [Jesus, [e] re- John IV.
ceiving intelligence of the fact,] set out for Galilee,
[f] divinely inspired with zeal for his work. [The special reason
for his thus quitting Judea, [1] was his being informed that reports had reached the jealous Pharisaical party at Jerusalem,
stating that "Jesus was now gaining and baptizing more followers than John !" [2] (although, in fact, Jesus did not baptize
at all in person, but only through the agency of his disciples ;)
[from which reports he concluded that their hostility would
operate as a still greater barrier to his efforts in that region
for the present.]
[4] In making this journey, his shortest route lay through
Samaria ; [5] and in his course he one day approached the town of
Shechem, [vulgarly pronounced *Sychar* by the Jews,] situated
near the tract of land which the patriarch Jacob bequeathed to
his favorite son Joseph, [6] where was a well attributed by tradition to the same patriarch. Upon reaching this spot therefore, Jesus, fatigued with the morning's travel on foot, sat
down at once beside the well, [to refresh himself with rest and
a draught of the cool water,] it being now about the sixth hour,
[i. e. midday ;] [8] while his disciples went on to the town itself,
to buy something for a slight meal. [7] Presently, a Samaritan
woman came out from the town, to fill her jar at the well ; and
Jesus [wishing to draw her into a conversation] requested of
her, "Let me have a drink from your water-jar." [9] The woman replied, "I wonder that you, who seem to be a Jew, should
ask a draught of water from me, a Samaritan !" (The Jews
and Samaritans disdain all intercourse with each other [when
they can avoid it].) [10] "Ah !" returned Jesus, [not noticing
her sarcastic allusion to the national feud,] "if you only knew
what a great privilege God is conferring upon you [by this in-

[a] Luke iii, 19. [b] Matt. xiv, 5. [c] Luke iii, 20. [d] Mark i, 14. [e] Matt. iv, 12. [f] Luke iv, 14.

28*

who it is that saith to thee, Give me to   JOHN IV.
drink, thou wouldest have asked of *him*, and
he would have given thee *living* water. ¹¹ The woman
saith unto him, Sir, thou hast nothing to draw with,
and the well is deep ; from whence then hast thou that
living water ? ¹² art thou greater than our father Jacob,
which gave us the well, and drank thereof himself and
his children and his cattle ? ¹³ Jesus answered and
said unto her, Whosoever drinketh of this water, shall
thirst again : ¹⁴ but whosoever drinketh of the water
that I shall give him, shall never thirst ; but the water
that I shall give him, shall be in him a well of water
springing up into everlasting life. ¹⁵ The woman saith
unto him, Sir, give *me* this water, that I thirst not
neither come hither to draw. ¹⁶ Jesus saith unto her,
Go call *thy husband*, and come hither. ¹⁷ The woman
answered and said, I have no husband. Jesus said
unto her, Thou hast well said, I have no husband :
¹⁸ for thou hast had *five* husbands, and he whom thou
now hast, is not thy husband ; in that saidst thou truly.
¹⁹ The woman saith unto him, Sir, I perceive that thou
art a prophet :—²⁰ our fathers worshiped in this mountain, and *ye* say that in Jerusalem is the place where
men ought to worship. ²¹ Jesus saith unto her, Woman, believe me, the hour cometh when ye shall neither
in this mountain nor yet at Jerusalem, worship the
Father. ²² *Ye* worship ye know not what ; *we* know
what we worship, for Salvation is of the Jews. ²³ But
the hour cometh and now is, when the true worshipers
shall worship the Father in spirit and in truth ; for the
Father seeketh such to worship him : ²⁴ God is a
Spirit, and they that worship him, must worship him
in spirit and in truth. ²⁵ The woman saith unto him,
I know that Messias cometh, (which is called Christ ;)
when he is come, he will tell us all things. ²⁶ Jesus
saith unto her, I that speak unto thee am he.

29

terview], and were but aware who the person is that **JOHN IV.**
thus asks you for a draught of water, [instead of declin-
ing the request] you would eagerly make a corresponding petition of him, and he would have granted you *living water.*"
11 To this the woman [not perceiving the force of his remark] rejoined, " Why, Sir, you have no bucket and rope to draw with,
and the well is too deep to reach the water without them ; how,
then, do you expect to get this *fresh water?* 12 Do you think
you are a person of more consequence than our ancestor Jacob,
who furnished us this well, and was content to drink from it himself with his whole family, as well as his cattle and sheep?" 13 Jesus
calmly endeavored to correct her by replying, " Still, every one that
takes a draught of water from this well, will soon grow thirsty again ;
14 but whoever partakes of the water which I propose to give, will
never again thirst for other means of supply.—No, the water which
I afford will itself become a perennial spring within him, bubbling
up with immortal blessedness !" 15 " I should like, Sir," said she
[sportively, still misapprehending him,] " that you would give *me*
some of this wonderful water, so that I should not get thirsty again,
nor need to come here and draw up water." 16 At this reply, Jesus
[resolving to impress her mind with a more serious sense of his
character] bade her, " Go, then, call your *husband,* and come back
with him here." 17 " I have no husband," said she confusedly.
" You may well say," returned Jesus, " that you ' have no husband ;'
—18 *you have been married no less than five times already, and the
man with whom you are now living, is not really your husband !*
You told the fact, [if you did mean to evade my direction.]"
19 " Sir," exclaimed she, [astounded at this exposure of what she
knew he could not naturally have been acquainted with,] " I see
clearly that you must be a prophet." 20 Then [wishing to divert
the conversation from the subject of her private irregularities, and
at the same time obtain his decision upon a question much contro-
verted between her nation and his countrymen,] she continued,
" Our ancestors Abraham and Jacob offered divine worship on this
mountain, [pointing to Mount Ger'izim, that towered near them ;]
but you Jews contend that in Jerusalem is the appointed spot for
the divine worship." 21 " Ah !" returned Jesus, " you may rely,
madam, upon my word, [to which you appeal as authority,] that
the eventful time is rapidly drawing nigh, when your entire nation
and mine will not have the privilege of worshiping our Heavenly
Father either upon this mountain or in Jerusalem. 22 Your countrymen perform divine worship in great ignorance as to its proper
mode and appointed place ; whereas the Jews have a much better
opportunity of knowing what is acceptable to God in this matter,
inasmuch as we are the chosen people from whom the Messianic
Deliverer is confessedly to spring. 23 But [aside from these comparatively trivial distinctions,] I assure you that the time is speedily
coming, nay, rather is now actually arrived, when [these *external,
anticipative* ceremonies are to be abolished, and] the genuine servants of our Heavenly Father must adopt the *spiritual* and *real* kind
of divine worship. And indeed this is the very essence of the worship which God has always claimed, and now especially demands ;
24 for being Himself by nature a pure SPIRIT, those who would worship
Him acceptably must do so in a directly *spiritual* manner." 25 " We
will soon know how this is," said the woman ; " for I am aware that
the Messiah " (meaning " Christ ") " is to appear before long, and he
will then fully resolve all such difficult questions." 26 Jesus replied,
" I who am now conversing with you, am that Messiah himself !"

[27] And upon this came his disciples, and   JOHN IV.
marveled that he talked with the woman ;
yet no man said, What seekest thou ? or, Why talkest
thou with her ? [28] The woman then left her waterpot,
and went her way into the city, and saith to the men,
[29] Come, see a man which told me all things that ever
I did ; is not this the Christ ?   [30] Then they went out
of the city, and came unto him.

[31] In the mean while his disciples prayed him saying, Master, eat.   [32] But he said unto them, I have
meat to eat that ye know not of.   [33] Therefore said
the disciples one to another, Hath any man brought
him aught to eat ?   [34] Jesus saith unto them, My meat
is to do the will of him that sent me, and to finish his
work.   [35] Say not ye, There are yet four months and
then cometh harvest ? behold, I say unto you, Lift up
your eyes and look on the fields ; for they are white
already to harvest.   [36] And he that reapeth receiveth
wages, and gathereth fruit unto life eternal ; that both
he that soweth and he that reapeth may rejoice together.   [37] And herein is that saying true, One soweth
and another reapeth : [38] I sent *you* to reap that whereon ye bestowed no labor ; other men labored, and ye
are entered into their labors.

[39] And many of the Samaritans of that city believed
on him for the saying of the woman which testified, He
told me all that ever I did.   [40] So when the Samaritans were come unto him, they besought him that he
would tarry with them : and he abode there two days.
[41] And many more believed, because of his own word;
[42] and said unto the woman, Now we believe, not because of *thy* saying ; for we have heard him ourselves,
and know that this is indeed the Christ, the Saviour
of the world.

30

²⁷ At this point, the conversation was interrupted   JOHN IV.
by Jesus's disciples returning with provision from
the town.   They wondered at finding their master
talking so familiarly with a Samaritan, especially a female, [in
so public a place;] but not one of them ventured to ask him
what he wished of her, or why he was speaking with her.

²⁸ She, however, [upon this announcement of himself as the
Messiah,] zealously ran back to the town, leaving her water-
jar behind [in her hurry and absence of mind], and cried out
to all her townsmen that she met, ²⁹ " Come quick with me, and
see a stranger, who has told me my whole history ! Is he the
Messiah, think you?" ³⁰ Roused by her earnestness, they sallied forth in numbers from the town, to see Jesus themselves.

³¹ In the mean time, the disciples pressed their Master to partake of the victuals they had brought ; ³² but he told them,
" I have a different kind of food to eat, of which you are little
aware." ³³ The disciples turned to each other with the question, " Can any person have brought him anything here to eat,
while we were gone?" ³⁴ Jesus then explained himself by
saying, " I relish better than my food, to fulfill His design, who
has sent me on my errand of mercy to this world. ²⁵ As you
were [looking at the grain fields by which we passed, you
were] saying, ' It is four months yet before harvest time ;' but
cast your eyes over yonder company of approaching townspeople,—that field of my moral culture is promising immediately
a spiritual harvest, [which you are to be employed in harvesting,] like the yellow crop of ripening grain. ³⁶ Now you know
harvest-labourers receive their appropriate wages, and in this
case they will gather in a harvest of souls for immortal blessedness ; so that I who have sowed, and you who will have har-
vested, may be glad alike [at the prospect of reaping a reward
for our toil]. ³⁷ For in this instance the adage holds true,
' One man sows, and another often reaps the crop.' ³⁸ I am
sending you to gather in a harvest which you have not toiled
to bring to maturity. Others have performed the work of religious preparation, and you now enter the field with the advantage of their previous labor."

³⁹ Several of the Samaritan inhabitants of the town, who
were drawing near, were already prepared for confidence in
Jesus by means of their townswoman's attestation—" He told
me my whole history." ⁴⁰ On coming up to him, therefore,
they pressed him to tarry with them ; and he so far complied
with their request, as to stay two days among them. ⁴¹ During this time, a great many more were induced by his discourses to avow their conviction of his Messiahship, ⁴² and remarked to their townswoman, " Our confidence in him is now
no longer based merely upon your statement; for we have
heard him ourselves, and are satisfied that he is indeed the
expected Deliverer of mankind, the Messiah himself."

§ 30.—*Christ Teaches publicly in Galilee.*

(Various Synagogues in the southern part of Galilee ; [*December* and
January ?] A. D. 26–7.)

⁴³ Now after two days he departed thence,   JOHN IV.
and went into Galilee ; ⁴⁴ (for Jesus himself
testified* that a prophet hath no honor in his own country :) ⁴⁵ then when he was come into Galilee, the Galileans received him, having seen all the things that he
did at Jerusalem at the feast ;† for they also went
unto the feast.

[MATT. IV, 17] From that time Jesus began ¹⁴ preach-   **Mark I.**
ing the gospel of the kingdom of God ¹⁵ and
saying, The time is fulfilled, and the kingdom of God
is at hand ; repent ye and believe the gospel.
¹⁵ And he taught in their synagogues, being   **Luke IV.**
glorified of all : ¹⁴ and there went out a fame
of him through all the region round about.

§ 31.—*The Nobleman's Son cured.*

(Cana and Capernaum ; [*January ?*] A. D. 27.)

⁴⁶ So Jesus came again into Cana of Gali-   `John IV.`
lee, where he made the water wine.‡ And
there was a certain nobleman, whose son was sick at
Capernaum : ⁴⁷ when he heard that Jesus was come
out of Judea into Galilee, he went unto him and besought him that he would come down and heal his
son ; for he was at the point of death. ⁴⁸ Then said
Jesus unto him, Except ye see signs and wonders, ye
will not believe. ⁴⁹ The nobleman saith unto him, Sir,
come down ere my child die. ⁵⁰ Jesus saith unto him,
Go thy way ; thy son liveth. And the man believed
the word that Jesus had spoken unto him, and he went
his way. ⁵¹ And as he was now going down, his ser-

---

* See Luke iv, 24, § 32.   † See chapter ii, 23, § 26.   ‡ § 23.

31

§ 30.—*Christ Teaches publicly in Galilee.*

(Various Synagogues in the southern part of Galilee; [*December* and *January?*]
A. D. 26–7.)

43 On the second day [after that on which he had thus   JOHN IV.
accepted the Shechemites' invitation], Jesus proceeded
on his way to Galilee. **44** This journey was made in full
view of the fact, (which he himself acknowledged [soon afterward],)
that a religious teacher is likely to receive comparatively little respect among his immediate countrymen, [on account of the familiarity generated by long association; yet there were other considerations in this case, which, to his mind, countervailed this disadvantage.] **45** Upon arriving at Galilee, however, the inhabitants
seemed generally disposed to give him a favorable reception; being
influenced by the miracles which many of them had seen him perform during the late Passover week at Jerusalem,—as they were
themselves accustomed to attend that festival.

14 [Having thus reached a field of labor where he had   **Mark I.**
reason to apprehend less hierarchal opposition,] *a* Jesus
now began with fresh ardor] to proclaim the subject of his mission, **15** declaring to the people at large, that "the
destined period of ancient prophecy had now transpired, and the
'Reign of the Divine Messiah' was close at hand!" and urging upon
them the duty of repentance and reformation, through a lively confidence in his announcements, [as a preparation for that
event.] **15** These exhortations he repeated wherever he   **Luke IV.**
went, in his weekly preaching in the several synagogues
[i. e. Jewish chapels] of that region, with such success
as to secure in general the respectful admiration of all his hearers.
14 The report of his arrival and discourses spread with rapidity over
the whole adjacent country, [exciting the universal interest of the
community.]

§ 31.—*The Nobleman's Son cured.*

(Cana and Capernaum; [*January?*] A. D. 27.)

46 In the course of the circuit of preaching thus entered   **John IV.**
upon, Jesus again visited Cana, where he had lately
changed the water into wine. Just at that time a certain officer [of high rank in the court of the tetrarch of Galilee]
happened to be in the village, who had a son lying very sick at Capernaum, [on the lake shore.] **47** Hearing of Jesus's arrival in Galilee from Judea, he betook himself to him, and entreated him to go
down there and cure his son, for he feared that he was at the point
of death. **48** To this request Jesus at first only replied, "Ah! you
[Jews] require miracle upon miracle, before you are willing to believe in me." **49** "O, dear Sir," said the distressed courtier, "do go
down with me, before my dear child dies!" **50** [Affected at his
earnest humility,] Jesus told him, "You may go; your son is convalescent." The grateful father, placing full reliance in Jesus's
words, set out for his home. **51** Before he had reached his house,

a Matt. iv, 17.

vants met him, and told him saying, Thy son   JOHN IV.
liveth. ⁵² Then inquired he of them the
hour when he began to amend; and they said unto
him, Yesterday at the seventh hour the fever left him:
⁵³ so the father knew that it was at the same hour in
the which Jesus said unto him, Thy son liveth; and
himself believed and his whole house. ⁵⁴ This is again
the second miracle that Jesus did, when he was come
out of Judea into Galilee.

§ 32.—*Christ, being rejected at Nazareth, fixes his
residence at Capernaum.*

([*January ?*] A. D. 27.)

  ¹⁶ And he came to Nazareth, where he had   **Luke IV.**
been brought up: and as his custom was, he
went into the synagogue on the sabbath-day, and stood
up for to read. ¹⁷ And there was delivered unto him
the book of the prophet Esaias: and when he had
opened the book, he found the place where it was
written,* ¹⁸ The Spirit of the Lord is upon me, because
he hath anointed me to preach the gospel to the poor;
he hath sent me to heal the broken-hearted, to preach
deliverance to the captives and recovering of sight to
the blind, to set at liberty them that are bruised, ¹⁹ to
preach the acceptable year of the Lord. ²⁰ And he
closed the book, and he gave it again to the minister,
and sat down; and the eyes of all them that were in
the synagogue were fastened on him: ²¹ and he began to say unto them, This day is this scripture fulfilled in your ears. ²² And all bare him witness, and
wondered at the gracious words which proceeded out
of his mouth:—and they said, Is not this Joseph's
son? ²³ And he said unto them, Ye will surely say

---

* Isa. lxi, 1, 2.

his domestics met him with the joyful news that "his **JOHN VI.** son was getting well!" ⁵² Upon his inquiring of them the precise time that he began to grow better, they told him, "Yesterday, just about the *seventh hour*, [i. e. at one o'clock, P. M.,] his fever was suddenly broken." ⁵³ The father, therefore, perceived that it coincided exactly with the time when Jesus told him that "his son was recovering." This fact established his own and his entire family's faith in the claims and doctrines of Jesus.—⁵⁴ This was now the second miracle that Jesus performed at this same village, the former one before going to Judea, and this latter after his return.

§ 32.—*Christ, being rejected at Nazareth, fixes his residence at Capernaum.*

([*January ?*] A. D. 27.)

16 In the progress of his tour, Jesus also visited Naza- **Luke IV.** reth, the village where he had spent his youthful years. On the Sabbath [after his arrival] he attended the religious services at the synagogue, as was his practice wherever he went, and [at the invitation of the presiding officer, he] rose and took his stand at the desk, for the purpose of reading to the congregation [the appointed portion of the prophetical writings, that followed the lesson out of the Pentateuch]. ¹⁷ The president caused the roll containing the prophecies of Isaiah to be handed to him, [directing him to the appropriate section for that day,] Accordingly, turning to the place indicated, Jesus read aloud this [opening clause of the] passage:—

> ¹⁸ " Jehovah's Spirit bids me prophesy :
> For with that holy unction, to my work
> He has inducted me, of bearing news
> Of joy to the afflicted exile souls.
> He has commissioned me, with words of hope
> To cure their tortured hearts ; to cry aloud,
> ' *Deliverance to the captives !* Soon will burst
> The bars that hold you dungeoned,' ¹⁹ and proclaim,
> ' The Jubilee of God's release is come !'
> When He will favor their abandoned cause."

20 Then furling the roll, he returned it to the sexton, and took his seat for the purpose of expounding the passage read, while every eye in the room was intent upon him. ²¹ He introduced his exposition by declaring, "This very day is the ultimate import of the portion of Scripture, which I have just read in your hearing, accomplished in me. ✿ ✿ ✿ " ²² Here [he paused, while] all his auditors exchanged tokens of applause, mingled with surprise, at the eloquent language and delightful sentiments that he uttered [in commenting on the prophecy. As he grew more personal, however, in the application of the text to his own character, their admiration became merged in their rising disaffection with his previous obscure condition among them ;] and the invidious whisper passed from one to another, " Is not this a son of Joseph, our late unobtrusive fellow-townsman? [Whence does this young man derive all these pretensions?]" ²³ Jesus [perceiving their captiousness] proceeded to

G   32*

unto me this proverb, Physician, heal thy-   LUKE IV.
self; whatsoever we have heard done in
Capernaum, do also here in thy country: 24 and he
said, Verily I say unto you, No prophet is accepted in
his own country. 25 But I tell you of a truth, many
widows were in Israel in the days of Elias,* when the
heaven was shut up three years and six months, when
great famine was throughout all the land; 26 but unto
none of them was Elias sent, save unto Sarepta, a city
of Sidon, unto a woman that was a widow: 27 and
many lepers were in Israel in the time of Eliseus the
prophet;† and none of them was cleansed, saving
Naaman the Syrian. 28 And all they in the synagogue,
when they heard these things, were filled with wrath;
29 and rose up and thrust him out of the city, and led
him unto the brow of the hill whereon their city was
built, that they might cast him down headlong:
30 but he, passing through the midst of them, went
his way.

13 And leaving Nazareth, he came and   **Matt. IV.**
dwelt in Capernaum, which is upon the sea-
coast, in the borders of Zabulon and Nephthalim:
14 that it might be fulfilled which was spoken by Esaias
the prophet saying,‡ 15 the land of Zabulon and the
land of Nephthalim, by the way of the sea, beyond
Jordan, Galilee of the Gentiles; 16 the people which
sat in darkness saw great light, and to them which sat
in the region and shadow of death, light is sprung up.

---

* 1 Kings xviii, 1, 45; xvii, 9.   † 2 Kings v, 1–14.   ‡ Isa. ix, 1, 2.
33

remark, "You are probably ready to object to me the **LUKE IV.**
common scornful saying, ' "Doctor, cure ·yourself!"—
the miracles that we have heard say you effected at Capernaum, let us see you perform here too, in your native town.'
24 Now [as to such a test," continued he, "in the first place,] let me
solemnly assure you, [I was well aware, in coming here,] that *no* religious teacher is likely to be cordially received in his native country,
[where he has always been familiarly known in his ordinary secular
capacity; so that your prejudice against me is no greater disproof
of my claims, than the neglect which the ancient prophets in general experienced from their countrymen was of the truth of their
message.] 25 But [in the second place, as regards my particular
course in this instance,] I must remind you of the remarkable fact,
that although there were many necessitous widows among the Israelites in the time of Elijah the prophet, when the dreadful famine ensued all over the country from the total absence of rain during the
period of three years and a half; 26 yet he was not directed to repair
to a single one of them, but, on the contrary, he retired to Zar'-
ephath, a· Phenician town, and there made his serviceable sojourn
with a Gentile widow. 27 Again, there· were lepers enough among
the Jews in the time of his successor Elisha's ministry; but instead
of relieving any of these, he cured only a foreigner, Naaman the
Syrian general. [You perceive, therefore, that the mercies of
God, and the miracles by which they are conveyed, ·have always
been granted solely to those who would be likely to appreciate
them.]" .
, 28 At this reflection upon· their unworthiness, [which they also
construed into a preference for the Gentiles above their own nation,]
the indignation of the audience swelled to such a pitch of frenzy,
29 that they rose up tumultuously, and after violently expelling Jesus
from the synagogue and town, hurried him forcibly up toward the
brink of a cliff rising from the slope on which the village is situated,
with the design of precipitating him off; 30 but Jesus, slipping from
among them [in the tortuous ascent, with which he was familiar],
effected his escape. .
13 Upon quitting Nazareth, [after this unceremonious **Matt. IV.**
treatment,] Jesus repaired to Capernaum, on the shore
of the lake Gennesareth, near the confines of the two
tribes of Zeb'ulon and Naph'tali, which he thenceforward made in
general his place of residence. 14 Thus was signally accomplished
the promise made by the prophet Isaiah:—

> 15 " [For as in former days the Lord debased,
> By the Assyrian's inroads,] all the tribe
> Of Naphtali, and [made thy country too,
> O] Zebulon, [full desolate,] and [bore
> Thy sons as trophies off, O]· Galilee
> Of motley race, along thy boisterous lake,
> And east from Jordan ; 16 [so in future times
> He'll make you all more highly favored far.
> Yes !] those benighted tribes shall feast their eyes
> With moral radiance ; though they dwell forlorn
> Amid the realms that sinful error spreads
> With pall as sable as 'death's dismal shade,'
> A heavenly Light shall dawn upon their path."

33*

§ 33.—*The Miraculous Draught of Fishes introduces the Definite Call of Peter and Andrew, and of James and John.*

(Lake Gennesareth, a little [south?] from Capernaum; [*January?*] A. D. 27.)

¹ And [MARK I, 16] as he walked, it came to pass **Luke V.** that as the people pressed upon him to hear the word of God, he stood by the lake of Gennesareth; ² and saw two ships standing by the lake, but the fishermen were gone out of them, and were washing their nets: ³ and he entered into one of the ships, which was Simon's, and prayed him that he would thrust out a little from the land; and he sat down and taught the people out of the ship.

⁴ Now. when he had left speaking, he said unto Simon, Launch out into the deep and let down your nets for a draught. ⁵ And Simon answering said unto him, Master, we have toiled all the night, and have taken nothing; nevertheless at thy word I will let down the net. ₆ And when [MARK I, 16] Simon and Andrew his brother had this done, they inclosed a great multitude of fishes: and their net brake: ⁷ and they beckoned unto their partners which were in the other ship, that they should come and help them; and they came and filled both the ships, so that they began to sink. ⁸ When Simon Peter saw it, he fell down at Jesus' knees, saying, Depart from me; for I am a sinful man, O Lord: ⁹ for he was astonished, and all that were with him, at the draught of the fishes which they had taken; ¹⁰ and so was also James and John the sons of Zebedee, which were partners with Simon.

¹⁹ And he saith unto [LUKE V, 10] Simon, Fear **Matt. IV.** not: follow me; and [LUKE V, 10] from henceforth I will make you fishers of men. ²⁰ And [LUKE V, 11] when they had brought their ships to land, they straightway left their nets and [LUKE V, 11] all, and followed him.

34

§ 33.—*The Miraculous Draught of Fishes introduces the Definite Call of Peter and Andrew, and of James and John.*

(Lake Gennesareth, a little [south ?] from Capernaum; [*January ?*] A. D. 27.)

¹ ªOn his way to Capernaum,ᴵ the peasantry **Luke V.**
crowded about Jesus, begging him to address them
on religious things. Accordingly he halted at the
shore of the lake Gennesareth, ² where he noticed two boats
hauled up on the beach, the fishermen who owned them having
left them, while engaged in washing off their nets. ³ Getting
into one of these, which belonged to Simon (Peter), he desired
him to push off the boat to a convenient distance from the
shore; and then, taking his seat on a bench of the boat, he
preached to the concourse in that situation.

⁴ After concluding his discourse, he said to Peter, "Now pull
out into deep water, and drop your net for a haul of fishes."
⁵ Peter, however, replied, "We have already worked hard
nearly all last night, Teacher, and have not caught any fish ;—
still, if you say so, ᵇ I will call my brother Andrew,ᴵ and we
will let out the net." ⁶ Upon doing so, they caught so great
a number of fish, when they brought the ends of the seine together, that it began to break with their weight; ⁷ so they
hastily beckoned to their comrades of the other boat, to come
out and help them secure the prize. The fish were so many
as to fill both boats, even to the danger of sinking them.
⁸ At the sight of this miracle, Peter fell in adoration at Jesus's
feet, suppliantly clasping his knees, and exclaiming, "O
sacred Sir, I am not fit to remain in your presence, such a
poor sinful mortal as I!"—⁹ for astonishment and awe had
seized upon him, as also upon the rest in the boat, ¹⁰ and even
upon those in the other boat, ⁹ at the preternatural haul of
fishes which they had just made at Jesus's dictation.

¹⁹ ᶜ "Be not alarmed,ᴵ" replied Jesus, addressing   **Matt. IV.**
ᶜ Peter ᴵ and his brother ; "but come, follow me as
disciples, and ᶜ henceforthᴵ I will cause you to become captivators of human souls [by the force of divine truth,
instead of mere fishermen]." ²⁰ ᵈ Upon making the land, therefore, they drew their boat up on the beach,ᴵ and at once aban-
doning their nets ᵈ and trade,ᴵ attached themselves permanently to him.

ª Mark i, 16 (first clause).   ᵇ Mark i, 16 (last clause).   ᶜ Luke v, 10.   ᵈ Luke v, 11.

34*

21 And going on [Mark I, 19] a little farther   MATT. IV.
from thence, he saw other two brethren,
James the son of Zebedee and John his brother, in a
ship with Zebedee their father, mending their nets;
and he called them: 22 and they immediately left the
ship and their father [Mark I, 20] with the hired servants,
and followed him.

§ 34.—A Demoniac restored to Sanity.

(Capernaum; [January?] A. D. 27.)

21 And they went into Capernaum: and   **Mark I.**
straightway on the sabbath-day he entered
into the synagogue and taught.   22 And [Matt. VII, 28] the
people were astonished at his doctrine; for he taught
them as one that had authority, and not as the
scribes.

23 And there was in their synagogue a man with an
unclean spirit; and he cried out [Luke IV, 33] with a loud
voice 24 saying, Let us alone; what have we to do with
thee, thou Jesus of Nazareth? art thou come to destroy us? I know thee who thou art, the Holy One
of God. 25 And Jesus rebuked him saying, Hold thy
peace, and come out of him: 26 and when the unclean
spirit had torn him [Luke IV, 35] and thrown him in the midst
and cried with a loud voice, he came out of him [Luke IV, 35]
and hurt him not. 27 And they were all amazed, insomuch that they questioned among themselves saying,
What thing is this? what new doctrine is this? for
with authority [Luke IV, 36] and power commandeth he
even the unclean spirits, and they do obey him [Luke IV, 36]
and come out. 28 And immediately his fame spread
abroad throughout all the region round about Galilee.

35

²¹ Going ᵃ a little farther¹ along the shore, he   MATT. IV.
saw the other two brothers, the boatmen ᵇ who
were Peter's associates,¹ James and John the sons
of Zebedee, in their boat, together with their father, occupied
in repairing their nets, [which had also been damaged by the
unusual haul of fishes.]   These two brothers, Jesus now summoned in like manner to be his constant attendants ; ²² and
they, promptly relinquishing their boat and implements to the
care of their father ᶜ and the assistance of the hired men,¹
likewise complied with the call.

§ 34.—A Demoniac restored to Sanity.

(Capernaum ; [January ?] A. D. 27.)

²¹ Upon the next sabbath after his arrival with his   **Mark I.**
disciples in Capernaum, Jesus attended the service
at the synagogue, where he expounded a passage of Scripture [by invitation].   ²² The tenor of his preaching agreeably surprised his audience, for it was with an air of authority far different from the tame and quibbling manner of
the scribes.

²³ There chanced to be present in the synagogue an individual afflicted with a [peculiar form of insanity, induced by]
diabolical control over his faculties.   [A fit coming upon him]
on this occasion, the fiend incited him to shriek ᵈ at the top
of his voice,¹ ²⁴ " Why do you not leave me and my colleagues
unmolested, O Jesus the Nazarene ?   Have you appeared, then,
to destroy our terrestrial power ?   I well know who you are,—
the Almighty's sacred Messiah !"   ²⁵ But Jesus sternly commanded the evil spirit, " Silence! miserable demon ;—quit
your victim instantly !"   ²⁶ At this mandate, the foul possessor
threw the epileptic into one of his violent convulsions ᵉ on the
floor,¹ and after causing him to howl with pain, released him
from his influence ᶠ without doing him any serious injury by
the spasm.¹ ²⁷ This unprecedented cure filled all the spectators with such astonishment and awe, that they exclaimed
inquiringly to each other, " What does this mean ! Here
seems to be an extraordinary preacher ; he lays his injunctions with ᵍ miraculous¹ authority upon evil spirits themselves, and obediently ᵍ they quit the possessed !"¹—²⁸ The
fame of Jesus [arising from this transaction] soon spread over
the whole adjacent country of Galilee.

ᵃ Mark i, 19.   ᵇ Luke v, 10.   ᶜ Mark i, 20.   ᵈ Luke iv, 33.   ᵉ Luke iv, 35.
     ᶠ Luke iv, 35.   ᵍ Luke iv, 36.

35*

§ 35.—*The Cure of Peter's Mother-in-law, and others.*

(Capernaum; [*January?*] A. D. 27.)

²⁹ And forthwith when they were come out   MARK I.
of the synagogue, they entered into the house
of Simon and Andrew, with James and John.   ³⁰ But
Simon's wife's mother lay sick of a [LUKE IV, 38] great
fever; and anon they tell him of her [LUKE IV, 38] and besought him for her : ³¹ and he came and [LUKE IV, 39] stood
over her and took her by the hand and [LUKE IV, 39] rebuked
the fever and lifted her up; and immediately the fever
left her, and she [LUKE IV, 39] arose and ministered unto
them.

³² And at even when the sun did set, they
brought unto him all that were diseased and them
that were possessed with devils; ³³ and all the city
was gathered together at the door : ³⁴ and he [LUKE IV, 40]
laid his hands on every one of them, and healed many that
were sick of divers diseases, and [MATT. VIII, 16] with his
word cast out many devils [LUKE IV, 41] crying out and saying, Thou art Christ the Son of God; and [LUKE IV, 41] he, re-
buking them, suffered not the devils to speak, because
they knew [LUKE IV, 41] that he was Christ :
¹⁷ that it might be fulfilled which was   **Matt. VIII.**
spoken by Esaias the prophet saying,*
Himself took our infirmities and bare our sicknesses.

§ 36.—*The First Tour of Galilee.*

([*February* and *March?*] A. D. 27.)

³⁵ And in the morning, rising up a great   **Mark I.**
while before day, he went out and departed
into a solitary place, and there prayed.   ³⁶ And Simon
and they that were with him followed after him :
³⁷ and when they had found him, they said unto him,
All men seek for thee; [LUKE IV, 42] and they stayed him,

---

* Isa. liii, 4.

36

§ 35.—*The Cure of Peter's Mother-in-law, and others.*

(Capernaum; [*January ?*] A. D. 27.)

²⁹ Upon leaving. the synagogue, after the con-   **MARK I.**
clusion of the services, Jesus accompanied Peter
and Andrew to their home, attended by his other
disciples, James and John. ³⁰ Peter's mother-in-law was at
this time confined to her bed with a ᵃ violent fever ; and upon
Jesus's entrance, the family immediately informed him respecting her, ᵃ requesting his aid in her case. ³¹ Accordingly,
[being shown into her apartment,] he approached her, and
ᵇ leaning over the couch, took her hand and raised her gently
up, ᵇ at the same time exerting his power in a few words for
the suppression of the fever ; which subsided so instantly that
she ᵇ arose well at once, and waited upon him and his disciples [at their supper].

³² After sunset, [which closed the sabbath,] and before it
grew dark, all the neighbors carried the sick and demoniac
members of their families to the house where Jesus was, ³³ in
such numbers that the whole town seemed to be collected before the door. ³⁴ All these invalids, laboring under every form
and stage of disease, he cured ᶜ by simply laying his hands
upon [the head of] each. He expelled the demons also ᵈ by
his simple mandate, ᵉ who shrieked as they quitted the mani-
acs, "You are the Messianic 'Son of God.'" But he ᵉ sternly
checked their vociferations, not giving them the opportunity
of divulging another syllable of their knowledge of his character ᵉ as the Messiah, [lest they might thereby accomplish
their malicious design of impeding his plans by a premature
disclosure.]

¹⁷ In this [relief of the maladies of those who   **Matt. VIII.**
applied to him, not without a sanatory effect upon
the souls of the patients], Jesus strikingly verified, in a physical sense, Isaiah's prediction concerning the Messiah :—

> " [Yet ah, infatuated souls !] it is
> *Our own* infirmities he borrows thus
> Upon himself!—our very woes removes,
> [Which sin has caused, by bearing them himself.]"

§ 36.—*The First Tour of Galilee.*

([*February* and *March ?*] A. D. 27.)

³⁵ Next morning, long before the break of day, Jesus   **Mark I.**
had risen and retired to a lonely spot at a distance
from the village, where he spent the hour of early dawn in private prayer. [He was soon missed, and] ᶠ a general search
was instituted by the inhabitants for him. ³⁶ His host Peter,
[gaining a slight clew from the family,] eagerly set out with the
other disciples in the direction they supposed their master had
taken, ³⁷ and at last discovered his retreat; when they told
him that " all the neighbors were anxiously searching after

ᵃ Luke iv, 38. ᵇ Luke iv, 39. ᶜ Luke iv, 40. ᵈ Matt. viii, 16. ᵉ Luke iv, 41. ᶠ Luke iv, 42.

that he should not depart from them.   ³⁸ And he   MARK I.
said unto them, Let us go into the next towns,
that I may preach [LUKE IV, 43] the kingdom of God there
also ; for therefore came I forth.

²³ And Jesus went about all Galilee, teach-   Matt. IV.
ing in their synagogues and preaching the
gospel of the kingdom, and healing all manner of sickness and all manner of disease among the people,
[MARK I, 39] and casting out devils.   ²⁴ And his fame went
throughout all Syria : and they brought unto him all
sick people that were taken with divers diseases and
torments, and those which were possessed with devils,
and those which were lunatic, and those that had the
palsy ; and he healed them : ²⁵ and there followed him
great multitudes of people from Galilee and from Decapolis and from Jerusalem and from Judea and from
beyond Jordan.

§ 37.—A Leper cured.

(Some town in Galilee; [*February* or *March ?*] A. D. 27.)

⁴⁰ And [LUKE V, 12] when he was in a certain city,   **Mark I.**
there came a leper [LUKE V, 12] full of leprosy to
him, [LUKE V. 12] who seeing Jesus, fell on his face, beseeching him, and kneeling down to him, and saying unto
him, If thou wilt, thou canst make me clean.   ⁴¹ And
Jesus, moved with compassion, put forth his hand and
touched him, and saith unto him, I will ; be thou clean :
⁴² and as soon as he had spoken, immediately the leprosy departed from him and he was cleansed. ⁴³ And
he straitly charged him and forthwith sent him away,
⁴⁴ and saith unto him, See thou say nothing to any
man ; but go thy way, show thyself to the priest and
offer for thy cleansing those things which Moses commanded,* for a testimony unto them.   ⁴⁵ But he went

---

* Lev. xiv, 2–32.

him, *a* and were exceedingly desirous that he would   MARK I.
remain with them permanently."| ³⁸ He, however,
replied, "Come, rather let us visit the *b* other towns
and| villages about here ; I *b.*must| proclaim the coming of the
' Reign of the divine Messiah ' there too, for you know that is
the design of my mission on earth."

²³ Accordingly, he made a circuit over the whole   Matt. IV.
of. Galilee, preaching the advent of the predicted
Messianic times in the different synagogues on his way, and
also curing the invalids and persons deprived of the use of any
of their physical faculties, *c* as well as demoniacs,| with whom
he met.   ²⁴ His fame rapidly spread ·through the whole ad-
:jacent portion of Syria ; insomuch that, wherever he went,
the people carried into his presence all those among them who
were afflicted with any bodily or mental disorder, such as persons confined to their bed by chronic and acute diseases, individuals laboring. under diabolical possession, lunatics and
paralytics.   All these he cured at once.   ²⁵ These public acts
gathered about him a crowd of adherents from Galilee and
Pere'a, especially [that section of the latter termed] the "Decap'olis," and even from Jerusalem and other parts of. Judea
Proper.

§ 37.—A Leper cured.

(Some town in Galilee ; [*February* or *March ?*] A. D. 27.)

⁴⁰ [While performing this tour,] *d* in one of the   Mark I.
towns,| a man *d* all covered| with an inveterate lep-
rosy came in his way, who, *d* as soon as he perceived him,|
[being acquainted with him by reputation,] ran toward him,
prostrating himself in the most humble manner before him,
suppliantly clasping his knees, and earnestly imploring him,
"O dear Sir ! [I understand] you can cure me of my foul disease; if you but please to exert your ability."   ⁴¹ Jesus, com-
passionating 'his case, touched him with the extended hand,
at the same time saying, "I please so to do ; be rid of your
unclean malady !"   ⁴² No sooner had he uttered the words,
than every trace of the man's leprosy disappeared.   ⁴³ Jesus
then dismissed him with this strict injunction, ⁴⁴ "Beware
that you do not divulge the author of this occurrence, [when
you appear at the Temple to get your cure certified ;] but go
directly, show yourself to the officiating priest, and present
the offerings enjoined by the Law ; so as to give public evidence of your purification."   ⁴⁵ On departing, however, the

a Luke iv, 42.   *b* Luke iv, 43.   *c* Mark i, 89.   *d* Luke v, 12.

37*

out and began to publish it much and to blaze   MARK I.
abroad the matter ; [LUKE V. 15] and great multitudes came together to hear and to be healed by him of their
infirmities, insomuch that Jesus could no more openly
enter into the city, but was without in desert places,
[LUKE V, 16] and prayed : and they came to him from every
quarter.

§ 38.—*Cure of a Paralytic.*

(Capernaum ; [close of *March?*] A. D. 27.)

[17] And [MARK II, 1] again he entered into Caper-   **Luke V.**
naum after some days ; and it was noised that he
was in the house : and straightway it came to pass on a
certain day, as he was teaching, that there were Pharisees and doctors of the law sitting by, which were
come out of every town of Galilee and Judea and
Jerusalem, [MARK II, 2] insomuch that there was no room to
receive them, no, not so much as about the door : and the
power of the Lord was present to heal them.

[18] And behold, [MARK II, 3] four men brought in a bed a
man which was taken with a palsy ; and they sought
means to bring him in and to lay him before him : [19] and
when they could not find by what way they might bring
him in, because of the multitude, they went upon the
housetop and [MARK II, 4] uncovered the roof where he was ;
and when they had broken it up, they let him down through
the tiling with his couch into the midst before Jesus.
[20] And when he saw their faith, he said unto him,
[MATT. IX, 2] Son, be of good cheer ; thy sins are forgiven
thee.   [21] And [MARK II, 6] certain of the scribes and the
Pharisees [MARK II, 6] sitting there began to reason [MATT. IX, 3]
within themselves saying, Who is this which speaketh
blasphemies ? who can forgive sins but God alone ?
[22] But when Jesus perceived [MARK II, 8] in his spirit their
thoughts, he answering said unto them, What [MATT. IX, 4]
evil reason ye in your hearts ?   [23] Whether is easier
38

man at once spread on every side the report of his cure   **MARK I.**
with all its circumstances.   Jesus therefore could no
longer safely enter the large towns in a public manner,
a on account of the increased and uncontrollable crowds whom the
fame of this incident drew around him there, with the design of
hearing him preach and being cured of their ailments; | but [per-
ceiving that this enthusiastic concourse would bring his mission to
a premature crisis,] he was obliged to continue his journey through
the more thinly-inhabited districts around, *b* where he could have
greater opportunity for private prayer; | yet even there multitudes
resorted to him from all directions.

§ 38.—*Cure of a Paralytic.*

(Capernaum ; [close of *March ?*] A. D. 27.)

[17c] After accomplishing the circuit of Galilee, Jesus re-   **Luke V.**
turned in a private manner to his chosen residence at
Capernaum; but so great was his celebrity, that it directly
became known that he was at home, and upon this notice,| *d* such
multitudes assembled there, that in a short time no one could get
near even the entrance of the house.| Jesus therefore commenced
discoursing to the crowd, which was also swelled by the attendance
of numerous Pharisees and other ecclesiastics, [who had been attracted by the fame of his teaching and miracles] from almost every
village of Galilee and Judea, as well as from Jerusalem, and were
now invited to take a seat within the house.

In the course of the teacher's remarks it became evident, that he
was ready to exert his divine ability for the cure of any invalids
present.   [18] Accordingly, *e* four men were soon seen to approach,
carrying a helpless paralytic upon a litter, whom they were trying
to convey into the house, in order to lay him before Jesus, [and thus
invite his curative aid.]   [19] Not being able to gain access, however,
on account of the crowd, they carried their patient up to the top
[of an adjoining house through its interior, and so across as far as
the rear balustrade separating the continuous roofing from that of
the gallery that projected over the inner court] of Jesus's mansion ;
f where they tore up the thatch covering of the gallery, after hav-
ing dug through and removed the thin coat of cement over it,| and
then lowered the litter with the invalid upon it, through the ori-
fice, at the feet of Jesus, [as he was preaching from the entrance
of the back hall to the people below, surrounded by the persons of
higher rank in the gallery and adjoining rooms.]   [20] Perceiving
the great confidence in his ability [to cure the paralytic, evinced
by this unusual pains on the part of his friends in approaching
him], Jesus addressed him with the kind assurance, "*g* Keep up
your courage, my friend ;| I pronounce your sins divinely par-
doned!"

[21] Upon this announcement, some of the ecclesiastics *h* sitting by|
began to conceive and even whisper such sentiments as these among
themselves, "Who is this, that presumes to utter such blasphemies?
is not the right to pardon human sin God's alone?"   [22] Jesus, in-
tuitively aware of these reflections in their minds, asked them,
"Why should you entertain such *i* invidious| thoughts.   [23] Which
of these two acts, think you, is the easier to accomplish,—to tell

a Luke v, 15.   *b* Luke v, 16.   *c* Mark ii, 1.   *d* Mark ii, 2.   *e* Mark ii, 3.
  f Mark ii, 4.   *g* Matt. ix, 2.   *h* Mark ii, 6.   *i* Matt. ix, 4.

38*

to say, Thy sins be forgiven thee, or to say,　LUKE V.
Rise up and [MARK II, 9] take up thy bed and
walk ?　24 But that ye may know that the Son of man
hath power upon earth to forgive sins, (he said unto
the sick of the palsy,) I say unto thee, Arise and take
up thy couch, and go unto thine house.　25 And immediately he arose up before them, and took up that
whereon he lay, and departed to his own house, glorifying God.　26 And [MATT. IX, 8] when the multitude saw it,
they were all amazed, and they glorified God [MATT. IX, 8]
which had given such power unto men, and were filled with
fear, saying, We have seen strange things to-day.

§ 39.—*The Call of Matthew.*

(Near the shore of Lake Gennesareth, not far from Capernaum;
[early in *April ?*] A. D. 27.)

13 And he went forth again by the sea-side ;　**Mark II.**
and all the multitude resorted unto him, and he
taught them.　14 And as he passed by [MATT. IX, 9] from
thence, he saw [LUKE V. 27] a publican, Levi, [MATT. IX, 9] named
Matthew, the son of Alpheus, sitting at the receipt of custom, and said unto him, Follow me : and he [LUKE V, 28]
left all, arose and followed him.

CHAPTER V.

THE SECOND YEAR OF OUR SAVIOUR'S MORE PUBLIC
MINISTRY.

§ 40.—*At his Second Passover, Christ Cures a Dis-*
abled Man, and Discourses to his Persecutors.

(Jerusalem; *Saturday, April 12,* A. D. 27.)

1 After this there was a feast of the Jews ;　**John V.**
and Jesus went up to Jerusalem.　2 Now
there is at Jerusalem, by the sheep-market, a pool which

this paralytic, [with the authority requisite to LUKE V.
make the declaration good,] 'Your sins are pardoned,'—or to bid him, [with a like effect,] 'get
up and walk away, *a* carrying with you the litter on which you
lie?'| [24] [If, then, they are both equally above human power,]
I will show you that as the 'Son of Man' I possess the power,
even while in this world, to pardon the sins of men.   Come,"
said he, addressing the paralytic, "get up, take your couch
and walk home with it." [25] Immediately, getting up in their
presence, the now-restored invalid took up the pallet and
handbarrow on which he had been lying, and walked away
with them to his home; praising God for his cure. [26] At this
sight, astonishment seized the bystanders, *b* especially the
populace,| who adored God, *b* for having manifested through
one who appeared to be human, such a divine capacity;| while
others were so overwhelmed with awe that they could only
exclaim, "This is the most extraordinary scene we ever witnessed!"

§ 39.—*The Call of Matthew.*

'(Near the shore of Lake Gennesareth, not far from Capernaum; [early in *April?*]
A. D. 27.)

[13] A few days after, Jesus made a short tour from **Mark II.**
the village along lake Gennesareth, where crowds
immediately gathered about him, at whose importunity he
addressed them on religious subjects. [14] Passing on a little
farther, he observed one Levi, *c*(surnamed also Matthew,)|
the son of Alphe'us, sitting in the toll-house [on the highway,
engaged in the collection of the duties levied on goods trans-
ported], and bade him "become his disciple." Matthew in-
stantly rose, *d* quitted his business,| and attached himself to
Jesus.

CHAPTER V.

THE SECOND YEAR OF OUR SAVIOUR'S MORE PUBLIC MINISTRY.

§ 40.—*At his Second Passover, Christ Cures a Disabled Man,
and Discourses to his Persecutors.*

(Jerusalem; *Saturday, April* 12, A. D. 27.)

[1] The festival of the Passover now drew near, and **John V.**
Jesus visited Jerusalem, [for the purpose of attending it.] [2] Now there is in the environs, near the "*Sheep-gate*"
[on the east side of the city], a certain bathing place, known

a Mark ii, 9.   *b* Matt. ix, 8.   *c* Matt. ix, 9.   *d* Luke v, 28.

39*

is called in the Hebrew tongue *Bethesda*,   JOHN V
having five porches.   ³ In these lay a great
multitude of impotent folk, of blind, halt, withered,
waiting for the moving of the water: ⁴ for an angel
went down at a certain season into the pool, and troubled
the water; whosoever then first after the troubling of
the water stepped in, was made whole of whatsoever
disease he had.   ⁵ And a certain man was there,
which had an infirmity thirty and eight years.   ⁶ When
Jesus saw him lie, and knew that he had been now a
long time in that case, he saith unto him, Wilt thou be
made whole ?   ⁷ The impotent man answered him, Sir,
I have no man, when the water is troubled, to put me
into the pool; but while I am coming, another steppeth
down before me.   ⁸ Jesus saith unto him, Rise, take
up thy bed and walk.   ⁹ And immediately the man was
made whole, and took up his bed and walked. And on
the same day was the sabbath: ¹⁰ the Jews therefore
said unto him that was cured, It is the sabbath-day; it
is not lawful for thee to carry thy bed.   ¹¹ He answered
them, He that made me whole, the same said unto me,
Take up thy bed and walk.   ¹² Then asked they him,
What man is that which said unto thee, Take up thy
bed and walk ?   ¹³ And he that was healed wist not
who it was; for Jesus had conveyed himself away, a
multitude being in that place.   ¹⁴ Afterward Jesus
findeth him in the temple, and said unto him, Behold,
thou art made whole ; sin no more, lest a worse thing
come unto thee.   ¹⁵ The man departed and told the
Jews that it was Jesus which had made him whole :
¹⁶ and therefore did the Jews persecute Jesus, and
sought to slay him, because he had done these things
on the sabbath-day.—¹⁷ But Jesus answered them, My
Father worketh hitherto, and I work.   ¹⁸ Therefore
the Jews sought the more to kill him, because he not
only had broken the sabbath, but said also that God

40

in the vernacular Syro-Chaldee by the name of JOHN V. *baith-hisdaw'*, [i. e. *House-of-Compassion*, or " Charity-Hospital,"] with five porticoes running around it.

³ These were occupied by great numbers of confirmed invalids, such as blind, crippled and consumptive persons, who reclined there in hopes of receiving a cure upon the agitation of the water,— ⁴ which was said to take place when an angel occasionally descended into the pool, and imparted such a virtue to its water, that whoever first bathed in it after this agitation, was perfectly cured of his complaint, whatever it might be. ⁵ Among these infirm persons was a man, who for thirty-eight years had been reduced to a state of complete helplessness by disease. ⁶ Jesus, as he passed by the spot, seeing this individual lying there, and being apprized that he had been thus bedridden for a long time, accosted him with the question, " You are desirous, I suppose, of being made well ?" ⁷ " O yes, sir," answered the poor invalid, " [I come here continually for that purpose ;] but I have no friend at hand to help me into the bath, when the water is agitated, and so, while I am slowly crawling there, some other patient, [less helpless than myself,] steps in before me, [and thus intercepts the benefit.]" ⁸ Jesus at once bade him, " Stand up! take your couch and walk home." ⁹ Restored to full vigor [by the miraculous power which accompanied the command], the man immediately rose, lifted his pallet, and walked away.

The day on which this occurrence took place chanced to be the sabbath; ¹⁰ this circumstance gave the invidious Jewish elders [who met him on his way,] a pretext to exclaim to the cured patient, " Do you not know it is the sabbath to-day ? It is contrary to the law for you to carry your bed!" ₁₁ The man made answer, " [I cannot help that ;] the person who cured me, told me to ' take up my couch and walk away with it,' [and I am doing as he bade me.]" ¹² They then asked him, " Who is it that presumed to give you such an order as to carry your couch about on the sabbath ?" ¹³ But the patient was unable to give the name of his benefactor, [not having learned it ; and he could not point him out,] as Jesus had by this time withdrawn himself from the crowd which the transaction had gathered at the place. ¹⁴ A day or two afterward, however, Jesus himself met him in the Temple, [whither he had repaired to offer a public recognition of the divine mercy in his cure,] and told him, " Observe, you have become a well man ; beware now, that you avoid your former sinful excesses, lest a more severe calamity befall you!" ¹⁵ [Having now identified his benefactor,] the man returned to the Jews who had questioned him, and told them, that " it was *Jesus*, who had cured him," [hoping to excuse his conduct by such eminent authority, as well as render due credit for the benefit received by him.] ¹⁶ But the malicious Jewish chiefs now began to persecute Jesus on this very account, and endeavored to secure his destruction, on the pretext that he had broken the sabbath by performing this cure.—¹⁷ To this allegation, Jesus simply replied, " My Father is incessantly engaged in the promotion of human happiness, and I but do the same." ¹⁸ This declaration incensed his opponents to still more violent desires for his death, for they now urged that he had not only violated the sab-

H   40*

was his Father, making himself equal with   JOHN V.
God.

19 Then answered Jesus and said unto them, Verily,
verily, I say unto you, The Son can do nothing of
himself, but what he seeth the Father do; for what
things soever he doeth, these also doeth the Son likewise: 20 for the Father loveth the Son, and showeth
him all things that himself doeth; and he will show
him greater works than these, that ye may marvel.
21 For as the Father raiseth up the dead and quickeneth them, even so the Son quickeneth whom he will:
22 for the Father judgeth no man, but hath committed
all judgment unto the Son; 23 that all men should hon-
or the Son, even as they honor the Father. He that
honoreth not the Son, honoreth not the Father which
hath sent him. 24 Verily, verily, I say unto you, He
that heareth my word and believeth on him that sent
me, hath everlasting life and shall not come into condemnation; but is passed from death unto life. 25 Verily, verily, I say unto you, The hour is coming and
now is, when the dead shall hear the voice of the Son
of God, and they that hear shall live: 26 for as the
Father hath life in himself, so hath he given to the
Son to have life in himself; 27 and hath given him
authority to execute judgment also, because he is the
Son of man. 28 Marvel not at this, for the hour is
coming in the which all that are in the graves shall
hear his voice 29 and shall come forth; they that have
done good, unto the resurrection of life; and they that
have done evil, unto the resurrection of damnation.
30 I can of mine own self do nothing: as I hear, I
judge; and my judgment is just: because I seek not
mine own will, but the will of the Father which hath
sent me. 31 If I bear witness of myself, my witness
is not true; 32 there is another that beareth witness
of me, and I know that the witness which he witness-

41

bath, but also committed blasphemy, by thus claiming **JOHN V.** equality with God as his proper Father.

19 Jesus answered these charges at length in the following address to the concourse, [and then left his adversaries to make what they might of their imputations:] " I do distinctly avow, that as the Son of God it is impossible for me to perform any act independently of Him, but I must follow exactly my Heavenly Father's example, by reason of the perfect identity of our natures. 20 Accordingly my Father, in His tender intimacy, has empowered me as His Representative [to perform all my official acts, at which some of you so cavil] ;—and the same sanction will yet enable me to effect such grander events, as will compel in you far different feelings of amazement. 21 Thus, as it is the omnipotent prerogative of the Father to restore the dead to life; precisely so will you soon behold the Son reanimate corpses at pleasure. 22 [Indeed, the same principle will prevail in the retribution that awaits the subjects of the Messiah's labors ;] for the Father does not design personally to dispense the award of temporal and eternal justice, but that judicial power is vested in the Son. 23 This will at last oblige all mankind to yield to the Son the same reverence accorded to the Father; although they may now disregard the Son, and thereby really cast contempt upon the Father, [whom they profess to venerate,] while they reject His Representative on earth. 24 Yet here I positively assure you, that whoever hearkens to my annunciations, and thus places full reliance in Him whom I am commissioned to represent, is in virtual possession of the immortal blessedness of the 'Messiah's Reign;' nor is he exposed to the sentence of those who do not share in that reign, having thereby transferred his position from a state of spiritual death and danger to one of moral prosperity. 25 And I further solemnly declare to you, that the time [of that stupendous exhibition of the invested power of the Son of God] is eventually coming,—yes, will be very soon foreshadowed by events of a like character,—when the mouldering dead of the human race will hear the sound of His archangel's trumpet; and at that summons, their sleeping dust will return to conscious animation. 26 For as the Father is [by divine attribute] the great source of vital existence, so also does He equally impart to his Son [in his earthly sphere, by virtue of their community of nature,] the same vivifying power. 27 In like manner is the peculiar province of pronouncing the divine judgments, intrusted to the latter in his appropriate character of the ' Son of Man.' 28 Look not with incredulous surprise upon this my declaration, that the time will finally arrive, when all the tribes of earth, who lie buried in their graves, will hear His summons 29 and issue from their long resting-places, such as have led lives of piety being then animated for a state of immortal happiness, while those that have been wicked will emerge to meet a doom of endless misery. 30 Nor [in this relation as the Judge of mankind,] can I act in a solitary and unsanctioned manner; I pass sentence according to the direct suggestions of the Deity, and my decisions must therefore be just; for [in my whole conduct as Mediator,] I constantly pursue, not any purposes of my own, but those of Him who has commissioned me on this errand. 31 Did I appeal to my own testimony alone in support of my claims, you might doubtless well object to me the common maxim, that 'a man's testimony concerning himself is not valid;' 32 but there is Another whose testimony corroborates mine, and His evidence in

41*

eth of me is true. ^{33} Ye sent unto *John*, and   JOHN V.
he bare witness unto the truth ; ^{34} but I receive not testimony from man ; but these things I say,
that ye might be saved : ^{35} he was a burning and a
shining light ; and ye were willing for a season to rejoice in his light. ^{36} But I have greater witness than
that of John ; for the works which the Father hath
given me to finish, the same works that I do bear witness of me, that the Father hath sent me ; ^{37} and the
Father himself which hath sent me, hath borne witness
of me : ye have neither heard his voice at any time,
nor seen his shape. ^{38} And ye have not his word
abiding in you ; for whom he hath sent, him ye believe
not : ^{39} search the scriptures, for in them ye think ye
have eternal life ; and they are they which testify of
me : ^{40} and ye will not come to me, that ye might have
life. ^{41} I receive not honor from men : ^{42} but I know
you, that ye have not the love of God in you. $_{43}$ I am
come in my Father's name, and ye receive me not ; if
another shall come in his own name, him ye will receive. ^{44} How can ye believe which receive honor
one of another, and seek not the honor that cometh
from God only ? ^{45} Do not think that I will accuse
you to the Father ; there is one that accuseth you,
even Moses, in whom ye trust : ^{46} for had ye believed
Moses, ye would have believed me, for he wrote of
me ; ^{47} but if ye believe not his writings, how shall ye
believe my words ?

§ 41. — *Christ Defends his Disciples for Plucking*
Grain on the Sabbath.

([On their Way to Galilee?] *Saturday, April* 19, A. D. 27.)

^{1} At that time Jesus went on the [LUKE VI, 1]   **Matt. XII.**
second sabbath-day [LUKE VI, 1] after the first
through the corn, and his disciples were a-hungered,
and began to pluck the ears of corn [MARK II, 23] as they
42

my behalf is perfectly irrefragable. [33] [In your pre-   **JOHN V.**
tended desire to ascertain the truth,] you sent a deputation to John the Baptist on the subject of the Messiah;
and he returned a righteous answer in my support. [34] I do not refer to this, because I have any need of human testimony to substantiate my claims; but merely say what I do concerning John,
from a desire to save you from your fatal unbelief, [even by that
means of conviction, if possible.] [35] He was indeed [all that you
called him,] a 'blazing, brilliant Light' in a religious sense, and
you were yourselves delighted with basking in his instructive radiance for a little while at first; [but how soon you forsook him, and
slighted his annunciations!] [36] Marked, however, as were his allu-
sions to me, I have a still stronger evidence in my behalf than that
of John; the very miracles and other acts, which my Father has
assigned me to accomplish here, testify [by their fulfillment in exact
accordance with His character and predictions, as well as by the
divine power required to effect them,] that He has commissioned
me to perform them. [37] Nay, my Father Himself, who has dispatched me on my mission, has given His direct testimony to my
character in descriptive announcements of old; although, it is true,
you have never heard Him audibly, nor seen Him ocularly appear,
in confirmation of my mission, [He having afforded you equally
positive communications of His mind on this subject.] [38] But it is
plain, His Word has no deep hold in your convictions [as to its true
import and application]; or you would not thus reject His Messenger as therein announced. [39] You do, I grant, take great pains in
examining the Scriptures as to their *literal* sense, because even you
are convinced that the means of securing immortal blessedness are
really contained in them, (although your carnal blindness prevents
your perceiving that they distinctly point to me;) [40] and yet you
inconsistently refuse to resort to me for the attainment of that very
blessedness. [41] I do not speak thus as courting human esteem by
gaining votaries; [42] but I would fain make you aware that genuine
love toward God is a stranger to your breasts. [43] This is proved by
the fact that you reject me, who come to you as my Father's representative; whereas if some one else should appear with his own
pretensions merely to sustain him, you would, as often before, cordially welcome him! [44] [This perversity of your judgment has its
origin in the worldliness of your feelings;] how can you hope to
exercise proper religious faith, when you are all so ambitious of
distinction among yourselves, and neglect the true moral distinction
which regards the divine approbation alone? [45] Yet do not infer from
this, that I am about to accuse you before my Father; no, [there is no
need of that, for]-there is one who already virtually charges you with
a most criminal heresy, and that one is the very Moses on whom you
so zealously rely. [46] But if you really had proper faith in him, you
would put confidence also in me; for he unequivocally refers to me in
his writings. [47] If, then, you so little believe what *he* has written, I
cannot expect you to give much credit to what I say."

§ 41.—*Christ Defends his Disciples for Plucking Grain on the
Sabbath.*

([On their Way to Galilee?] *Saturday, April* 19, A. D. 27.)

[1] As Jesus was passing along through some fields of   **Matt. XII.**
ripe barley, attended by his disciples, *a* on the follow-
ing Sabbath,| the latter, being somewhat hungry, pulled off a few

a Luke vi, 1.

42*

went, and to eat, [LUKE VI, 1] rubbing them in   MATT. XII.
their hands: ² but when the Pharisees saw
it, they said unto him, Behold, thy disciples do that
which is not lawful to do upon the sabbath-day.   ³ But
he said unto them, Have ye not read* what David did,
when he [MARK II, 25] had need and was a-hungered, and
they that were with him; ⁴ how he entered into the
house of God, [MARK II, 26] in the days of Abiathar the high-
priest, and did [LUKE VI, 4] take and eat the show-bread,
[LUKE VI, 4] and gave also to them that were with him, which
was not lawful† for him to eat, neither for them which
were with him, but only for the priests?   ⁵ Or have
ye not read in the law,‡ how that on the sabbath-days
the priests in the temple profane the sabbath, and are
blameless? ⁶ but I say unto you, that in this place is
one greater than the temple.   ⁷ But if ye had known
what this meaneth,‖ I will have mercy and not sacrifice, ye would not have condemned the guiltless.
[MARK II, 27] And he said unto them, The sabbath was made for
man, and not man for the sabbath: ⁸ for the Son of man
is Lord even of the sabbath-day.

§ 42.—*The Cure of the Withered Hand.*

([Capernaum?] *Saturday, April* [26?], A. D. 27.)

¹ And [MATT. XII, 9] when he was departed thence,   **Mark III.**
he entered again [LUKE VI, 6] on another sabbath
into the synagogue, [LUKE VI, 6] and taught.   And there
was a man there which had a withered [LUKE VI, 6] right
hand: [LUKE VI, 7] and the scribes and Pharisees [MATT. XII, 10]
asked him saying, Is it lawful to heal on the sabbath-days?
² And they watched him, whether he would heal him
on the sabbath-day; that they might accuse him.
³ And he [LUKE VI, 8] knew their thoughts, and saith unto

---

* 1 Sam. xxi, 1–6. † Lev. xxiv, 9. ‡ Num. xxviii, 9, 10, 18, 19.
‖ Hosea vi, 6; compare 1 Sam. xv, 22.

heads of the grain near them, and were eating the   MATT. XII.
kernels *a* which they rubbed out in their hands,|
[as was the common practice with travelers.]
[2] A number of Pharisees close by, who had noticed this act, immediately came up to the party and exclaimed to Jesus, "See,
you are allowing your disciples to violate the sabbath by that
kind of manual labor!" [3] "Well," replied Jesus, "did you
never read in the Scriptures, what King David and his men
once did, when they were pressed by hunger? [4] how he went
into the Tabernacle, *b* in the younger days of that Abi'athar
whose subsequent history as High-Priest so much depended
upon this incident,| and *c* took| the loaves of 'Show-Bread'
from Ahim'elech's hands, sharing in eating them with his comrades, although it was contrary to the law for any person whatever to eat them except the priests. [5] Again, have you not
noticed the directions of that Law, in observance of which the
priests constantly infringe the rest otherwise required on the
sabbath, by offering the sacrifices in the Temple on that day?
and yet they are guilty of no crime. [6] Now let me tell you, a
much greater personage than any of the priests is concerned
in the present transaction. [7] If you had only *d* ascertained| the
true force of that passage,—

    'To Me the promptings of a heart humane
    Are dearer far than costly sacrifice,'—

you would not thus have charged my innocent disciples with
impiety, [in simply appeasing their hunger.] *e* You ought to
have known, that the sabbath was instituted for the benefit of
mankind, and not man created merely to observe that ordi-
nance;| [8] and [such being its provisional nature,] I have cer-
tainly the right, as the divinely-deputed 'Son of Man,' to
modify its strictness as I think proper."

§ 42.—*The Cure of the Withered Hand.*

([Capernaum ?] *Saturday, April* [26 ?], A. D. 27.)

[1] *f* Having proceeded on his journey,| Jesus once   **Mark III.**
more resorted to the synagogue *f* of the place to
which he came,| *g* on a subsequent sabbath, and discoursed to
the assembly.| There was present a man whose *g* right| hand
had become shriveled and useless by disease; *h* certain Phari-
sees and other ecclesiastics, therefore, who were there,| [know-
ing his practice,] *i* put this question to Jesus, "whether it were
lawful to cure a complaint on the sabbath?"| [2] watching his
answer and conduct upon the suggestion, in hopes of finding
an occasion of charging him with violating the sabbath, by
recommending and performing such an act on that day.
[3] *j* Well aware of their secret intentions,| he bade the afflicted

a Luke vi, 1.   *b* Mark ii, 26.   *c* Luke vi, 4.   *d* Matt. ix, 13.   *e* Mark ii, 27.
f Matt. xii, 9.   *g* Luke vi, 6.   *h* Luke vi, 7.   *i* Matt. xii, 10.   *j* Luke vi, 8.

the man which had the withered hand,   MARK III.
[LUKE VI, 8] Rise up and stand forth [LUKE VI, 8]
in the midst: and he arose and stood forth.   ⁴ And he saith
unto them, [LUKE VI, 9] I will ask you one thing: Is it lawful to do good on the sabbath-days, or to do evil?
to save life, or to kill? but they held their peace.
[MATT. XII, 11] And he said unto them, What man shall there be
among you, that shall have one sheep, and if it fall into a pit
on the sabbath-day, will he not lay hold on it and lift it out?
[12] how much then is a man better than a sheep! wherefore it
is lawful to do well on the sabbath-days.   ⁵ And when he
had looked round about on them with anger, being
grieved for the hardness of their hearts, he saith unto
the man, Stretch forth thine hand: and he stretched
it out; and his hand was restored whole as the other.
⁶ And the Pharisees [LUKE VI, 11] were filled with madness,
and went forth and straightway took counsel with the
Herodians against him, how they might destroy him.

§ 43.—*Multitudes are Cured of their Diseases.*

(Lake Gennesareth, near Capernaum; [early in] *May,* A. D. 27.)

⁷ But [MATT. XII, 15] when Jesus [MATT. XII, 15] knew it, he
withdrew himself with his disciples to the sea: and a
great multitude from Galilee followed him, and from
Judea ⁸ and from Jerusalem and from Idumea and from
beyond Jordan; and they about Tyre and Sidon, a
great multitude, when they had heard what great things
he did, came unto him.   ⁹ And he spake to his disciples, that a small ship should wait on him, because of
the multitude, lest they should throng him: ¹⁰ for
he had healed [MATT. XII, 15] all; insomuch that they
pressed upon him for to touch him, as many as had
plagues; ¹¹ and unclean spirits, when they saw him,
fell down before him, and cried saying, Thou art the
Son of God. ¹² And he straitly charged them that
they should not make him known.

44.

man " *a* rise up and ! stand out *a* in the middle of MARK III.
the floor,"! [that all might see what was about to
occur.] *a* The patient having taken his stand as
directed,! ⁴ Jesus then said to his inquirers, " Before I answer
your question, *b* let me ask you another,! Which is the more
lawful act on the sabbath, to confer a *benefit* or to do an *injury ?*
—to save human life, [as I am engaged in doing,] or destroy
it, [as you seek to do?" Confounded at this reflection upon
themselves,] they made no reply. *c* "Suppose," continued he,
" one of you were to own a single sheep, and it should chance
to fall into a dangerous hole on the sabbath ; would you not
take hold and lift it out immediately?! *d* how much rather,
then, ought one to relieve a human being, who is of such superior importance to a sheep! It is evidently right, therefore,
to perform such good acts as a cure on the sabbath."!   ⁵ Then
looking around upon his captious auditors, with a feeling of
indignation mingled with pain at the callous blindness of their
minds [in resisting so natural a conclusion,] he turned to the
patient and directed him to "straighten out his hand." The
virtue attending the command enabled the man at once to
perform it, his hand being restored *e* to perfect soundness like
the other.!   ⁶ No sooner had the Pharisees, *f* who were now
more furiously exasperated by their refutation than ever,! left
the house, than they began to *f* plot among themselves,! and
concert measures with the " Herodians " for the destruction
of Jesus.

§ 43.—*Multitudes are Cured of their Diseases.*

(Lake Gennesareth, near Capernaum ; [early in] *May*, A. D. 27.

⁷ Jesus, *g* learning that this violent conspiracy was forming
against him,! retired with his disciples to the shore of the lake
Gennesareth. He was followed thither by vast crowds not
merely from Galilee, but also from Judea generally, ⁸ as well
as from Jerusalem, and even from Idume'a and Pere'a ; multitudes, too, from Tyre and Sidon and their vicinity, hearing the
fame of his miracles, resorted to him. ⁹ The concourse at last
obliged him to request his disciples to get one of their boats
ready for his reception, while he preached to the throng, so
that he might not be uncomfortably crowded ; ¹⁰ for, as he
cured all the diseased who came, every one who had any complaint was so anxious to get near and touch him, that there
was a general rush upon him. ¹¹ Demoniacs also, as soon as
they saw him, fell on the ground before him, shrieking out,
" You are the Son of God !" ¹² These evil spirits, however, he
strictly and repeatedly commanded, [as he was expelling
them,] not to disclose his full character in this public
manner.

a Luke vi, 8.   *b* Luke vi, 9.   *e* Matt. xii, 11.   *d* Matt. xii, 12.
e Matt. xii, 13.   *f* Luke vi, 11.   *g* Matt. xii, 15.

44*

17 That it might be fulfilled which was   **Matt. XII.**
spoken by Esaias the prophet saying,*
18 Behold my servant whom I have chosen, my beloved in whom my soul is well pleased : I will put my
Spirit upon him, and he shall show judgment to the
Gentiles.   19 He shall not strive nor cry, neither shall
any man hear his voice in the streets : 20 a bruised
reed shall he not break, and smoking flax shall he not
quench; till he send forth judgment unto victory.
21 And in his name shall the Gentiles trust.

§. 44.—*After a Night spent in Prayer, Christ Selects
his Twelve Apostles.*

(A Mountain near Capernaum; [*May ?*] A. D. 27.]

12 And it came to pass in those days, that   **Luke VI.**
he went out into a mountain to pray, and
continued all night in prayer to God.   13 And when it
was day, he called unto him his disciples [MARK III, 13]
whom he would, and they came unto him : and of them he
chose twelve, whom also he named *apostles* ; [MARK III, 14]
that they should be with him, and that he might send them
forth to preach, [15] and to have power to heal sicknesses, and
to cast out devils.   [MATT. X, 2] Now their names are these:
The first 14 Simon (whom he also named Peter) and
Andrew his brother, James [MATT. X, 2] the son of Zebedee
and John [MARK III, 17] his brother, (and he surnamed them
Boanerges, which is, The sons of thunder,) Philip and Bartholomew, 15 Matthew [MATT. X, 3] the publican and Thomas, James the son of Alpheus and Simon called *Ze-
lotes*, 16 and Judas the brother of James [MATT. X, 3] (or
Lebbeus whose surname was Thaddeus) and Judas Iscariot,
which also was the traitor.

* Isa. xlii, 1–4.

45

¹⁷ In these circumstances was signally fulfilled the **Matt. XII.**
prediction of the prophet Isaiah,—

¹⁸ "Behold, the times of the Messiah come!—
That Minister by Heaven's high patronage
Sustained, his great commission to fulfill;
The peerless favorite of My sanctioning love!
My Spirit's influence he shall enjoy,
To herald forth My will to all mankind.
Yet meek his temper and his words will be,—
¹⁹ No clamor, pompous shouts nor loud debate
Will mark his passage in life's thoroughfare.
²⁰ But, though his accents bland will meet the ear
Of all the sorrowing, (like the lenient hand
That spares to snap a shattered walking-reed,)
Nor quench the latent hope of comfort there,—
A faintly glimmering spark of smoldering wick;
Still he will vindicate triumphantly
The sovereign method of My saving grace.
[For never will his mission flag nor fail,
Sustained by power divine in human hands,
Until eventually o'er all the earth
He will establish the celestial plan,]
²¹ And distant Gentiles learn to look to him,
With hopes obedient in his gracious words."

§ 44.—*After a Night spent in Prayer, Christ Selects his Twelve
Apostles.*

(A Mountain near Capernaum; [*May ?*] A. D. 27.)

¹² About this time, Jesus ascended alone a mountain   **Luke VI.**
in the vicinity, where he remained all the night, en-
gaged in private meditation and prayer. ¹³ At day-light
he summoned his disciples, *a* having previously directed such as he
wished to repair to him at that time, | and selected from among them
twelve, on whom he imposed the title of *Apostles* [i. e. envoys];
b appointing them to be his constant companions and messengers to
proclaim his doctrines, | *c* and empowering them to cure diseases and
exorcise demons. | The names of these twelve were as follows:—

{ ¹⁴ SIMON I., whom he surnamed Peter, *d* (being the first disciple that he adopted;) |
{ ANDREW [his Greek name], Peter's brother;
{ JAMES I., } *e* the sons of Zebedee, (which two brothers he used to call the *Boan'-*
{ JOHN;   }   *ērgets'*, [the Galilean pronunciation of the Syro-Chaldee words *Be-*
         nai' Rĕgāz', " sons of commotion "] or " sons of thunder," [on account of their
         impetuous temper];) |
{ PHILIP [his Greek name];
{ NATHANAEL, surnamed Bartholomew [i. e. son-of-Tolmai];
{ ¹⁵ LEVI, otherwise called Matthew, *f* formerly a *Por'titor* [i. e. sub-collector of Ro-
{   man customs];|
{ THOMAS [from the Hebrew *tĕōm'*, i. e. " twin"];
{ JAMES II., the [supposed] son of Alphe'us;
{ SIMON II., *g* known as the "Ca'nanite" ([from the Syro-Chaldee *canawn'*, i. e.
   jealous],| from his having belonged to that party of " Zealots " [against relig-
   ious innovation among the Jews]);
{ ¹⁶ JUDE I., another brother of the last James, *f* surnamed Lebbe'us and likewise
{   Thadde'us;|
{ JUDAS II., distinguished by the epithet of the "Iscariot" [from the Hebrew *Ish-
   Kĕriŏth'*, i. e. " man of Ke'rioth," that being his native place], (who eventually
   became the base betrayer *g* of his Master.)|

a Mark iii, 13.   *b* Mark iii, 14.   *c* Mark iii, 15.   *d* Matt. x, 2.
     e Mark iii, 17.   *f* Matt. x, 3.   *g* Matt. x, 4.

45*

[17] And he came down with them and   LUKE VI.
stood in the plain; and the company of his
disciples and a great multitude of people out of all
Judea and Jerusalem, and from the sea-coast of Tyre
and Sidon, which came to hear him and to be healed
of their diseases; [18] and they that were vexed with
unclean spirits: and they were healed. [19] And the
whole multitude sought to touch him; for there went
virtue out of him, and healed them all.

§ 45.—*The Sermon on the Mount.*

(Near Capernaum; [*May?*] A. D. 27.)

[1] And seeing the multitudes, he went up   **Matt. V.**
into a mountain; and when he was set, his
disciples came unto him: [2] and he opened his mouth
[LUKE VI, 20] to his disciples, and taught them saying,
[3] Blessed are [LUKE VI, 20] ye the poor in spirit, for theirs
is the kingdom of heaven;* [6] blessed are they which
do hunger and thirst [LUKE VI, 21] now after righteousness,
for they shall be filled; [4] blessed are they that mourn,
for they shall be comforted;† [LUKE VI, 21] blessed are ye
that weep now, for ye shall laugh; [5] blessed are the meek,
for they shall inherit the earth;‡ [9] blessed are the
peace-makers, for they shall be called the children of
God; [7] blessed are the merciful, for they shall obtain
mercy; [8] blessed are the pure in heart, for they shall
see God; [10] blessed are they which are persecuted for
righteousness' sake, for theirs is the kingdom of heav-
en; [11] blessed are ye when men shall [LUKE VI, 22] hate
you and revile you and persecute you, and shall
[LUKE VI, 22] separate you from their company, and say all
manner of evil against you falsely for my sake;
[12] rejoice [LUKE VI, 23] in that day and be exceeding glad,

---

* See Isa. lxvi, 2; lvii, 15.   † Compare Isa. lxi, 2.
‡ See Psa. xxxvii, 11.

¹⁷After having made choice of these, he descended LUKE VI.
with them to a more level part of the mountain, where
he stood surrounded by the rest of his disciples, together
with a great concourse of people from the whole of Judea, including
numbers from Jerusalem, as well as from the maritime district of
Tyre and Sidon, who had resorted thither, to hear him discourse
and be cured of their multifarious complaints, ¹⁸among them numbers severely afflicted with demoniacal possession. ¹⁹Indeed such
divine efficacy was manifestly exerted by him, in fully relieving all
these cases, that the entire crowd was eager to touch him, so as to
experience this curative virtue.

§ 45.—*The Sermon on the Mount.*

(Near Capernaum; [*May ?*] A. D. 27.)

Subject: GOSPEL TRUTHS, IN CONTRAST WITH THE ARROGANT HY-
POCRISY OF THE PHARISEES.

. ¹Perceiving the great concourse that was gathered **Matt. V.**
about him, Jesus moved to an eminence [which gave
him a convenient command of the gentle slope] of the
mountain, and taking his seat there, addressed them at length,
a directing his remarks especially to his immediate disciples ǀ who
stood nearer to him. ²The following is the substance of his discourse :—
³"Happy are those *a* of you ǀ who 'feel their spiritual poverty !'
for to such are held out the blessings of the 'Reign of the Divine
Messiah.' ⁶Yes, happy those who embrace the divine precepts with
the avidity of a hungry and thirsty man ! for their spiritual appetite is about to be satisfied. ⁴Happy the 'sorrowing' for sin ! for
soon will their hearts be 'cheered' with the promised relief. *b* Yes,
happy they who for the present penitently weep ! for they will yet
laugh for joy at pardon. ǀ
⁵"Happy are the 'patient !' for they have the promise of spirit-
ually 'recovering the realm' of the Messiah. ⁹Yes, happy they who
studiously promote peace, [and mildly observe it even under injury] !
for such may well be entitled *children of God*, [whose forbearance
they imitate.] ⁷Happy, too, are the compassionate ! for they will
receive compassion at the divine hand. ⁸Happy, in fine, are they
whose hearts are holy and sincere ! for they will be admitted to the
presence of God.
¹⁰"Nor less happy are those that are persecuted for their adher-
ence to pious duty ! for such is the distinctive lot on earth of the
subjects of the 'Reign of the Divine Messiah.' ¹¹Yes, happy may
you account yourselves, when an ungodly world shall pursue you
with *c* malice and ǀ insult *c* and rejection ǀ and persecution and de-
famatory denunciations in every possible form of groundless
charges, on account of your attachment to me *c* as the Messiah ! ǀ
¹²Rejoice, therefore, with great delight *d* on such occasions ǀ for,
mark, I promise you, your bliss will [thereby be enhanced, so as to]
make ample amends, in the life to come; and [you may derive
assurance from the fact, that] in a similar way your predeces-

a Luke vi, 20.   *b* Luke vi, 21.   *c* Luke vi, 22.   *d* Luke vi, 23.

46*

cheek, turn to him the other also; [40] and if   MATT. V.
any man will sue thee at the law and take
away thy coat, let him have thy cloak also; [41] and
whosoever shall compel thee to go a mile, go with him
twain.—[43] Ye have heard that it hath been said,* Thou
shalt love thy neighbor, and hate thine enemy: [44] but
I say unto you, Love your *enemies*, bless them that
curse you, do good to them that hate you, and pray
for them which despitefully use you and persecute
you;—[42] give to him that asketh thee, and from
him that would borrow of thee, turn not thou away,—
[LUKE VI, 30] and of him that taketh away thy goods, ask them
not again.   [46] For if ye love them which love you, what
reward have ye? do not even [LUKE VI, 32] sinners the
same? [47] and if ye salute your brethren only, what do
ye more than others? do not even the publicans so?
[LUKE VI, 33] And if ye do good to them which do good to you,
what thank have ye? for sinners also do even the same; [34] and
if ye lend to them of whom ye hope to receive, what thank
have ye? for sinners also lend to sinners, to receive as much
again: [35] but love ye your *enemies*, and do good and lend,
hoping for nothing again; and your reward shall be great, even
[45] that ye may be the children of your Father which
is in heaven; [LUKE VI, 35] for he is kind unto the unthankful
and to the evil: for he maketh his sun to rise on the evil
and on the good, and sendeth rain on the just and on
the unjust: [48] be ye therefore [LUKE VI, 36] merciful, even
as your Father which is in heaven, is [LUKE VI, 36]
merciful.

[1] Take heed that ye do not your alms be-.   Matt. VI.
fore men, to be seen of them; otherwise ye
have no reward of your Father which is in heaven.
[2] Therefore when thou doest thine alms, do not sound
a trumpet before thee, as the hypocrites do in the syna-

---

* Lev. xix, 18.

left one too for him to inflict a similar affront,' rather   MATT. V.
than violently resent it; ⁴⁰ and if some one should feel
disposed to prosecute you unjustly, and thus deprive
you of 'the *tunic* [i. e. shirt] that you wear,' still, [sooner than liti-
gate about the matter,] let him take your *mantle* too; ⁴¹ likewise,
if a public courier should press you [together with your horse, ve-
hicle or whatever,] into his service to carry him on a mile,—[then,
rather than resist his compulsion,] travel two miles with him at
once.

⁴³ "Another principle inculcated in the Mosaic law is, '*Love your
fellow*' Jew, from which you have unjustifiably inferred, that you
are to 'hate every one else as an enemy.'   ⁴⁴ But *I* tell *a* all of you
that hear me, ǀ 'love' even your *enemies;* yes, you must return kindness to such as bear you ill-will, you must bless those that curse you,
you must pray in the behalf of all who maltreat and persecute you,
—⁴² and in like manner you must [when you can spare it,] freely
give to a needy person what he asks of you, and cheerfully lend him
what he may wish to borrow of you, [even though there be no immediate prospect of repayment,] instead of turning upon your heel
at his petition; *b* nay, in many cases the spirit of charity will forbid
your sternly demanding back your property, even when wrongfully
taken.   ⁴⁶ For suppose you should 'love' those who love you, [and
carry the duty no farther,] what peculiar reward could you expect
c from the divine favor?ǀ—do not the very 'Tax-gatherers,' *c* those
proverbial extortioners, ǀ do as much as this?   ⁴⁷ And if you do kindly greet your national friends merely, what superior morality is
there in that act?—do not even the *c* wicked ǀ Gentiles practice the
same custom?   *d* And though you were to confer kindnesses upon
such only as have conferred the like upon you, what special credit
is it to you?—the vilest sinners do the very same.ǀ   *e* And if you
should do no more than lend to those from whom you expect to receive back, what is there remarkably praiseworthy in that?—the
veriest sinners lend to sinners with the prospect of receiving a full
equivalent.ǀ   *f* On the contrary, you ought to love your very enemies, showing them kindness and lending to such as you cannot
anticipate will be able to repay you; then will your future recompense be great, ǀ ⁴⁵ as the children [by evident imitation] of the
f Supreme ǀ Benefactor, who affords His earthly blessings even to
the thankless wicked, making His sun rise for them as well as for
the pious, and showering down the rain of heaven upon the field
of the righteous and that of the unrighteous alike.   ⁴⁸ For in this
duty your motive should be, to resemble the perfect *g* benignity ǀ of
your Heavenly Father.

¹ "[In opposition to the practice of the vulgarly re-   **Matt. VI.**
puted saints,] be careful not to perform your acts of
piety in a public and showy manner; for if you neg-
lect this admonition, you are not entitled to any reward in the consideration of your Heavenly Father.   ² Accordingly, when you bestow charity, never proclaim it [as it were, like a king's herald,]
'with a flourish of trumpets in front' of you, after the fashion of
the would-be-liberal, when they meet the necessitous in a synagogue or street, their chief motive being to gain the applause of the

. *a* Luke vi, 27. *b* Luke vi, 30.   *c* Luke vi, 32.   *d* Luke vi, 33   *e* Luke vi, 34.
        f Luke vi. 35,   *g* Luke vi, 36.

gogues and in the streets, that they may   MATT. VI.
have glory of men ; (verily I say unto you,
They *have* their reward :) [3] but when thou doest alms,
let not thy left hand know what thy right hand doeth ;
[4] that thine alms may be in secret, and thy Father,
which seeth in secret, himself shall reward thee openly.—[5] And when thou prayest, thou shalt not be as the
hypocrites are ; for they love to pray standing in the
synagogues and in the corners of the streets, that they
may be seen of men ; (verily I say unto you, They *have*
their reward :) [6] but thou, when thou prayest, enter into
thy closet, and when thou hast shut thy door, pray to
thy Father which is in secret ; and thy Father, which
seeth in secret, shall reward thee openly.   [7] But when
ye pray, use not vain repetitions, as the heathen do ;
for they think that they shall be heard for their much
speaking : [8] be not ye therefore like unto them ; for
your Father knoweth what things ye have need of
before ye ask him.—[16] Moreover when ye fast, be not
as the hypocrites, of a sad countenance ; for they disfigure their faces, that they may appear unto men to
fast ; (verily I say unto you, They *have* their reward :)
[17] but thou, when thou fastest, anoint thine head and
wash thy face ; [18] that thou appear not unto men to
fast, but unto thy Father which is in secret ; and thy
Father, which seeth in secret, shall reward thee
openly.

[1] Judge not, that ye be not judged ;   **Matt. VII.**
[LUKE VI, 37] condemn not, and ye shall not be condemned : [2] for with what judgment ye judge, ye shall
be judged ; and with what measure ye mete, it shall
be measured to you again. [LUKE VI, 37] Forgive, and ye
shall be forgiven : [38] give, and it shall be given unto you ;
good measure, pressed down and shaken together and running
over, shall men give into your bosom.   [3] And why behold-
est thou the *mote* that is in thy brother's eye, but

bystanders:—I assure you, such hypocrites will find **MATT. VI.**
[to their sorrow,] that this applause is their only reward. ³ On the contrary, when *you* bestow charity,
be rather as private as if you did not wish to 'let your left hand
know what your right is doing;' ⁴ and for this genuine benevolence
your Heavenly Father, who observes all that passes in private, will
hereafter reward you publicly.

⁵ "Again, when you pray, do not resemble these seeming devo-
tees, who love so much to stand praying at the corners of the city
thoroughfares, where they can the more effectually attract the notice of others;—let me solemnly assure you, such pretenders will
have that notice for their sole reward. ⁶ On the contrary, when *you*
pray [at your personal devotions], retire rather to some secret place,
and having closed the door against all human observation, pray with
undivided sincerity to your Heavenly Father, who marks all your
private conduct, and will eventually reward you publicly. ⁷ Moreover, be not verbose in your prayers, like heathen worshipers, who
appear to imagine that their petitions will be successful in proportion to their prolixity; ⁸ never imitate them, therefore, in this absurd
practice,—for prayer is not designed to inform your Heavenly Father
of your wants by their tedious recital, since He is already perfectly
acquainted with them, before you supplicate Him to relieve them.

¹⁶ "In like manner, when you fast, never imitate the lugubrious
and slovenly air of the hypocrites to whom I have alluded; for they
merely render their personal appearance unsightly, in order that
others may observe that they are fasting;—I tell you assuredly, they
will receive no other reward. ¹⁷ On the contrary, when *you* fast,
appear as usual, anointing your head and washing your face; ¹⁸ so
as not to seem to others as if you were fasting, being content that
your Heavenly Father is aware of it, who witnesses what you do in
private, and will in the end bestow your appropriate reward.

¹ "[In further contrast with the cynical spirit of that **Matt. VII.**
class,] I enjoin upon you, not to sit in judgment on the
character, and demeanor of others, lest they do the
same to you; *a* be slow to condemn them of faults, and you may
then expect that the same forbearance will be extended to you:|
² for depend upon it, they will judge you strictly according to your
own decisions, and deal out censure to you in full proportion to your
own severity. *a* In like manner, be ready to excuse the offenses of
others against you, and you will then be likely to find a placable
disposition exercised toward your own frailties;| *b* and likewise be
liberal in conferring favors, so that you may experience a like generosity in turn: yes, in this way, your beneficiary neighbors will
repay your candor and good nature with 'good measure, packed
down, well shaken and full to overflowing, poured into your lap.'|
^{3, 4} [Your own imperfections ought to incite you to this charity in
estimating others' motives:] why should you so captiously fix your
attention upon the mere 'splintery *speck*' of a foible in the eye of

a Luke vi, 37.   *b* Luke vi, 38.

considerest not the *beam* that is in thine   MATT. VII.
own eye? ⁴ or how wilt thou say to thy
brother, Let me pull out the mote out of thine eye;
and behold, a beam is in thine own eye? ⁵ thou hypocrite, first cast out the beam out of thine own eye;
and then shalt thou see clearly to cast out the mote
out of thy brother's eye.—¹² Therefore all things whatsoever ye would that men should do to you, do ye even
so to them; for this is the law and the prophets.

ˏ ¹⁵ Beware of false prophets, which come to you in
sheep's clothing, but inwardly they are ravening
wolves: ¹⁶ ye shall know them by their fruits: Do
men gather grapes of thorns, or figs of thistles?
¹⁷ even so every good tree bringeth forth good fruit,
but a corrupt tree bringeth forth evil fruit: ¹⁸ a good
tree cannot bring forth evil fruit, neither can a corrupt
tree bring forth good fruit: ²⁰ wherefore, by their fruits
ye shall know them.   ²¹ Not every one that saith unto me, Lord, Lord, shall enter into the kingdom of
heaven; but he that *doeth the will* of my Father
which is in heaven: ²⁴ therefore whosoever [LUKE VI, 47]
cometh to me and heareth these sayings of mine, and
doeth them, I will liken him unto a wise man, which
[LUKE VI, 48] digged deep and built his house upon a *rock;*
²⁵ and the rain descended, and the floods came, and the
winds blew, and [LUKE VI, 48] the stream beat [LUKE VI, 48]
vehemently upon that house; and it fell not, for it was
founded upon a rock: ²⁶ and every one that heareth
these sayings of mine, and doeth them *not*, shall be
likened unto a foolish man, which [LUKE VI, 49] without a
foundation built his house upon the *sand;* ²⁷ and the
rain descended, and the floods came, and the winds
blew and beat upon that house; and [LUKE VI, 49] immediately it fell, and great was the fall of it.

¹ When he was come down from the   **Matt. VIII.**
mountain, great multitudes followed him.

51

another's morality, and with an air of self-compla-   MATT. VII.
cent friendship offer to extract it; when in fact there
is a monstrous '*beam*' of a fault in the eye of your
own moral habits, which-you totally overlook? ⁵ Let all such hypocritical censors first purge their own moral vision of its heinous
blurs, and then perhaps they will be better qualified to detect and
remove the lesser failings of their fellow-men.—¹² In short, [regu-
late your conduct and temper in this and all other cases arising under the mutual relations of life, by the following golden rule,] *Act
toward others just as you would wish them to act toward you* in like
circumstances; for this indeed is the essence of [all the precepts on
such topics in] the whole ' Law and Prophets,' as I have exemplified.

¹⁵ " Finally, [although you are to be thus charitable in your judgment of others,] I still caution you against all such erroneous and
faithless teachers of religion; for they approach you [in a garb of
woolen mantles,] as if they were the gentle sheep, whose fleeces
they wear, but in their hearts they are prowling wolves !—¹⁶ and I
will give you an unerring mark by which you may distinguish them :
it is their *conduct*. Now you know, each species of tree and shrub
is recognized by means of its peculiar kind of *fruit;* so that we
never expect to 'gather a *a* crop of figs from a thorn-tree,'¹ nor to
'pick a bunch of grapes from off a *a* brier-bush,' such as the *cal-
trop;*' ¹⁷, ¹⁸ because excellent fruit grows only upon choice trees.
²⁰ Thus men's actions will certainly indicate their moral character,
as fruit does the kind of tree that bore it.

²¹ " In conclusion, [I warn you, my hearers, that on account of
the necessity of this agreement of deportment with profession,] it
does not follow that every one who salutes me as his 'Revered
Teacher,' will really be admitted under the ' Reign of the Divine
Messiah ;' but only those who actually perform the will of my Heavenly Father, *b* as enjoined by me.l   ²⁴ I would therefore compare,
c for your profit,l the person who *c* after resorting to me and listening to my instructions as I am now giving them,l thereupon *complies* with them, to a prudent man, that in building his house *d* digs
down deepl until he reaches the solid rock, on which he then lays
the foundation ; ²⁵ thus when the winter sets in, the rain may pour
down, and the brooks swell *d* with the freshet,l. while the winds
rage and dash *d* the stream with furyl against the building,—but all
combined *d* can never shakel down such a house, because it is firmly built on a foundation-rock. ²⁶ On the contrary, every one that
hears these my injunctions without obeying them, resembles some
silly person, that builds his dwelling flat upon the sandy *e* soil, without any foundation-stones at all;l ²⁷ so that when the wintry storm
drives such a torrent against the building, it falls *e* at oncel with a
tremendous crash,—an utter wreck !"

¹ After concluding this discourse, Jesus descended   **Matt. VIII.**
the hill, followed by the great throng that heard it.

a Luke vi, 41.   *b* Luke vi, 46.   *c* Luke vi, 47.   *d* Luke vi, 48.   *e* Luke vi, 49.

•

§ 46.—*The Centurion's Servant cured.*

(Capernaum; [*May?*] A. D. 27.]

¹ Now when he had ended all his sayings   **Luke VII.**
in the audience of the people, he entered
into Capernaum.   ² And a certain centurion's servant,
who was dear unto him, was [Matt. VIII, 6] at home sick
[Matt. VIII, 6] of the palsy, grievously tormented and ready to
die : ³ and when he heard of Jesus, he sent unto him
the elders of the Jews, beseeching him that he would
come and heal his servant.   ⁴ And when they came to
Jesus, they besought him instantly saying, That he
was worthy for whom he should do this ; ⁵ for he loveth our nation, and he hath built us a synagogue.
⁶ Then Jesus went with them.   And when he was
now not far from the house, the centurion sent friends
to him, saying unto him, Lord, trouble not thyself : for
I am not worthy that thou shouldest enter under my
roof ; ⁷ wherefore neither thought I myself worthy to
come unto thee ; but say in a word [Matt. VIII, 8] only,
and my servant shall be healed : ⁸ for I also am a man
set under authority, having under me soldiers, and I
say unto one, Go, and he goeth ; and to another, Come,
and he cometh ; and to my servant, Do this, and he
doeth it.   ⁹ When Jesus heard these things, he marveled at him, and turned him about and said unto the
people that followed him, [Matt. VIII, 10] Verily I say unto
you, I have not found so great faith, no, not in Israel.
[Matt. VIII, 13] And Jesus said unto the centurion, Go thy way ;
and as thou hast believed, so be it done unto thee.   ¹⁰ And
they that were sent, returning to the house, found the
servant [Matt. VIII, 13] in the self-same hour whole that had
been sick.

52

§ 46.—*The Centurion's Servant cured.*
(Capernaum; [*May ?*] A. D. 27.)

[1] On his return to Capernaum, immediately after **Luke VII.**
the above public exposition of his doctrines, Jesus
was met at the entrance of the village [2] by a message on the behalf of a certain *centurion* [i. e. captain of about
one hundred men]. This military officer had *a* at his house
a male domestic, highly esteemed by him, who was *a* confined
to his bed by so severe an attack of a paralytic nature, attended
with excruciating pain, that he was likely to die unless speedily relieved. [3] Hearing of Jesus's ability to cure diseases, the
centurion prevailed upon a number of the Jewish elders to
wait upon Jesus,—[hoping that they would have more influence than himself,]—with the urgent request, that he would
"come and save his servant's life." [4] Accordingly, repairing
to Jesus, they earnestly solicited his aid in the case, adding
[as a special inducement in the centurion's favor,] that "he
was an individual worthy of such a benefit, [5] being a great
friend of their nation and religion, and even the person who
had built the village-synagogue for their use." [6] Jesus *b* assented to their request, and as he was accompanying them
for the purpose of fulfilling it, some of the centurion's friends
met him at a short distance from the house, whom he had dispatched [upon further consideration] to say to Jesus for him,
"Dear Sir, do not give yourself the trouble of coming in person, for I am not deserving of having you visit my residence,—
[7] and on that account I did not consider myself a fit person to
prefer my request to you, but procured the intervention of others; if you will but speak to that effect *c* in a single word, my
servant will at once be cured: [8] just as even I, in the exercise
of the military authority with which I am invested, can bid
one of my subalterns, 'Go yonder,' and he goes there directly;
or command another, 'Come here,' and he does so; or indeed
order one of my ordinary servants to 'perform this or that
piece of work,' and he obeys on the spot.'" [9] Surprised at hearing a message expressing so much confidence coming from
such a quarter, Jesus turned to the elders and populace accompanying him, declaring, *d* "Assuredly! I tell you, I have not
met with such a decided exhibition of faith in me anywhere
among the whole Jewish people!" [e] He then bade the centurion through his friends, "Return; it shall be done to you as
you have believed!" [10] Upon regaining the house, the messengers found the patient recovering *e* from the very moment
of that announcement.

a Matt. viii, 6.   b Matt. viii, 7.   c Matt. viii, 8.
        d Matt. viii, 10.   e Matt. viii, 13.

§ 47.—*The Widow's Son restored to Life.*

(Nain; [*May?*] A. D. 27.)

[11] And it came to pass the day after,   LUKE VII.
that he went into a city called Nain ; and
many of his disciples went with him, and much people.
[12] Now when he came nigh to the gate of the city,
behold, there was a dead man carried out, the only son
of his mother, and she was a widow ; and much people of the city was with her.   [13] And when the Lord
saw her, he had compassion on her, and said unto her,
Weep not : [14] and he came and touched the bier ; and
they that bare him stood still : and he said, Young
man, I say unto thee, Arise : [15] and he that was dead
sat up and began to speak ; and he delivered him to
his mother.   [16] And there came a fear on all ; and
they glorified God saying, That a great prophet is risen
up among us ; and, That God hath visited his people :
[17] and this rumor of him went forth throughout all
Judea and throughout all the region round about.

§ 48.—*John's Message to Christ.*

(Castle of Mache'rus, and Galilee [in the vicinity of Nain and Ca-pernaum?] ; [*June?*] A. D. 27.)

[18] And the disciples of John showed him [MATT. XI, 2]
in the prison of all these [MATT. XI. 2] works of Christ : [19] and
John, calling unto him two of his disciples, sent them
to Jesus, saying, Art thou he that should come ? or
look we for another ?   [20] When the men were come
unto him, they said, John Baptist has sent us unto
thee, saying, Art thou he that should come ? or look
we for another ?   [21] And in that same hour he cured
many of their infirmities and plagues and of evil spirits, and unto many that were blind he gave sight :
[22] then Jesus answering said unto them, Go your way
and tell John what things ye have seen and heard ;

53

§ 47.—*The Widow's Son restored to Life.*

(Nain; [*May ?*] A. D. 27.)

[11] On the next day, Jesus made a journey to the LUKE VII.
neighboring town of Nain, attended by his disciples,
(the Apostles as well as numerous others,) and followed by a large company of the populace in general. [12] As he was
approaching the gate of the town, suddenly a funeral procession
appeared, who were conveying out for interment the corpse of a
youth, an only son of his widowed mother, while a large assemblage
of the townspeople were following the body to the grave. [13] Touched
at the sight of the doubly-bereaved mother's affliction, the compassionate Teacher approached her with the consoling words, "Cease
your tears." [14] Then advancing still nearer and placing his hand
upon the bier, that the bearers might stop and let it down, he thus
addressed the deceased, "Young man, I bid you, Rise up alive!"
[15] The lifeless youth immediately [returned to animation, and] sitting upright commenced to speak, when Jesus [beckoning the
mourner,] consigned him to his overjoyed mother's arms.

[16] Awe seized the minds of all the beholders, who began to praise
God [for this manifest interposition of His power,] exclaiming, "A
remarkable Prophet has surely arisen in our midst!" and others
declared, that "Jehovah had evidently now regarded His chosen
people with the long-promised mercy!" [17] The report of this miracle of Jesus spread [from Galilee] through the whole of Judea and
all the country adjacent.

§ 48.—*John's Message to Christ.*

(Castle of Mache′rus, and Galilee [in the vicinity of Nain and Capernaum ?]; [*June ?*]
A. D. 27.)

[18] Certain disciples of John the Baptist, becoming acquainted with
these wonderful transactions *a* of Jesus, | hastened with the news to
their master, *a* at that time confined in prison, | [in order to satisfy
their minds by his authority, concerning the true character of one
who wrought such miracles, and yet seemed disinclined to lay claims
to the Messiahship. [19] After listening to their doubts, which his
own testimony had failed to remove, John determined to refer them
to Jesus himself;] accordingly summoning two of the most influential of them, he dispatched them to him, with directions to ask him,
"Are you the promised Messiah, or are we still to look for some one
else to appear in that character?" [20] Upon reaching Jesus, the
messengers stated their errand and proposed the question as they
had been directed. [21] [Instead of replying to them directly,] he
immediately engaged himself in curing the great numbers of pa-
tients in the crowd about him, of all their chronic and acute diseases, also restoring to sanity the demoniacs among them, and conferring a recovery of sight upon numerous blind persons. [22] He then
turned to John's messengers with this answer, "Go and carry back
word to your master, what you have just now heard and seen me

a Matt. xi, 2.

how that the blind see, the lame walk, the   LUKE VII.
lepers are cleansed, the deaf hear, the dead
are raised, to the poor the gospel is preached : ²³ and
blessed is he whosoever shall not be offended in me.

²⁴ And when the messengers of John were departed,
he began to speak unto the people concerning John,
What went ye out into the wilderness for to see? a
reed shaken with the wind? ²⁵ But what went ye out
for to see? a man clothed in soft raiment? behold,
they which are gorgeously appareled and live delicate-
ly, are in kings' courts. ²⁶ But what went ye out for
to see? a *prophet?* yea, I say unto you, and much
more than a prophet. ²⁷ This is he of whom it is
written,* Behold, I send my messenger before thy
face, which shall prepare thy way before thee ;
[MATT. XI, 14] and if ye will receive it, this is Elias which was
for to come: [15] he that hath ears to hear, let him hear.
²⁸ For I say unto you, Among those that are born of
women, there is not a greater prophet than John the
Baptist ; but he that is least in the kingdom of God, is
greater than he. [LUKE XVI, 16] The law and the prophets
were until John; since that time the kingdom of God is
preached [MATT. XI, 12] until now, [LUKE XVI, 16] and every man
presseth into it [MATT. XI, 12] by force. ²⁹ And all the people
that heard him, and the publicans, justified God, being
baptized with the baptism of John ; ³⁰ but the Pharisees and lawyers rejected the counsel of God against
themselves, being not baptized of him. ³¹ And the
Lord said, Whereunto then shall I liken the men of
this generation, and to what are they like ? ³² they are
like unto children sitting in the market-place, and calling one to another and saying, We have piped unto
you, and ye have not danced ; we have mourned to
you, and ye have not wept: ³³ for John the Baptist

---

* Mal. iii, 1.

doing; tell him that [the ancient prophecies are being **LUKE VII.**
fulfilled:] the blind are regaining their sight, the deaf
their hearing, the lame the use of their feet, lepers are
losing their defilement, corpses are restored to life, and in short the
glad tidings of salvation are proclaimed to the humblest classes of
society!—²³ happy indeed is he who does not waver in his confidence
in me, [as you seem inclined to do, on account of my unpretending
manner!]"

²⁴ As soon as John's messengers had departed, Jesus took up the
discussion of the Baptist's character, before the assembled crowd,
asking them, "What kind of a person did you use to resort to the
'Desert of Judea,' with the expectation of finding John to be?—a
man fickle as a flimsy reed rocking about in the breeze? ²⁵ Well,
[if his was a different temper from that,] what sort of a man *did*
you go there to see?—was it some one clothed in a fine suit? No!
you well know that such as wear sumptuous dresses and indulge in
similar luxury, are only to be found in the proud palaces of royalty.
²⁶ What description of person then, I still ask, did you go out there
to get a sight of?—was it a prophet? Yes indeed, I tell you, and
one with a far more exalted mission than any of the ancient prophets; ²⁷ for he is the very person of whom one of them thus writes,
[in the behalf of Jehovah,]—

'Mark! I will send an envoy in advance,
To smooth a passage for' your 'royal march.'

And he is indeed, *a* as I wish that all classes who hear me! *b* were
but willing! *a* to notice attentively,! *b* the identical 'second Elijah'!
whose coming is predicted [by the same prophet]. ²⁸ Observe what
I say: a more distinguished prophet than John the Baptist has never
arisen among men; and yet the humblest individual under the [ful-
ly-developed] 'Reign of the Divine Messiah' will far surpass him [in
spiritual knowledge]. *c* For the 'Law and Prophets' were your sole
religious guides until the coming of John, but since the commencement of his ministry, the actual advent of that 'Reign' has been
proclaimed! *d* [with a clearness gradually increasing] up to the present hour,! *c* when the whole common people seem eager to rush!
d with impetuous zeal into it,—[and it is destined to unfold to complete distinctness.]!

²⁹ "Yes, when they first heard John preach, the general mass of
the populace, and even the hard-hearted Tribute-collectors, thank-
fully fell in with the divine arrangements, by penitently submitting
to the baptism which he prescribed; ³⁰ but the perverse Pharisees
and conceited public expounders of the Law have thwarted the divine economy respecting their salvation, by spurning his baptism.
³¹ I am almost at a loss how to represent adequately the [inconsist-
ency of conduct exhibited in this matter by these] characters of the
present day;—³² I can only compare their capriciousness to that
often witnessed among boys sitting at play in a town square, when
they vociferously complain to some of their sulky mates, 'We have
tried' every means to please you, and yet you refuse to join our
sport!—first we "fluted" for you, but you would not dance to the
music!" and then we "wailed for you, but you neither cried *e* nor
lacerated yourselves"! in concert!' ³³ Just so [fault-finding are
these persons:] first appeared John, who abjured the usual comforts

a Matt. xi, 15; *b* Matt. xi, 14; *c* Luke xvi, 16; *d* Matt. xi, 12. *e* Matt. xi, 17.

came neither eating bread nor drinking   LUKE VII.
wine, and ye say, He hath a devil ; ³⁴ the
Son of man is come eating and drinking, and ye say,
Behold, a gluttonous man and a wine-bibber, a friend
of publicans and sinners : ³⁵ but Wisdom is justified of
all her children.

²⁰ Then began he to upbraid the cities   **Matt. XI**
wherein most of his mighty works were
done, because they repented not: ²¹ Wo unto· thee,
Chorazin! wo unto thee, Bethsaida! for if the mighty
works which were done in you had been done in Tyre
and Sidon, they would have repented long ago in sackcloth and ashes ; ²² but I say unto you, It shall be more
tolerable for Tyre and Sidon at the day of judgment,
than for you : ²³ and thou, Capernaum, which art exalted unto heaven, shalt be brought down to hell! for
if the mighty works which have been done in thee,
had been done in Sodom, it would have remained until
this day ; ²⁴ but I say unto you, That it shall be more
tolerable for the land of Sodom [MATT. X, 15] and Gomorrah
in the day of judgment, than for thee.

§ 49.—*Kind Offices of a Woman to Christ at a Pharisee's Table.*

(Galilee [on the way from the vicinity of Nain toward Capernaum?] ;
[*June?*] A. D. 27.)

³⁶ And one of the Pharisees desired him   **Luke VII.**
that he would eat with him ; and he went
into the Pharisee's house, and sat down to meat : ³⁷ and
behold, a woman in the city, which was a sinner, when
she knew that Jesus sat at meat in the Pharisee's
house, brought an alabaster-box of ointment, ³⁸ and
stood at his feet behind him weeping, and began to
wash his feet with tears, and did wipe them with the
hairs of her head, and kissed his feet and anointed
them with the ointment. ³⁹ Now when the Pharisee

of life; and directly they cried out, 'He is a demoniac!'   LUKE VII.
—34 then when the 'Son of Man' has now appeared,
and partakes of the ordinary kinds of fare; him they
are equally ready to stigmatize by exclaiming, 'See, he is a glutton
and drunkard, an associate of tax-gatherers and like miscreants!'
35 But [cavil as they may,] the course that heavenly wisdom pursues
in this as in all other cases, needs no vindication in the minds of
such as have imbibed its true spirit.''

20 Then calling to mind [the indignities and want of. **Matt. XI.**
a hearty reception that he had experienced (especially
from the higher classes) in] the towns of that vicinity,
which had witnessed the greater part of his miracles wrought, Jesus thus reproached them [in terms of melancholy indignation],
because they had not penitently embraced his teachings: 21 ''Alas
for you, Chorazin and Bethsaida! for had the miracles that have
been effected in your midst, been wrought in the pagan cities of
Tyre and Sidon, I doubt not that long ere this, they would have
convinced the inhabitants of their duty of [conforming with my
claims by] repenting of their sins, a sitting! [if needs be,] with the
sackcloth of grief about them and the ashes of mourning upon their
heads: 22 but O! I warn you, a less aggravated doom will be pronounced upon the heathen Tyrians and Sidonians in the final judgment, than upon you! 23 And thou too, O Capernaum, that hast
been raised to heaven [as it were, by the privilege of my special
residence], wilt yet be swallowed up in the deepest oblivion of the
grave; for had the city of Sodom itself been favored with the warning miracles which thy residents have witnessed, it would doubtless be standing to this hour, [spared by timely repentance:] 24 but
O! I repeat it, a more direful judgment [temporal and eternal,]
impends over thee, than was even visited upon the guilty Sodom
b and Gomorrah!'' |

§ 49.—*Kind Offices of a Woman to Christ at a Pharisee's Table.*
(Galilee [on the way from the vicinity of Nain toward Capernaum?] ; [*June ?*] A.D.27.)

36 A few days afterward, a certain Pharisee invited **Luke VII.**
Jesus to partake of a meal at his house.   Accepting the
invitation, he took a place on the couch around the
table, [although the host did not appear very cordial in the reception of his guest.] 37 While he was reclining at the meal, a certain
female of the town, who was notorious for the general irregularity
of her past life, learning that he was there, repaired thither with a
vase of perfumed unguent in her hand; 38 and taking her station
behind him, where she could bend over his feet, [that lay extended
upon the margin of the couch and unsandaled,] she bedewed them
with her penitential tears, and then wiping them with the hair of
her head, she kissed them with affectionate reverence, and anointed them with the perfumery in the vase. 39 The Pharisee host,

a. Luke x, 13.   b Matt. x, 15.

55*

which had bidden him, saw it, he spake LUKE VII.
within himself saying, This man, if he
were a *prophet*, would have known who and what manner of woman this is that toucheth him; for she is a
sinner : ⁴⁰ and Jesus answering said unto him, Simon,
I have somewhat to say unto thee ; and he saith, Master, say on. ⁴¹ There was a certain creditor which
had two debtors, the one owed five hundred pence, and
the other fifty ; ⁴² and when they had nothing to pay,
he frankly forgave them both : tell me therefore, which
of them will love him most ? ⁴³ Simon answered and
said, I suppose that he to whom he forgave most : and
he said unto him, Thou hast rightly judged. ⁴⁴ And
he turned to the woman, and said unto Simon, Seest
thou this woman ? I entered into thine house, *thou*
gavest me no water for my feet, but *she* hath washed
my feet with tears, and wiped them with the hairs of
her head ; ⁴⁵ thou gavest me no kiss, but this woman,
since the time I came in, hath not ceased to kiss my
feet ; ⁴⁶ mine head with oil thou didst not anoint, but
this woman hath anointed my feet with ointment :
⁴⁷ wherefore I say unto thee, Her sins which are many
are forgiven, for she loved much ; but to whom little
is forgiven, the same loveth little. ⁴⁸ And he said
unto her, Thy sins are forgiven. ⁴⁹ And they that sat
at meat with him, began to say within themselves,
Who is this that *forgiveth sins* also ? ⁵⁰ And he said
to the woman, Thy faith hath saved thee ; go in peace.

§ 50.—*The Second Tour of Galilee.*

([*June* to *September?*] A. D. 27.)

¹ And it came to pass afterward, that he **Luke VIII.**
went throughout every city and village,
preaching and showing the glad tidings of the kingdom of God : and the twelve were with him, ² and
certain women which had been healed of evil spirits

observing the occurrence, made this comment upon   LUKE VII.
it in his mind, "Surely if this man were a real prophet, he would have known [by inspired intuition,] what
a wicked-character this woman is, who is thus contaminating him
by her touch!" [40] [Aware of the reflections that were passing in
the bosom of his host,] Jesus addressed him thus: "Simon, I have
a simple question I would like to ask you." "Well, Teacher," returned he, "let me hear it." [41] "It is this," rejoined Jesus: "A
certain capitalist had two debtors, one of whom owed him five
hundred *dena'rii* [i. e. about $75,] and the other fifty [i. e. about
$7 50]; [42] and neither of them having wherewith to pay their re-
spective debts, he generously released them both from their entire
obligation: now, which of these two persons, should you expect,
would cherish the greater degree of affectionate gratitude toward
him?" [43] "I should think," replied the Pharisee, "it ought to be
he who had the larger debt released to him." "Precisely so," responded Jesus. [44] Then partly facing the woman, [as he turned in
raising himself up from his elbow,] he continued to his host, "Do
you observe this woman? When I entered your dwelling, you did
not supply me with the customary water for washing my feet;
whereas this woman has been moistening them with her tears, and
wiping them with her hair. [45] *You* offered me no kiss of welcome;
but *she* has been incessantly kissing my feet, almost since I entered
the house. [46] You did not perfume my head with ointment, [in token of gladness at my presence;] whilst she has been anointing my
feet with perfumery. [47] Therefore [on your own admission, this
conduct on her part proves,] I tell you, that her past sins, and those
aggravated ones too, are all divinely pardoned, inasmuch as she has
evinced a corresponding [depth of grateful] *love;* whereas he who
has experienced but little of the pardoning mercy of God, is seen to
display a proportionally small degree of affection." [48] Then addressing the penitent, he directly assured her, "I pronounce your sins
entirely remitted!" [49] At this announcement the other guests whispered among themselves, "Who is this man, that assumes even to
pardon sins!" [50] [Undisturbed by these invidious remarks,] Jesus
merely told the woman, "*Your* confidence in my full authority has
been your salvation from the effects and guilt of sin: you may now
retire with [the happy consciousness of] the divine favor."

§ 50.—*The Second Tour of Galilee.*

([*June to September ?*] A. D. 27.)

[1] Immediately after this, Jesus commenced another   **Luke VIII.**
circuit in Galilee, visiting each town and village, and
preaching wherever he went the joyful tidings of the
advent of the "Reign of the Divine Messiah;" being attended in
these labors by his twelve apostles, [2] and accompanied in his journey
by several females, whom he had cured of maladies and demoniacal

K   56*

and infirmities, Mary called Magdalene   LUKE VIII.
(out of whom went seven devils,) ³ and
Joanna the wife of Chuza, Herod's steward, and Su-
sanna and many others; which ministered unto him
of their substance.

§ 51.—*The Restoration of a Demoniac to Sanity, with
the connected Incidents.*

(Capernaum; [*October ?*] A. D. 27.)

¹⁹ And they went into a house; ²⁰ and the   **Mark III.**
multitude cometh together again, so that
they could not so much as eat bread: ²¹ and when his
friends heard of it, they went out to lay hold on him;
for they said, He is beside himself.

²² Then was brought unto him one pos-   **Matt. XII.**
sessed with a devil, blind and dumb; and
he healed him, insomuch that the blind and dumb both
spake and saw: ²³ and all the people were amazed and
said, Is not this the son of David? ²⁴ But when the
Pharisees [MARK III, 22] and the scribes which came down from
Jerusalem heard it, they said, This fellow [MARK III, 22]
hath Beelzebub, and doth not cast out devils but by Beelzebub the prince of the devils. ²⁵ And Jesus knew
their thoughts, and [MARK III, 23] called them unto him and
said unto them [MARK III, 23] in parables, Every kingdom
divided against itself is brought to desolation, and every
city or house divided against itself shall not stand;
²⁶ and if Satan cast out Satan, he is divided against
himself; how shall then his kingdom stand? [MARK III, 23]
How can Satan cast out Satan? [LUKE XI, 18] because ye say
that I cast out devils through Beelzebub. ²⁷ And if I by
Beelzebub cast out devils, by whom do your children
cast them out? therefore they shall be your judges:
²⁸ but if I cast out devils by the Spirit of God, then
[LUKE XI, 20] no doubt the kingdom of God is come unto

possession,—namely, Mary [distinguished by the **LUKE VIII.**
surname of she] "of Mag'dala," (from whom
he had exorcised seven demons;) ³ Joannah, the
wife of Chuzah steward of Herod An'tipas; and Susannah, together with a number of others [of less note]. These females
gratefully combined to supply his fare out of their private
means.

§ 51.—*The Restoration of a Demoniac to Sanity, with the con-nected Incidents.*

(Capernaum; [*October ?*] A. D. 27.)

¹⁹ When the party arrived home after this tour, **Mark III.**
²⁰ so great crowds once more assembled immediately thither, that they had no opportunity even to
refresh themselves by a repast. ²¹ The immediate relatives of
Jesus, learning this, set out from their residence for his, with
the view of insisting upon his taking the needed refreshment
and repose; [and arriving at the entrance of the house they
begged the crowd to disperse,] declaring that "the people were
taxing his enthusiasm beyond the bounds of prudence."

²² Meanwhile, there had been brought to him a **Matt. XII.**
man afflicted with mental derangement, the result
of diabolical influence, and attended with the loss
of sight as well as of speech. This person he cured of his three-
fold malady, so completely ²³ that the populace standing by
exclaimed in utter amazement, "Can this [miracle-working
teacher] be other than the promised 'Descendant of David'?"

²⁴ On the contrary the Pharisees *a* and certain scribes at that
time present from Jerusalem,¹ who [stood by and] heard the
people express themselves thus, told them, "[Did you not notice the remark of this pretender's relatives just now concerning his insanity?] He could not appear thus to exorcise demons, if he were not in league with Baal'zebub their ringleader, *a* by being a demoniac himself!!" ²⁵ Aware of their
malevolent reflections, Jesus *b* pointedly¹ addressed them *b* with
this comparison,¹ "Any empire whose rulers or citizens are
embroiled in a civil war with each other, cannot escape speedy
ruin; and every family whose members are at bitter variance
among themselves, must soon be broken up: ²⁶ just so, if one
fiend is exorcising another, *c* as you affirm is the case with me,¹
Satan's dominion must be in a state of anarchy *d* and about
to fall in hopeless ruins.¹ ²⁷ Again, if *I* exorcise demons by
the aid of Baal'zebub, then by whose help, I ask, do *your own
followers* profess to exorcise them?—so you see, their practice retorts your calumny. ²⁸ If, however, I am exorcising demons by the *e* power l of the *Divine Spirit*, then *e* evidently l the
'Reign of the Divine Messiah' is already come among you.

a Mark iii, 22. *b* Mark iii, 23. *c* Luke xi, 18. *d* Mark iii, 26. *e* Luke xi, 20.

you. [Luke XI, 21] When a strong man armed   MATT. XII.
keepeth his palace, his goods are in peace;
²⁹ or else how can one enter into a strong man's house
and spoil his goods, except [Luke XI, 22] a stronger than he
first [Luke XI, 22] come upon him and overcome him and bind
the strong man? and then he will spoil his house.
³⁰ He that is not with me, is against me; and he that
gathereth not with me, scattereth abroad.   ³¹ Wherefore I say unto you,· All manner of sin and blasphemy
shall be forgiven unto men; but the blasphemy against
the *Holy Ghost* shall not be forgiven unto men : ³² and
whosoever speaketh a word against the Son of man, it
shall be forgiven him; but whosoever speaketh against
the Holy Ghost, it shall not be forgiven him, neither
in this world neither in the world to come : [Mark III, 30]
(because they said, He hath an unclean spirit.)   ³⁴ O generation of vipers, how can ye, being evil, speak good
things? (for out of the abundance of the heart, the
mouth speaketh : ³⁵ a good man, out of the good treasure of the heart, bringeth forth good things; and an
evil man, out of the evil treasure, bringeth forth evil
things :) ³⁶ but I say unto you, That every idle word
that men shall speak, they shall give account thereof
in the day of judgment; ³⁷ for by thy words thou shalt
be justified, and by thy words thou shalt be condemned.
³⁸ Then certain of the scribes and of the Pharisees
[Luke XI, 16] tempting him answered saying, Master, we
would see a sign [Luke XI, 16] from heaven from thee.
³⁹ But [Luke XI, 29] when the people were gathered thick together, he answered and said to them, An evil and adul-
terous generation seeketh after a sign, and there shall
no sign be given to it but the sign of the prophet Jonas ; ⁴⁰ for as Jonas was three days and three nights
in the whale's body,* so shall the Son of man be three

---

* Jonah i, 17; ii, 10.

[29] Surely, 'an enemy cannot successfully enter MATT. XII.
the mansion *a* securely guarded[by its herculean
owner in full armor, unless he *b* burst upon him
with an overpowering force, strip him of his boasted panoply,[
and bind his robust limbs; then he can proceed to plunder his
furniture and valuables:' [so I could not thus wrest victims
from Satan's grasp, did I not assail him with superior power.
[30] Besides, the common adage holds true of me in this case,]
'Whoever is not decidedly on a man's side, is really his oppo-
nent; he that is not engaged in contributing to a person's object, does in effect detract from it:' [so, inasmuch as I am not
manifestly a coöperator in Satan's cause, I must be his actual
antagonist.] [31, 32] Accordingly, I solemnly declare to you, that
although every other offense and insult committed against me
as the 'Son of Man,' may be pardoned [upon due repentance];
yet this blasphemy, *c* of which you have now been guilty, in
alleging that I am acting under diabolical influence,[thus im-
peaching the character of the Holy Spirit [in connection with
whom I am acting], is totally unpardonable in this world, and
will subject its perpetrator to *d* eternal[condemnation hereafter. [34] You brood of malicious detractors! it is in vain to
expect you to say anything good and right, [either on this or
any other occasion,] while you are so corrupt in soul: for it is
but the spontaneous outgushing of the heart, that the lips utter; [35] so that the pious person alone pronounces excellent
sentiments, drawn from the store of generous emotions *e* within him,[—whilst the wicked man pours forth only the rancorous language of a heart replete with depravity. [36] Ah! I tell
you, each human being will be held to a strict account in the
final judgment, for every word of wanton calumny that they
may have spoken upon earth; [37] yes, according to the moral
character of your own previous words will then be your ac-
quittal or condemnation."
    [38] Upon hearing these caustic remarks, some of the Pharisees
and scribes, [at whom they were aimed,] *f* prompted by the
secret motive of subjecting him to an embarrassing test,[artfully replied, "Teacher, we would be glad just now to see you
work some miracle *f* affecting the *sky*,[[in confirmation of
your authority.]", [39] "Yes," retorted Jesus, *g* turning to the
assembled crowd,["these corrupt and godless men of the present day are always demanding some fresh sensible warrant of
my mission; but no such superfluous portent will be afforded
them. They shall only see an event parallel to that which
occurred to the prophet Jonah; [40] namely, as Jonah's preservation alive within the maw of the sea monster, during parts
of three days and the included nights, *h* was an evidence to the
Ninevites [of the genuineness of his prophetical character];[
so will my claims as the 'Son of Man' be established by my

a Luke xi, 21.   *b* Luke xi, 22.   *c* Mark iii, 30.   *d* Mark iii, 29.
e Luke vi, 45.   *f* Luke xi, 16.   *g* Luke xi, 29.   *h* Luke xi, 30.

days and three nights in the heart of the   MATT. XII.
earth.   ⁴¹ The men of Nineveh shall rise
in judgment with this generation and shall condemn it;
because they repented at the preaching of Jonas,* and
behold, a greater than Jónas is here : ⁴² the queen of
the south shall rise up in the judgment with this generation and shall condemn it ; for she came from the
uttermost parts of the earth to hear the wisdom of Solomon,† and behold, a greater than Solomon is here.

⁴³ When the unclean spirit is gone out of a man, he
walketh through dry places, seeking rest, and findeth
none ; ⁴⁴ then he saith, I will return into my house
from whence I came out : and when he is come, he
findeth it empty, swept and garnished. ⁴⁵ Then goeth
he and taketh with himself seven other spirits more
wicked than himself, and they enter in and dwell there :
and the last state of that man is worse than the first.
Even so shall it be also unto this wicked generation.

²⁷ And it came to pass, as he spake these   Luke XI.
things, a certain woman of the company
lifted up her voice and said unto him, Blessed is the
mother that bare and nursed thee. ²⁸ But he said,
Yea, rather blessed are they that hear the word of
God and keep it.

⁴⁶ While he yet talked to the people, be-   Matt. XII.
hold, his mother and his brethren stood
without, desiring to speak with him, [MARK III, 31] and sent
unto him, calling him, [LUKE VIII, 19] but could not come at him
for the press. ⁴⁷ Then one said unto him, Behold, thy
mother and thy brethren stand without, desiring to
speak with thee. ⁴⁸ But he answered and said unto
him that told him, Who is my mother? and who are
my brethren? ⁴⁹ And he [MARK III, 34] looked round about
on them which sat about him, and stretched forth his hand

---

* Jonah iii, 5.   † 1 Kings x, 1.

[resurrection from the tomb, after] remaining with-　MATT. XII.
in the bosom of the earth the same length of time.
41 Nay, those very inhabitants of ancient Nineveh
will seem to rise at the final judgment to the condemnation of this
vile race; for *they* did repent upon hearing the admonitory proclamation of Jonah, whereas a far more distinguished messenger than
Jonah is now addressing this impenitent age. 42 That 'queen of
Sheba' too, on the south of us, who made Solomon a visit from the
extremity of Arabia, expressly in order to be an ear-witness of his
famed wisdom, will then appear in condemnatory contrast with the
present age; for an infinitely greater sage than Solomon is here
[conveying his instruction, and yet they disregard him."

43 Then drawing an illustration of the condition and fate of his
calumniators, from the cure just effected by him, Jesus continued,
"According to your own belief,] a foul fiend, upon his expulsion
from a possessed person, ranges disconsolate through some barren
region, in quest of relief [from the anguish of guilt that torments
him, by a shelter in some human tenement; 44 and to save your
credit, upon the relapse of a demoniac whom you profess to have
rendered sane, you say of the exorcised demon in such a case, that]
being unsuccessful in the search, he resolves to return to his late
victim, and take up his quarters there. [Be that as it may,] such
a fiend, if at his return he find that former abode untenanted [by
any better occupant], but swept clean and put in order [as if for his
reception]; 45 he will then assuredly go forth [to the general rendezvous of his comrades,] and associate with him perhaps seven
other demons, worse, it may be, than himself, [for the secure possession of such an inviting residence,] and these all repairing thither
will enter and permanently occupy that mansion;—in the state of
him whose mind is the theatre of such an occupancy, 'the latter
evil is greater than the former.' Precisely such will become the
condition of the abandoned race who now hear me; [the incipient
conviction forced upon them by my previous preaching and miracles, by being resisted will but increase their guilty obduracy, which
not even the required miracle would remove.]"

27 In the course of these remarks, a certain woman　Luke XI.
among the crowd [carried away with enthusiastic admiration,] interrupted him by exclaiming, "Happy must
be the mother that bore and nursed you, [in the possession of so
eloquent a son!]" 28 "But more happy still," returned he, "are
such as *obey* the divine communications that they are now hearing."

46 By the time that he had about concluded these　Matt. XII.
popular addresses, his mother and brothers had arrived, anxious to see and speak with him, but were
obliged to stand in the street, *a* on account of the throng that block-
ed up the entrance, | *b* and prevented even their messengers from
reaching him. | 47 Some one near him informed him of the fact,
48 but he replied by saying *c* to the surrounding concourse, | "My
mother and brothers, you say!—Whom do you think I regard as my
nearest relatives?" 49 Then *d* looking round upon the circle of his
followers sitting about him, | and pointing to his disciples, he an-

a Luke viii, 19.　　*b* Mark iii, 31.　　*c* Mark iii, 33.　　*d* Mark iii, 34.

59*

toward his disciples, and said, Behold, my　　**MATT. XII.**
mother and my brethren! ⁵⁰ for whosoever
shall do the will of my Father which is in heaven, the
same is my brother and sister and mother.

³⁷ And as he spake, a certain Pharisee be-　　**Luke XI.**
sought him to dine with him; and he went
in and sat down to meat: ³⁸ and when the Pharisee
saw it, he marveled that he had not first washed before dinner. ³⁹ And the Lord said unto him, Now do
ye Pharisees make clean the *outside* of the cup and
the platter, but your *inward* part is full of ravening
and wickedness: ⁴⁰ ye fools, did not he that made that
which is without, make that which is within also?
⁴¹ but rather give alms of such things as ye have
[MATT. XXIII, 26] within the cup and platter; and behold, all
things are clean unto you. ⁴² But wo unto you, Pharisees! for ye tithe mint and rue [MATT. XXIII, 23] and anise
and cummin and all manner of herbs, and pass over
[MATT. XXIII, 23] the weightier matters of the law, judgment,
[MATT. XXIII, 23] mercy and faith and the love of God; these
ought ye to have done, and not to leave the other un-
done: [MATT. XXIII, 24] ye blind guides, which strain at a gnat,
and swallow a camel. ⁴⁴ Wo unto you, scribes and Pharisees, hypocrites! for ye are as graves which appear
not, and the men that walk over them are not aware
of them; [MATT. XXIII, 27] ye are like unto whited sepulchres,
which indeed appear beautiful outward, but are within full of
dead men's bones and of all uncleanness: [28] even so ye also
outwardly appear righteous unto men, but within ye are full
of hypocrisy and iniquity.

⁴⁵ Then answered one of the lawyers and said unto
him, Master, thus saying, thou reproachest *us* also.
⁴⁶ And he said, Wo unto you also, ye lawyers! for ye
lade men with burdens grievous to be borne, and ye
yourselves touch not the burdens with one of your
fingers. ⁵² Wo unto you, lawyers! for ye have taken
60

swered, "See, here are the members of my [spirit- **MATT. XII.**
ual] family! [50] Yes, and not only these, but every
one else that *complies with the will of my Heavenly
Father* a as made known by me, l is nearer to my heart than my
mere earthly kindred."

[37] While Jesus was making these observations, one of **Luke XI.**
the Pharisees present invited him to partake of dinner
[i. e. the noon lunch] with him. Accepting the offer,
Jesus entered his house, and at once took his place on the couch
before the table. [38] The Pharisee noticed with marks of cynical
surprise that his guest did not perform the usual ablutions before
the repast. [39] [Aware of these reflections in his host's mind, and
observing that the domestics were very particular in rubbing the
exterior surface of the dishes set on the table, in order to free them
from any accidental impurity,] Jesus made this cutting comment:
"Aye! you b hypocritical! Pharisees are extremely nice in making
the *outside* of your drinking cups and b preserve! plates clean, but
quite overlook the fact that the *inside* is filled with the fruits of extortionate improbity! [40] Dolts that you are! to act as if the outside
and the inside of a dish were not made alike, and for equal cleanli-
ness. [41] I would advise all such c blear-eyed! persons, first to cleanse
the inside of their dish of its moral defilement, by bestowing a portion c of its contents! in charity; and then, c whether the outside
be ceremonially lustrated or not, l the whole will be pure for you
[in the divine estimation]. [42] Alas for you d hypocritical scribes
and! Pharisees! who in your zeal for paying the tithe of your entire
produce, even down to mint and rue d and dill and cummin! and
every other insignificant herb, do yet neglect d the far more important injunctions of the divine law, such as! justice and d compassion
toward men, and faith and! love toward God; while you should not
omit the former, you are most imperatively bound to attend to these
latter. e And [so you undertake not merely to practice, but also to
teach religion,] yourselves as unfit as 'stark blind guides' are to
conduct travelers; you are always 'straining out the wine-flies' one
moment, and then 'gulping down some camel' the next. l [44] Yes,
you false-hearted scribes and Pharisees! you are like concealed
graves, over which persons tread unaware of their liability to pol-
lution, f or like whitewashed tombs, which on the outside indeed
look fresh and fair, but inside are choked with corpses' bones and
hideous foulness; l g just so you [by your ablutions and scrupulous
observances,] seem uncommonly sanctimonious and upright exter-
nally to human sight, but at heart you are all hypocrisy and knavish ungodliness." l

[45] Here he was interrupted by one of the professional expounders
of the Law, who replied, "By making such sweeping denunciations
as these, Teacher, you insult *us* likewise." [46] "Yes," returned Jesus, "I say, alas for you lawyers too! for [by the rigorous construction and additions put by you upon the ceremonial Law,] you load
your fellow-men with intolerable religious burdens, but do not raise
a single finger toward bearing them yourselves. [52] In this way,
you h lock up the entrance to the 'Reign of the Divine Messiah' in
others' faces, l by taking away from them its key of true religious

---

a Luke viii, 21.   b Matt. xxiii, 25.   c Matt. xxiii, 26.   d Matt. xxiii, 23.
e Matt. xxiii, 24.   f Matt. xxiii, 27.   g Matt. xxiii, 28.   h Matt. xxiii, 13.

away the key of knowledge, [Matt. XXIII, 13]   LUKE XI.
and shut up the kingdom of heaven against men;
ye entered not in yourselves, and them that were entering in ye hindered.

53 And as he said these things unto them, the scribes
and the Pharisees began to urge him vehemently, and
to provoke him to speak of many things; 54 laying
wait for him, and seeking to catch something out of
his mouth, that they might accuse him.

§ 52.—*Discourses to the Disciples and Multitude.*

(Capernaum; [*October ?*] A. D. 27.)

1 In the mean time, when there were   Luke XII.
gathered together an innumerable multi-
tude of people, insomuch that they trode one upon another, he began to say unto his disciples first of all,
Beware ye of hypocrisy.

13 And one of the company said unto him, Master,
speak to my brother, that he divide the inheritance
with me. 14 And he said unto him, Man, who made
me a judge or a divider over you? 15 And he said
unto them, Take heed and beware of covetousness;
for a man's life consisteth not in the abundance of the
things which he possesseth. 16 And he spake a parable unto them saying, The ground of a certain rich
man brought forth plentifully: 17 and he thought within himself saying, What shall I do, because I have no
room where to bestow my fruits? 18 And he said,
This will I do: I will pull down my barns and build
greater; and there will I bestow all my fruits and my
goods: 19 and I will say to my soul, Soul, thou hast
much goods laid up for many years; take thine ease,
eat, drink and be merry. 20 But *God* said unto him,
Thou fool, this night thy soul shall be required of thee:
then whose shall those things be which thou hast pro-

61

knowledge; so that you both refuse to enter there   LUKE XI.
yourselves, and prevent such others as would from
entering."

⁵³ In consequence of these severe reflections upon them, the
copyists and interpreters of the Law and the Pharisees generally conceived [a deadly grudge against Jesus, and concerted]
the project of proposing various difficult questions to him for
unpremeditated solution, ⁵⁴ with the design of slyly watching
his answers, to catch some unguarded expression from his lips,
which might be used as a ground of ecclesiastical or civil
accusation.

§ 52.—Discourses to the Disciples and Multitude.

(Capernaum; [October ?] A. D. 27.)

¹ The repast being concluded, [Jesus returned   **Luke XII.**
to his own residence; but while he was on his way
thither,] so great a concourse of people gathered
about him, as well nigh to trample upon one another. As he
was addressing a caution to his disciples, to "shun by all
means the hypocritical doctrines of the Pharisees," ¹³ one of
the assembled crowd interrupted him with this request,
"Teacher, my brother refuses to settle our father's estate with
me; have the goodness to interpose your authority, by requiring him to allow me my share." ¹⁴ Jesus replied [by a sharp
rebuke of his cupidity and misconception of the Messiah's of-
fice], "Who, sir, ever 'constituted me a civil judge or arbitra-
tor' in your secular matters?" ¹⁵ Then addressing the concourse generally, he proceeded, "Take warning [from this ex-
ample], and guard against a grasping disposition, remembering
that the happiness of life does not depend upon the amount
of one's possessions; [but true enjoyment flows only from a
contented use of a sufficiency for one's actual wants.] ¹⁶ He
next went on to illustrate the folly of reliance upon gain by
the following instance: "The farm of a certain opulent man
yielded so unusually plentiful a return one season, ¹⁷ as to
make him at a loss in his mind, how to find room for stor-
ing away all the produce. ¹⁸ At last he resolved to tear down
his barns and build more capacious ones, in which to deposit
his whole crop and other effects; ¹⁹ and then [in his self-
gratulation at his worldly prospects,] he said to himself, 'I
have now plenty of provisions stored up to last me a good
many years to come; I will sit down contented, and eat and
drink what I like, and take my fill of comfort.' ²⁰ [Little did
he think that] God was at that hour preparing for him the
summons [of His providence], 'Stupid sensualist! surrender
your earthly existence this very night!—and who will then

61*

vided? ²¹ So is he that layeth up treas-   LUKE XII.
ure for himself, and is not rich toward
God.

²² And he said unto his disciples, Therefore I
say unto you, Take no thought for your life, what
ye shall eat; neither for the body, what ye shall
put on: ²³ the life is more than meat, and the body
is more than raiment. ²⁴ Consider the ravens: for
they neither sow nor reap, which neither have
store-house nor barn; and God feedeth *them:* how
much more are ye better than the fowls! ⁶ Are
not five sparrows sold for two farthings? and not
one of them is forgotten before God; ⁷ fear not
therefore, ye are of more value than many sparrows: but even the very hairs of your head are
all numbered; [LUKE XXI, 18] there shall not a hair of
your head perish. ²⁵ And which of you with taking thought can add to his stature one cubit?
²⁶ if ye then be not able to do that thing which
is least, why take ye thought for the rest?
[MATT. VI, 28] And why take ye thought for raiment?
²⁷ consider the lilies how they grow; they toil
not, they spin not; and yet I say unto you, that
Solomon in all his glory was not arrayed like
one of these: ²⁸ if then God so clothe the grass,
which is to-day in the field and to-morrow is cast
into the oven; how much more will he clothe
you, O ye of little faith! ²⁹ And seek not ye
what ye shall eat or what ye shall drink [MATT. VI, 31]
or wherewithal ye shall be clothed, neither be ye of
doubtful mind; ³⁰ (for all these things do the nations of the world seek after; and your Father
knoweth that ye have need of these things:) ³¹ but
rather seek ye [MATT. VI, 33] *first* the kingdom of God
[MATT. VI, 33] and his righteousness, and all these things

enjoy what you have amassed?'   21 Such is the fate   LUKE XII.
of him who accumulates wealth for his own purposes
merely, neglecting [those heavenly riches which
would be insured by] the consecration of his property to God."

22 Then applying the subject to his more immediate disciples, he
continued, " In view of this'[inability of earthly possessions to secure permanent happiness], I charge you, never suffer yourselves
to be distressed with solicitude, as to how you shall obtain food for
sustaining life or clothing for the body.   23 Is not your life itself a
more eminent bestowment than the means of subsistence, and your
body a more valuable gift than clothing for it?—[surely then He
who has already conferred the greater blessing, will not withhold
the less.]   24 Consider for a moment the condition of *a* the birds that
fly through the air,l the very crows, [those outcasts from human
interest;] *they* have no fields to sow or reap, nor harvest to gather
into grain-cellars or barns, and yet *a* your Heavenly Father l supplies
food [by the arrangements of nature] for these unfurnished creatures;—certainly you are of vastly more importance than the wild
feathered tribes.   6 [Nor is the universality of the divine care its
only feature; it is so particular also in its application, that] not one
of the very sparrows, that sell in market for the insignificant price
of *b* two for an *assa'rius* [i. e. 1½ cents], orl two *assa'rit* [i. e. 3
cents] for five, *b* perishes l unheeded by *b* your Heavenly Father,l
the all-superintending Deity ;—7 then assuredly, you who are so in-
comparably more important in the scale of creation than mere sparrows, need not be alarmed [lest your safety as well as wants be not
provided for.   No indeed; for the divine care is so minute, that]
the very hairs of your head may be said to be individually counted
in His *c* preserving l economy.   25 Is any one of you able, by exercising his most anxious ingenuity, to increase his stature by a single
foot, [as he grows up to manhood, or by the least part of one? his
physical form becomes developed by the providential course of nature, independently of his own will;] 26 if therefore you have no
control over a matter so trivial as this, of what use is it to be under
great concern about the other particulars of your life? *d* Again,
why need you occasion yourselves uneasiness respecting a due supply of *clothing* for your persons?l—27 learn a lesson from the lilies,
that grow and bloom without culture *d* in the open meadow; l *they*
neither toil for a subsistence, nor spin a dress to wear, and yet I aver
that King Solomon, in all the splendor of his unrivaled court, was
never arrayed in apparel of such gorgeous hues as deck one of these
flowers of spontaneous growth.   28 If, then, the God of providence
thus sumptuously adorns the very plants of the common, that blossom one day, and wither the next into mere fuel for the baking-jar,
He will far more certainly clothe you His human creatures, who
nevertheless betray such a prevalent want of confidence in Him.
29 Do not therefore *e* anxiously l inquire, 'How shall we get food and
drink *e* and clothing,'l as if you had any occasion to be thus in suspense: 30 for [you ought to feel rebuked, to remember that] it is a
universal trait of *heathen* nations, to be engrossed in temporal cares;
but *you* should bethink yourselves that your *f* Heavenly l Father is
aware of your physical necessities, [and will provide for them, if you
trust yourselves in His hands.]   31 Consequently, the true course for
you to pursue in this matter is, to make it your FIRST endeavor to
become members of the ' Reign of the Divine Messiah,' and participants in the genuine holiness that He enjoins, and then you may

a Mat. vi, 26.   *b* Mat. x, 29.   *c* Lu. xxi, 18.   *d* Mat. vi, 28.   *e* Mat. vi, 31.   *f* Mat. vi, 32.

shall be added unto you.   [MATT. VI, 34] Take   **LUKE XII.**
therefore no thought for the morrow; for the
morrow shall take thought for the things of itself: sufficient
unto the day is the evil thereof.   33 Sell that ye have,
and give alms : [MATT. VI, 19] lay not up for yourselves treasures upon earth, where moth and rust doth corrupt, and
where thieves break through and steal; but provide yourselves bags which wax not old, a treasure in the
heavens that faileth not, where no thief approacheth,
neither moth [MATT. VI, 20] nor rust corrupteth : 34 for
where your treasure is, there will your heart be
also.

1 There were present at that season   **Luke XIII.**
some that told him of the Galileans, whose
blood Pilate had mingled with their sacrifices.   2 And
Jesus answering said unto them, Suppose ye that
these Galileans were sinners above all the Galileans,
because they suffered such things ?   3 I tell you, Nay ;
but except ye repent, *ye* shall all likewise perish.
4 Or those eighteen, upon whom the tower in Siloam
fell and slew them, think ye that they were sinners
above all men that dwelt in Jerusalem ?   5 I tell you,
Nay ; but except *ye* repent, ye shall all likewise perish.   6 He spake also this parable : A certain man
had a fig-tree planted in his vineyard; and he came
and sought fruit thereon, and found none.   7 Then
said he unto the dresser of his vineyard, Behold, these
three years I come seeking fruit on this fig-tree and
find none : cut it down ; why cumbereth it the ground ?
8 And he answering said unto him, Lord, let it alone
this year also, till I shall dig about it, and dung it :
9 and if it bear fruit, well ; and if not, then after that
thou shalt cut it down.

63

rest assured that a supply for all these earthly require- **LUKE XII.**
ments will be superadded to the spiritual blessings that
you will thence derive. *a* So you have no cause to be
distressed with care for the wants of a coming day; when that future arrives, it will be abundant time to consider its temporal exigencies, [and there is One who will then provide for them;]l 'every
day has troubles enough of itself,' [without borrowing any from the
next. 33 Thus, rather than imitate the acquisitiveness of this man
whom I just now reproved;] you would do well to dispose of your
property, [if it be a hinderance to you in espousing my persecuted
cause,] and distribute the proceeds in charity; by which course you
will deposit them in a celestial purse that will never wear out.   And,
b instead of accumulating wealth here on earth, where the moth may
ruin your store of clothing, or the worm eat up your stock of grain,
or the thief come and dig through the walls of your dwelling, and
steal away your hoard of money;l acquire an unfailing treasure in
heaven, which is exposed to none of these accidents. 34 Then [you
will not be distracted from attention to your spiritual interests by secular pursuits; but] 'where your property lies, there your feelings will
be enlisted too,' [namely, in the concerns of the heavenly world.]"

1 Some of the company present from Judea on this **Luke XIII.**
occasion informed Jesus of [an atrocity that had lately occurred to] certain Galileans, whom Pilate had
executed [for being concerned in an insurrectionary movement at
Jerusalem, butchering them while engaged at the very altar, and
thus] mingling their blood with that of the sacrificial animals they
were then offering [in the temple court; hoping by the recital to
gain his sympathy against the oppressor]. 2 Jesus, however, [in-
stead of expressing any opinion whatever in this respect, made use
of the occurrence to correct an uncharitable opinion prevalent
among the Jews respecting such calamities, and] replied, " Do you
suppose that those Galilean sufferers were more heinous sinners
than any of their fellow-countrymen, and that on this account they
came to such a miserable end? 3 Such an inference, let me tell
you, would be far from just; for [your entire nation has so grievously departed from God, that] unless you speedily repent and re-
form, a like fate will overtake you all! 4 Again, you may imagine
that those eighteen persons, who were recently crushed to death by
the fall of the tower at the fountain of Shilo'ah, had transgressed
the divine Law in some more flagrant manner than any other inhabitant of Jerusalem; 5 but that was not necessarily true, for [once
more I warn you, that your whole city has so flagitiously offended Jehovah, by its irreligion and rejection of me, that] unless you avert the
blow by a timely repentance, an equally signal ruin awaits you all!"

6 He then proceeded to enforce the admonition by the following
illustration: " Suppose a proprietor has a fig-tree planted in his
vineyard, and [at the usual age for bearing,] he goes expecting to
get fruit from it, but is disappointed by finding it barren. 7 He naturally says to his gardener, 'See, this is the third year since I set
out this fig-tree, and now when I have come to gather the fruit, I
find it does not bear at all! cut it down at once; what is the use of
its occupying the ground, [and so excluding other products, without
yielding any fruit itself!]' 8 But the forbearing gardener intercedes,
'Still, master, let it stand this one year more, till I give it another
trial, by loosening and enriching the soil around it; 9 perhaps it will
bear fruit next season,—but if it should not, then [I'll not plead for
it any longer, and] you may cut it down.'"—*a* Mat. vi, 34. *b* Mat. vi, 19.

§ 53.—*Parables addressed to the Populace.*

(Lake Gennesareth, near Capernaum; [*October?*] A. D. 27.)

[1] The same day went Jesus out of the   **Matt. XIII.**
house, and sat [MARK IV, 1] again to teach by
the sea-side : [2] and great multitudes were gathered
together unto him [LUKE VIII, 4] out of every city, so that he
went into a ship and sat; and the whole multitude
stood on the shore.   [3] And he spake many things unto them in parables saying, [MARK IV, 3] Hearken; Behold,
a sower went forth to sow : [4] and when he sowed,
some seeds fell by the wayside, [LUKE VIII, 5] and were
trodden down, and the fowls came and devoured them
up ; [5] some fell upon stony places, where they had not
much earth, and forthwith they sprung up, because
they had no deepness of earth, [6] and when the sun was
up, they were scorched, and because they had no root
[LUKE VIII, 6] and lacked moisture, they withered away ;
[7] and some fell among thorns, and the thorns sprung
up and choked them, [MARK IV, 7] and they yielded no fruit :
[8] but other fell into good ground, and [MARK IV, 8] sprang
up and increased and brought forth fruit, some a hundred-fold, some sixty-fold, some thirty-fold.   [LUKE VIII, 8]
And when he had said these things, he cried, [9] Who hath
ears to hear, let him hear.

[24] Another parable put he forth unto them saying,
The kingdom of heaven is likened unto a man which
sowed good seed in his field; [25] but while men slept,
his enemy came and sowed tares among the wheat,
and went his way : [26] but when the blade was sprung
up and brought forth fruit, then appeared the tares
also.   [27] So the servants of the householder came and
said unto him, Sir, didst not thou sow good seed in
thy field? from whence then hath it tares? [28] He
said unto them, An enemy hath done this.   The ser-

64

§ 53.—*Parables addressed to the Populace.*

(Lake Gennesareth, near Capernaum; [*October ?*] A. D. 27.)

[1] Leaving his residence again in the course of the afternoon of the same day, Jesus repaired to the shore of the lake Gennesareth, and took a seat there, [a] for the purpose of instructing the populace! [2] that constantly thronged around him, [b] from the neighboring villages,| [whenever he appeared abroad.] Presently, the crowd became so great as to oblige him [in order to escape their pressure,] to get into a boat, and while seated in it a short distance out on the water, to address the concourse standing on the shore. [3] He thus discoursed to them at length, conveying his instructions in an allegorical style, as follows: "Suppose a husbandman goes out into his field to sow some grain; the success of different portions of the seed will be various. [4] Some of it, for instance, is scattered along the beaten pathway; this is [c] partly trodden to pieces by the passers-by,| and what escapes this fate, the [c] wild| birds that come along pick up and devour. [5] Another portion, it may be, falls upon a stony spot, where there is not a sufficiency of soil; this shallowness of the earth makes its sprouts appear above ground the more quickly, [6] but when the sun shines out hot after the rainy weather, the shoots are soon scorched, and wither away, on account of their want of roots, [d] to supply them with moisture.| [7] Another part, perhaps, is cast among a patch of thorn roots; and these sprouting up [e] along with it,| soon choke it, [f] so that it never comes to anything.| [8] But the rest of the seed probably drops on good soil, [g] where it comes up well, grows thriftily,| and yields an ample return, varying from thirty to sixty and even a hundred fold, [according to circumstances.]—[9] 'Let every one that has ears to hear with,'" [h] added Jesus emphatically,| "'hear and understand' this instruction."

[24] Another illustration that he made use of was this: "The 'Reign of the Divine Messiah' may be compared to a farmer, who sows good grain in his field; [25] but in the dead of the night, some one, who owes him a grudge, goes and scatters *darnel* seeds over the sown field, and escapes unobserved. [26] As soon, however, as the shooting grain begins to blossom, and the heads to set, the darnel too becomes apparent among it. [27] So the farmer's workmen come and tell him, 'Master, you sowed good clean grain in your field, did you not? where then has all this darnel come from?' [28] But he answers them, 'Some ill-disposed person has done this mischief.' The men

Matt. XIII.

---

[a] Mark iv, 1.   [b] Luke viii, 4.   [c] Luke viii, 5.   [d] Luke viii, 6.
[e] Luke viii, 7.   [f] Mark iv, 7.   [g] Mark iv, 8.   [h] Luke viii, 8.

L

64*

vants said unto him, Wilt thou then that   MATT. XIII.
we go and gather them up ?   ²⁹ But he
said, Nay ; lest while ye gather up the tares, ye root
up also the wheat with them : ³⁰ let both grow together
until the harvest, and in the time of harvest I will say
to the reapers, Gather ye together first the tares, and
bind them in bundles to burn them ; but gather the
wheat into my barn.

²⁶ And he said, So is the kingdom of God   **Mark IV.**
as if a man should cast seed into the ground,
²⁷ and should sleep and rise night and day, and the
seed should spring and grow up, he knoweth not how ;
²⁸ for the earth bringeth forth fruit of herself, first the
blade, then the ear, after that the full corn in the ear :
²⁹ but when the fruit is brought forth, immediately he
putteth in the sickle, because the harvest is come.

³¹ Another parable put he forth unto   **Matt. XIII.**
them saying, [MARK IV, 30] Whereunto shall we
liken the kingdom of God ? or with what comparison shall we
compare it ? The kingdom of heaven is like to a grain
of mustard-seed, which a man took and sowed in his
field : ³² which indeed is the least of all seeds ; but
when it is grown, it is the greatest among herbs, and
becometh a tree, [MARK IV, 32] and shooteth out great branches ;
so that the birds of the air come and lodge in the
branches [MARK IV, 32] and under the shadow thereof.

³³ Another parable spake he unto them : [LUKE XIII, 20]
Whereunto shall I liken the kingdom of God ? The kingdom of heaven is like unto leaven, which a woman
took and hid in three measures of meal, till the whole
was leavened.

³⁴ All these [MARK IV, 33] and many such things spake
Jesus unto the multitude in parables, [MARK IV, 33] as they
were able to hear it ; and without a parable spake he not
unto them ; ³⁵ that it might be fulfilled which was

65

then naturally say, 'If you like, we will go at   MATT. XIII.
once and pull it all out.'   ²⁹ But he replies,
'No, do not weed out the darnel now, by any
means; lest in doing so, you should tear up the grain by the
roots along with it.   ³⁰ Let them both grow together till the
harvest: and then I will direct the reapers to collect first the
darnels [as they cut them down], and bind them up by themselves into bundles for fuel, but to gather up the
grain and store it in my barn.'—²⁶ [There is an-   **Mark IV.**
other analogy in this comparison,]" continued Je-
sus: "The 'Reign of the Divine Messiah' [in its
patient labors for the salvation of men, calmly waiting for the
results in due time of the force of truth under the divine blessing, yet prepared to take advantage of every hopeful indica-
tion,] resembles the husbandman in committing his grain to
the earth, ²⁷ and then [resting in secure expectation of a crop,]
going to bed at night and rising in the morning as usual, while
the seed is sprouting and growing, without his [assisting or]
comprehending the process.   ²⁸ For the soil yields its products
by its own germinating property; first bringing forth the tender blade, then expanding the head of grain, and finally ma-
turing the plump kernel in the head.   ²⁹ But as soon as the
crop shows itself fit for harvesting, [the husbandman's time
for action returns, and] he immediately sends out the reapers
with their sickles into the harvest-field."

³¹ A third illustration employed was this: **Matt. XIII.**
"The 'Reign of the Divine Messiah' [in its sure
progress, from the smallest beginnings,] may
also be compared to a grain of mustard-seed, which one takes
and plants in his garden: ³² it is itself among the smallest
kinds of seeds [common among us], but [a] being sown, it comes
up,| grows and spreads out into one of our largest plants, be-
ing often quite a little tree in size and shape, [a] and sending
out considerable branches,| so as to afford no little shelter for
the roving birds under its foliage."

³³ "In like manner," added he, "the 'Reign of the Divine
Messiah' resembles [in this its gradually disseminative character,] a housewife, that takes a piece of fermented dough,
and kneads it with three se'ahs [i. e. about one bushel] of
flour, by the diffusion of which the whole mass is ultimately
fermented."

³⁴ In this way, Jesus delivered his instructions to the people
by the means of figurative representations, carefully avoiding
any more explicit mode of communication in public, [b] which
they were not then in a fit state of mind to appreciate.|
³⁵ This method of teaching, too, was in accordance with that
proposed by the sacred writer in the Psalms,—

a Mark iv, 32.   *b* Mark iv, 33.

65*

spoken by the prophet saying,* I will　MATT. XIII.
open my mouth in parables, I will utter
things which have been kept secret from the foundation of the world.　³⁶ Then Jesus sent the multitude
away, and went into the house.

§ 54.—*Explanation of the Parables.*

(Capernaum; [*October ?*] A. D. 27.)

¹⁰ And [MARK IV, 10] when he was alone, the disciples
[MARK IV, 10] that were about him with the twelve, came and
said unto him, Why speakest thou unto them in parables? [LUKE VIII, 9] What might this parable be?　¹¹ He answered and said unto them, Because it is given unto
you to know the mysteries of the kingdom of heaven,
but to them [MARK IV, 11] that are without it is not given.
¹³ Therefore speak I to them in parables ; because they
seeing see not, and hearing they hear not, neither do
they understand : ¹⁴ and in them is fulfilled the prophecy of Esaias which saith,† By hearing ye shall hear,
and shall not understand ; and seeing ye shall see, and
shall not perceive : ¹⁵ for this people's heart is waxed
gross, and their ears are dull of hearing, and their eyes
they have closed ; lest at any time they should see
with their eyes, and hear with their ears, and should
understand with their heart, and should be converted,
and I should heal them, [MARK IV, 12] and their sins should
be forgiven them. [LUKE X, 23] And he turned him unto his
disciples and said privately, ¹⁶ But blessed are *your* eyes,
for they see ; and your ears, for they hear : ¹⁷ for verily I say unto you, That many prophets and righteous
men [LUKE X, 24] and kings have desired to see those things
which ye see, and have not seen them ; and to hear
those things which ye hear, and have not heard them.
[MARK IV, 13] Know ye not this parable? and how then will ye

---

* Psa. lxxviii, 2.　　　† Isa. vi, 9, 10.

> "With various *examples* I will speak,   Matt. XIII.
> Rehearsing ancient things in meaning deep."

36 These discourses being concluded, he dismissed the assembled people, and retired to his own residence in the village.

§ 54.—*Explanation of the Parables.*

(Capernaum; [*October ?*] A. D. 27.)

10·a As soon as Jesus was withdrawn [from the populace into his own house], the apostles and several other of his special adherents came and asked him, "What is your object in addressing the people in such figurative language? b Please explain to us the meaning of the emblem of the *Sower.*" 11 "I use this mode of illustration," replied he, "because to *you* alone belongs the privilege of clearly understanding the mysterious developments [that will hereafter take place] under the 'Reign of the Divine Messiah;' [such a full revelation of] its plans being withheld from the c uninitiated mass, who are not prepared for the disclosure.] 13 On this account, I discourse to them by means of symbolical illustrations suited to their [mental condition, which is a] state of 'seeing, and yet not perceiving; of hearing, and still not understanding,' [by reason of their disinclination to religious truth.] 14 Thus, what the prophet Isaiah declared [of his own countrymen], holds true of this race,—

> 'You hear my words, but comprehend them not;
> You see, but fail my errand to perceive:
> 15 For this incorrigible people's heart
> Is stupid grown to spiritual things,—
> Their inward ears obtuse refuse to hear
> God's truth, they close the eye-sight of their souls;
> Resolved they will not be convinced thereby,
> To change their evil ways, and pardon find.'

16 On the contrary, happy are you, whose eyes are privileged to see intelligently the divine economy, and whose ears are enabled to hear understandingly its saving doctrines! 17 Yes, I tell you, many an ancient prophet and saint d and even prince has earnestly longed to witness the scenes which you are now favored to behold, and to listen to the developments of sacred knowledge which you are now permitted to hear; but they did not live in an age to gratify their desire.

e "But do you not really understand the illustration of the 'Sower'? how then can you be relied on to comprehend other

a Mark iv, 10.   b Luke viii, 9.   c Mark iv, 11.   d Luke x, 24.   e Mark iv, 13.

66*

know all parables?   ¹⁸ Hear ye therefore   MATT. XIII.
the parable of the sower : [MARK IV, 14] The
sower soweth the word of God.   ¹⁹ This is he which received seed by the way-side ; when any one heareth
the word of the kingdom and understandeth it not, then
cometh the wicked one, and catcheth away that which
was sown in his heart ; [LUKE VIII, 12] lest he should believe
and be saved : 20 but he that received the seed into stony
places, the same is he that heareth the word, and anon
with joy receiveth it, ²¹ yet hath he not root in himself
but dureth for a while, for when tribulation or persecution ariseth because of the word, by and by he is
offended : ²² he also that received seed among the
thorns, is he that heareth the word [LUKE VIII, 14] and goeth
forth, and the care of this world and the deceitfulness
of riches [MARK IV, 19] and the lusts of other things entering in
choke the word, and he becometh unfruitful : ²³ but he
that received seed into the good ground, is he that
heareth the word [MARK IV, 20] and receiveth it [LUKE VIII, 15]
in an honest and good heart and understandeth it, which
also beareth fruit [LUKE VIII, 15] with patience and bringeth
forth, some a hundred-fold, some sixty, some thirty.

[MARK IV, 21] And he said unto them, ¹⁵ Neither   **Matt. V.**
do men light a candle and put it [LUKE XI, 33] in
a secret place, neither under a bushel [MARK IV, 21] or under
a bed, but on a candlestick ; and it giveth light unto
all that are in the house.   ¹⁴ *Ye* are the light of
the world : a city that is set on a hill cannot be
hid ; ¹⁶ let *your* light so shine before men, that they
may see your good works, and glorify your Fa-
ther which is in heaven.   ²² The light
of the body is the eye : if therefore   **Matt. VI.**
thine eye be single, thy whole body
shall be full of light, [LUKE XI, 36] having no part dark, as
when the bright shining of a candle doth give thee light ;
²³ but if thine eye be evil, thy whole body shall be full
67

allegorical communications [such as I shall have oc-   MATT. XIII.
casion to make in public]?¹   ¹⁸ However, listen to
its interpretation : a The Sower signifies the promul-
gator l b of the gospel; l   ¹⁹ the parts of the field sown along the pathway, represent such persons as do not give sufficient heed to the instructions concerning the 'Messiah's Reign,' to comprehend them
when heard ; in consequence of which, when Satan comes [with his
deceptive insinuations], he is thus enabled to efface the slight impression made by religious truth upon their mind, [like a bird
snatching up seed from the surface of the ground.] ²⁰ The stony
part of the field denotes those hearers, who indeed receive my instructions with enthusiasm at first, ²¹ but [in consequence of not
allowing them to take a deep hold upon their judgments and purposes,] like seed rooting in shallow soil, they make but fickle and
temporary converts; so that when troubles or persecutions subsequently arise to them on account of their espousal of my cause, [be-
ing unfortified against these,] they are soon discouraged and abandon their faith. ²² The thorny portion of the field corresponds to
another class of hearers, who, c on leaving my presence, l suffer a too
earnest solicitude about their temporal affairs, and an excessive desire of wealth, d and an undue attachment to other earthly interests
and pleasures, to absorb their attention, l to the exclusion of the para-
mount pursuits of religion, [like weeds choking up a plant] until it
becomes unproductive. ²³ The good soil that is sown upon, however,
is emblematical of such hearers, as e gladly receive l the divine instruction f into minds well prepared to appreciate [and improve] it, l
and who consequently exhibit the f permanent l fruits of it in their
conduct; like grain that bears a hundred, sixty or thirty fold, [ac-
cording to the quality of the soil.]

¹⁵ "On the same principle [of expecting some useful   Matt. V.
effect to follow an action]," continued Jesus, "no one
lights a lamp, and then covers it over with a mo'dius
[i. e. a peck measure, nearly,] g or any other such utensil, l nor puts
it h in a hiding place, l g as under the couch ; l but places it on a can-
dela'brum [i. e. a lamp-stand], that it may afford its light to the
family g and guests. l   ¹⁴ In like manner, you, my disciples, are designed to be the moral illuminators of the world, and therefore, like
a city built upon a hill, which is conspicuous far and near, [unob-
scured by any intercepting object,] ¹⁶ you also should send forth the
radiance of your religious precepts [in every direction, from the
eminence of station to which you are raised, enforcing them by an
example of holy living]; so that all within the circle of your influence may witness your distinguished but unostentatious piety, and
may thus be constrained to honor and serve your Heavenly Father,
[who has enabled you thus to attest His truth.] ²² Now   Matt. VI.
you know, 'the eye serves for a light to the body,' [and
upon its healthy state depends the correctness of one's
physical movements;] just so, when the eye of your soul's intention
is sound and susceptible to the light of conviction, your whole
mental system will be illuminated with a clear perception of
sacred things, i as free from moral dimness in every part as a room
lighted by a brilliant lamp; l ²³ but whenever this spiritual eye is
diseased [with prejudice, or beclouded with unholy motives], the
entire frame of the moral powers becomes enshrouded in error

a Mark iv, 14.   b Luke viii, 11.   c Luke viii, 14.   d Mark iv, 19.   e Mark iv, 20.
f Luke viii, 15.   g Luke viii, 16.   h Luke xi, 33.   i Luke xi, 36.

of darkness : if therefore the light that is   MATT. VI.
in thee be darkness, how great is that
darkness ! [LUKE XI, 35] take heed therefore.—
26 For there is nothing covered, that shall not   Matt. X.
be revealed ; and hid, that shall not be known :
27 what I tell you in darkness, that speak ye in light ;
and what ye hear in the ear [LUKE XII, 3] in closets, that
preach ye upon the house-tops.   24 And he   Mark IV.
said unto them, Take heed [LUKE VIII, 18] how
ye hear ; and unto you that hear, shall more be given :
12 for whosoever hath, to him shall be   Matt. XIII.
given, and he shall have more abundance ;
but whosoever hath not, from him shall be taken away
even that he [LUKE VIII, 18] seemeth to have.

36 And his disciples came unto him saying, Declare
unto us the parable of the tares of the field.   37 He
answered and said unto them, He that soweth the good
seed is the Son of man, 38 the field is the world, the
good seed are the children of the kingdom, but the
tares are the children of the wicked one, 39 the enemy
that sowed them is the devil, the harvest is the end of
the world, and the reapers are the angels : 40 as therefore the tares are gathered and burned in the fire, so
shall it be in the end of this world ; 41 the Son of man
shall send forth his angels, and they shall gather out
of his kingdom all things that offend, and them which
do iniquity, 42 and shall cast them into a furnace of
fire ; there shall be wailing and gnashing of teeth :
43 then shall the righteous shine forth as the sun in
the kingdom of their Father.   Who hath ears to hear,
let him hear.—47 Again the kingdom of heaven is like
unto a net, that was cast into the sea and gathered of
every kind, 48 which, when it was full, they drew to
shore, and sat down and gathered the good into vessels,
but cast the bad away : 49 so shall it be at the end of
the world ; the angels shall come forth and sever the

and depravity. *a* Beware, | therefore, lest the religious MATT. VI.
light with which you are now favored, be withdrawn
and leave you to spiritual darkness, [by reason of a failure on your part to improve it aright; for should such a change
occur,] how much more aggravated [will be the spiritual delusion in
which you will be involved, by a perversion of such light as you now
enjoy!] 26 [If you would avoid such a fate, you must be Matt. X.
diligent in disseminating the principles inculcated upon
you:] for in this as in other matters, 'there is no affair so
private as will not some time be disclosed, nor anything so obscure
as not to be ultimately known with public certainty;' 27 so that
whatever explanations I now give you in the darkness of privacy,
you are to declare eventually in the blaze of noon-day, and the truths
you are hearing whispered, as it were, in your ear *b* in the retirement
of a secret room, | you must soon preach with all the publicity of a
'proclamation from the roof of the house.' 24 Be care- Mark IV.
ful, then, to heed what you now hear from me;
12 for upon the improvement which you as well as my Matt. XIII.
other hearers make of my communications, depends
the bestowal of additional instruction: whoever makes
a good use of the religious knowledge he already has, will receive an
increase of it; but he that neglects to do so, will soon experience
the total loss of what he *c* fancies he still | possesses."

36 His disciples then begged him to "explain to them the meaning
of the allegory of the *Darnels* in the field of grain." 37 He did so by
replying, "The husbandman, who sows the good grain, represents the
'Son of Man;' 38 the field typifies the world of mankind [and specially
the Jewish community]; the good seed is an emblem of the true
members of the 'Messiah's Reign;' the darnels denote the wicked;
39 the enemy, that sows them, means Satan; the harvest-time corresponds to the termination of the terrestrial existence of the human
race, [and in a local application to the conclusion of the Jewish com-
monwealth]; and the reapers answer to angels, [or in the particular
instance referred to, they signify the providential agents in the final
catastrophe]. 40 Accordingly, as the darnels are gathered and consumed for fuel, just so at the conclusion of human probation [either
in general or specially], 41 the 'Son of Man' will commission his appointed instruments to collect from among the professed members
of his 'Reign' all the teachers of pernicious doctrines, and all who
have led irreligious lives, 42 and hurl them into the flaming furnace
of [temporal and] eternal perdition;—there will their anguish be
vented in fruitless lamentation and grating of the teeth! 43 But at
that [final] distinction in the destiny of mortals, the true saints will
be invested, in the [consummation of the] 'Reign of [the Divine
Messiah'—then become that of] their Heavenly Father,—with a
glory like that of the resplendent sun. 'Let every one having ears
to hear with, hear and understand' these solemn truths.

47 "[In respect to this same feature of the mixed character of its
apparent members on earth,] the 'Reign of the Divine Messiah'
may likewise be compared to a fisherman's drag-net, which is
dropped out in the lake, and encloses fish of every kind promiscu-
ously; 48 but when a sufficient number have thus been caught, it is
hauled ashore, and the men [getting out of the boat and] sitting down
on the beach, select the good fish out and put them in baskets, while
they throw the worthless ones away. 49 A similar distinction will
take place at the final judgment, [and in a subordinate sense, at the
overthrow of this nation;] the appointed angels will go among the

a Luke xi, 35.   *b* Luke xii, 3.   *c* Luke viii, 18.

wicked from among the just, [50] and shall   MATT. XIII.
cast them into the furnace of fire ; there
shall be wailing and gnashing of teeth.

[44] Again the kingdom of heaven is like unto treasure
hid in a field ; the which when a man hath found, he
hideth, and for joy thereof goeth and selleth all that he
hath, and buyeth that field.—[45] Again the kingdom of
heaven is like unto a merchantman seeking goodly
pearls ; [46] who, when he had found one pearl of great
price, went and sold all that he had, and bought it.—
[51] Jesus saith unto them, Have ye understood all these
things ?   They say unto him, Yea, Lord.   [52] Then
said he unto them, Therefore every scribe which is
instructed unto the kingdom of heaven, is like unto a
man that is a householder, which bringeth forth out of
his treasure things new and old.

[53] And it came to pass, that when Jesus had finished
these parables, he departed thence.

§ 55.—*Passage across the Lake Gennesareth, with the connected Incidents.*

([*October ?*] A. D. 27.)

[18] Now when Jesus saw great multitudes   **Matt. VIII.**
about him, [MARK IV, 35] the same day, when the
even was come, he gave commandment to depart unto
the other side [LUKE VIII, 22] of the lake.   [19] And [LUKE IX, 57]
as they went in the way, a certain scribe came and said
unto him, Master, I will follow thee whithersoever
thou goest.   [20] And Jesus saith unto him, The *foxes*
have holes, and the *birds of the air* have nests ; but
the *Son of man* hath not where to lay his head.
[21] And [LUKE IX, 59] he said unto another of his disciples,
[LUKE IX, 59] Follow me.   But he said unto him, Lord, suffer me first to go and bury my father.   [22] But Jesus
said unto him, Follow me ; and let the dead bury their

69

motley assembly of human characters, and separate   **MATT. XIII.**
the wicked from the holy, [50] and plunge the former
into the flaming furnace of everlasting perdition,—
where ceaseless cries and teeth ground together in despair will be
the fit expression of their misery!

[44] "In view of these momentous results, the 'Reign of the Divine
Messiah,' [as regards the importance of possessing a veritable interest in it,] may be illustrated by a large sum of money secreted in
a field, which some person accidentally finding, conceals the discovery at which he is so overjoyed, until he has gone [to the owner
of the land where it lies,] and purchased the lot of ground,—even
if he has to part with all his property, [in order to procure the means
to buy it.]

[45] "To use another figure, [of the same import, the participants
of] the 'Reign of the Divine Messiah' may be compared to a traveling merchant, who is in search of fine pearls; [46] meeting with one
pearl of exceeding value [offered at a comparatively low price,] he
immediately disposes of all he is worth, so as to enable him to purchase it."

[51] After making these explanations, Jesus asked his disciples, "Do
you now understand all these illustrations?"   "Yes, Master," replied they, "we do."   [52] "Well," returned he, "[if you really comprehend them, take this admonition for their use:] Every religious
teacher, who is properly instructed to fulfill his part in the 'Reign
of the Divine Messiah,' should be like the prudent head of a family,
who produces [for each day's consumption,] out of his store [of provisions, supplies consisting both of] articles recently procured from
the market, as well as [of stock laid in] long before."

[53] When he had finished these allegorical instructions, Jesus left
his residence [and the village, for the purpose of making an excur-
sion in the neighborhood].

§ 55.—*Passage across the Lake Gennesareth, with the connected Incidents.*

([*October ?*] A. D. 27.)

[18][a] Toward evening of the same day,[1] Jesus, observ-   **Matt. VIII.**
ing that great numbers of people were gathering about
him [in his walk], proposed to his disciples, to [b] take
a boat at the lake and cross over, [in order to escape the press.]

[19][c] While they were on their way to the lake,[1] a certain scribe
[among those who had gathered about him, fearful of losing so
favorable an opportunity for attaching himself to one from whose
fortunes he hoped to acquire much personal aggrandizement,] approaching exclaimed, "Teacher, *I* am willing to attend you as a constant disciple in all your travels."   [20] Jesus [perceiving that he was
actuated by selfish expectations which would be disappointed,] told
him, "[You must make up your mind, in that case, to submit to my
privations:] the very foxes have their burrows, and the wild birds
their nests [and roosts]; but the 'Son of Man' has no settled home
'in which to rest his head at night.'"—[21] Another of the company,
[d] upon being bidden by Jesus to "become his disciple,"[1] requested
of him, "Master, only permit me to go and arrange my father's funeral,
[of whose death I have just heard;] and I will immediately return
and attend you constantly."   [22] But Jesus [apprehensive that the
delay would prove fatal to his resolution of discipleship,] told him,
" Leave the burial of their deceased relatives to those who are

[a] Mark iv, 35.   [b] Luke viii, 22.   [c] Luke ix, 57.   [d] Luke ix, 59.

dead : [LUKE IX, 60] but go *thou* and preach the   MATT. VIII.
kingdom of God.

⁶¹ And another also said, Lord, I will fol-   Luke IX.
low thee ; but let me first go bid them farewell
which are at home at my house.   ⁶² And Jesus
said unto him, No man having put his hand to the
plow, and looking back, is fit for the kingdom of
God.

²³ And when [MARK IV, 36] they had sent away   Matt. VIII.
the multitude and he was entered [MARK IV, 36]
even as he was into a ship, [LUKE VIII, 22] they launched forth,
and his disciples followed him ; [MARK IV, 36] and there
were also with him other little ships.   ²⁴ But [LUKE VIII, 23]
as they sailed, he was [MARK IV, 38] in the hinder part of the
ship, asleep [MARK IV, 38] on a pillow : and behold, there
arose a great tempest in the sea, insomuch that the
ship was covered with the waves ; [LUKE VIII, 23] and they
were in jeopardy.   ²⁵ And his disciples came to him and
awoke him saying, Lord, save us ; [MARK IV, 38] carest
thou not that we perish ?   ²⁶ Then he arose and rebuked the winds and [LUKE VIII, 24] the raging of the sea ;
[MARK IV, 39] and the wind ceased, and there was a great
calm.   And he saith unto them, Why are ye fearful,
O ye of little faith ?   ²⁷ But the men [MARK IV, 41] feared
exceedingly and marveled, saying, What manner of man
is this, that even the winds and the sea obey him !

§ 56.—*The Cure of Two Demoniacs.*

(South-eastern shore of the Lake Gennesareth, near Gad'ara :
[*October ?*] A. D. 27.)

¹ And they came over unto the other side -   Mark V.
of the sea, into the country of the Gadarenes
[MATT. VIII, 28] and Gergesenes.   ² And when he was come
out of the ship, immediately there met him [MATT. VIII, 28]
coming out of the tombs [MATT. VIII, 28] two men with unclean spirits, [MATT. VIII, 28] exceeding fierce, so that no man

70

spiritually dead, [by being engrossed in the con-   **MATT. VIII.**
cerns of this life;] but do *you* come and *a* engage at
once in [the more important work of] preaching the
advent of the 'Reign of the Divine Messiah,' [for which task I will
shortly have need of you.]"ᴵ

⁶¹ A third [upon a similar requirement,] begged,   **Luke IX.**
"First allow me, Master, to go and bid adieu to my
family, and I will return immediately and attend you."
⁶² But Jesus answered him in like manner, "No one that undertakes a religious office and then suffers his mind to be diverted by
temporal engagements, is [any more] qualified for usefulness in the
'Reign of the Divine Messiah' [than a farmer that 'takes hold of the
plow, and attempts to guide its course by looking at the furrow
behind him']."

²³ [Upon his arrival at the shore of the lake,] *b* dis-   **Matt. VIII.**
missing the crowd that followed him,ᴵ he entered a
boat *b* at once,ᴵ accompanied by his special disciples,
b and attended by a number of the rest in other boats.ᴵ ²⁴ *c* While
they were making the passage,ᴵ Jesus [wearied with the exertions
of the day, *d* leaning his head upon the seat] in the stern of the
boat, with [one of the cushions from the rowers' benches for] a pillow,ᴵ *c* fellᴵ fast asleep. Meanwhile *e* a furious gale of windᴵ suddenly
c sweptᴵ over the lake, and the water began to heave so violently,
that the waves *e* dashedᴵ into the boat, and it was *e* in imminent
danger of being filled at once.ᴵ ²⁵ The disciples therefore hastily
waked Jesus, crying out, "Master, *f* Master!ᴵ *d* do you not care at
all for our safety?ᴵ O rescue us [in some way from our peril], or
we shall instantly be drowned!" ²⁶ Upon this appeal he awoke,
and [to show his power over the elements of nature, he] exclaimed,
"Wind, be quiet! Waves, cease to roll!" Instantly, *f* the gale
lulled, the billows were smoothed,ᴵ and a total calm succeeded.
Then addressing his disciples, he reproved their vociferous fears by
asking, "What makes you so cowardly? Why have you no more
confidence in my preserving care?" ²⁷ They, however, *g* were completely awe-struck, andᴵ could only express their astonishment by
exclaiming *g* to one another,ᴵ "What a mighty Being *g* indeedᴵ is
this, whose commands the very wind and waves obey!"

§ 56.—*The Cure of Two Demoniacs.*

(South-eastern shore of the Lake Gennesareth, near Gad'ara; [*October ?*] A. D. 27.)

¹ When they had reached the opposite shore of the   **Mark V.**
lake, they landed *h* near the [site of the ancient] city of
the Ger'gashites, nowᴵ within the bounds of the town
of Gad'ara. ² Scarcely had Jesus quitted the boat, when *h* twoᴵ demoniacs *i* from the latter townᴵ rushed out of the ruined sepulchres

---

a Luke ix, 60.   *b* Mark iv, 36.   *c* Luke viii, 23.   *d* Mark iv, 38.   *e* Mark iv, 37.
f Luke viii, 24.   *g* Mark iv, 41.   *h* Matt. viii, 28.   *i* Luke viii, 27.

might pass by that way, ³ who [Luke VIII, 27] had   **MARK V.**
devils long time, and ware no clothes, neither
abode in any house, but had their dwelling among the
tombs; and no man could bind them, no, not with
chains : ⁴ because that [Luke VIII, 29] oftentimes it had caught
them and they had been often [Luke VIII, 29] kept bound with
fetters and chains, and the chains had been plucked
asunder by them, and the fetters broken in pieces;
neither could any man tame them : ⁵ and always
[Luke VIII, 29] driven of the devil into the wilderness, night
and day they were in the mountains and in the tombs,
crying and cutting themselves with stones.   ⁶ But
when they saw Jesus afar off, they ran [Luke VIII, 28] and
fell down before him and worshiped him, ⁷ and cried with
a loud voice and said, What have we to do with thee,
Jesus, thou Son of the Most High God ? ⁸ (for he said
unto them, Come out of the men, ye unclean spirits :)
[Matt. VIII, 29] art thou come hither to torment us ?   ⁷ We adjure thee by God, that thou torment us not [Matt. VIII, 29],
before the time.   ⁹ And he asked them, What is your
name ?   And they answered saying, Our name is,
Legion; for we are many.   ¹⁰ And they besought
him much, that he would not send them away out of
the country [Luke VIII, 31] into the deep.   ¹¹ Now there
was there nigh unto the mountains, [Matt. VIII, 30] a good
way off from them, a great herd of swine feeding; ¹³ (they
were about two thousand :) ¹² and all the devils besought him saying, [Matt. VIII, 31] If thou cast us out, send
us into the swine, that we may enter into them.   ¹³ And
forthwith Jesus gave them leave ; and the unclean
spirits went out and entered into the swine : and the
herd ran violently down a steep place into the sea, and
were choked in the sea.

¹⁴ And they that fed the swine fled, and told
in the city and in the country [Matt. VIII, 33] everything,
and what was befallen to the possessed of the devils.   And

71 .

close by toward him. [3] These persons, [a] having ˈMARK V. been severely afflicted in this manner for some time, [had become so ungovernably frantic that they] tore off their clothes, abandoned their homes, and re- sorted to these tombs for shelter, [b] where their raving fury rendered it unsafe for travelers to pass near them.| [4] Their relatives, [c] when they perceived one of these frequent attacks coming on,| had often confined them with fetters and manacles, [e] and guarded them closely;| but [they had at length relin- quished all measures of restraint, for] the maniacs had broken their irons with the superhuman strength of madness, which it was impossible to subdue, [5] and [c] under the impulse of the delirious fiend had wildly returned to [the same haunts among the ruins on] the uninhabited shore, where they| constantly roamed night and day through the deserted sepulchres cut in the adjacent rocks, screaming and gashing themselves with stones, [in their melancholy lunacy.] [6] No sooner did they see Jesus at a distance, than they ran and prostrated them- selves before him, [7] at the same time shrieking aloud, " O, let us alone, Jesus, thou Son of God Almighty!" [8] But Jesus com- manded the foul demons to " quit the possessed." [7] They still shrieked out, " O! [d] is it for this purpose you have come in this region?| We implore you, in the name of God, do not torture us [by an expulsion from human tenements], [d] before the ap- pointed time [of general judgment]!"| [9] Jesus then asked the miserable fiends, " By what name do you call yourselves?" The demons replied [through the instrumentality of the ma- niacs], " We may be called a *Legion* [the name of a battalion of troops, among the Romans], for there are a great number of us who have taken possession of this man." [10] At the same time they repeated their earnest entreaty that he would not order them to quit that region of country, [e] for [they thus hoped to escape the torments of a banishment to] the pit of perdition.| [11] There chanced to be a large drove of swine just then grazing [f] at a distance| toward the cliffs along the shore, [13] consisting of some two thousand. [12] The demons therefore begged [through the same medium], that " [g] if he expelled them,| he would allow them to take possession of these ani- mals." [13] This permission being immediately given, they quitted the [faculties of the] men and seized upon [those of] the hogs, causing the [h] whole| drove to rush headlong off the heights into the lake, where they were soon drowned.
　[14] The men tending the swine while feeding, [i] who wit- nessed the transaction,| fled with dismay and reported in the city as well as all along the country [through which they passed], what had befallen their charge, [j] and the occur-

a Luke viii, 27.　　*b* Matt. viii, 28.　　*c* Luke viii, 29.　　*d* Matt. viii, 29.
e Luke viii, 31.　　*f* Matt. viii, 30.　　*g* Matt. viii, 31.　　*h* Matt. viii, 32.
　　i Luke viii, 34.　　　　　　　　*j* Matt. viii, 33.

[Matt. VIII, 34] the whole city went out to see what   **Mark V.**
it was that was done.   ¹⁵ And they come to
Jesus, and see them that were possessed with the
devil and had the legion, sitting [Luke VIII, 35] at the feet
of Jesus and clothed and in their right mind : and they
were afraid.   ¹⁶ And they that saw it, told them how
it befell to them that were possessed with the devils,
and also concerning the swine.   ¹⁷ And [Luke VIII, 37] the
whole multitude of the country of the Gadarenes round about,
when they [Matt. VIII, 34] saw him, began to pray him to depart out of their coasts ; [Luke VIII, 37] for they were taken
with great fear.   ¹⁸ And when he was come into the ship,
they that had been possessed with the devils prayed
him that they might be with him : ¹⁹ howbeit Jesus
suffered them not but saith unto them, Go home to
your friends, and tell them how great things the Lord
hath done for you, and hath had compassion on you.
²⁰ And they departed, and began to publish in Decapolis how great things Jesus had done for them : and all
men did marvel.

²¹ And when Jesus was passed over again by ship
unto the other side, much people gathered unto him ;
[Luke VIII, 40] for they were all waiting for him : and he was
nigh unto the sea.   [Matt. IX, 1] And he came into his own
city.

§ 57.—*Matthew's Feast, and the connected Incidents.*

(Capernaum ; [*November ?*] A. D. 27.)

¹⁰ And [Luke V, 29] Levi made him a great feast   **Matt. IX.**
in his own house : and it came to pass, as Jesus
sat at meat in the house, behold, many publicans and
sinners came and sat down with him and his disciples ;
[Mark II, 15] for there were many, and they followed him.
¹¹ And when [Luke V, 30] their scribes and the Pharisees
saw it, they said unto his disciples, Why eateth your
Master with publicans and sinners ?   ¹² But when
72

rence that had happened to the demoniacs.| [15]This roused ᵃthe whole neighborhood| to go and see what had taken place ; and upon reaching Jesus, they saw the late demoniacs now sitting quietly and humbly ᵇ at their Benefactor's feet,| with their clothes adjusted decently, and in the possession of their reason.   At this spectacle the visitants were struck with amazement and awe, [16] which were heightened as the bystanders, who had witnessed the whole occurrence, narrated to them how the demoniacs ᶜ had been restored,| and the animals destroyed.   [17] ᵈ The dread [of a repetition of such an event, which, however beneficial to others, they felt to be a warning infliction upon themselves,]| induced ᵈthe entire inhabitants of that region| to entreat Jesus to withdraw from their vicinity.   [18] As he was entering the boat ᵈ to return immediately to the other side of the lake,| [in compliance with this request,] the recovered demoniacs begged him to allow them to accompany him ; [19] but he refused and ᵉ dismissed them| by replying, "Go home to your friends, and relate to them what a mercy Jehovah has effected for you." [20] Accordingly, they returned and proclaimed, ᶠnot only in their own town but| through the whole of the Decap'olis, what Jesus had done for them,—the recital causing universal astonishment.

[21] Having embarked in the boat, Jesus crossed the lake again, and on reaching the opposite shore, he found a large concourse of people collected [to receive him, who had been there some time], ᵍin expectation of his return.| ʰBut [as it was too late to address them further, dismissing them,] he retired to his residence in Capernaum.|

MARK V.

§ 57.—*Matthew's Feast, and the connected Incidents.*

(Capernaum ; [*November ?*] A. D. 27.)

[10]Not long after the above occurrences, ⁱMatthew (otherwise named Levi) gave a large entertainment at his own house in honor of his Master,| to which a great number of " publicans " and ⁱ other| persons of hitherto sinful character, were invited, being [the former associates of the host, and] ʲgenerally adherents to the cause of his new Master,| and took their places at the banquet along with Jesus and his twelve disciples. [11] [As the company were retiring from the house after the party had broken up,] the Pharisees ᵏand scribes of the village,| ˡwho had observed what was going on,| asked the disciples ᵏin a sneering under-tone,| "What makes your Teacher ᵏtake you to| eat and drink in company with such immoral persons as Tax-gatherers?" [12] Jesus,

Matt. IX.

a Matt. viii, 34.   b Luke viii, 35.   c Luke viii, 36.   d Luke viii, 37.
e Luke viii, 38.   f Luke viii, 39.   g Luke viii, 40.   h Matt. ix, 1.
i Luke v, 29.   j Mark ii, 15.   k Luke v, 30.   l Mark ii, 16.

Jesus heard that, he said unto them, They   MATT. IX.
that be whole, need not a physician, but
they that are sick; [13] for I am not come to call the
righteous, but sinners, to repentance.

[MARK II, 18] And the disciples of John and of the Pharisees
used to fast: [14] then came to him the disciples of John,
saying, Why do we and the Pharisees fast oft [LUKE V, 33]
and make prayers, but thy disciples fast not? [15] And
Jesus said unto them, Can [LUKE V, 34] ye make the children of the bride-chamber mourn, as long as the bridegroom is with them? [MARK II, 19] as long as they have the
bridegroom with them, they cannot fast; but the days will
come, when the bridegroom shall be taken from them,
and then shall they fast.

[LUKE V, 36] And he spake also a parable unto them: [16] No
man putteth a piece of new cloth unto an old garment;
for that which is put in to fill it up, taketh from the
garment, and the rent is made worse, [LUKE V, 36] and the
piece that was taken out of the new, agreeth not with the old.—
[17] Neither do men put new wine into old bottles; else
the bottles break, and the wine runneth out, and the
bottles perish: but they put new wine into new bottles,
and both are preserved.—[39] No man also   Luke V.
having drunk old wine, straightway desireth
new; for he saith, The old is better.

§ 58.—*While going to Resuscitate Jaï'rus's Daughter,
Jesus cures a Woman of her Hem'orrhage.*

(Capernaum; [*November?*] A. D. 27.)

[22] And [MATT. IX, 18] while he spake these things   **Mark V.**
unto them, behold, there cometh one of the
rulers-of-the-synagogue, Jairus by name; and when
he saw him, he fell at his feet [23] and besought him
greatly saying, My [LUKE VIII, 42] one only little daughter,
[LUKE VIII, 42] about twelve years of age, lieth at the point of

73

overhearing the sly cavil, turned to them with this **MATT. IX.**
answer, "Because 'persons that are in good health
have no occasion for a physician's aid, it is only such
as are unwell that require his services;' [13] and just so, my mission
does not lead me to invite the *would-be-saints* a to repentance,| but
such as are ready to confess themselves sinners."

[14] bThis happened to be a day which the disciples of John the
Baptist as well as the Pharisees were observing as a season of private
fasting;| some of those, therefore, cthat had put the above question,|
being former adherents of John, inquired, "But why, when we the
disciples of John, and clikewise| the Pharisees generally, are in the
habit of fasting frequently, cand [making our season of abstinence
one] of special prayer,| do your followers neglect this duty, cand
attend such feasts instead?"| [15] "Can dyou expect,|" replied Jesus,
"that the *par'anymphs* [i. e. friends of the bridegroom, who super-
intended the wedding,] should efast| in token of mourning during
the wedding week, while ethey have| the Bridegroom in their com-
pany? eCertainly not.| The time, however, draws near, when the
Bridegroom is to be removed from them; and then they will have
a fit occasion to fast for grief."

[16] [To vindicate more fully in the minds of all his hearers this
propriety of suiting actions to the exigencies of one's case,] fJesus
propounded to them the following figurative representation [of the
unprepared state of his disciples for such severe requirements]:|
"No one sews on a patch of ffresh| undressed cloth to mend a hole
in an old cloak; for in that case, the new piece would fnot only
match ill with the old dress,| but its rigidity would also tear out the
edges of the old and pliant cloth, and so only enlarge the gap.

[17] ["On the same principle of adaptation," continued he,] "nobody sets away new wine in old skin-casks; for if one did, the wine
[in working] would burst the weak and inelastic skins, and thus not
only destroy them, but run away itself. The true way, of course, is
to put up new wine in new skins, and so [by having them corre-
spond,] both are saved.

[39] "[To impose such austerities upon my disciples at **Luke V.**
this stage of preparation," concluded Jesus, "would be as
unwise] as if a person, having just drank well-cured wine,
should directly call for some fresh *must* [i. e. grape-juice] in preference, [that had not yet settled nor been clarified. Such a thing no
one thinks of doing,] for everybody would say at once, 'The wine
properly cured is more delicious.'"

§ 58.—*While going to Resuscitate Jaï'rus's Daughter, Jesus cures a Woman of her Hem'orrhage.*

(Capernaum; [*November ?*] A. D. 27.)

[22] gAs Jesus was thus discoursing to the bystanders,| **Mark V.**
[on his way home,] a certain one of the directors of the
synagogue of the place, by the name of Jaï'rus, came by
[in eager search for him], and upon thus discovering him, prostrated
himself at his feet, [23] and earnestly entreated him to "go to his
residence, and lay his restoring hand upon his honly| daughter,
habout twelve years of age,| whom he left in the agonies of death,

a Luke v, 32.　　b Mark ii, 18.　　c Luke v, 33.　　d Luke v, 34.
e Mark ii, 19.　　f Luke v, 36.　　g Matt. ix, 18.　　h Luke viii, 42.

death; I pray thee, come and lay thy hands   MARK V.
on her, that she may be healed, and she shall
live.   24 And Jesus [MATT. IX, 19] arose and went with him;
and much people followed him and thronged him.

25 And a certain woman which had an issue of blood
twelve years, 26 and had suffered many things of many
physicians and had spent all that she had, and was
nothing bettered, but rather grew worse, 27 when she
had heard of Jesus, came in the press behind and
touched [MATT. IX, 20] the hem of his garment; 28 for she
said [MATT. IX, 21] within herself, If I may touch but his
clothes, I shall be whole: 29 and straightway the fountain of her blood was dried up, and she felt in her body
that she was healed of that plague.   30 And Jesus, immediately knowing in himself that virtue had gone out
of him, turned him about in the press and said, Who
touched my clothes?   31 And [LUKE VIII, 45] when all denied,
Peter and his disciples said unto him, Thou seest the
multitude thronging thee, and sayest thou, Who touched
me?   [LUKE VIII, 46] And Jesus said, Somebody hath touched
me: for I perceive that virtue is gone out of me.   32 And he
looked round about to see her that had done this thing:
33 but the woman [LUKE VIII, 47] when she saw that she was
not hid, fearing and trembling, knowing what was done
in her, came and fell down before him and told him
[LUKE VIII, 47] before all the people all the truth, [LUKE VIII, 47]
for what cause she had touched him, and how she was healed
immediately.   34 And he said unto her, Daughter,
[LUKE VIII, 48] be of good comfort; thy faith hath made thee
whole: go in peace, and be whole of thy plague.

35 While he yet spake, there came from the ruler-
of-the-synagogue's house certain which said, Thy
daughter is dead; why troublest thou the Master any
further?   36 As soon as Jesus heard the word that was
spoken, he saith unto the ruler-of-the-synagogue, Be
not afraid; only believe, [LUKE VIII, 50] and she shall be made
74

a and who by this time, he feared, had quite expired ;| Mark V.
or he was sure she would then be revived."   ²⁴ Jesus
acceded to his request, and *b* set out| to accompany him,
b attended by his disciples,| and followed by so great a crowd of peo-
ple as almost to block up *c* his passage.|

²⁵ In the concourse was a certain female, who had been afflicted
with an intermittent hem'orrhage for twelve years,—²⁶ and had en-
dured every sort of medical treatment by various physicians, ex-
pending all her little property *d* in their fees,| without realizing any
benefit from their prescriptions, but finding her complaint rather
aggravated, *d* so that she had resigned all hopes of a cure ;|—²⁷ just
now learning that Jesus [of whose wonderful power over diseases
she had heard,] was passing near, she hastened thither, and forcing
her way through the crowd, came behind him near enough to touch
the *e* bottom fringe| of his mantle ; ²⁸ for she said *f* to herself,| "If I
can but touch the *f* mere edge| of his dress, I shall receive a cure."
²⁹ From the very instant that she did so, she felt her disorder entirely removed, [although she was then suffering under its influence.] ³⁰ Jesus, being conscious of the miraculous influence that
had emanated from him, instantly turned round in the crowd, and
asked, "Who is it that just now touched my cloak?" ³¹ *g* All that
were very near, denied having done so, and Peter,| in the name of
the other disciples, replied, *g* "Master,| you see how the throng are
crowded *g* close about| you, and it is hard telling who in particular
touched you." *h* "Some one certainly touched me with a special
design ; for I felt a curative influence exerted by me," returned
Jesus,| ³² as he looked around in search of her who had done so.
³³ The woman, therefore, *i* perceiving that she had not escaped his
notice,| came trembling with the apprehension of being chided for
[her conduct, in obtaining thus covertly] the cure of which she was
conscious, and falling prostrate before him acknowledged the whole
truth concerning herself, *i* stating to him before the whole populace
for what reason she had touched him, and how she had been in-
stantly cured.| ³⁴ Upon this avowal, Jesus mildly told her, *j* "You
need not be so alarmed,| madam ; your confidence in me has been
the means of restoring you to health. You may now retire with
the happy assurance of the divine favor, and that your troublesome
complaint will never return."

³⁵ While he was saying thus, *k* a messenger| from the director-of-
the-synagogue's family came up and told him, "Your daughter has
just breathed her last; it is not worth while to give the Teacher
any further trouble in coming to the house." ³⁶ But Jesus, upon
hearing this announcement, immediately bade the disconsolate
father, "Be not discouraged ; only keep up your confidence in my

a Matt. ix, 18.   *b* Matt. ix, 19.   *c* Luke viii, 42.   *d* Luke viii, 43.
e Matt. ix, 20.   *f* Matt. ix, 21.   *g* Luke viii, 45.   *h* Luke viii, 46.
i Luke viii, 47.   *j* Luke viii, 48.   *k* Luke viii, 49.

whole. [38] And he cometh to the house of the   MARK V.
ruler-of-the-synagogue : [37] and he suffered
no man to follow him, save Peter and James and John
the brother of James, [LUKE VIII, 51] and the father and the
mother of the maiden : [38] and [MATT. IX, 23] Jesus came into the
ruler's house, and seeth the tumult, [MATT. IX, 23] the people
making a noise, and [MATT. IX, 23] the minstrels that wept and
wailed greatly : [39] and when he was come in, he saith
unto them, [MATT. IX, 24] Give place; why make ye this ado
and weep? the damsel is not dead, but sleepeth.
[40] And they laughed him to scorn, [LUKE VIII, 53] knowing
that she was dead. But when he had put them all out,
he taketh the father and the mother of the damsel and
them that were with him, and entereth in where the
damsel was lying: [41] and he took the damsel by the
hand and said unto her, *Talitha-cumi;* which is, being
interpreted, Damsel, (I say unto thee,) arise. [42] And
(LUKE VIII, 55] her spirit came again, and straightway the
damsel arose and walked; for she was of the age of
twelve years. [43] And he commanded that something
should be given her to eat.—[42] And [LUKE VIII, 56] her
parents were astonished with a great astonishment;
[43] and he charged them straitly that no man should
know it : [MATT. IX, 26] but the fame hereof went abroad into
all that land.

§ 59.—*Two Blind Men and a Dumb Demoniac cured.*

(Capernaum; [*November?*] A. D. 27.)

[27] And when Jesus departed thence, two   **Matt. IX.**
blind men followed him, crying and saying,
Thou son of David, have mercy on us. [28] And when
he was come into the house, the blind men came to
him : and Jesus saith unto them, Believe ye that I am
able to do this? They said unto him, Yea, Lord.
[29] Then touched he their eyes, saying, According to

75.

ability, *a*and she will yet be revived.!'' ³⁸On MARK V.
reaching the dwelling, ³⁷Jesus allowed none of his
followers to attend him within, except Peter and
the brothers James and John. ³⁸As he entered, he observed
the professional mourners *b* and the rest of the assembly generally,‖ making a great ado with their lamentations and inces-
sant howling dirges, accompanied with the *c* sound of flutes
b and lacerations of themselves [in token of violent grief] for
the deceased ;‖ ³⁹and bade them, *d* "Stand aside,‖ and cease
your tears and din ; the girl is not really dead [so as to be
beyónd restoration], she is merely sleeping as it were."
⁴⁰But they only treated his words with incredulous derision,
e aware that she was actually dead,‖ [and thinking that there
was now no hope.] He, however, proceeded to turn the whole
troop of mourners out of the house, and then taking with him
only the girl's parents and the three disciples that entered
with him, went into the room where the corpse was. ⁴¹Tak-
ing hold of her hand, he pronounced these words, *teleethaw'
koo'mee*, (the Syro-Chaldee for, " *Girl, rise !*"), ⁴²upon which
f her soul returned to the body,‖ and she instantly rose up and
walked about the room. ⁴³Jesus then directed her parents to
give her some food, [to show her complete restoration to
health.] ⁴²Utter astonishment seized *g* the parents‖ at their
daughter's reanimation, *h* and the report of the occurrence
spread all over that region of country;‖ ⁴³although Jesus
strictly charged them to let none but the family know it.

§ 59.—*Two Blind Men and a Dumb Demoniac cured.*

(Capernaum ; [*November ?*] A. D. 27.)

²⁷As Jesus was leaving Jaï'rus's house, two blind Matt. IX.
men followed him, loudly imploring him, " Merci-
fully restore our sight, O ' Descendant of David !'"
²⁸No sooner had he entered his residence, [to which he hastened in order to escape the throng,] than the blind men came
to him, repeating their entreaty. In answer to his interrogation, " Have you full confidence in my ability to effect a cure
for you?" they replied, " Yes, indeed, Master, we have."
²⁹Then touching their eyes, he said, " It shall be done to you

---

a Luke viii, 50.   *b* Luke viii, 52.   *c* Matt. ix, 23.   *d* Matt. ix, 24.
e Luke viii, 53.   *f* Luke viii, 55.   *g* Luke viii, 56.   *h* Matt. ix, 26.

your faith, be it unto you. ³⁰ And their   MATT. IX.
eyes were opened : and Jesus straitly
charged them saying, See that no man know it.
³¹ But they, when they were departed, spread abroad
his fame in all that country.

³² As they went out, behold, they brought to him a
dumb man possessed with a devil : ³³ and when the
devil was cast out, the dumb spake ; and the multitudes
marveled saying, It was never so seen in Israel.
³⁴ But the Pharisees said, He casteth out devils through
the prince of the devils.

§ 60.—*Second Rejection of Christ at Nazareth.*

([*December?*] A. D. 27.)

¹ And be went out from thence, and came   **Mark VI.**
into his own country ; and his disciples fol-
low him. ² And when the sabbath-day was come, he
began to teach in the synagogue : and many hearing him were astonished saying, From whence hath
this man these things ? and what wisdom is this which
is given unto him, that even such mighty works are
wrought by his hands ? ³ Is not this the [MATT. XIII, 55]
carpenter's son, the son of Mary, the brother of James
and Joses and of Juda and Simon ? and are not his
sisters [MATT. XIII, 56] all here with us ? [MATT. XIII, 56] Whence
then hath this man all these things? And they were offended at him. ⁴ But Jesus said unto them, A prophet
is not without honor, but in his own country and among
his own kin and in his own house. ⁵ And he could
there do no mighty work, [MATT. XIII, 58] because of their
unbelief, save that he laid his hands upon a few sick
folk and healed them. ⁶ And he marveled because of
their unbelief.

76

as you believe it may." ³⁰ Instantly they recov-   MATT. IX.
ered the perfect use of their eyes ; upon which he
sternly charged them, "Take care that you let no
person know who has done this for you!" ³¹ But as soon as
they had gone out of doors, they commenced to proclaim the
author of their cure through the whole country.

³² Scarcely had these men left the house, when some neigh-
bors entered, bringing to Jesus a person that had become dumb
in consequence of demoniacal possession. ³³ He expelled the
demon, upon which the dumb man immediately recovered the
faculty of speech, greatly to the astonishment of the bystanders, who exclaimed, "Certainly such a wonderful instance of
cure has never been witnessed in our nation before!". ³⁴ The
malignant Pharisees, however, repeated their blasphemous detraction, "He exorcises demons by collusion with their ringleader!"

§ 60.—*Second Rejection of Christ at Nazareth.*

([*December ?*] A. D. 27.)

¹ Leaving Capernaum, Jesus soon afterward made   **Mark VI.**
a visit once more to Nazareth his former home, at-
tended by his twelve disciples. ² On the sabbath
succeeding his arrival, having attended at the synagogue, he
accepted an invitation to address the congregation. Many of
his hearers were greatly surprised at his discourse, remarking
to each other, "Why does this upstart assume all this authority. Whence does he derive these sage maxims [that he thus
affects to be inspired with,] and the power to effect the miracles attributed to him? ³ Is not this the young man that we
used to see at work *a* with his father Joseph the carpenter?!
Why, [yes, the family are nothing remarkable :] his mother is
one Mary, and he has several [half-]brothers, James and Simon
and Jude and Joses, [whom we have known from boys ;] and
there are some of his own sisters that have grown up to womanhood among us, *b* [besides the younger children.] We think
but little of such pretenders!!" In this way they slighted
his claims, and scorned his instructions. ⁴ But he merely replied to their captiousness by saying, "[I told you once before,
that I did not expect much success with you, for] I knew
that 'a religious teacher is nowhere so little likely to gain a
favorable hearing, as among his own townsmen and relatives
and family.'" ⁵ This prejudice, therefore, was so great an
obstacle *c* to confidence in him, that none applied to him for
the exertion of his miraculous aid, except a few invalids, whom
he restored to health by laying his hand upon them. ⁶ Still,
he could not but wonder at their perverse incredulity, [after
the many proofs they had had of his mission.]

a Matt. xiii, 55.   *b* Matt. xiii, 56.   *c* Matt. xiii, 58.

§ 61.—*Third Circuit in Galilee, in extension of which the Apostles are detached with Instructions.*

([*January* to *March ?*] A. D. 28.)

[35] And Jesus went about all the cities and   **Matt. IX.**
villages, teaching in their synagogues, and
preaching the gospel of the kingdom, and healing every
sickness and every disease among the people.   [36] But
when he saw the multitudes, he was moved with compassion on them, because they fainted and were scattered abroad, as sheep having no shepherd : [37] then
saith he unto his disciples, The harvest truly is plente-
ous but the laborers are few ; [38] pray ye therefore the
Lord of the harvest, that he will send forth laborers
into his harvest.

[1] And when he had called [Luke IX, 1] together   **Matt. X.**
unto him his twelve disciples, he [Mark VI, 7]
began to send them forth by two and two, and gave them
power against unclean spirits, to cast them out, and to
heal all manner of sickness and all manner of disease.
[5] These twelve Jesus sent forth, and commanded them
saying, Go not into the way of the Gentiles, and into
any city of the Samaritans enter ye not ; [6] but go
rather to the lost sheep of the house of Israel : [7] and
as ye go, preach saying, The kingdom of heaven is at
hand.   [8] Heal the sick, cleanse the lepers, raise the
dead, cast out devils ; freely ye have received, freely
give.   [9] Provide neither gold nor silver nor brass in
your purses, [Mark VI, 8] no bread, [10] nor scrip for your
journey, neither two coats neither shoes, [Mark VI, 9] (but
be shod with *sandals*,) nor yet staves, [Mark VI, 8] (save a
staff only :) [Luke X, 4] and salute no man by the way.   [11] And
into whatsoever city or town ye shall enter, inquire
who in it is worthy, and there abide till ye go thence ;
[Luke X, 7] go not from house to house : [8] and into whatsoever

77 ·

§ 61.—*Third Circuit in Galilee, in extension of which the Apostles are detached with Instructions.*

([*January to March ?*] A. D. 28.)

³⁵ Soon after this, Jesus set out on a third tour through **Matt. IX.** the cities and villages of Galilee, [availing himself of the privilege of] discoursing in the synagogues wherever he went, to preach the doctrines of the "Messiah's Reign," and [accompanying his instructions with confirmatory miracles, by] relieving every variety of disease or impaired faculties. ³⁶ Observing [the deplorable want of sound religious teaching among the mass of] the people who gathered everywhere about him, that in this respect they were like sheep that had no shepherd, and were therefore torn in pieces [by their wolves of hierarchal sectaries], and left to stray into every pernicious error, he was deeply touched with sympathy for their spiritual destitution, ³⁷ and remarked to those of his disciples who attended him, "This harvest of religious effort is truly vast and inviting, but on the other hand how few are we the reapers engaged in harvesting it! ³⁸ This ought to prompt you to entreat its Divine Proprietor to furnish a more adequate force of reapers to enter His harvest-field."

¹ [In pursuance of this idea, he resolved to enlarge the **Matt. X.** compass of the tour he was then making, by employing them in subsidiary excursions in various directions.] Accordingly having *a* assembled^l his twelve apostles all together, he commissioned them to go *b* in pairs^l, to different sections of the country, and propagate his doctrines, at the same time conferring upon them *a* miraculous^l authority to expel demons, as well as power to cure every description of physical disorder and weakness. ⁵ The tenor of this commission ran as follows: "You are not now to visit any of the adjacent Gentile districts, nor to carry your message to any of the inhabitants of Samaria; ⁶ but you must confine your labors for the present to the pure descendants of Israel, who are now like sheep [abandoned by their pastors and] wandering far from the true fold. ⁷ As you travel from place to place, your great errand is, to announce publicly everywhere, 'The "Reign of the Divine Messiah" rapidly draws near!' ⁸ [In confirmation of your prophetic authority to make this declaration,] you are to perform suitable miracles, such as curing the sick, restoring lepers, and expelling demons; and as you have been invested with this miraculous endowment gratuitously by me, so you must employ it in the alleviation of human misery without requiring any pay for so doing. ⁹ You are to prepare no outfit for a leisurely and pleasure-taking journey, as by supplying yourselves with a *c* well-filled purse, or stowing your belt with cash, whether gold, silver or copper, *d* or taking along any food, ^l ¹⁰ or carrying with you a traveling knapsack, or taking a change of clothes, or providing *cal'cei* [i. e. shoes covering the whole foot] *e* instead of simple sandals, or furnishing yourselves with a walking-stick, *f* if you chance not to have one in your hand; *e* nor are you allowed to linger for passing lengthy salutations to any one on the road. ¹¹ [Trusting to a more providential method of obtaining your supplies as you need,] you must inquire, when you reach any town or village, what resident of it is a suitable person to give you entertainment; and continue your quarters there—*g* without going from one house to another [in search of more agreeable ac-

a Luke ix, 1.   *b* Mark vi, 7.   *e* Luke x, 4.   *d* Luke ix, 3.
    e Mark vi, 9.   *f* Mark vi, 8.   *g* Luke x, 7.

city ye enter, and they receive you, eat such things   Matt. X.
as are set before you; [10] for the workman is
worthy of his meat. [12] And when ye come into a
house, salute it [Luke X, 5] by first saying, Peace be to this
house: [13] and if the house be worthy, [Luke X, 6] and the
son of peace be there, let your peace come upon it : but
if it be not worthy, let your peace return to you. [14] And
whosoever shall not receive you nor hear your words,
when ye depart out of that house or city, shake off the
dust of your feet [Mark VI, 11] for a testimony against them :
[Luke X, 11] notwithstanding, be ye sure of this, that the kingdom of God is come nigh unto them. [40] He that receiveth
[Luke X, 16] and heareth you, receiveth me ; and he that
receiveth me, receiveth him that sent me : [Luke X, 16]
and he that despiseth you, despiseth me ; and he that despiseth
me, despiseth him that sent me [41] he that receiveth a
prophet in the name of a prophet, shall receive a prophet's reward ; and he that receiveth a righteous man in
the name of a righteous man, shall receive a righteous
man's reward ; [42] and whosoever shall give to drink
unto one of these little ones, a cup of cold water only,
in the name of a disciple, verily I say unto you, he
shall in no wise lose his reward.

[1] And it came to pass when Jesus had   **Matt. XI.**
made an end of commanding his twelve disciples, he departed thence to teach and to preach in
their cities. [12] And they went out [Luke IX, 6]   **Mark VI.**
through the towns, and preached [Luke IX, 6] the
gospel, that men should repent : [13] and they cast out
many devils, and anointed with oil many that were
sick and healed them [Luke IX, 6] everywhere.

78

commodations]¹—as long as you stay in the place, MATT. X.
ᵃ contenting yourselves with the fare that is thus
afforded yóu:¹ ¹⁰[nor need you feel any hesitation
in availing yourselves of such hospitality, for] 'every workman is entitled to his wages,'. [and you have as just a claim
for support from those who enjoy your religious services.]
¹² When you enter a dwelling [to which you are thus directed],
salute its inmates ᵇ by saying simply, 'May blessings rest upon
this household!'¹—¹³ and then, if the ᶜ occupants¹ be persons
suitable for the reception of the blessings, your wish will be
accomplished; but if they be unworthy of them, it will merely
be rendered of no effect. ¹⁴ And in case any individual ᵈ or
town¹ should thus refuse to entertain you or attend to your
message, then as you leave that person's house or that town,
shake the dust from your feet, ᵈ and as you stand in the thoroughfare, proclaim,¹ ᵉ 'We wipe off the very dust of your street
that clings to our feet,¹ ᶠ as a sign that we abandon you¹ [as
unworthy of any further efforts to reform]: ᵉ still, you may
depend, our message will prove true, that "The 'Reign of the
Divine Messiah' rapidly draws near" even to *you;* [although,
if you continue impenitent, it will be but in national and
eternal judgment!]¹ ⁴⁰ [Never forget, therefore, your high
authority:] whoever welcomes *you* ᵍ and your announcements,¹
welcomes *me* whom you now represent, and in like manner
welcomes also *Him* who has charged me with my mission;
ᵍ but whoever rejects you, equally rejects me, and consequently Him whose ambassador I am.¹ ⁴¹ And I assure you,
that every person who [in such case] entertains a religious
teacher or saint, purely on account of that sacred character,
will receive an eternal recompense. ⁴² Yes, no one that fur-
nishes one of these disciples with a draught of cool ʰ water¹
merely, when thirsty, because of, their adherence to me, will
ever fail of a large reward [for even that slight act of kind-
ness]."

¹ Having delivered these instructions to his apos- Matt. XI.
tles, Jesus set out afresh to complete his tour of
reformatory preaching through the cities of Galilee. ¹² They also immediately proceeded to exe- Mark VI.
cute their mission, proclaiming to the inhabitants
ⁱ of every village in their course,¹ the duty of repentance ⁱ as a preparation for the Messiah's reception,¹ ¹³ and
supporting their exhortations by expelling demons in numerous instances, and curing invalids ⁱ universally¹ without any
other application than a simple anointing with oil.

a Luke x, 8.	*b* Luke x, 5.	*c* Luke x, 6.
d Luke x, 10.	*e* Luke x, 11,	*f* Mark vi, 11.
g Luke x, 16.	*h* Mark ix, 41.	*i* Luke ix, 6.

§ 62.—*Herod Beheads John the Baptist, and thinks him Revived in the person of Christ.*

(Mache'rus [and Galilee?; *March?*] A. D. 28.)

²¹ And when a convenient day was come, MARK VI. that Herod on his birthday made a supper to his lords, high-captains and chief-estates of Galilee; ²² and when the daughter of the said Herodias came in and danced, and pleased Herod and them that sat with him, the king said unto the damsel, Ask of me whatsoever thou wilt, and I will give it thee : ²³ and he sware unto her, Whatsoever thou shalt ask of me, I will give it thee, unto the half of my kingdom. ²⁴ And she went forth and said unto her mother, What shall I ask ? And she said, The head of John the Baptist. ²⁵ And she came in straightway with haste unto the king, and asked saying, I will that thou give me by and by in a charger, the head of John the Baptist. ²⁶ And the king was exceeding sorry : yet for his oath's sake and for their sakes which sat with him, he would not reject her : ²⁷ and immediately the king sent an executioner and commanded his head to be brought ; and he went and beheaded him in the prison, ²⁸ and brought his head in a charger and gave it to the damsel, and the damsel gave it to her mother. ²⁹ And when his disciples heard of it, they came and took up his corpse, and laid it in a tomb, [MATT. XIV, 12] and went and told Jesus.

¹⁴ And king Herod heard of him, (for his name was spread abroad,) [LUKE IX, 7] and he was perplexed; and he said [MATT. XIV, 2] unto his servants, That John the Baptist was risen from the dead, and therefore mighty works do show forth themselves in him : ¹⁵ others said, That it is Elias ; and others said, That it is a prophet, or as one of the [LUKE IX, 8] old prophets [LUKE IX, 8] risen again : ¹⁶ but when

79

§ 62.—*Herod Beheads John the Baptist, and thinks him Revived in the person of Christ.*

(Mache'rus [and Galilee?; *March ?*] A. D. 28.)

21 [John the Baptist meanwhile was confined in **MARK VI.** prison, as before related.] But on the festive occasion of a sumptuous banquet which Herod An'tipas made upon his birthday, and to which he invited the nobility of his court and his generals, together with the other prominent men of Galilee, **22** Salo'mè, the daughter [by a former husband] of the same Herodias [at whose instigation John was imprisoned], came *a* into the room! and performed a [*pantomime*] dance for the entertainment of the company, which so delighted Herod and the party generally, that in his extravagance he promised the girl, "I will make you a present of whatever you request of me." **23** And [to convince her that he was in earnest in his praise,] he assured her with a solemn oath, "I will actually give you whatever you ask, even if it should be of the value of half of my dominions." **24** [Full of girlish delight at the offer, but not knowing how best to avail herself of it,] she ran to her mother with the news, and asked her, "What gift shall I request?" [Seizing the opportunity to accomplish her long-cherished spite,] she told her daughter to "request the head of John the Baptist." **25** Eagerly hastening back to her uncle, she preferred as her request, "I want you to give me on the spot, the head of John the Baptist on a dish." **26** The Tetrarch immediately repented the rash privilege he had given her; but he was ashamed to deny her, after he had sworn before all the company to do as she desired. **27** He therefore immediately dispatched one of his *speculato'res* [i. e. body-guard, who acted as executioners], with orders to bring the head of John. **28** The officer accordingly went and beheaded him in the prison; and having brought the head in a dish, he presented it to the girl, who carried it to her mother. **29** Some of John's disciples, learning their teacher's fate, came to the dungeon, and taking up his headless body, carried it to a sepulchre, [where they interred it decently.] *b* They then went and informed Jesus [of his forerunner's murder].|

14 *c* Shortly after this event,| the fame of Jesus, that was spread far and wide [by his own and his disciples' *d* doings,| during their circuit], reaching Herod, he observed *e* to his officials,| "I really think this person must be John the Baptist come to life again, and that [his supernatural character enhanced by] this resurrection enables him to effect such miracles as are reported to take place." *d* This perplexing suspicion was [rendered the more harassing to his mind by being] suggested by the comments of the populace [upon his conduct toward John].| **15** Others, however, expressed their belief, that "Jesus was the returned 'Elijah;'" while still others conjectured that "he was one of the *f* ancient| prophets, *f* that had reappeared in a resuscitated body."| **16** But Herod, after

a Matt. xiv, 6.   *b* Matt. xiv, 12.   *c* Matt. xiv, 1.
d Luke ix, 7.   *e* Matt. xiv, 2.   *f* Luke ix, 8.

Herod heard thereof, he said, [LUKE IX, 9] Who   MARK VI.
is this of whom I hear such things?   It is
John whom I beheaded; he is risen from the dead.
[LUKE IX, 9] And he desired to see him.

§ 63.—*Upon the Return of the Apostles, Christ Retires with them across the Lake, where he Feeds more than Five Thousand persons.*

(Capernaum and North-eastern Coast of the Lake Gennesareth, near
Bethsaida-in-Pere'a; [*Thursday, March 25 ?*] A. D. 28.)

30 And the apostles gathered themselves together
unto Jesus, and told him all things, both what they
had done and what they had taught.   31 And he said
unto them, Come ye yourselves apart into a desert
place, and rest a while; (for there were many coming
and going, and they had no leisure so much as to eat :)
32 and [MATT. XIV, 13] when Jesus heard of the death of John,
they departed [JOHN VI, 1] over the sea of Galilee, into a desert place [LUKE IX, 10] belonging to the city called Bethsaida
by ship privately;   33 and the people [MATT. XIV, 13] heard
thereof and saw them departing, and many knew him
and ran afoot thither out of all cities, [JOHN VI, 2] because
they saw his miracles which he did on them that were diseased,
and out-went them and came together unto him.
34 And Jesus, when he came out, saw much people,
and was moved with compassion toward them, because
they were as sheep not having a shepherd : [JOHN VI, 3]
and he went up into a mountain, and there he sat with his
disciples; and he began to teach them many things
[LUKE IX, 11] of the kingdom of God, and healed them that had
need of healing.

35 And when the day was now far spent, his disciples
came unto him and said, This is a desert place, and
now the time is far passed : 36 send them away, that
they may go into the country round about and into
the villages, and [LUKE IX, 12] lodge and buy themselves
80

being apprized of their various explanations, persisted   MARK VI.
[in declaring his conviction,] that "he was none other
than John the Baptist, whom he had beheaded, but
who had now revived;" *a* although he confessed he was puzzled to
know how it could be so. This [unaccountable air of Christ's appearance and performances,] made him desirous of satisfying himself by seeing him personally. |

§ 63.—*Upon the Return of the Apostles, Christ Retires with them across the Lake, where he Feeds more than Five Thousand persons.*

(Capernaum and North-eastern Coast of the Lake Gennesareth, near Bethsaida-in-Pere'a; [*Thursday, March 25 ?*] A. D. 28.)

30 When the apostles had accomplished their respective missions, they returned to their Master, and reported to him what incidents they had met with, detailing all the miracles they had performed, as well as the instructions they had given publicly. 31 Their arrival at their home attracted such numbers of people, who were incessantly coming [to gratify their curiosity or receive instruction and physical relief,] and as constantly retiring [after having obtained their purpose], that the fatigued Teacher and his disciples had not even leisure left them to refresh themselves with a repast. The inconvenience attending this press of company, *b* together with the report which Jesus had just received of Herod's procedure and of his sentiments concerning himself, [and which made him desirous of avoiding a contact with the Tetrarch at a time so calculated to excite the seditious tendencies of the people,] | induced him to propose to his apostles to " accompany him in a private manner without the crowd, to some retired spot where they could rest themselves a little while." 32 Accordingly, quitting the village, they took a boat at the lake, and crossing over by themselves, landed on the opposite uninhabited shore, *c* not far from the city of Bethsaida in Pere'a. |
33 The crowd, however, when they saw them leaving the village,—most of them being aware of their destination,—followed them, *d* for the purpose of witnessing a repetition of the miraculous cures which Jesus had performed upon the sick ; | and [not being able to obtain a passage in boats across the lake,] great numbers from all the neighboring towns ran by land [around the head of the lake], and reaching the other side before the boat, presented themselves to him on its arrival. 34 Upon landing, therefore, he was affected with a deep sympathy for the religious wants of the vast concourse whom he saw about him, inasmuch as they were like sheep destitute of a shepherd ; and *e* ascending an eminence close by, he took a seat there with his disciples, | and delivered an extended discourse to the people *f* concerning the " Reign of the Divine Messiah," at the same time curing such of them as required relief from disease. |
35 As evening was now coming on, his *g* twelve | disciples approached and reminded him, that " the region where they were was quite uninhabited, and it was already getting late ; 36 so that it was perhaps best to dismiss the crowd, in order that they might repair to the adjoining hamlets and villages, and purchase for themselves some

_a_ Luke ix, 9.   _b_ Matt. xiv, 13.   _c_ Luke ix, 10.   _d_ John vi, 2.
_e_ John vi, 3.   _f_ Luke ix, 11.   _g_ Luke ix, 12.

bread; for they have nothing to eat. ³⁷ He   MARK VI.
answered and said unto them, [MATT. XIV, 16]
They need not depart; give ye them to eat. And they say
unto him, Shall we go and *buy* two hundred pennyworth of bread, and give them to eat? [JOHN VI, 5] He
saith unto Philip, *Whence* shall we buy bread that these may
eat? [6] (and this he said to prove him; for he himself knew
what he would do.) [7] Philip answered him, Two hundred
pennyworth of bread is not *sufficient* for them, that every one
of them may take a little. ³⁸ He saith unto them, How
many loaves have ye? go and see. And when they
knew, [JOHN VI, 8] one of his disciples, Andrew, Simon Peter's
brother, saith unto him, [9] There is a lad here which hath five
barley-loaves and two small fishes; but what are they among
so many? [LUKE IX, 13] We have no more, except we should go
and *buy* meat for all this people. [MATT. XIV, 18] He said, Bring
them hither to me.   ³⁹ And he commanded them to make
all sit down by companies upon the green grass; ⁴⁰ and
they sat down in ranks, by hundreds and by fifties:
⁴¹ and when he had taken the five loaves and the two
fishes, he looked up to heaven, and blessed and brake
the loaves, and gave them to his disciples to set before
them; and the two fishes divided he among them all,
[JOHN VI, 11] as much as they would: ⁴² and they did all eat
and were filled.   [JOHN VI, 12] He said unto his disciples,
Gather up the fragments that remain, that nothing be lost:
⁴³ and they took up twelve baskets full of the fragments
and of the fishes, [JOHN VI, 13] which remained over and above
unto them that had eaten. ⁴⁴ And they that did eat of
the loaves, were about five thousand men, [MATT. XIV, 21]
beside women and children.

¹⁴ Then those men, when they had seen   **John VI.**
the miracle that Jesus did, said, This is of a
truth that Prophet* that should come into the world.—
⁴ And the passover, a feast of the Jews, was nigh.

---

* Deut. xviii, 15.

food; as they had evidently brought no provision **Mark VI.**
with them." ³⁷ "Well," replied he, *ᵃ* "there is
no necessity for dismissing the people; I just furnish them with food yourselves on the spot." *ᵇ* "Yes," returned they, I " [that would do, if we had it here to furnish;]
but would you have us go and purchase enough to supply *ᶜ* this
large company I with a meal?" *ᵈ* He then asked Philip,
"Where can you purchase food enough for them all?" I
ᵉ (This question was put with the design of testing his and the
other disciples' faith, [and not of obtaining information;] for
he well knew himself what plan he was about to adopt for
meeting the emergency.) I *ᶠ* Philip answered, I "Two hundred
dena'rii [i. e. about $30] would hardly buy bread enough to
give each of them a morsel." ³⁸ "Well," said Jesus, "how
much bread have you here? just go and ascertain." After
searching among the whole assembly, *ᵍ* Andrew, the brother
of Simon (Peter), reported as the result, I *ᶜ* "We can find no
one that has any provisions here at all, I *ʰ* except a single young
man, and he has I *ᶜ* only I five *ʰ* barley biscuits I and a couple of
ʰ little I fishes cooked; *ʰ* but what is that toward supplying so
many persons? I" *ⁱ* Jesus, however, replied, "Bring them here
to me." I ··³⁹ He then directed his disciples to " bid the people
recline upon the *ʲ* abundant I green grass of the place, in groups
[of an oblong form,] ⁴⁰ consisting of one hundred persons wide
by fifty deep." As soon as this arrangement was effected,
⁴¹ he took the five biscuits in his hands, and looked up toward
the sky while he pronounced the blessing, he then broke them
and handed the pieces to the apostles, directing them to distribute the subdivisions in turn to the people. *ᵏ* In the same
way I he divided the two fishes also among them all, ⁴² *ᵏ* the
victuals miraculously sufficing for the appetites of the whole. I
When they had all eaten till they were satisfied, *ˡ* he told his
disciples, " Collect the remaining fragments, that nothing be
wasted." I ⁴³ Accordingly, they picked up all the bits of the
five biscuits and two little fishes, that were left after all had
eaten their fill, and these were enough to fill *twelve baskets.*
⁴⁴ The number of the persons who partook of the meal was
ᵐ about I five thousand men, *ᵐ* besides numerous women and
children. I

··¹⁴ The people who had witnessed this miracle of **John VI.**
Jesus, exclaimed, " Surely, this is the Messianic
' Prophet' who is to appear among us!"—⁴ This in-
cident occurred shortly before the Jewish festival of the
Passover.

a Matt. xiv, 16.   *ᵇ* Matt. xiv, 17.   *c* Luke ix, 13.   *d* John vi, 5.   *e* John vi, 6.
f John vi, 7.   *g* John vi, 8.   *h* John vi, 9.   *i* Matt. xiv, 18.
j John vi, 10.   *k* John vi, 11   *l* John vi, 12.   *m* Matt. xiv, 21.

§ 64.—*In Returning, Christ Walks upon the Water.*

(Lake and Plain of Gennesareth, and Capernaum : [*Thursday* and
Friday?] *March* [25 and 26?], A. D. 28.)

22 And [John VI, 15] when Jesus therefore per-   **Matt. XIV.**
ceived that they would come and take him by
force, to make him a king, straightway he constrained
his disciples to get into a ship and to go before him
unto the other side [Mark VI, 45] unto Bethsaida, while he
sent the multitudes away : 23 and when he had sent the
multitudes away, he went up into a mountain apart to
pray ; and when the evening was come, [John VI, 16] his
disciples went down unto the sea, [17] and entered into a ship,
and went over the sea toward Capernaum : and it was now
dark, and he was there alone. 24 But the ship was now
in the midst of the sea, tossed with waves ; for the
wind was contrary. [Mark VI, 48] And he saw them toiling
in rowing, 25 and [John VI, 19] when they had rowed about five
and twenty or thirty furlongs, in the fourth watch of the
night Jesus went unto them, walking on the sea,
[Mark VI, 48] and would have passed by them : 26 and when
the disciples saw him walking on the sea, [John VI, 19] and
drawing nigh unto the ship, they were troubled saying, It
is a spirit ; and they cried out for fear. 27 But straightway Jesus spake unto them saying, Be of good cheer :
it is I ; be not afraid. 28 And Peter answered him and
said, Lord, if it be thou, bid me come unto thee on the
water. 29 And he said, Come. And when Peter was
come down out of the ship, he walked on the water, to
go to Jesus : 30 but when he saw the wind boisterous,
he was afraid ; and beginning to sink, he cried saying,
Lord, save me. 31 And immediately Jesus stretched
forth his hand and caught him, and said unto him, O
thou of little faith, wherefore didst thou doubt ?
32 And when they were come into the ship, the wind

82

§ 64.—*In Returning, Christ Walks upon the Water.*

(Lake and Plain of Gennesáreth, and Capernaum.; [*Thursday* and *Friday ?*] *March* [25 and 26?], A. D. 28.)

²² *a* Perceiving [from the enthusiasm produced **Matt. XIV.** by this miracle in the minds of the assembly,] that the mass of the people were just ready to rise in civil rebellion, and [whether he would or not,] proclaim him as their king [to free their nation from its foreign yoke, and that such would inevitably be the result if he afforded them an opportunity] ;| Jesus immediately ordered his twelve disciples to get into the boat by themselves, and cross over the lake *b* to Bethsaida-in-Galilee,| leaving him to follow as soon as he should have dismissed the concourse. ²³ Accordingly, having dismissed his large audience [*c* with suitable parting admonitions|], he ascended a summit of the adjoining range of hills by himself, for the purpose of private prayer. It was nearly dark *d* when the disciples pushed out| in the boat upon the water, *e* steering their course for the opposite shore in the direction of Capernaum,| ²⁴ and, on getting fairly out into deep water, *e* night set in upon them,| while at the same time a *f* strong| head wind sprung up, which raised the waves and made their progress slow and dangerous. Meanwhile, Jesus continued alone on shore, *g* but [in the dim distance] he observed them tossed about in their little boat by the rough sea,| ²⁵ and about the fourth *watch* of the night [i. e. 3 o'clock A. M.], *h* when they had only been able to make a headway of some twenty-five or thirty *stadia* [i. e. between 3 and 3¼ miles] from shore,| he left the mountain and came toward them walking upon the surface of the water, *g* and seemed disposed to pass by them.| ²⁶ But upon seeing him thus walking along over the water *h* near the boat,| the disciples were terrified and screamed out for fear, "O! yonder is a spectre!" ²⁷ The familiar voice of Jesus, however, immediately quieted their alarm, as he said, "It is only I; be not frightened." ²⁸ Peter [in order to satisfy himself of the identity of Jesus,] replied, "Master, if it is really you, give me the leave [and ability] to walk out to you on the water." ²⁹ "You may come," returned Jesus. So getting out of the boat, Peter commenced to walk out over the water toward his Master; ³⁰ but seeing the waves roll high with the wind, he soon became frightened, and as he immediately began to sink, he called out, "O! Master, save me from drowning." ³¹ Jesus at once stretched out his hand and caught him, at the same time saying, "O you distrustful one! what made you doubt my sustaining power?" ³² No sooner had they got again into the boat

a John vi, 15.   *b* Mark vi, 45.   *c* Mark vi, 46.   *d* John vi, 16.
e John vi, 17.   *f* John vi, 18.   *g* Mark vi, 48.   *h* John vi, 19.

ceased : [JOHN VI, 21] and immediately the ship ⸻ MATT. XIV.
was at the land whither they went.   33 Then
they that were in the ship, [MARK VI, 51] were sore amazed
in themselves beyond measure, and came and worshiped
him saying, Of a truth thou art the Son of God;
[MARK VI, 52] for they considered not the miracle of the loaves,
for their heart was hardened.

34 And when they were gone over, they came into
the land of Gennesaret : 35 and when the men of that
place had knowledge of him, they sent out into all that
country round about, and brought unto him [MARK VI, 55]
in beds all that were diseased, [MARK VI, 55] where they heard
he was ; [56] and whithersoever he entered into villages or cities
or country, they laid the sick in the streets, 36 and besought
him that they might only touch the hem of his garment: and as many as touched, were made perfectly
whole.

22 The day following, when the people   John VI.
which stood on the other side of the sea, saw
that there was none other boat there save that one
whereinto his disciples were entered, and that Jesus
went not with his disciples into the boat, but that his
disciples were gone away alone ; 24 when the people
therefore saw that Jesus was not there, neither his
disciples, 23 (howbeit there came other boats from Tiberias nigh unto the place where they did eat bread
after that the Lord had given thanks ;) 24 they also took
shipping and came to Capernaum, seeking for Jesus.

§ 65.—*Christ's Discussion in the Synagogue, and its
Effects upon his Followers.*

(Capernaum; *Saturday, March* [27 ?] A. D. 28.)

59 (These things said he in the synagogue, as he taught
in Capernaum.)—25 And when they had found him on
the other side of the sea, they said unto him, Rabbi, when
83

a with the rest,| than the gale instantly ceased;   MATT. XIV.
b and the boat directly reached the shore toward
which they were going.| ³³ They, however, were
so completely astounded [at the two-fold miracle], that they prostrated themselves in the boat before him, exclaiming, " Surely you are the Messianic '*Son of God!*'"   *c* Their surprise showed that they had been made none the wiser [as to his character] by the miraculous multiplication of the victuals ; for their minds seemed stupid [to a just apprehension of this subject].|

   ³⁴ Having thus crossed the lake, *d* they landed| on the Plain of Gennesareth.   *e* Immediately upon their quitting the boat,| ³⁵ the inhabitants of that vicinity, learning who it was that had made them a visit, dispatched messengers *f* to pass rapidly| through the whole adjacent country ; so that the people flocked *f* to the place where they heard that he was,| bringing with them all their sick *f* upon litters,| to be cured.   *g* All the cities and villages through which he passed [on his way home,] brought out their sick into the town-squares,| ³⁶ and the invalids begged of him the privilege of merely touching the fringe of his cloak, [in the confident expectation of being thereby restored to health ;] and all that did so were cured.

   ²² On the next morning [after the day on which the   **John VI.** multitude had been miraculously supplied with food], as
they stood on the eastern shore of the lake, [they found
their plans frustrated with regard to Jesus, and were in doubt what course to pursue ; for] they knew that there was at that time no boat there, besides the single one in which the disciples had embarked, and they had noticed that he did not accompany them in that boat, they having left the shore alone in it : ²⁴ [they wondered therefore what had become of him,] as they did not find him there, nor could learn that his disciples [had returned to take him off, nor indeed that either of them] were anywhere in the vicinity. ²³ Seeing, however, the numerous boats that had now arrived at the scene of the last evening's meal, from the city of Tiberias, [to which the report of the miracle had spread, and concluding that he must have taken passage in one of them on their way back for his home,] ²⁴ they also hailed some of them, and thus returned to Capernaum in search of Jesus.

§ 65.—*Christ's Discussion in the Synagogue, and its Effects upon his Followers.*

(Capernaum ; *Saturday, March* [27 ?] A. D. 28.)

⁵⁹ [The next day after his return being the Sabbath,] Jesus repaired to the synagogue, ²⁵ where some of those who had come [the day before] from the opposite side of the lake in search of him, now found him. [On seeing him among the assembly, they made their way to him] and inquired, " Teacher, when did you arrive

---

a Mark vi, 51.   *b* John vi, 21.   *c* Mark vi, 52.   *d* Mark vi, 53.
     e Mark vi, 54.   *f* Mark vi, 55.   *g* Mark vi, 56.

camest thou hither?   ²⁶ Jesus answered   JOHN VI.
them and said, Verily, verily I say unto you,
Ye seek me, not because ye saw the miracles, but because ye did eat of the loaves and were filled : ²⁷ labor
not for the meat which perisheth, but for that meat
which endureth unto everlasting life, which the Son
of man shall give unto you ; for him hath God the
Father sealed.   ²⁸ Then said they unto him, What
shall we do, that we might work the works of God ?
²⁹ Jesus answered and said unto them, This is the work
of God, that ye *believe* on him whom he hath sent.
³⁰ They said therefore unto him, What *sign* showest
thou then, that we may see, and believe thee ? what
dost thou work ?   ³¹ Our *fathers** did eat manna in the
desert ; as it is written,† He gave them bread from
heaven to eat.   ³² Then Jesus said unto them, Verily,
verily I say unto you, *Moses* gave you not that bread
from heaven ; but my Father giveth you the *true*
bread from heaven : ³³ for the bread of God is he
which cometh down from heaven, and giveth life unto
the world.

³⁴ Then said they unto him, Lord, evermore give
us this bread.   ³⁵ And Jesus said unto them, *I* am
the bread of life : he that cometh to me, shall never
hunger ; and he that believeth on me, shall never
thirst.   ³⁶ But I said unto you, That ye also have
seen me, and believe not.   ³⁷ All that the Father
giveth me, shall come to me ; and him that cometh
to me, I will in no wise cast out : ³⁸ for I came down
from heaven, not to do mine own will, but the will
of him that sent me ; ³⁹ and this is the Father's will
which hath sent me, that of all which he hath given
me, I should lose nothing, but should raise it up again
at the last day ; ⁴⁰ and this is the will of him that sent

---

* Exod. xvi, 15.   † Psa. lxxviii, 24.

here?"   ²⁶ To this question he replied [in a manner   JOHN VI.
which led to a lengthened discourse on his part, concerning the benefits of his mission to those who rightly appre-
ciated it : " I am well aware of your motives," said he, " and] I solemnly avow my settled conviction, that you are induced to cultivate
an adherence to me, not from [a sincere confidence in my true character, based upon] the miracles which you have seen me perform, but
simply because, having just now been supplied with an abundant meal
by me, you hope for a repetition of similar worldly advantage. · ²⁷ On
the contrary, I charge you to be very little solicitous about acquiring
the perishable sustenance of your animal natures, but to bend your
most intense efforts toward the attainment of that spiritual sustenance, which will nourish your souls with immortal blessedness, and
which the 'Son of Man' is now ready to impart to you. Yes, [from him
alone is this higher blessing to be derived, for] him has his Divine Father specially commissioned for this purpose on earth."   ²⁸ "What services, then, must we render to God," inquired they, "in order so to fulfill the deeds enjoined by him, [as to secure His more peculiar favor,
and the blessings that are dependent upon it?]"   ²⁹ "The great duty
which He requires," replied Jesus, "is, *to rely implicitly upon me* as His
ambassador."   ³⁰ "But what proof of authority have you exhibited to
us," asked some of the leading men of the synagogue, [who had not
witnessed the late miracle,] " the sight of which could warrant us in
such a confidence in your character? Where is the public miracle
wrought by you to substantiate your claims?   ³¹ Our ancestors were
supplied with *manna* during their migration in the 'Desert,' and [in
reference to this direct sanction of Jehovah to the mission of Moses,]
the Psalmist says,—

> '[Though] He had showered manna for their food,
> And thus supplied them with *celestial* bread :'—

[we would have *you* afford us some equally irrefragable proof of your
mission.]"   ³² "Still," returned Jesus, " Moses himself did not furnish
your forefathers with even that *physical* kind of ' celestial food;' [for
it really was the gift of God, and therefore no such miraculous act on
Moses's part as you demand of me :] but I here declare, that my Father
is now offering you the true spiritual kind of ' celestial food,' [which
the other but prefigured.]   ³³ Yes, the genuine ' *Food from on high*'
is none other than That which has descended from Heaven, and imparts the highest life to mankind."

³⁴ Here the common people [misapplying his language to some
means of temporal sustenance,] exclaimed, "Teacher, we wish you
would supply us with this food more constantly than even Moses did
the manna anciently !"   ³⁵ Jesus then distinctly declared his meaning,
" *I am myself that ' Life-giving Food;'* whoever applies to me with
sincere confidence, need never more feel the cravings of unsatisfied
spiritual appetite.   ³⁶ *You* however, as I have often told you, although
you have seen enough of me—were you candid, do not properly believe in me.   ³⁷ Yet, [I shall not be destitute of success in my proffers ;
for] my Father will reward my labors by inclining and enabling some
portion of mankind to apply to me [through His gracious influences],
and I assure you, I will never reject any one that honestly applies to
me [for spiritual relief, whatever may be his circumstances] .   ³⁸ No,
for the very purpose of my descending from Heaven to earth, was to
accomplish not so much any purpose of my own [in a terrestrial ca-
pacity], as those of Him whose agent I am ;   ³⁹ and His design is, that I
should never abandon to destruction whatever part of the human race
is thus committed to my care, but should resuscitate every such person
to a blissful immortality at the final judgment.—⁴⁰ Nay, it is even His

84*

me, that every one which seeth the Son　JOHN VI.
and believeth on him, may have everlasting life, and I will raise him up at the last day.

⁴¹ The Jews then murmured at him, because he
said, I am the bread which came down from heaven ;
⁴² and they said, Is not this *Jesus* the son of Joseph,
whose father and mother we know ? how is it then
that he saith, I came down from heaven ?　⁴³ Jesus
therefore answered and said unto them, Murmur
not among yourselves.　⁴⁴ No man can come to me,
except the Father which hath sent me draw him,
(and I will raise him up at the last day :)　⁴⁵ it is
written in the prophets,* And they shall be all taught
of God ; every man therefore that hath heard, and
hath learned of the Father, cometh unto me : ⁴⁶ not
that any man hath seen the Father, save he which
is of God, he hath seen the Father.　⁴⁷ Verily,
verily I say unto you, He that believeth on me,
hath everlasting life : ⁴⁸ I am that bread of life :
⁴⁹ your *fathers* did eat manna in the wilderness, and
are dead ; ⁵⁰ this is the bread which cometh down
from heaven, that a man may eat thereof, and *not*
die : ⁵¹ I am the living bread which came down from
heaven ; if any man eat of this bread, he shall live
forever ; and the bread that I will give is my *flesh*,
which I will give for the life of the world.

⁵² The Jews therefore strove among themselves
saying, How can this man give us his *flesh* to eat ?
⁵³ Then Jesus said unto them, Verily, verily I say
unto you, Except ye eat the flesh of the Son of man
and drink his blood, ye have no life in you ; ⁵⁴ whoso
eateth my flesh and drinketh my blood, hath eternal
life, and I will raise him up at the last day : ⁵⁵ for
my flesh is meat indeed, and my blood is drink in-

---

* Isa. liv, 13.

wish, that [not a few merely, but] *every one* whom the
message of His Son may reach, provided he confides in
that Son for that purpose, should enjoy immortal bliss,
and every such person will I actually thus resuscitate : [so that it
is evidently not my intention to repel any humble applicant.]"

⁴¹ At this assertion of Jesus, "I am the Food which has descended
from on high," the Jewish leaders vented their dissatisfaction by remarking in a captious undertone, ⁴² " Is not this pretender Jesus, the
son of Joseph ? The whole town are well acquainted with his parents
[as unpretending persons, and know his earthly extraction]. What
right, then, has he to assert, 'I am come down from Heaven?'"
⁴³ Jesus replied to these their cavils, "You have no reason to whisper
such querulous observations to one another. ⁴⁴ [My divine origin is
proved by the coöperation of God with the labors of my mission ;
for] no one possesses the requisite disposition to apply to me for salvation, without the assisting influences of the Spirit of my Father who
has commissioned me, [upon his moral affections and will ; yet these
attracting influences some will experience,] and such persons it is
whom I will finally resuscitate to immortal bliss. ⁴⁵ Moreover, [this
doctrine of divine influences is in accordance with what] the prophet
Isaiah declares,—

> ' [Your people] all in heavenly lore will be
> Apt scholars, by Jehovah's Spirit taught ;'—

and in realizing this promise, every one who thus listens to God's instruction and becomes His disciple, can only do so by applying to me.
⁴⁶ Certainly [such knowledge could not be acquired in any more
immediate way ; for] no mere human being has ever personally beheld the Supreme Father, such manifestations being the exclusive
privilege of Him who has just arrived from the intimate society of
his Father, [and is therefore alone qualified by that direct intercourse to be the channel of human communication with Him.] ⁴⁷ And
by virtue of this my character it was, that I declared, that ' every one
who confides in me, is thereupon made a partaker of immortal blessedness.' ⁴⁸ And for this reason, I repeat, I AM THE LIFE-GIVING FOOD
for the soul. ⁴⁹ Your forefathers, I grant, ate *manna* in the ' Desert,'
—but they all *died* nevertheless ; ⁵⁰ whereas this, of which I speak,
is a different kind of food coming from the skies, expressly that all
who partake of it, may *escape* death, [and that of a more grievous na-
ture]. ⁵¹ In a word, *I* am this vital food, of heavenly origin; whoever partakes of which, will live forever [in the highest sense] ; and
the food which I thus design to furnish, is none other than *my own
body;* which I will soon offer [as a sacrifice], to retrieve the spiritual
life of the human race."

⁵² At this announcement, his opponents among the Jewish hierarchy turned the dispute upon his adherents of the lower class, by
asking them in derision, "Now how will you explain the absurdity,
that he.' is going to give us the flesh of his body to eat ' ?" ⁵³ To this
heartless scoff Jesus merely replied, "[Reject my declarations as
you may, yet] I solemnly warn you, that unless you thus spiritually
eat the flesh of the 'Son of Man,' and drink his blood, [by partaking
through faith of the benefits of his sacrificial atonement,] you must
remain totally devoid of the elements of spiritual life. ⁵⁴ He who does
partake of these, however, thereby enters upon the enjoyment of
that life, and him will I revive to enjoy its blessedness forever, at
the resurrection of the final judgment; ⁵⁵ for [by their sacrificial virtue thus received,] my flesh becomes the genuine aliment, and my
blood the only reviving draught, [which the soul's moral nature re-

deed. ⁵⁶ He that eateth my flesh and   JOHN VI.
drinketh my blood, dwelleth in me, and I
in him: ⁵⁷ as the living Father hath sent me, and I
live by the Father; so he that eateth me, even he
shall live by me. ⁵⁸ *This* is that bread which came
down from heaven; not as your *fathers* did eat
manna, and *are dead;* he that eateth of this bread
shall *live forever.*

⁶⁰ Many therefore of his disciples, when they had
heard this, said, This is a hard saying; who can
hear it? ⁶¹ When Jesus knew in himself that his
disciples murmured at it, he said unto them, Doth
this offend you? ⁶² what and if ye shall see the Son
of man ascend up where he was before? ⁶³ It is *the
Spirit* that quickeneth; the *flesh* profiteth nothing:
the words that I speak unto you, they are spirit and
they are life. ⁶⁴ But there are some of you that
believe not. (For Jesus knew from the beginning
who they were that believed not, and who should
betray him.) ⁶⁵ And he said, Therefore said I unto
you,* that no man can come unto me, except it were
given unto him of my Father. ⁶⁶ From that time
many of his disciples went back and walked no more
with him.

⁶⁷ Then said Jesus unto the twelve, Will *ye* also
go away? ⁶⁸ Then Simon Peter answered him, Lord,
to whom shall we go? *thou* hast the words of eternal
life; ⁶⁹ and we believe and are sure that thou art that
Christ, the Son of the living God. ⁷⁰ Jesus answered
them, Have not I chosen you twelve, and one of you
is a *devil?* ⁷¹ (He spake of Judas Iscariot the son of
Simon; for he it was that should betray him, being one
of the twelve.)

---

* Verse 44.

quires.]   ⁵⁶ He who thus participates in the benefits of my passion, becomes thereby united to me by spiritual relationship and resemblance, and conversely I with him, [as intimately as our physical natures would be incorporated together by his literally subsisting upon my actual flesh and blood;] ⁵⁷ and just as my being is blended by a unity of nature with that of my self-existent Father whose commission I bear, in a corresponding manner does that individual also, who thus appropriates the efficacy of my bodily sacrifice, subsist spiritually through the union thereby established with me. ⁵⁸ In this sense am I the Food that has descended from Heaven, a far more vitalizing aliment than the *manna* on which your ancestors subsisted, but which did not secure them from the doom of mortality; for the recipient of this Food will possess immortal bliss."

JOHN VI.

⁶⁰ [Upon his leaving the synagogue, after having concluded these remarks,] numbers of his more general followers who had heard them, [dissatisfied on account of their disagreement with their own preconceived opinions concerning the Messiah,] peevishly observed to one another, "Tough doctrine this! Who is to listen with patience to such intimations [of a Messiah that has dropped from the clouds, and yet is to be tamely made away with]?" ⁶¹ Jesus, aware that some of his adherents were covertly caviling at his declarations, thus expostulated with them: "Why should you take offense at what I have said? ⁶² Suppose you were to see the 'Son of Man' (as you really will one day) in the very act of ascending to the place of His former abode, —[would you then doubt my heavenly origin]? ⁶³ As to your misapprehension of my declaration, that I am to offer my body for the world's redemption, I must remind you that the *spiritual influences* thus procured, are what vitalize the moral powers of the soul, whereas the mere sacrificial *flesh* evidently could not at all answer that purpose; and viewed in this light it is, that my language addressed to you becomes replete with spiritual and life-giving significancy. ⁶⁴ Yet I know that there are some of you, who are too much prejudiced [by notions of the Messiah's triumphant career], to put any faith in my doctrines [of his propitiatory character, however clearly explained]." This he said because he was aware all along from his first connection with his followers, who were the ones among them that possessed no genuine faith in his true character, and indeed knew what very individual [of his immediate disciples themselves,] would eventually become his betrayer. ⁶⁵ "It is in view of this [natural alienation of the human heart to my spiritual precepts]," continued Jesus, "that I just now told you, that 'no person possesses the indispensable inclination for applying to me for spiritual blessings, unless the requisite influences be afforded to him by my Father, [enabling him to do so.]'" ⁶⁶ Upon the enforcement of this spiritual test of discipleship, many of his former adherents deserted him, and were no longer found among his followers.

⁶⁷ [This defection at once becoming apparent, Jesus asked the twelve Apostles, "Tell me, are *you* too disposed to abandon me?" ⁶⁸ Simon (Peter) ardently answered in the name of the rest, "To what other teacher, dear Master, should we resort in preference? Certainly your instructions alone conduct to immortal blessedness. ⁶⁹ Yes, we are confident, nay certain, that you are indeed the MESSIAH, even *the* '*Son of God*' himself!" ⁷⁰ "Ah," returned Jesus, "surely I have selected you twelve as my special attendants; and yet [despite your expression of attachment,] *one* out of your small number is a very demon!" ⁷¹ In this declaration he referred to Judas "of Ke'rioth," (he whose father's name was Simon,) one of the twelve, who in the issue became his betrayer to his enemies.

CHAPTER VI.

THE THIRD YEAR OF CHRIST'S MORE PUBLIC MINISTRY.

PORTION I.

CHRIST'S SUBSEQUENT STAY IN GALILEE.

(Time, *six months.*)

§ 66.—*Christ avoids attending this Third Passover at Jerusalem.*

([Capernaum?] *Sunday, March* 28, A. D. 28.)

¹ After these things Jesus walked in   **John VII.**
Galilee; for he would not walk in Jewry,
because the Jews sought to kill him.

§ 67.—*Confutation of Pharisaic Superstitions concerning Lustration.*

([Capernaum? early in] *April,* A. D. 28.)

¹ Then came together unto him the Phari-   **Mark VII.**
sees and certain of the scribes, which came
from Jerusalem : ² and when they saw some of his
disciples eat bread with defiled (that is to say, with
unwashen) hands, they found fault, ³ (for the Pharisees and all the Jews, except they wash their hands
oft, eat not, holding the tradition of the elders; ⁴ and
when they come from the market, except they wash,
they eat not; and many other things there be, which
they have received to hold, as the washing of cups
and pots and brazen vessels and tables :) ⁵ then the
Pharisees and scribes asked him, Why walk not thy
disciples according to the tradition of the elders, but eat
bread with unwashen hands? ⁶ He answered and said
unto them, Well hath Esaias prophesied of you hypocrites, as it is written,* This people [Matt. XV, 8] draweth

---

* Isa. xxix, 13.

CHAPTER VI.

THE THIRD YEAR OF CHRIST'S MORE PUBLIC MINISTRY.

PORTION I.

CHRIST'S SUBSEQUENT STAY IN GALILEE.

(Time, *six months*.)

§ 66.— *Christ avoids attending this Third Passover at Jerusalem.*

([Capernaum?] *Sunday, March* 28, A. D. 28.)

¹ [On account of the public excitement in Judea   **John VII.**
Proper relative to him] at this time, Jesus deemed
it prudent to defer his annual visit to Jerusalem,
and confine his travels for the present to Galilee; because [he
was apprized] of a plot which the leading Jews of the metropolis had laid for his destruction.

§ 67.— *Confutation of Pharisaic Superstitions concerning Lustration.*

([Capernaum? early in] *April*, A. D. 28.)

¹ ªWhile Jesus was thus continuing in Galilee,   **Mark VII.**
on one occasion certain Scribes of the Pharisaical
party, who had paid him a visit from Jerusalem,
² jealously watched some of his disciples partaking of a meal
with "unhallowed" (i. e. unwashed) hands. ³ (The Pharisees,
it must be observed, and indeed the Jews generally, never eat
without having first carefully washed their hands by rubbing
each in the other, in strict observance of the traditional injunctions of the ancient doctors: ⁴ and even when they return
from any place of public intercourse, the Pharisees are in the
habit of washing their persons more or less thoroughly before
they eat, [being apprehensive lest they may have acquired some
accidental impurity by contact with the common people.]
Besides these, there are various other traditional observances
with which they strictly comply, such as their endless ablutions of drinking-cups, pitchers, copper vessels and couches
for meals.) ⁵ Accordingly, they demanded of him, "Why do
your disciples thus neglect to conform to the prescriptions of
the ancient doctors as handed down to us, in taking their
meal without having first washed their hands?" ⁶ In reply,
Jesus told them in a tone of stern rebuke, "Most appropriately
does the declaration of the prophet Isaiah apply to such hypocrites as you, [when he represents Jehovah as saying of his
countrymen,]—

ª Matt. xv, 1.

87*

nigh unto me with their mouth, and honoreth   MARK VII.
me with their lips; but their heart is far
from me : ⁷ howbeit, in vain do they worship me,
teaching for doctrines the commandments of men.
⁸ For laying aside the commandment of *God*, ye hold
the tradition of *men*, as the washing of pots and cups;
and many other such like things ye do.   ⁹ And he said
unto them, Full well ye reject the commandment of
God, that ye may keep your own tradition : ¹⁰ for
Moses said, * Honor thy father and thy mother, and
† Whoso curseth father or mother, let him die the death;
¹¹ but *ye* say, If a man shall say to his father or mother,
It is *Corban*, (that is to say, a gift,) by whatsoever thou
mightest be profited by me, he shall be free : ¹² and ye
suffer him no more to do aught for his father or his
mother; ¹³ making the word of God of none effect
through your tradition, which ye have delivered : and
many such like things do ye.   ¹⁴ And when he had
called all the people unto him, he said unto them,
Hearken unto me every one of you and understand :
¹⁵ there is nothing *from without* a man, that entering
into him, can defile him; but the things which come
out of him, those are they that defile the man : ¹⁶ if
any man have ears to hear, let him hear.

¹² Then came his disciples, and said unto   **Matt. XV.**
him, Knowest thou that the Pharisees were
offended, after they heard this saying?   ¹³ But he
answered and said, Every plant which my heavenly
Father hath not planted, shall be rooted up.   ¹⁴ Let
them alone : they be blind leaders of the blind; and if
the blind lead the blind, both shall fall into the ditch.
[MARK VII, 17] And when he was entered into the house from the
people, ¹⁵ then answered Peter and said unto him, Declare unto us this parable.   ¹⁶ And Jesus said, Are *ye*

---

* Exod. xx, 12.   † Exod. xxi, 17.

'—— this nation outwardly alone   **MARK VII.**
a Approaches Me in worship,¹ with their lips
Pronouncing solemn praise, while in their heart
They're far estranged from loyalty to Me,
⁷ And all their show of reverence for Me
The vain dictation of a human rule !'—

⁸ for you scrupulously cling to traditional human injunctions, to the prejudice of the divine commands; as is evinced by your punctiliously rinsing household utensils, and innumerable ceremonies of a like futile character. ⁹ Take for instance," continued he, " the following case out of many, in which you *b* even¹ violate a plain requirement of the *Almighty*, in favor of your own traditional maxims : ¹⁰ *c* Jehovah delivered¹ through Moses this sacred injunction, ' Revere your father and mother both in feeling and conduct,' and [added this penalty for an infraction of that law,] ' Let any one that utters abusive or prejudicial language concerning his father or mother, be put to death summarily.' ¹¹ But *you*, on the contrary, institute this rule, ' If any person tells his father or mother, " The article of money or goods " (whatever it may be), " which you wish me to contribute to your relief, is *Korbawn'* [a Hebrew term meaning *gift*], (i. e. a consecrated *offering* to God), he is thereby exempted from the duty of contributing it ;' ¹² and [by allowing this principle to apply to anything that might be given in aid of his parents,] you excuse him from all obligation to provide for them. ¹³ In this manner you do away with the whole force of a direct command of God, by your traditional maxims ; and by some similar casuistry you manage to evade well-nigh every moral precept of the divine law !"

¹⁴ Then calling the crowd that stood by, to come near, he observed to them, " I wish you all to hear and understand me distinctly [in this matter of ablutions]. ¹⁵ It is nothing external which a person *takes into d* his mouth,¹ that can really pollute him, but it is what *issues from d* his mouth,¹ that alone has this effect. ¹⁶ Therefore, ' let every one that has ears to hear with, hear and understand ' my meaning !"

¹² His disciples had by this time gathered about him,   **Matt. XV.**
and were asking him, " Are you aware that the Pharisees are exceedingly incensed, at hearing the strictures you have just passed upon them ?" ¹³ " Well," replied Jesus, " [I cannot help that.] Every plant of religious doctrine that my Heavenly Father has not authorized to be planted in His moral garden, must be torn up by the roots in the prosecution of my work. ¹⁴ But give yourselves no concern for their approval or censure : they are ' stark-blind guides to equally blind travelers ' in the paths of religious knowledge ; and you know, ' when one blind man undertakes to guide another, they are both sure to tumble into some pit.' "

¹⁵ *e* As soon as he was alone in his house with his disciples,¹ Peter, in the name of the rest, [as they had all been greatly surprised at his remarks concerning the unimportance of the kind of one's food in point of ceremonial purity,] requested him to " explain to them the meaning of his apothegm on that subject." ¹⁶ " What !" re-

a Matt. xv, 8.   *b* Matt. xv, 3.   *c.* Matt. xv, 4.   *d* Matt. xv, 11.   *e* Mark vii, 17.

also yet [Mark VII, 18] so without understand-   Matt. XV.
ing? [17] do not ye yet understand that whatsoever [Mark VII, 18] thing from without entereth in at the
mouth, [Mark VII, 18] cannot defile him; because it entereth
not into his heart, but goeth into the body, and is cast
out into the draught, [Mark VII, 19] cleansing all meats?
[18] But those things which proceed out of the mouth,
come forth from the heart, and they defile the man;
[19] for out of the heart proceed evil thoughts, murders,
adulteries, licentiousness, thefts, [Mark VII, 22] covetousness,
wickedness, deceit, lasciviousness, an evil eye, false witness,
blasphemies, [Mark VII, 22] pride, foolishness: [20] these are
the [Mark VII, 23] evil things which [Mark VII, 23] come from
within, and defile a man; but to eat with unwashen
hands defileth not a man.

§ 68.—*The Demoniac Daughter of a Syro-Phenician Woman Cured.*

(North-western part of Galilee; [*April?*] A. D. 28.)

[21] Then Jesus went thence and departed into the
coasts of Tyre and Sidon, [Mark VII, 24] and entered into
a house, and would have no man know it; but he could not
be hid: [22] and behold, a woman of Canaan, [Mark VII, 26]
(the woman was a Greek, a Syrophenician by nation,) [25] whose
young daughter had an unclean spirit, heard of him, and came
out of the same coasts, and cried unto him saying,
Have mercy on me, O Lord, thou son of David; my
daughter is grievously vexed with a devil. [23] But he
answered her not a word. And his disciples came and
besought him saying, Send her away; for she crieth
after us. [24] But he answered and said, I am not sent
but unto the lost sheep of the house of Israel. [25] Then
came she and worshiped him saying, Lord, help me.
[26] But he answered and said, [Mark VII, 27] Let the *children*
first be filled; for it is not meet to take the children's
89

turned Jesus, "are *you* too still *a* so! dull of appre-   **MATT. XV.**
hension? [17] Have you failed to perceive, after
my explicit language, that whatever *a* external!
aliment is taken into one's mouth, passes into the stomach
merely, and is thus eliminated from the system, *b* without coming into contact with the mind! *a* so as to have any polluting
effect upon it?! [18] But on the other hand, the sentiments which
the mouth utters, proceed from the mind, and these are what
really defile one's nature. [19] For it is from the inner workings
of the soul, that all criminal thoughts and purposes emanate;
such as *c* impiety;!—murder, *c* malice,! injuries, abusive and *c* arrogant! language,—adultery and inchastity,—theft, false testimony and *c* deceit,—avarice and envy.! [20] These *d* vile internal!
dispositions *d* exhibited by any one,! are what really stain his
character; but to eat with unpurified hands, has no such contaminating influence."

§ 68.—*The Demoniac Daughter of a Syro-Phenician Woman
Cured.*

(North-western part of Galilee; [*April ?*] A. D. 28.)

[21] [Finding himself opposed by the Pharisees at Capernaum,
who were exasperated at the above pointed rebuke,] Jesus
quitted the village, and took a journey toward the confines of
Phenicia. *e* Arriving one day at a house near the frontiers, he
entered and claimed the rights of hospitality,—privately, however, as he did not wish his coming to be publicly known in
the place. [This injunction of secrecy upon his host was in-
effectual, for] the fact of his presence was soon circulated
through the neighborhood.! [22] *f* Incited by the report of his
character,! a certain *g* Gentile! woman, a native Phenician,
f who had a little daughter afflicted with demoniacal possession,! came from across the border, and getting within speaking distance, [as he was prosecuting his journey the next day,]
she loudly implored him, "Pity me, O Sir, 'Descendant of David,' and *g* cure my daughter,! who is suffering severely from
diabolical possession!" [23] But he [paid seemingly no attention
to her entreaties, and] proceeded on his way, without giving
her a word of reply. Presently his disciples came up, and
begged him to "gratify her request, for she was following them
with loud and pathetic entreaties." [24] "But then," replied
Jesus, "my personal mission is exclusively to the poor straying sheep of Jacob's posterity." [25] By this time the afflicted
woman had reached them, and throwing herself before him,
she besought him, "O dear Sir, do afford me your curative aid
for my daughter!" [26] Jesus still returned, *h* "You must wait
till the [Jews, the] proper *children* of the family of divine
choice, are first supplied with the food of religious blessings.!
These provisions must not be taken away from the children,

a Mark vii, 18.   *b* Mark vii, 19.   *c* Mark vii, 22.   *d* Mark vii, 23.
e Mark vii, 24.   *f* Mark vii, 25.   *g* Mark vii, 26.   *h* Mark vii, 27.

bread, and to cast it to *dogs*. ²⁷ And she MATT. XII.
said, Truth, Lord; yet the dogs [MARK VII, 28]
under the table eat of the [MARK VII, 28] children's *crumbs*,
which fall from their master's table. ²⁸ Then Jesus
answered and said unto her, O woman, great is thy
faith : [MARK VII, 29] for this saying go.thy way; be it unto
thee even as thou wilt : [MARK VII, 29] the devil is gone out
of thy daughter. And her daughter was made whole
from that very hour. [MARK VII, 30] And when she was
come to her house, she found the devil gone out, and her
daughter laid upon the bed.

§ 69.—*After Curing a Deaf Stammerer and Many
other Invalids, Christ Feeds a Multitude of over
Four Thousand.*

(The Decap'olis; [*May ?*] A. D. 28.)

³¹ And again departing from the coasts   **Mark VII.**
of Tyre and Sidon, he came [MATT. XV, 29] nigh
unto the sea of Galilee, through the midst of the coasts
of Decapolis ; [MATT. XV, 29] and went up into a mountain, and
sat down there. ³² And they bring unto him one that
was deaf and had an impediment in his speech ; and
they beseech him to put his hand upon him. ³³ And
he took him aside from the multitude, and put his finger into his ears, and he spit and touched his tongue ;
³⁴ and looking up to heaven, he sighed and saith unto
him, *Ephphatha*, that is, Be opened. ³⁵ And straightway his ears were opened, and the string of his tongue
was loosed, and he spake plain. ³⁶ And he charged
them that they should tell no man : but the more he
charged them, so much the more a great deal they
published it ; ³⁷ and were beyond measure astonished,
saying, He hath done all things well ; he maketh both
the deaf to hear, and the dumb to speak.

90

and thrown to the '*dogs*' [of Gentiles]." ²⁷"O   MATT. XII.
Sir!" responded she, "that is true; but yet the
very dogs *a* under the table! are allowed to catch
whatever crumbs their master's *a* children! let fall in eating."
²⁸ [On hearing this declaration of humble perseverance,] Jesus
replied to her, "Madam, your confidence in me is so great,
that *b* on account of this expression of it, I bid you depart
with your petition satisfied:! it is as you desire; *b* the demon
has left your daughter!"! *c* Upon returning to her home,! the
woman found that her daughter had been restored to sanity
from the very time of this answer, *c* and was now quietly reposing on a couch.!

§ 69.—*After Curing a Deaf Stammerer and Many other Invalids,*
Christ Feeds a Multitude of over Four Thousand.

(The Decap'olis ; [*May ?*] A. D. 28.)

³¹ After a short stay in the district of Galilee   **Mark VII.**
that borders on Phenicia, Jesus returned to the
lake Gennesareth, and crossing it, passed over
within the bounds of the Decap'olis. *d* Here he ascended an
eminence of the hills that skirt the lake, and took a seat
there, [in order to deliver instruction to the company that
gathered about him.! ³² After the conclusion of the discourse,]
some neighbors brought before him a man whom disease had
deprived of hearing, as well as rendered unable to speak without great difficulty, with the request that he would lay his
restoring hand upon the sufferer. ³³ Accordingly, taking the
invalid aside from the pressure of the crowd, Jesus first put
his fingers in the man's ears, and next, having spit upon the
ground, he touched the patient's tongue with a little of the
clay thus formed; ³⁴ he then raised his eyes toward heaven, and
with a sigh [of commiseration for the man's unhappy condition,] pronounced this word, *effathah'* [Syro-Chaldee for "*open*
thyself"], i. e. "Ears and tongue, recover your natural func-
tions!" ³⁵ Instantly the patient was restored to the faculty
of hearing, and the obstruction in his voice was removed, so
that he spoke readily and distinctly. ³⁶ Jesus then enjoined
upon the man and his friends not to mention the author of
his cure; but this strict charge seemed only to cause them to
proclaim the circumstances the more publicly. The miracle
being thus known by the whole surrounding concourse, ³⁷ excited among them the most lively emotions of surprise; so
that they exclaimed with enthusiastic admiration of Jesus,
"He is constantly bestowing blessings: he enables the very
deaf to hear, and the dumb to speak!"

a Mark vii, 28.   *b* Mark vii, 29.   *c* Mark vii, 30.   *d* Matt. xv, 29.

90*

³⁰And great multitudes came unto him, **Matt. XV.**
having with them those that were lame,
blind, dumb, maimed, and many others, and cast them
down at Jesus' feet; and he healed them: ³¹insomuch
that the multitude wondered, when they saw the dumb
to speak, the maimed to be whole, the lame to walk, and
the blind to see; and they glorified the God of Israel.

³²Then [Mark VIII, 1] the multitude being very great and
having nothing to eat, Jesus called his disciples unto him
and said, I have compassion on the multitude, because
they continue with me now three days and have
nothing to eat; and I will not send them away fasting
[Mark VIII, 3] to their own houses, lest they faint in the way,
[Mark VIII, 3] (for divers of them came from far.) ³³And his
disciples say unto him, *Whence* should we have so
much bread in the wilderness, as to fill so great a
multitude ? ³⁴And Jesus saith unto them, How many
loaves have ye ? And they said, Seven, and a few
little fishes. ³⁵And he commanded the multitude to
sit down on the ground : ³⁶and he took the seven
loaves and the fishes, and gave thanks, and brake them
and gave to his disciples, and the disciples to the multitude ; ³⁷and they did all eat and were filled, and they
took up of the broken meat that was left, seven baskets full ; ³⁸(and they that did eat, were four thousand
men, beside women and children.) ³⁹And he sent
away the multitude.

§ 70.—*The Pharisees and Sadducees again Demanding a confirmatory Portent, Christ Cautions his
Disciples against their Doctrines.*

(West Shore of the Lake Gennesareth near Dalmanu'tha, and North-
east Shore not far from Bethsaida-in-Pere'a; [*May?*] A. D. 28.)

³⁹And [Mark VIII, 10] straightway he took ship [Mark VIII, 10]
with his disciples, and came into the coasts of Magdala
91

³⁰ The report of this cure attracted great num- **Matt. XV.**
bers of people, who came bringing with them all
their friends that were crippled, deaf-and-dumb,
distorted in their limbs, or afflicted with any other physical
disability, and placed them at the feet of Jesus for relief. All
these he cured with such a manifest exertion of superhuman
power, ³¹ that the crowd in their astonishment at hearing the
dumb speak, and witnessing decrepit limbs restored to vigor,
cripples walking about, and blind persons in possession of
their sight, were led to praise Jehovah [for these tokens of
regard for His chosen people].

³² *A day or two after this, observing that an immense number of people had collected around him, and that they were
unsupplied with victuals, | Jesus called his disciples and re-
marked to them, "I feel much concerned for this concourse:
they have attended me now these three days, till their little
stock of provisions is exhausted; and I am reluctant to dis-
miss them hungry *b* to their homes, | lest their strength should
fail them on the road, *b* as some of them have come from a
long distance." | ³³ "Well," returned the disciples, "we do
not see where any one can procure food enough to supply such
a multitude *c* out here, | where there is not a house in sight."
³⁴ "How much bread have you here?" asked Jesus. "Only
seven biscuits," replied they, "and five small fishes." ³⁵ He
then directed the concourse to recline on the ground for a
meal, ³⁶ and taking in his hands the seven biscuits, after pronouncing "the blessing," he broke them, and handed the fragments to his disciples, to distribute them in turn to the people. The same was done with the little fishes. ³⁷ [These
scanty provisions held out so preternaturally, that] all present
ate their fill, and of the bits that remained after the meal,
there were gathered up seven baskets full. ³⁸ The number
that partook of the repast was *d* about | four thousand men,
besides numerous women and children. ³⁹ The meal being
over, Jesus dismissed the people.

§ 70.—*The Pharisees and Sadducees again Demanding a confirmatory Portent, Christ Cautions his Disciples against their
Doctrines.*

(West Shore of the Lake Gennesareth near Dalmanu'tha, and North-east Shore not
far from Bethsaida-in-Pere'a; [*May ?*] A. D. 28.]

³⁹ As soon as the company had dispersed, Jesus crossed the
lake in a boat *e* with his disciples, and landed at the out-
skirts of the village of Dalmanu'tha, | adjacent to the town

a Mark viii, 1.   b Mark viii, 3.   c Mark viii, 4.
          d Mark viii, 9.   e Mark viii, 10.

[Mark VIII, 10] at the parts of Dalmanutha. ¹ The   **Matt. XVI.**
Pharisees also with the Sadducees came
[Mark VIII, 11] forth, and began to question with him, and
tempting desired him that he would show them a sign
from heaven. ² He answered and said unto them,
When it is evening, ye say, It will be fair weather, for
the sky is red ; ³ and in the morning, It will be foul
weather to-day, for the sky is red and lowering ;
[Luke XII, 54] when ye see a cloud rise out of the west, straightway ye say, There cometh a shower, and so it is ; [55] and when
ye see the south wind blow, ye say, There will be heat, and
it cometh to pass: O ye hypocrites, ye can discern the
face of the *sky* [Luke XII, 56] and of the *earth;* but can ye
not discern the signs of [Luke XII, 56] this time? [57] Yea,
and why even of yourselves judge ye not what
is right? ²⁵ Agree with thine adversary   **Matt. V.**
quickly, [Luke XII, 58] that thou mayest be delivered from him, while thou art in the way with him
[Luke XII, 58] to the magistrate ; lest at any time the adversary deliver thee to the judge, and the judge deliver thee to the officer, and thou be cast into prison:
²⁶ verily I say unto thee, Thou shalt by no means come
out thence, till thou hast paid the uttermost
farthing. [Mark VIII, 12] And he sighed deeply   **Matt. XVI.**
in his spirit, and saith; ⁴ A wicked and adul-
terous generation seeketh after a sign ; and there shall
no sign be given unto it, but the sign of the prophet
Jonas.

And he left them, and [Mark VIII, 13] entering into the
ship again, departed [Mark VIII, 13] to the other side. ⁵ And
when his disciples were come to the other side, they
had forgotten to take bread, [Mark VIII, 14] neither had they
in the ship with them more than one loaf. ⁶ Then Jesus
said unto them, Take heed and beware of the leaven
of the Pharisees and of the Sadducees, [Mark VIII, 15] and
of the leaven of Herod. ⁷ And they reasoned among

92

of Mag'dala. [1] Here he was met by a party of   **Matt. XVI.**
Pharisees and Sadducees *a* from the village,| who
[incited by the report of his recent miracles,]
came and insidiously asked him to exhibit, for their satisfaction some palpable prodigy of a celestial nature.   [2] To this requirement Jesus replied, "When evening comes on, you often
remark to one another, 'It is going to be fair weather: the
sky looks red;' [3] and early in the morning, [you frequently
draw with equal correctness the opposite conclusion,] 'We
shall have a stormy day, for the sky is lowery with purplish
clouds.' *b* So, when you mark the thunder-cloud spring up in
the west, you predict, 'There is a shower coming on!' which
indeed occurs:| *c* and when you observe a stiff *Notus* [i. e.
south-west breeze] blowing, you confidently say, 'This will
bring a Sirocco heat!' [i. e. an oppressively warm and moist
wind;] and so it actually turns out.| What inconsistent ob-
servers you are! you can prognosticate the weather well enough
from the indications of the *d* natural| elements ; how comes it
then that you are so unable to apprehend the premonitions of
your future history *d* afforded by present occur-
rences?| [25] *e* Why indeed can you not even learn   **Matt. V.**
an admonitory lesson from your own policy in civil
matters?| When summoned by a prosecutor at law, [to ap-
pear before the magistrate and answer to his just claims upon
you,] you are well aware of the necessity of settling his demand while you are on your way with him *f* to court, by taking
pains| to effect some compromise *f* that will release you from
his warrant;| if you would not be forcibly arraigned before the
magistrate, who will then become your judge, and pass you
over into the hands of the ' *Collector*,' [26] to be kept by him in
jail till you pay the very last fraction of the account. [I tell
you, if you were wise, you would be equally prompt in seeking
to escape the condign penalty, that I am continually intimating impends over you for neglect of the divine
claims.]" [4] *g* Then sighing deeply, he concluded,| **Matt. XVI.**
"This wicked and profligate race of men are for-
ever requiring additional miracles; but [as I said some time
since,] no such evidence will be afforded them, except an
event parallel to that which occurred to the prophet Jonah."
    Leaving his artful adversaries with this rebuff, Jesus *h* en-
tered the boat again and returned to the eastern side of the
lake.| [5] Upon arriving at the opposite shore, the disciples
discovered that owing to their forgetful neglect to bring food
along with them, *i* they had only a single biscuit in the boat.|
[6] Accordingly, as Jesus began to *j* charge them,| "Beware of
the leaven of the Pharisees and Sadducees, *j* as well as of the
Herodians!"| [7] they concluded that he referred to their over-

---

a Mark viii, 11.   *b* Luke xii, 54.   *c* Luke xii, 55.   *d* Luke xii, 56.   *e* Luke xii, 57.
f Luke xii, 58.   *g* Mark viii, 12.   *h* Mark viii, 13.   *i* Mark viii, 14.   *j* Mark viii, 15.

themselves saying, It is because we have   MATT. XVI.
taken no bread.   8 Which when Jesus
perceived, he said unto them, O ye of little faith, why
reason ye among yourselves, because ye have brought
no bread? [MARK VIII, 17] perceive ye not yet? 9 do ye not
yet understand? [MARK VIII, 17] have ye your heart yet hardened? [18] having eyes, see ye not? and having ears, hear ye not?
neither remember the five loaves of the five thousand,
and how many baskets ye took up? [MARK VIII, 19] They
say unto him, Twelve. 10 Neither the seven loaves of
the four thousand, and how many baskets ye took up?
[MARK VIII, 20] And they said, Seven. [21] And he said unto them,
11 How is it that ye do not understand that I spake it not
to you concerning *bread*, that ye should beware of the
leaven of the Pharisees and of the Sadducees? 12 Then
understood they how that he bade them not beware of
the leaven of *bread*, but of the *doctrine* of the Pharisees
and of the Sadducees.

§ 71.—*A Blind Man Cured.*

(Bethsaida of Pere'a; [*May ?*] A. D. 28.)

22 And he cometh to Bethsaida: and   **Mark VIII.**
they bring a blind man unto him and besought him to touch him; 23 and he took the blind
man by the hand and led him out of the town, and
when he had spit on his eyes and put his hands upon
him, he asked him if he saw aught. 24 And he looked
up and said, I see *men* (as trees) walking. 25 After
that he put his hands again upon his eyes, and made
him look up; and he was restored and saw every man
clearly. 26 And he sent him away to his house saying, Neither go into the town, nor tell it to any in the
town.

93

sight, and whispered to each other, "He says   Matt. XVI.
this because we have brought no bread with
us." [8] Aware of their thoughts, Jesus chidingly
asked them, "What makes you talk so earnestly among yourselves concerning your omission to bring along with you a
supply of bread, you distrustful ones! [9] Have you not yet arrived at a comprehension of my providential care? [a] Are
your moral perceptions and feelings still so obtuse, that you
can neither see my deeds with your eyes, nor hear my words
with your ears, [so as to appreciate their spirit?]| Have you
forgotten the five biscuits that I distributed among the five
thousand?—do you remember how many baskets full of fragments you gathered up on that occasion?" [b] "Yes," replied
they, "there were *twelve*."| [10] [c] "And when I divided| the
seven biscuits among the four thousand," continued he, "how
many baskets of pieces did you then collect?" [c] "*Seven*,"
answered they.| [d] "Well, then," returned he,| [11] "how comes
it, [after such exhibitions of my provident power,] that you
should now fail to perceive that I had no need of referring to
literal bread in telling you to beware of the *leaven* of the
Pharisees and Sadducees?" [12] They then understood that he
did not mean, that they were to avoid supplying themselves
with fermented bread, but that they must shun the religious
maxims of the Pharisees and others.

§ 71.—*A Blind Man Cured.*

(Bethsaida of Pere'a; [*May ?*] A. D. 28.)

[22] When Jesus had proceeded as far as Beth-   **Mark VIII.**
saida-in-Pere'a, some of the inhabitants brought
before him a man whom disease had deprived of
his eye-sight, with the request that he would restore his vision
by his curative touch. [23] Accordingly, taking the blind man
by the hand, he led him out of the village, [in order to avoid
the crowd;] and then, having spit upon his eyelids and laid
his hands on them, he asked the patient, whether he could see
anything? [24] The man upon raising his eyes to ascertain, answered, "I believe I can distinguish something like men
around me, but they look to me like trees, except that they
appear to be walking about." [25] Then having placed his hands
again upon the patient's eyes, Jesus bade him look up again.
Upon his doing so, his sight was fully restored, so that he saw
all the bystanders distinctly. [26] Jesus now dismissed him to
his home, at the same time charging him, "not to enter the
village in going, nor mention the occurrence to any of its
residents."

a Mark viii, 18.   *b* Mark viii, 19.   *c* Mark viii, 20.   *d* Mark viii, 21.

§ 72.—*A Second Profession of Faith in him by the Apostles, leads Christ to Predict his Passion and the Trials of his Followers.*

(Vicinity of Cesare'a-Philip'pi ; [*May*,] A. D. 28.)

13 When Jesus [MARK VIII, 27] went out and **Matt. XVI.** his disciples, he came into the coasts of Cesarea-Philippi : [LUKE IX, 18] and it came to pass, as he was alone praying, his disciples were with him; and he asked his disciples [MARK VIII, 27] by the way saying, Whom do men say that I, the Son of man, am ? 14 And they said, Some say that thou art John the Baptist; some, Elias ; and others, Jeremias, or one of the [LUKE IX, 19] old prophets [LUKE IX, 19] risen again. 15 He saith unto them, But whom say *ye* that I am ? 16 And Simon Peter answered and said, Thou art the *Christ*, the Son of the living God. 17 And Jesus answered and said unto him, Blessed art thou, Simon Bar-jona ; for *flesh and blood* hath not revealed it unto thee, but my *Father* which is in heaven : 18 and I say also unto thee, That thou art *Peter*, and upon this *rock* I will build my church, and the gates of hell shall not prevail against it. 19 And I will give unto thee the keys of the kingdom of heaven : and whatsoever thou shalt bind on earth, shall be bound in heaven ; and whatsoever thou shalt loose on earth, shall be loosed in heaven. 20 Then charged he his disciples that they should tell no man that he was Jesus the Christ.

21 From that time forth began Jesus to show unto his disciples, how that he must go unto Jerusalem, and suffer many things, [MARK VIII, 31] and be rejected of the elders and chief-priests and scribes, and be killed, and be raised again the third day ; [MARK VIII, 32] and he spake that saying openly. 22 Then Peter took him, and began to rebuke him saying, Be it far from thee, Lord ; this

94

§. 72.—*A Second Profession of Faith in him by the Apostles, leads Christ to Predict his Passion and the Trials of his Followers.*

(Vicinity of Cesare′a-Philip′pi; [*May*,] A. D. 28.)

13 As Jesus was advancing, *a* together with his disci-   **Matt. XVI.**
ples, among the villages around Cesare′a-Philip′pi, *b* he
retired to a secluded spot for private prayer; and being rejoined by them [at the conclusion of his devotions], he asked
them *a* in proceeding on, "Whom do the *b* populace call me?"
14 They replied, "Some say you are John the Baptist come to life
again, and others take you to be the returning Elijah, while still
others think you must be Jeremiah or some other one of the *c* ancient
prophets revived." 15 "And whom do *you* hold me to be?" inquired he in continuation. 16 Simon (Peter) warmly replied in the
name of the rest, "You are the *Messiah*, even the 'Son of the ever-
living God'!" 17 "Yes," returned Jesus, "and happy are you,
Simon Bar-Jonah [(i. e. *Jonah's Son*, in Hebrew), in being of this
conviction]; for certainly no human teaching [corrupt as it is all
around us,] has ever fixed this important discovery in your mind,
but you have been convinced by the miracles which my Heavenly
Father is performing through me. 18 Therefore I now declare to
you, that, as your adopted name is PETER, [(i. e. *Rock*, in Greek,)
of a like character is the acknowledgment which you have just
made of my nature: for] upon the *rock* of this essential doctrine as
a foundation, will I build the temple of my universal Church, so
firmly that the most malignant force of all her fiendish foes shall
never be able to overturn the structure. 19 To you [in common
with your fellow-apostles, whose spokesman you are in this confession,] I will intrust the [administration of the affairs of the 'Reign
of the Divine Messiah,' giving you jointly the] key of the gospel
edifice: so that whatever persons or ordinances you bolt out from
the pale of my earthly Church, will also be excluded in the counsels
of Heaven; and those characters or measures to which you unbar
an entrance into the community of my followers here below, will
likewise be admitted to the divine ratification." 20 He then strictly
enjoined upon them all, not to avow in public [as yet] their conviction that he was the Messiah,
21 [Deeming their minds well prepared by the confidence thus
expressed in him, so as not to be shaken in their constancy by an
intimation of his approaching fate, and that a reference to such a
painful subject would also correct whatever prospects they might
still entertain of earthly happiness, as likely to accrue from their
connection with him;] Jesus now began to disclose to his disciples
more distinctly the important truth, that [in the execution of his
sacrificial work] *d* as the "Son of Man," it was requisite for him
soon to visit Jerusalem, and there, after enduring the utmost viru-
lence *e* and scorn of the Jewish leaders, hierarchy and ecclesiastics,
at last submit to be put to an ignominious death at their instiga-
tion; but that on the third day afterward he would revive. 22 *f* As
he was freely discoursing on this subject to them, Peter, laying his
hand on his Master's arm, began to check these melancholy apprehensions by officiously exclaiming, "Heaven forbid, dear Master,

a Mark viii, 27.   *b* Luke ix, 18.   *c* Luke ix, 19.
d Mark viii, 31.   *e* Luke xvii, 25.   *f* Mark viii, 32.

shall not be unto thee.   ²³ But he turned   MATT. XVI.
[MARK VIII, 33] about and looked on his disciples,
and said unto Peter, Get thee behind me, Satan; thou
art an offense unto me: for thou savorest not the things
that be of God, but those that be of men.

[MARK VIII, 34] And when he had called the people unto him
with his disciples also, ²⁴ then said Jesus unto his disciples [LUKE IX, 23] and to them all, If any man will come after
me, let him deny himself and take up his cross [LUKE IX, 23]
daily and follow me: ²⁵ for whosoever will save his
life, shall lose it; and whosoever will lose his life for
my sake [MARK VIII, 35] and the gospel's, shall find it: ²⁶ for
what is a man profited, if he shall gain the whole world,
and lose his own soul, [LUKE IX, 25] or be cast away? or
what shall a man give in exchange for his soul?
[MATT. X, 32] Whosoever therefore shall confess me before men,
him will I confess also before my Father which is in heaven
[LUKE XII, 8] and before the angels of God; [MATT. X, 33] but whosoever shall deny me [MARK VIII, 38] and be ashamed of me and
of my words [MATT. X, 33] before men [MARK VIII, 38] in this adul-
terous and sinful generation, [MATT. X, 33] him will I also deny
before my Father which is in heaven: ²⁷ for the Son of man
shall come in [LUKE IX, 26] his own glory and in the glory of
his Father with his angels; and then he shall reward
every man according to his works; ²⁸ verily I say
unto you, There be some standing here which shall
not taste of death, till they see the Son of man coming
in his kingdom [MARK IX, 1] with power.

§ 73.—*The Transfiguration.*

([Mount Hermon?] *May,* A. D. 28.)

¹ And after six [LUKE IX, 28] or eight days   **Matt. XVII.**
Jesus taketh Peter, James and John his
brother, and bringeth them up into a high mountain

that such a tragical event should occur to you!—"   MATT. XVI.
[23] Jesus turned round [toward Peter at this incredulous interruption], *a* and perceiving the other disciples animated with the same carnal spirit, l he cut short his imperti-
nence by sternly bidding him, "Take your proper place as a submissive follower, and do not attempt to obtrude upon me your satanic
suggestions! Your advice would prove an obstacle to my mission,
for it proceeds from a heart not imbued with the purposes of God,
but actuated by worldly notions."

[24] [Apprehensive lest this expectation of temporal advantage might
still cling to the minds of his followers,] Jesus *b* called about him the
general mass of his customary adherents in addition to his twelve disciples, l and proceeded to instruct them *c* all l as follows : "Whoever
will be my *d* true l disciple, must renounce his own earthly gratifica-
tion, and be willing to hazard *c* daily l even an ignominious death in
my service ; [25] and I warn you all, that any one who abandons my
cause through anxiety to secure his life, will thereby really sacrifice
[all that is valuable in] it, while he that adheres to me *e* and my gospel l at the risk of his very life, will thus most effectually insure its
highest interests. [26] Now [the proverb teaches you, that] 'a person
would be no gainer, were he to acquire the whole earth, and lose his
life in the attainment ;' and [if the adage further asks,] 'Where is the
equivalent that a man can give to purchase back his life?' [I may
say with even greater emphasis, There is nothing that can compen-
sate him for the ruin of his *endless* existence. [27] Be assured that these
everlasting consequences infallibly depend upon fidelity or apostasy
in my cause :] *f* for it is that person who unflinchingly avows his attachment to me in the face of human opposition, that I will acknowledge as my faithful follower in the presence of an assembled universe ; l *g* but whoever allows himself to be overcome by the scorn and
persecution of the profligate and sin-hardened race with which he is
surrounded, so as to desert or reject me and my injunctions, that person will find himself likewise rejected by me as unworthy in the final
judgment. l Yes, the 'Son of Man' [persecuted and slighted as he may
be now], will hereafter reappear as the Judge of mankind, invested
with the glorious majesty of the Godhead, *h* which he will then be
seen to share in common with his Divine Father, l and surrounded by
his retinue of *h* celestial l angels ; and at that grand adjudication of
human characters, will he assign the awards of eternity to each individual suited to that person's earthly conduct. [28] *i* Nay," continued
Jesus, l "I solemnly assure you, that ere the eyes of not a few of those
who now stand here listening to me, shall close in death, they will
have beheld [a scene that may fitly represent the final retributions of
that day; for (at the destruction of Jerusalem) they will gaze upon]
the 'Son of Man' as he returns [in a similar but subordinate sense]
to consummate his 'Reign' with *i* divine authority l over Jewish op-
position] !"

§ 73.—*The Transfiguration.*

([Mount Hermon ?] *May,* A. D. 28.)

[1] On the sixth day after *j* the above disclosure of   Matt. XVII.
the scheme of his mission, l selecting Peter and the
brothers James and John as his *k* sole l attendants,
Jesus set out for an ascent of *j* the l very lofty mountain in that region,

a Mark viii, 33.   *b* Mark viii, 34.   *c* Luke ix, 23.   *d* Matt. x, 38.
e Mark viii, 35.   *f* Matt. x, 32.   *g* Mark viii, 38.   *h* Luke ix, 26.
    i Mark ix, 1.   *j* Luke ix, 28.   *k* Mark ix, 2.

apart, [2] and [LUKE IX, 29] as he prayed, was   MATT. XVII.
transfigured before them ; and his face
did shine as the sun, and his raiment was white as the
light, [MARK IX, 3] so as no fuller on earth can white them.
[3] And behold, there appeared unto them Moses and
Elias talking with him ; [LUKE IX, 31] who appeared in glory,
and spake of his decease which he should accomplish at Jerusalem. [32] But Peter and they that were with him, were
heavy with sleep; and when they were awake, they saw his
glory and the two men that stood with him. [4] Then
[LUKE IX, 33] as they departed from him, answered Peter and
said unto Jesus, Lord, it is good for us to be here; if
thou wilt, let us make here three tabernacles, one for
thee, and one for Moses, and one for Elias : [MARK IX, 6]
(for he wist not what to say; for they were sore afraid.)
[5] While he yet spake, behold, a bright cloud over-
shadowed them ; [LUKE IX, 34] (and they feared as they entered into the cloud;) and behold, a voice out of the
cloud which said, This is my beloved Son in whom I
am well pleased ; hear ye him : [6] and when the disciples heard it, they fell on their face and were sore
afraid. [7] And [LUKE IX, 36] when the voice was past, Jesus
came and touched them, and said, Arise and be not
afraid. [8] And when they had lifted up their eyes,
they saw no man save Jesus only.

[9] And as they came down from the mountain, Jesus
charged them saying, Tell the vision to no man, until
the Son of man be risen again from the dead.
[LUKE IX, 36]. And they told no man in those days any of those
things which they had seen: [MARK IX, 10] and they kept that
saying with themselves, questioning one with another what
the rising from the dead should mean. [10] And his disciples asked him saying, Why then say the scribes that
Elias must first come ? [11] And Jesus answered and
said unto them, Elias truly shall first come and restore
all things ; [12] but I say unto you, That Elias is come
96

[probably Mount Hermon. Arrived at one of the MATT. XVII.
lower summits,] *a* while he was engaged in private
devotion! [at a short distance from the three dis-
ciples], ² his whole physical appearance underwent a remarkable
change; his countenance becoming radiant [with such unearthly
light, that it shone] like the sun, and his dress assuming a brilliancy
b like that of dazzling snow, surpassing the whiteness which any
bleaching of human art could effect. | ₃ Presently there could be dis-
tinguished *c* amid a halo [of celestial radiance that floated near],|
d two other| bright forms, those of the departed Moses and Elijah,
who commenced a conversation with Jesus, *c* on the subject of the
violent death by which he was soon to close his mission at Jerusalem.|
e During their Master's devotions, Peter and the two other disciples
had fallen into a doze through fatigue; but being roused [by the
voices near them], they looked up and saw the resplendency that en-
circled him, and recognized [by their conversation] the two persons
who were now standing beside him. | ⁴*f* Bewildered with astonish-
ment and the awe that checked the utterance of the others,| Peter
cried out to Jesus, *g* as soon as the celestial visitors had retired,| "O
Teacher, what a privilege it is for us to be in so favored a spot as this!
Give us leave to erect three booths here, one for your own residence,
another for Moses, and the third for Elijah; [that we may perpetually
enjoy such heavenly visits!]" ⁵ While these expressions of wild delight were escaping his lips, suddenly a brilliant cloud enveloped the
whole company, *h* making the disciples shudder as it passed over
them;| from the midst of which there issued a Voice that declared,
"This is My dear and only Son, on whom rests my fondest approval!
Hearken to his instructions!" ⁶ As they heard these words, the disciples fell prostrate to the earth in reverential terror, [and continued
in this suppliant posture,] ⁷ till Jesus approaching gently touched
them, bidding them "rise and lay aside their alarm." ⁸ Upon this
assurance, they stood up, and on looking around, they saw no one
present with them except Jesus himself.
 ⁹ As they were descending the mountain, Jesus charged them,
"not to relate what they had just seen to any person, until the
'Son of Man' had revived from the tomb;" *i* an injunction which
they observed by a strict secrecy for the prescribed period,| *j* although
they had quite a discussion among themselves at the time, to know
what their Master meant by "reviving from the tomb,"| [an ex-
pression which they failed after all to comprehend as yet. ¹⁰ Not
daring to question him directly on the subject, they resolved to ask
him to explain a difficulty which the appearance of the glorified
saints to their sight had raised in their minds during the discussion;] accordingly one of their number inquired of him, "Are the
public Expounders of the Law correct, when they tell us that Elijah
must appear before the Messiah comes? [If so, was not his visit
with you just now a prestige of the speedy establishment of your
empire?]" ¹¹ "Yes," replied Jesus, "an Elijah *is* to come before
that event, and his office is to set everything right [in the moral
attitude of the popular mind respecting that event] ; ¹² but that
Elijah, I assure you, has *already* appeared among us, and his coun-

a Luke ix, 29.   *b* Mark ix, 3.   *c* Luke ix, 31.   *d* Luke ix, 30.   *e* Luke ix, 32.
f Mark ix, 6.   *g* Luke ix, 33.   *h* Luke ix, 34.   *i* Luke ix, 36.   *j* Mark ix, 10.

P   96*

already, and they knew him not, but have   MATT. XVII.
done unto him whatsoever they listed:
likewise, [MARK IX, 12] as it is written of him,* shall also the
Son of man suffer of them [MARK IX, 12] many things and be
set at naught.   ¹³ Then the disciples understood that he
spake unto them of John the Baptist.

§ 74.—*Cure of a Demoniac, whom the Disciples had
Failed to Restore to Sanity.*

(Vicinity of Cesare′a-Philip′pi ; *May*, A. D. 28.)

¹⁴ And [LUKE IX, 37] on the next day, when he   **Mark IX.**
came [LUKE IX, 37] down from the hill to his disciples he saw a great multitude about them, and the
scribes questioning with them.   ¹⁵ And straightway
all the people, when they beheld him, were greatly
amazed, and running to him saluted him.   ¹⁶ And he
asked the scribes, What question ye with them ?
¹⁷ And one of the multitude [MATT. XVII, 14] kneeling down
to him, answered and said, Master, I have brought unto
thee my [LUKE IX, 38] only son, which hath a dumb spirit ;
¹⁸ and wheresoever he taketh him, he teareth him,
[LUKE IX, 39] and bruising him hardly departeth from him ;
[MATT. XVII, 15] for he is lunatic and sore vexed, and he
[LUKE IX, 39] suddenly crieth out and foameth and gnasheth
with his teeth and pineth away :   ²² and oft-times it
hath cast him into the fire and into the waters, to destroy him.   ¹⁸ And I spake to thy disciples that they
should cast him out, and they could not.   ¹⁹ He answereth him and saith, O faithless generation, how
long shall I be with you ? how long shall I suffer you ?
—Bring him unto me.   ²⁰ And they brought him unto
him : and [LUKE IX, 42] as he was yet a-coming, when he saw
him, straightway the spirit tare him ; and he fell on

---

* See especially Isa. liii ; Dan. ix, 26.

trymen, instead of recognizing him properly, have **MATT. XVII.** inflicted-suffering and death upon him at their caprice. In like manner is the 'Son of Man' also about to be the sport of their *a* mockery and utmost malice, in fulfillment of ancient prophecy."[1] 13 From this explanation, the disciples perceived that he was speaking to them of John the Baptist, as being the predicted Elijah.

§ 74.—*Cure of a Demoniac, whom the Disciples had Failed to Restore to Sanity.*

(Vicinity of Cesare'a-Philip'pi ; *May*, A. D. 28.)

14 Upon returning to the rest of the disciples *b* the **Mark IX.** next day,[1] Jesus found them surrounded by a large concourse of people, among whom were several Scribes engaged in a warm dispute with the disciples. 15 Seeing him approach so unexpectedly yet opportunely, the assembly rushed toward him with surprise and delight, saluting him with a reverent welcome. 16 [Perceiving that some special cause must have attracted such a crowd,] he demanded of the Scribes, "What were you disputing about just now with my disciples?" 17 In reply, a man *c* came forward[1] from among the crowd, and *c* suppliantly prostrating himself before him,[1] *d* cried out,[1] "I was bringing my *d* only[1] son, with the design of presenting him before you to be cured.—*d* I beg you,[1] *e* have pity on him,[1] and *d* relieve him[1] of the *e* epilepsy[1] with which he is so severely afflicted as frequently to deprive him of the power of speech. His disease is the result of the influence of a demon with which he is possessed; 18 and when a fit comes on, the fiend *f* causes him immediately to shriek dreadfully[1] [in his inarticulate way], and throws him into convulsions, in which he dashes himself on the ground, grinds his teeth together, and froths at the mouth: 22 oftentimes the demon impels him to throw himself into the flames, or else to rush into the water, as if to destroy him outright, *f* and clings to him with such pertinacity that[1] he is worn to a skeleton *f* with violent paroxysms.[1] —18 [Not being able to find you,] I *g* presented him[1] to your disciples for relief; but they were unable to effect an expulsion." 19 Upon this information, Jesus reprovingly exclaimed to his disciples, "How distrustful you are, [not to exercise reliance on my power, though absent, enough to enable you to perform a cure !]— can I be always with you, [to effect cures in person, without your ever learning to have full confidence, so as to act in my name ?]" *h* Next turning to their opponents, he exclaimed, "What a perverse set of men are you,[1] [to cavil at the failure !]—must I continually put up with your malicious detraction?" Then addressing the petitioner, he said, "Bring *i* your son[1] *h* here[1] to me !" 20 No sooner had they brought him within sight of Jesus, than the fiend threw him into a spasm, that made him roll on the ground, the foam

a Mark ix, 12.	*b* Luke ix, 37.	*c* Matt. xvii, 14.
d Luke ix, 38.	*e* Matt. xvii, 15.	*f* Luke ix, 39.
g Matt. xvii, 16.	*h* Matt. xvii, 17.	*i* Luke ix, 41.

the ground and wallowed foaming. ²¹ And   MARK IX.
he asked his father, How long is it ago
since this came unto him? And he said, Of a child :
²² but if thou canst do anything, have compassion on
us and help us. ²³ Jesus said unto him, If thou canst
believe,—all things are possible to him that believeth.
²⁴ And straightway the father of the child cried out
and said with tears, Lord, I believe ; help thou mine
unbelief. ²⁵ When Jesus saw that the people came
running together, he rebuked the foul spirit saying
unto him, Thou dumb and deaf spirit, I charge thee
come out of him, and enter no more into him. ²⁶ And
the spirit cried and rent him sore and came out of
him : and he was as one dead ; insomuch that many
said, He is dead. ²⁷ But Jesus took him by the hand
and lifted him up, [LUKE IX, 42] and delivered him again to
his father ; and he arose [MATT. XVII, 18] cured from that very
hour. [LUKE IX, 46] And they were all amazed at the mighty
power of God.

²⁸ And when he was come into the house, his dis-
ciples asked him privately, Why could not *we* cast
him out ? [MATT. XVII, 20] And Jesus said unto them, Because
of your *unbelief.* ⁵ And the apostles said   **Luke XVII.**
unto the Lord, Increase our faith. ⁶ And
the Lord said, If ye had faith as a *grain of mustard-
seed,* ye might say unto this sycamine-tree, Be thou
plucked up by the root, and be thou planted in the sea ;
and it should obey you : [MATT. XVII, 20] and nothing shall be
impossible unto you. ²⁹ And he said unto   **Mark IX.**
them, This kind can come forth by nothing
but by *prayer and fasting.*
   98

oozing from his mouth. 21 To Jesus's inquiry, "How   MARK IX.
long has he been afflicted with this lunacy?" the father
replied, "Ever since he was a small boy.—22 O Sir, if
your ability can indeed reach such an inveterate case, do in compassion relieve him and thereby me!" 23 "Yes," returned Jesus,
"[I can easily afford you your desire,] if *you* on your part will but
exercise a corresponding degree of confidence in my ability; for [I
would have you aware of this great truth, that] *all needed blessings
may be realized by him who trusts the Divine power and goodness for
them*." 24 At this offer, the agonized parent exclaimed with tears
[of earnest sincerity falling from his eyes], "I do indeed confide in
you; O then, render me the craved relief for my son, distrustfully
though I just now expressed myself!"

25 Perceiving that the crowd was pressing toward the spot, Jesus
sternly charged the demon to "quit the patient, (whom he had reduced to the condition of a deaf mute,) and never again attack
him!" 26 After causing the sufferer to shriek and go into a terrible
convulsion, the fiend relinquished his grasp, leaving the subject so
utterly prostrated and corpse-like, that many of the by-standers
were confident "he was dead." 27 But Jesus, taking his hand, as-
sisted him to rise upon his feet, and then presented him, *a* per-
fectly restored to health from that instant,| *b* to his father.| *c* All
who witnessed the cure, were astonished at this manifest exertion
of divine power.|

28 As soon as their Master had withdrawn into the house [where
he was temporarily lodging], the disciples *d* came to him| privately
with this question, "What was the reason why *we* were unable to
expel that demon?" He replied, *e* "It was on account of your
want of faith| [in the efficiency of my power as dele-
gated to you]." 5 The mortified apostles apologet-   Luke XVII.
ically responded, "Master, by your indulgent encouragement, we will endeavor to exercise a more perfect confidence
in your ability for the future." 6 "Ah!" returned Jesus, "[you
are not even now sensible of the extent of your deficiency in this
respect. For] *e* I assure you,| had you faith [of the genuine char-
acter, even though it were so limited in its application that it might
seem small] as a grain of mustard-seed, you might, in its assurance,
bid this sycamore-tree [probably pointing to one that overshaded
the dwelling,] 'be torn up by the roots without human hands, and
plant itself in the unstable sea,' and the power of God would accomplish your behest; *e* or you might even command yonder mountain [pointing apparently to Mount Hermon, on which he had
spent the last night,] to 'be transported to another spot,' and it
would change its site at once: indeed, [with such unwavering
reliance upon divine aid,] no task would baffle you.|

29 However," concluded he, "the faith requisite for the   Mark IX.
expulsion of demons, as in the case just now, [can only
be attained in connection with such a devotional spirit, as] is the
fruit of frequent prayer, and [with that mortification of the natural
inclinations to which] fasting, [when religiously observed, so emi-
nently contributes.]"

a Matt. xvii, 18.   *b* Luke ix, 42.   *c* Luke ix, 43.
                    d Matt. xvii, 19.   *e* Matt. xvii, 20.

98*

§ 75.—*Christ again Predicts his Passion.*

(On his Passage through northern Galilee; [*June?*] A. D. 28.)

³⁰ And they departed thence and passed   MARK IX.
through Galilee; and he would not that any
man should know it.   ³¹ For [LUKE IX, 43] while they wondered every one at all things which Jesus did, he taught his
disciples and said unto them, [LUKE IX, 44] Let these sayings
sink down into your ears: for the Son of man is delivered
into the hands of men, and they shall kill him; and
after that he is killed, he shall rise the third day.
[MATT. XVII, 23] And they were exceeding sorry: ³² but they
understood not that saying, and were afraid to ask
him.

§ 76.—*The Sacred Half-Shekel miraculously Provided.*

(Capernaum; [*June?*] A. D. 28.)

²⁴ And when they were come to Caper-   **Matt. XVII.**
naum, they that received tribute-money
came to Peter and said, Doth not your master pay
tribute?   ²⁵ He saith, Yes.   And when he was come
into the house, Jesus prevented him saying, What
thinkest thou, Simon? of whom do the kings of the
earth take custom or tribute; of their own *children*,
or of *strangers?*   ²⁶ Peter saith unto him, Of strangers.
Jesus saith unto him, Then are the children free:
²⁷ notwithstanding, lest we should offend them, go thou
to the sea and cast a hook, and take up the fish that
first cometh up; and when thou hast opened his mouth,
thou shalt find a piece of money; that take and give
unto them for me and thee.

99

§ 75.—*Christ again Predicts his Passion.*

(On his Passage through northern Galilee ; [*June ?*] A. D. 28.)

[30] Jesus now crossed over into Galilee with his   MARK IX.
disciples, avoiding public notice as much as possible. [As they were traveling southward through
the country,] [31] *a* his followers' minds being still excited with
the amazement produced by his recent wonderful acts,[l] Jesus
declared to his disciples *b* in the most impressive manner,[l]
that "the 'Son of Man' would shortly fall into the power of
those by whom his life would be taken ; but that on the third
succeeding day, he should return to life." *c* This statement
filled them with great grief [l] [at the calamity which it seemed
to forebode] ; [32] yet they did not apprehend their Master's full
meaning, nor did they venture to ask him *d* to resolve the
mystery,[l] [lest he might reprehend them for their dullness of
understanding.]

§ 76.—*The Sacred Half-Shekel miraculously Provided.*

(Capernaum ; [*June ?*] A. D. 28.)

[24] Upon their arrival at Capernaum, one of   Matt. XVII.
the collectors of "the *didrach'ma*" [(i. e. about
30 cents,) or *half-shekel* tax for the Temple,]
meeting Peter [near the house which the rest of the party
had entered], asked him, "Your Teacher pays the Temple-
tax, does he not?" [25] "Yes," replied Peter, ["he always
does so ;"] and as he was entering the house, [to report the
demand to his Master,] Jesus anticipated him with this question, "Simon, what is your opinion? from whom are kings in
the custom of exacting capitation or other taxes,—from their
own children, or from their subjects [who are not members
of their family]?" [26] "From their subjects, I should certainly say," answered Peter. "Then," returned Jesus, "their
children are evidently exempt from such a demand ; [and I as
the Son of God ought not therefore be required to pay a tax
for His Temple.] [27] However, lest we should give these collectors and their hierarchal employers an opportunity to find
fault ; do you just go down to the Lake, and drop in a hook
and line ; draw out the fish that first rises [to catch the bait],
and when you have opened its throat, you will find in it a
stater [i. e. about 60 cents], which you may take and pay to
the collectors for your own tax as well as mine."

a Luke ix, 43.   *b* Luke ix, 44.   *c* Matt. xvii, 23.   *d* Luke ix, 45.

§ 77.—*Christ Exhorts his Contentious Disciples to Mutual Deference and Forbearance.*

(Capernaum; [*June?*] A. D. 28.)

[MATT. XVIII, 1] At the same time came the dis-   **Mark IX.**
ciples unto Jesus: ³³ and being in the house
he asked them, What was it that ye disputed among
yourselves by the way? ³⁴ But they held their peace:
for by the way they had disputed among themselves
who should be the greatest. [LUKE IX, 47] And Jesus perceiving the thought of their heart, again asked them;
[MATT. XVIII, 1] and they answered, We were saying, Who is the
greatest in the kingdom of heaven? ³⁵ And he sat down
and called the twelve, and saith unto them, If any man
desire to be first, the same shall be last of all and servant of all.   ³⁶ And he took a child and set him in the
midst of them: and when he had taken him in his
arms, he said unto them, [MATT. XVIII, 3] Except ye be converted and become as little children, ye shall not enter into
the kingdom of heaven: [4] whosoever therefore shall humble
himself as this little child, the same is greatest in the kingdom of heaven; [LUKE IX, 48] for he that is least among you all,
the same shall be great.   ³⁷ Whosoever shall receive one
of such children in my name, receiveth me; and whosoever shall receive me, receiveth not me, but him that
sent me.

³⁸ And John answered him saying, Master, we saw
one casting out devils in thy name, and he followeth
not us; and we forbade him, because he followeth not
us.   ³⁹ But Jesus said, Forbid him not; for there is
no man which shall do a miracle in my name, that can
lightly speak evil of me: ⁴⁰ for he that is not against
us, is on our part.   ⁴² And whosoever shall offend one
of these little ones that believe in me, it is better for
him that a millstone were hanged about his neck, and
he were cast into the sea: [MATT. XVIII, 7] woe unto the

100

§ 77.—*Christ Exhorts his Contentious Disciples to Mutual Deference and Forbearance.*

(Capernaum; [*June ?*] A. D. 28.)

³³ When the disciples had *a* assembled again¦ in the   **Mark IX.**
house [on Peter's return after satisfying the collector's
claim], Jesus asked them, "What question was it that
you were discussing so earnestly together, as we were walking toward
the village [this morning]?" ³⁴ They were reluctant to answer,[being
aware that they merited a reproof;] for they had been disputing, which
of them should have the highest post [under the anticipated "Reign
of the Divine Messiah]." *b* But their Master had noticed their selfish
altercation,¦ and as he pressed the inquiry, *a* they at length faltered
out a confession, that the subject of their debate was, "who among
them was destined to the chief eminence in his approaching empire?"¦
³⁵ To this question, Jesus, having taken a seat, and gathered them all
close about him [for special instruction], replied, "If any of you is ambitious of being foremost in rank, he will gain the truest eminence
among my followers, by taking the most lowly position, and seeking
to promote the interests of the rest." ³⁶ Then *c* inviting¦ a child, who
was near, to come to him, he placed him in the middle of the circle,
and throwing his arms complacently about him, he told them, *d* "I
solemnly assure you, that until you lay aside your present worldly sentiments, and adopt the unambitious simplicity that characterizes
children, you will none of you ever be admitted to the privileges of the
'Reign of the Divine Messiah.'¦ *e* Therefore it is he who is willing to
take a subordinate place like this child, that will become the most
honored under that 'Reign;'¦ *f* the one seemingly the most insignificant among you being really the chief [in commendable qualities].¦
³⁷ And [as connected with this duty of humility, I would remind you,
that] whoever treats with a kindly welcome a person of such a child-
like spirit, as being my follower, thereby in effect exhibits an equal
regard for me whom such a one represents; nor for me alone, but
also for Him whose Ambassador I am."

³⁸ [At this injunction of a catholic spirit,] John observed inquir-
ingly, [as if to gain his Master's approval for such an exception,]
"Teacher, we came across a man lately, who was attempting to exorcise demons by assuming the authority to pronounce your name as a
talisman; and we immediately forbade his doing so, because he did
not accompany us as your follower." ³⁹ But Jesus replied, "You ought
not to have prohibited him; for you may depend, there is no person,
capable of thus performing a miracle in my name, that can readily be
induced to join the general detraction against me. ⁴⁰ And indeed,
[you should have perceived, that] whoever does not side with the
party opposed to my cause, does in reality espouse it. ⁴² [You must be
careful, therefore, not to check the well-meant acts of such individuals, lest you endanger their incipient attachment to me; for I warn
you, that] if any one should be the means of wantonly discouraging or
diverting even the most insignificant of my followers, [whose faith in
me may be as little confirmed as the strength of this child,] a more
miserable doom hereafter awaits that instrument of apostasy, than
[he would here experience,] were he plunged into the *g* heart of the¦
sea, with a *g* huge¦ mill-stone [i.e such an upper mill-stone as is turned
by an ass] hung round his neck! *h* It is indeed inevitable that incen-
tives to defection from my cause should arise [through the pressure of
circumstances induced by human depravity]; but alas for that per-

<hr>

a Matt. xviii, 1.   *b* Luke ix, 47.   *e* Matt. xviii, 2.   *d* Matt. xviii, 3.
e Matt. xviii, 4.   *f* Luke ix, 48.   *g* Matt. xviii, 6.   *h* Matt. xviii, 7.

world because of offenses! for it must needs   MARK IX·
be that offenses come; but woe to that man by
whom the offense cometh! ^{49} For every one shall be
salted with fire, and every sacrifice shall be salted
with salt. ^{50} Salt is good; but if the salt have
lost his saltness,. wherewith will ye season it?
[MATT. V, 13] it is thenceforth [LUKE XIV, 35] neither fit for
the land, nor yet for the dunghill; but men cast it out
[MATT. V, 13] to be trodden under foot: ye are the salt of the
earth.   Have salt in yourselves, and
have peace one with another. ^{10} Take   **Matt. XVIII.**
heed that ye despise not one of these
little ones; for I say unto you, That in heaven their
angels do always behold the face of my Father which
is in heaven.

^{15} Moreover, [LUKE XVII, 3] take heed to yourselves: if thy
brother shall trespass against thee, go and tell him his
fault between thee and him alone; if he shall hear thee,
thou hast gained thy brother : [LUKE XVII, 3] and if he repent, forgive him. ^{16} But if he will not hear thee, then
take with thee one or two more, that in the mouth of
two or three witnesses* every word may be established : ^{17} and if he shall neglect to hear them, tell it
unto the church; but if he neglect to hear the church,
let him be unto thee as a heathen man and a publican :
^{18} verily I say unto you, Whatsoever ye shall bind on
earth, shall be bound in heaven; and whatsoever
ye shall loose on earth, shall be loosed in heaven.
^{19} Again I say unto you, That if two of you shall
agree on earth as touching anything that they shall
ask, it shall be done for them of my Father which is
in heaven; ^{20} for where *two or three* are gathered
together in my name, there am I in the midst of
them.

---

* See Deut. xix, 15.

son, none the less, in whose corrupt will originates the MARK IX.
provocation !! 49 [Yes, my followers must be subjected
to a severe ordeal:] for, as every sacrificial offering is required to be sprinkled with salt, [before it can be presented to God;]
so is each one of my disciples to be *seasoned*, as it were, by their fiery
trials [here for final acceptance in heaven. 50 Now, you know, the
proverb says,] ' Salt is an excellent thing for seasoning purposes; but
should the salt used in flavoring food become itself insipid, by what
seasoning could its saltness be restored?'—*a* it is evidently worthless
for any use, except that of being thrown out over the walk,| *b* for it is
not even fit for manuring the soil.| *a* Just so, *you* are to be the salt of
society,| [to imbue it with the principles of my religion, and thus not
merely render your own lives an acceptable oblation to God, but also
infuse a like sanctifying influence into others' minds. And to effect
this,] you must retain the salt of spirituality in your hearts, being especially careful to preserve harmony among yourselves, [which so emi-
nently promotes religious steadfastness. 10 To avoid Matt. XVIII.
all collisions therefore, which would lead any to abandon my cause,] beware of treating with disparagement any one of these
my followers, however inferior they may appear; for I assure you, that
in the celestial world the representative angels of even the least noted
among them, are ever high in the favor of my Heavenly Father.

15 "[A like spirit of *c*cautious| forbearance should be exercised even
toward offenders, lest a too great severity should precipitate their
fall.] Should it happen, therefore, that any one of your religious associates should [so far yield to frailty as to] commit a willful injury
against you, [the true measures of redress which you are to take, are
as follows :] First repair to him frankly, and calmly endeavor to con-
vince him of his misconduct *c*by a suitable admonition| in private ; in
case he heeds your remonstrance-*c* and penitently acknowledges his
fault, you are to forgive him sincerely,|—and by this course you will
have won him back to rectitude and fellowship. 16 Should he with-
stand your efforts, however, to correct him in this way, you must then
go to him again, taking with you one or two other members of your
fraternity, [whose counsels would be likely to be influential with him;]
so that 'by the testimony of two or three witnesses the whole evidence
may be confirmed' [respecting his duty and reparation]. 17 Should he
also prove contumacious under their reproof, you are next to lay the
matter before the congregation [of saints to which you belong, and
obtain their decision respecting it] ; and if he continues refractory
against their sentence likewise, you are [finally, but not till then, to
cease to treat him with fraternal association, and are] to regard him
as an irreligious man like a heathen or tax-gatherer. 18 [In such cases
of excision from your brotherhood,] I assure you [the subject of it in-
curs the fearful weight of the authority with which I lately declared
you invested in a corporate capacity], that ' whatever persons you
bolt out from the pale of my earthly Church, will also be excluded in
the counsels of heaven ;' and the same is true of admission. 19 And
furthermore I assure you that [so far from the whole religious assembly with which you are connected being invariably necessary to be
present, in such ecclesiastical determinations as are contemplated by
this grant of jurisdiction], in case only two of you [are able to meet
for the deliberation, and they] concur in any such measure concerning my Church here on earth, their decision and prayer for its accomplishment shall be effectual through my Heavenly Father's rati-
fying power; 20 for in fine, wherever even so small a number as two

---

a Matt. v, 13.   *b* Luke xiv, 35.   *c* Luke xvii, 3.

21 Then came Peter to him and said,   MATT. XVIII.
Lord, how oft shall my brother sin
against me, and I forgive him? till *seven* times?
22 Jesus saith unto him, I say not unto thee, Until
seven times [LUKE XVII, 4] in a day; but, Until *seventy
times seven.*   23 Therefore is the kingdom of heaven
likened unto a certain king which would take account
of his servants; 24 and when he had begun to reckon,
one was brought unto him which owed him ten thousand talents; 25 but forasmuch as he had not to pay,
his lord commanded him to be sold and his wife and
children and all that he had, and payment to be made:
26 the servant therefore fell down and worshiped him
saying, Lord, have patience with me, and I will pay
thee all; 27 then the lord of that servant was moved
with compassion, and loosed him and forgave him the
debt.   28 But the same servant went out and found
one of his *fellow-servants*, which owed him a hundred
pence; and he laid hands on him and took him by the
throat, saying, Pay me that thou owest; 29 and his
fellow-servant fell down at his feet, and besought him
saying, Have patience with me, and I will pay thee
all; 30 and he would not, but went and cast him into
prison, till he should pay the debt.   31 So when his
fellow-servants saw what was done, they were very
sorry, and came and told unto their lord all that was
done: 32 then his lord, after that he had called him,
said unto him, O thou wicked servant, I forgave thee
all that debt, because thou desiredst me; 33 shouldest
not thou also have had compassion on thy fellow-servant, even as I had pity on *thee?*   34 And his lord was
wroth and delivered him to the tormentors, till he
should pay all that was due unto him: 35 so likewise
shall my heavenly Father do also unto *you*, if ye from
your hearts forgive not every one his brother their
trespasses.

102

or three of my sincere followers may be con- MATT. XVIII.
vened to carry out the purposes of my religion, ———————
my divine presence is guarantied [to crown
their proceedings with success."
²¹ Wishing to know how far this lenity toward offenders was
to extend,] Peter, approaching more closely, asked, "Master,
how often may one of my brother disciples, who has inflicted
an injury upon me, be forgiven ᵃ on profession of penitence,|—
as many as seven times?" ²² Jesus replied, "I do not mean
merely to say that you must forgive him [with great patience,
even were it] seven times ᵃ in one day ;| but indefinitely oftener,
even seventy times seven, [if he afford you occasion.] ²³ In respect to this feature of clemency, the 'Reign of the Divine
Messiah' itself may be compared to some king, who might
wish to settle accounts with his fiscal officers. ²⁴ In execution
of this purpose, one of them is brought before him, who is deficient [it may be an enormous amount, as] ten thousand *talents*
[i. e. of silver, about $9,000,000]. ²⁵ As he has no means of
making up the arrearage, his sovereign orders him to be sold
into bondage, together with his wife and children, and all his
property likewise to be confiscated, and the proceeds to be applied toward liquidating the debt. ²⁶ At this rigid sentence,
the culprit officer prostrating himself humbly before his royal
master, begs him, 'Indulge me with time [to settle my af-
fairs], and I will try to pay you the full amount.' ²⁷ Pitying
his case, the king releases him from custody, and remits the
entire sum due. ²⁸ Now suppose this same officer goes out
from the scene of this discharge, and meeting one of his fellow
officers, who chances to owe him the trifling sum of one hundred
dena'rii [i. e. about $15], he seizes him by the throat, fiercely
bidding him, 'Pay me instantly what you owe me!' ²⁹ The
poor fellow falls before him, imploring him in like manner,
'Allow me a little time [to collect in what is owing me,] and
I will pay you the whole amount.' ³⁰ But the creditor refuses,
and in default of immediate payment goes and gets him thrown
into jail, to lie there till he shall pay the debt. ³¹ The associate officers, witnessing the transaction, are so shocked at the
creditor's inhumanity, that they indignantly report it to their
sovereign, who immediately summons him before him, and
thus addresses him, 'Vile menial, I compassionately canceled
my large claim against you, at your earnest entreaty : ³³ why
then, did you not treat your fellow officer with a like commiseration?' ³⁴ Then revoking the late discharge, his incensed
master commands him to be incarcerated till a payment of the
full amount shall be enforced.—³⁵ In a similar vindictive manner," concluded Jesus, will your Heavenly Father conduct himself toward *you* [as to your own crimes against Him], if you do
not each cordially forgive your fellow the misdemeanors committed against you, [but acknowledged with sorrow.]"

ᵃ Luke xvii, 4.

102*

§ 78.—*The Mission of the Seventy.*

([Capernaum?]; [early in *September ?*] A. D. 28.)

¹ After these things, the Lord appointed   **Luke X.**
other* seventy also, and sent them two and
two before his face into every city and place whither
he himself would come.   ² Therefore said he unto
them, ³ Go your ways ; behold, I send you forth as
lambs among wolves : [Matt. X, 16] be ye therefore
wise as serpents, and harmless as doves.   ⁶ Give   **Matt. VII.**
not that which is holy unto the dogs, neither
cast ye your pearls before swine, lest they trample
them under their feet, and turn again and
rend you.   ²³ But when they persecute you   **Matt. X.**
in this city, flee ye into another : for verily
I say unto you, Ye shall not have gone over the cities
of Israel, till the Son of man be come.   ²⁴ The disciple is not above his master, nor the servant above his
lord, [John XIII, 16] neither he that is sent greater than he that
sent him ; ²⁵ it is enough for the disciple [Luke VI, 40] that
is perfect, that he be *as* his master, and the servant as
his lord : if they have called the master of the house
Beelzebub, how much more shall they call them of his
household !   ²⁶ Fear them not therefore.

§ 79.—*Christ's Final Departure from Galilee for Je-rusalem, with the Incidents on the Journey.*

(Galilee and Samaria ; latter part of *September,* A. D. 28.)

² Now the Jews' feast of tabernacles was   **John VII.**
at hand : ³ his brethren therefore said unto
him, Depart hence and go into Judea, that thy disciples also may see the works that thou doest : ⁴ for
there is no man that doeth anything in secret, and he

---

* Compare §§ 44, 61.

§ 78.—*The Mission of the Seventy.*

([Capernaum!]; [early in *September?*] A. D. 28.)

[1] Some time after these occurrences, [being about to   **Luke X.** travel in a somewhat new district,] Jesus appointed seventy of his most reliable followers, exclusive of the previously nominated Apostles, and sent them in pairs by various routes in advance of him, [to prepare the inhabitants of each town and region for his intended visit.] [2] The charge that he delivered to them was of the following purport: [3] Go forth [to your assigned sphere of labor, remembering that] I am sending you like defenseless sheep among prowling wolves; *a* it behooves you therefore, to conduct yourselves with the circumspection of the serpent, coupled with the inoffensiveness of the dove.[1] [6] [Exercise the   **Matt. VII.** discretion of the proverb, in the reserved communication of the precious truths of your sacred message to men of unholy and groveling minds,] 'not to deal out the consecrated flesh of sacrifices to profane dogs; nor offer pearls to swine, who would only trample the jewels in the mire with their feet, and then turning round with disappointed voracity tear in pieces the luckless donors.' [23] Yet, [doubtless, despite your utmost care,   **Matt. X.** you will often be assailed with opposition; and] when the inhabitants of one town malignantly reject your message, then you must make your escape to the next town on your route;—I assure you, you will not have more than time enough to complete the circuit of the cities of Judea and Pere'a, before the consummation of the mission of the 'Son of Man.' [24] [But you must not be disheartened by persecution: you know,] 'no disciple is of greater importance than his teacher, nor the slave than his master, *b* nor an ambassador than the principal;'[1] [25] but the highest lot that a subordinate, *c* however faithful,[1] can expect, is to share the fortunes of his superior: since my adversaries have nicknamed *me*, the head of the family, *Baal'zebub*, how much more likely will they be to stigmatize *you*, the members of that family! [26] Do not lose your courage, therefore, [if you *should* be subjected to a like treatment with myself.]"

§ 79.—*Christ's Final Departure from Galilee for Jerusalem, with the Incidents on the Journey.*

(Galilee and Samaria; latter part of *September*, A. D. 28.)

[2] The Jewish Festival of "Tabernacles" was now approaching; accordingly [3] Jesus's younger [half-]brothers, [5] although not convinced [as yet] of his full character as the Messiah, still [hoping to derive much temporal advantage from his evident rank as a prophet,] [3] urged him, "The best course for you to take, is to quit this section of country, [where your popularity is waning], and visit Judea; so as to give your adherents there an opportunity of witnessing the miracles which you are engaged in effecting, [and thus increase their attachment as well as number:] [4] it is certainly bad policy for any one, who desires to gain personal celebrity, to perform his official acts in comparative obscurity; you should exhibit the signal miracles you are

a Matt. x, 16.   *b* John xiii, 16.   *c* Luke vi, 40.

himself seeketh to be known openly; if   JOHN VII.
thou do these things, show thyself to the
world : ⁵(for neither did his brethren believe in him.)
⁶ Then Jesus said unto them, *My* time is not yet come,
but *your* time is always ready ; ⁷ the world cannot hate
you, but *me* it hateth, because I testify of it that the
works thereof are evil : ⁸ go *ye* up unto this feast ; *I*
go not up yet unto this feast, for my time is not yet
full come. ⁹ When he had said these words unto
them, he abode still in Galilee : ¹⁰ but when his brethren were gone up, then went he also up unto the feast ;
not openly, but as it were in secret.

⁵¹ And it came to pass, when the time   **Luke IX.**
was come that he should be received up,
he steadfastly set his face to go to Jerusalem, ⁵² and
sent messengers before his face : and they went and
entered into a village of the Samaritans, to make ready
for him ; ⁵³ and they did not receive him, because his
face was as though he would go to Jerusalem. ⁵⁴ And
when his disciples James and John saw this, they said,
Lord, wilt thou that we command fire to come down
from heaven and consume them, even as Elias did ?*
⁵⁵ But he turned and rebuked them and said, Ye know
not what manner of spirit ye are of: ⁵⁶ for the Son of
man is not come to *destroy* men's lives, but to *save*
them. And they went to another village.

¹¹ And it came to pass, as he went to   **Luke XVII.**
Jerusalem, that he passed through the
midst of Samaria and Galilee. ¹² And as he entered
into a certain village, there met him ten men that
were lepers, which stood afar off : ¹³ and they lifted
up their voices and said, Jesus, Master, have mercy
on us. ¹⁴ And when he saw them, he said unto them,
Go show yourselves unto the priests.† And it came

---

* 2 Kings i, 10, 12.   † See Levit. xiii, 46 ; Num. v, 2, 3.

achieving, to the public at the metropolis." ⁶To   JOHN VII.
this misconceived advice, Jesus replied, "No fa-
vorable occasion for my visiting Judea has yet occurred this year, but *you* have always an opportunity of repairing thither without any apprehension; ⁷ for an irreligious
community like that, is not likely to molest you in your stay
among them, [since your sentiments and plans so well coin-
cide with their own,]—but for *me* they entertain an implaca-
ble hatred, because I am in the habit of reproving their wicked
practices. It is well enough for you to attend the coming Festival; but I shall not accompany you thus publicly, for the suitable period is not just yet arrived, [when I can judiciously go
thither.]" ⁹ With this vindication of his course, he continued
still for several days in Galilee; ¹⁰ but soon after his brothers
had left for the capital, he also [found himself so situated that
he] ventured to make the visit, by avoiding all publicity, and
traveling in as retired a manner as possible.

⁵¹ Accordingly, as the time for his predicted as-   Luke IX.
cension was now not far distant, Jesus finally *a* quit-
ted Galilee, | and resolutely turned his steps toward
Jerusalem. ⁵² On his journey, he adopted the plan of sending
some of his disciples in advance to the various villages of Samaria through which he was to pass, in order that they might
privately prepare accommodations for him. ⁵³ On one occasion, upon the application of his messengers at a certain village, the inhabitants refused to entertain him, because he was
directing his course toward Jerusalem, [a place of worship for
which they entertained the most rancorous jealousy.] ⁵⁴ At
this exhibition of inhospitable scorn, two of his disciples, the
brothers James and John, were so incensed, that they proposed, "Master, with your authorizing leave, we will bid the
lightning fall from heaven, and consume this village of heathen miscreants!—just as Elijah once did." ⁵⁵ But Jesus
turned to them with this rebuke, "Ah, you little think what
an unholy temper such resentment betrays!—⁵⁶ the 'Son of
Man' has not visited the earth for the purpose of destroying
human life, but to *rescue* man from endless death." He
therefore calmly proceeded with his disciples to the next
village.

¹¹ In continuing his journey toward Jerusa-   Luke XVII.
lem, while passing through the middle of Sa-
maria, after leaving Galilee, ¹² as he was entering a certain village, ten men afflicted with leprosy met him,
but keeping at the prescribed distance, [to prevent contami-
nation. ¹³ They immediately recognized him,] and cried out,
"O Master Jesus, in compassion cure us!" ¹⁴ On seeing from
whom the request came, Jesus bade them acquiescingly, "Go
and show yourselves to the priests [of your respective vil-
lages]." No sooner had they started to obey the direction,

a Matt. xix, 1.

to pass, that as they went, they were   LUKE XVII.
cleansed.   ¹⁵ And one of them, ¹⁶ (and he
was a *Samaritan*,) ¹⁵ when he saw that he was healed,
turned back, and with a loud voice glorified God,
¹⁶ and fell down on his face at his feet, giving him
thanks.   ¹⁷ And Jesus answering said, Were there not
ten cleansed? but where are the *nine*? ¹⁸ there are
not found, that returned to give glory to God, save
this stranger.   ¹⁹ And he said unto him, Arise, go thy
way; thy faith hath made thee whole.

CHAPTER VI.—PORTION II.

CHRIST'S SUBSEQUENT ITINERANCY THROUGH JUDEA AND PERE'A.

(Time, *six months less one week*.)

§ 80.—*Christ's Public Teaching at the Festival of Tabernacles, with the Connected Incidents.*

(Jerusalem, the Temple, [Court of the Women?]; *Wednesday, September 24, to Sunday, September 28, A. D. 28*.)

¹¹ Then the Jews sought him at the feast,   **John VII.**
and said, Where is he? ¹² And there was
much murmuring among the people concerning him:
for some said, He is a good man; others said, Nay,
but he deceiveth the people: ¹³ howbeit no man spake
openly of him, for fear of the Jews.

¹⁴ Now about the midst of the feast, Jesus went up
into the temple and taught: ¹⁵ and the Jews marveled
saying, How knoweth this man letters, having never
learned? ¹⁶ Jesus answered them and said, My doctrine is not *mine*, but his that sent me: ¹⁷ if any man
will do his will, he shall know of the doctrine, whether
it be of God or whether I speak of myself: ¹⁸ he that
speaketh of himself, seeketh his own glory; but he

than they were restored from their contagious malady. 15 One of their number,—16 who chanced moreover to be a Samaritan,—15 on finding himself recovered, hastened back to his benefactor, loudly praising God as he
went, 16 and falling prostrate at Jesus's feet, humbly poured out his
grateful acknowledgments for the merciful cure   17 Jesus rejoined
[in a tone of surprise to the bystanders], "Were there not *ten* of
them that were restored?—where, then, are the other nine? 18 Are
none of them to be found, that are disposed to return and give to
God the praise of their recovery, except this single foreigner?"
19 Then addressing the thankful patient, he said, "You may now
rise and return home; it is your confidence in me that has restored
you to health."

LUKE XVII.

CHAPTER VI.—PORTION II.

CHRIST'S SUBSEQUENT ITINERANCY THROUGH JUDEA AND PERE'A.

(Time, *six months less one week.*)

§ 80.—*Christ's Public Teaching at the Festival of Tabernacles,
with the Connected Incidents.*

(Jerusalem, the Temple, [Court of the Women?]; *Wednesday, September* 24, to
Sunday, September 28, A. D. 28.)

11 When the Festival began, the Jewish leaders instituted a search for Jesus, [with the design of executing
their plot against him, supposing he would be likely to
be present. As they went around through the crowd in this manner, inquiring, "Where is that pretender?"] 12 the populace began
to whisper among themselves concerning him; some remarking,
"I believe he is really a good man," while others as strenuously
objected, "Far from it; he is a popular impostor!" 13 None of his
partisans, however, dared profess their sentiments *publicly* in his
favor, being restrained by their fear of the Jewish hierarchy, [who
were evidently bent upon his destruction.]
14 Having waited till the Festival had half-way progressed, Jesus
now appeared at the capital, and immediately proceeding to the
[Women's] Court of the Temple, commenced instructing the people
assembled there. 15 [The depth of thought and information displayed in] his discourse, surprised the Jews of the higher class who
heard him, and suggested the inquiry, "How comes he to be so expert
in theological science, without having ever received a literary educa-
tion?" 16 To the disparaging tone of this remark, Jesus rejoined,
"The doctrines which I deliver, are not my own unsupported assertions, but are prescribed and corroborated by Him whose messenger
I am. 17 Let but a person comply with the will of God [as made
known by me,] and his experience will soon satisfy him whether my
instructions are of a divine origin, or the suggestions of my own
fancy. 18 Besides, every one whose teaching is thus merely self-
prompted, is observed to aim at enhancing his own fame; whereas
he who studies to promote the honor of Him whose legate he is,
cannot be other than a trust-worthy teacher, and entirely unaffected

John VII.

that seeketh his glory that sent him, the   JOHN VII.
same is true, and no unrighteousness is in
him.   ¹⁹ Did not Moses give you the law, and yet
none of you keepeth the law? why go ye about to
kill me? The people answered and said, Thou hast
a devil; who goeth about to kill thee? ²¹ Jesus
answered and said unto them, I have done one work,
and ye all marvel. ²² Moses therefore gave unto
you circumcision,* (not because it is of Moses, but of
the fathers;) † and ye on the sabbath-day circumcise
a man : ²³ if a man on the sabbath-day receive circumcision, that the law of Moses should not be
broken ; are ye angry at me, because I have made a
man every whit whole on the sabbath-day ? ²⁴ Judge
not according to the appearance, but judge righteous
judgment.

²⁵ Then said some of them of Jerusalem, Is not
this he whom they seek to kill? ²⁶ but lo, he speaketh
boldly, and they say nothing unto him. Do the rulers
know indeed that this is the very Christ? ²⁷ howbeit
we know this man whence he is; but when Christ
cometh no man knoweth whence he is. ²⁸ Then
cried Jesus in the temple, as he taught, saying, Ye
both know me and ye know whence I am : and I am
not come of myself, but he that sent me is true,
whom ye know not; ²⁹ but I know him, for I am
from him, and he hath sent me.

³⁰ Then they sought to take him; but no man laid
hands on him, because his hour was not yet come.
³¹ And many of the people believed on him and said,
When Christ cometh, will he do more miracles than
these which this man hath done ? ³² The Pharisees
heard that the people murmured such things concern-

---

* Levit. xii, 3.   † Gen. xvii, 10; xxi, 4.

by any sinister motive.—[19] [Your objections of im-   JOHN VII.
morality against me," continued Jesus, "are utterly
inconsistent with your own conduct.] Was it not Moses,
[—whose injunctions I am constantly upholding,—] that delivered to
your forefathers the Law? and yet [with all your loud professions of regard for his precepts,] every one of your hierarchal party is in the habit
of grossly violating those divine statutes. [If you entertain such a
reverence for that sacred canon, let me ask you one question,] Why
are you all the time trying to *murder me*, in defiance of it?" [20] "You
must be out of your senses," scornfully replied the [disaffected part of
the] crowd; "who is 'trying to murder you?'" [21] Jesus proceeded,
[overlooking the people's misapplication of his charge to themselves
instead of their leaders: "Just look at the frivolous nature of your
cavils; for instance,] the signal cure that I effected some time since in
this city, only gave your Council an occasion of indignant surprise,
[because it was performed on the sabbath.] [22] But Moses himself (or
rather, in conformity with the patriarchal institution that was of established authority long prior to his legislation) enjoined the rite of
circumcision upon your nation, in so obligatory a manner that you
never wave the ceremony [though the prescribed day for its observance should fall] on the sabbath. [23] If, then, you scrupulously attend
to this custom even on the sabbath, lest the Mosaic law should be in-
fringed, [by the neglect of so slight a sanatory regulation in its appointed season; why should you thus bitterly inveigh against me for
restoring a man's *entire* physical system to health on that day? [24] You
should not decide so rashly upon a superficial view of one's conduct,
but according to an impartial consideration [of the facts and bear-
ings in the case.]"

[25] A cluster of citizens of Jerusalem, [who stood by and noticed
this fearless exhibition of himself on the part of Jesus,] observed
aloud to one another, "Is not this the person whom our chief men
are anxious to seize and put to death? [26] Look, there he is, publicly discoursing, without one of them so much as interfering by a
word of reply! I wonder if the San'hedrim have actually come to
the conclusion that he is the Messiah, [that they let him thus alone!
[27] They are very much deluded, if they think so; for] we all know too
well the particulars of this pretender's parentage and residence for
that;—whereas when the Messiah appears, his origin will not be so
vulgarly known." [28] Knowing the cavils which these persons were
making, Jesus, in the midst of his instructions in the Temple, exclaimed with a loud voice, that they might hear, "Yes indeed, you are
acquainted with me and know my extraction, [in a human relation;]
yet have I not appeared at my own bidding, for there is a veracious Being who has given me my [like truthful] commission;—He it is whom
you do *not* know [by an appreciation of His purposes and claims, and
therefore you fail to recognize my higher relation to Him]. [29] *I* know
Him perfectly, for it is from [the co-equality of] His own society that
I am now arrived as His commissioner on earth!"

[30] [Learning that Jesus was in the city,] his adversaries endeavored
to discover some pretext for apprehending him, but did not as yet succeed in arresting him, [being providentially hindered] until the destined time for the consummation of his [expiatory] office should arrive. [31] Numbers of the populace, however, entertained great confidence in him, which they expressed in such private remarks as these,
"Could we expect the Messiah, on his appearance, to perform a greater
number of signal miracles than those which he has effected?" [32] Gaining information [through its members of the more inimical Pharisai-

ing him ; and the Pharisees and the chief- JOHN VII.
priests sent officers to take him.

³³ Then said Jesus unto them, Yet a little while am
I with you, and then I go unto him that sent me:
³⁴ ye shall seek me, and shall not find me ; and where
I am, thither ye cannot come. ³⁵ Then said the
Jews among themselves, Whither will he go, that
we shall not find him? will he go unto the dispersed
among the Gentiles, and teach the *Gentiles?* ³⁶ what
manner of saying is this that he said, Ye shall seek
me, and shall not find me ; and where I am, thither
ye cannot come?

³⁷ In the last day, that great day of the feast, Jesus
stood and cried saying, ²⁸ Come unto me, Matt. XI.
all ye that labor, and are heavy laden, and
I will give you rest: ²⁹ take my yoke upon you and
learn of me, for I am meek and lowly in heart ; and
ye shall find rest unto your souls: ³⁰ for my yoke is
easy, and my burden is light. ³⁷ If any John VII.
man thirst, let him come unto me and
drink: ³⁸ he that believeth on me, as the Scripture
hath said,* out of his heart shall flow rivers of living
water: ³⁹ (but this spake he of the Spirit, which they
that believe on him should receive ; for the Holy
Ghost was not yet given, because that Jesus was not
yet glorified.)

⁴⁰ Many of the people therefore, when they heard
this saying, said, Of a truth this is the Prophet:†
⁴¹ others said, This is the Christ: but some said,
Shall Christ come out of *Galilee?* ⁴² hath not the
Scripture said,‡ that Christ cometh of the seed of
David, and out of the town of Bethlehem, where
David was? ⁴³ So there was a division among the

---

* Isa. lv, 1; lviii, 11; compare xliv, 3.   † Deut. xviii, 18.
‡ Isa. xi, 1; Jer. xxiii, 5; Micah v, 2; see 1 Sam. xvi, 1.

cal party,] that such sentiments concerning Jesus were **JOHN VII.** currently whispered among the people, the San'hedrim dispatched officers with orders to arrest him.

³³ [A day or two afterward, being apprised of the hostile movements of the hierarchy with reference to him,] Jesus addressed to them this public warning, [in the temple,] "It is but a little while longer that I am to remain among you, before I return to Him who has sent me on my mission. [You need not therefore take such pains to hasten me out of the way. ³⁴ When I am gone from earth,] long and anxiously will you look for me [in the character of a Messiah to arise and deliver you from the calamities with which your nation will be visited]; but your search [for such an appearance] will be in vain! for to that [celestial] abode whither I am about to retire, *you* [in your present ungodly state of mind] can never gain access to find me." ³⁵ The puzzled leaders turned to each other with the sneering question, "Where is he going, that 'we shall not be able to find him?' Does he intend to repair to the expatriated Jews that live scattered among the Gentiles, and to instruct the heathen too! ³⁶ And then, what does he mean by saying, 'You will look for me, but search in vain; to that region whither I am about to withdraw, you can never gain access?'"

³⁷ On the eighth day of the Festival, the last and most pompously celebrated of all, Jesus [took a conspicuous station in the Temple court, and there] proclaimed aloud this inviting appeal, ²⁸ "Yield yourselves to my instruction, O all ye poor **Matt. XI.** souls, who are so wearily toiling under your grievous burden [of legal ceremonies, rendered still more oppressive by traditional observances superimposed]; and I will point out to you a far more easy mode of relief [from the sins for which you thus seek to atone]. ²⁹ Yes, assume the yoke of my doctrines, and become *my* disciples—a teacher of a mild and condescending spirit, [the very opposite of your rigid haughty scribes,]—and then will you gain repose for your sin-worn souls; ³⁰ for the yoke of my precepts is one well adapted to your strength and circumstances, and the burden of the duties I enjoin, is light to be borne."

³⁷ [Then adverting to the festive ceremony of bringing **John VII.** the water from the Fountain of Shilo'ah into the temple, which was being performed at the time, Jesus with a loud voice continued his exhortation,] "Whoever is thirsty [for more heavenly draughts than these,] I bid apply to me, and he may then drink all he desires. ³⁸ If a person will but confide in my claims, in him will be realized the promises of Scripture; for in his heart [will thereupon be opened a spring of celestial influences, from which] shall gush forth the perennial streams of sacred bliss!" ³⁹ By this intimation, Jesus specially referred to the unprecedented effusion of the Holy Spirit which believers in him were soon to experience,—a manifestation of divine influence that was reserved until after his own ascension.

⁴⁰ Impressed by these appeals, numbers of the populace were led to remark, "This teacher must certainly be the 'Prophet' [foretold by Moses]." ⁴¹ Others declared, "He is the Messiah himself!" but this view was combatted by a third class, who urged, "What! is the Messiah to arise out of Galilee? ⁴² Do not the Scriptures declare that he is to be a descendant of King David, and a native of Bethlehem, David's paternal village?" ⁴³ Thus there was a conflict

people because of him :   ⁴⁴ and some of   JOHN VII.
them would have taken him ; but no man
laid hands on him.

⁴⁵ Then came the officers to the chief-priests and
Pharisees; and they said unto them, Why have ye
not brought him ?   ⁴⁶ The officers answered, Never
man spake like this man.   ⁴⁷ Then answered them
the Pharisees, Are *ye* also deceived ?   ⁴⁸ have any of
the rulers or of the Pharisees believed on him ?
⁴⁹ but this people who knoweth not the law, are
cursed.   ⁵⁰ Nicodemus saith unto them, (he that
came to Jesus by night,* being one of them,)   ⁵¹ Doth
our law † judge any man, before it hear him and know
what he doeth ?   ⁵² They answered and said unto
him, Art thou also of Galilee ? search and look ; for
out of Galilee ariseth no prophet.

⁵³ And every man went unto his own house.—
¹ Jesus went unto the Mount of Olives.   **John VIII.**

§ 81.—*The Adulteress Pardoned.*

(Jerusalem, the Temple, [Court of the Women ?]; *Monday, Sept. 29,*
A. D. 28.)

² And early in the morning he came again into the
temple: and all the people came unto him; and he
sat down and taught them.   ³ And the scribes and
Pharisees brought unto him a woman taken in adultery; and when they had set her in the midst, ⁴ they
say unto him, Master, this woman was taken in adultery : ⁵ now Moses in the law ‡ commanded us that
such should be stoned ; but what sayest *thou?*   ⁶(This
they said tempting him, that they might have to accuse
him.)   But Jesus stooped down and with his finger
wrote on the ground, as though he heard them not.

---

* See § 26.   † Compare Deut. i, 16, 17; xvii, 4; xix, 15, 18.
‡ Deut. xxii, 21-24; Levit. xx, 10.

of opinion among them on the subject. ⁴⁴ Some [of JOHN VII. the more violent of them, being partisans of the Pharisaical leaders,] were for arresting Jesus, but none of them found a favorable opportunity for effecting their design.

⁴⁵ Indeed the very officers sent out for this express purpose, now returned unsuccessful to the assembled San'hedrim, and on being demanded, "Why have you not seized and brought him hither?" ⁴⁶ they could only reply, "We [had not the hardihood to do it; for we must confess, we] never heard a man discourse so eloquently and forcibly as he, in all our lives!" ⁴⁷ "What," returned the Pharisees with indignant scorn, "are *you* too seduced by him? ⁴⁸ Show us a single [well-informed person, as a member of the San'hedrim, or any] one of the Pharisees, that has any faith in his pretensions! ⁴⁹ As for this stupid rabble, [who alone believe him,] they are an execrable set, that know nothing about the requirements or prophecies of Scripture!" ⁵⁰ [Disgusted with this profane outrage upon just procedure,] Nicodemus, one of the members, (the same person who once visited Jesus by night,) mildly demurred, ⁵¹ "But then, is it in accordance with our Law, to condemn the accused person, without having first given him an opportunity to be heard in self-defense, or having even distinctly ascertained his crime?" ⁵² To this, the Pharisees, [still more exasperated at meeting with opposition from one of their own council,] retorted with a sneer, "Are *you* too one of this pretender's Galilean admirers? Search the Scriptures a little more carefully, and you will see that no prophet can have arisen out of Galilee, [according to any of their predictions."

⁵³ As the deliberations of the San'hedrim were now without an object, through the failure of the officers, their meeting broke up,] and the members repaired to their respective places of abode.—¹ [The last day of the Festival being thus John VIII. closed,] Jesus also retired [to his usual lodgings at Bethany, just] across the Mount of Olives.

§ 81.—*The Adultress Pardoned.*

(Jerusalem, the Temple, [Court of the Women?] ; *Monday, Sept.* 29, A. D. 28.)

² On the following morning, Jesus repaired to the Temple again by early light, whither the mass of the populace soon assembled, to listen to the instructions which, taking his seat, he communicated to them. ³ While thus occupied, a party of Scribes and other Pharisees approached him, bringing in their custody a woman who had just been apprehended for the crime of conjugal infidelity; and placing her in the middle of the circle as they stood around him, ⁴ they thus artfully addressed him, "Teacher, this female was detected this morning under such circumstances as to demonstrate that she had just been guilty of adultery. ⁵ Now the Mosaic statutes enjoin upon us, to cause such criminals to be stoned to death. What is your decision in the case?" ⁶ Their object in this inquiry was, [to make a handle out of the sentence which they supposed he could not fail to give, in order] to embroil him with the civil authorities; or [in the failure of such a verdict, to implicate him] before the San'hedrim [for heresy against the Law]. Jesus, however, [without returning any direct answer,] merely bent over as he sat, and drew marks with his finger on the sand.

⁷ So when they continued asking him, he ⎯ JOHN VIII.
lifted up himself and said unto them, He
that is *without sin* among you, let him first cast a stone
at her. ⁸ And again he stooped down and wrote on
the ground. ⁹ And they which heard it, being convicted by their own conscience, went out one by one,
beginning at the eldest even unto the last; and Jesus
was left alone, and the woman standing in the midst.
¹⁰ When Jesus had lifted up himself, and saw none
but the woman, he said unto her, Woman, where are
those thine accusers? hath no man condemned thee?
¹¹ She said, No man, Lord.   And Jesus said unto her,
Neither do *I* condemn thee; go,—and sin no more.

§ 82.—*Further Public Teaching of Christ, with the
Violent Issue of the ensuing Discussion.*

(Jerusalem, the Temple, Court of the Women; *Tuesday* and *Wednesday, September* 30 and *October* 1, A. D. 28.)

¹² Then spake Jesus again unto them, ²⁰ in the
treasury, as he taught in the temple, ¹² saying, I am
the light of the world; he that followeth me, shall not
walk in darkness, but shall have the light of life.
¹³ The Pharisees therefore said unto him, Thou hearest
record of *thyself;* thy record is not true. ¹⁴ Jesus
answered and said unto them, Though I bear record
of myself, yet my record is true : for I know whence
I came and whither I go; but *ye* cannot tell whence I
come and whither I go. ¹⁵ *Ye* judge after the flesh, *I*
judge no man; ¹⁶ and yet if I judge, my judgment is
true; for I am not alone, but I and the Father that
sent me.   ¹⁷ It is also written in your law,* that the
testimony of two men is true : ¹⁸ I am one that bear
witness of myself; and the Father that sent me,
beareth witness of me. ¹⁹ Then said they unto him,

---

* Deut. xvii, 6; xix, 15.

7 But as they persisted in their question, he at length   JOHN VIII.
raised himself up, and with pointed emphasis thus
replied to them, "If there is one among you, who has
never been guilty of a similar offense, let him hurl the *first* stone
upon the culprit!" 8 Then bending over again, he continued to
trace marks on the sand. 9 At this significant retort, the prosecuting
hearers, convicted by the very consciousness of their own shameful
lasciviousness, slunk away one by one, the more distinguished no
less than those of the lowest class; so that presently Jesus was left
alone with the woman standing in the middle of the open space
[formed by the bystanding crowd]. 10 On rising upright, Jesus, seeing no one near him except the woman, asked her, "Woman, where
are those accusers of yours? Has no one of them demanded that you
be stoned to death?" 11 "No one, sir," replied she. "Then," returned
Jesus, "neither will I. Retire; but never hereafter repeat your
crime!"

§ 82.—*Further Public Teaching of Christ, with the Violent Issue of the ensuing Discussion.*

(Jerusalem, the Temple, Court of the Women; *Tuesday* and *Wednesday, September*
30 and *October* 1, A. D. 28.)

12 On the next day Jesus repaired in like manner to the Temple, for
the purpose of instructing the people; 20 taking his seat in that part
[the "Women's Court"] which contained the sacred treasure-chests,
he thus addressed the crowd that gathered about him, 12 "I am the
moral Light of mankind, having appeared in order that every one
who becomes my disciple, may grope no longer in the fatal darkness
of sinful error, but [guiding his footsteps by the radiance of my doc-
trines] may ever enjoy the life-giving beams of heavenly truth!"
13 To this, the Pharisees standing near scoffingly replied, "But you
are bearing testimony in *your own* commendation; such evidence is
never admitted as valid." 14 "Yes," returned Jesus, "I do indeed
testify in my own behalf, but nevertheless my testimony is valid, inasmuch as [the peculiar necessity of the case renders it an exception
to ordinary rules; for] I alone know [of myself] my origin and mission, and [am therefore the proper person to] reveal these facts to
you, who cannot otherwise become fully aware of them. 15 [Besides,
as this objection of yours shows,] you have a faulty habit of arguing
according to one's mere external appearance, with judgments warped
by passion and prejudice; whereas I charitably refrain from passing
sentence upon any one as yet. 16 Yet were I to exercise this my prerogative of pronouncing upon human characters, my decisions would
be correct and warrantable, being [based upon very different principles from yours; for (which proves the unsoundness of your objection, in the second place,) I am] not alone in anything that I do, but
my Father who has given me my commission, is identified with me in
all its execution. 17 Now it is a principle of your own Law, that the
concurrent testimony of two persons in any matter shall be valid;
18 so in this case, I give in my evidence concerning the character of
my mission, and my Father, who sent me to perform it, Himself
corroborates my statements [by the miracles which His power enables me to effect]." 19 "Where is this father of yours, [that we
may procure his testimony?]" insultingly asked his opponents.
"Ah!" replied Jesus, "it is indeed evident that you are neither
willing to appreciate me, nor have any heartfelt acquaintance with
my Father; for did you acknowledge my claims, you would then

Where is thy Father ?   Jesus answered,   JOHN VIII.
Ye neither know me nor my Father ; if
ye had known me, ye should have known my
Father also. ²⁰ These words spake Jesus : and no
man laid hands on him, for his hour was not yet
come.

²¹ Then said Jesus again unto them, I go my way,
and ye shall seek me, and shall die in your sins ;
whither I go, ye cannot come.   ²² Then said the
Jews, Will he kill himself? because he saith, Whither
I go, ye cannot come.   ²³ And he said unto them, *Ye*
are from beneath, *I* am from above ; *ye* are of this
world, *I* am not of this world :   ²⁴ I said therefore
unto you, that ye shall die in your sins ; for if ye believe not that I am he, ye shall die in your sins.
²⁵ Then said they unto him, Who art thou ?   And
Jesus saith unto them, Even the same that I said
unto you from the beginning.   ²⁶ I have many things
to say and to judge of you : but he that sent me, is
true ; and I speak to the world those things which I
have heard of him.   ²⁷ (They understood not that he
spake to them of the Father.)   ²⁸ Then said Jesus
unto them, When ye have lifted up the Son of man,
then shall ye know that I am he, and that I do
nothing of myself ; but as my Father hath taught me,
I spea these things.   ²⁹ And he that sent me is with
me ; the Father hath not left me alone : for I do
always those things that please him.

³⁰ As he spake these words, many believed on him.
³¹ Then said Jesus to those Jews which believed on
him, If ye continue in my word, then are ye my
disciples indeed ;   ³² and ye shall know the truth,
and the truth shall make you free.   ³³ They answered
him, We be Abraham's seed, and were never in
bondage to any man ; how sayest thou, Ye shall be
110

alone recognize my Father whom I represent." 20 Al- **JOHN VIII.**
though these remarks of Jesus were so plainly uttered
in a public place, no person as yet laid violent hands
on him, [an overruling Providence guarding him,] until the destined
hour of the last tragic scene should arrive.

21 Accordingly, [not meeting with serious molestation,] Jesus continued his public instructions [on the next day also, and in the course
of them remarked to some of his opponents who stood listening with
wily malignity], "Full soon, I again warn you, will I depart from your
midst, and then will you long for my appearance : but [as you have rejected my relief,] you will perish under the full penalty of your guilt.
Then to those abodes whither I am about to return, you can never
gain admittance!" 22 This solemn reproof, the Jewish hierarchy [to
whom it was addressed] endeavored to turn into ridicule [by the
coarse witticism], "Perhaps he intends to commit suicide? he says,
'That region whither I am about to go, you will not enter.' [If he
hurries himself out of the world, doubtless we shall not follow him!"
23 Without noticing this malicious jeer,] Jesus proceeded, "[Alas for
you! the variance of your dispositions coincides but too well with that
of your origin from mine, in causing an irreparable divergence in our
destiny ; for] you are of mere earthly extraction and kindred carnal
passions, while I am of heavenly origin and incorrupt affinities. 24 On
this account it was that I told you, 'You will perish under the full
penalty of your guilt ;' for unless you do yield yourselves to a reliance upon my claims, you will perish most miserably with the
weight of all your sins upon you!" 25 His opponents hereupon asked,
[rather in contempt than for information,] "Pray, who are you,
[that you threaten thus to destroy us?" To this question,] Jesus
emphatically replied, "I am just what I keep telling you I am [the
Son of God.—26 But it is vain for me to meet your frivolous quibbles
any further]. There are indeed numerous topics of information
and reproof with reference to yourselves, which I might discuss before you ; but [in your present perverse state of mind, I shall content myself with this single refutation of your cavils, that] as He
who has sent me on my mission is beyond all suspicion veracious,
so [my message is also true, since] I simply communicate to men
that intelligence, [learned by intimacy with him,] which he has
commissioned me to declare." 27 The manner in which his hearers
received this announcement, showed that they were unwilling to
understand him as speaking of his Heavenly Father. 28 To this incredulity, Jesus replied, "[Contemned as I am now, yet] when you
shall have elevated the 'Son of Man' [not to the royal dignity which
you demand in the Messiah, but on the cross], then you will be convinced that I am what I profess to be, not a self-instigated actor, but
making my denunciations in pursuance of the instructions of my
Father ; 29 who having sent me on my mission, does not leave me
single-handed in its accomplishment, [but constantly accompanies
me with his corroborating power,]—thus evincing His complacency
in my acts."

30 While Jesus was uttering these last remarks, numbers of the crowd
were impelled [by the force of the argument contained in them,] to
avow their credence of his claims and character. 31 To these believers
in him, he observed, "If you continue faithful to your confidence in
my declarations, you will ripen into genuine disciples, 32 and acquire
such an experimental knowledge of sacred truth as taught by me, that
it will free you from the trammels of superstition and sin." 33 [The unbelieving Pharisees, however, anxious to undermine this frank ex-

made free? [34] Jesus answered them, JOHN VIII.
Verily, verily I say unto you, Whoso-
ever committeth sin, is the servant of sin. [35] And
the servant abideth not in the house forever, but
the Son abideth ever; [36] if the Son therefore shall
make you free, ye shall be free indeed. [37] I know
that ye are Abraham's seed ; but ye seek to kill me,
because my word hath no place in you: [38] I speak
that which I have seen with my Father; and ye
do that which ye have seen with *your* father.
[39] They answered and said unto him, Abraham is
our father. Jesus saith unto them, If ye *were* Abraham's children, ye would do the works of Abraham :
[40] but now ye seek to kill me, a man that hath told you
the truth, which I have heard of God; this did
not Abraham : [41] ye do the deeds of your father.
Then said they to him, We be not born of licentiousness ; we have one Father, even God. [42] Jesus
said unto them, If God were your Father, ye would
love me : for I proceeded forth and came from God ;
neither came I of myself, but he sent me. [43] Why
do ye not understand my speech ? even because ye
cannot hear my word. [44] Ye are of your father
the devil, and the lusts of your father ye will do :
he was a murderer from the beginning, and abode
not in the truth, because there is no truth in him ;
when he speaketh a lie, he speaketh of his own,
for he is a liar and the father of it : [45] and because
I tell you the truth, ye believe me not. [46] Which
of you convinceth me of sin ? and if I say the truth,
why do ye not believe me ? [47] He that is of God,
heareth God's words; ye therefore hear them not,
because ye are not of God. [48] Then answered the
Jews and said unto him, Say we not well, that
thou art a Samaritan and hast a devil ? [49] Jesus
answered, I have not a devil : but I honor my Father;
111

pression of faith on the part of the people, began to   JOHN VIII.
carp at his phraseology, by torturing it into an invidious national reflection:] "We are the free-born
descendants of Abraham," said they, "and have never in all our
lives been in bondage to any master; why then do you talk of 'lib-
erating' us?" ·³⁴ "But nevertheless," returned Jesus, "I solemnly
assure you, that whoever practices sin, becomes its *slave;* [and this
is a far more debasing tyranny than any political subjugation.]
³⁵ Now a slave has not the privilege of remaining perpetually in the
house of his master, [being liable to be sold away at any time;] but
a son is entitled to permanent membership in the family: ³⁶ so that
if I, the Son [and Heir of my Heavenly Father's property], grant
you manumission from the service of sin, [and consequent adoption
into the divine family,] then you will become spiritually free in a
truer sense [than if rescued from physical thraldom]. ³⁷ I grant
that you are the literal posterity of Abraham, but [alas, what de-
generate sons!] you are even plotting my death [incited by the vile
passions] in your hearts, which refuse to admit my benignant doctrines. ³⁸ Thus while I am declaring the message imbibed in my
Father's society, you are but executing the lessons instilled by *your*
[Satanic] father." ³⁹ [Not knowing exactly how to take this imputation,] they answered, "We acknowledge no other progenitor than
Abraham." "Were you indeed the true-hearted posterity of Abraham," returned Jesus, "you would imitate his conduct. ⁴⁰ But instead of that, you are at this very moment meditating my murder,
whose only offense is that I am delivering to you those lessons of
truth with which I have been intrusted from the intimacy of God;
Abraham was very far from acting thus. ⁴¹ You are therefore evidently carrying out the conduct of your [Satanic] father." [Still un-
decided as to his allusion respecting their parentage,] they now responded, "[If you do not refer to our natural lineage, we would yet
have you know,] we are no spurious offspring of idolatrous worship;
we acknowledge but one spiritual Father, God Himself." ⁴² "Ah!"
rejoined Jesus, "if God were indeed your properly recognized Father,
you would not fail to love *me* also, who am come to you commissioned from His presence,—and not in my own authority, unsanctioned by Him, [as you represent.] ⁴³ Why is it, that you are so
dull in apprehending my language respecting your parentage?—it
is only because you do not pay sufficient attention to my statements
in general, to understand them. ⁴⁴ [In plain words then,] you are
the moral progeny of Satan, and are therefore ready to carry out
his purposes; for Satan was a *murderer* at the very outset of human
history, and moreover he so continually swerves from truth, that
he is *falsehood* itself. When therefore *he* speaks a lie, he utters but
the spontaneous product of his own thoughts, for he not only uses
mendacity, but is its very originator; ⁴⁵ and [it is by reason of this
his paternity of falsehood in your congenial minds, that] when *I* announce to you what is *true*, you refuse to credit me. ⁴⁶ Yet who among
you can convict me of a deviation from truth?—if then I tell you truth,
why should you not believe me? ⁴⁷ [Why, do I say?—it is because] the
true child of God [as I, in my earthly mission,] listens to the divine instructions, and you, not being His children, heed them not [as delivered by me]." ⁴⁸ Here the Jewish leaders, [losing their temper,] could
only turn the force of his refutation by the taunt, "Ha! we are about
right, in calling you a Samaritan heretic, a mad-cap instigated by a
demon!" ⁴⁹ [To this burst of scurrility,] Jesus mildly replied, "I am
no demoniac, but evince my sanity by aiming to promote my Father's

and ye do dishonor me : [50] and I seek not   JOHN VIII.
mine own glory; there is one that seek-
eth and judgeth. [51] Verily, verily I say unto you,
If a man keep my saying, he shall never see death.
[52] Then said the Jews unto him, Now we know that
thou hast a devil.   Abraham is dead, and the prophets ; and thou sayest, If a man keep my saying, he
shall never taste of death : [53] art thou greater than
our father Abraham, which is dead? and the prophets
are dead ; whom makest thou thyself? [54] Jesus
answered, If I honor myself, my honor is nothing ;
it is my Father that honoreth me, of whom ye say,
that he is your God : [55] yet ye have not known him ;
but *I* know him, and if I should say, I know him not,
I shall be a liar like unto you ; but I know him, and
keep his saying. [56] Your father Abraham rejoiced
to see my day ; and he saw it, and was glad. [57] Then
said the Jews unto him, Thou art not yet fifty years
old, and hast thou seen Abraham? [58] Jesus said
unto them, Verily, verily I say unto you, Before
Abraham was, I am. [59] Then took they up stones
to cast at him : but Jesus hid himself, and went
out of the temple, going through the midst of them,
and so passed by.

§ 83.—*The Seventy Return with a Report of Success,*
which Inspires their Master with Joy.

([Mount of Olives?] ; [early in] *October*, A. D. 28.)

[17] And the seventy returned again with **Luke X.**
joy saying, Lord, even the devils are subject unto us through thy name. [18] And he said unto
them, I beheld Satan as lightning fall from heaven.
[20] Notwithstanding in this rejoice not, that the spirits
are subject unto you ; but rather rejoice because your
names are written in heaven.

112·

glory; yet in spite of this, you on the other hand are
slandering me with invectives. ⁵⁰ Well, [vent your
abusive epithets, if you will!] I am not now concerned
to vindicate my own honor; there is One who takes care of this, and
will deal out due retribution [for indignities offered to me! ⁵¹ Yes, and
neither will respect shown to me lose its appropriate reward; for] I
solemnly assure you, that whoever practically adheres to my instructions, will never more experience [spiritual and (its resulting) eter-
nal] death." ⁵² [Determined to neutralize the influence of his inviting
announcements,] his Jewish foes here again interrupted him with the
rude exclamation, "Now at any rate, it is evident that you are a crazy
demoniac! for Abraham has been dead for centuries, and not one of
the prophets has escaped the same fatality; and yet you have the
hardihood to assert, 'Whoever observes my instructions, will never
die at all!' ⁵³ Are *you* a greater personage than our ancestor Abraham,
who himself yielded to the common lot of mortals? or are you en-
dowed with superior power to that of the ancient prophets, who were
alike unable to ward off the doom of dissolution? Pray, whom do you
make yourself out to be?" ⁵⁴ [To this distortion of his remarks,] Jesus
returned, "[I will wave the question of comparative superiority for
the present:] were the honor of my legation a matter that I arrogate
to myself, it would be worthless; but [as I have intimated to you,] it is
freely bestowed upon me by my Father, ⁵⁵ a Being of whom, despite
your professions that He is the object of your filial worship, you betray
a woful ignorance. I however am intimate in all His plans and feelings, and were I to shrink from avowing my acquaintance with Him,
I would be as false-hearted as yourselves; yes, I know him perfectly,
and [the very reverse of you] I am even now observing His injunc-•
tions in my message to you.—⁵⁶ [Do you ask, what is my rank? Let
me tell you to your shame,] your progenitor Abraham himself exulted
with longing hope as he looked forward to the period of my advent;
yes, he actually beheld it [in the anticipative visions of faith], and
his bosom glowed with sacred rapture at the [prospective] scene!"
⁵⁷ "Why," said the Jewish leaders, [pretending to understand him as
referring to a cotemporaneous witnessing of his own person,] "you
are not yet fifty years of age, at the utmost; and do you pretend to
have personally seen Abraham?" ⁵⁸ "I solemnly assure you," returned Jesus, "that indefinitely before Abraham was born, my existence extends!" ⁵⁹ At this [declaration of his divine preëxistence,] his
opponents, [pretending to deem him guilty of blasphemy,] furiously
caught up some stones that chanced to be lying near, for the purpose
of hurling them at him; but Jesus escaped their missiles, by burying
himself in the very midst of the crowd, and thus quitting the Temple.

JOHN VIII.

§ 83.—*The Seventy Return with a Report of Success, which In-spires their Master with Joy.*

([Mount of Olives?]; [early in] *October*, A. D. 28.)

¹⁷ Soon after these events, the seventy messengers, having accomplished their tour, returned to their Master, and
reported their success in such joyful terms as these, "Master, the very demons were submissive to our exorcising use of your
authoritative name!" ¹⁸ "Yes," returned Jesus, "when I sent you
forth, I foresaw that [in the issue of the spiritual contest which you
were entering,] Satan's dominion would be as speedily and irretrievably broken, as if he had been precipitated from his realms of the sky
by a flash of lightning down to his native hell! ²⁰ Still, you should not
so much rejoice on this account, that demons yield to your invested

Luke X.

²¹ In that hour Jesus rejoiced in spirit   LUKE X.
and said, I thank thee, O Father, Lord of
heaven and earth, that thou hast hid these things
from the wise and prudent, and hast revealed them
unto babes: even so, Father; for so it seemed good
in thy sight.—²² All things are delivered to me of my
Father: and no man knoweth who the Son is, but
the Father; and who the Father is, but the Son and
he to whom the Son will reveal him.

§ 84.—*Christ Answers a Lawyer by Defining the Duty of Love to One's Neighbor.*

(Environs of Jerusalem; [middle of *October?*] A. D. 28.)

²⁵ And behold, a certain lawyer stood up, and
tempted him saying, Master, what shall I do to
inherit eternal life? ²⁶ He said unto him, What is
written in the law? how readest thou? ²⁷ And he
answering said,* Thou shalt love the Lord thy God
with all thy heart and with all thy soul and with all
thy strength and with all thy mind, and thy neighbor
as thyself. ²⁸ And he said unto him, Thou hast
answered right; this do, and thou shalt live. ²⁹ But
he, willing to justify himself, said unto Jesus, And
who is my *neighbor?* ³⁰ And Jesus answering said,
A certain man went down from Jerusalem to Jericho,
and fell among thieves, which stripped him of his
raiment and wounded him, and departed, leaving him
half dead. ³¹ And by chance there came down a
certain priest that way, and when he saw him, he
passed by on the other side; ³² and likewise a Levite,
when he was at the place, came and looked on him,
and passed by on the other side; ³³ but a certain
Samaritan, as he journeyed, came where he was:

---

* See Deut. vi, 5, and Levit. xix, 18.

authority; but rather glory in the assurance that your LUKE X.
individual names are inscribed upon the register of celestial citizenship."

21 Under the complacent emotions produced by this favorable result
of the deputation, Jesus uttered the following prayer of exultation :
"I bless Thee, my Father, the universal Sovereign, that although
Thou leavest the self-styled learned in divine things to their real ignorance, Thou dost yet impart such lessons of heavenly science to the
unassuming docility of these mere infants in religious lore. Most fervently is this Thy wise condescension to be adored, O Father, that it
has pleased Thee so to do!" 22 [Then turning to his disciples, in order
to give them a correct idea of the channel through which they derived these blessings, he remarked,] "All [the knowledge relative to
my Heavenly Father's purposes for effecting man's salvation,] is intrusted to me [to communicate in my divine embassy]: so that no
person can have any true conception of the relation that subsists between my Father and His Son [in this important work], except ourselves the two parties alone, and such human beings as may be en-
lightened on the subject by the voluntary information imparted by
the Son, [the sole Representative of God to mankind.]"

§ 84.—*Christ Answers a Lawyer by Defining the Duty of Love to
One's Neighbor.*

(Environs of Jerusalem ; [middle of *October ?*] A. D. 28.)

25 [In the course of the popular instruction with which Jesus now
occupied himself,] on one occasion a certain jurist fell in with him ;
who put this question to him, with the design of ensnaring him [into
some remark that might be turned to his prejudice], "Teacher, by
the observance of which of the divine injunctions shall I the most certainly secure immortal blessedness?" 26 To this Jesus replied by another interrogation, "What do you find written in [that portion of]
the divine Law?" [pointing to the motto of the *phylac'tery* worn on
the lawyer's dress.] 27 "It is these commands," responded the other :
"'Devote to Jehovah your God the supreme affection of your heart
and service of your life;' and, 'Love your fellow with the same kindly
concern for his welfare as you entertain toward yourself.'" 28 "Well,"
returned Jesus, "you have furnished a correct answer to your own
question. You have only to observe faithfully these precepts, and
you will assuredly obtain the blessedness for which you inquire."

29 Anxious to make out some plausibility, nevertheless, in his
question, the expounder of the law now asked, [as if for further information,] "Whom, then, am I to consider as my 'fellow' in this
command?" 30 To this Jesus replied by the following illustration:
"A certain Jew made a journey from his residence at Jerusalem to
the city of Jericho; and [in passing through the lonely intervening
tract,] he was attacked by a party of the banditti infesting that
region, who, having robbed him of his very clothes, and severely
wounded him [in his attempts at self-defense], then made off with
the booty, leaving the poor fellow for dead on the ground. 31 While
he lay in this hapless state, a certain priest chanced to pass along
the road; but on noticing the lifeless creature, he haughtily pursued
his journey without stopping to relieve him. 32 In like manner, a
Levite, on arriving at the spot, merely approached the unconscious
sufferer, and after casting a curious glance upon him, passed on.
33 But at length a Samaritan traveler came up to the place where

113*

and when he saw him, he had compassion   LUKE X.
on him, ³⁴ and went to him and bound up
his wounds, pouring in oil and wine, and set him on
his own beast and brought him to an inn, and took
care of him : ³⁵ and on the morrow, when he departed,
he took out two pence and gave them to the host, and
said unto him, Take care of him; and whatsoever
thou spendest more, when I come again, I will repay
thee.   ³⁶ Which now of these three, thinkest thou,
was *neighbor* unto him that fell among the thieves?
³⁷ And he said, He that showed mercy on him.
Then said Jesus unto him, Go, and do *thou* likewise.

§ 85.—*A Visit with Martha and Mary.*

(Bethany; [former part of *November?*] A. D. 28.)

³⁸ Now it came to pass, as they went, that he
entered into a certain village : and a certain woman
named Martha received him into her house. ³⁹ And
she had a sister called Mary, which also sat at Jesus'
feet and heard his word : ⁴⁰ but Martha was cumbered
about much serving, and came to him and said, Lord,
dost thou not care that my sister hath left me to serve
alone? bid her therefore that she help me. ⁴¹ And
Jesus answered and said unto her, Martha, Martha,
thou art careful and troubled about many things :
⁴² but *one* thing is needful; and Mary hath chosen
that good part which shall not be taken away from
her.

§ 86.—*Directions concerning Prayer.*

([Mount of Olives?]; [late in *November?*] A. D. 28.)

¹ And it came to pass, that as he was   LUKE XI.
praying in a certain place, when he ceased,
one of his disciples said unto him, Lord, teach us to

114

the unfortunate man lay extended, and [despite his na-   LUKE X.
tional animosity,] his sympathy was touched at the
sight ; ³⁴ he approached the senseless outcast, and [find-
ing signs of life,] bandaged his wounds, after dressing them with a
healing mixture of oil and wine. [Having thus restored the sufferer
to animation,] he lifted him up, laid him on his own mule, and
having carried him to the nearest *caravan'serai* [i. e. public house,]
he stayed there and took care of him during the night. ³⁵ On the
next morning, as he was preparing to continue his journey, the
generous stranger took out two *dena'rii* [i. e. about 30 cents] from
his purse, and handing them to the keeper of the *caravan'serai*,
told him, ' Nurse this invalid [carefully, till he is entirely well];
and whatever additional expense you incur [in attending upon his
wants], I will reimburse to you on my return.' ³⁶ Now which of
these travelers," asked Jesus, "would seem to you to be acting the
part of a ' fellow' to the individual maltreated by the robbers?"
³⁷ " Why," replied the lawyer, "it would be the one that extended
to him the benevolent relief." " Well, then," rejoined Jesus, "do
you in your future conduct imitate his humane spirit !"

§ 85.—*A Visit with Martha and Mary.*

(Bethany ; [former part of *November ?*] A. D. 28.)

³⁸ After spending some time with his disciples in such excursions
[of instruction in the neighborhood of the metropolis], Jesus visited
the little village of Bethany ; where he was welcomed to the hospitable residence of a certain female named Martha, [at which he
had often before been entertained.] ³⁹ She had a sister named
Mary, who taking her seat along with the disciples at their Master's
feet, [while he was delivering his instructions to those assembled in
the house,] listened with avidity to his communications. ⁴⁰ Martha,
however, was too much taken up with her domestic labors to allow her
an opportunity for this, and [vexed at her sister's seeming leisure,]
she applied to Jesus with this expostulation, " Master, is it a matter
of indifference to you, that my sister has left the burden of the
house-work upon me alone? Do bid her take hold with me !"
⁴¹ But Jesus reprovingly replied to her complaint, " Martha ! Mar-
tha ! you give yourself much needless anxiety and disturbance
about your various family concerns. ⁴² There is really but *one* interest that is of vital importance ; and Mary has selected precisely
that most excellent pursuit, nor must she be diverted from it."

§ 86.—*Directions concerning Prayer.*

([Mount of Olives ?] ; [late in *November ?*] A. D. 28.]

¹ As Jesus was on his way [toward the metropolis,   LUKE XI.
after leaving the hospitable residence of the two sisters
at Bethany], he turned aside from the path to a retired
spot for private prayer ; and on having finished his devotions, he
was accosted by one of his disciples, who accompanied him, with
this request, " Master, will you favor us [in addition to your previous instructions,] with some *form* of prayer [adapted to our relation as your disciples]? in the same manner as John the Baptist used

114*

pray, as John also taught his disciples.   LUKE XI.
2 And he said unto them, When ye pray,
say [MATT. VI, 9] after this manner, Our Father which art
in heaven, hallowed be thy name : thy kingdom come ;
thy will be done, as in heaven, so in earth. 3 Give us
day by day our daily bread : 4 and forgive us our sins,
for we also forgive every one that is indebted to us ;
and lead us not into temptation, but deliver us from
evil. [MATT. VI, 13] For thine is the kingdom and the power
and the glory, forever. Amen. [14] For if [MARK XI, 25] (when
ye stand praying) [MATT. VI, 14] ye forgive men their trespasses,
your heavenly Father will also forgive you ; but if ye forgive
not men their trespasses, neither will your Father forgive your
trespasses.

5 And he said unto them, Which of you shall have
a friend, and shall go unto him at midnight and say
unto him, Friend, lend me three loaves : 6 for a friend
of mine in his journey is come to me, and I have
nothing to set before him ? 7 And he from within
shall answer and say, Trouble me not : the door is
now shut, and my children are with me in bed ; I cannot rise and give thee. 8 I say unto you, Though he
will not rise and give him because he is his *friend*,
yet because of his *importunity* he will rise and give
him as many as he needeth : 9 and I say unto *you*,
Ask, and it shall be given you ; seek, and ye shall
find ; knock, and it shall be opened unto you : 10 for
every one that asketh, receiveth ; and he that seeketh,
findeth ; and to him that knocketh, it shall be opened.
11 If a son shall ask bread of any of you that is a
father, will he give him a stone ? or if he ask a fish,
will he for a fish give him a serpent ? 12 or if he shall
ask an egg, will he offer him a scorpion ? 13 if ye then,
being evil, know how to give good gifts unto your
children, how much more shall your heavenly Father
give the Holy Spirit to them that ask him ?

115

to furnish outlines of prayer to his followers." ² In 　LUKE XI.
compliance with their desire, Jesus said to them : "In
your [social] worship, you will find it profitable to
frame your supplications after the following

"MODEL OF PRAYER.

"Our Heavenly Father, mayest Thou be universally adored, and
"Thy 'Messiah's Reign' be speedily established, till all mankind
"shall conform to Thy will with the same delight as do celestial
"beings! ³ Grant us daily the supplies of life, ⁴ and pardon, [we
"beseech Thee,] our sins, even as we forgive the offenses of others
"toward ourselves ; and moreover, do Thou protect us from all en-
"ticements, that we be not again overcome by transgression. *a* [[For
"these favors, we humbly ascribe to Thee supreme and eternal do-
"minion and majesty ! *Amen.*]]|

b "The duty (expressed above) of forgiving all your fellow-mor-
tals their faults toward yourselves, [when acknowledged with regret,] is an indispensable condition in order to your receiving par-
don at the hands of God." |

⁵ Jesus then proceeded [to illustrate the necessity of *earnestness*
in prayer, in the following manner] : "Suppose one of you should
repair to the house of some friend, at the unseasonable hour of
midnight, with this request, 'Neighbor, have the kindness to lend
me three biscuits ; ⁶ a friend of mine on a journey has just arrived
at my house, and I have not a morsel to give him to eat.' ⁷ Suppose now, your friend, at whose door you are knocking, should reply to you from the inside, 'Can you not get along without putting
me to that trouble? The door is bolted fast, and my children are
all in bed, as well as I ; so that I should have to get up and supply
you myself, which I cannot well do at this hour.' ⁸ If notwithstanding this repulse, the man outside persists in his request, before long the other, who could not be induced on the mere strength
of friendship, will yet, I warrant you, be prevailed upon by his
pertinacity, to get up and help him to whatever he requires. ⁹ On
the same principle [of the success of assiduous application], I charge
you, Entreat your Almighty Friend [with fervency that will not be
denied, for the spiritual food you crave], and it will certainly be
granted you; search [with indefatigable diligence in the ways of
His grace], and you will not fail eventually to discover the blessings you need; knock [vigorously at the door of His promises], and
it will soon be opened to meet your wants : ¹⁰ for no one ever thus
applies to Him in vain.

¹¹ "Suppose again, one of you who is a parent, should be asked
by his child for a piece of bread, would he present him with [some-
thing as unsatisfactory as] a stone, in reply?—much less would he
offer him [anything as hurtful as] a serpent instead of a fish, ¹² or
a scorpion for an egg! ¹³ If *you*, then, with all the error and evil
tendencies of your human nature, are yet capable of bestowing what
is suitable upon your children, how much more likely is your *Heavenly* Father, [who is all perfection,] to confer *c* that best of all
gifts, | the influence of the Holy Spirit, upon those that implore it
of Him !"

a Matt. vi, 13.　　　 *b* Matt. vi, 14, 15.　　　 *c* Matt vii, 11.

§ 87.—*A Blind Man Cured.*

(Jerusalem ; *Saturday, November* 27, A. D. 28.)

¹ And as Jesus passed by, he saw a man **John IX.** which was blind from his birth : ² and his disciples asked him saying, Master, who did sin, this man or his parents, that he was born blind ? ³ Jesus answered, Neither hath this man sinned nor his parents ; but that the works of God should be made manifest in him : ⁴ I must work the works of him that sent me, while it is day ; the night cometh, when no man can work : ⁵ as long as I am in the world, I am the light of the world. ⁶ When he had thus spoken, he spat on the ground, and made clay of the spittle, and he anointed the eyes of the blind man with the clay, ⁷ and said unto him, Go, wash in the pool of Siloam, (which is by interpretation, *Sent.*) He went his way therefore and washed, and came seeing.

⁸ The neighbors therefore, and they which before had seen him that he was blind, said, Is not this he that sat and begged ? ⁹ Some said, This is he : others said, He is *like* him : but he said, I *am* he. ¹⁰ Therefore said they unto him, How were thine eyes opened ? ¹¹ He answered and said, A man that is called Jesus made clay and anointed mine eyes, and said unto me, Go to the pool of Siloam and wash : and I went and washed, and I received sight. ¹² Then said they unto him, Where is he ? He said, I know not.—¹⁴ And it was the sabbath-day when Jesus made the clay and opened his eyes.

116

§ 87.—*A Blind Man Cured.*

(Jerusalem; *Saturday, November* 27, A. D. 28.)

[1] [Soon after reaching the capital,] as Jesus was **John IX.** passing along [one of its streets], he observed a beggar sitting there, who had been entirely blind from his very birth. [2] [As the afflicted man, hearing the sound of the footsteps of the company, implored their charity, repeating the tale of his sufferings from want of sight,] the disciples asked their Master, "Whose sin was the judicial cause of this man's being born blind, his own or that of his parents?" [3] Jesus replied, "[You quite misconceive the moral design of Providence in this man's blindness;] it is not an infliction for sin either on the part of himself or his parents, but is intended to be the occasion of an exhibition of the miraculous agency of God in his relief. [4] Accordingly, as His Representative on earth, it behoves me to be continually engaged in performing these acts of His enjoined upon me, while the day of my mission lasts; for it will soon close in a tragic '*night*—that hour unpropitious for all labor.' [5] So long, however, as I remain among men, I will not cease to be their [bodily as well as spiritual] illuminator." [6] With these remarks, ordering the blind man to approach, he spit upon the ground, and having thus formed a paste of clay, applied it as an ointment to the patient's eye-lids, [7] and then bade him, "Go and wash [your eyes] in the Fountain of Shilo'ah" (a Hebrew name equivalent to *Sent* [i. e. a *gushing* forth of water]). On obeying the direction, the blind man retired from the ablution with perfect vision.

[8] Seeing his altered appearance, his neighbors who had formerly known him as a blind pauper, now exclaimed to one another, "Is not this the man that used to sit along the streets begging?" [9] Some replied, "It is surely the same;" and others, "He is certainly very much like him." The man himself, however, assured them, "I am the very person." [10] "How then," asked they, "have your eyes come to be capable of sight?" [11] "A person whom they call Jesus," replied he, "applied a salve of clay to my eyes, and told me to 'go to the Fountain of Shilo'ah, and wash them;' and on doing so, I gained my eye-sight." [12] They then asked him, "Where is that person?" But he could only answer, "I do not know [where he has gone by this time]."—[14] The day on which this cure was effected was the sabbath.

§ 88.—*The Investigation before the San'hedrim, with Christ's Discourses on the Subject.*

(Jerusalem; *Sunday, November* 28, A. D. 28.)

¹³ They brought to the Pharisees him   JOHN IX. that aforetime was blind. ¹⁵ Then again the Pharisees also asked him how he had received his sight : he said unto them, He put clay upon mine eyes, and I washed, and do see. ¹⁶ Therefore said some of the Pharisees, This man is not of God, because he keepeth not the sabbath-day : others said, How can a man that is a sinner do such miracles? and there was a division among them. ¹⁷ They say unto the blind man again, What sayest thou of him, that he hath opened thine eyes? He said, He is a prophet. ¹⁸ But the Jews did not believe concerning him, that he had been blind and received his sight, until they called the parents of him that had received his sight : ¹⁹ and they asked them saying, Is this your son, who ye say was born blind?—how then doth he now see? ²⁰ His parents answered them and said, We know that this is our son, and that he was born blind ; ²¹ but by what means he now seeth we know not, or who hath opened his eyes we know not : he is of age, ask him ; he shall speak for himself. ²² (These words spake his parents, because they feared the Jews ; for the Jews had agreed already, that if any man did confess that he was Christ, he should be put out of the synagogue : ²³ therefore said his parents, He is of age ; ask him.) ₂₄ Then again called they the man that was blind, and said unto him, Give God the praise ; we know that this man is a sinner. ²⁵ He answered and said, Whether he be a sinner or no, I know not ; one thing I know, that whereas I was blind, now I see. ²⁶ Then said they to him again, What did

117

§ 88.—*The Investigation before the San'hedrim, with Christ's Discourses on the Subject.*

(Jerusalem; *Sunday, November 28, A. D. 28.*)

13 The next day, the late blind man was examined before the San'hedrim, [with special reference to the alleged violation of the sabbath in his cure]. 15 The court repeated the question [before asked by his neighbors,] "How came you to see?" to which he answered as before, "My benefactor applied some clay to my eyes, and after washing them, I found myself possessed of sight." 16 Some of the members (being of the Pharisaical party) hereupon insisted, "This pretended teacher cannot be a divine ambassador, for he does not observe the divine ordinance of the sabbath;" while others [of more liberal views] urged in reply, "But how could a vile impostor perform such miracles as this?" A division of opinion therefore ensued among them.

17 [Being thus baffled in their attempt to impeach Jesus directly,] his enemies now returned to the man who had been the subject of the cure, with this interrogation, "What do *you* think concerning him, in having cured you of blindness on the sabbath?" [hoping to make out a collusion between them, and thus destroy the evidence for the cure.] The man frankly declared, "I believe he is a prophet." 18 The hostile Pharisees accordingly employed this avowal, as an argument for refusing to credit the man's assertion that he was born blind, unless his parents should be summoned and vouch for the fact. Having sent for them, therefore, 19 they demanded of them in a brow-beating tone, "Is this your son whom you are prepared to testify to, as having been born blind? How then has he of late become possessed of sight?" 20 The parents made answer, "He is indeed our son, and was certainly born blind; 21 but we are unable to say by what means he is now possessed of sight, nor have we any personal knowledge of any one's having enabled him to use his eyes. He is of age, however, and can readily answer your questions for himself." 22, 23 The parents were thus guarded in their reply [to the latter part of the question], from fear of the Jewish hierarchy; for they were aware that the San'hedrim had passed a resolution, that any person who should publicly acknowledge the Messiahship of Jesus, should incur the penalty of religious excommunication [in the second degree.

24 Failing in this direction], the prosecutors again summoned the late blind man for cross-questioning, and thus exhorted him [with a view to make him implicate himself by a further avowal], "Confess now the truth concerning your cure in the fear of the Omniscient; for we have positive knowledge that this Jesus to whom you attribute it, is a flagitious impostor." 25 [Indignant at this imputation upon his benefactor,] the man retorted, "That he is such a character, I am yet to be convinced; but of this one thing I am certain, at all events, that I used to be blind, but I now have the perfect use of my eyes: [and this is proof enough in the case for me!]" 26 They then asked him more in detail, [as if to fairly canvass the matter, but really in order to catch at some discrepancy or improbability,] "What operation did he perform upon you?

JOHN IX.

117*

he to thee? how opened he thine eyes? John IX.
²⁷ He answered them, I have told you
already, and ye did not hear; wherefore would ye
hear it again? will ye also be his disciples? ²⁸ Then
they reviled him and said, Thou art his disciple; but
we are Moses' disciples: ²⁹ we know that God spake
unto Moses; as for this fellow, we know not from
whence he is. ³⁰ The man answered and said unto
them, Why, herein is a marvelous thing, that ye know
not from whence he is, and yet he hath opened mine
eyes: ³¹ now we know that God heareth not sinners;
but if any man be a worshiper of God and doeth his
will, him he heareth: ³² since the world began, was it
not heard that any man opened the eyes of one that
was born blind; ³³ if this man were not of God, he
could do nothing. ³⁴ They answered and said unto
him, Thou wast altogether *born* in sins, and dost thou
teach us? And they cast him out.

³⁵ Jesus heard that they had cast him out: and
when he had found him, he said unto him, Dost thou
believe on the Son of God? ³⁶ He answered and
said, Who is he, Lord, that I might believe on him?
³⁷ And Jesus said unto him, Thou hast both seen him,
and it is he that talketh with thee. ³⁸ And he said,
Lord, I believe: and he worshiped him. ³⁹ And
Jesus said, For judgment I am come into this world;
that they which see not, might see, and that they
which see, might be made blind. ⁴⁰ And some of the
Pharisees which were with him heard these words,
and said unto him, Are *we* blind also? ⁴¹ Jesus said
unto them, If ye were blind, ye should have no sin:
but now ye say, We see; therefore your sin re-
maineth.

¹ Verily, verily I say unto you, He that en-   John X.
tereth not by the door into the sheep-fold,
but climbeth up some other way, the same is a thief

118

by what process did he cure your eyes?"   ²⁷ The man JOHN IX.
scornfully replied to these quibbles, "I have told you
once already, how he did it; but you would not listen
to such a means as being efficacious. Why do you ask me to repeat
the account? is it because you have a mind to become his followers
yourselves?"   ²⁸ [This cutting jeer was too much for their pretended sincerity, and] they broke out at once in a torrent of invectives, "*You* are his proselyte; we are disciples of Moses: ²⁹ for we
know that Moses was divinely inspired, but this pretender has come
from nobody knows what source of authority!"   ³⁰ "Strange indeed," sarcastically rejoined the man, "that you should not know
his origin, when he has the ability to give me eye-sight! ³¹ It is
very certain that God does not regard 'flagitious impostors,' so as to
enable them to perform such miracles; it is only those that piously
conform to the will of God, that are thus honored. ³² Such a wonder was never heard of before, as any one's bestowing eye-sight
upon a person born blind; ³³ and surely if this teacher were not a
messenger from God, he could not perform such an act."   ³⁴ [Irri-
tated beyond measure at this bold refutation from an inferior,]
the opposing party furiously exclaimed, "You low-lived wretch,
marked by sin at your very birth! have you the effrontery to attempt to instruct *us?*" and in their rage they ordered him to be
violently thrust out [of their presence, following up the expulsion
by a sentence of excommunication against him as an adherent of
Jesus.

³⁵ In the course of the day], Jesus, being apprized of the man's
ignominious ejection by the San'hedrim, met him [in the street],
and thus accosted him, "Have you faith in the Messianic 'Son of
God'?" ³⁶ The man assentingly asked, "Can you inform me concerning him, dear sir; I would gladly confide in him."   ³⁷ Jesus
then plainly announced himself to him, "You *have* seen him; yes,
it is himself that now speaks to you!"   ³⁸ [Overwhelmed with emotions of joyful conviction,] the man cried out, "O yes, Master, I do
believe in you!" at the same time prostrating himself in humble
adoration before him.   ³⁹ Jesus turned to the by-standers with this
remark, [to which the illustration before them gave point,] "One
great object of my mission to mankind, is to [furnish a discrimina-
tive] test [of] their moral character, and [as the result of the choice
of receiving or rejecting me thus afforded them,] to bestow spiritual
sight upon those who are blind from mere ignorance, and develop
the real blindness of those who fancy they see religious things
clearly."   ⁴⁰ A number of Pharisees, who had now gathered around
the place, stung by this reflection upon themselves, contemptuously
asked him, "It may be, you would insinuate that *we* too are poor
blind ignoramuses?" ⁴¹ [To this braggart challenge,] Jesus returned with dignified emphasis, "If you *were* simply blind for want
of information, your misapprehension of me might admit of some
apology; but inasmuch as you repel all conviction by the bigoted
claim, 'We are the well-enlightened,' your unbelief becomes an un-
mitigated crime!"

¹ [Then addressing the crowd, Jesus thus depicted their JOHN X.
Pharisaical teachers,] "I solemnly assure you, that whatever person [especially in insinuating himself among the
flock of God's people as a religious pastor,] avoids entering the sheep-
fold through [a preparatory acceptance of me] the true wicket-gate,
but clambers over into the fold by some clandestine passage, is no

118*

and a robber; [2] but he that entereth in by ┃JOHN X.
the door, is the shepherd of the sheep: [3] to
him the porter openeth, and the sheep hear his voice,
and he calleth his own sheep by name and leadeth them
out; [4] and when he putteth forth his own sheep, he
goeth before them, and the sheep follow him, for they
know his voice; [5] and a stranger will they not follow,
but will flee from him; for they know not the voice
of strangers. [6] This parable spake Jesus unto them;
but they understood not what things they were which
he spake unto them. [7] Then said Jesus unto them
again, Verily, verily I say unto you, *I* am the door of
the sheep: [8] all that ever came before me are thieves
and robbers; but the sheep did not hear them: [9] I am
the door; by me if any man enter in, he shall be
saved, and shall go in and out, and find pasture.
[10] The thief cometh not but for to steal and to kill and
to destroy; I am come that they might have life, and
that they might have it more abundantly. [11] I am the
good shepherd: the good shepherd giveth his life for
the sheep; [12] but he that is a hireling and not the
shepherd, whose own the sheep are not, seeth the wolf
coming, and leaveth the sheep and fleeth; and the
wolf catcheth them and scattereth the sheep: [13] the
hireling fleeth, because he is a hireling and careth not
for the sheep. [14] I am the good shepherd, and know
my sheep, and am known of mine: [15] as the Father
knoweth me, even so know I the Father; and I lay
down my life for the sheep. [16] And other sheep I
have, which are not of this fold; them also I must
bring, and they shall hear my voice, and there
shall be one fold and one shepherd. [17] Therefore
doth my Father love me, because I lay down my
life, that I might take it again: [18] no man taketh
it from me, but I lay it down of myself; I have
power to lay it down, and I have power to take it

119

better than a stealthy thief: [2] whereas the genuine JOHN X.
shepherd is shown by his going frankly in at the
proper entrance. [3] The door-keeper admits the latter as of legitimate authority, and the sheep listen to his familiar voice; and when he calls those of the sheep that belong
to him by their accustomed names, they recognize the sound,
and readily follow him. [4] Having thus led them out, he goes
before them through the pastures, the sheep obediently following the wonted voice of their master; [5] but instead of following a stranger, they will run from him in alarm at the un-
familiar sound of his call." [6] Perceiving, however, that the
auditors at whom this allegory was chiefly aimed, were indis-
posed to apply it [thus concisely expressed,] to themselves,
[7] Jesus proceeded [to repeat it more in detail: "In plain terms,
despite your prejudices], I assure you, *I* am the true Door to the
sheep-fold of God's genuine worshipers; [8] and all [you Pharisaic
pastors], who up to my time have usurped the charge of His
flock, are mere thievish intruders,—to whose harsh mandates
His true sheep have accordingly refused to yield a cordial as-
sent. [9] But whoever enters the fold through me, the legitimate portal of admission to the divine favor, will thereby be
secured from spiritual thieves, and enjoy access at will to the
pastures of life-giving grace. [10] On the other hand, the false
teacher, like a roving marauder, only pounces upon the fold in
order to steal and butcher and destroy its inmates; whereas
my errand is to impart to them *life* of a higher and more abundant character than they now enjoy. [11] Yes, I am the benignant Chief-shepherd himself, such a one as is ready to hazard
his own life for the preservation of the flock, [12, 13] and no hireling under-shepherd [such as you], who cares not for the safety
of sheep that do not belong to him, but when he sees some
[pernicious error like a] ravenous wolf approach, abandons
the flock, with coward venality, to be torn in pieces and scattered by the fierce beast. [14] Not so do I, the kind-hearted
Shepherd, who am endeared to the flock that is my own, by a
mutual intimacy of spirit [15] like that which subsists between
my Father and myself; for I am actually about to sacrifice my
life to retrieve them from their spiritual peril. [16] Yes, and not
the flock of this nation only will I thus redeem; I anticipate
another flock [the Gentiles], which I must annex, so soon as
they learn to obey my voice, and then there will be but one
general fold, under a single chief-shepherd. [17] This consummation of my mission by the resignation of my life in the behalf of man,—but soon to resume it,—meets the highest complacency of my Father, being voluntary on my part; [18] for no
being whatever compels me to the sacrifice,—I freely exercise my privilege of surrendering my life, and will equally
regain it by the energy of my own nature; and in all this
earthly career, I am fulfilling the grand purport of those

again : this commandment have I received   JOHN X.
of my Father.

[19] There was a division therefore again among the
Jews for these sayings : [20] and many of them said, He
hath a devil and is mad ; why hear ye him ? [21] others
said, These are not the words of him that hath a devil :
can a devil open the eyes of the blind ?

§ 89.—*Christ's Discourses at the Festival of Dedication.*

(Jerusalem, the Temple, Solomon's Portico; between the *Tuesdays,*
November 30, and *December* 7, A. D. 28.),

[22] And it was at Jerusalem the feast of the dedication, and it was winter : [23] and Jesus walked in the
temple in Solomon's porch. [24] Then came the Jews
round about him, and said unto him, How long dost
thou make us to doubt? if thou be the Christ, tell us
plainly. [25] Jesus answered them, I told you, and ye
believed not; the works that I do in my Father's
name, they bear witness of me : [26] but ye believe not,
because ye are not of my sheep. As I said unto you,
[27] my sheep hear my voice, and I know them, and
they follow me : [28] and I give unto them eternal life,
and they shall never perish, neither shall any pluck
them out of my hand ; [29] my Father which gave them
me is greater than all, and none is able to pluck them
out of my Father's hand : [30] I and my Father are one.
[31] Then the Jews took up stones again to stone him.
[32] Jesus answered them, Many good works have I
showed you from my Father ; for which of those
works do ye stone me? [33] The Jews answered him
saying, For a *good* work we stone thee not, but for
blasphemy, and because that thou, being a man,
makest thyself God. [34] Jesus answered them, Is it

120

instructions delivered to me in the intimacy of my JOHN X.
Father's counsels."

19 Here a diversity of opinion again arose among the
audience, respecting the truthfulness of this discourse; 20 many de-
crying him in the debate by such impatient remarks as these, "Non-
sense! he is merely uttering the ravings of a demon! Why listen to
him?" 21 While others pleaded, "But these declarations are not
the incoherent language of a demoniac. Besides, can a demoniac
exercise the sacred power of bestowing sight upon the blind?"

§ 89.—*Christ's Discourses at the Festival of Dedication.*

(Jerusalem, the Temple, Solomon's Portico; between the *Tuesdays, November* 30,
and *December* 7, A. D. 28.)

22 The anniversary of the Renewal of the Temple services having
arrived, [Jesus remained at Jerusalem; 23 and] one day as he was
walking about under the shelter of Solomon's Portico, 22 (it being
the season of the winter rains,) 24 a party of the hierarchal Jews
clustered around him with this interrogation, [by which they hoped
to elicit some ground of inculpation,] "How long do you intend to
keep our minds in suspense as to your character? Tell us at once
in so many words, Are you the Messiah?" 25 [To this insidious du-
plicity,] Jesus replied, "I have already told you [time and again],
who I am; but you would not believe my declaration,—yet the very
miracles that I am continually performing by my Father's authority,
are of themselves sufficient evidence of my character as His representative; 26 but you are determined not to credit my claims, for you
have evidently no affinity with my flock [in docility nor consequently
in discipleship]. On the contrary, as I lately assured you, 27 my true
sheep listen with a teachable spirit to the voice of my instructions,
and while I acknowledge them as mine [by the bestowal of spiritual
blessings], they reciprocate my care by following me with obedient
steps; 28 and thus I lead them forth to the reception of immortal
blessedness at my pastoral hand,—a privilege which will preserve
them evermore [from spiritual famine, malady or death]; and of
which no ruthless prowler will be suffered to deprive them against
their will, by snatching them from my protective fold. 29 No! for
my Father, whose gracious Spirit wins them to my care, is more
powerful than all their foes combined, so that no being whatever
can wrest them from *His* loved embrace; 30 and in their salvation,
I am identified with my Father by a unity of nature."

31 At this announcement, some of the Jewish hierarchy in a transport of fanaticism again caught up stones, which they were about
to hurl at him [as a blasphemer; when others less violent interposed, that they might accomplish their designs more securely by
other means]. 32 Jesus meantime calmly met their fury with this
only remonstrance, "Many are the beneficent deeds, that I have
publicly performed among you as my Father's Delegate; for which
of these would ye now stone me?" 33 [In tones still quivering with
rage,] his assailants scowled back the reply, "It is for no *good* act
which you have *ever* done, that we would fain stone you, but for
your daring blasphemy in arrogating *divinity* to yourself, a mere
man!" 34 "As to any such claim being criminal on my part," returned Jesus, "what will you say to the declaration of your own
Scriptures,—

S

not written in your law,* I said, Ye are . JOHN X.
gods ? ³⁵ If he called them gods unto
whom the word of God came, (and the scripture
cannot be broken;) ³⁶ say ye of him whom the
Father hath sanctified and sent into the world, Thou
blasphemest; because I said, I am the Son of God ?
³⁷ If I do not the works of my Father, believe me
not: ³⁸ but if I do, though ye believe not me, believe the works; that ye may know and believe
that the Father is in me, and I in him.   ³⁹ Therefore
they sought again to take him; but he escaped out
of their hand.

§ 90.—*Christ Withdraws from Jerusalem, and Gains more Converts.*

(Bethany-beyond-Jordan; *December*, A. D. 28.)

⁴⁰ And he went away again beyond Jordan, into the
place where John at first baptized; and there he
abode.   ⁴¹ And many resorted unto him and said,
John did no miracle; but all things that John spake
of this man were true.   ⁴² And many believed on
him there.

§ 91.—*The Revivification of Lazarus.*

(Bethany [near Jerusalem]; [*January ?*] A. D. 29.)

¹ Now a certain man was sick named **John XI.**
Lazarus, of Bethany the town of Mary
and her sister Martha.   ³ Therefore his sisters sent
unto him saying, Lord, behold, he whom thou lovest
is sick.   ⁴ When Jesus heard that, he said, This
sickness is not unto death, but for the glory of God,
that the Son of God might be glorified thereby.

* Psa. lxxxii, 6.

'Mark now [your sentence] published from on High, JOHN X.
[Ye magistrates who persevere in fraud:
Although] you occupy the rank of *gods*,—
[In honor raised above the menial mass,—
Yea, in their sight are all with majesty
Supreme as if Jehovah's offspring, clothed; . . .]'?

35 Since, then, Jehovah here addresses His subjects with the full title of '*gods*,' in the very language of that Holy Writ itself, whose propriety you cannot question; 36 why should you charge me, the Father's consecrated Legate to mankind, with blasphemy, in calling myself the Son of God? 37 If indeed I do not perform acts in keeping with my Father's, then you are at liberty to withhold your confidence from me; 38 but inasmuch as I do perform such acts, I call upon you to yield your credence, if not on the strength of my personal declarations, yet at least to the evidence of my miraculous acts,—and thus consent to acknowledge with conviction, that I and my Father are blended in action as in nature." 39 This plea of Jesus, however, only served to incite his opponents [on account of the impression they perceived it was making upon the populace,] to another effort to arrest him on the spot; but the attempt was frustrated by Jesus availing himself of the confusion it created, to slip out of their reach.

§ 90.—*Christ Withdraws from Jerusalem and Gains more Converts.*

(Bethany-beyond-Jordan; *December*, A. D. 28.)

40 [The Festival of Dedication being over,] Jesus retired from the capital, [to allow the rage of his enemies to abate;] and again visited the tract of country on the eastern shore of the Jordan, around Bethany, the scene of a part of John the Baptist's early ministrations. Here he spent several weeks in teaching and performing miracles; 41 while multitudes flocked about him, under the impulse of sentiments which they expressed in such terms as these, "John [although unquestionably a great prophet,] performed no miracles as this Teacher does, but his prophetic testimony [as to his Successor's superiority] has certainly been verified in him." 42 [Being thus prepossessed in favor of Jesus,] great numbers of them soon became fully convinced of his Messiahship.

§ 91.—*The Revivification of Lazarus.*

(Bethany [near Jerusalem]; [*January?*] A. D. 29.)

1 [While Jesus was thus engaged in Pere'a,] a certain John XI. inhabitant of the village of Bethany-in-Judea, by the name of Lazarus, the brother of the friendly sisters Martha and Mary, chanced to fall dangerously ill. 3 Accordingly, his sisters [in the hope of thus securing a cure,] sent the following word to Jesus, "Master, our brother—dear, we know, to yourself as well as to us—is very sick. [Can you not hasten to his relief?]" 4 On receiving this intelligence, Jesus merely observed, "This illness of his will not terminate [as to its permanent issue,] in his death, but is destined to result in a stupendous exhibition of the divine power, by which the glory of the 'Son of Man' will be enhanced."

121*

⁵ Now Jesus loved Martha and her sister JOHN XI.
and Lazarus. ⁶ When he had heard there-
fore that he was sick, he abode two days still in the
same place where he was.

⁷ Then after that saith he to his disciples, Let us
go into Judea again. ⁸ His disciples say unto him,
Master, the Jews of late sought to stone thee ; and
goest thou thither again ? ⁹ Jesus answered, Are
there not twelve hours in the day ? if any man walk
in the day, he stumbleth not, because he seeth the
light of this world ; ¹⁰ but if a man walk in the night,
he stumbleth, because there is no light in him.
¹¹ These things said he : and after that he saith unto
them, Our friend Lazarus *sleepeth;* but I go that I
may awake him out of sleep. ¹² Then said his disciples, Lord, if he sleep, he shall do well. ¹³ (Howbeit Jesus spake of his death ; but they thought that
he had spoken of taking of rest in sleep.) ¹⁴ Then
said Jesus unto them plainly, Lazarus is dead ; ¹⁵ and
I am glad for your sakes that I was not there, to the
intent ye may believe ; nevertheless let us go unto
him. ¹⁶ Then said Thomas (which is called Didymus)
unto his fellow-disciples, Let us also go, that we may
die with him.

¹⁷ Then when Jesus came, he found that he had lain
in the grave four days already. ¹⁸ (Now Bethany
was nigh unto Jerusalem, about fifteen furlongs off :)
¹⁹ and many of the Jews came to Martha and Mary,
to comfort them concerning their brother. ²⁰ Then
Martha, as soon as she heard that Jesus was coming,
went and met him ; but Mary sat still in the house.
²¹ Then said Martha unto Jesus, Lord, if thou hadst
been here, my brother had not died : ²² but I know
that even now, whatsoever thou wilt ask of God,
God will give it thee. ²³ Jesus saith unto her, Thy
brother shall rise again. ²⁴ Martha saith unto him,

122

[5] [The message, however, in reality deeply touched his sympathy,] for he felt a great affection for the whole family; [6] but he deemed it prudent [not to alarm them by expressing his concern] on hearing the sickness, [and important engagements required him] still to remain where he was for the present.

[7] On the second day after the arrival of the news, [having now dispatched all that was urgent in his business in that region,] Jesus proposed to his disciples that they should " return into Judea." [8] But they thus remonstrated against such a course, " Why, Teacher, the Jewish hierarchy were so very lately bent on stoning you, and will you venture among them again?" [9] Jesus replied [in the enigmatical but piquant language of the adage], "Does not each day contain its fixed number of twelve hours? and 'if a traveler journey during these hours of day-light, he advances with security,' enjoying the beams of the natural sun on his path; [10] whereas, if he waits till the inopportune season of night, he will unavoidably stumble over some fatal obstruction in the dark: [just so, if I industriously proceed to my providential sphere of labor during the appointed time of my sojourn on earth, I need be apprehensive of no mishap; but if I timidly defer the performance of whatever good task comes in my way, until it is entirely pleasant for me to undertake it, ere that opportunity may arrive, the auspicious but limited period of my mission will have closed, when I will be disappointed of any successful prosecution of its interests." [11] Perceiving that the disciples failed to apprehend the force of his reply,] Jesus added in explanation, " Our friend Lazarus is ' asleep,' and I am going to awake him." [12] " Certainly then, Master," rejoined they, " if he is enjoying a quiet slumber, he will recover ; [and there is therefore no call for your hazarding yourself in Judea to cure him.]" [13] Jesus corrected this misapprehension of his language, [14] by telling them in plain terms, " Lazarus is dead. [15] Our absence at his decease, however, is a matter of joy to me, on *your* account ; as it will afford an opportunity of enlarging your confidence in me [by his resuscitation]. But now let us go where he is." [16] At this expression of settled determination, Thomas (otherwise called Did'y-mus [i. e. the " *Twin*," in Hebrew and Greek respectively,]) exclaimed to his fellow-disciples [with affectionate bluntness, " Well, if our Master will run the risk of his life among his enemies,] let us go with him and share his fate !"

[17] On arriving at the village of Bethany (in Judea, [18] about 15 *sta'dia* [i. e. nearly 1¼ miles] from Jerusalem), [17] Jesus ascertained, —[19] from the numbers of Jews who were repairing from Jerusalem to the residence of Martha and Mary, in order to condole with them for the loss of their brother,—[17] that Lazarus had been buried now four days [both extremes included]. [20] No sooner had Martha [who happened to be out of doors engaged in some domestic concern,] heard that Jesus was approaching, than she hastened to the outskirts of the village to meet him; but Mary [being uninformed of his coming,] continued sitting in silent grief within the house. [21] On reaching Jesus, Martha said to him, " Master, had you only been here at our request, you might have prevented my brother's death; [22] yet I am aware that even now [the assurance you sent us may be verified, for] whatever petition you may make to God in our behalf, will doubtless be granted you." [23] Jesus reassured her, " Your brother will certainly revive." [24] " Ah yes," rejoined Martha, " I know he will revive at the final resurrection; [but he

I know that he shall rise again in the resur-   JOHN XI.
rection at the last day.   25 Jesus said unto
her, *I* am the resurrection and the life: he that believeth in me, though he were dead, yet shall he live;
26 and whosoever liveth and believeth in me, shall
never die.   Believest thou this?   27 She saith unto
him, Yea, Lord; I believe that thou art the Christ
the Son of God, which should come into the world.
28 And when she had so said, she went her way, and
called Mary her sister secretly saying, The Master
is come, and calleth for thee.   29 As soon as she heard
that, she arose quickly and came unto him: 30 (now
Jesus was not yet come into the town, but was in that
place where Martha met him.)   31 The Jews then
which were with her in the house and comforted her,
when they saw Mary that she rose up hastily and
went out, followed her saying, She goeth unto the
grave to weep there.   32 Then when Mary was come
where Jesus was and saw him, she fell down at his
feet, saying unto him, Lord, if thou hadst been here,
my brother had not died.   33 When Jesus therefore
saw her weeping and the Jews also weeping which
came with her, he groaned in the spirit and was
troubled, 34 and said, Where have ye laid him? They
say unto him, Lord, come and see.   35 Jesus wept.
36 Then said the Jews, Behold how he loved him!
37 And some of them said, Could not this man, which
opened the eyes of the blind, have caused that even
this man should not have died?   38 Jesus therefore
again groaning in himself, cometh to the grave; (it
was a cave, and a stone lay upon it:) 39 Jesus said,
Take ye away the stone.   Martha, the sister of him
that was dead, saith unto him, Lord, by this time he
is offensive; for he hath been dead four days.
40 Jesus saith unto her, Said I not unto thee, that if
thou wouldest believe, thou shouldest see the glory of

123

is lost to us on earth!]" ²⁵ Jesus then more dis-   JOHN XI.
tinctly declared, "*I* am the author of that resurrec-
tion and the procurer not only of the life which it
ushers in, but of all other; whoever therefore confides in me,
even though he must die corporeally, shall enjoy a spiritual
and blissful immortality,—²⁶ nor will any living being that
confides in me, perish forever either in soul or body. Do you
fully credit this? [Then why be apprehensive lest I shall not
redeem my pledge in reference to your brother, since I am
competent to a resuscitation so much higher and more general?]" ²⁷ Martha [still not clearly discerning the drift of his
remarks,] could only respond with fervent devotion, " Yes indeed, Master; I do believe that you are no less than the Messiah, even the 'Son of God' so long expected to appear!"
²⁸ With these words she hastened back, [animated by the an-
ticipation of relief,] and summoned her sister Mary, telling
her privately, "The Teacher is just entering the village, and
wishes to see you!" ²⁹ On hearing this intelligence, Mary at
once rose up and hastened out to meet him; ³⁰ for Jesus had
not yet come within the village, but remained still in the
same spot where Martha had first met him. ³¹ Her Jewish
visitors meanwhile, who were condoling with her in the house,
seeing Mary rise abruptly and leave the room, whispered to
each other, "She is going out to the sepulchre, to weep there;"
they therefore followed [in order to mourn with her]. ³² But
Mary, on reaching Jesus, immediately threw herself in dependent grief at his feet, sobbing out [in a half-reproachful, half-
imploring tone], "O Master, if you had only been present, my
brother's life would have been saved!" ³³ At the sight of
Mary's tears of anguish, with her Jewish companions also
weeping around her, Jesus was so deeply affected that he with
difficulty restrained his emotions ³⁴ sufficiently to inquire,
"Where is he buried?" The friends replied, " We will show
you his tomb, sir;" ³⁵ and as they led the way, the tender sympathy of Jesus for the distressed family found vent in a flood
of silent tears. ³⁶ The Jewish visitors, on witnessing his emotion, remarked in a low tone to each other, "He is weeping!
how dear a friend must Lazarus have been to him!" ³⁷ But
others less respectful retorted captiously, "Why, then, could
not he who pretends to have so lately bestowed sight upon the
man born blind, have prevented his friend's decease, [if he
really loved him so much?" ³⁸ Without noticing this caviling whisper—so soon to be refuted,—] Jesus proceeded to the
tomb,—which was a sepulchral cave hewn in the face of a rock,
with a slab of stone set up to close the entrance,—and in a
voice still choked with emotion, ³⁹ bade the attendant friends,
"Remove the stone door;" upon which Martha [supposing he
wished merely to take a look at the remains of his friend,] interposed the remark, "Master, the corpse is by this time offensive, being now buried parts of four days." ⁴⁰ But Jesus chid-

God ? ⁴¹Then they took away the stone   JOHN XI.
from the place where the dead was laid.
And Jesus lifted up his eyes and said, Father, I thank
thee that thou hast heard me : ⁴²and I knew that
thou hearest me always; but because of the people
which stand by, I said it, that they may believe that
thou hast sent me. ⁴³And when he thus had spoken,
he cried with a loud voice, Lazarus, come forth.
⁴⁴And he that was dead came forth, bound hand and
foot with grave-clothes ; and his face was bound about
with a napkin. Jesus saith unto them, Loose him,
and let him go. ⁴⁵Then many of the Jews which
came to Mary, and had seen the things which Jesus
did, believed on him : ⁴⁶but some of them went their
ways to the Pharisees, and told them what things
Jesus had done.

§ 92.—The Determination of the San'hedrim.

(Jerusalem; [January ?] A. D. 29.)

⁴⁷ Then gathered the chief-priests and the Pharisees a council, and said, What do we ? for this man
doeth many miracles : ⁴⁸if we let him thus alone, all
men will believe on him ; and the Romans shall come
and take away both our place and nation. ⁴⁹And
one of them named Caiaphas, being the high-priest
that same year, said unto them, Ye know nothing at
all, ⁵⁰nor consider that it is expedient for us that one
man should die for the people, and that the whole
nation perish not. ⁵¹(And this spake he not of himself, but being high-priest that year, he prophesied
that Jesus should die for that nation ; ⁵²and not for
that nation only, but that also he should gather together
in one the children of God that were scattered abroad.)
⁵³ Then from that day forth they took counsel together
for to put him to death.

124

ingly replied to her, "Did I not tell you, that if you would
only confide in my competency and faithfulness, you
should witness a display of divine power in this case?"
⁴¹ The friends, thus reassured, removed the stone from the entrance of
the vault where the deceased lay, and Jesus then raising his eyes toward heaven, uttered the following pathetic ejaculation, "Father, I
bless Thee for [seconding my designs in this case by] Thy effective approval: ⁴² yes, *I* indeed need not this evidence that Thou always regardest my invocations]—even when mentally expressed—with rati-
fying concurrence] : but I now pray audibly to Thee, on account of
the crowd that stand around me, so that Thy public attestation may
convince them that I am [no Satanic agent, but] Thy true Messenger
[accredited by palpable tokens of Thy aid]." ⁴³ After this brief adjura-
tion, Jesus exclaimed in a loud tone of authority, "Lazarus, come
forth !" ⁴⁴ Instantly the reanimated corpse issued from the sepulchre,
with his feet and hands still wrapped in the grave-clothes, and the
napkin yet fastened around his eye-brows. Jesus now directed the
friends to "disencumber him of these habiliments, that he might
return home as usual."

⁴⁵ Numbers of [the better disposed part of] Mary's Jewish companions in grief, witnessing this miracle of Jesus, were led by it to a
full admission of his character ; ⁴⁶ but some of the rest, being partisans of the Pharisaical leaders, went and invidiously reported the
whole matter to them.

§ 92.—*The Determination of the San'hedrim.*
(Jerusalem ; [*January ?*] A. D. 29.)

⁴⁷ On receiving these reports of Jesus's proceedings, the Pharisaical
hierarchy convened the San'hedrim [for the purpose of deliberating
on the subject], and thus introduced the business of the meeting,
"What measures had we better take with reference to this impostor,
who is gaining such celebrity by the magical wonders that he is constantly effecting? ⁴⁸ If we let him go on with merely the slack strictures that we have thus far contented ourselves with passing upon him,
the whole populace will be led away by his trickery, [and in their enthusiastic confidence in his Messiahship will presently proclaim him
their king ;] and then the jealous Romans will overwhelm us [indis-
criminately with their forces, and in their vengeance at the rebellion
will] raze our city and blot out our nation !" ⁴⁹ One of their number,
Caiaphas, who was also High Priest at that time, [after listening to this
puzzled yet anxious inquiry, which betrayed the timorous spirit of the
speakers,] boldly delivered his own opinion of the propriety of rigorous
measures, in the following reproachful terms, "You are very short-
sighted [in your hesitating proposal under the present emergency],
⁵⁰ not to consider that it would be good policy for us to cause this individual to be put to death at once, and thereby secure the safety of the
populace, rather than allow the entire nation to be destroyed by his
seditious means!" ⁵¹ In this violent harangue, he unconsciously uttered
an important prophetic sentiment, namely that Jesus *should die on the
behalf of the nation ;*—⁵² nor was this prediction of which he, as bearing
the typical office of High Priest, was providentially made the appropriate though unworthy instrument, confined in its extent to the Jewish
nation, but received its full accomplishment in the subsequent incor-
poration of all God's children, scattered in heathen countries also, into
one family.—⁵³ This counsel [so decidedly expressed and from so high a
source,] swayed the assembly to the adoption of a resolution, from that
time vigorously prosecuted, that they would procure the death of Jesus.

§ 93.—*Christ Retires from the neighborhood of Jeru-salem, and afterward Attracts numerous Followers beyond the Jordan.*

(Ephron and Pere'a; [*January* and *February ?*] A. D. 29.)

⁵⁴ Jesus therefore walked no more openly 　JOHN XI.
among the Jews; but went thence unto a
country near to the wilderness, into a city called
Ephraim, and there continued with his disciples.
¹ And he arose from thence and cometh into 　Mark X.
the coasts of Judea, by the farther side of
Jordan: and the people resort unto him again; and
as he was wont, he taught them again, [MATT. XIX, 2] and
healed them there.

§ 94.—*A Female Cured of Spinal Paral'ysis.*

(Pere'a; [latter part of *February ?*] A. D. 29.)

¹⁰ And he was teaching in one of the 　Luke XIII.
synagogues on the sabbath: ¹¹ and behold,
there was a woman which had a spirit of infirmity
eighteen years, and was bowed together, and could in
no wise lift up herself. ¹² And when Jesus saw her,
he called her to him and said unto her, Woman, thou
art loosed from thine infirmity: ¹³ and he laid his
hands on her: and immediately she was made straight,
and glorified God. ¹⁴ And the ruler-of-the-synagogue
answered with indignation, because that Jesus had
healed on the sabbath-day, and said unto the people,
There are six days in which men ought to work; in
them therefore come and be healed, and not on the
sabbath-day. ¹⁵ The Lord then answered him and
said, Thou hypocrite! doth not each one of you on the
sabbath loose his ox or his ass from the stall, and lead
him away to watering? ¹⁶ and ought not this woman,
being a daughter of Abraham, whom Satan hath bound,
125

§ 93.—*Christ Retires from the neighborhood of Jerusalem, and afterward Attracts numerous Followers beyond the Jordan.*

(Ephron and Pere'a; [*January* and *February ?*] A. D. 29.)

 54 [Being apprized of this definitive resolve on   JOHN XI. the part of the San'hedrim for his destruction,] ——————— Jesus judged it imprudent for him to travel for the present in so exposed a manner near the metropolis; he therefore left Bethany, and repaired with his disciples to a town by the name of Ephron, situated on the north-western edge of the Desert of Judea. After remaining there for a few weeks, ¹ he crossed over into Pere'a, [designing   **Mark X.** thence to proceed southward] on the eastern shore ——————— of the Jordan, just out of the confines of Judea. He was followed, wherever he went, by crowds of people, whom he instructed as usual, ᵃ and cured of their diseases.|

§ 94.—*A Female Cured of Spinal Paral'ysis.*

(Pere'a; [latter part of *February ?*] A. D. 29.)

¹⁰ [In the course of this itinerancy,] as Jesus   **Luke XIII.** was teaching one sabbath in a synagogue of that ——————— region, ¹¹ there chanced to be present a woman afflicted by demoniacal influence with a nervous weakness in the back, of eighteen years' continuance, which had bent her body together to such a degree that she was totally unable to stand erect. ¹² Seeing the invalid, Jesus compassionately said to her, "Woman, I pronounce you cured of your disease!" ¹³ at the same time laying his restoring hand upon her. Instantly she was enabled to stand up straight, and poured forth her acknowledgments to God for her cure. ¹⁴ The President of the Synagogue, however, vexed at Jesus for having effected the cure on the sabbath, [yet not daring to reprehend him directly,] told the people in a scolding tone, "There are six working days in the week, during which all kinds of labor must be performed; if you wish to receive cures, apply on one of those days, and not on the sabbath." ¹⁵ To this bigoted reflection upon himself, Jesus replied, "What a hypocritical direction! is not every one of you in the habit of letting your beasts of burden out of their stalls on the sabbath, and driving them to the watering-place? ¹⁶ Was it not much more suitable, then, for me to release this female,— [not merely of a higher order of creation, but of the highest class of human beings,] a descendant of Abraham,—crippled by a Satanic spell these eighteen years, from her physical dis-

a Matt. xix, 2.

lo, these eighteen years, be loosed from LUKE XIII.
this bond on the sabbath-day ? ¹⁷ And
when he had said these things, all his adversaries were
ashamed : and all the people rejoiced for all the glorious things that were done by him.

§ 95.—*Christ Sets out leisurely for Jerusalem, Teaching on the Way.*

(Pere'a ; [close of *February ?*] A. D. 29.)

²² And he went through the cities and villages,
teaching and journeying toward Jerusalem. ²³ Then
said one unto him, Lord, are there few that be saved ?
And he said unto them, ²⁴ Strive to enter in at the
strait gate : [MATT. VII, 14] because strait is the gate, and narrow is the way, which leadeth unto life, and few there be that
find it ; [13] for wide is the gate, and broad is the way, that
leadeth to destruction, and many there be which go in thereat.
For many, I say unto you, will seek to enter in, and
shall not be able : ²⁵ when once the Master of the house
is risen up and hath shut to the door, and ye begin to
stand without and to knock at the door, saying, Lord,
Lord, open unto us ; and he shall answer and say unto
you, I know you not whence ye are. ²⁶ Then shall
ye begin to say, We have eaten and drunk in thy presence, and thou hast taught in our streets : [MATT. VII, 22]
Lord, Lord, have we not prophesied in thy name? and in thy
name have cast out devils? and in thy name done many wonderful works? ²⁷ But he shall say, I tell you, I know
you not whence ye are ; depart from me, all ye work-
ers of iniquity. ²⁸ There shall be weeping and gnashing of teeth, when ye shall see Abraham and Isaac and
Jacob and all the prophets, in the kingdom of God, and
you yourselves thrust out : ²⁹ and they shall come
from the east and from the west and from the north
and from the south, and shall sit down in the kingdom

126

ability on the sabbath?" [17] Refuted by this rejoinder, his opponents hung their heads in confusion, while the people unanimously expressed their gladness at this another of his signal achievements.

LUKE XIII.

§ 95.—*Christ Sets out leisurely for Jerusalem, Teaching on the Way.*

(Pere'a; [close of *February ?*] A. D. 29.)

[22] Jesus now directed his course toward Jerusalem, [still keeping on the eastern side of the Jordan, and] publicly instructing the inhabitants of the towns and villages in his route. [23] On one of these occasions, he was accosted by a querulous hearer with this question, "Sir, are [we to infer from your statements, that] only a few [of our chosen people] are to be participants in the immunities of the Messiah's Reign'?" [Without deigning to gratify directly the curiosity of this inquiry,] Jesus exhorted all those around him in the following terms: [24] "[Your great concern should be, to] strain every nerve [so to advance in the path of the divine requirements], that you may individually gain admission through that narrow portal; *a* for the lane by which the mansion of eternal felicity is approached, is hemmed in [by God's restrictive rules], and the very entrance to that access is contracted [to the close dimensions of His commands],—so that comparatively few of you, I fear, will search out that narrow passage!; *b* while on the other hand, a spacious avenue with wide-spread gates conducts to the abode of perdition, and crowds, alas! turn from the highway of human life into that fatal thoroughfare. Yes, numbers [of your deluded countrymen, I warn you,] will eventually [essay, with fond self-righteous hopes, to] claim admittance to the sacred residence of final bliss, but without success; [25] for from the decisive hour, when [at the close of each one's day of earthly probation,] the divine Proprietor shall rise [from his seat of hospitable invitation to his festive board,] and bolt the door [as at nightfall against all tardy guests], thereafter though you [with too late repentance should arrive for entertainment, and] standing outside commence to rap for admission, with the familiar address, 'Dear Sir, open the door, we pray you, to let us in!' yet will He disdain your entreaties with the cool reply, 'I wish no acquaintance with such unseasonable comers!' [26] [In your application to me] *c* at that solemn day of adjudication, you [who now reject me] may attempt to claim [my recognition by pleading as well-known friends, 'But, dear Sir, do not hesitate to admit us; do you not recollect we used to be on intimate terms with you?]—we have taken many a meal with you, and [are your countrymen who] have often heard you discourse publicly in our streets;' *c* yes, [some of you may perhaps represent yourselves as my actual followers,] declaring, 'Why, Master, by your authority we were formerly enabled to utter prophecies, exorcise demons, and effect a variety of miracles; [surely you will not now exclude us!]' [27] But such intruders will only hear the Master-of-the-house say from within, 'I tell you, I believe not a word of your pretensions. Begone; you are bent on mischief!'—*d* for I will then [be your inexorable Judge, and] repudiate any acquaintance or company with all you that practice unholiness. [28] At that rejection, [great will be your disappointment]—so bitter as to be expressed only by the tears of despair and teeth ground together in anguish,—when you behold [29] the myriads of redeemed saints assembling from all quarters of the earth, and reclining at the banquet of endless delight in the 'Reign

a Matt. vii, 14.   *b* Matt. vii, 13.   *c* Matt. vii, 22.   *d* Matt. vii, 23.

of God ; [MATT. VIII, 12] but the children of the LUKE XIII.
kingdom shall be cast out into outer darkness:
³⁰ and behold, there are last, which shall be first ; and
there are first, which shall be last.

§ 96.—*The Insidious Warning against Herod.*

(Pere'a; [close of *February ?*] A. D. 29.)

³¹ The same day there came certain of the Phari-
sees saying unto him, Get thee out and depart hence ;
for Herod will kill thee. ³² And he said unto them,
Go ye and tell that *fox*, Behold, I cast out devils and
I do cures to-day and to-morrow, and the third day I
shall be perfected ; ³³ nevertheless, I must walk to-
day and to-morrow and the day following; for it cannot be that a prophet perish out of Jerusalem.

§ 97.—*While Taking a Meal with an eminent Pharisee, Christ Cures a Dropsical Patient, and Discourses to the Company concerning Modesty, Charity, and the necessity of a Prompt Compliance with
the Offers of the Gospel.*

(Pere'a; [beginning of *March ?*] A. D. 29.)

¹ And it came to pass, as he went into **Luke XIV.**
the house of one of the chief Pharisees to
eat bread on the sabbath-day, that they watched him.
² And behold, there was a certain man before him
which had the dropsy : ³ and Jesus answering spake
unto the lawyers and Pharisees, saying, Is it lawful to
heal on the sabbath-day ? ⁴ And they held their peace.
And he took him and healed him, and let him go :
⁵ and answered them saying, Which of you shall have
an ass or an ox fallen into a pit, and will not straightway pull him out on the sabbath-day ? ⁶ And they
could not answer him again to these things.

127

of the Divine Messiah,' [28] in company with all the   LUKE XIII.
holy patriarchs and prophets; while you, *a* the ex-
pectant heirs of that ' Reign ' by national selection, |
will yourselves be excluded from its mansion for your present im-
penitence *a* into the out-door darkness of privation. | [30] Yes, mark
you this, that [in the moral discriminations and awards of that
period,] the relative position of many of you [Jews with respect to
Gentiles,] will be precisely reversed as to the favor of God!''

§ 96.—*The Insidious Warning against Herod.*

(Pere'a ; [close of *February* ?] A. D. 29.)

[31] On the same day with the above discourse, a party of Pharisaical emissaries [of Herod An'tipas, who was jealous of Jesus's
popularity,] came to him with this hypocritical advice, "You had
better make haste out of Herod's territory, for he is concerting your
death." [Aware of their artifice,] Jesus replied, "Just go back and
tell that *fox*, that [he need not put himself to such trouble to get
rid of so inoffensive a person as I; for] I am only going to expel
demons and cure diseases a day or two longer in his dominions, and
after a very limited time I am about to finish my career. [33] But I
shall have a few days yet in which to continue my itinerancy; for
it is scarcely possible for any prophet to perish elsewhere than in
Jerusalem!"

§ 97.—*While Taking a Meal with an eminent Pharisee, Christ Cures a Dropsical Patient, and Discourses to the Company concerning Modesty, Charity, and the necessity of a Prompt Compliance with the Offers of the Gospel.*

(Pere'a ; [beginning of *March* ?] A. D. 29.)

[1] Having accepted an invitation tendered him one   Luke XIV.
sabbath [in the course of this journey,] by one of the
managers of the synagogue of the town where he
chanced to be, who was a Pharisee, to take a place at his board in
company with his host's associates, who closely watched his movements [with the desire of detecting some ground of disparage-
ment], [2] Jesus noticed a man afflicted with the dropsy, [who had
silently placed himself in his view, in hopes of a cure. [3] Aware of
this captious state of mind,] Jesus accosted the Pharisaical Jurists
about him with this question, "Is it allowable to cure a disease on
the sabbath?" [4] They, however, [fearful of committing themselves
by an answer that might be refuted,] made no reply. Jesus, therefore, touching the invalid, cured him, and then dismissed him.
[5] He now turned to the company with this answer to his own question, "Suppose one of you had a beast of burden that should fall
into a well-pit on the sabbath, would he not immediately extricate
it?" [6] His opponents were unable to object a word of reply to this
vindication of his conduct.

a Matt. viii, 12.

127*

⁷ And he put forth a parable to those   LUKE XIV.
which were bidden, when he marked how
'they chose out the chief rooms; saying unto them,
⁸ When thou art bidden of any man to a wedding, sit
not down in the highest room; lest a more honorable
man than thou be bidden of him, ⁹ and he that bade
thee and him, come and say to thee, Give this man
place, and thou begin with shame to take the lowest
room : ¹⁰ but when thou art bidden, go and sit down in
the lowest room; that when he that bade thee cometh,
he may say unto thee, Friend, go up higher : then
shalt thou have worship in the presence of them that
sit at meat with thee : ¹¹ for whosoever exalteth himself shall be abased, and he that humbleth himself shall
be exalted.   ¹² Then said he also to him that bade
him, When thou makest a dinner or a supper, call not
thy friends nor thy brethren neither thy kinsmen nor
thy rich neighbors; lest they also bid thee again, and
a recompense be made thee; ¹³ but when thou makest
a feast, call the poor, the maimed, the lame, the blind ;
¹⁴ and thou shalt be blessed; for they cannot recompense thee, for thou shalt be recompensed at the resurrection of the just.

¹⁵ And when one of them that sat at meat with
him heard these things, he said unto him, Blessed
is he that shall eat bread in the kingdom of God.
¹ And Jesus answered and spake unto   Matt. XXII.
them again by parables, and said, ² The
kingdom of heaven is like unto a certain king, which
made a marriage for his son, [LUKE XIV, 16] and bade many;
³ and sent forth his servants [LUKE XIV, 17] at supper-time,
to call them that were bidden to the wedding : and
they would not come.   ⁴ Again he sent forth other
servants saying, Tell them which are bidden, Behold,
I have prepared my dinner; my oxen and my fatlings
are killed, and all things are ready : come unto the
128

⁷Observing how anxious the guests were to   Luke XIV.
select the most honorable positions at the table,   ——————
Jesus addressed to them this maxim, ⁸ "When
you are invited by any one hereafter to a festive banquet,
never recline in the most conspicuous place, lest a more distinguished guest than yourself be invited, ⁹ and your host
should come and tell you, "Make room for this gentleman at
the head of the table;' and thus you be obliged to surrender
your place, and submit to the mortification of taking a less
honorable one. ¹⁰ But on being invited, do you rather go to
the foot of the table and there recline, so that when your host
enters the room, he may say to you, 'Friend, you are entitled
to a place farther up;' and thus you will secure the respect
of your fellow guests. ¹¹ [For in this as in all other matters,
a man is sure to find at last his proper level,] assuming vanity
being depressed, while retiring worth is elevated."

¹² He next turned to the host with this advice, "For the
future, when you prepare a convivial meal, rather than invite
your friends, relatives and wealthy neighbors, in the prospect
of their returning you the favor, ¹³ do you call in beggars,
cripples, lame and blind persons; ¹⁴ and your genuine benevolence will then be blessed with the assurance, that, although
these penniless persons cannot repay you themselves, yet you
will be rewarded when the righteous dead shall rise to their
eternal bliss."

¹⁵ Here one of the auditors at the table exclaimed [with
affected piety], "Yes, happy indeed are we [Jews], who are
privileged with the assurance of sharing in that feast under
the 'Reign of the Divine Messiah,' [both here
and hereafter!" ¹ With the design of correct-   **Matt. XXII.**
ing this self-complacent bigotry,] Jesus replied   ——————
by the following illustration [of the dealings of God with
their nation]: ² "The 'Reign of the Divine Messiah' may be
compared to the case of some king, who makes a sumptuous
feast at his son's wedding, ³ and sends his domestics around
with *a* numerous| invitations to his guests. But on their de-
clining the first call, ⁴ he sends other domestics *b* at the ap-
pointed hour,| to importune them with the more special mes-
sage, 'I assure you, my feast is all ready, with its dressed
bullocks and fatlings; do not delay to attend the wedding
festivities.' *c* The guests, however, as if by concert, still beg

---

a Luke xiv, 16.   *b* Luke xiv, 17.   *c* Luke xiv, 18.

marriage.   5 But [Luke XIV, 18] they all with   MATT. **XXII.**
one consent began to make excuse: the first
said unto him, I have bought a piece of ground, and I must
needs go and see it; I pray thee have me excused; [19] and
another said, I have bought five yoke of oxen, and I go to prove
them; I pray thee have me excused; [20] and another said, I
have married a wife, and therefore I cannot come: so they
made light of it, and went their ways, one to his farm,
another to his merchandise; 6 and the remnant took his
servants, and entreated them spitefully, and slew them.
7 But when the king heard thereof, he was wroth; and
he sent forth his armies, and destroyed those murderers, and burned up their city.   8 Then saith he to his
servants, The wedding is ready; but they which were
bidden were not worthy: 9 go ye therefore into the
highways, and as many as ye shall find, [Luke XIV, 21] the
poor and the maimed and the halt and the blind, bid to the
marriage.   [Luke XIV, 22] And the servant said, Lord, it is done
as thou hast commanded, and yet there is room.   [23] And the
lord said unto the servant, Go out into the highways and
hedges, and compel them to come in; that my house may be
filled.   10 So those servants went out into the highways,
and gathered together all as many as they found, both
bad and good; and the wedding was furnished with
guests.   11 And when the king came in to see the
guests, he saw there a man which had not on a wedding-garment: 12 and he saith unto him, Friend, how
camest thou in hither, not having a wedding-garment?
And he was speechless.   13 Then said the king to the
servants, Bind him hand and foot, and take him away
and cast him into outer darkness: there shall be weeping and gnashing of teeth.   14 For many are called,
but few are chosen.

129

to be excused, one assigning as his apology, MATT. **XXII.**
that ' he is just about purchasing a farm, and
is obliged to visit it immediately,' | *a* another,
that ' he has just engaged` five yoke of oxen, and has to go
and try them,' | *b* and another, that ' he is just celebrating his
nuptials, and therefore cannot leave home ;' | [5] and with these
pretexts, they carelessly go about their private concerns ;—
[6] while the rest of the invited carry their insult so far as to
seize the messengers, and maltreat and even kill them.   [7] At
the report of those of his servants who escape, the enraged
sovereign dispatches his troops instantly, who take summary
vengeance on the murderers, ravaging their city with fire and
sword.   [8] He then says to his domestics, ' My feast is all ready,
but the unworthy guests who slighted my invitations, shall
not *c* taste a morsel of it; | [9] do you therefore *d* hasten | out
into the thoroughfares *d* as well as lanes of the city, | and call
in *d* here | to the festival all the *d* beggars, cripples, lame and
blind | that you can meet with.' *e* The servants returning
with the report that their ' master's orders are obeyed, but
that there is still room to spare,' | *f* he then directs them to
' go out once more into the highways as well as hedged paths
around the city, and *insist* upon the coming in of all they
find ;' | [10] so they sally forth and gather together all the home-
less creatures that they come across, good and bad promiscu-
ously, till the house is at length filled with guests.—[11] Suppose now the king on entering the banquet-room to greet his
guests, should espy a fellow there, who has neglected to array
himself in the appropriate marriage-dress [provided from the
royal wardrobe for all] ; [12] he would at once ask him, ' Sirrah !
what business have you in here, without the nuptial apparel
on ?'   The wretch has not a word of excuse to offer ; [13] so the
monarch bids his attendants, ' Here, bind this intruder hand ·
and foot, and then take and hurl him into the darkness out
of doors !'—there will his doom be one of anguish expressible
only by tears and grated teeth ! [14] For many," concluded
Jesus, " are the guests· *invited* to the feast of the ' Messiah's
Reign,' but comparatively few of them are its finally selected
participants."

a Luke xiv, 19.   *b* Luke xiv, 20.   *c* Luke xiv, 24.
d Luke xiv, 21.   *e* Luke xiv, 22.   *f* Luke xiv, 23.

§ 98.—*Resolute Self-denial Requisite for true Discipleship.*

(Pere'a; [early in *March ?*] A. D. 29.)

25 And there went great multitudes with **Luke XIV.**
him : and he turned and said unto them,
26 If any man come to me, and hate not his father and
mother and wife and children and brethren and sisters,
yea, and his own life also, he cannot be my disciple.
28 For which of you intending to build a tower, sitteth
not down first and counteth the cost, whether he have
sufficient to finish it ?　29 lest haply after he hath laid
the foundation, and is not able to finish it, all that behold it begin to mock him 30 saying, This man began
to build, and was not able to finish.　31 Or what king
going to make war against another king, sitteth not
down first and consulteth, whether he be able with ten
thousand to meet him that cometh against him with
twenty thousand ?　32 or else while the other is yet a
great way off, he sendeth an embassage and desireth
conditions of peace.　33 So likewise whosoever he be
of you that forsaketh not all that he hath, he cannot be
my disciple.—35 He that hath ears to hear, let him
hear.

§ 99.—*The Gospel specially Seeks to Reclaim those that are Conscious of their Alienation from God.*

(Pere'a; [early in *March ?*] A. D. 29.)

1 Then drew near unto him all the publi- **Luke XV.**
cans and sinners, for to hear him : 2 and
the Pharisees and scribes murmured saying, This
man receiveth sinners, and eateth with them.
10 And he answered, For the Son of man **Luke XIX.**
is come to seek and to save that which
130

§ 98.—*Resolute Self-denial Requisite for true Discipleship.*

(Pere'a; [early in *March ?*] A. D. 29.)

·25 As Jesus proceeded on his journey, attended by **Luke XIV.**
vast crowds of seeming devotees, he turned to them
with this admonition: 26 "If any person undertakes
to be my disciple, without holding in subordination [to the devotion due to me and my cause,] his affection for all his earthly relatives even the dearest,—yes, and his concern for his own life itself;
he cannot become my *a* genuine[1] follower. 28 [Draw a lesson from
the forethought of common life:] Suppose one of you were design-
ing to erect a country-seat; would he not previously sit down ·[to
his writing-tablet,] and calculate the probable cost, so as to ascertain whether he could command funds enough for the purpose?
29 [Certainly;] for he would be anxious to avoid the mortification
of being obliged to leave the work uncompleted through a failure
of means, after [he had committed himself by] laying the foundation, and then having every passer-by jeer him as they behold the
monument of his folly. 30 'This simpleton began to build a house,
but could not finish it!' 31 On the same principle [of precaution],
if some king were on the eve of marching to engage in battle with
a hostile prince, should he not calmly deliberate first, whether with
his army of, say, ten thousand men he is in adequate force to encounter his antagonist, who is at the head, it may be, of a body of
twenty thousand? 32 and in case he finds his troops insufficient,
then, long before he meets his rival, he dispatches ambassadors to
him, suing for terms of peace. 33 In imitation of this spirit of
prudence," concluded Jesus, "let no one of you 35 (for I wish 'every
one who has ears, to hear' and apply this advice to himself) 33 attempt to become my disciple, who has not fully made up his mind
to renounce all his most cherished possessions, [should they come
into conflict with his duty toward me.]"

§ 99.—*The Gospel specially Seeks to Reclaim those that are Conscious of their Alienation from God.*

(Pere'a; [early in *March ?*] A. D. 29.)

1 [Advancing a little farther,] Jesus was surrounded **Luke XV.**
by all the "Publicans" and similar flagitious characters of the region, eager to listen to his instructions.
2 His attention to these persons so offended the fastidious bigotry
of the Pharisaical Scribes standing near, that they whispered scoffingly to each other, "This loose-principled teacher does not scruple
to admit the vilest wretches to his audience, and even associate
with them at meals [and in other familiar relations!" 3 From the as-
persion couched under this remark,] Jesus vindicated
himself by the following reply: 10 "[And very prop- **Luke XIX.**
erly,] for the 'Son of Man's' express errand to earth
is, to seek after and rescue the sinful race of man from the spiritual

a Matt. x, 37.

was lost.   ³ And he spake this parable unto   **Luke XV.**
them saying, ⁴ What man of you having a
hundred sheep, if he lose one of them, doth not leave
the ninety and nine in the wilderness, and go after that
which is lost, until he find it ? ⁵ and when he hath
found it, he layeth it on his shoulders, rejoicing.
⁶ And when he cometh home, he calleth together his
friends and neighbors saying unto them, Rejoice with
me ; for I have found my sheep which was lost : ⁷ I
say unto you, that likewise joy shall be in heaven
over one sinner that repenteth, more than over ninety
and nine just persons which need no repentance ;
[MATT. XVIII, 14] even so it is not the will of your Father which
is in heaven, that one of these little ones should perish.
⁸ Either what woman having ten pieces of silver, if
she lose one piece, doth not light a candle, and sweep
the house, and seek diligently till she find it ?   ⁹ And
when she hath found it, she calleth her friends and her
neighbors together saying, Rejoice with me, for I have
found the piece which I had lost : ¹⁰ likewise I say
unto you, There is joy in the presence of the angels
of God over one sinner that repenteth.

¹¹ And he said, A certain man had two sons : ¹² and
the younger of them said to his father, Father, give
me the portion of goods that falleth to me ; and he
divided unto them his living.   ¹³ And not many days
after, the younger son gathered all together and took
his journey into a far country, and there wasted his
substance with riotous living : ¹⁴ and when he had
spent all, there arose a mighty famine in that land ;
and he began to be in want.   ¹⁵ And he went and
joined himself to a citizen of that country ; and he
sent him into his fields to feed swine : ¹⁶ and he would
fain have filled himself with the husks that the swine
did eat ; and no man gave unto him.   ¹⁷ And when he
came to himself, he said, How many hired servants of

exposure into which they have erred. ³ᵃ Just imagine   **Luke XV.**
your own feelings! (to employ a comparison), ⁴ if one
of you should own a hundred sheep, and one of them
were to ᵃ stray away! and get lost; would he not [as soon as he
missed it,] leave the ninety-nine others on the spot, even though
in an uninhabited plain destitute of protection, and hasten away
ᵃ to the surrounding hills, ! to hunt up the fugitive? ⁵ And when
he succeeds in finding it, ᵇ I warrant you, ! he secures it from future
wandering by laying it on his shoulder, with a heart filled with a
ᵇ keener delight on account of its recovery, than he feels even for
the possession of the ninety-nine that did not stray; ! ⁶ and on
reaching his home, he assembles all his friends and neighbors,
[who had heard of his loss,] with these joyful tidings, 'Be glad
with me, for I have found my lost sheep!' ⁷,¹⁰ In like manner, I
assure you, there is a thrill of joy pervading the angelic residents
of heaven on account of a single penitent sinner, that seems to
eclipse even the complacency experienced toward a multitude of
persons whose holy lives call for no reformation; ᶜ nor is my Heavenly Father willing that any one, even so insignificant as these
'Publicans,' should perish [without an effort to retrieve him.!
⁸ The same interest in behalf of men's souls, may also be illustrated
by the case of] a woman, who chances to mislay one of ten
drachmas [i. e. a silver coin current for about 15 cents] that she
had ; does she not light a lamp, sweep her house all over, and
search into every crevice and corner with the utmost assiduity, till
she finds it ? ⁹ and then with what delight does she call upon all
her female friends and neighbors to 'rejoice with her for the recovery of her lost money !' "
  ¹¹ [To exhibit more clearly the injustice of the Pharisees, prejudice at his concern for the spiritual welfare of the lower classes,]
Jesus proceeded with the following illustration: "A certain wealthy
farmer had two sons, ¹² the younger of whom, on attaining adult
age, said to him, 'Father, I wish you would make over to me in
advance the share of your property which is entailed to me as an
inheritance, [and let me try my fortune with it.]' So the indulgent parent divided his estate between them, [the elder son still
remaining with his father as before.] ¹³ In a few days, the younger
son converted all his property into cash, and traveled into a foreign
country, where he soon dissipated it in profligacy. ¹⁴ Having thus
squandered all his fortune, a severe famine occurred in the region
where he was, which still further drained his resources; ¹⁵ and [in
the extremity of his destitution,] he was at last compelled to hire
himself out to a resident of the town, who sent him to the degrading
employment of feeding his swine in the country. ¹⁶ Here he [was
so ill-fed himself, that he] would many a time gladly have ap-
peased the cravings of hunger with the very *carob*-pods that formed
the provender of the hogs; but his rigorous master denied him
even this pitiful privilege. ¹⁷ At length the poor wretch, sobered
by his affliction, [came to his senses as to the deplorable condition
to which he had reduced himself by his vicious excesses, and with
penitent regret for his folly,] thus reflected: 'How many hired
men in my father's employ have a superabundance of food, while I

ᵃ Matt. xviii, 12.   ᵇ Matt. xviii, 13.   ᶜ Matt. xviii, 14.

131*

my father's have bread enough and to   LUKE XV.
spare, and I perish with hunger!   ¹⁸ I will
arise and go to my father, and will say unto him,
Father, I have sinned against Heaven and before
thee, ¹⁹ and am no more worthy to be called thy son ;
make me as one of thy hired servants.   ²⁰ And he
arose and came to his father : but when he was yet a
great way off, his father saw him, and had compassion
and ran and fell on his neck and kissed him.   ²¹ And
the son said unto him, Father, I have sinned against
Heaven and in thy sight, and am no more worthy to
be called thy son.   ²² But the father said to his servants, Bring forth the best robe and put it on him, and
put a ring on his hand and shoes on his feet ;   ²³ and
bring hither the fatted calf and kill it, and let us eat
and be merry :   ²⁴ for this my son was dead, and is
alive again ; he was lost, and is found : and they began to be merry.   ²⁵ Now his elder son was in the
field ; and as he came and drew nigh to the house, he
heard music and dancing :   ²⁶ and he called one of the
servants, and asked what these things meant.   ²⁷ And
he said unto him, Thy brother is come ; and thy father
hath killed the fatted calf, because he hath received
him safe and sound.   ²⁸ And he was angry and would
not go in ; therefore came his father out and entreated
him.   ²⁹ And he answering said to his father, Lo, these
many years do I serve thee, neither transgressed I at
any time thy commandment and yet thou never gavest
me a *kid*, that I might make merry with my friends :
³⁰ but as soon as this thy son was come, which hath
devoured thy living with harlots, thou hast killed for
him the fatted calf.   ³¹ And he said unto him, Son,
thou art ever with me, and all that I have is thine ;
³² it was meet that we should make merry and be glad :
for this thy brother was dead, and is alive again ; and
was lost, and is found.

132

am here starving to death! ¹⁸ I will instantly LUKE XV.
start for home, and frame my entreaties to my
father, [when I reach him, in these words, which
he surely cannot reject,] "Father, I have acted wickedly toward God in neglecting to observe your parting admonitions!
¹⁹ and by my disobedient profligacy I have unfitted myself to
be regarded as your son; I only beg you will treat me as one
of your hired men."' ²⁰ Accordingly he returned to his father, who caught a glimpse of him in the distance, and with
compassion [at his altered appearance,] hastened to meet him,
embracing him in his arms and kissing him with paternal
fondness. ²¹ The humbled son began his premeditated confession, ²² but the father [gladdened by his unhoped-for return, interrupted him in the care of supplying his evident
wants, and] bade his domestics, 'Bring the choice robe out
of the house, and put it on him, and fetch a ring for his finger,
and sandals for his feet; ²³ and then run and take the fat calf
out of the stall and dress it, and we will have a merry feast:
²⁴ for this is my long-lost son just returned,—after I had given
him up for dead, it is as if he had come to life again!'
²⁵ While they were thus rejoicing, the elder son, who had
been out in the field at work, on coming near the house,
heard unusual sounds, as if of a musical concert and dancing
in token of some joyful occurrence; ²⁶ so calling one of the
domestics, he asked him 'what it all meant?' ²⁷ 'Why,' rejoined the servant, 'your brother has arrived, and your father
has slaughtered the fat calf for a sumptuous meal, because he
has got back safe and sound.' ²⁸ At this news, the elder
brother was offended [on account of the attention shown the
new comer], and sulkily kept out of the house; so that presently his father came out and invited him in. ²⁹ He then
peevishly replied to his father's solicitation, '*I* have been now
working for you so many years, without ever disobeying you,
and yet you never gave me so much as a kid for a feast with
my friends; ³⁰ but no sooner has this young scape-grace arrived, after having swallowed up his patrimony in debauchery,
than you slaughter the fat calf for his entertainment!' ³¹ 'My
dear son,' soothingly returned the father, 'I constantly enjoy
your company at home, and all my property is at your service
[as my heir]; ³² but it is suitable to the peculiar joyfulness
of the occasion, for me to make a feast with special hilarity,
when this your long-lost brother, whom we had thought to be
dead, has returned to us alive.'"

132*

§ 100.—*The Prudence of securing God's Favor by a Devout use of the Privileges of Life.*

(Pere'a; [early in *March?*] A. D. 29.)

[1] And he said also unto his disciples, **Luke XVI.** There was a certain rich man which had a steward; and the same was accused unto him, that he had wasted his goods. [2] And he called him and said unto him, How is it that I hear this of thee? give an account of thy stewardship; for thou mayest be no longer steward. [3] Then the steward said within himself, What shall I do? for my lord taketh away from me the stewardship: I cannot dig; to beg I am ashamed.—[4] I am resolved what to do, that when I am put out of the stewardship, they may receive me into their houses. [5] So he called every one of his lord's debtors unto him, and said unto the first, How much owest thou unto my lord? [6] And he said, A hundred measures of oil. And he said unto him, Take thy bill, and sit down quickly, and write *fifty*. [7] Then said he to another, And how much owest thou? And he said, A hundred measures of wheat. And he said unto him, Take thy bill, and write *fourscore*.—[8] And the lord commended the unjust steward, because he had done wisely; for the children of this world are in their generation wiser than the children of light: [9] and I say unto *you*, Make to yourselves friends of the mammon of unrighteousness; that when ye fail, they may receive you into everlasting habitations. [10] He that is faithful in that which is least, is faithful also in much; and he that is unjust in the least, is unjust also in much; [11] if therefore ye have not been faithful in the unrighteous mammon, who will commit to your trust the true riches? [12] and if ye have not been faithful in that which is another man's, who shall give you

133

§ 100.—*The Prudence of securing God's Favor by a Devout use of the Privileges of Life.*

(Pere'a ; [early in *March ?*] A. D. 29.)

[1] [After having thus vindicated his concern for the   **Luke XVI.**
salvation of the " Publicans,"] Jesus now turned to
his followers with this lesson, [drawn from the thrifty
though iniquitous policy of that class :] "A certain wealthy person
had a steward against whom one [of his other domestics] brought
him the accusation, that he was squandering his employer's property by embezzlement. [2] On receiving this information, his master
summoned him with this stern demand, 'What rascality is this I
hear concerning your administration? Make out a full account of
your stewardship; you must vacate that office immediately.' [3] [As-
tounded by this summary ejection,] the steward deliberated thus,
'What business shall I take up, now that my employer removes
me from my office? I have not the strength to dig for a livelihood;
[I have no trade,] and should have to beg my bread, which is too
shameful to think of.—[4] [A thought strikes me, and] I'll try the
project instantly; so that when I am turned out of my stewardship, I shall have some friends to welcome me to their homes.'
[5] Accordingly, summoning each of his master's debtors separately,
he asked the first, 'How much do you owe my employer?' [6] The
man replied, 'One hundred *baths* [i. e. about 900 gallons] of olive-
oil.' 'Well,' returned the steward, 'just sit down here and sign
your obligation to pay *fifty*.' [7] He then reduced another's debt, in
like manner, from one hundred *cors* [i. e. about 1450 bushels] of
grain to eighty, [and so on with the rest of the debtors. [8] Being
subsequently informed of this artifice on the part of the steward,]
his master was struck with the fellow's ingenuity, villanous as it
was, in thus managing to secure himself friends. In this way it
is," proceeded Jesus, " that mere wordly men evince oftentimes
greater tact than the subjects of divine instruction, in their respective designs. [9] I therefore enjoin upon you, [especially the
affluent 'Publicans' among you,] to secure friends now, by a religious appropriation of your wealth—too often the gains of dis-
honesty,—who may welcome you to the hospitality of their everlasting mansions, when your earthly resources shall have failed
you. [10] Now one that shows a prudent fidelity [—unlike the per-
fidy of the steward, though resembling his cunning reserva-
tion of means—] in the disbursement of a small amount, will be
equally discreet in the discharge of a more important trust, and
if he is recreant to an inferior confidence, he will be so to the
greater one; [11] therefore if at the day of final awards, you be found
faithless to the deposit of the spurious wealth of earth, [—instead
of striving, by its scrupulous devotion to pious interests, to show
your sorrow for its unholy acquisition,—] will you be likely to be
intrusted with the genuine riches of the skies? [12] nay, if you prove
treacherous [—like the dishonest steward—] to Another's estate,
[committed to your charge as trustees of the divine conferments,]
will you be presented with property of *your own* [to take care of,

133*

that which is your own ? ^{13} No servant   LUKE XVI.
can serve two masters : for either he will
hate the one, and love the other ; or else he will hold
to the one, and despise the other : ye cannot serve
God and mammon.

§ 101.—*Salvation not connected with Wealth.*

(Pere'a ; [early in *March ?*] A. D. 29.)

^{14} And the Pharisees also, who were covetous, heard
all these things ; and they derided him. ^{15} And he
said unto them, Ye are they which justify yourselves
before men ; but God knoweth your hearts : for that
which is highly esteemed among men, is abomination
in the sight of God.—^{19} There was a certain rich man,
which was clothed in purple and fine linen, and fared
sumptuously every day : ^{20} and there was a certain
beggar named Lazarus, which was laid at his gate, full
of sores, ^{21} and desiring to be fed with the crumbs
which fell from the rich man's table ; moreover the
dogs came and licked his sores. ^{22} And it came to
pass that the beggar died, and was carried by the
angels into Abraham's bosom.   The rich man also
died, and was buried ; ^{23} and in hell he lifted up his
eyes, being in torments, and seeth Abraham afar off
and Lazarus in his bosom : ^{24} and he cried and said,
Father Abraham, have mercy on me, and send Lazarus that he may dip the tip of his finger in water, and
cool my tongue ; for I am tormented in this flame.
^{25} But Abraham said, Son, remember that thou in thy
life-time receivedst thy good things, and likewise
Lazarus evil things ; but now he is comforted, and
thou art tormented : ^{26} and besides all this, between
us and you there is a great gulf fixed ; so that they
which would pass from hence to you, cannot ; neither
can they pass to us, that would come from thence.

134

in the inalienable possessions of eternity? [13] From
this entire illustration," concluded Jesus, "you may
moreover derive this lesson, that] as it is impossible LUKE XVI.
for any domestic to serve with ardor two masters at the same time,
—because he will of necessity revolt at the commands of one, while
he cheerfully executes the opposite requirements of the other; or
at least he will diligently effect the purposes of the latter, and
merely hurry through those of the former in a slighting way;—
so it is equally out of the question for you to become the genuine
servants of God, while you are votaries at heart of the idol of
wealth."

§ 101.—*Salvation not Connected with Wealth.*

(Pere'a; [early in *March ?*] A. D. 29.]

[14] This discourse on the subordinate use of riches was overheard
by the Pharisees standing near, who, in order to screen their own
avaricious character, indulged in open derision of its author. [15] Jesus therefore addressed to them this reproof, "*You* are always ready
to assert yourselves blameless in the eyes of God, but that Being is
intimately acquainted with the iniquity of your hearts; and thus
the objects of human applause are often the most offensive to
God."
[19] [Jesus then proceeded to illustrate still further the true religious position of the different classes of his hearers by the following
case:] "Let us take a certain opulent individual [as a fair instance
of earthly regard], who reveled in all the luxury of magnificent
paraphernalia of purple *byssus* [i. e. a peculiar cotton, of silk-like
fineness,] and splendid banquets daily; [20] and contrast with his the
case of a certain indigent person by the name of Lazarus, who was
carried in a helpless ulcerous condition to the portal of his rich
neighbor's palace [as a favorable resort for alms]—[21] glad to swallow
the fragments that were left from the feasts within, while [his only
physicians were] the stray dogs [that in return for a share of his
scanty meal,] dressed his sores with their tongues. [22] Soon the diseased mendicant was released from his earthly sufferings, and [though
his absence was scarcely noticed perhaps among men, yet] angels escorted his spirit to the society of Abraham in bliss. Shortly afterward
the rich man too met the same lot of mortals, and his burial was celebrated with pompous mourning: [23] but far different was his condition
in the other world,—there he lifted his eyes amid the agony of perdition, and beheld Abraham far removed from him, and Lazarus in
honored company with the beatified patriarch. [24] Then he begged
aloud, 'Father Abraham, in pity to me send Lazarus, if but to moisten
the tip of his finger and cool my tongue parched by these fiery torments of *Hadès*' [i. e. the place of departed spirits among the an-
cients]. [25] But Abraham decliningly bade him, 'Recollect, my once-
termed child, that you received all the blessings you could desire during your life-time, while Lazarus suffered severe privations; but now
[the just award balances your fortunes,—] he is solaced [with immortal bliss, the meed of patient piety], while you are anguished
[with the deserved doom of irreligious prodigality]. [26] Nor is the
relief you crave practicable; there is a wide chasm interposed by
the Almighty's decree between our respective regions [i. e. between
Paradise, the abode of the righteous, and *Gehen'na*, the flaming
dungeon of the wicked; in the intermediate *Hadès* of the Jews],

²⁷ Then he said, I pray thee therefore,　LUKE XVI.
father, that thou wouldest send him to my
father's house: ²⁸ for I have five brethren; that he
may testify unto them, lest they also come into this
place of torment. ²⁹ Abraham saith unto him, They
have Moses and the prophets; let them hear them.
³⁰ And he said, Nay, father Abraham, but if one went
unto them from the dead, they will repent. ³¹ And he
said unto him, If they hear not Moses and the prophets, neither will they be persuaded, though one rose
from the dead.

§ 102.—*The Messiah already come.*

(Pere'a; [former part of *March ?*] A. D. 29.)

²⁰ And when he was demanded of the　**Luke XVII.**
Pharisees, when the kingdom of God
should come, he answered them and said, The kingdom of God cometh not with observation; ²¹ neither
shall they say, Lo here! or, Lo there! for behold, the
kingdom of God is *within* you.

§ 103.—*Perseverance and Humility in Prayer.*

(Pere'a; [former part of *March ?*] A. D. 29.)

¹ And he spake a parable unto them to　**Luke XVIII.**
this end, that men ought always to pray
and not to faint; ² saying, There was in a city a judge,
which feared not God, neither regarded man: ³ and
there was a widow in that city; and she came unto
him saying, Avenge me of mine adversary. ⁴ And he
would not for a while: but afterward he said within
himself, Though I fear not God nor regard man, ⁵ yet
because this widow troubleth me, I will avenge her;
lest by her continual coming she weary me. ⁶ And
the Lord said, Hear what the unjust judge saith; ⁷ and
shall not *God* avenge his own elect, which cry day and

impassable to those on either side.' ²⁷ 'Then I im-   LUKE XVI.
plore you,' continued the hopeless wretch in his address, 'at least to dispatch him ²⁸ to warn the five
brothers whom I left ²⁷ at home, ²⁸ that they may avoid this region
of torment, [by a different line of moral conduct from myself.]'
²⁹ The sainted patriarch replied, 'They have warnings enough in
the writings of Moses and the prophets; let them heed *their* admonitions.' ³⁰ [Dreading their hapless company,] the miserable being
still urged, 'Alas! father Abraham, I fear they will disregard those
monitions like myself; but were one to revisit them from the grave,
they would surely repent at his warning.' ³¹ But Abraham thus cut
off his importunity, 'If they heed not the Scriptures, they would
not be convinced of their danger, even if one *should* rise from the
grave to warn them!'"

§ 102.—*The Messiah already come.*

(Pere'a; [former part of *March ?*] A. D. 29.)

²⁰ Shortly afterward, being asked by a knot of   **Luke XVII.**
Pharisees, who still dogged his steps, "when the
'Reign of the Divine Messiah' was to be ushered in,
[which he had been so long intimating?]" Jesus replied, "Cease
to imagine that his 'Reign' is to be introduced with the emblazoned
parade of earthly royalty, ²¹ or that occasion will be given for [am-
bitious partisans to proclaim the progress of his triumphal career
through the land by] shouting, '[Rally to the Messiah's standard!]
Here is his camp pitched! Yonder city has yielded to his prowess!'
—no; mark what I say, the 'Messiah's Reign' has *already* begun
unheeded in your very midst."

§ 103.—*Perseverance and Humility in Prayer.*

(Pere'a; [former part of *March ?*] A. D. 29.)

¹ [In the course of the instruction which Jesus   **Luke XVIII.**
was now improving every moment to impress upon
his disciples' minds,] he made use of the following
illustration to enforce the duty of praying with undiscouraged assiduity [for relief from persecution]: ² "There was a magistrate in
a certain town, who was [of such unblushing corruption as to
seem] neither actuated in his public and private conduct by a reverence for God nor respect for the rights of men; ³ and there was
also in the same place a widow, who had occasion to resort to
him with this petition, 'Will your highness vindicate my cause
against the unjust charge of my prosecutor at law?' ⁴ For a while
he refused to redress her wrong, but at last he thus reflected, 'To
be sure, everybody knows that I do not care a straw for equity
either human or divine; ⁵ but still I had better render this woman
satisfaction, to escape being plagued by her perpetually teasing
me.' ⁶ Observe now," continued Jesus, "the conclusion of even
the iniquitous magistrate; ⁷ and will not *God*, then, [the righteous
Judge of the universe,] see that justice is done His maltreated saints,
[the special objects of His favor,] when they entreat Him with
persevering earnestness?—even though he seem to protract their

night unto him, though he bear long   LUKE **XVIII.**
with them? ⁸ I tell you that he will
avenge them speedily.—Nevertheless when the Son
of man cometh, shall he find faith on the earth?

⁹ And he spake this parable unto certain which
trusted in themselves that they were righteous, and
despised others : ¹⁰ Two men went up into the temple
to pray; the one a Pharisee, and the other a publican.
¹¹ The Pharisee stood and prayed thus with himself,
God, I thank thee, that I am not as other men are, extortioners, unjust, adulterers, or even as this publican :
¹² I fast twice in the week, I give tithes of all that I
possess. ¹³ And the publican, standing afar off, would
not lift up so much as his eyes unto heaven, but smote
upon his breast saying, God be merciful to me a sinner. ¹⁴ I tell you, this man went down to his house
justified rather than the other : for every one that exalteth himself, shall be abased ; and he that humbleth
himself, shall be exalted.

§ 104.—*The Doctrine of Divorce.*

(Pere'a; [former part of *March?*] A. D. 29.)

³ The Pharisees also came unto him,   **Matt. XIX.**
tempting him and saying unto him, Is it
lawful for a man to put away his wife for every cause?
⁴ And he answered and said unto them, Have ye not
read,* that he which made them at the beginning,
made them male and female, ⁵ and said,† For this
cause shall a man leave father and mother, and shall
cleave to his wife ; and they twain shall be one flesh?
⁵ wherefore they are no more twain, but one flesh.
What therefore *God* hath joined together, let not *man*
put asunder. ⁷ They say unto him, Why did *Moses*
then command‡ to give a writing of divorcement, and

---

* Gen. i, 27.   † Gen. ii, 24.   ‡ Deut. xxiv, 1.

deliverance. ⁸ I assure you, He *will* execute con-   LUKE **XVIII.**
dign redress on their behalf.—Yet, [despite this
prospect of requital,] I fear that when the 'Son of
Man' appears [in his vindictive providence, to inflict the threatened
retribution], He will find but few in this hardened land, possessed
of faith [enough to save them from the terrible fate of the im-
penitent] !''

⁹ Then turning to a number [of Pharisees] who stood near, he
exposed their presumptuous self-righteousness, which led them to
look with sovereign contempt upon the moral character of others;
by the following illustration [of the appropriate temper of prayer]:
¹⁰ ''Two men once entered the [Israelites' Court of the] Temple to
perform their devotions, one of whom was a Pharisee, while the
other was a 'Publican.' ¹¹ The former in proud prominence stood
up to pray [virtually if not literally in the following strain of self-
complacent superciliousness]: 'O God, I praise Thee that I am not
of the sinful character of other men, being neither extortionate,
dishonest, unchaste, nor vile like yonder ''Publican!'' ¹² I fast
strictly twice a week [i. e. on Mondays and Thursdays], and pay
tithes of all my property and income. ✿ ✿ ✿' ¹³ The poor 'Publican,' on the contrary, modestly took his station in some obscure
corner of the sacred court, and scarcely venturing through conscious unworthiness to lift his eyes toward heaven, he struck his
hand upon his breast in deep contrition, penitently ejaculating, 'O
God, have mercy upon my sinful soul!' ¹⁴ I assure you, the latter
worshiper returned home absolved by the divine approval instead of
the other; for 'arrogant vanity is sure to be depressed to its proper
level of contempt, while unassuming merit is elevated in honor.' ''

§ 104.—*The Doctrine of Divorce.*

(Pere'a; [former part of *March ?*] A. D. 29.)

³ [During this journey of Jesus,] some of the at-   **Matt. XIX.**
tendant Pharisees proposed this insidious question to
him, '' Is it allowable for a husband to divorce his
wife for any slight pretext?'' ⁴ Jesus replied, ''Have you never
read in the Mosaic account, that man's Creator formed originally
a single male and a single female of the race, ⁵ and pronounced
the decree, that 'for this reason [the mutual dependence of the
sexes], a man will quit even his parents' society, and adhere with
affectionate association to his wife, [their interests being so identi-
fied] that they shall be regarded as one and the same person?'
⁶ Thus [after union by marriage], they no longer remain two iso-
lated individuals, but constitute a social unit for all the affairs of
life; and therefore let no human authority presume for trivial
reasons to sever those whom the *Almighty* has so solemnly united!''
⁷ '' Why then,'' rejoined the Pharisees, ''did Moses [under the divine
sanction] enact, that a man might dismiss his wife by simply giving

U   136*

to put her away?   ⁸ He saith unto them,   MATT. XIX.
Moses, because of the hardness of your
hearts, suffered you to put away your wives; but from
the beginning it was not so. ⁹ And I say unto you,
Whosoever shall put away his wife, except it be for
adultery, and shall marry another, committeth adultery; and whoso marrieth her which is put away, doth
commit adultery; [MARK X, 12] and if a woman shall put
away her husband, and be married to another, she committeth
adultery.

[10] And in the house ¹⁰ his disciples say unto him, If
the case of the man be so with his wife, it is not good
to marry. · ¹¹ But he said unto them, All men cannot
receive this saying, save they to whom it is given:
¹² for there are some eunuchs, which were so born;
and there are some, which were made so of men; and
there be some, which have made themselves so for
the kingdom of heaven's sake: he that is able to receive it, let him receive it.

§ 105.—*Commendatory Reception of Infants.*

(Pere'a; [former part of *March ?*] A. D. 29.)

¹³ And they brought young children to   **Mark X.**
him, that he should touch them [MATT. XIX, 13]
and pray: and his disciples rebuked those that brought
them. ¹⁴ But when Jesus saw it, he was much displeased, and [LUKE XVIII, 16] called them unto him and said
unto them, Suffer the little children to come unto me,
and forbid them not: for of such is the kingdom of
God; ¹⁵ verily I say unto you, Whosoever shall not
receive the kingdom of God as a little child, he shall
not enter therein. ¹⁶ And he took them up in his arms,
put his hands upon them and blessed them; [MATT. XIX, 15]
and departed thence.

137

her a certificate of divorcement?"　[8] "Moses,"　**MATT. XIX.**
returned Jesus, " allowed your nation to divorce
wives in this manner, because it was [one of
their deep-rooted customs to do so in a more arbitrary way,
which they clung to with such tenacious prejudice, that they
would have rebelled at its abrogation entirely, in] their de-
graded inability to appreciate a more humane regulation; but
such was not the primeval conception [of the marriage-bond
on the part of its great Designer].　[9] Therefore I now declare
to you, [in the true construction of the matrimonial relation,]
that whoever repudiates his wife for any other than the sole
cause of conjugal infidelity, and then marries another woman,
commits adultery; and whoever marries a woman so divorced, is
equally guilty of the same crime, [a] as is also the woman herself.l"
　[10] [b] When the disciples were alone in the house with their
Master,l they renewed the discussion by remarking with [b] inquiring surprise,l "If this be the unalterable arrangement
of wedlock, it is unsafe to marry at all, [as a man would
be without resource against deception in his wife.]"　[11] "It
is not every person," replied Jesus, "that is capable of the
continence which you prescribe; but few have the faculty of
complete celibacy.　[12] Some men are naturally incapable of
marriage; others are so by human barbarity; while a third
class voluntarily undergo this deprivation, in order to give
their untrammeled attention to the promotion of the [f] Reign
of the Divine Messiah.'　My religion [does not insist upon
abstinence from the connubial state, but] merely permits
those to submit to the privation, who are constitutionally or
religiously adapted to it."

§ 105.—*Commendatory Reception of Infants.*

(Pere'a; [former part of *March ?*] A. D. 29.)

　[13] [c] About the same time,l some parents [who had　**Mark X.**
great faith in the holiness of Jesus's character,] presented to him their [d] youngl children, in order to secure the virtue of an imposition of his hands [c] and the blessing of
his prayers;l but the disciples [on witnessing what they deemed
an idle act of concern for those so young,] repelled them with the
charge of intrusion.　[14] Jesus, however, reprovingly bade his
hasty disciples, "Let the children approach me without hin-
drance, for of characters gentle and simple-hearted as those in-
nocents is the 'Reign of the Divine Messiah' to be composed;
[15] and I solemnly assure you, that unless a person be initiated
into it with the tender docility of a babe, he will never share
its privileges."　[16] Then, after folding them in his arms, and
pronouncing his benediction upon their infantile spirits, as he
placed his hand upon their little heads [in token of guardian
influence], [e] he proceeded on his journey.l

a Mark x, 12.　*b* Mark x, 10.　*c* Matt. xix, 13.　*d* Luke xviii, 15.　*e* Matt xix, 15.

§ 106.—*The Visit of a Rich Young Man leads Christ to Discourse on the Prejudicial influence of Wealth upon Piety, and the Rewards of Self-Denying Exertions in Religious Duty.*

(Pere'a; [second week in] *March;* A. D. 29.)

¹⁷ And when he was gone forth into the   MARK X.
way, there came [LUKE XVIII, 18] a certain ruler
running and kneeled to him, and asked him, Good
Master, what [MATT. XIX, 16] good thing shall I do that I
may inherit eternal life ?   ¹⁸ And Jesus said unto him,
Why callest thou me *good?* there is none good but
one, that is, God. [MATT. XIX, 17] But if thou wilt enter into
life, ¹⁹ thou knowest the commandments.*   [MATT. XIX, 18]
He saith unto him, Which? Jesus said, Do not commit
adultery, Do not kill, Do not steal, Do not bear false-
witness, Defraud not, Honor thy father and mother ;
[MATT. XIX, 19] and, Thou shalt love thy neighbor as thyself.
²⁰ And he answered and said unto him, Master, all
these *have* I observed from my youth [MATT. XIX, 20] up;
what lack I yet?   ²¹ Then Jesus beholding him loved
him, and said unto him, One thing thou lackest:
[MATT. XIX, 21] if thou wilt be perfect, go thy way, sell whatsoever thou hast, and give to the poor, and thou shalt
have treasure in heaven ; and come, take up the cross,
and follow me.   ²² And he was sad at that saying, and
went away grieved : for he had great possessions.
²³ And when Jesus [LUKE XVIII, 24] saw that he was very sor-
rowful, he looked round about, and saith unto his disciples, How hardly shall they that have riches enter into
the kingdom of God !   ²⁴ And the disciples were astonished at his words. But Jesus answereth again and
saith unto them, Children, how hard is it for them that

---

* Exod. xx, 12-17; Levit. xix, 18.

§ 106.—*The Visit of a Rich Young Man leads Christ to Discourse on the Prejudicial influence of Wealth upon Piety, and the Rewards of Self-Denying Exertions in Religious Duty.*

(Pere'a; [second week in] *March;* A. D. 29.)

[17] While Jesus was prosecuting his route, a cer-　MARK X.
tain *a* distinguished member of the Jewish hier-
archy,| [a comparatively young man for that
honor,] came running toward him, and prostrating himself
reverently before him, made this inquiry, "Most excellent
Teacher, I wish to be informed, what *b* specially conducive
ordinance| I must observe, in order to attain immortal bless-
edness the most certainly?" [18] [To this flattering address,]
Jesus replied, "Why do you apply so unrestricted an epithet
to me? there is no being who is ' *excellent*' [in the absolute
sense], except God Himself." [19] He then referred him to the
religious observance of the divine commands, *c* as the ap-
pointed mode of attaining his desire.| *d* "But which of these,"
rejoined the other,| [" am I to regard as chiefly important?"]
" I mean particularly those of the Decalogue," returned Jesus,
citing a number of its commandments, *e* and annexing the
great injunction of universal *humanity* as the crowning duty
toward one's fellow-men.| [20] The inquirer pleaded, "I *have*
strictly obeyed all these precepts from my earliest youth;
f what then is there still deficient in my preparation?"|
[21] Casting an admiring look at him, *g* on hearing this| [ingen-
uous offer to comply with any further requirement, which
nevertheless betrayed a large degree of misconception as to
his own character and request], Jesus blandly told him, "There
g yet| exists a capital defect in your devotion of yourself to
God: *h* in order to be complete in this respect,| you must at
once sell *h* all| your property, and bestow it in charity,—thus
exchanging it for the truer wealth of celestial bliss; then you
must carry out your self-consecration to religion by becoming
my exclusive disciple, even at the risk of your life." [22] [Un-
prepared for so stern a condition,] the seeker retired with a
dejected air at the disappointment of his fond hopes; for he
could not make up his mind to part with the extensive property which he owned.

[23] Jesus now turned to his disciples, and improved the incident, by remarking, "With what difficulty can the wealthy
become members of the ' Reign of the Divine Messiah!' "
[24] Seeing his disciples astonished [by understanding the declaration as totally exclusive], Jesus explained himself further
[by varying the expression], "How difficult it is to induce
those who rely upon wealth [with tenacious cupidity as the

a Luke xviii, 18.　　*b* Matt. xix, 16.　　*c* Matt. xix, 17.　　*d* Matt. xix, 18.
e Matt. xix, 19.　　*f* Matt. xix, 20.　　*g* Luke xviii, 22.　　*h* Matt. xix, 21.

138*

trust in riches to enter into the kingdom   **MARK X.**
of God ! ²⁵ it is easier for a camel to go
through the eye of a needle, than for a rich man to
enter into the kingdom of God.   ²⁶ And they were
astonished out of measure, saying among themselves,
Who then can be saved ?   ²⁷ And Jesus looking upon
them saith, With men it is impossible, but not with
God ; for with God all things are possible.

²⁸ Then Peter began to say unto him, Lo, *we* have
left all, and have followed thee ; [MATT. XIX, 27] what shall
we have therefore ?   ²⁹ And Jesus answered and said,
Verily I say unto you, ²⁸ That ye which   **Matt. XIX.**
have followed me, in the *regeneration* when
the Son of man shall sit in the throne of his glory, ye
also shall sit upon twelve thrones, judging the twelve
tribes of Israel.: ²⁹ and every one that hath forsaken
houses or brethren or sisters or father or mother or wife
or children or lands for my name's sake [MARK X, 29] and
the gospel's, shall receive a hundred-fold [MARK X, 30] now
in this time, houses and brethren and sisters and mothers and
children and lands with persecutions, and shall inherit everlasting life [MARK X, 30] in the world to come.

⁷ But which of you having a servant   **Luke XVII.**
plowing or feeding cattle, will say unto
him by and by, when he is come from the field, Go
and sit down to meat ; ⁸ and will not rather say unto
him, Make ready wherewith I may sup, and gird thyself and serve me, till *I* have eaten and drunken ; and
afterward *thou* shalt eat and drink ?   ⁹ Doth he thank
that servant, because he did the things that were commanded him ?   I trow not.   ¹⁰ So likewise *ye*, when
ye shall have done all those things which are commanded you, say, We are unprofitable servants ; we
have done that which was our duty to do.

¹ For the kingdom of heaven is like unto   **Matt. XX.**
a man that is a householder, which went out
139

source of happiness], to comply with the terms of ad- **Mark X.**
mission under the 'Messiah's Reign.'   25 I pronounce
it 'an easier matter to thrust the huge body of a *camel*
through a *needle's* eye,' than to get a rich man of such a disposition
into that 'Reign.'"   26 *a* The disciples still more astonished [at
hearing this seeming asseveration of utter impossibility], exclaimed
to each other, "What [rich person, or indeed almost any] one, can
expect, then, to attain this salvation? 27 Jesus assured them with
an impressive look, "To *human* ability it is indeed impracticable;
but the task does not exceed the influence of the Almighty to accomplish."

28 Here Peter, [in the consciousness of being at least untrammeled by this disqualification,] accosted his Master thus, "*We* your
chosen disciples have at all events relinquished our little earthly all
to attend upon your steps; *b* what remuneration shall we receive! [in
the apportionment of the favors of your 'Reign?']"

29 Jesus replied, "I assure you, that you, 28 who have **Matt. XIX.**
thus attached yourselves to me, will be rewarded for
all your sacrifices—in the [sequel of that scheme of moral resuscitation which is being provided for the Jewish nation, and which
will be consummated at the physical] renovation of mankind, when
the 'Son of Man' will assume his glorious throne of adjudication,—
by being yourselves likewise seated, as it were, on the twelve
thrones of [that distinguished bliss to which your apostolical rank
and labors shall have elevated you, an eminence that will exhibit
you as the representatives of the patriarchal] heads of the twelve
tribes of the Israelites.   29 And indeed every one who relinquishes his
earthly relatives and possessions in order to consecrate himself to
my cause, will be abundantly requited for his self-denial [by the
dearer joys of religion] *c* in this life, accompanied though they be
with external persecution, and will hereafter attain immortal
blessedness."

7 [Jesus then proceeded to guard his disciples **Luke XVII.**
against the vein of self-complacency which Peter's
remark discovered, by the following illustration:]
"Suppose one of you had a servant employed in agriculture or attending to cattle; on his returning home from work, would you
tell him, 'You may pass in immediately, and take your meal,' when
you have not yourself eaten? 8 would you not rather bid him, 'Get
my meal ready, and prepare yourself to wait on me while I eat,
and then take your own repast?' 9 The master, I warrant you,
does not feel himself under any obligation to return thanks to the
servant for fulfilling his commands; 10 and on the same principle,
you too, after accomplishing all my service enjoined upon you,
should humbly confess yourselves as 'being servants not entitled to
any special desert, having merely done your duty.'"

1 [These remarks on the subject of the anticipations **Matt. XX.**
of his votaries, Jesus closed by the following illustration, calculated to exhibit the gratuitousness of any
recompense: "The distribution of final awards in] the 'Reign of
the Divine Messiah,' may be compared with the conduct of a land-
holder, who went out early in the morning to hire laborers to work

---

a Matt. xix, 25.   *b* Matt. xix, 27.   *c* Mark x, 30.

early in the morning to hire laborers into   MATT. **XX.**
his vineyard : [2] and when he had agreed
with the laborers for a penny a day, he sent them into his
vineyard.   [3] And he went out about the third hour,
and saw others standing idle in the market-place, [4] and
said unto them, Go ye also into the vineyard ; and
whatsoever is right, I will give you : and they went
their way.   [5] Again he went out about the sixth and
ninth hour, and did likewise.   [6] And about the eleventh
hour he went out and found others standing idle, and
saith unto them, Why stand ye here all the day idle ?
[7] They say unto him, Because no man hath hired us.
He saith unto them, Go ye also into the vineyard ;
and whatsoever is right, that shall ye receive.   [8] So
when even was come, the lord of the vineyard saith
unto his steward, Call the laborers, and give them
their hire, beginning from the last unto the first.
[9] And when they came that were hired about the eleventh hour, they received every man a penny : [10] but
when the first came, they supposed that they should
have received more ; and they likewise received every
man a penny.   [11] And when they had received it, they
murmured against the good-man of the house [12] saying, These last have wrought but one hour, and thou
hast made them equal unto us, which have borne the
burden and heat of the day.   [13] But he answered one
of them and said, Friend, I do thee no wrong; didst
not thou agree with me for a penny ? [14] take that thine
is, and go thy way : I will give unto this last, even as
unto thee ; [15] is it not lawful for me to do what I will
with mine own? is thine eye evil because I am good ?
[16] So [MATT. XIX, 30] many that are the last shall be first, and
the first last : for many be called, but few chosen.

140

in his vineyard ; ² and having bargained with a   MATT. **XX.**
number for a *dena'rius* [i. e. about 15 cents]
per day, he set them to work.   ³ Going out again about
the *third hour* [i. e. 9 o'clock A. M.], he saw some other
workmen standing unemployed in the public square, ⁴ and
engaged them too to work in his vineyard, promising them
' a fair compensation for their work.'   ⁵ In like manner he went
out at the *sixth* and *ninth hours* [i. e. at noon and 3 o'clock
P. M.], and made similar engagements.   ⁶ Finally, going out
about the *eleventh hour* of the day [i. e. at 5 o'clock P. M.],
he found other workmen still standing there, and on asking
them, ' why they were standing there, idle all the day long ?'
⁷ they replied, ' Because no person has hired us ;' so he sent
them too into his vineyard, engaging to ' pay them what was
right for their labor.'   ⁸ After sundown, the proprietor told his
foreman to ' summon the workmen and pay them their wages,
beginning with those last hired, and so proceeding to those
first engaged.'   ⁹ The men who had been hired at the *eleventh
hour*, on coming forward, were paid a *dena'rius* apiece ; ¹⁰ upon
which those who were the first to begin their day's work, expected to be paid more, but they too only got a *dena'rius* each.
¹¹ At this remuneration, they began to complain against the
proprietor, ¹² that ' the last comers, who had worked but a
single hour, were paid an equal amount with themselves, who
had toiled through the whole heat of the day !'   ¹³ But their
employer thus remonstrated with one of them, ' Friend, I am
doing you no wrong ; did you not agree with me at a *dena'rius*
for a day's work?   ¹⁴ Take your wages then, and retire satisfied ; it is my pleasure to pay this last comer just the same
that I give you.   ¹⁵ Have I not a right to act as I choose in
the bestowal of my own money? why then should you grow
envious at my liberality ?'—¹⁶ In a way not unlike this," concluded Jesus, " will *a* many, who may be last [in embracing
my Gospel,] be finally promoted to the first place [in its rewards, on account of their diligence] ; while some that have
been my earliest followers, will come far behind them [by a
failure to improve their precedence] ; for numerous are those
that are invited to the field of labor, but the *approved* candidates for its honors will be comparatively few."

a Matt. xix, 30.

140*

§ 107.—*Christ a third time Predicts his Passion.*

(Pere'a [opposite Jericho?]; [*Friday?*] *March* [11?], A. D. 29.)

³² And they were in the way, going up to   **Mark X.**
Jerusalem; and Jesus went before them:
and they were amazed; and as they followed, they
were afraid.   And he took again the twelve [MATT. XX, 17]
disciples apart in the way, and began to tell them what
things should happen unto him ³³ saying, Behold, we
go up to Jerusalem; [LUKE XVIII, 31] and all things that are
written by the prophets° concerning the Son of man shall be
accomplished: and the Son of man shall be delivered
unto the chief-priests and unto the scribes and they shall
condemn him to death, and shall deliver him to the Gentiles; ³⁴ and they shall mock him [LUKE XVIII, 32] and spitefully entreat him and shall scourge him and shall spit upon
him and shall kill him: and the third day he shall rise
again.   ³⁴ And they understood none of   **Luke XVIII.**
these things; and this saying was hid from
them, neither knew they the things which were spoken.

§ 108.—*The Ambitious Request on the behalf of
James and John.*

(Pere'a [opposite Jericho?]; [*Friday?*] *March* [11?], A. D. 29.)

²⁰ Then came to him the mother of Zebe-   **Matt. XX.**
dee's children with her sons, worshiping
him and desiring a certain thing of him.   ²¹ And he
said unto her, What wilt thou?   She saith unto him,
Grant that these my two sons may sit the one on thy
right hand and the other on the left in thy kingdom.
²² But Jesus answered and said, Ye know not what ye
ask: are ye able to drink of the cup that I shall drink
of, and to be baptized with the baptism that I am baptized with?   They say unto him, We are able.   ²³ And
he saith unto them, Ye shall drink indeed of my cup,

° See especially Isa. liii.

141

§ 107.—*Christ a third time Predicts his Passion.*

(Pere'a [opposite Jericho?]; [*Friday ?*] *March* [11?], A. D. 29.)

[32] As Jesus now more directly bent his steps to-   **Mark X.**
ward Jerusalem, his disciples [apprehensive of danger there awaiting them,] followed their Master in
great alarm, lagging in the rear with astonishment [at his
hardihood in venturing thither. Seeing their timid reluct-
ance], he took the twelve Apostles *a* aside on the road, and
once more informed them of his approaching fate in the following explicit terms : [33] "You perceive we are visiting Jerusalem, *b* where the predictions of the ancient Prophets concerning me are about to be fulfilled. The 'Son of Man' is
soon to be betrayed into the malicious power of the hierarchy,
who will capitally condemn him, and then hand him over to
the Gentile authorities [i. e. the Roman *Proc'urator*], [34] to be
treated with the most shameful mockery, *c* insults and even
spitting upon, and then lashed and put to death *d* by crucifixion : but on the third ensuing day [both ex-
tremes included,] he will revive."—[34] The disci-   **Luke XVIII.**
ples, however, still failed to comprehend their
Master's meaning, their mind being too much obscured [by
preconceived anticipations of an opposite character, to allow
them] to realize the force of these mournful premonitions.

§108.—*The Ambitious Request on the behalf of James and John.*

(Pere'a [opposite Jericho?]); [*Friday ?*] *March* [11?], A. D. 29.)

[20] [On the announcement of this contemplated   **Matt. XX.**
journey of Jesus, Salo'mè,] the mother of *e* James
and John the sons of Zebedee, *e* was instigated
by them, to come to him attended by themselves, and prostrating herself before him urge this petition, *e* "Teacher, I
desire that you would grant me a favor." [21] "What do you
wish me to do for you?" returned he. "That you would
allow these my two sons," said she, "to occupy the chief
posts of honor in your expected monarchy." [22] "Ah !" responded Jesus, "you are little aware how sorrowful a boon
you are asking for your sons. Are you willing," continued he,
addressing them directly, "to quaff the bitter cup [of martyr-
dom] that I am about to drain, and to be overwhelmed with
the trials which I am shortly to undergo ?" "Yes," replied
they inconsiderately, "we will volunteer to share your fortunes." [23] Jesus forbearingly rejoined, "You will indeed be
honored with a slight experience of my hardships ; but I
cannot consistently bestow the honorary emoluments of my

a Matt. xx, 17.   *b* Luke xviii, 31.   *c* Luke xviii, 32.   *d* Matt. xx, 19.   *e* Mark x, 35.

and be baptized with the baptism that I   MATT. **XX.**
am baptized with : but to sit on my right
hand and on my left, is not mine to give, but it shall
be given to them for whom it is prepared of my
Father.

²⁴ And when the ten heard it, they were moved with
indignation against the two brethren.   ²⁵ But Jesus
called them unto him and said, Ye know that the
princes of the Gentiles exercise dominion over them,
and they that are great exercise authority upon them :
²⁶ but it shall not be so among *you ;* but whosoever
will be great among you, let him be your minister ;
²⁷ and whosoever will be chief among you, let him be
your servant : ²⁸ even as the Son of man came not to
be ministered unto, but to minister, and to give his life
a ransom for many.

§ 109.—*Two Blind Men Cured.*

(Jericho ; [*Friday ?*] *March* [11 ?], A. D. 29.)

⁴⁶ And they came [LUKE XVIII, 35] nigh to   **Mark X.**
Jericho ; [LUKE XIX, 1] and Jesus entered and
passed through it.   And as he went out of Jericho with
his disciples and a great number of people, blind Bar-
timeus the son of Timeus [MATT. XX, 30] and another blind
man sat by the highway-side begging : ⁴⁷ and when
they heard [LUKE XVIII, 36] the multitude pass by, they asked
what it meant.   [³⁷] And when they told them that it was
Jesus of Nazareth, they began to cry out and say,
Jesus, thou son of David, have mercy on us.   ⁴⁸ And
many [LUKE XVIII, 39] which went before charged them, that
they should hold their peace : but they cried the more
a great deal, Thou son of David, have mercy on us.
⁴⁹ And Jesus stood still and commanded them to be
called ; and they call the blind men saying unto them,
Be of good comfort, rise ; he calleth you.   ⁵⁰ And they,

142 .

'Reign,' otherwise than [upon those faithful ad- MATT. XX.
herents for whose finally-approved qualifica-
tions] the meed is reserved in my Heavenly Father's plan of rewards."

²⁴ The ten other Apostles who listened to this request, were
highly incensed at the two brothers, [who had preferred it for
the sake of gaining the supremacy;] ²⁵ and Jesus, noticing
their displeasure, called them around him, and thus lectured
them all on the subject: "Among heathen nations, you know,
potentates rule their subjects with despotic sway, and those
in high station are anxious to display their authority over in-
feriors. ²⁶, ²⁷ But such a lordly spirit must not exist in the
bosom of your fraternal society; on the contrary, whoever
aims to be chief and foremost among you, must seek for eminence [in his brethren's affection, and superiority in service-
ableness to them], by becoming the most ready to subserve
their wants and wishes: ²⁸ thus imitating the example of
your Master the 'Son of Man,' who has himself visited the
earth, not to be the pampered object of menial attendance,
but to serve the vital interests of mankind, by devoting himself as a sacrificial ransom for the forfeited souls of the wide
world."

§ 109.—*Two Blind Men Cured.*

(Jericho; [*Friday ?*] *March* [11 ?], A. D. 29.)

⁴⁶ The travelers now [crossed the Jordan, and]   **Mark X.**
were approaching the city of Jericho, ᵃ through
which they passed I [without stopping]. As Jesus
was leaving the city with his disciples, accompanied by a large
crowd [whom his arrival had attracted], ᵇ two I blind men,
one [of whom was a well-known character], "blind Bar-
Time'us" (i. e. *Time'us's Son* [a Hebrew patronym'ic]), were
sitting along the road begging; ⁴⁷ and hearing ᶜ the sound of
an unusual crowd passing by, they asked some one "what
was its occasion?" I ᵈ Being informed I that "'Jesus the Nazarene' was passing by," [of whose fame they had learned,]
they set up an imploring shout, ᵇ "Master I Jesus, 'Heir of
David,' compassionate our case I" ⁴⁸ The ᵉ crowd I ᶠ that went
ahead I contemptuously told them to cease their clamor; but
they vociferated still the more resolutely, "'Heir of David,' in
pity relieve us!" ⁴⁹ [On arriving opposite the spot,] Jesus
halted and ordered the suppliants to be ᵍ brought to him; I
accordingly his attendants went to the blind men, and summoned them with this kind invitation, "Take courage and
rise; he is calling you!" ⁵⁰ So the poor fellows throwing off
their tattered robes, [to be unimpeded in their steps, got up

---

ᵃ Luke xix, 1.   ᵇ Matt. xx, 30.   ᶜ Luke xviii, 36.   ᵈ Luke xviii, 37.
ᵉ Matt. xx, 31.   ᶠ Luke xviii, 39.   ᵍ Luke xviii, 40.

casting away their garments, rose and came   MARK X.
to Jesus. ⁵¹ And Jesus answered and said   ——————
unto them, What will ye that I should do unto you?
The blind men said unto him, Lord, that we might receive our sight.   ⁵² And Jesus [MATT. XX, 34] had compassion on them, and touched their eyes: and said unto them,
[LUKE XVIII, 42] Receive your sight: go your way ; your faith
hath made you whole.   And immediately they received
their sight, and followed Jesus in the way, [LUKE XVIII, 43]
glorifying God: and all the people, when they saw it, gave.
praise unto God.

§ 110.—*The Visit at Zacche'us's House, and Dis-*
course on Religious Fidelity.

(Western suburbs of Jericho; [*Friday* evening to *Sunday* morning?] *March* [11–13?], A. D. 29.)

 ² And behold, there was a man named   **Luke XIX.**
Zaccheus, which was the chief among the   _
publicans, and he was rich.   ³ And he sought to see
Jesus who he was ; and could not for the press, because he was little of stature : ⁴ and he ran before and
climbed up into a sycamore-tree to see him ; for he
was to pass that way.   ⁵ And when Jesus came to the
place, he looked up and saw him, and said unto him,
Zaccheus, make haste and come down ; for to-day I
must abide at thy house.   ⁶ And he made haste and
came down, and received him joyfully.   ⁷ And when
they saw it, they all murmured saying, That he was
gone to be guest with a man that is a sinner.   ⁸ And
Zaccheus stood and said unto the Lord, Behold, Lord,
the half of my goods I give to the poor ; and if I have
taken anything from any man by false accusation, I
restore him fourfold.   ⁹ And Jesus said unto him, This
day is salvation come to this house, forasmuch as he
also is a son of Abraham.

 ¹¹ And as they heard these things, he added and
143

and made their way to Jesus. ⁵¹ He then asked them, **MARK X..**
"What do you wish of me?"　"O honored Sir," replied
they, "we pray you to enable us to see!"　⁵² *a* Com--
miserating their hapless lot,ǀ Jesus *a* touched their eyes,ǀ telling
them, "You may retire *b* restored ;ǀ your faith has been the means
of your gaining your eye-sight."　Instantly they were enabled to
exercise perfect vision; and [overwhelmed with gratitude, they]
followed their benefactor along the road, *c* praising God for their
cure, as did also all the crowd who witnessed it.ǀ

§ 110.—*The Visit at Zacche'us's House, and Discourse on Religious Fidelity.*

(Western suburbs of Jericho ; [*Friday* evening to *Sunday* morning ?] *March* [11–13 ?],
A. D. 29.)

　²[As Jesus was proceeding through the outskirts　**Luke XIX.**
of the city of Jericho,] a certain wealthy Receiver-
General of the Roman tribute, Zacche'us by name,
³ being very anxious to become acquainted by sight with the great
Teacher [concerning whom he had heard so much], but failing to
catch a glimpse of him through the crowd on account of his own
diminutive stature, ⁴ ran some distance in advance along the road
by which Jesus was about to leave [the city], and climbed up a
sycamore-tree, in order to get a fair sight of him.　⁵ On reaching
the spot, Jesus casting his eye up into the tree, espied Zacche'us;
and [being divinely aware of his favorable disposition,] called out
to him, "Zacche'us, make haste down out of the tree, [and conduct me to your home!]　I am purposed to make you a visit for the
[rest of the] day."　⁶ Accordingly, Zacche'us descended with joyful
expedition, eager to welcome so revered a guest to his hospitality:
⁷ The aristocratic bystanders, however, all indulged in ill-suppressed
sneers, at Jesus's having " put up at the house of a person of so infamous a profession !"　⁸ [This invidious reflection having reached
his ears,] Zacche'us made the following generous proposal of amend-
ment to his newly-adopted Master, [near whom he stood listening
to his instructions, after the introductory offices of hospitality were
over, "In proof of my sincerity in embracing your doctrines]
Teacher, I here offer to bestow one-half of my property upon the
destitute ; and if any person can show that I have ever extorted
anything from him by unfairness in official dealings, I pledge myself
to indemnify him to four times the amount."　⁹ [Struck with the
frank devotion of his host, and to rebut the calumnious scoff of the
proud Pharisees,] Jesus declared in his presence, "This very day
has this family attained deliverance from their sins; for I pronounce
this its head reinstated as a genuine descendant of Abraham."
　¹¹ Perceiving that these remarks [on the immediate blessing of
his host,] excited in the minds of his listening followers the anticipation that his "Reign" was on the eve of being ushered in [with
regal demonstrations,] Jesus annexed the following illustration,
[for the purpose of dissipating such an inference,] to which his
present approach to Jerusalem might [otherwise seem to give some

a Matt. xx, 34.　　*b* Luke xviii, 42.　　*c* Luke xviii, 43.

143*

spake a parable, because he was nigh to   LUKE XIX.
Jerusalem, and because they thought that
the kingdom of God should immediately appear : ¹²he
said therefore, A certain nobleman went into a far
country to receive for himself a kingdom, and to return : ¹³ and he called his ten servants, and delivered
them [MATT. XXV, 14] his goods : [15] and unto one he gave five
talents, to another two, and to another one ; (to every man according to his several ability;) and said unto them, Occupy
till I come : [MATT. XXV, 16] and straightway took his journey.
¹⁴ But his citizens hated him, and sent a message after
him saying, We will not have this man to reign over
us.   [MATT. XXV, 16] Then he that had received the five talents,
went and traded with the same, and made them other five
talents ; [17] and likewise he that had received two, he also
gained other two : [18] but he that had received one, went and
digged in the earth, and hid his lord's money.   ¹⁵ And it
came to pass, that [MATT. XXV, 19] after a long time when he
was returned, having received the kingdom, then he
commanded these servants to be called unto him, to
whom he had given the money, that he might know
how much every man had gained by trading.   ¹⁶ Then
came the first [MATT. XXV, 20] that had received five talents,
saying, Lord, thy five talents have gained ten talents.
¹⁷ And he said unto him, Well, thou good servant ; because thou hast been faithful in a very little, [MATT. XXV, 21]
I will make thee ruler over many things : enter thou into the
joy of thy lord ; have thou authority over ten cities.
¹⁸ And the second [MATT. XXV, 22] that had received two talents came and said, Lord, thou deliveredst unto me two talents;
behold, I have gained two other talents besides them.   ¹⁹ And
he said likewise to him, [MATT. XXV, 23] Well done, good and
faithful servant ; thou hast been faithful over a few things, I
will make thee ruler over many things : enter thou into the
joy of thy lord ; be thou also over five cities.   ²⁰ And
another [MATT. XXV, 24] which had received the one talent came

144

countenance, as if about to] be a designed occa-   LUKE XIX.
sion : [12] "A certain Person of princely lineage,"
said he, " undertook a journey to a distant country for the purpose of being invested with the rank of royalty
[accruing to him], and of then returning [to take possession
of the kingdom thus confirmed to him]. [13] Accordingly, summoning several of his principal officers, he intrusted each of
them with a sum of money [a] in proportion to their respective
capacities! [for managing property, say], to one [a] five! *minœ*
[i. e. about $77,] [a] to another two [i. e. about $31], and to the
rest a single *mina* [i. e. about $15] apiece ;! at the same time
giving them this charge, ' Employ this deposit in business, till
I return.' [14] After his departure, a number of ill-affected citizens sent a deputation to follow him [to the seat of the supreme government], with representations that ' they were extremely solicitous not to have him appointed as their king ;'
but he pursued his errand, and succeeded in securing his title
to the throne. [15] On his return [b] after a considerable period
of absence,! he ordered his officers, to whom he had committed the several sums, to be summoned before him, to render their [b] account of the investment of the funds.! [16] Accordingly, the principal agent, on appearing in his presence,
reported himself thus, [c] with the cash in his hand,! ' Master,
with the [c] five! *minœ* which you intrusted to my discretion, I
have gained in trade [c] five! more, as you may see ;' [17] to which
the Prince replied, ' Well done ! you are an industrious minister; and as you have been faithful in discharging a slight
trust, [d] I will honor you with a greater one ; you shall par-
ticipate the joyful elevation of your Master in dignity,! by
being promoted to the viceroyship of ten cities in my realms.'
[18] Then came the next in order of capital, and reported a
corresponding profit of [e] two additional! *minœ ;* [19] which account met a like gracious acceptance from his Master, and
was rewarded with the principality of that number of other
cities. [20] Lastly appeared one of those who had received a
single *mina* in charge, who muttered out the following state-

---

a Matt. xxv, 15.   *b* Matt. xxv, 19.   *c* Matt. xxv, 20.
     d Matt. xxv, 21.   *e* Matt. xxv, 22.

V   144*

saying, Lord, behold here is thy talent, Luke XIX.
which I have kept laid up in a napkin
[Matt. XXV, 25] in the earth: ²¹ for I feared thee, because
[Matt. XXV, 24] I knew thee that thou art an austere man; thou
takest up that thou layedst not down, and reapest that
thou didst not sow. ²² And he saith unto him, Out of
thine own mouth will I judge thee, thou wicked
[Matt. XXV, 26] and slothful servant: thou knewest that I
was an austere man, taking up that I laid not down, and
reaping that I did not sow? ²³ Wherefore then gavest
not thou my money into the bank, that at my coming I
might have required mine own with usury? ²⁴ And
he said unto them that stood by, Take from him the
talent, and give it to him that hath ten talents; ²⁵(and
they said unto him, Lord, he *hath* ten talents:) ²⁶ for
I say unto you, That unto every one which hath, shall
be given, [Matt. XXV, 29] and he shall have abundance; and
from him that hath not, even that he hath shall be
taken away from him: [Matt. XXV, 30] and cast ye the unprofitable servant into outer darkness; there shall be weeping
and gnashing of teeth. ²⁷ But those mine enemies, which
would not that I should reign over them, bring hither
and slay them before me.

²⁸ And when he had thus spoken; he went before,
ascending up to Jerusalem.

§ 111.—*Christ's Arrival and Feast at Bethany.*

(*Sunday, March* 13, A. D. 29.)

⁵⁵ And the Jews' passover was nigh at　**John XI.**
hand: and many went out of the country up
to Jerusalem before the passover, to purify themselves.
⁵⁶ Then sought they for Jesus, and spake among them-
selves, as they stood in the temple, What think ye?
that he will not come to the feast? ⁵⁷ Now both the
chief-priests and the Pharisees had given a command-

145

ment of his proceedings, 'Master, [21] I was aware   LUKE XIX.
of your crabbed temper, as being a person likely
to "pick up what you never placed in the spot,"
and "reap a field that you did not sow;" I was therefore apprehensive lest you might exact too rigorously of me, [20] and
have kept your identical money safely wrapped up in a napkin
[a] and concealed from theft in a hole under ground.| Here is
the *mina* that belongs to you, [without loss or change.]'
[22] 'Faithless varlet,' replied the Master, 'I will convict your
slothful treachery from your own surly statements; acquainted
with my griping disposition, were you!—[23] then why did you
not seek to conciliate me, by diligently putting out my money
on interest at the broker's, so that on coming back, I might
get what I committed to you, together with its avails?' [24] He
then directed the bystanding officers, 'Take away the *mina*
from this lazy menial, and bestow it upon the possessor of the
ten *minæ;*' [25] and in answer to their remonstrative suggestion,
'Master, *he* seems already to have enough without this largess,'
[26] the Sovereign vindicated his procedure by declaring [as the
fixed policy of his administration], 'Whoever makes a good
use of the faculties and advantages he has, shall be rewarded
with an extra bounty; but he that neglects to improve his
trust, will be deprived of all.' [27] [He then proceeded to inflict due retribution, by bidding his attendants,] [b] 'Seize yonder worthless wretch, and plunge him into the gloomy exile
[of perdition], where bitter wails and teeth grated in despair
will be his endless portion;| and as for those inimical citizens
who opposed my elevation to royalty, drag them in here, and
execute them before my eyes.'"
[28] Having spent the day [succeeding his arrival] in such
discourses as these, Jesus left the hospitable mansion of Zacche'us [on the second morning], to proceed on his journey to
Jerusalem.

§ 111.—*Christ's Arrival and Feast at Bethany.*

(*Sunday, March* 13, A. D. 29.)

[55] As the Jewish festival of the Passover was now   John XI.
at hand, to which crowds of Jews were assembling
from all parts of the country at Jerusalem a few
days in advance, in order to [qualify themselves for partici-
pating in its solemnities by] the prescribed lustrative ceremonies; [56] the people began to inquire doubtfully of each
other, as they stood within the precincts of the Temple, looking anxiously around for Jesus, "Think you, he will by any
means venture to attend the Paschal festival?' [57] This solicitude was enhanced by a proclamation issued by the San'hedrim,

---

a Matt. xxv, 25.   *b* Matt. xxv, 30.

ment, that if any man knew where he were,   JOHN XI.
he should show it, that they might take
him.—¹ Then Jesus, six days before the   **John XII.**
passover, came to Bethany, where Lazarus
was which had been dead, whom he raised from the
dead.   ⁹ Much people of the Jews therefore knew
that he was there: and they came, not for Jesus' sake
only, but that they might see Lazarus also, whom he
had raised from the dead.   ¹⁰ But the chief-priests
consulted that they might put Lazarus also to death;
¹¹ because that by reason of him many of the Jews
went away and believed on Jesus.

² There they made him a supper, [MATT. XXVI, 6] in the
house of Simon the leper; and Martha served : but Lazarus was one of them that sat at the table with him.
³ Then took Mary [MATT. XXVI, 7] an alabaster-box containing a pound of ointment of spikenard, very costly,
[MARK XIV, 3] and she brake the box, and poured it on his head
[MATT. XXVI, 7] as he sat at meat, and anointed the feet of
Jesus, and wiped his feet with her hair : and the house
was filled with the odor of the ointment.   ⁴ Then saith
one of his disciples, (Judas Iscariot Simon's son, which
should betray him,) [MATT. XXVI, 8] To what purpose is this
waste ?   ⁵ Why was not this ointment sold for three
hundred pence, and given to the poor ?   [MARK XIV, 5] And
they murmured against her.   ⁶ (This he said, not that he
cared for the poor; but because he was a thief, and
had the bag and bare what was put therein.)   ⁷ Then
said Jesus, Let her alone ; [MATT. XXVI, 10] why trouble ye
the woman? for she hath wrought a good work upon me:
[MARK XIV, 8] she hath done what she could ; [MATT. XXVI, 12] for
in that she hath poured this ointment on my body, against
the day of my burying hath she kept this.   ⁸ For the
poor always ye have with you, [MARK XIV, 7] and whenso-
ever ye will ye may do them good ; but *me* ye have not
146

ordering that if any person were cognizant of the   JOHN XI.
whereabouts of Jesus, he should give them immediate
notice, that they might arrest him. 1 [Undeterred by   John XII.
these formidable designs,] Jesus pursued his journey,
and on the fifth day preceding the commencement of
the Paschal celebration [i. e. four whole days intervening between
the respective dates], he reached Bethany, the village where Lazarus, whom he had lately resuscitated when deceased, resided. 9 His
arrival there being quickly rumored in the metropolis, great numbers of its inhabitants flocked thither, not merely for the purpose
of visiting Jesus, but also from a curiosity to see Lazarus, the subject of this miraculous revivification. 10 This notoriety incited the
jealous San'hedrim to deliberate upon some project for the destruction of Lazarus also; 11 as numbers of the Jews of the capital were
falling off from the Pharisaical party, and yielding their faith to
Jesus from the persuasive influence of the miracle in the case of
Lazarus.

2 On the evening of his arrival at Bethany, as Jesus was partaking
of an entertainment, provided in special honor of him, *a* at the
house of a certain Simon, [formerly] a leper,l at which Martha
waited upon the table, and her brother Lazarus was one of the invited guests; 3 *b* their sister l Mary *c* approached l with an alabaster
vase of aromatic ointment in her hand, containing a *libra* [i. e.
about ¾ of a pound] of the most costly pure oil of *spikenard,* and
d breaking the neck of the flask,l she anointed the *e* head l and feet
of Jesus with its contents, having first wiped off [the dust from]
the latter with the hair of her head, as [they projected behind him
beyond the edge of the couch *c* on which] he reclined.l While the
perfume of the exquisite unguent was diffused through the whole
house, 4 Judas "Iscariot" (the son of Simon, and one of the disciples,
the same person that soon became his Master's betrayer) exclaimed
e to the rest of the disciples l *f* with indignation at the sight,l
5 *e* "Why was this waste of the ointment committed?l it might have
been sold for *g* more than l two hundred *dena'rii* [i. e. about $30],
and the proceeds distributed among the necessitous." 6 He made
this captious remark, not from any feeling of charity for the poor,
but because he was the thievish purser of the company of the Apostles, and was in the habit of pilfering their contributions to the
poor fund. 7 Jesus, however, *h* on learning this impatience,l calmly
replied, "Do not interfere with the good woman *i* by pestering her
with censure upon her conduct; she has really performed a praiseworthy office for mel *j* to the extent of her means,l by anointing
j my person beforehandl for burial. 8 As to the poor, you have
them constantly in your midst, *k* and may relieve them whenever
you wish;l but you will not be perpetually favored with *my* personal company. *l* Accordingly, [as a reward for this female's affectionate improvement of the opportunity of my presence,] I assure

a Matt. xxvi, 6.   *b* John xi, 2.   *c* Matt. xxvi, 7.   *d* Mark xiv, 3.
e Mark xiv, 4.   *f* Matt. xxvi, 8.   *g* Mark xiv, 5.   *h* Matt. xxvi, 10.
i Mark xiv, 6.   *j* Mark xiv, 8.   *k* Mark xiv, 7.   *l* Matt. xxvi, 13.

always.   [MATT. XXVI, 13] Verily I say unto   JOHN XII.
you, Wheresoever this gospel shall be preached
in the whole world, there shall also this that this woman
hath done, be told for a memorial of her.

--------•--------

CHAPTER VI.—PORTION III.

CHRIST'S LAST SOJOURN AT JERUSALEM, UP TO HIS FOURTH
PASSOVER.

(Time, *three days.*)

§ 112.—*Christ's Public Entry into Jerusalem.*

(Road from Bethany to Jerusalem; *Monday, March* 14, A. D. 29.)

¹ And [JOHN XII, 12] on the next day, when   **Matt. XXI.**
they drew nigh unto Jerusalem, and were
come to Bethphage [LUKE XIX, 29] and Bethany, unto the
Mount of Olives, then sent Jesus two disciples ² saying unto them, Go into the village over against you,
and straightway ye shall find an ass tied, and a colt
with her [MARK XI, 2] whereon never man sat; loose them
and bring them unto me : ³ and if any man say aught
unto you, ye shall say, The Lord hath need of them ;
and straightway he will send them.   ⁶ And the disciples went, and [MARK XI, 4] found the colt tied by the door
without, in a place where two ways met ; and they loose him.
[5] And certain of them that stood there said unto them, What
do ye, loosing the colt?   And they did as Jesus commanded
them : [MARK XI, 6] and they let them go.   ⁷ And [MARK XI, 7]
they brought the ass and the colt, and put on them their
clothes, and they set him thereon.   ⁴ All this was done,
that it might be fulfilled which was spoken by the
prophet saying, ⁵ Tell ye the daughter of Sion,
[JOHN XII, 15] Fear not : behold, thy King cometh unto thee,
meek and sitting upon an ass and a colt the foal of an ass.

147

you, that in whatever quarter of the whole globe the JOHN XII. Gospel I am now establishing shall be hereafter proclaimed, this generous act of hers will be embraced in its publication, as an unfading reminiscence of her."|

CHAPTER VI.—PORTION III.

CHRIST'S LAST SOJOURN AT JERUSALEM, UP TO HIS FOURTH PASSOVER.

(Time, *three days.*)

§ 112.—*Christ's Public Entry into Jerusalem.*

(Road from Bethany to Jerusalem; *Monday, March* 14, A. D. 29.)

1 *a* On the day following his arrival at Bethany, | Matt. XXI. Jesus set out for Jerusalem; and on approaching the city, having reached the confines of the little village of Beth'phagè, situated near the ridge of the Mount of Olives, he dispatched two of his disciples in advance, 2 directing them, " Go into yonder village in front of you, and on entering it you will soon discover an ass tied there, with a colt by her side, *b* on which no person has ever ridden; | untie them both, and bring them here to me. 3 If any one makes any objection to your procedure, *c* asking you 'what you are about, untying the beasts ?'| tell him, 'Our Master has occasion for their use;' and he will give you permission at once to take them." 6 The disciples setting off, *d* found the animals as Jesus had told them, before a door at a fork of the road,| fulfilled their errand, *e* satisfying the owners with the answer they were directed to make,| and then leading the ass and colt to their Master, spread their cloaks upon the backs of both, and mounted Jesus *f* upon the latter,| [leading the other as a relay by his side.]—4 All these particulars were attended to in fulfillment of the concurrent predictions of the prophets Isaiah and Zechariah :—

5 " Let Zion's daughter, fair Jerusalem,
　　Be told in that auspicious day the news,
　　'Attend! your long-expected Saviour comes !' "

g " Exult with fearless joy exuberant
　　At that propitious era,| blooming maid
　　That circlest Zion's heights with virgin grace,
　　[Yea, shout thy welcome, fair Jerusalem :]
　　For lo! your promised King will then approach
　　Your walls, [a righteous Saviour from your woes]—
　　Yet lowly is his mien, he rides an ass,
　　A colt which still its mother trots beside."

a John xii, 12. 　　*b* Luke xix, 30. 　　*c* Luke xix, 31. 　　*d* Mark xi, 4.
　　e Mark xi, 5, 6. 　　*f* Luke xix, 35. 　　*g* John xii, 15.

16 (These things understood not his disciples **John XII.**
at the first; but when Jesus was glorified,
then remembered they that these things were written
of him, and that they had done these things unto
him.)

8 And [LUKE XIX, 36] as he went, a very great **Matt. XXI.**
multitude [JOHN XII, 12] that were come to the
feast, when they heard that Jesus was coming to Jerusalem,
spread their garments in the way; others cut down
branches from the [JOHN XII, 13] palm-trees and strewed
them in the way: 9 and [LUKE XIX, 37] when he was come
nigh, even now at the descent of the Mount of Olives, the
multitudes that went before and that followed,
[LUKE XIX, 37] began to rejoice and praise God with a loud voice
for all the mighty works that they had seen; [JOHN XII, 17] the
people therefore that was with him when he called Lazarus
out of his grave and raised him from the dead, bare record:
[18] for this cause the people also met him, for that they heard
that he had done this miracle; and cried, saying, Hosanna
to the Son of David; Blessed is [JOHN XII, 13] the King
of Israel that cometh in the name of the Lord;
[LUKE XIX, 38] Peace in heaven; Hosanna in the highest.
19 The Pharisees therefore said among **John XII.**
themselves, Perceive ye how ye prevail
nothing? behold, the world is gone after him.
39 And some of the Pharisees from among **Luke XIX.**
the multitude said unto him, Master, rebuke thy disciples. 40 And he answered and said unto
them, I tell you, that if these should hold their peace,
the *stones* would immediately cry out!

41 And when he was come near, he beheld the city
and wept over it, 42 saying, If thou hadst known, even
thou, at least in this thy day, the things which belong
unto thy peace! but now they are hid from thine eyes:
43 for the days shall come upon thee, that thine enemies shall cast a trench about thee and compass thee

148

¹⁶ The disciples were not aware at the time, of the   John XII.
significance of these circumstances, but after the
ascension of Jesus, this verification of ancient
prophecy, by these acts of theirs, occurred to their minds.

⁸ ᵃ As Jesus thus rode along, I a very great con-   Matt. XXI.
course of persons, ᵇ whom the report of his intended visit to Jerusalem I ᶜ had attracted to meet
him I ᵇ as they were repairing thither to attend the festival, I en-
thusiastically spread their cloaks along the road; while others
cut off boughs from the adjacent ᶜ palm-trees, I and strewed
them in his path.   ⁹ ᵈ While the procession was thus nearing
the western slope of the Mount of Olives, I the whole crowd of
Jesus's adherents, as well those who preceded as those who followed him, set up a shout ᵈ of adoring joy at the top of their
voices, exclaiming with rapture at the recollection of the numerous miracles that they had seen him effect I—ᵉ especially
the revivification of Lazarus from the tomb, which the attendant throng eagerly recounted, I ƒ most of them having joined his
present retinue on account of the fame of this miracle, I—" Hosanna [i. e. " be now propitious," a Hebrew ejaculation of sacred
delight] be ascribed to the ' Heir of David !'   Praised be the
predicted ᶜ King of Israel, I who is now come ! ᵍ glorious blessing be his meed I among the heavenly choir I"
¹⁹ The invidious Pharisees, however, [being ap-   John XII.
prized in the city of this honorary welcome of Jesus
by the populace,] tauntingly exclaimed to their more lenient
colleagues of the San'hedrim, " There, you see how little progress your tardy policy is making ; look, the whole
country is crazy after him !"   ³⁹ Indeed some of   Luke XIX.
the Pharisaical emissaries who were mingled with
the crowd itself that surrounded Jesus, impatiently urged him,
" Teacher, do check these vociferations of your followers !"
⁴⁰ But he emphatically replied to their sinister suggestion,
" [No, no ! let them shout ;] I tell you that if these human
voices should refrain their acclamations, God would animate
the very stones to proclaim my triumph, [were there no other
means of celebrating this predicted march I]"
⁴¹ As Jesus drew near to the city, he shed tears, as he foresaw the deplorable fate which the impenitence of its inmates
would ere long bring upon it,] ⁴² exclaiming with desponding
tenderness, " O, if thou didst but appreciate in this so oppor-
tune a crisis in thy history, [cherished metropolis of this once
heaven-chosen land,] what course of conduct [toward me]
would be conducive to thy welfare !—but, alas ! thou art even
at this auspicious moment incorrigibly blind to thy best interests.   ⁴³ For soon the calamitous period will overtake thee,
when besieging troops will rear a hostile rampart around thy

a Luke xix, 36.   b John xii, 12.   c John xii, 13.   d Luke xix, 37.
e John xii, 17.   ƒ John xii, 18.   g Luke xix, 38.

round and keep thee in on every side,' LUKE XIX. 44 and shall lay thee even with the ground and thy children within thee; and they shall not leave in thee one stone upon another; because thou knewest not the time of thy visitation.

§ 113.—*Christ's Proceedings in the Temple.*

(Jerusalem; *Monday, March* 14, A. D. 29.)

10 And when he was come into Jerusa- **Matt. XXI.** lem, all the city was moved saying, Who is this? 11 And the multitude said, This is Jesus the prophet of Nazareth of Galilee. 12 And Jesus went into the temple of God, and cast out all them that sold and bought in the temple, and overthrew the tables of the money-changers and the seats of them that sold doves; [MARK XI, 16] and would not suffer that any man should carry any vessel through the temple: 13 and said unto them, It is written, My house shall be called [MARK XI, 17] of all nations the house of prayer; but ye have made it a den of thieves. 14 And the blind and the lame came to him in the temple; and he healed them. 15 And when the chief-priests and scribes saw the wonderful things that he did, and the children crying in the temple and saying, Hosanna to the Son of David; they were sore displeased, 16 and said unto him, Hearest thou what these say? And Jesus saith unto them, Yea; have ye never read, Out of the mouth of babes and sucklings thou hast perfected praise?

17 And [MARK XI, 11] when he had looked round about upon all things, and now the even-tide was come, he left them and went out of the city into Bethany [MARK XI, 11] with the twelve; and he lodged there.

149

walls, and hem thee in with a strict blockade on every   LUKE XIX.
side, [44] until having captured thee by storm, they shall
demolish thy structures after the butchery of thy inhabitants, not leaving 'one stone of thy edifices standing upon another;' [all this overthrow will befall thee,] because thou now re-
fusest to recognize the favorable presence of thy celestial Deliverer."

§ 113.—*Christ's Proceedings in the Temple.*

(Jerusalem ; *Monday, March 14, A. D. 29.*)

[10] No sooner had Jesus thus entered Jerusalem, than   **Matt. XXI.**
the whole city was thrown into a fever of excitement,
strangers inquiring, " Who is this personage that has
arrived ?" [11] and the crowd that escorted him replying, " It is the
Prophet Jesus, a citizen of Nazareth in Galilee." [12] Jesus, however,
continued his course directly to the Temple, and immediately addressed himself to the task of expelling a second time all the dealers
within its precincts, overturning the counters of the money-changers
and the seats of the traders in doves, *a* and forbidding any person
to make it a thoroughfare for [the transit or deposit of articles of]
merchandise: | [13] [these summary measures were accompanied by
this statement of his authority to the awe-struck intruders,] " The
word of God declares," said he,—

" ' My Temple is to be a place of prayer
b For all mankind, e'en Gentile worshipers ;' |

but *you* [by your knavish traffic,] have turned it into—

' —— a cave of mere banditti ——.' "

[14] [During the rest of the day, numerous] persons, afflicted with
chronic blindness or lameness, resorted to Jesus, who continued in
the Temple teaching, and were entirely cured by his miraculous
power. [15] The Pharisaical hierarchy, however, on witnessing these
miracles effected by him, and listening to the children's acclamations [caught from the lips of his older adherents] still resounding
in the Temple, " *Hosanna* for the ' Heir of David !' " were so incensed, [yet dared not attempt any violence on account of his popularity,] [16] that they sneeringly exclaimed to him, "Do you hear
what an uproar those urchins are making about you?" "Yes,"
replied Jesus, "[I do ; and if you object to their acclamations,]
let me ask you, if you have never read in the Scriptures this declaration,—

' [Yet] e'en the weakness of the infant's voice,
In artless praise proclaims Thy mighty skill?' "

[17] *c* After having thus surveyed the Temple | [and cleared it of
its profanations], Jesus retired [from the plaudits of the crowd, lest
he might seem to foster their tendency to invest him with royalty],
and issuing from the city *c* at nightfall, | returned to Bethany to
spend the night there, *c* attended by his Apostles. |

a Mark xi, 16.   *b* Mark xi, 17.   *c* Mark xi, 11.

§ 114.—*The Symbolical Fate of the Barren Fig-tree.*

(Jerusalem and Bethany; *Tuesday* and *Wednesday, March* 15 and 16, A. D. 29.)

^{18} Now in the morning, as he returned   MATT. XXI.
[MARK XI, 12] from Bethany into the city, he
hungered: ^{19} and when he saw a fig-tree in the way
[MARK XI, 13] afar off having leaves, he came to it, [MARK XI, 13]
if haply he might find anything thereon; and found nothing
thereon but leaves only, [MARK XI, 13] (for the time of figs
was not yet;) and said unto it, Let no fruit grow on thee
henceforward forever.   [MARK XI, 14] And his disciples
heard it. And presently the fig-tree withered away.

[MARK XI, 15] And they come to Jerusalem: and   Luke XXI.
Jesus went into the temple, ^{37} and in the day-
time he was teaching in the temple; ^{38} and all the
people came early in the morning to him in the temple,
for to hear him: ^{37} and at night he went out and abode
in the mount that is called the Mount of Olives.
^{47} And he taught daily in the temple. But   Luke XIX.
the chief-priests and the scribes and the
chief of the people [MARK XI, 18] heard it, and sought to
destroy him, ^{48} and could not find what they might do:
[MARK XI, 18] for they feared him; for all the people were
very attentive to hear him, [MARK XI, 18] because all the
people was astonished at his doctrine.

[MARK XI, 20] And in the morning, as they   Matt. XXI.
passed by, they saw the fig-tree dried up from
the roots: ^{20} and when the disciples saw it, they marveled, [MARK XI, 21] and Peter called to remembrance saying
unto him, Master, behold how soon is the fig-tree
[MARK XI, 21] which thou cursedst withered away! ^{21} Jesus
answered and said unto them, [MARK XI, 22] Have faith in
God: verily I say unto you, If ye have faith and doubt
not, ye shall not only do this which is done to the fig-

150

§ 114.—*The Symbolical Fate of the Barren Fig-tree.*

(Jerusalem and Bethany; *Tuesday* and *Wednesday, March* 15 and 16, A. D. 29.)

[18] Early [a] on the following day, as the com-   MATT. XXI.
pany were leaving Bethany | on their way back
to the city, Jesus began to feel very hungry.
[19] On seeing a fig-tree standing alone by the road-side [b] at a
distance, which seemed flourishing, | he went up to it [b] in the
prospect of getting something to eat from it; | but [b] upon
reaching it, | he found none [of the common winter's fruit
hanging on it, nor any signs of the early summer fruit], but
merely leaves,—[which gave promise of precocity at first
sight,] [b] although the regular season for fig-gathering had not
yet arrived. | [Seizing upon the incident to impress a warn-
ing upon his disciples' minds,] [c] as they stood listening to
him, | he pronounced this solemn sentence, "Let [c] no person
ever be able to gather | any fruit from this tree hereafter!"—
The fig-tree immediately began to wither and die.
[37] [d] Having proceeded on his way, | Jesus occu-   Luke XXI.
pied himself [as a systematic scheme for the two
days to come,] [38] in instructing the multitudes
who flocked to hear him in the Temple during the day-time,
[37] and withdrawing to pass the night at Bethany,
just across the Mount of Olives. [47] As he was   Luke XIX.
thus discoursing to-day, the Jewish hierarchy,
[e] being informed of his public acts and doctrines, | were anxious
to devise [e] some method | for his destruction; [48] but [e] dared not
execute any such design, | as the entire populace attended his
preaching with devoted [c] admiration. |
[20] [f] On the next morning, | as the disciples, [f] on   Matt. XXI.
their way with their Master from Bethany to the
city, | were passing by the fig-tree against which
he had uttered the malediction the day before, they were as-
tonished to see it blasted [f] down to the very roots. | [g] Peter |
calling the attention of Jesus to its sudden blight, [21] he replied by the following exhortation: [h] "You ought to have
greater confidence in the Almighty's power | [as possessed by
me, than your surprise at this result of my command be-
trays]. I deliberately assure you, that if you did but exercise an unwavering faith [in my efficacy to second your acts],
you might yourselves not merely perform such a slight miracle as has occurred in the case of this fig-tree; but should
you [in the discharge of your delegated duties,] bid yonder
mountain [pointing to the Mount of Olives, whose summit
lay just in advance of them] [i] be lifted up and hurled into the

a Mark xi, 12.   b Mark xi, 13.   c Mark xi, 14.   d Mark xi, 15.
e Mark xi, 18.   f Mark xi, 20,   g Mark xi, 21.   h Mark xi, 22.

150*

tree, but also if ye shall say unto this   MATT. XXI.
mountain, Be thou removed, and be thou
cast into the sea; it shall be done, [MARK XI, 23] and ye
shall have whatsoever ye say: 22 and [MARK XI, 24] therefore
I say unto you, All things whatsoever ye shall [MARK XI, 24].
desire when ye ask in prayer, believing [MARK XI, 24] that ye
receive them, ye shall receive.

§ 115.—*Being Questioned as to his Authority by the San'hedrim, Christ Illustrates their Heinous Impenitence toward him.*

(Jerusalem, the Temple, [Court of the Women?] *Wednesday, March 16, A. D. 29.*)

23 And when he was come [MARK XI, 27] again into the temple, the chief-priests [MARK XI, 27] and the scribes and the elders of the people came unto him, as he was [MARK XI, 27] walking in the temple teaching [LUKE XX, 1] the people and preaching the gospel, and said, By what authority doest thou these things, and who gave thee this authority? 24 And Jesus answered and said unto them, I also will ask you one thing, which if ye tell me, I in like wise will tell you by what authority I do these things: 25 the *baptism of John*, whence was it; from *heaven*, or of *men?* And they reasoned with themselves saying, If we shall say, From heaven; he will say unto us, Why did ye not then believe him? 26 but if we shall say, Of men; we fear the people [LUKE XX, 6] will stone us: for all hold John as a prophet [MARK XI, 32] indeed. 27 And they answered Jesus and said, We cannot tell. And he said unto them, Neither tell I you by what authority I do these things.

28 But what think ye? A certain man had two sons; and he came to the first and said, Son, go work to-day in my vineyard. 29 He answered and said, I will not; but afterward he repented and went. 30 And he came to the second and said likewise: and he

151

sea,'ᵃ without allowing the least doubt to enter your
minds!·[as to the virtue of the authority with which
I have invested you], the fact would certainly take
place. ²² ᵇ For in general, I pledge you the assurance,! that whatever suitable request you make of God, fully reposing upon His
ᵇ actual! acceptance of your petition [for my sake], will thereupon
infallibly be granted you."

MATT. XXI.

§ 115.—*Being Questioned as to his Authority by the San'hedrim,
Christ Illustrates their Heinous Impenitence toward him.*

(Jerusalem, the Temple, [Court of the Women!]; *Wednesday, March* 16, A. D. 29.)

²³ Continuing his journey, Jesus proceeded ᶜwith his disciples!
directly to the Temple ᶜagain, and as he was walking around its
courts,! instructing ᵈthe populace in the doctrines of his gospel,!
he was met by [a deputation of] the hierarchy from the San'hedrim,
who [as having jurisdiction over theological matters,] accosted him
with the [seemingly candid] question, "By virtue of what authority
do you take upon you to teach and act thus publicly? who has empowered you·to do so?" ²⁴ [Instead of gratifying their expectations of being furnished with a ground of accusation by a direct
avowal of his Messianic character,] Jesus made this reply, "Let
me in turn ask you a simple question, before I answer yours:
²⁵ Whence did *John the Baptist* derive his authority to exercise his
public ministry,—from a divine or human source?" [At a loss for
an answer], the inquirers consulted among themselves [a few moments, how to get over the dilemma]; "for," deliberated they, "if
we reply, 'He, was divinely commissioned,' he will at once retort,.
'Then why did you not credit his testimony [concerning me]?'
²⁶ and if on the other hand we should answer, 'He acted in a
merely human uninspired capacity,' we have reason to dread the.
indignation of the populace, (ᵉperhaps a shower of stones,!) as
they universally consider John to have been a ᶠgenuine! prophet.'·
²⁷ So they [concluded to state themselves unable to solve the problem, and] returned to Jesus with this answer, "We do not know
whence he derived his authority." [Penetrating the falsehood of
this acknowledgment,] Jesus responded, "Then I shall not tell.
you either, by what authority *I* claim to be empowered in my public acts."

²⁸ [Resolved, however, not to let the occasion pass without ad-
monishing them of their contumacious spirit with regard to his
claims, Jesus proposed this illustration to them:] "Now give me
your opinion as to the following case: A parent had two sons, to
one of whom he went one day with the injunction, 'My son, I wish
you to go and work to-day in my vineyard.' ²⁹ But the son declared in reply, 'I shall not do so;' afterward, however, he repented
of his filial disobedience, and went to the appointed task. ³⁰ [Still
undiscouraged,] the father impartially applied to the other with
the like requirement; and *he* readily assented, "Yes sir, I will do

ᵃ Mark xi, 23.   ᵇ Mark xi, 24.   ᶜ Mark xi, 27.
ᵈ Luke xx, 1.   ᵉ Luke xx, 6.   ᶠ Mark xi, 32.

answered and said, I go, sir; and went MATT. XXI.
not. ³¹ Whether of them twain did the
will of his father? They say unto him, The first.
Jesus saith unto them, Verily I say unto you, That
the publicans and the harlots go into the kingdom of
God before *you :* ³² for John came unto you in the way
of righteousness, and ye believed him not; but the
publicans and the harlots believed him; and ye, when
ye had seen it, repented not afterward, that ye might
believe him.

³³ Hear another parable: There was, a certain
householder, which planted a vineyard and hedged it
round about and digged a wine-press in it and built a
tower, and let it out to husbandmen, and went into a
far country [Luke XX, 9] for a long time. ³⁴ And when the
time of the fruit drew near, he sent his servants to the
husbandmen, that they might receive the fruits of it:
³⁵ and the husbandmen took his servants, and beat one,
and killed another, and stoned another, [Mark XII, 3] and
sent him away empty. ³⁶ Again he sent other servants
more than the first; and they did unto them likewise.
[Luke XX, 13] Then said the lord of the vineyard, What shall
I do? ³⁷ but [Mark XII, 6] having yet therefore one son, his
well-beloved, last of all he sent unto them his son, saying, They will reverence my *son,* [Luke XX, 13] when they
see him. ³⁸ But when the husbandmen saw the son,
they said among themselves, This is the heir; come,
let us kill him, and let us seize on his inheritance:
³⁹ and they caught him, and cast him out of the vine-
yard, and slew him. ⁴⁰ When the lord therefore of
the vineyard cometh, what will he do unto those husbandmen? ⁴¹ They say unto him, He will miserably
destroy those wicked men, and will let out his vineyard unto other husbandmen, which shall render him
the fruits in their seasons. ⁴² Jesus saith unto them,
⁴³ Therefore say I unto you, The kingdom of God shall

so immediately,' but nevertheless he did not   MATT. XXI.'
actually set about the work.   ³¹ Now which of
these two sons really complied with his father's
commands?" "The former, certainly," replied the hierarchal
emissaries. "And in the same way," rejoined Jesus, "the vilest
characters precede *you* in entering the 'Reign of the Divine Messiah!' ³² John the Baptist [as you dare not deny,] appeared in'
your midst, enforcing his holy precepts by a blameless example; yet you withhold credence from his declarations: whereas
the most profane and dissolute classes of society have yielded
their faith to his annunciations. Thus you [unlike the former
son,] have refused to repent subsequently of your stubborn-
rejection of his divine teachings."

³³ [In order to impress their minds with a deeper sense of
their atrocious treatment of him as God's Messenger,] Jesus
proceeded to propound to them another illustration, as follows :
" A certain land-owner planted a vineyard on his premises, in-
closing it with a tight hedge, furnishing it with a deep vat for
the wine-press, and building a guard-house within it [for protection against all intruders; and having thus provided it with
every convenience], he leased it out for a term of years to a company of gardeners, while he traveled abroad. ³⁴ When the season
of vintage arrived, he sent of course a number of his domestics
to the tenants, to receive his proportion of the crop [as the stipu-
lated rent]; ³⁵ but the villanous occupants seized the messengers
and handled some of them so severely, that they were glad to escape with their lives, while they pelted others away with stones,
a without paying any of them the least part of the dues.| ³⁶ The
landlord patiently sent still another set of domestics, but these
were treated with still more *b* shameful abuse,| so that some of
them even *c* died| of their *d* wounds.| ³⁷ At last the forbearing
owner *e* resolved| to dispatch to the rebellious tenants his *f* dear.
and only son,| supposing that 'they would *e* certainly' show his
own son due respect.' ³⁸ But no sooner had the young man'
come within sight, than the miscreants deliberated thus among
themselves, 'See, yonder comes the landlord's heir; come, let,
us kill him on the spot, and then we shall have no one to dispute our possession of the estate.' ³⁹ [This infamous measure
prevailed;] they seized him, beat him out of the vineyard, and
then murdered him outright. ⁴⁰ Now when the proprietor returned, what punishment do you imagine he would inflict upon
those gardeners?" ⁴¹ "He would undoubtedly execute the
wretches summarily, and let out the vineyard to worthier tenants, who would pay him the due produce," replied the hierarchal deputation; [not suspecting the drift of the illustration.]
⁴³*g* "Certainly he would," rejoined Jesus,| "and on the same
principle, I declare to you, that [unless you repent, all share

a Mark xii, 3.   *b* Mark xii, 4.   *c* Mark xii, 5.   *d* Luke xx, 12.
      e Luke xx, 13.   *f* Mark xii, 6.   *g* Mark xii, 9.

be taken from *you*, and given to a na-   MATT. XXI.
tion bringing forth the fruits thereof.

[Luke XX, 16] And when they heard it, they said, God forbid.
[17] And he beheld them and said, 42 Did ye never read in
the scriptures,* The stone which the builders rejected,
the same is become the head of the corner : this is the
Lord's doing, and it is marvelous in our eyes ?   44 And
whosoever shall fall on this stone, shall be broken ;
but on whomsoever it shall fall, it will grind him to
powder.

45 And when the chief-priests and Pharisees had
heard his parables, they perceived that he spake of
them ; 46 but when they sought to lay hands on him,
they feared the multitude, because they took him for a
prophet : [Mark XII, 12] and they left him and went their way.

§ 116.—*The Insidious Question of the combined Pharisees and Herodians concerning Tribute-Money.*

(Jerusalem, the Temple, [Court of the Women ?] *Wednesday, March*
16, A. D. 29.)

15 Then went the Pharisees and took   Matt. XXII.
counsel how they might entangle him in
his talk : 16 and they [Luke XX, 20] watched him and sent
out unto him their disciples with the Herodians,
[Luke XX, 20] which should feign themselves just men ; that
they might take hold of his words, that so they might deliver
him unto the power and authority of the governor. [Mark XII, 14]
And when they were come, they asked him saying, Master,
we know that thou art true and teachest the way of
God in truth, neither carest thou for any man ; for
thou regardest not the person of men : 17 tell us therefore, What thinkest thou ? is it lawful to give tribute
unto Cesar, or not ? [Mark XII, 15] shall we give, or shall we
not give ? 18 But Jesus perceived their wickedness and

---

* Psa. cxviii, 22, 23.

in] the 'Reign of the Divine Messiah' will be taken   MATT. XXI.
from you and bestowed upon a [Gentile] race, who
will yield a more suitable return for its privileges."
a [Struck with the fearful import of their own concession,] they
faltered out the deprecation, "May such a fate never befall our
chosen nation!"! ⁴²Jesus then drove home [the conviction for
which an opening was thus made, by] this forcible retort, b sharp-
ened by his piercing glance:! "What prophetic import, then, [if you
disclaim such a base refusal of God's messengers,] do you assign to
that passage of His word, which you have often read,—

> ' A stone once spurned as shapeless, for the walls
> Of Thy theocracy's most honored fane,
> By blear-eyed architects of princely pride,—
> I now am reared to grace its buttress chief,
> The corner-block that props and crowns the whole;
> The Almighty's scheme has wrought the glorious change,
> So wondrous to the eye of erring man?'

⁴⁴Ah! whoever jostles against this Corner-Stone [in fool-hardy
prejudice at its prominent position], will himself be bruised in his
spiritual interests [by the collision]; but direst woe to those upon
whom it may fall [with the weight of the divine judgments for its
contempt], for it will surely crush them to atoms!"
⁴⁵The Pharisaical hierarchy, who listened to these allegories,
aware that they were the persons aimed at by them, ⁴⁶racked their
ingenuity to devise some mode of violently arresting Jesus c at once;!
but deterred by a fear of exasperating the populace, who universally esteemed him as a divine Prophet, d they were compelled to
retire and leave him unmolested.!

§ 116.—*The Insidious Question of the combined Pharisees and
Herodians concerning Tribute-Money.*

(Jerusalem, the Temple, [Court of the Women!] *Wednesday, March 16, A. D. 29.*)

¹⁵[This failure of success being reported to the   **Matt. XXII.**
San'hedrim,] the Pharisees and "Herodians" [i. e.
partisans of Herod An'tipas] among that body formed
a coalition, for the purpose of conceiving some plot, to entrap Jesus
[into some declaration that might be employed to his injury.]
¹⁶Accordingly, they concerted the scheme of dispatching, e on some
chosen opportunity, a few artful persons! of their number, e who
under the specious guise of conscientious inquirers after truth,
should inveigle him into an expression of opinion, which would
enable them to seize and commit him to the secular tribunal,! [as
guilty of civil treason.] These insidious emissaries therefore f approached him! with this question, "Teacher, we are convinced
that you are a veracious prophet, interpreting the divine precepts
correctly, and biased neither by human fear nor favor in your determinations: [we have therefore resolved to consult you on a difficult point of duty. ¹⁷Will you be so kind as to] favor us with
your opinion, as to whether it is right for us [the professed subjects
of Jehovah alone,] to pay tribute to the Gentile emperor?" ¹⁸See-
ing through their sinister mask at a glance, Jesus replied, "Why

a Luke xx, 16.   b Luke xx, 17.   c Luke xx, 19.
d Mark xii, 12.   e Luke xx, 20.   f Mark xii, 14.

said, Why tempt ye me, ye hypocrites? MATT. XXII.
¹⁹ Show me the *tribute-money.* And
they brought unto him a penny. ²⁰ And he saith unto
them, Whose is this image and superscription?
²¹ They say unto him, Cesar's. Then saith he unto
them, Render therefore unto Cesar the things which
are Cesar's, and unto God the things that are God's.
²² When they had heard these words, [LUKE XX, 26] they
could not take hold of his words before the people; and they
marveled [LUKE XX, 26] at his answer, and held their peace,
and left him and went their way.

§ 117.—*Artful Question of the Sadducees concerning
the Resurrection.*

(Jerusalem, the Temple, [Court of the Women?] *Wednesday, March
16, A. D. 29.*)

²³ The same day came to him the Sadducees, (which
say that there is no resurrection,) and asked him ²⁴ saying, Master, Moses said,* If a man die having no
children, his brother shall marry his wife and raise up
seed unto his brother. ²⁵ Now there were with us
seven brethren : and the first, when he had married a
wife, deceased, and having no issue, left his wife unto
his brother ; ²⁶ likewise the second also [MARK XII, 21] took
her, and died, neither left he any seed ; and the third
[MARK XII, 21] likewise, unto the seventh ; [LUKE XX, 31] and
they left no children, and died: ²⁷ and last of all the
woman died also. ²⁸ Therefore in the resurrection,
whose wife shall she be of the seven? for they all
had her. ²⁹ Jesus answered and said unto them, Ye
do err, not knowing the scriptures nor the power of
God : 30 for [LUKE XX, 34] the children of this world marry and
are given in marriage ; but in the resurrection they neither
marry nor are given in marriage : [LUKE XX, 36] neither can

---

* Deut. xxv, 5.

are you trying thus to insnare me, you hypo-   MATT. XXII.
crites! [19] Just show me one of the coins demanded as a capitation-tax." Accordingly,
they exhibited a *dena'rius* [i. e. a Roman piece of money,
equivalent to about 15 cents]. [20] He then asked them, "Whose
effigy and name is this stamped upon it?" [21] "The Roman
emperor's," [probably Tiberius, who was then reigning,] answered they. "Then all you have to do," returned Jesus, "is
to accord to the emperor what he is entitled to [on its very
face], and at the same time devote to Jehovah the spiritual
service that is *His* due."

[22] [a] Foiled in their hope of detecting some slip in his public
expressions, which would afford them a pretext for turning
the popular voice against him, the artful agents were forced
to retire with admiration at his ready sagacity, [a] being unable
to meet his answer.

§ 117.—*Artful Question of the Sadducees concerning the Resur-
rection.*

(Jerusalem, the Temple, [Court of the Women?] *Wednesday, March* 16, A. D. 29.)

[23] On the same day with the above discussion, a number of
the Sadducees, a sect who reject the doctrine of the resurrection of the human body hereafter, approached Jesus with the
following artful question: [24] "Teacher, Moses directed [b] [in
the code of laws which he drew up for] our nation, that in
case a [c] married man dies without an heir, his brother must
marry the widow by right of affinity, and so continue his
brother's family. [25] Now there were seven brothers among
our countrymen, the eldest of whom having married, died
without issue; thus leaving his widow to be married by the
next oldest brother. [26] He too died childless, and in turn the
third, and so on through the entire seven, [d] without having
any offspring. [27] Finally, the widow also died. [28] Now to
which of the seven brothers will she belong as a wife at the
resurrection, seeing they all were married to her?" [29] [With
prompt facility] Jesus refuted their fallacy by replying, "What
an egregious error you make in your doctrines, by misapply-
ing such passages of Scripture, and failing to appreciate the
all-wise power of God [to effect the details of the resurrection! [30] Let me correct all such gross misconception of that
event] : [e] in this life indeed, persons are wedded to each
other; but in the state of being which supervenes at the
final resurrection, the matrimonial relation has no place with
either sex, the constitutions of [f] the finally blest being then
[refined from such earthly attributes,] like those of angelic

a Luke xx, 26.   b Mark xii, 19.   c Luke xx, 28.
d Mark xii, 22.   e Luke xx, 34.   f Luke xx, 35.

they die any more; but are as the angels - MATT. XXII.
of God in heaven, [LUKE XX, 36] and are the
children of God, being the children of the resurrection.
[31] But as touching the resurrection of the dead, have
ye not read [MARK XII, 26] in the book of Moses that which
was spoken unto you by God, [MARK XII, 26] in the bush
saying,* [32] I am the God of Abraham and the God of
Isaac and the God of Jacob? God is not the God of
the *dead*, but of the *living*; [LUKE XX, 38] for all live unto
him. · [MARK XII, 27] Ye therefore do greatly err. [33] And
when the multitude heard this, they were astonished
at his doctrine. [39] Then certain of the   Luke XX.
scribes answering said, Master, thou hast
well said.

§ 118.—*The Lawyer's Curious Question concerning
the Relative Importance of the Divine Commands.*

(Jerusalem, the Temple, [Court of the Women?] *Wednesday, March*
16, A. D. 29.)

[MATT. XXII, 34] But when the Pharisees had heard   **Mark XII.** ·
that he had put the Sadducees to silence, they
were gathered together. [28] And one of the scribes
[MATT. XXII, 35] which was a lawyer, came, and having heard
them reasoning together, and perceiving that he had
answered them well, asked him, [MATT. XXII, 35] tempting
him, Which is the first commandment of all [MATT. XXII, 36]
in the law? [29] And Jesus answered him, The first of
all the commandments is,† Hear, O Israel: The Lord
our God is one Lord: [30] and thou shalt love the Lord
thy God with all thy heart and with all thy soul and
with all thy mind and with all thy strength: this is the
first [MATT. XXII, 38] and great commandment. [31] And the
second is like, namely this,‡ Thou shalt love thy
neighbor as thyself: there is none other commandment

° Exod. iii, 6.   † Deut. vi, 4, 5.   ‡ Lev. xix, 18.

beings *a* of immortal nature.¹ ³¹ As regards the   MATT. XXII.
[doctrine of the reunion of the bodies of the departed with their surviving spirits at the] general
resurrection, which you dispute, I would ask if you have never
read that passage *b* in the very writings of Moses [to which you
appeal, namely], in his account of the flaming bush,¹ where Jehovah
declared to him, and thereby to you, ³² 'I am [your ancestral Deity,]
the God whom Abraham, Isaac and Jacob worshiped?' Now [no
one will be so hardy as to deny that] Jehovah is the God of living
beings, not of corpses; [and therefore if He in the time of Moses,
centuries after these patriarchs' decease, still maintained a present
relation toward them as their Deity (for He says, 'I *am*,' not, *was*,)
then certainly they must have been yet alive in some important
sense, which could have been no other than that their spirits sur-
vived.] *c* Consequently it is evident that your sect has departed
widely from the truth of revelation on this subject;¹ *d* and it follows, that [not only those patriarchs, but] the whole human race
continue their existence with respect to God,¹ after it has ceased
among men.]" ³³ The bystanding crowd, who listened to this [refu-
tation of the Sadducees on their own ground], were struck with
Jesus's skill in instruction; *e* and some of the scribes present, [in
their delight at seeing their adversaries worsted in argument,] exclaimed, "Teacher, you have ably answered them!"¹

§ 118.—*The Lawyer's Curious Question concerning the Relative Importance of the Divine Commands.*

(Jerusalem, the Temple, [Court of the Women?] *Wednesday, March* 16, A. D. 29.)

²⁸ *f* The Pharisees being apprised that Jesus had   **Mark XII.**
silenced their rivals the Sadducees, flocked to the
spot¹ [for the purpose of concerting some question
themselves with which more successfully to confound him]. *g* One
of their number, who was versed in the law,¹ animated by the
well-aimed reply of Jesus in the controversy at which he had been
just now present, undertook *g* to embarrass him¹ by the following
question: *h* "Teacher,¹ which of the divine injunctions *h* in the
'Law'¹ is the most important?" ²⁹ Jesus replied, "The most essential precept is this: 'Hearken, ye tribes of Israel: Jehovah our
God is the sole Deity, and claims the undivided homage of His people; ³⁰ therefore you must yield Him the supreme affection of your
hearts and service of your lives.' ³¹ The second duty in importance
to this is as follows, resembling and growing out of the former:
'Love your fellow with the same kindly concern for his welfare, as
you entertain toward yourself.' These two constitute the chief

a Luke xx, 36.   *b* Mark xii, 26.   *c* Mark xii, 27.   *d* Luke xx, 38.
e Luke xx, 39.   *f* Matt. xxii, 34.   *g* Matt. xxii, 35.   *h* Matt. xxii, 36.

greater than these ; [MATT. XXII, 40] on these   MARK XII.
two commandments hang all the law and the
prophets. ³² And the scribe said unto him, Well, Master, thou hast said the truth : for there is one God, and
there is none other but he ; ³³ and to love him with all
the heart and with all the understanding and with all
the soul and with all the strength, and to love his neighbor as himself, is more than all whole burnt-offerings
and sacrifices. ³⁴ And when Jesus saw that he answered discreetly, he said unto him, Thou art not far
from the kingdom of God.

§ 119.—*Christ Silences all further Interrogatories, by*
proposing an Embarrassing Question concerning the
Paternity of the Messiah.

(Jerusalem, the Temple, [Court of the Women ?] *Wednesday, March*
16, A. D. 29.)

⁴¹ While the Pharisees were gathered   **Matt. XXII.**
together, Jesus asked them, [MARK XII, 35]
while he taught in the temple, ⁴² saying, What think ye of
Christ? whose son is he? They say unto him, The
son of David. ⁴³ He saith unto them, How then doth
David in [MARK XII, 36] the Holy Spirit call him Lord, saying [LUKE XX, 42] in the book of Psalms,* ⁴⁴ The Lord said
unto my Lord, Sit thou on my right hand, till I make
thine enemies thy footstool ? ⁴⁵ if David then [MARK XII, 37]
himself call him *Lord,* how is he his *son?* ⁴⁶ And no
man was able to answer him a word, neither durst any
man from that day forth ask him any more questions.
[MARK XII, 37] And the common people heard him gladly.

---

* Psa. cx, 1.

requirements of God, ^a and form the basis of the
entire teaching of the 'Law' as well as of the   MARK XII.
'Prophets.'|"   ³² "Yes, indeed," returned the
jurist, [his narrow views yielding before this lofty morality,]
"there is only one true God ; and, as you say, ³³ to observe
these two precepts in their appropriate spirit, is, it must be
confessed, a more acceptable devotion to Him than to offer
ever so many *hol'ocausts* [i. e. animals, every piece of whose
carcasses is burnt in sacrifice] and sacrificial services."
³⁴ Struck with this candid perception of religious truth [in so
unlooked-for a quarter], Jesus rejoined, " [Profit by the pursuance of such sentiments as you have just now expressed,
and] you are very nearly prepared for an admittance into the
'Reign of the Divine Messiah !' "

§ 119.—*Christ Silences all further Interrogatories, by proposing
an Embarrassing Question concerning the Paternity of the
Messiah.*

(Jerusalem, the Temple, [Court of the Women ?] *Wednesday, March* 16, A. D. 29.)

⁴¹ Resolved to improve the present concourse   Matt. XXII.
of the Pharisees about him, [in order to expose
the shallowness of their captious pretensions
to knowledge,] Jesus in turn now put this question to them,
^b appropriately to the instructions which he was at the time
giving to the people :| ⁴² " Tell me, what opinion do you
^b learned men! entertain with reference to the Messiah ; that
is, whose descendant is he to be ?"   " King David's, certainly,"
replied they.   ⁴³ " How, then," retorted Jesus, " when David
himself, in the inspired composition ^c of the Psalms,| says re-
specting him,—

> ⁴⁴ ' Jehovah to my Liege His word has passed :
> " At length in state be seated at My right,
>   My throne's Anointed representative;
>   For I meanwhile will all your foes subdue,
>   As captives bowed beneath the victor's foot!" '—

⁴⁵ thus entitling him as his own Divine *Sovereign*,—can he be
[merely] his lineal *descendant* and therefore inferior ?"   ⁴⁶ Unable to solve this problem, the confused opponents of Jesus
made not a word of reply ; and [warned by this public defeat,
his adversaries of every sect] were careful for the future not
to venture upon any question to him.   ^d Great crowds of the
populace, however, still continued to listen with delight to
his discourses.|

a Matt. xxii, 40.   b Mark xii, 35.   c Luke xx, 42.   d Mark xii, 37.

§ 120.—*Christ Denounces the Hypocrisy of the Hierarchy.*

(Jerusalem, the Temple, [Court of the Women ;] *Wednesday, March 16, A. D. 29.*)

[1] Then spake Jesus to the multitude   **Matt. XXIII.**
and to his disciples, [2] saying, The scribes
and the Pharisees sit in Moses' seat; [3] all therefore
whatsoever they bid you observe, that observe and do:
but do not ye after their works; for they say, and do
not.   [4] For they bind heavy burdens and grievous to
be borne, and lay them on men's shoulders; but they
themselves will not move them with one of their fingers.   [5] But all their works they do for to be seen of
men : they make broad their phylacteries and enlarge
the borders of their garments, [6] and [Luke XX, 46] desire to
walk in long robes, and love the uppermost rooms at feasts
and the chief seats in the synagogues [7] and greetings
in the markets, and to be called of men, *Rabbi, Rabbi.*
[8] But be not *ye* called Rabbi; for *one* is your Master,
even Christ, and all ye are brethren : [9] and call no
man your *father* upon the earth; for *one* is your
Father which is in heaven : [10] neither be ye called
masters ; for one is your Master, even Christ : [11] but
he that is greatest among you, shall be your servant; [12] and whosoever shall exalt himself, shall be
abased ; and he that shall humble himself, shall be
exalted.

[14] Woe unto you, scribes and Pharisees, hypocrites !
for ye devour widows' houses, and for a pretence
make long prayer : therefore ye shall receive the
greater damnation. [15] Woe unto you, scribes and
Pharisees, hypocrites ! for ye compass sea and land to
make one proselyte ; and when he is made, ye make
him twofold more the child of hell than yourselves.
[16] Woe unto you, ye blind guides ! which say, Whoso-

157

§ 120.—*Christ Denounces the Hypocrisy of the Hierarchy.*

(Jerusalem, the Temple, [Court of the Women ;] *Wednesday, March* 16, A. D. 29.)

·1 Jesus now took occasion to *a* introduce into the
instruction which he was giving the populace,| the
following remarks [suggested by the above alterca-
tion], calculated to guard his auditors, *b* especially his own disciples,|
[against indulging in unwarrantable sentiments either of extreme
prejudice or customary admiration respecting his opponents:] 2 "The
Pharisaical scribes, you must never forget, occupy the position of
Moses's representatives as religious teachers ; 3 it therefore becomes
you to heed and obey their instructions, [when thus derived from the
Scriptures.] Yet, on the other hand, you must not follow their *example;* for they do not practice their own precepts of duty. 4 For
instance, [you may see their inconsistent exemption of themselves
from obligation, even in ceremonial matters,] in their habit of rigidly
exacting of others the most severe traditional observances, like crush-
ing bundles piled upon men's shoulders, while they excuse themselves
from laying a finger of participation upon the same task. 5 All the
good deeds that they do pretend to perform, are done merely for the
sake of ostentation, [and their whole demeanor is studied with the
same view of courting human applause.] Thus, they enlarge their
phylac'teries [i. e. lockets worn upon the person, containing verses
from the Scriptures], and widen the fringes of their *a* long mantles,
in which they love so much to stalk abroad,| [in affectation of zeal
for such marks of piety ;] 6 and they are fond of reclining at the head
of the table in entertainments, and of being seated in the front row in
the synagogue ; 7 and their vanity is also flattered by reverential salu-
tations in the public thoroughfares, as well as by being addressed by
others in the pompous title of '*Rabbi*' [i. e. *My Teacher*, in Hebrew].
8, 10 But *you* must not seek such appellations of arrogant eminence ;
for you have but one Oracle in sacred teaching, namely, [myself,] the
Messiah, and you are all on a level [of private judgment in your
friendly fraternity, being obliged to succumb to no man's dictation
as to religious truth. 9 On the same ground of equality], you ought
not to dignify any mortal with the title of '*Father*' [in spiritual dog-
matism over you] ; for you have only one Father, whose word is your
law, namely, your Heavenly Father. 11 On the contrary, if any one
is more distinguished in position or attainments among you, he is
rather to be emulous in serving the rest with a superior assiduity ;
12 for [in the discriminations of my administration the unfailing
maxim will hold true, that] 'overweening pride is sure to be humbled, while unambitious worth is promoted.' "

14 [Then turning to the parties themselves thus animadverted upon,
who stood near, Jesus continued his strictures by the following direct
rebuke :] "Shame and retribution on such hypocrites as you Pharisaical scribes! your nefarious embezzlement of widows' property—[of
which you have gained the control by the confidence inspired] by your
pretended piety in protracted and frequent devotions,—will ere long
meet with the aggravated punishment it deserves. 15 Specious miscreants you are, who 'traverse sea and land' with indefatigable zeal,
to win a single proselyte to your religion ; and after you have [gained
over some heathen to Judaism, and especially to your own sect,] you
only render him twice as fit for perdition as yourselves, [by your
bigoted tenets!] 16 What miserable sophistry do you teach your

Matt. XXIII.

---

a Mark xii, 38.　　　　*b* Luke xx, 45.

157*

ever shall swear by the *temple*, it is   MATT. XXIII.
nothing; but whosoever shall swear
by the *gold* of the temple, he is a debtor : ¹⁷(ye fools
and blind! for whether is greater the gold, or the
temple that sanctifieth the ·gold ?) ¹⁸ and whosoever
shall swear by the *altar*, it is nothing; but whosoever sweareth by the *gift* that is upon it, he is guilty :
¹⁹(ye fools, and blind! for whether is greater the gift,
or the altar that sanctifieth the gift ?) ·²⁰ Whoso
therefore shall swear by the altar, sweareth by it and
by all things thereon; ²¹ and whoso shall swear by
the temple, sweareth by it and by him that dwelleth
therein.   ²⁹ Woe unto you, scribes and Pharisees,
hypocrites! because ye build the tombs of the prophets and garnish the sepulchres of the righteous, ³⁰ and
say, If *we* had been in the days of our fathers, we
would not have been partakers with them in the
blood of the prophets; ³¹ wherefore ye be witnesses
unto yourselves, that ye are the *children* of them
which killed the prophets, [LUKE XI, 48] for ye build their
sepulchres; ³² fill ye up then the measure of your
fathers.   ³³ Ye serpents, ye generation of vipers, how·
can ye escape the damnation of hell ?   ³⁴ Wherefore
[LUKE XI, 49] also said the wisdom of God, Behold, I send
unto you prophets and wise men and scribes; and
some of them ye shall kill and crucify, and some of
them shall ye scourge in your synagogues and persecute them from city to city : ³⁵ that upon you may
come all the righteous blood shed upon the earth
[LUKE XI, 50] from the foundation of the world, from the
blood of righteous Abel * unto the blood of Zacharias
son of Barachias,† whom ye slew between the temple
and the altar; ³⁶ verily I say unto you, All these
things shall come upon this generation.   ³⁷ O Jerusa-

---

* See Gen. iv, 8.   † See 2 Chron. xxiv, 21.

pupils, that 'an oath taken "by the sacredness   MATT. XXIII.
of the Temple," is of no importance,' [and may
therefore be broken with innocence ;] but that
' if one vows in the penalty of the *gold* devoted to the Temple, he
is solemnly bound to fulfill his promise !' [17] Stupid and stark-
blind guides to the spiritual traveler !—which is entitled to the
higher reverence, the mere gold contributed to the Temple, or
the Temple itself which imparts to the gold all its reputed sanctity ? [18] And in the same way you inculcate that ' an oath rati-
fied by an appeal to the altar [of burnt-offerings], is of no force ;'
but that ' if one swears by a pledge of the offering laid upon the
altar, he must forfeit its value, in case of a failure.' [19] Blear-eyed
blockheads ! not to see that it is equally true in this case, [20] that
whoever makes oath by the altar, virtually includes an appeal to
the sanctity of all its contents ; [21] while any one who swears by
the Temple, appeals at the same time to the Divine Inmate to
whom it is dedicated. [29] Your hollow-hearted piety appears, too,
in your rebuilding the tombs of the ancient prophets, and beau-
tifying the monuments of former saints ; [30] exclaiming with pretended sorrow, ' Had we lived in the days of our forefathers who
were their cotemporaries, we would not have participated with
them in the martyrdom of these holy men :' [31] when in fact,
[by your persecuting malice toward me,] you, who repair these
worthies' sepulchres, convict yourselves as genuine descend-
ants [a] concurring in the acts | of your ancestors, who slew them,
[—both being at heart parties in the murder, just as when one
person kills a man, and another buries up his body.] [32] Thus
are you filling to the brim whatever was deficient in the vessel
of your ancestors' crimes, till it shall overflow the measure of
the divine forbearance ! [33] how then, you desperate brood of
malignant vipers, can you escape the condign doom of irre-
trievable woe ? [34] [As a full test of this your incorrigible tem-
per,] [b] God, in His supreme wisdom, | has resolved to favor you
with the mission of [b] Apostolic | teachers of inspired knowl-
edge ; yet I am aware that you will put some of these to death,
even by the barbarous mode of crucifixion ; while on others
you will inflict the ignominy of public lashes, and persecute
the rest from one town to another. [35] Thus you will be visited
with the full penalty [of consummated guilt, the retribution
demanded] for the bloodshed of all previous saints, from the
murder of Abel down to that of Zechariah the son of [Jehoi'-
ada or] Barachi'ah, whom your nation butchered between the
Temple and the [great] Altar ; [36] yes, I assure you, the punishment for all these unrepented atrocities will be exacted of your
countrymen within the present generation !

[37] "O Jerusalem, Jerusalem," concluded Jesus, [as he mournfully foresaw the ruin which their impenitence would soon
bring upon them,] "the murderess of the prophets, and mal-

a Luke xi, 48.   *b* Luke xi, 49.

lem, Jerusalem, thou that killest the   MATT. XXIII.
prophets and stonest them which are
sent unto thee, how often would I have gathered thy
children together, even as a hen gathereth her chickens
under her wings ; and ye would not!   ³⁸ Behold, your
house is left unto you desolate ; ³⁹ for I say unto you,
Ye shall not see me henceforth, till [LUKE XIII, 35] the time
come when ye shall say, Blessed is he that cometh in
the name of the Lord.

§ 121.—*The Preference of the Widow's Trifling Gift.*

(Jerusalem, the Temple, Court of the Women ; *Wednesday, March* 16, A. D. 29.)

⁴¹ And Jesus sat over against the treas-   **Mark XII.**
ury ; and [LUKE XXI, 1] he looked up and beheld
how the people cast money into the treasury : and
many that were rich cast in much.   ⁴² And there came
a certain poor widow, and she threw in *two mites*,
which make a farthing : ⁴³ and he called unto him his
disciples and saith unto them, Verily I say unto you,
That this poor widow hath cast more in than all they
which have cast into the treasury ; ⁴⁴ for all they did
cast in of their abundance [LUKE XXI, 3] unto the offerings
of God, but she of her want did cast in all that she had,
even all her living.

§ 122.—*After gratifying the Request of some Proselytes for an Interview, Christ Retires from Public.*

(Jerusalem, the Temple, Court of the Gentiles; *Wednesday, March* 16, A. D. 29.)

²⁰ And there were certain Greeks among   **John XII.**
them, that came up to worship at the feast :
²¹ the same came therefore to Philip, which was of
Bethsaida of Galilee, and desired him saying, Sir, we
would see Jesus.   ²² Philip cometh and telleth An-

treater of the divine messengers sent to thee, how
gladly would I ever have collected thy inhabitants
into the security of my followers, with an affec-
tionate concern like that of the hen, as she screens her tender brood
under her wings! but, alas! thou hast continually refused my pro-
tecting care. [36] And now, [in return for rejecting me, mark me,
you who are its citizens, the metropolis that constitutes] your cherished home, with its proud Temple will shortly be reduced to a
desolate ruin, [on my desertion;] [39] nor, I warn you, will I ever
henceforth return [to bless your anxious gaze with my delivering
presence], unless a penitent hour shall come when you can greet
my message with the welcome,—

MATT. XXIII.

> 'Glad homage be the meed of him who comes,
> Expected long, Vice-gerent of the skies!'"

§ 121.—*The Preference of the Widow's Trifling Gift.*

(Jerusalem, the Temple, Court of the Women; *Wednesday, March* 16, A. D. 29.)

[41] As Jesus was sitting [in the Court of the Women],
engaged in these discussions, he [a] chanced to cast his
eyes toward the chests that stood opposite him for
the reception of the sacred fund, into which the numbers who attended the Festival were continually dropping their [a] voluntary
contributions [for the support of the Temple services], many of
the wealthier Jews ostentatiously flinging in large sums of money.
As he continued looking at the crowd of offerers, [42] [b] he observed
among them a widow, evidently in indigent circumstances, approach the coffer and drop into it two *lepta* [a minute bronze coin],
(together making only a *quadrans* [i. e. about 2 mills] in value.)
[43] [Struck with the unaffected generosity of the woman,] he called
his disciples, and remarked to them, "I assure you, yonder poor
widow has made a proportionally greater donation than any of the
other contributors: [44] for all the rest have merely given what they
could easily spare from their superabundance; whereas she, poor
as she is, has thrown into the treasury her very last means of
subsistence!"

Mark XII.

§ 122.—*After gratifying the Request of some Proselytes for an Interview, Christ Retires from Public.*

(Jerusalem, the Temple, Court of the Gentiles; *Wednesday, March* 16, A. D. 29.)

[20] Among the concourse of visitors at the Festival
were a party of Hellenistic "Proselytes of the Gate"
[i. e. Gentiles speaking Greek, partially initiated into
Judaism], who resorted thither for divine worship. [21] These persons not being allowed admittance into the inner part of the Tem-
ple-inclosure, where Christ was at this time teaching,] seeing Philip
(of Bethsaida-in-Galilee), [whom they recognized as belonging to
the company of his Master, in the Outer Court,] approached him
with this request, "We wish, sir, to have an interview with Jesus."
[22] Philip immediately went [into the Women's Court, where the rest
of the disciples were with their Master, and reported this intimation
to his townsman Andrew, and they then both announced it to Jesus

John XII.

_a_ Luke xxi, 1.   _b_ Luke xxi, 2.

drew : and again, Andrew and Philip tell   JOHN XII.
Jesus.   [23] And Jesus answered them saying, The hour is come, that the Son of man should
be glorified : [24] verily, verily I say unto you, Except
a corn of wheat fall into the ground and *die*, it abideth
alone; but if it die, it bringeth forth much fruit.
[25] He that loveth his life, shall lose it ; and he that
hateth his life in this world, shall keep it unto life
eternal : [26] if any man serve me, let him follow me ;
and where I am, there shall also my servant be : if
any man serve me, him will my Father honor.—
[27] Now is my soul troubled; and what shall I say ?
Father, save me from this hour ? but for this cause
came I unto this hour.   [28] Father, glorify thy name.
Then came there a voice from heaven saying, I
have both glorified it and will glorify it *again.*
[29] The people therefore that stood by and heard it,
said that it thundered.   Others said, An angel spake
to him.   [30] Jesus answered and said, This voice came
not because of *me*, but for *your* sakes.   [31] Now is
the judgment of this world ; now shall the prince of
this world be cast out.   [32] And I, if I be lifted up
from the earth, will draw all men unto me.   [33](This
he said signifying what death he should die.)   [34] The
people answered him, We have heard out of the law*
that Christ abideth *forever;* and how sayest thou,
The Son of man must be lifted up ? who is this Son
of man ?   [35] Then Jesus said unto them, Yet a little
while is the light with you : walk while ye have the

---

* See 2 Sam. vii, 13 ; Psa. cx, 4; Dan. ii, 44.

himself. [23] Jesus accordingly [went out to the petition- JOHN XII.
ers, and to satisfy their curiosity as to the emoluments of
his adherents], made to them the following remarks:
"The destined hour for the elevation of the 'Son of Man' [to the most
glorious exhibition of his character], is indeed well nigh arrived: [24] yet
let me call your serious attention to the fact, that unless a kernel of
grain planted in the ground *decay* in the process of germination, it
must remain solitary and unproductive ; but on the other hand its
seemingly perishing in this manner becomes the means of its subsequent growth and prolific increase at harvest; [—and just so, my un-
promising sleep among the dead is requisite in order to the glorious
progress of my mission. [25] As regards your own expectation of advantage from a connection with my career, let me tell you, in accordance
with this principle, that] whoever declines espousing my cause from
attachment to the safety and comfort of his present life, will infallibly
incur the loss of its higher interests for hereafter ; while he that disre-
gards the security of his earthly existence in competition with fidelity
to me, will thereby most effectually guard its eternal welfare. [26] If
therefore any one becomes an adherent to my service, he must consent to follow me in all my fortunes; and then in whatever circumstances and station the issue of my enterprise shall place me, as my
constant attendant he will be a partner in my company and condition: it is on those that thus serve me, that my Father will confer the
eventual honors of my Administration."
[27] [Here for a moment overwhelmed with the sudden prospect of the
agony to which he had just alluded as awaiting himself, Jesus burst
forth into the passionate exclamation,] "Already is my spirit seized
with gloomy perturbation ! [To what prayer can I run for relief from
the terrors that assail me?] O my Father, shall I implore Thee to spare
me the fearful ordeal [of judicial atonement]?—but no! for that great
purpose itself [of enduring it,] it was, that I have presented myself to
this trying anguish [of vicarious passion]. [28] I will only ask Thee, Father, Secure Thy honor in my mission by whatever mode Thou seest
best." Immediately there was heard a response from the sky, "Yes, I
have thus far promoted My glory [by the influences connected with the
arrangements for the Messiah's coming], and I will still further enhance My praise [by the results flowing from the accomplishment of
that scheme] !" [29] At the sound of these ominous words, the bystanding populace declared, "Hark ! it thunders." But a few others [who
had heard more distinctly,] were confident that "it was an angel
speaking to Jesus." [30] He, however, explained the matter by remarking, "The celestial declaration you have just heard was not so much
designed for *my* satisfaction, as for the confirmation of your faith in
me." [31] [Then drawing encouragement from the evident impression
made upon the auditors by this attesting portent, Jesus proceeded in
a more exulting strain,] "The crisis of my great condemnatory contest with the corrupt nature and practices of a sinful race, is now close
at hand, in which its Satanic ringleader is to receive a fatal sentence
of expulsion from his sovereignty; [32] yes, [the most forbidding circumstance of my expiatory inflictions,] must become the very means of my
certain triumph,] for by being reared aloft above the earth, I shall the
more effectually attract universal attention and homage." [33] By this
last observation Jesus hinted at his destined mode of death upon the
cross, [but left his hearers to pursue for the present their favorite interpretation of the Messiah's exaltation to kingly power.] [34] The
crowd, however, [in their misconceived views on the subject,] captiously rejoined, "Why, *we* have been accustomed to learn from the

light, lest darkness come upon you ; for　JOHN XII.
he that walketh in darkness knoweth
not whither he goeth : 36 while ye have light, believe in the light, that ye may be the children of
light.

These things spake Jesus, and departed and did
hide himself from them. 37 But though he had
done so many miracles before them, yet they believed not on him ; 38 that the saying of Esaias
the prophet might be fulfilled which he spake,*
Lord, who hath believed our report, and to whom
hath the arm of the Lord been revealed ? 39 therefore they could not believe, because that Esaias said
again,† 40 He hath blinded their eyes and hardened
their heart ; that they should not see with their
eyes nor understand with their heart, and be converted, and I should heal them : 41 these things said
Esaias, when he saw his glory and spake of him.
42 Nevertheless among the chief-rulers also many
believed on him ; but because of the Pharisees they
did not confess him, lest they should be put out of
the synagogue : 43 for they loved the praise of men
more than the praise of God.—44 Jesus cried and
said, He that believeth on me, believeth not on me,
but on him that sent me ;‡ 45 and he that seeth
me, seeth him that sent me.‖ 46 I am come a light
into the world, that whosoever believeth on me
should not abide in darkness.¶ 47 And if any man
hear my words and believe not, I judge him not ;**
for I came not to judge the world, but to save the
world :†† 48 he that rejecteth me and receiveth not

---

* Isa. liii, 1.　† Isa. vi, 10.　‡ See chap. v, 23, 38 ; compare viii, 42, 47.
‖ See chap. v, 19, 36, 37 ; compare viii, 29 ; x, 25, 30, 38.
¶ See chap. viii, 12 ; compare ix, 5 ; xii, 35.　** See chap. v, 45.
†† See chap. iii, 17 ; compare v, 24 ; viii, 51.

Scriptures, that the Messiah is to continue *perpetually*   John XII.
[in his personal office upon earth] ; what do you mean
then by saying that ' the " Son of Man" must be reared
aloft' [and borne away to heaven]! What kind of a 'Son of Man' would
that be ?" [35] [Without directly meeting this prejudice,] Jesus admonished them in reply, " Only a little while longer is the Light to remain among you : be careful then to go about [in the execution of your duties], while this light beams upon your pathway, lest a premature night [of unillumined ignorance] overtake you, ere you have performed the needful task ; and whoever then attempts to walk about in the dark, [as you are now doing,] must surely miss his way. [36] Therefore, while you are favored with the teaching of the present Light, confide in the instructions thus imparted, and then alone you will truly become well-informed sharers of religious day."

Having finished these public discourses, Jesus departed from the Temple, and thenceforth secluded himself from the concourse resorting there. [37] Indeed, [his intercourse with the people at large was now evidently no longer of any avail, for] although he had effected so many stupendous miracles in their very sight, they still persisted in [either utterly rejecting, or else as hopelessly] misinterpreting his sacred character. [38] This treatment of him, however, was a striking verification of the ancient prophecy of Isaiah,—

> ' And yet, despite these intimations plain,
> Who of my countrymen will credit me ?—
> Few in His actions scan the power divine ;
> So false the notions of expectant pride !"

[39] Of this [disregard of the Messiah's true characteristics,] their failure to confide in him was the natural consequence ; just as the same prophet had indicated in another passage,—

> [40] " Their inward ears obtuse refuse to hear
> God's truth, they close the eyesight of their souls ;
> Resolved they will not be convinced thereby,
> To change their evil ways, and pardon find."

[41] These premonitory declarations Isaiah had uttered long ago, as he prophetically contemplated the times of the Messiah, who was the theme of his predictions. [42] Still, [amid this general incredulity,] a considerable number even of the chief men of the nation secretly believed in Jesus's claims, although on account of the [predominance of the] Pharisaical party, they did not publicly avow their convictions, lest they might incur the threatened penalty of excommunication ; [43] [and this ignominious trial,] their minds, being attached more strongly to the good opinion of their fellow men than to the approbation of God, [were not prepared to brave.—[44] This unbelief, moreover, Jesus himself had reproved by his public instructions, which also afforded additional evidence of his mission ; for] he had distinctly declared in substance, that " he who confided in him, did not so much give credence to *him* merely, as thereby evince his faith in Him whose Messenger he was," [45] inasmuch as " whoever was a spectator of his [miraculous and doctrinal] acts, did therein really witness those of Him whose commission he bore [as Representative and equal] ;"— [46] that " he had appeared on earth as a Teacher to illuminate the minds of men, and thus preserve all who would rely upon his instructions, from continuing in the darkness of depraved ignorance ;" [47] although " if any one should disbelieve his annunciations after hearing them, *he* [Christ] would not need to pass sentence of retribution himself upon him at the time," " as it was not the object of his terrestrial mission to condemn mankind, but to save their souls ;" [48] for " those

my words, hath one that judgeth him ; * the   JOHN XII.
word that I have spoken, the same shall
judge him in the last day.† ⁴⁹ For I have not spoken
of myself; but the Father which sent me, he gave me
a commandment, what I should say, and what I should
speak :‡ ⁵⁰ and I know that his commandment is life
everlasting ; ‖ whatsoever I speak therefore, even as
the Father said unto me, so I speak.¶

§ 123.—*Christ minutely Predicts the signal Destruction of persecuting Jerusalem, and Warns his Followers of the final Judgment.*

(Mount of Olives; *Wednesday, March* 16, A. D. 29.)

¹ And Jesus went out and departed   **Matt. XXIV.**
from the temple : and his disciples came
to him for to show him the buildings of the temple,
[LUKE XXI, 5] how it was adorned with goodly stones and gifts.
² And Jesus said unto them, See ye not all these
things ? verily I say unto you, [LUKE XXI, 6] The days will
come in the which there shall not be left here one stone
upon another, that shall not be thrown down. ³ And
as he sat upon the Mount of Olives [MARK XIII, 3] over
against the temple, the disciples [MARK XIII, 3] Peter and
James and John and Andrew came unto him privately
saying, Tell us, *when* shall these things be ? and
what shall be the *sign* of thy coming and of the end
of the world ? ⁴ And Jesus answered and said unto
them, Take heed that no man deceive you : ⁵ for
many shall come in my name saying, I am Christ ;
and shall deceive many ; [LUKE XXI, 8] and the time draweth
near: go ye not therefore after them. ⁶ And ye shall hear
of wars and rumors of wars : see that ye be not

○ See chap. viii, 50.   ‡ See chap. v, 30; vii, 16; viii, 28.
† Compare chap. iii, 19; ix, 41.   ‖ See chap. v, 39.
¶ Compare chap. vii, 28, 29; viii, 26.

that disallowed his claims and rejected his declara- JOHN XII.
tions, had another judge, namely the announcement
itself which he had often made to them, [49] to the effect
that ' he did not utter promulgations of his own prompting, but that
his Father who had dispatched him on his mission, had instructed
him what injunctions and communications to make,' [48] and this
statement [being a sufficient basis for their belief,] would prove the
ground of such person's condemnation at the final judgment;" [50] and
he had virtually added, that " being fully confident that immortal
bliss could be secured through his Father's prescriptions alone, he
had closely conformed his communications with those directions."

§ 123.—*Christ minutely Predicts the signal Destruction of persecuting Jerusalem, and Warns his Followers of the final Judgment.*

(Mount of Olives; *Wednesday, March* 16, A. D. 29.)

[1] Having thus despondingly quitted the Temple **Matt. XXIV.**
[for the last time, as Jesus was slowly wending his
way toward Bethany], his followers collected about
him, and [as they ascended the Mount of Olives, which commands
the view of the whole city,] one of them [in admiration at the im-
posing sight of the Temple edifice just opposite,] pointed it out with
national pride, *a* exclaiming, " Teacher, look again at the huge
stones! *b* of dazzling whiteness, *a* of which yonder vast structure is
composed, *b* with its walls gorgeously hung with costly offerings! !"
[2] Jesus, however, impressively checked these fond expressions by replying, " Gaze [with delight a little longer, if you will,] upon all
those *c* splendid buildings; but mark the solemn prediction which
I here make to you, *d* The calamitous period is rapidly drawing
near, when *not a single stone on that site will be left unrazed upon
another !*"
[3] Having by this time reached the top of the hill, as he sat down,
e in full view of the Temple, [to muse and discourse upon the topic,]
e the brothers Peter and Andrew, together with James and John,
approached him privately with this inquiry, "*f* Teacher, let us hear
when this wonderful catastrophe is to occur?—tell us by what *token*
we may anticipate the eventful time of the public demonstration of
your power, that is thus to consummate the present order of things?"
[4] [With the design of sobering this curiosity, and at the same time
setting the important subjects they had thus confounded, in their
true light,] Jesus replied *g* by the following admonitory discourse to
his followers about him: " I caution you against being led astray [in
your anticipations respecting the mode and time of this my public
manifestation]: [5] for numerous impostors will presently appear
among you, who by assuming my Messianic character, *h* and proclaiming that ' that destined period has arrived,' will delude not a
few of their countrymen to the belief of their claims; *h* but do not
you become their partisans. [6] Neither suffer your minds to be agitated with apprehensions of this event's immediate occurrence, on
account of the civil commotions, warlike encounters and threatened vengeance *i* for insurrections, with which your ears will soon
be saluted in various quarters of the land; for a great many such

a Mark xiii, 1.   b Luke xxi, 5.   c Mark xiii, 2.
d Luke xxi, 6.   e Mark xiii, 3.   f Luke xxi, 7.
g Mark xiii, 5.   h Luke xxi, 8.   i Luke xxi, 9.

troubled; for all these things must Matt. **XXIV.**
[Luke XXI, 9] first come to pass, but the end
is not yet.   ⁷ For nation shall rise against nation, and
kingdom against kingdom; and there shall be famines
and pestilences and earthquakes in divers places
[Mark XIII, 8] and troubles; [Luke XXI, 11] and fearful sights and
great signs shall there be from heaven: ⁸ all these are the
beginning of sorrows.

   ¹⁷ But beware of men: for [Luke XXI, 12]   **Matt. X.**
before all these they shall lay their hands on you
and persecute you, and they will deliver you up to the
councils [Luke XXI, 12] and into prisons, and they will
scourge you in their synagogues; ¹⁸ and ye shall be
brought before governors and kings for my sake,
[Luke XXI, 13] and it shall turn to you for a testimony
against them and the Gentiles.   ¹⁹ But when they
deliver you up, take no thought [Mark XIII, 11] beforehand
how or what ye shall speak [Luke XII, 11] or what thing
ye shall answer, [Mark XIII, 11] neither do ye premeditate; but
whatsoever shall be given you in that hour, that speak ye:
for it shall be given you in that same hour what ye
shall speak; [Luke XXI, 15] I will give you a mouth and wisdom, which all your adversaries shall not be able to gainsay
nor resist: ²⁰ for it is not ye that speak, but the Spirit
of your Father which speaketh in you.—³⁴ Think not
that I am come to send peace on earth; I came not
to send peace, but a sword [Luke XII, 51] and division: [49] I
am come to send fire on the earth, and what will I, if it be
already kindled? ³⁵ for I am come to set a man at variance against his father, and the daughter against her
mother, and the daughter-in-law against her mother-
in-law; ³⁶ and a man's foes shall be they of his own
household: [Luke XII, 52] for from henceforth there shall be
five in one house divided, three against two, and two against
three.   ⁹ Then shall they deliver you up   **Matt. XXIV.**
to be afflicted: [Mark XIII, 12] the brother

163

alarming incidents are to take place previous to **MATT. XXIV.** the expected *consummation* of your people's destiny, which is not to transpire so soon as you imagine. ⁷No, there will be one part of the nation arrayed in hostile force against another, and this one of its chieftains involved in deadly feud against that one; while famine here, pestilence there, and *a* tremendous! earthquakes elsewhere all over the country will add their horrors *b* to the distractions of those times, !—*a* and, besides other terrific providential occurrences, the very skies will exhibit frightful portents of impending disaster :! ⁸yet all these dire calamities are but the first slight heavings of the fatal throes which will finally ensue to this devoted community!

¹⁷ "But *c* before these ominous events shall transpire, **Matt. X.** trials¡ [will occur to yourselves, which] will require your greatest firmness and circumspection, [in order to preserve your religious integrity uninjured,] against the malicious plans of wicked men. For you will be *c* subjected to the most violent persecution,! by being impeached before the San'hedrim, lacerated with stripes in the very synagogues, *c* incarcerated in dungeons,! ¹⁸ and arraigned before rulers even of royal authority, all simply in consequence of your adherence to me; but [if you faithfully endure these inflictions,] you will thereby afford the most effective proof both to your Jewish and Gentile persecutors, of the truth of the religion you profess. ¹⁹ But when your fellow-citizens thus treacherously criminate you, *d* I wish you particularly to remember! that you need be under no concern *d* to *premeditate*! the form or matter of any *d* defense of yourselves;! you have only to rely upon the inspired *e* eloquence and sagacity with which I! will furnish you on the occasion *e* so effectually that none of your opponents will be able to refute or invalidate your reasoning;! ²⁰ for you will not be left in those critical moments to the unaided powers of your own minds, but your language will be prompted and energized by the influences of the *f* Holy! Spirit, [which your Heavenly Father will afford you on my behalf.]—³⁴ You are not to suppose [from my own patient demeanor], that the first effects of my mission will be to produce harmony among those to whom it comes; on the contrary, my advent to this nation will be the signal for unsheathing the sword *g* of disunion, ! *h* and inflaming the fire-brand of strife between two classes of its inhabitants!—nay, that torch is already lighted [in the enmity manifested against myself], and I cannot wish that the occasion were avoided.! ³⁵ For the immediate result of my coming will be, to introduce such a disparity of sentiment between the most intimate relatives, by converting some of them to my religion, that children will often be found arrayed in bitter opposition to parents, or parents against their children; ³⁶ so that one [of my followers] will not seldom find the members of his own family his most formidable and violent enemies, [on account of his faith. ⁹ In the alienations of **Matt. XXIV.** that period,] one of your own *i* parents, brothers or friends! will perfidiously expose you to the persecuting magistrates, and *j* even your children thus turn against you! and cause the death of *i* some of their parents;! indeed, you must expect to be detested [as fanatics] by all your acquaintances, even the re-

a Luke xxi, 11.   *b* Mark xiii, 8.   *c* Luke xxi, 12.   *d* Luke xxi, 14.
e Luke xxi, 15.   *f* Mark xiii, 11.   *g* Luke xii, 51.   *h* Luke xii, 49.
i Luke xxi, 16.   *j* Mark xiii, 12.

shall betray the brother to death, and the ·Matt. **XXIV.**
father the son; and children shall rise up
against their parents, and shall kill [Luke XXI, 16] some of
you : and ye shall be hated of all nations for my
name's sake. ¹⁰·And then shall many be offended,
and shall betray one another and shall hate one another. ²⁸ And [Luke XII, 4] I say unto you, my   **Matt. X.**
friends, Fear not them which kill the *body*,
but are not able to kill the *soul ;* but rather fear him
which is able to destroy both soul and body in hell.·
¹³ But he that shall endure unto the end,· **Matt. XXIV.**
the same shall be saved : [Luke XXI, 19] in
your patience possess ye your souls : [Luke XII, 32] fear not,
little flock ; for it is your Father's good pleasure to give you
the kingdom. ¹⁴ And this gospel of the kingdom shall
be preached in all the world, for a witness unto all.
nations ; and then shall the end come.

¹⁵ When ye therefore shall see [Luke XXI, 20] Jerusalem
compassed with armies, and the abomination of desolation,
spoken of by Daniel the prophet, stand in the holy
place [Mark XIII, 14] where it ought not, (whoso readeth, let
him understand ;) [Luke XXI, 20] then know that the desolation thereof is nigh. ¹⁶ Then let them which be in
Judea, flee into the mountains ; [Luke XXI, 21] and let them
which are in the midst of it, depart out ; and let not them that·
are in the countries, enter thereinto : ¹⁷ let him which is
on the house-top, not come down [Mark XIII, 15] into the
house neither enter therein, to take anything out of his
house : ¹⁸ neither let him which is in the field, return
back to take his clothes : [Luke XVII, 32] remember Lot's wife.ᵒ

ᵒ Gen. xix, 26.

lentless Gentiles, in consequence of your profession of my name. [10] The hardships of this opposition, in which each one will have the prospect of
MATT. XXIV.
being betrayed some day through the malevolence of his former
friends, will cause many of my adherents to apostatize
from my cause; [28] but I admonish you, *a* my followers, I
that instead of being terrified out of your fidelity by the
Matt. X.
force of human persecution, which can reach no farther, at the utmost, than to the destruction of the *body*, you must shun with trembling care the dreadful doom that will overtake [Jewish and other]
apostates, at the hand of Him who can not only destroy the body [by
such judgments as we have been contemplating], but
also plunge the soul in endless perdition ! [13] Those
of my adherents, however, who persevere in their
Matt. XXIV.
allegiance to me even under the most extreme discouragement and
persecutions, will eventually experience deliverance [from that awful
two-fold fate, as well as from the trials and inflictions caused by their
Jewish enemies] ; *b* maintain your constancy, therefore, and thus
preserve your safety I [both in that crisis and for eternity]. *c* Neither
be alarmed [as to the final success of the cause which you have es-
poused] ; for though a small and feeble band now, [you are yet the
objects of divine complacence, and] it is the certain purpose of your
Heavenly Father to instate you triumphantly in the full privileges
of His 'Messiah's Reign' [on earth and hereafter.]I [14] And in fulfillment of this design, the gospel in which I am now proclaiming this
'Reign,' will be published to the world at large, by you the witnesses
to all mankind of its truth, before that crowning catastrophe shall
occur, which will close the present Dispensation [of Judaism].

[15] "So soon *d* however, I as you shall see *e* Jerusalem invested with
besieging troops, I (for eventually will be seen that idolatrous symbol
—the sure harbinger of wide-spread desolation wherever it appears
[*i. e.* the silver eagles on the tops of the Roman standards, images
which the soldiers worshiped as sacred]—intimated by the prophet
Daniel, reared in defiance within the precincts of the interior in-
closure of the Temple, *d* profaning that hallowed spot by its ruthless impiety, I) *e* then," continued Jesus, I (and let every one who
peruses this account of his solemn prediction, mark well its striking
language,) "*e* be apprised that the great catastrophe of your nation
will no longer be delayed ;I [16] therefore, upon the occurrence of
that signal presage, let every one of you that shall be residing in
the country of Judea [Proper], escape with all dispatch to the hills
beyond its borders, *f* and if any happen to be within the city itself,
let them instantly quit it, as they value their lives, while those
who live in the neighboring villages must not venture to enter it
for any purpose. I [17] [Such indeed should be your haste to save
yourselves from the sudden closing in of the blockading army, that
on its approach,] a person on one of the housetops of the city will
not have time to descend and carry away his effects within, [but
must run with his household for the walls over the adjoining roofs;]
[18] nor must the laborer in the field return to his house, for the sake
of securing any of his property, even his clothing, [but must hurry
his family away with the utmost speed: *g* if you should linger to
secure these inferior concerns], you might be overtaken by a fate
as melancholy as the memorable one that befell Lot's wife, I [as she
turned a wistful gaze back to the doomed city she was leaving ;]

---

a Luke xii, 4.   *b* Luke xxi, 19.   *c* Luke xii, 32.   *d* Mark xiii, 14.
e Luke xxi, 20.   *f* Luke xxi, 21.   *g* Luke xvii, 32.

[LUKE XXI, 22] For these be the days of ven-　MATT. XXIV.
geance, that all things which are written*
may be fulfilled. ¹⁹ And woe unto them that are
mothers in those days ! ²⁰ but pray ye that your flight
be not in the winter neither on the sabbath-day :
²¹ for then shall be great tribulation [LUKE XXI, 23] in the
land and wrath upon this people, such as was not since
the beginning of the world to this time, no, nor ever
shall be. [LUKE XXI, 24] And they shall fall by the edge of
the sword, and shall be led away captive into all nations ;
and Jerusalem shall be trodden down of the Gentiles, until
the times of the Gentiles be fulfilled.† ²² And except
those days should be shortened, there should no
flesh be saved ; but for the elect's sake those days
shall be shortened. [LUKE XVII, 22] And he said unto the
disciples, The days will come, when ye shall desire to see
one of the days of the Son of man, and ye shall not see it :
²³ then if any man shall say unto you, Lo, here is
Christ ! or, There ! believe it not. ²⁴ For there
shall arise false Christs and false prophets, and
shall show great signs and wonders ; insomuch that,
if it were possible, they shall deceive the very
elect : [MATT. XXIV, 12] and because iniquity shall abound,
the love of many shall wax cold : 25 behold, I have told
you before. ²⁶ Wherefore if they shall say unto
you, Behold, he is in the desert ! go not forth ;
Behold, he is in the secret chambers ! believe it
not : ²⁷ for as the lightning cometh out of the east,
and shineth even unto the west ; so shall also the
coming of the Son of man be [LUKE XVII, 24] in his
day. [37] And they answered and said unto him, Where,
Lord ? And he said unto them, ²⁸ For wheresoever

---

* See particularly Dan. ix, 26 ; Deut. xxviii, 49-67.
† Compare especially Ezek. xxxvii, 21.

a for that will be the overwhelming period of **MATT. XXIV.**
divine retribution upon this guilty metropolis, in
which the full denunciations of prophecy will be
executed.| [19] But woe to those females in that terrible emergency,
whose delicate circumstances or tender infants prevent their speedy
removal! [20] You will need also most earnestly to entreat the God
of providence, that your flight at that juncture may not occur during
the inclemency of the winter rains, nor fall upon the sacred sabbath,
[which would so materially impede your escape, the former circumstance by the inconvenience and hardship of the season, and the
latter by a just scrupulousness as to violating the day:] [21] For that
will be a time of the most general and unprecedented distress *b* in
this land, and retributive suffering to its inhabitants,| that has ever
happened since the creation of the world *c* by its divine Governor|
down to the present time, and one not to be at all equaled by the
rigors of any similar catastrophe in the future: *d* a calamity that
will result in the most unsparing butchery of yonder citizens, and
their miserable slavery as prisoners of war among all nations, while
Jerusalem itself will then be trodden with galling occupancy by the
exulting heel of the profane Gentile [Romans and other infidel con-
querors], until the prophetical term of this heathen sway shall have
fully elapsed.| [22] So severe, indeed, will be the exterminating ruin
of that crisis, that were it protracted to the full fury of human designs, it must involve the universal destruction of the Jewish race;
but for the sake of preserving the redeemed [Christian] portion from
the same massacre and proscription, the continuance of that fell period
will be abbreviated *e* by Almighty providence.|

[23] "At the time of that melancholy catastrophe," continued Jesus,
"if any person should announce to you that 'the Messiah has appeared in this place or that!' place no confidence in these assertions;
[to such popular excitements you will then be peculiarly liable,] for
f it will not be very long after my departure before you will earnestly
wish for the time of my judicial appearance, [in the prospect of being thereby relieved from the persecution which you will be called
to endure,] and that expected event will seem hopelessly delayed:|
[24], [11] [acting upon the similar anticipations of your countrymen, then
wrought up to their highest prevalence,] various pretended Messiahs
and self-styled prophets will spring up, who will exhibit apparent
miracles and prodigies, so artfully as to deceive, if possible, my chosen
followers themselves,—indeed, their delusive pretensions will succeed with but too many of even these, [12] who will suffer their attachment to me to be cooled by the general irreligion of those times.
[25] Observe, I have *g* fully| put you on your guard against such im-
postors; [26] so that if a report comes to you, that 'the Messiah has
been discovered out in the lonesome country!' do not run with the
crowd to see, or if it be said, 'He is to be found in a certain private
room!' never credit it: [27] for unexpected—but obvious, to all [the
doomed inhabitants of this city], as the lightning that flashes from
the east along the whole sky to the west, will be that appointed
'coming of the "Son of Man!"'"

[28] *h* Here the disciples [still undivested of their notions of a pompous manifestation,] inquired, "In what locality, then, *is* this your
triumphant appearance to be made?" Jesus correctively evaded
their curiosity by the proverbial reply,| " 'Wherever the carcass [of
the Jewish victim of despoliation] lies, to that spot will the vultures

a Luke xxi, 22.	*b* Luke xxi, 23.	*c* Mark xiii, 19.	*d* Luke xxi, 24.
e Mark xiii, 20.	*f* Luke xvii, 22.	*g* Mark xiii, 23.	*h* Luke xvii, 37.

the carcass is, there will the eagles   MATT. **XXIV.**
be gathered together.

²⁹ Immediately after the tribulation of those days,
shall the sun be darkened, and the moon shall
not give her light,* and the stars shall fall from
heaven,† and the powers of the heavens shall be
shaken :‡ [LUKE XXI, 25] and upon the earth there shall be
distress of nations with perplexity; the sea and the waves
roaring; [26] men's hearts failing them for fear and for looking after those things which are coming on the earth.
³⁰ And then shall appear the sign of the Son of
man in heaven; and then shall all the tribes of
the earth mourn,‖ and they shall see the Son of
man coming in the clouds of heaven¶ with power
and great glory: ³¹ and he shall send his angels
with a great sound of a trumpet, and they shall
gather together his elect from the four winds, from
one end of heaven to the other.   [LUKE XXI, 28] And
when these things begin to come to pass, then look up
and lift up your heads; for your redemption draweth nigh.
³² Now learn a parable of the fig-tree [LUKE XXI, 29] and
all the trees: When their branch is yet tender and
putteth forth leaves, ye know that summer is nigh;
³³ so likewise ye, when ye shall see all these things,
know that [LUKE XXI, 31] the kingdom of God is near,
even at the doors: ³⁴ verily I say unto you, *This
generation shall not pass, till all these things be*

---

* Compare Isa. xiii, 10.   † Compare Isa. xxxiv, 4.
‡ Compare Isa. xiii, 13.   ‖ See Dan vii, 13.
¶ Compare Zech. xii, 12.

[of Roman devastation] flock ;' [they will therefore mainly pounce upon the metropolis, but they will also plunder and lacerate the country of Judea at large.]

MATT. **XXIV.**

²⁹ " Immediately consequent upon the distress of that final campaign," resumed Jesus, " [will occur a state of things in this country, to which may be applied the figurative language of Scripture, (applicable in its full sense only to the final dissolution of nature,) that]—

> ' A night of terror o'er the nation hangs
> As dark as if [the constellated lights
> Of heaven were vail'd with murky clouds,]
> The sun were in his radiant path eclipsed,
> And e'en the moon refused her kindly ray,'—

> ' The very stars, that else had gleam'd for hope,
> Across the sky political, shall drop '

> ' Amid the general shock of state, as if
> Jehovah's arm the vault of heaven rock'd ;'

a [or as it is elsewhere prefigured,]—

> ' Thereafter I will bring to pass events
> Tremendous as celestial prodigies,'

([whether they be, as the prophet intimates,]—

> ' As if the sun to blackness were obscured,
> And fouler blood displaced the moon eclipsed,'

[or affect only the stars, as in other intimations,])

> ' And presages terrestrial, [such as blood
> And flames and curling smoke, all causeless seen
> Along the ground, precursors sure of woe,]'

equally ominous with the roar of the boisterous billows to those exposed to their fury. The dire occurrences [fitly represented by these natural commotions,] will occasion an anxious dismay among the subjects of them, | *b* that will leave them only to breathless terror and despair in prospect of the misfortunes about to fall upon their land !|
³⁰ At that awful exigency will be exhibited to all Jewish eyes the [national judgments that will betoken, in a moral sense, that] expected ' "Son of Man's" appearance on the clouds of the sky,' invested with retributive power befitting such a sublime manifestation; [scenes that will cause such general consternation that in a more doleful sense,]—

> ' Each family throughout the land will wail '

³¹ [in bitter anguish at the inevitable blow; nor will that appearance of His be wanting in the attendant angels suitable to the grandeur of the occasion,] for He will then dispatch the appropriate agents [of His providential designs], with signs of warning clear as the world-wide tones of the trumpet [for the final assemblage of the human race], to gather to a place of safety His chosen followers from every quarter of the country. *c* So soon, therefore, as you shall descry the first distinct occurrence of these ominous symptoms, you may then pluck up courage, assured that your rescue [from present as well as impending afflictions] is close at hand. |
³² [" Respecting the particular *time* of this catastrophe—as well as of the final one which it prefigures," continued Jesus,] "you may learn this lesson of inference : when you notice the young twigs of the fig *d* or any other tree| sprouting and leafing out, you are aware *e* without further information| that the summer season is approaching ;
³³ on the same principle [of arguing consequences from preliminary developments,] upon discerning the preparatory incidents which I

a Luke xxi, 25.   *b* Luke xxi, 26.   *c* Luke xxi, 28.   *d* Luke xxi, 29.   *e* Luke xxi, 30.

fulfilled. ³⁵ Heaven and earth shall   MATT. **XXIV.**
pass away, but my words shall not
pass away. ³⁶ But of that day and hour knoweth no
man, no, not the angels of heaven, [MARK XIII, 32] neither
the Son, but my Father only. ³⁷ But as the days of
Noe were, so shall also the coming of the Son of man
be : ³⁸ for as in the days that were before the flood,
they were eating and drinking, marrying and giving in
marriage, until the day that Noe entered into the ark,
³⁹ and knew not until the flood came and took them
all away : [LUKE XVII, 28] likewise also as it was in the days
of Lot ; they did eat, they drank, they bought, they sold,
they planted, they builded ; [29] but the same day that Lot
went out of Sodom, it rained fire and brimstone from heaven,
and destroyed them all : so shall also the coming of
the Son of man be. [LUKE XVII, 34] I tell you, in that night
there shall be two men in one bed ; the one shall be taken,
and the other shall be left : ⁴⁰ then shall two be in the
field ; the one shall be taken, and the other left :
⁴¹ two women shall be grinding at the mill ; the one
shall be taken, and the other left. ³⁴ And   **Luke XXI.**
take heed to yourselves, lest at any time
your hearts be overcharged with surfeiting and drunk-
enness and cares of this life, and so that day come
upon you unawares ; ³⁵ for as a snare shall it come on
all them that dwell on the face of the whole earth :
³⁶ watch ye therefore and pray always, that ye may
be accounted worthy to escape all these things that
shall come to pass, and to stand before the Son of
man ; [MARK XIII, 33] for ye know not when the time is.
⁴³ But know this, that if the good-man   **Matt. XXIV.**
of the house had known in what watch
the thief would come, he would have watched and
would not have suffered his house to be broken up :
⁴⁴ therefore be ye also ready ; for in such an hour
as ye think not, the Son of man cometh.

167

have mentioned in detail, you should thus be ap-   MATT. **XXIV.**
prised that the *a* establishment of the 'Reign of the
Divine Messiah'! [upon the runs of your national
polity] is imminently nigh. ³⁴ I solemnly declare to you that the identical generation of men now living here shall not have become ex-
tinct, ere the entire course of events to which I have thus far (primarily) alluded, will be consummated ; ³⁵ and you may rest assured,
that 'were the sky and earth to fade into naught,' my assertions shall
never fail! ³⁶ But the exact date of the final catastrophe of your nation (and of the world) no finite being knows, not even the celestial
angels, *b* nor the incarnate Son himself! [of his human ability] ; it is a
secret reserved for the immediate counsels of my Almighty Father,
[and therefore I must not divulge it, although in my divine capacity
I am privy to it.] ³⁷ This only will I tell you, that as in Noah's time,
³⁸ just before the flood, the families about him [despite his continued
admonitions,] were [busied with all security and levity in the ordinary indulgences of life,] taking their usual meals and contracting
marriages, up to the very day that Noah entered the ark,—³⁹ careless
of the threatened deluge which instantly overwhelmed them all ; *c* or
as in the days of Lot, the inhabitants of Sodom were [thoughtlessly
immersed in their temporal affairs,] attending to their meals, their
bargains, their farms and their houses, ! *d* but the very day on which
Lot quitted the city, the lightning kindled [their bituminous soil],
and sunk them in the flaming lake :! ³⁷ equally unsuspected beforehand [in both these future events] will be the decisive manifestation
of the 'Son of Man.' ⁴⁰ So [mysterious to the unexpecting will be
the providential discriminations of each period,] that of *e* two men
sleeping together at night upon the same couch,! or of two laborers
together in the field by day, ⁴¹ or of two women turning the same
handmill, the one [an unbeliever, and therefore unprepared,] will be
overtaken by the destruction, while the other [if a Christian] will
escape, [in the one case, by flight, in the other, by divine salvation.]-
³⁴ Hence, you must exercise an unceasing circum-   Luke **XXI.**
spection over yourselves, lest you suffer your minds
to be stupefied [as in those ancient examples,] by luxurious revelry,
and become so engrossed in worldly concerns, that the tremendous
crisis [in either sense] take you by surprise ; ³⁵ for stealthy as a
trap will it spring upon the fancied safety of the inhabitants of
this land [in its primary fulfillment, and in its secondary, of the
whole world] : ³⁶ you will therefore need [amid this general un-
concern,] to waken your spiritual energies, and maintain your vigilance against the uncertain arrival of these events, by unceasing
prayer, in order that you may personally so preserve your Christian character, as to escape the impending calamities and stand ac-
quitted at this [as at the final] judicial appear-
ance of the 'Son of Man.' ⁴³ Now you know, if a   **Matt. XXIV.**
householder were aware at what hour of the night
a thief was about to attempt a burglary upon him, he would sit up
to guard his house from being broken open ; ⁴⁴ on the same principle of defense, do you hold yourselves in constant readiness for
that expected encounter,—and so much the more cautiously, because in some *unexpected* hour the 'Son of Man' will surely appear."

<hr />

a Luke xxi, 31.   *b* Mark xiii, 32.   *c* Luke xvii, 28.
d Luke xvii, 29.   *e* Luke xvii, 34.

41 Then Peter said unto him, Lord,   **Luke XII.**
speakest thou this parable unto us, or even
to all?   42 And the Lord said, 37 What I   **Mark XIII.**
say unto *you*, I say unto *all*, Watch.
34 For the Son of man is as a man taking a far journey, who left his house, and gave authority to his servants, and to every man his work ; and commanded
the porter to watch.   45 Who then is a   **Matt. XXIV.**
faithful and wise servant, whom his lord
hath made ruler over his household, to give them meat
in due season?   46 Blessed is that servant whom his
lord, when he cometh, shall find so doing : 47 verily I
say unto you, That he shall make him ruler over all
his goods.   48 But and if that evil servant shall say in
his heart, My lord delayeth his coming ; 49 and shall
begin to smite his fellow-servants, and to eat and drink
with the drunken ; 50 the lord of that servant shall
come in a day when he looketh not for him and in an
hour that he is not aware of, 51 and shall cut him
asunder, and appoint him his portion with the hypocrites [Luke XII, 46] and unbelievers : there shall be weeping and gnashing of teeth.   47 And that   **Luke XII.**
servant which knew his lord's will, and
prepared not himself neither did according to his will,
shall be beaten with *many* stripes ; 48 but he that knew
not, and did commit things worthy of stripes, shall be
beaten with *few* stripes : for unto whomsoever much is
given, of him shall be much required ; and to whom men
have committed much, of him they will ask the more.
42 Watch therefore ; for ye know not what   **Matt. XXIV.**
hour your Lord doth come, [Mark XIII, 35] at
even or at midnight or at the cock crowing or in the morning : [36] lest coming suddenly, he find you sleeping.—
1 Then shall the kingdom of heaven be   **Matt. XXV.**
likened unto ten virgins, which took their
168

41 Here Peter inquired, "Master, do you design this illustration for the warning of us your particular disciples, simply, or for all your followers generally?" **42** Jesus replied, **37** "The charge of watchfulness that I am giving to you, I enjoin upon all my followers [in every age, in order to be prepared against the occurrence of these two eventful periods particularly; and this state of watchfulness, in a general sense, can only be attained by a continual preparation, on the part of each person, to meet the close of his probation, whenever it may come]: **34** for my position with respect to them in the interim will be like that of some master of a family, who upon taking a journey to a distant country, bids adieu to his family, after having confided the management of his property to his domestics, assigning each his appropriate duties, and charging the porter to keep a strict guard at the door during his absence.   **45** Your station as **Matt. XXIV.** Christians [and especially that of my Apostles and subsequent teachers in my Church] resembles the door-keeper's, or that of some faithful and discreet servant, whom his master appoints as foreman over the other domestics, empowering him to pay them their stated wages.   **46** Fortunate indeed will it be for such a servant, if his master on his return find him faithfully discharging his trust! **47** I warrant you, he will promote him to the entire charge of his estate. **48** But should that servant grow remiss, thinking that 'his master was so long in returning, [that no special vigilance was requisite at the time,]' **49** and so begin [to abuse his delegated authority,] maltreating the other domestics and carousing[with his master's property]in company with the profligate; **50** depend upon it, his master will return in an unlooked-for moment, surprising him when he is least aware, **51** and after lashing him well nigh to death, will consign him to the miserable lot [of dungeons or ironed drudgery,] that all such *a* recreant! falsifiers of their former character, merit: yes, the doom [that awaits you, if like that delinquent slave you prove faithless to your duty as guardians and overseers of the Church amid the overhanging dangers of whatever period, will be one of remediless suffering when involved in your fellows' fall, and of endless anguish in the retributions of eternity,] fitly symbolized by the wails of torture and teeth clenched in agonized despair, [which the usual punishments produce upon such culprits.]   **47** And in these vindictive inflictions, my followers, if faithless, will suffer the most severely, [as seen more emphatically in the awards of the final judgment,—and especially those who are highest in authority;] just as the servant who is fully acquainted with his master's departing orders, and yet neglects to execute them in preparation for his return, would be punished with the greatest number of lashes; **48** while the rest who were comparatively ignorant of the commands they were transgressing in their remissness, would meet a lighter penalty: for in this as in other commissions of trust, the requirement, and consequently the guilt of failure, is in proportion to the bestowment.   **42** It behooves you, therefore, to be continually on the lookout for *your* Master's reappearance, since you cannot tell at what particular time it will occur,—*b* whether he will return at the *evening watch* or that of *midnight, cock-crowing* or *dawn* [i. e. during the respective quarters from sunset to sunrise] of the intervening night;! *c* else, on his arrival he may catch you napping.!

Luke XII.

Mark XIII.

Luke XII.

Matt. XXIV.

1 "The dispensation of the immunities of the 'Reign of the Divine Messiah' at such a critical period, [and   **Matt. XXV.**

a Luke xii, 46.   *b* Mark xiii, 35.   *c* Mark xiii, 36.

Y   168*

lamps and went forth to meet the bride-　MATT. XXV.
groom.　² And five of them were wise,
and five were foolish : ³ they that were foolish took
their lamps, and took no oil with them ; ⁴ but the
wise took oil in their vessels with their lamps.
⁵ While the bridegroom tarried, they all slumbered
and slept : ⁶ and at midnight there was a cry made,
Behold, the bridegroom cometh ; go ye out to meet
him ; ⁷ then all those virgins arose, and trimmed their
lamps.　⁸ And the foolish said unto the wise, Give us
of your oil ; for our lamps are gone out : ⁹ but the
wise answered saying, Not so ; lest there be not
enough for us and you : but go ye rather to them that
sell, and buy for yourselves.　¹⁰ And while they went
to buy, the bridegroom came ; and they that were
ready, went in with him to the marriage : and the
door was shut.　¹¹ Afterward came also the other
virgins saying, Lord, Lord, open to us : ¹² but he
answered and said, Verily I say unto you, I know you
not.　³⁵ Let *your* loins be girded about,　Luke XII.
and your lights burning ; ³⁶ and ye yourselves like unto men that wait for their lord, when he
will return from the wedding ; that when he cometh
and knocketh, they may open unto him immediately.
³⁷ Blessed are those servants, whom the lord when he
cometh shall find watching ; verily I say unto you,
that he shall gird himself, and make them to sit down
to meat, and will come forth and serve them : ³⁸ and
if he shall come in the second watch, or come in the
third watch, and find them so, blessed are those servants.　¹³ Watch therefore, for ye know　Matt. XXV.
neither the day nor the hour wherein the
Son of Man cometh.

³¹ When the Son of Man shall come in his glory,
and all the holy angels with him, then shall he sit
upon the throne of his glory ; ³² and before him shall

especially in the personal awards of eternity,] will resemble the case of ten virgins in the festivities of **MATT. XXV.** a wedding, whose office it was to take the lanterns, and form the procession to escort the bride, when the bridegroom came to conduct her to his house for solemnizing the nuptials. 2 Five of these bridal companions were discreet young women, and the other half were silly girls, 3 who, when they got their lanterns ready at evening, never thought of furnishing themselves with an additional supply of oil to replenish them; 4 while the more prudent ones, on leaving their homes for that of the bride, took the precaution to carry with them each a little can of oil besides that contained in their lanterns. 5 As usual, it was quite late before the bridegroom made his appearance, the girls meanwhile all began to nod with drowsiness, and at length fell into a doze; 6 from which they were suddenly aroused at midnight by the startling shout, ' Ho! the bridegroom is coming,—let the bride's retinue advance to meet him!'. 7 Thereupon the maidens all sprang up, and hastily trimmed their lamps afresh, preparing to sally out: 8 in the emergency, the negligent ones begged of the thoughtful, ' Let us have a little of your oil, our lanterns have burned out;' 9 but the others replied, ' If we spare you any, there will hardly be enough left for ourselves; you had better go to the oil-shops, and buy some for yourselves.' 10 So away they hastened to purchase it,—but while they were gone, the bridegroom arrived, those who were all ready of course accompanied him home, passing within to the nuptial scene, and the door was closed after them. 11 Presently the rest of the maidens arriving at the house, entreated its master to ' admit them;' 12 but he only returned them answer, ' I certainly know nothing about such stragglers; you cannot have belonged to my suite.'—

35 [It will be equally too late for *you*, my followers in **Luke XII.** general, to prepare for my arrival when that time of (special, individual or universal) trepidation comes;] you must therefore stand momentarily equipped in soul, 36 as the domestics of one of the bridesmen, on an occasion like the above, should do at home, 35 with their lights all burning, 36 against the return of their master from the festivities of the wedding party, and thus ready to open the door for him instantly when he knocks. 37, 38 Fortunate will be the servants in this instance, whom their Master, at whatever hour of that night [which represents the respective periods of the probation of this nation, of each person and of the human race,] He may return, shall find thus vigilantly awaiting Him; I assure you, He will in turn become their servant, at a banquet [of joyful security, first on earth, and finally in heaven], to which He will at once invite them! 13 Maintain, therefore, a **Matt. XXV.** constant wakefulness of expectant preparation for that great event, the moment of which I have declared to be so uncertain with you.

31 " But when [in the highest sense of that expression," concluded Jesus,] " the ' Son of Man' shall make His *last* universal advent, clothed with the celestial majesty of His full judicial power, and openly attended by His angelic ministers in its execution, *then* [in His consummated triumph,] He will be seated on His august throne of retribution, 32 while in His presence will be assembled all the members of the human family that have ever lived; and He will separate them into two classes [according to their individual moral character], as a shepherd would part the sheep in his

be gathered all nations : and he shall   MATT. XXV.
separate them one from another, as a
shepherd divideth his sheep from the goats ; [33] and he
shall set the sheep on his right hand, but the goats on
the left.   [34] Then shall the King say unto them on
his right hand, Come, ye blessed of my Father, inherit the kingdom prepared for you from the foundation of the world : [35] for I was a-hungered, and ye
gave me meat ; I was thirsty, and ye gave me drink ;
I was a stranger, and ye took me in ; [36] naked, and ye
clothed me ; I was sick, and ye visited me ; I was in
prison, and ye came unto me.   [37] Then shall the righteous answer him saying, Lord, when saw we thee a-hungered, and fed thee ? or thirsty, and gave thee drink ?
[38] when saw we thee a stranger, and took thee in ?
or naked, and clothed thee ? [39] or when saw we thee
sick, or in prison, and came unto thee ?   [40] And the
King shall answer and say unto them, Verily I say unto
you, Inasmuch as ye have done it unto one of the
least of these my *brethren*, ye have done it unto me.
[41] Then shall he say also unto them on the left hand,
Depart from me, ye cursed, into everlasting fire, prepared for the devil and his angels : [42] for I was a-hungered, and ye gave me no meat ; I was thirsty,
and ye gave me no drink ; [43] I was a stranger, and
ye took me not in ; naked, and ye clothed me not ;
sick and in prison, and ye visited me not.   [44] Then
shall they also answer him saying, Lord, when
saw we thee a-hungered or athirst or a stranger or
naked or sick or in prison, and did not minister unto
thee ? [45] Then shall he answer them saying, Verily
I say unto you, Inasmuch as ye did it not to one of
the least of these, ye did it not to me.   [46] And these
shall go away into everlasting punishment, but the
righteous into life eternal.
   170

flock from the goats, [33] ranging the sheep in honor toward the right, but the goats at the left.   MATT. XXV. [34] Then will He, as Sovereign arbiter of all human destiny, announce an award like this to those upon his right, 'Approach, ye candidates for My Father's beatific honors, and share henceforth in full fruition the immortal privileges of My "Reign," which have been provided for you all ever since the original creation of man upon earth.' [35] [And as some of the characteristic evidences of their qualification for such an exalted meed, He will declare to them,] 'When I was hungry, *you* were those that supplied me with food; in my thirst, you relieved me; as I wandered a homeless exile, you received me hospitably; [36] you furnished me with the clothing of which I was destitute; you compassionately attended my sickness; your friendly visits cheered me in the prison to which persecution had consigned me.' [37-39] These sainted blest will no doubt modestly ask, [in surprise that any seemingly slight acts of benevolence on their part should be construed into such high praise,] 'When, Master, did we ever perform these offices for you?' [40] He will then [develop the true worth of every such minute service, by the] reply, '[Although you may not have had an opportunity of rendering these attentions to Me personally, yet,] as you have shown similar unaffected marks of regard for My followers, were it but in the case of one of the humblest of them, you have virtually done the same to Me, [on whose account you have done so.]' [41] Turning next to those upon His left, the Eternal Judge will thus pronounce their final doom, 'Reprobate guilty, be exiled from the delights of My presence into the perpetual flames of perdition, which were designed only for Satan and his fellow-demons!—[42] in My hunger, thirst, [43] expatriation, scantiness of clothing, sickness or imprisonment, *you* refused to extend to me the needed succor, [which it was in your power to afford.]' [44] And if they shall attempt to excuse themselves by a denial that 'they had ever witnessed Him [personally] in such necessitous circumstances, and failed to relieve Him;' [45] the ready answer will meet them, 'By turning a deaf ear to like wants in the person of some one of my humble followers, you have, in principle, declined to succor me whom they represented on earth.' [46] This latter class, accordingly, will be sentenced to everlasting punishment, while the holy will be admitted to endless bliss."

¹ And it came to pass, when Jesus had · **Matt. XXVI.**
finished all these sayings, he said unto
his disciples, ² Ye know that after two days is the
feast of the passover, and the Son of man is betrayed
to be crucified.

§ 124.—*Plots for Christ's Apprehension.*

(Jerusalem; *Thursday, March* 17, A. D. 29.)

³ Then assembled together the chief-priests and the
scribes and the elders of the people unto the palace of
the high-priest, (who was called Caiaphas,) ⁴ and
consulted that they might take Jesus by subtilty,
and kill him : ⁵ but they said, Not on the feast-day,
lest there be an uproar among the people.

¹⁴ Then [JOHN XIII, 2] the devil having now put it into his
heart, one of the twelve, called Judas Iscariot, went
unto the chief-priests [LUKE XXII, 4] and captains ¹⁵ and·
said unto them, What will ye give me, and I will deliver him unto you? · And they [LUKE XXII, 5] were glad, and
covenanted with him for thirty pieces of silver. ¹⁶And
[LUKE XXII, 6] he promised, and from that time he sought
opportunity to betray him [LUKE XXII, 6] unto them in the
absence of the multitude.

171

[1] Having thus concluded the discourse [on **Matt. XXVI.** the subject of his future comings], Jesus continued on his way to Bethany, warning his disciples, [whose minds still required preparation for the tragic issue to which his stay with them was now rapidly converging,] [2] "You are aware, that on the day after to-morrow the Passover follows *a* the first of the 'Days of Unleavened Bread ;'I at that festival the 'Son of Man' will be betrayed into the hands of those who are to crucify him !''

§ 124.—*Plots for Christ's Apprehension.*

(Jerusalem; *Thursday, March* 17, A. D. 29.)

[3] [On the next day,] the members of the San'hedrim held a private meeting at the mansion of Caiaphas the High-priest, [4] in which they consulted *b* with great solicitudeI as to the most feasible stratagem for getting Jesus within their grasp, and putting him to death ; [5] but [their deliberations resulted in no definite plan, for] it was the general opinion that any violent measures just at the present time, while the people were assembled for the Passover, were not safe, lest the populace, who generally favored him, might make a riot in his defense.

[14] [Some vague rumor, however, of this anxious debate on the part of the San'hedrim having reached] Judas " of Ke'rioth,'' one of the apostles, *c* with diabolical cupidityI [excited at the prospect of turning it to his own advantage, he] immediately repaired to the place where they were in session, [15] and made this proposal *d* through the Prefect of the TempleI [i. e. military officer having charge of its precincts, whose subordinates he found in attendance], "What reward will you give me, if I will engage to deliver Jesus slyly into your hands?" *e* Delighted at the offer,I they agreed to pay him thirty *silverlings* [i. e. *staters*, making about $18], for the service. Judas *f* accepted these terms,I [16] and from that moment he was continually watching a safe opportunity to execute his treachery, *f* in the absence of the popular throng.I

a Luke xxii, 1.   *b* Mark xiv, 1.   *c* Luke xxii, 3.
d Luke xxii, 4.   *e* Mark xiv, 11.   *f* Luke xxii, 6.

171*

CHAPTER VI.—PORTION IV.

THE INCIDENTS OF CHRIST'S PASSION.

(Time, *three days.*)

§ 125.—*Christ's Preparation for his Fourth Passover.*

(Bethany and Jerusalem; *Thursday, March* 17, A. D. 29.)

⁷ Then came the [MARK XIV, 12] first day - **Luke XXII.**
of unleavened bread, when the passover
must be killed: [MATT. XXVI, 17] and the disciples came to Jesus;
⁸ and he sent Peter and John saying, Go and prepare
us the passover, that we may eat.   ⁹ And they said
unto him, *Where* wilt thou that we prepare?   ¹⁰ And
he said unto them, Behold, when ye are entered into
the city, there shall a man meet you bearing a pitcher
of water; follow him into the house where he entereth in: ¹¹ and ye shall say unto the good-man of the
house, The Master saith unto thee, [MATT. XXVI, 18] My
time is at hand; where is the guest-chamber, where I
shall eat the passover [MATT. XXVI, 18] at thy house with my
disciples?   ¹² And he shall show you a large upper
room furnished [MARK XIV, 15] and prepared; there make
ready.   ¹³ And they went and found as he had said
unto them; and they made ready the passover.

§ 126.—*The Passover Meal, with the connected Incidents and Discourses.*

(Jerusalem; *Thursday* evening, *March* 17, A. D. 29.)

¹⁴ And [MARK XIV, 17] in the evening when the hour was
come, he sat down and the twelve apostles with him.
[JOHN XIII, 1] Now before the feast of the passover, when Jesus
knew that his hour was come that he should depart out of this
world unto the Father, having loved his own which were in

CHAPTER VI.—PORTION IV.

THE INCIDENTS OF CHRIST'S PASSION.

(Time, *three days.*)

§ 125.—*Christ's Preparation for his Fourth Passover.*

(Bethany and Jerusalem; *Thursday, March* 17, A. D. 29.)

[7] The ensuing day was *a* the first of! the "Days **Luke XXII.** of Unleavened Bread" [i. e. 14th of Nisan], on which the law required the paschal lamb to be slaughtered; [8] accordingly, Jesus *b* summoned! two of his disciples, Peter and John, and bade them, "Go into the city and get the Passover supper ready for us to eat to-night." [9] To their inquiry, "In what house do you wish us to prepare it?" [10] he replied by directing them, "Go to the city, and, observe! as soon as you enter it, a man will meet you, carrying a jar of water; follow him to the first house that he enters with the water, [11] and say to the master of it, 'Our Teacher bade us say to you, *c* "My time is limited [for the consummation of my earthly sojourn, and consequently for the celebration of this Passover preceding it, and the nearness of its expiration does not allow me a more leisurely provision for the occasion]; I have therefore a mind to partake of the Passover at your house :! please tell me which is your guests' apartment, in which I may prepare to eat it with my disciples?"' [12] He will thereupon show you a large attic room furnished [with couches and every other convenience], *d* ready for our reception ;! there prepare the meal." [13] The two disciples proceeded *e* to the city,! found everything just as Jesus had told them, and made the arrangements for the paschal supper according to his directions.

§ 126.—*The Passover Meal, with the connected Incidents and Discourses.*

(Jerusalem; *Thursday* evening, *March* 17, A. D. 29.)

[14] *f* Toward evening,! Jesus set out for the city, accompanied by the rest of the disciples, and at the usual hour for the paschal supper [i. e. soon after dark] took his place at the table thus prepared, surrounded by the entire number of his apostles. *g* Being already perfectly aware that the destined period for his departure from this world to his heavenly home was close at hand, his affections turned with increasing tenderness at this last interview toward those who had adhered to him

---

a Mark xiv, 12.　　*b* Matt. xxvi, 17.　　*c* Matt. xxvi, 18.　　*d* Mark xiv, 15.
e Mark xiv, 16,　　*f* Mark xiv, 17.　　　　　　　　　　　　　*g* John xiii, 1,

172*

the world, he loved them unto the end : ¹⁵ and LUKE **XXII.**
he said unto them, With desire I have
desired to eat this passover with you before I suffer ;
¹⁶ for I say unto you, I will not any more eat thereof,
until it be fulfilled in the kingdom of God. ¹⁷ And
he took the cup, and gave thanks, and said, Take
this, and divide it among yourselves.

²⁴ And there was also a strife among them,
which of them should be accounted the greatest.
² And supper being ended, ³ Jesus know- **John XIII.**
ing that the Father had given all things
into his hands, and that he was come from God, and
went to God ; ⁴ he riseth from supper, and laid aside
his garments, and took a towel and girded himself ;
⁵ after that, he poureth water into a basin, and began
to wash the disciples' feet, and to wipe them with
the towel wherewith he was girded. ⁶ Then cometh
he to Simon Peter : and Peter saith unto him,
Lord, dost thou wash my feet ? ₇ Jesus answered
and said unto him, What I do, thou knowest not
now ; but thou shalt know hereafter. ⁸ Peter saith
unto him, Thou shalt never wash my feet. Jesus
answered him, If I wash thee not, thou hast no part
with me. ⁹ Simon Peter saith unto him, Lord, not
my *feet* only, but also my *hands* and my *head.*
¹⁰ Jesus saith to him, He that is washed, needeth
not save to wash his feet, but is clean every whit ;
and ye are clean, but not *all :* ¹¹ (for he knew who
should betray him ; therefore said he, Ye are not
all clean.) ¹² So after he had washed their feet,
and had taken his garments, and was set down again,
he said unto them, Know ye what I have done to you ?
¹³ Ye call me Master and Lord ; and ye say well, for
so I am : ¹⁴ if I then, your Lord and Master, have
washed your feet, ye also ought to wash one another's
feet ; ¹⁵ for I have given you an example, that ye

in his earthly career, | 15 and prompted this remark to his disciples, as they reclined about him, "I have felt a more than ordinary desire to be spared to partake this one more paschal meal in company with you, before I undergo my [expiatory] passion ; 16 for I assure you, I shall never again share in such an occasion, until I enjoy its highest accomplishment in [the celestial banquets of] the 'Reign of the Divine Messiah.'" 17 He then introduced the exercises of the paschal solemnity by taking up the [first] cup of wine, and after pronouncing the usual benediction over it, he passed it round to 'his disciples, saying, "Take this cup, and share its contents among you."

LUKE XXII.

24 There had just occurred an altercation among the disciples, as to which of them was entitled to the preëminence in rank ; 2 Jesus therefore, at this stage of the supper, 3 conscious of the responsible mission which his Heavenly Father—from whom he had come, and to whom he was about so shortly to return—had so plenarily intrusted to him, 4 arose from the supper table, [with the design of checking this ambitious spirit of his apostles by a last emphatic act of authority,] and laying aside his upper garment, he took a towel and wound it about his waist, [in the manner of a servant preparing to wait upon the company in the ceremony then in order of performing the ablution connected with the paschal meal.] 5 Then pouring some water into the ewer, he set about washing the feet of the disciples [as they lay projected beyond the edge of the couches,] and wiping them dry with the ends of the towel about him. 6 As he came to (Simon) Peter in his turn, the latter [astonished at such condescension,] exclaimed, "What, Master, are you washing my feet?" 7 Jesus replied, "The design of the present action on my part, you may not just now understand, but wait, and it shall be explained to you presently." 8 Peter, however, persisted in [his reluctance, earnestly] declaring, "I can never consent to have you degrade yourself by washing *my* feet." "If you do not suffer me to wash you [spiritually, and in token of that relation of dependence, submit to this ablution]," significantly returned Jesus, "you deprive yourself of the badge of my discipleship." 9 [Overcome by this appeal to his attachment,] Peter now as eagerly exclaimed, "O Master, then wash not my feet only, but my hands and my face too." 10 "Nay," replied Jesus, "you know, when one has *bathed* before supper, he has only occasion to wash off his feet on coming to the table, being entirely clean in other respects ; just so, you my disciples are all [morally] clean [by the purifying influence of my grace in general, although your hearts still need that cleansing from the special sin of ambition, which this ablution of your feet is designed to symbolize],—not all of you, however." 11 Jesus made this exception, "You are not all pure [in intention and feeling]," because he recognized among them his purposed betrayer. 12 So as soon as he had finished washing their feet all around, and resumed his garment and place at the table, he thus explained his conduct: "Are you aware of the meaning of the act which I have just performed upon you?—13 You are in the habit of calling me 'Teacher' and 'Master;' and very properly, for such I am. 14 Now since I, your Teacher and Master, have condescended to the menial task of washing your feet, you surely ought to be willing to perform similar kind offices, if need be, toward each other; 15 I have just now set you a conspicuous example, to teach you to be mutually as affectionate and obliging among yourselves, as I am toward you.

John XIII.

should do as I have done to you. ^{25} And   **Luke XXII.**
he said unto them, The kings of the
Gentiles exercise lordship over them, and they that
exercise authority upon them, are called benefac-
tors ; ^{26} but *ye* shall not be so : but he that is greatest
among you, let him be as the younger ; and he that
is chief, as he that doth serve. ^{27} For whether is
greater he that sitteth at meat, or he that serveth ?
is not he that sitteth at meat ? but I am among you
as he that serveth.—^{28} Ye are they which have continued with me in my temptations : ^{29} and I appoint
unto you a kingdom, as my Father hath appointed
unto me ; ^{30} that ye may eat and drink at my table in
my kingdom, and sit on thrones judging the twelve
tribes of Israel. ^{17} If ye know these   **John XIII.**
things, happy are ye if ye *do* them. ^{18} I
speak not of you all ; I know whom I have chosen :
but that the scripture may be fulfilled,* He that
eateth bread with me, hath lifted up his heel against
me ; ^{19} now I tell you before it come, that when it is
come to pass, ye may believe that I am he. ^{21} When
Jesus had thus said, he was troubled in spirit, and
[MARK XIV, 18] as they sat and did eat, Jesus testified and
said, Verily, verily I say unto you, that one of you
[MARK XIV, 18] which eateth with me, shall betray me,
^{22} Then the disciples looked one on another, doubting
of whom he spake. ^{22} And they were   **Matt. XXVI.**
exceeding sorrowful, and began every one
of them to say unto him, Lord, is it I ? [MARK XIV, 19] and
another said, Is it I? ^{23} And he answered and said, He
that dippeth his hand with me in the dish, the same shall
betray me. ^{24} The Son of man goeth, as it is written of
him ;† but woe unto that man by whom the Son of man
is betrayed ! it had been good for that man if he had not

---

* Psa. xli, 9.   † Compare John xiii, 18, above.

²⁵ Gentile monarchs, indeed, tyrannize over their **Luke XXII.** subjects, and their populaces generally entitle their haughtiest oppressors their most glorious benefactors ; ²⁶ but with your association a far different principle is to prevail : whoever is a superior among you, must conduct himself with the humility of the lowest ; and your chief should have all the complaisance of a servant. ²⁷ For which is the higher, in rank, the person reclining at a feast, or the domestic waiting at the table ?—surely the former ; yet I, your sovereign, have assumed among you the position of a servant, [and therefore, he among you who aims at preëminence, must imitate my example. ²⁸ As to your hopes of aggrandizement, however, I will say this much, that] to you, who shall have faithfully adhered to me in all the trials of my earthly mission, ²⁹ I will appoint a rank corresponding with the royal dignity which my Father confers upon me ; ³⁰ namely, you shall be privileged to eat and drink at the [general] table of my [spiritual] blessings in my approaching Messianic 'Reign'[both on earth and hereafter], and [specially] be exalted to a station [in your apostolate] parallel with that of throned judges over the twelve tribes of Israel. ¹⁷I **John XIII.** have now clearly pointed out your duty [of conformity with me in reciprocal condescension] ; you will therefore only expect to be blessed [with a participation in my exaltation,] by a close observance of this my precept. ¹⁸ Yet [in the expectations of rewarded fidelity on your part, which I thus express,] I do not include your entire number ; I am too well aware of the dispositions and designs of each of those whom I have chosen as my Apostles, [and therefore cognizant of the intended treachery of one of them, to be so indiscriminate in my remarks respecting them ;] such a faithless exception, however, is but a second verification of the declaration of Scripture,—

> ' [Yea,—viler still, alas !—my very friend,
> My intimate, my honored confidant,]
> The boon companion plighted at my board,
> Uplifts the vicious heel to lay me low.'

¹⁹ I forewarn you now of this future treachery respecting me, so that when it actually transpires, [instead of being thrown into consternation,] you may only derive from it a greater confidence in my supernatural character [as the Messiah]."

. ²¹ ^a As the supper was progressing [by the partaking of the bitter herbs and sauce, which now succeeded], the company still reclining,| Jesus, his mind becoming oppressed with the mournful circumstance to which he had just alluded, earnestly declared to his disciples, " I solemnly repeat it, one of your number, ^b whose hand is now extended with the rest to the food upon the table, | ^a as he eats with me, | is about to betray me." ²² ^c Overwhelmed with grief at this direct announcement, · they looked with blank amazement at each other, utterly at a loss to divine which he referred to ; ^d and then the anxious whisper was circulated, who among them could possibly be the culprit ?| ²²Soon the agitated inquiry ^eburst from **Matt. XXVI.** one lip after another, "Master, is it I ?" "or I ?"|— ²³ but Jesus only replied to their solicitude, " It is some one ^f among you twelve, | who is now dipping his fingers with me into the sauce-dish, that will be my betrayer. ²⁴ The ' Son of Man' is indeed about to depart [from earth] in the manner predicted in the Scriptures, but alas, none the less, for that man by whose instrumentality his betrayal shall be effected ! better had it been for such a one's eternal

---

_a Mark xiv, 18.   _b Luke xxii, 21, (last clause.)   _c Matt. xxvi, 22.
_d Luke xxii, 23.   _e Mark xiv, 19.   _f Mark xiv, 20.

been born. ^{23} Now there was leaning on   **John XIII.**
Jesus' bosom one of his disciples whom
Jesus loved; ^{24} Simon Peter therefore beckoned to
him, that he should ask who it should be of whom he
spake : ^{25} he then, lying on Jesus' breast, saith unto
him, Lord, who is it ? ^{26} Jesus answered, He it is
to whom I shall give a sop, when I have dipped it :
and when he had dipped the sop, he gave it to Judas
Iscariot the son of Simon. ^{25} Then   **Matt. XXVI.**
Judas (which betrayed him) answered
and said, Master, is it I ? He said unto him, Thou
hast said. ^{27} And after the sop Satan en-   **John XIII.**
tered into him. Then said Jesus unto him,
That thou doest, do quickly. ^{28} Now no man at the
table knew for what intent he spake this unto him :
^{29} for some of them thought, because Judas had the
bag, that Jesus had said unto him, Buy those things
that we have need of against the feast; or, that he
should give something to the poor. ^{30} He then, having received the sop, went immediately out : and it
was night.

^{31} Therefore when he was gone out, Jesus said, Now
is the Son of Man glorified, and God is glorified in
him : ^{32} if God be glorified in him, God shall also
glorify him in Himself, and shall straightway glorify
him. ^{33} Little children, yet a little while I am with
you : ye shall seek me ; and as I said unto the Jews,*
Whither I go, ye cannot come, so now I say to *you.*
^{36} Simon Peter said unto him, Lord, *whither* goest
thou ? Jesus answered him, Whither I go, thou canst
not follow me now ; but thou shalt follow me afterward. ^{37} Peter said unto him, Lord, *why* cannot I follow thee now ? I will lay down my life for thy sake.
^{38} Jesus answered him, Wilt thou lay down thy life for

---

* See chap. vii, 34.

welfare, had he never existed." ²⁴ [In the per-   John XIII.
plexity which this hint deepened without reliev-
ing,] (Simon) Peter privately beckoned to one of
the disciples [John], ²³ who reclined next to Jesus in front—
the favorite of his Master,—²⁴ to inquire of Jesus, who the individual might be, to whom he referred? ²⁵ Accordingly, leaning back on his Master's breast, he whispered in his ear, "Master, which of us is it?" Jesus replied in the same confidential
manner, "It is he to whom I will give a morsel, after I have
dipped it in the sauce." ²⁶ Then sopping a piece of the herbs
in the sauce, he handed it to Judas "of Ke'rioth" (son of one
Simon). ^a The justly suspicious Judas [thus directly noticed,]
was constrained, | ³⁰ on receiving the sop, ^a to echo [falteringly
the general question], "Is it I, Teacher?" to which his Master
promptly rejoined [in an undertone], "Even so." | ²⁷ Then,
while the traitor's fiendish purpose was only concentrated to a
more resentful determination by this pointed detection, Jesus
continued to him in a loud voice, "What you have to do then,
be at once about, if you must!" ²⁸ None of the rest of the
company understood the import of this ambiguous direction;
²⁹ the most thought, that as Judas was purser to the consocia-
tion, Jesus had told him in the preceding whisper, to "purchase some article needed for to-morrow's ceremonies," or
else had bidden him make a donation to the poor for some
purpose. ³⁰ [Full of guilty animosity,] Judas immediately left
the room, it being now considerably after dark.

³¹ Relieved by this withdrawal, Jesus exultingly exclaimed,
[at the prospect of a speedy accomplishment of his mission,]
"Now is the 'Son of Man' on the eve of his glorious distinction [through the triumphant results of his approaching death],
and the Almighty is to be honored by his means; ³² then, as
such praise will accrue to God from his passion, reciprocally
also will God raise him to glory with Himself, and thus will
his celestial glorification be shortly consummated!—³³ My
dearest disciples," continued he, "I am to remain among you
but a very short time longer; when I am gone, you will often
anxiously look for my return, but, as I lately told the hierarchy, 'To that place whither I am about to withdraw, you
cannot have access,' so [for a different reason] I now tell
you."

³⁶ Here (Simon) Peter interrupted him by asking, "Master,
where are you going?" Jesus repeated in reply, "Where I
am presently going, you cannot have the privilege of following me just now, but you will one day follow me thither [at
death]." ³⁷ "But why, Master," continued Peter, "may I
not follow you even now, [through every peril?]—I am ready
to risk my very life in your defense." ³⁸ "Would you indeed
be willing to venture your life in my behalf?" returned Jesus:

a Matt. xxvi, 25.

my sake? verily, verily I say unto thee, JOHN XIII.
The cock shall not crow, till thou hast denied me thrice. 31 Then saith Jesus Matt. XXVI.
unto them, All ye shall be offended be-
cause of me this night; for it is written,* I will smite
the Shepherd, and the sheep of the flock shall be
scattered abroad. 32 But after I am risen again, I
will go before you into Galilee. 33 Peter answered
and said unto him, Though all men shall be offended
because of thee, yet will I never be offended.
31 And the Lord said, Simon, Simon, be- Luke XXII.
hold, Satan hath desired to have you,
that he may sift you as wheat; 32 but I have prayed
for thee, that thy faith fail not: and when thou art
converted, strengthen thy brethren. 33 And he said
unto him, Lord, I am ready to go with thee both into
prison and to death. 34 And he said, I tell thee,
Peter, the cock shall not crow [MARK XIV, 30] twice this
day, [MARK XIV, 30] even in this night, before that thou
shalt thrice deny that thou knowest me. [MARK XIV, 31]
But he spake the more vehemently, If I should die with thee,
I will not deny thee in any wise. Likewise also said they all.
35 And he said unto them, When I sent you without
purse, and scrip and shoes,† lacked ye anything?
And they said, Nothing. 36 Then said he unto them,
But now he that hath a purse, let him take it, and
likewise his scrip; and he that hath no sword, let
him sell his garment and buy one. 37 For I say unto
you, that this that is written must yet be accomplished in me,‡ And he was reckoned among the
transgressors; for the things concerning me have an
end. 38 And they said, Lord, behold, here are two
swords. And he said unto them, It is enough.

---

* Zech. xiii, 7.   † See § 61.   ‡ Isa. liii, 12.

"ah! Peter, [you little know your own heart;] I sol- **John XIII.**
emnly warn you, that the cock will not have crowed for
morn, before you have disowned me as many as three
times!'' 31 Then turning to the disciples generally, **Matt. XXVI.**
he continued, "You will all be staggered in your adhesion to me this very night; for the catastrophe predicted by Scripture concerning me, is now about to occur,—

'["Leap from thy scabbard, sword of wrath divine
Provoked by human sin, and glut thy edge
In expiation in the Shepherd's heart
Who leads My people!" cries Jehovah's voice,—
"His, who alone, though man, my Equal is;]
Strike down the guardian shepherd at a blow,
And lo! on all sides flee the frighted sheep,—
[Yet will I spare and soothe the straying lambs."]'

32 Still, I will rise again from the fatal stroke, and will then precede
you to a certain spot in Galilee." 33 Hereupon Peter reiterated his res-
olute attachment by declaring, "If everybody else were actually to
be estranged from you, I am certain I would not."
31 But his Master checked his self-confidence by telling **Luke XXII.**
him, "Simon, Simon, mark me, Satan longs to get all
of you under the full power of his temptations to apostasy, and then he
would sift your hearts as severely as grain is winnowed, [which would
reveal far more of the chaff of selfish distrust in me than you imagine,
and might prove your ruin; nor will you escape entirely unscathed
from his snares.] 32 But I have had occasion to pray particularly for
you [in view of this trial], that your confidence in me might not then
desert you; I shall therefore charge you especially with the task of encouraging the wavering faith of your associate disciples, so soon as you
shall have recovered from your own defection." 33 "O! Master," returned Peter, "[so far from alienation by adversity,] I am ready at any
moment to attend you even to prison, or to death itself." 34 "Peter!"
replied Jesus, "once more I solemnly tell you, that in the course of
this identical night, the cock will not have crowed *a* twice for dawn, I
before you will three several times deny all acquaintance with me."
"*b* No, no, Master," insisted Peter the more vehemently, "if I had to
die with you for it, I would never disavow you." The rest of the disciples too made similar professions of constancy. I
35 Jesus then proceeded to impress their minds more deeply with a
sense of the perils awaiting them. "When I sent you out on your
preaching tour," said he, "without purse, wallet or shoes, did you experience any inconvenience from the want of them?" "No," answered
they, "scarcely any." 36 "But in the coming emergency, on the contrary," rejoined he, "whoever has a well-stored purse, will have need
to take it with him [in the vicissitudes through which you will pass],
and so too of his wallet; and if any traveler through the dangerous
scenes before you, is destitute of a dagger for defense, he had better sell
his very cloak and buy one, than go unarmed. 37 For I assure you, that
the Scriptural intimation has yet to be accomplished in my case,—

'E'en yields he to be reckon'd with the vile,
In infamy by man, in doom by Heaven;'

yes, every minute prediction concerning me is to be fully verified."
38 "Master," said the disciples, [who had been searching among their
garments for weapons,] "here are two daggers." "Never mind
[about supplying yourselves literally with arms]," returned he;
"that will do on that subject."

a Mark xiv, 30.   *b* Mark xiv, 31.

Z

26 And as they were eating, Jesus **Matt. XXVI.**
took bread, and blessed it, and brake it
and gave it to the disciples, and said, Take, eat;
this is my body [1 Cor. XI, 24] which is broken for you:
this do in remembrance of me.   27 And he took the
cup, and gave thanks, and gave it to them saying,
Drink ye all of it; 28 for this is my blood of the
new testament, which is shed for many for the
remission of sins: [1 Cor. XI, 25] this do ye, as oft as ye
drink it, in remembrance of me.   29 But I say unto
you, I will not drink henceforth of this fruit of
the vine, until that day when I drink it new with
you in my Father's kingdom.

1 Let not your heart be troubled; ye **John XIV.**
believe in *God*, believe also in *me*.   2 In
my Father's house are many mansions; (if it
were not so, I would have told you;) I go to
prepare a place for you: 3 and if I go and prepare a place for you, I will come again and receive you unto myself; that where I am, there ye
may be also: 4 and whither I go ye know, and
the way ye know.   5 Thomas saith unto him, Lord,
we know not *whither* thou goest; and how can
we know the *way?*   6 Jesus saith unto him, *I* am
the way and the truth and the life; no man cometh
unto the Father but by me.   7 If ye had known
me, ye should have known my *Father* also; and
from henceforth ye know him and have seen him.
177

²⁶ While they were partaking of the more substan-   **Matt. XXVI.**
tial parts of the supper, [i.e. the bread and flesh of the
other sacrifices accompanying the lamb itself, after the second cup of
wine,] Jesus taking a cake of the unleavened biscuit in his hands, pronounced the customary benediction over it, and then breaking it in
pieces, distributed a portion to each of the disciples, with this touching
remark and injunction, "Take and eat this fragment of bread, which
represents my body *a* so soon to be yielded by me¹ *b* to be lacerated [by
crucifixion, as a vicarious sacrifice] on your behalf; and [in your future religious meetings] perform this ceremony in commemoration of
me¹ [as at once your Friend and Redeemer]."—^{27 c} In a similar manner, after the supper was concluded¹ [by the eating of the paschal lamb
itself], Jesus took up the [third] cup of wine, and pronouncing the
usual blessing over it, he passed it round among them, telling them
d as they all in turn partook of its contents,¹ "Drink likewise this
wine; ²⁸ it betokens my own blood, which, as a seal of the *New* Covenant [of the gospel,] instituted by me, I am about to pour forth freely
for the entire human race, in expiation of their sins: *e* whenever,
therefore, [in the ecclesiastical arrangements by which you may be
favored with the privilege,] you may partake of such a cup, observe
this social act as a remembrance of me. [in this my sacrificial relation
to you. ²⁹ As for myself,] I distinctly forewarn you, that I shall never
from this hour again have an opportunity like this of joining with you
in a draught of the produce of the vine, until that period *f* shall arrive,¹
when in company with you I shall forever drink it fresh [by consummation,] amid the blessedness of the 'Reign of the Divine Messiah'
in my Father's presence."

¹ [After the repast was finished, while they continued   **John XIV.**
reclining at the table, Jesus proceeded to fortify his disciples' minds against the shock which they were soon to experience,
by the following parting counsels:] "Do not suffer yourselves to be
agitated [with despondency in view of my intimations of departure];
renew your confidence in the protection of God, and call to mind the
many evidences you have had of my ability [and promptness to exercise that unfailing succor in your behalf]. ² Now in my Father's [ce-
lestial] home, to which I am about to go, there are abundant resi-
dences [for you also, as well as for all beside];—had there not been ample room there for you too, I would long since have ingenuously told
you so, [and not deceived you up to this late period of my personal service, by the hope of attending me into all the triumphant scenes of my
career;]—and I am now but going in advance to fit up an apartment
there for each of you: ³ so when I have arrived there and prepared an
abode for you [by the qualifying influences of my intercessions and
mediatory grace in your behalf during probation], I will then return
to you, [initially by the natural summons that relieves each of you
from his earthly detention, and fully at the general resurrection,] and
take you home with myself; and thus, where my course shall permanently terminate, there you too will eventually accompany me, [no
more to separate.] ⁴ What place of withdrawal I refer to, you certainly by this time well know [from my frequent intimations to you
respecting heaven as connected with my departure], and you are
quite as well aware of the avenue thither, [namely, by me, as I have
often told you.]"

⁵ Here, Thomas, [disinclined to acquiesce in a remark which he
failed to comprehend,] interposed the question, "Master, you have
not even told us where you intend to go, and how should we know the

---

a Luke xxii, 19.   *b* 1 Cor. xi, 24.   *c* Luke xxii, 20.
d Mark xiv, 23.   *e* 1 Cor. xi, 25.   *f* Luke xxii, 18.

⁸ Philip saith unto him, Lord, show
us the Father, and it sufficeth us.

⁹ Jesus saith unto him, Have I been so long time
with you, and yet hast thou not known *me*, Philip?
he that hath seen *me*, hath seen the *Father;* and
how sayest thou then, Show us the Father? ¹⁰ Believest thou not that I am *in* the Father, and the
Father in me? the words that I speak unto you,
I speak not of myself; but the Father, that dwelleth in me, he doeth the works : ¹¹ believe me that
I am in the Father, and the Father in me ; or else
believe me for the very works' sake. ¹² Verily,
verily, I say unto you, He that believeth on me,
the works that I do shall he do also : and greater
works than these shall he do ; because I go unto
my Father. ¹³ And whatsoever ye shall ask in
my name, that will I do ; that the Father may
be glorified in the Son : ¹⁴ if ye shall ask anything
in my name, I will do it. ¹⁵ If ye love me, keep
my commandments : ¹⁶ and I will pray the Father,
and he shall give you another Comforter, that he
may abide with you forever, ¹⁷ even the Spirit of
truth, whom the world cannot receive, because it
seeth him not neither knoweth him ; but *ye* know
him, for he dwelleth *with* you, and shall be *in* you :
¹⁸ I will not leave you comfortless ; I will come to
you. ¹⁹ Yet a little while, and the world seeth me
no more ; but ye see me : because I live, ye shall
178

way thither?" ⁶ "I myself," responded Jesus, [with an   JOHN XIV.
emphasis that left no uncertainty as to his destination,]
" am the true and life-giving Way [of approach to Heaven]; no human being gains access to the Father, save through my mediation.
⁷ Your intimacy with me, therefore, ought to have given you all a definite acquaintance with the character of my Father, and from this moment [set it down as an ascertained fact, that in all His relations cog-
nizable by finite capacities] you are thus acquainted with Him, and
have in fact seen Him [in me his incarnate Representative.]" ⁸ "Master," said Philip, [with a blunt curiosity to reduce the subject to a
more distinct apprehension,] "just exhibit to us some visible manifestation of the Father's person, and we shall rest satisfied [that we have
gained an actual perception of Him]." ⁹ "What!" returned Jesus,
"after I have lived familiarly with you all for several years, have you,
Philip, still remained unacquainted with *me*, [who am identical with
Him?] I tell you, whoever has seen me, has really beheld the Father
in that very sight; how then can you consistently ask me to ' afford
you a gaze at the Father?' [since all that is visible in His nature, is
palpable in myself.] ¹⁰ Do you doubt that I am involved in my Father's being, and He conversely embodied in me?—[let my doings
themselves convince you of the correlation between us:] the very
doctrines which I deliver to you are not self-originated, [but proceed
primarily from my Father; and in like manner] He, [by His God-
head] inhering in my person, effects all my miracles. ¹¹ Fully settle
it, then, in your convictions, that between my Father and myself
there subsists an entire, and most intimate union [in nature, purpose and conduct, each implying the other in all respects;—even if
you fail to rely upon my assertion to that effect, yet] surely you must
be impelled, by witnessing the miracles which I perform, to repose
implicit confidence in me as His plenary agent.

¹² "The result of such confidence in me," continued Jesus, [resum-
ing his former topic,] " will be in respect to these very miracles, that
the person [among you] exercising it, will be enabled to effect even
more stupendous acts [in his Apostolical delegation,] than ever I have
done; ¹³ in short, whatever you [my Apostolical representatives, and
in a subordinate degree every follower of mine] shall pray for on my
behalf [i. e. as authorized for the promotion of my cause], I will effect
in that exercise of my [divine] prerogative, by which my Father's
praise is so directly secured through the representative power of His
Son,—¹⁴ I say *every* such request of yours, however great, shall be accomplished by my personal mediation. ¹⁵ [In order to realize this fulfillment of your petitions, however,] you must faithfully observe all my
precepts, as upon this proof of love toward me [can you alone claim my
interest in you. ¹⁶ Then in entering upon my intercessory office,] I
will second your prayers before my Father, and He will grant you another [divine] Helper [especially in the arduous duties of your mis-
sion], an effectual substitute in my absence, to be your perpetual companion [within]; ¹⁷ namely, the Holy Spirit,—that impressive Exposi-
tor of sacred truth, whom the mass of mankind, from their distorted
perception and corrupt ignorance of moral things, are unable to admit to the control of their minds; but whose influences *you* begin to
apprehend, since He even now hovers continually near you, ready to
be enshrined presently in the full occupancy of your breasts. ¹⁸ I shall
therefore by no means leave you in bereavement [of the *consolations*
of my presence], for I am indeed only about to approach you the more
closely [by the greater intimacy of the representative Spirit, secured
by my departure, and finally by taking you to myself]. ¹⁹ In a little

178*

live also. ²⁰ At that day ye shall know   JOHN XIV.
that I am in my Father, and ye in
me, and I in you. ²¹ He that hath my commandments and keepeth them, he it is that loveth me ;
and he that loveth me, shall be loved of my Father,
and I will love him and will manifest myself to
him. ²² Judas saith unto him (not Iscariot), Lord,
how is it that thou wilt manifest thyself unto *us*,
and not unto the *world ?* ²³ Jesus answered and
said unto him, If a man love me, he will keep
my words ; and my Father will love him, and we
will come unto him and make our abode with him.
²⁴ He that loveth me not, keepeth not my sayings :
and the word which ye hear is not mine, but the
Father's which sent me. ²⁵ These things have I
spoken unto you, being yet present with you ; ²⁶ but
the Comforter, which is the Holy Ghost, whom
the Father will send in my name, he shall teach
you all things, and bring all things to your remembrance whatsoever I have said unto you. ²⁷ Peace
I leave with you, my peace I give unto you ; not
as the world giveth, give I unto you : let not your
heart be troubled, neither let it be afraid. ²⁸ Ye
have heard how I said unto you, I go away and
come again unto you ; if ye loved me, ye would rejoice, because I said, I go unto the Father, for my
Father is greater than I : ²⁹ and now I have told
you before it come to pass, that when it is come
to pass, ye might believe. ³⁰ Hereafter I will not
talk much with you ; for the prince of this world
cometh, and hath nothing in me : ³¹ but that the
world may know that I love the Father ; and as

while hence, this world is to behold me no more as its
occupant, but *you* will still continue to behold me [in
your recollection and spiritual conceptions]; and in the
issue, your steps too will follow me to that immortal bliss for which I
shall survive, and to which I shall thereby admit you.   20 The occurrence of this my revivification will at length compel your own minds
to the just apprehension of the important relation, which [I have just
declared to you that] I sustain as intimately connected with the Father, and [thereafter you will soon become fully aware] that I am also
identified [in sympathy and object] with yourselves, and you reciprocally [in love and labor] with me.   21 It is those only, however, who
treasure up and faithfully practice my precepts, that possess a genuine
love for me, and such accordingly will be loved by my Father; I too
will entertain a most tender love toward them, and will express it by
satisfactory disclosures of my character to them [in the intimacy of
communion through the Spirit]." 22 Here Jude (not he "of Ke'rioth")
[but the other disciple of that name,—in surprise at the limited development of his career which he supposed Jesus to be contemplating by
this remark,] inquired, "But why, Master, are you going to confine
the exhibition of your Messianic character to us, instead of publicly announcing yourself to the world?" 23 Jesus replied, [evasively leading
his mind to the correct appreciation of what it concerned him to know,
"What I stated was this, that] whoever loves me, will observe my injunctions, and as he would thus secure my Father's love also, we will
both of us then visit him [in the special internal manifestations of sacred love], and indeed take up our abode permanently with him [in
the constant influence of the indwelling Spirit].   24 On the contrary,
that person who has no real love for me, will evince his want of it by a
disregard of my precepts, [so that any further revelation of myself to
him, would be unavailing;] and [such a one need never hope to enjoy the spiritual company of my Father, since] the precepts to which
you are listening from my mouth, are not originally mine, but issued
by my Father whose commission I bear, [and therefore a contempt
for them must be regarded as a slighting of Him.]

25 "I have thought it proper to make these intimations to you while
I yet continue in your midst, [although well aware of your liability to
misunderstand and forget them;] 26 but the inward Helper, the Holy
Spirit to whom I referred as about to be sent by the Father in my stead
and authority, will more efficiently teach you all these truths, and
clearly remind you of all my teachings.—27 Before taking my leave of
you, I now bequeath to you my blessing—I impart the blessing of my
own bliss to your hearts; no such empty presents as this world affords,
do I bestow upon you, [but the priceless gift of my grace.]   I therefore again charge you, let not your minds be disturbed by anxiety or
fear, in view of my departure: 28 recollect what I just now told you,
that 'I am but going, soon to return to you;' now your affection for
me ought to make you glad on my account, that I am going to my
Father, whose position is so much more exalted than mine [in my
present sphere].   29 My great object, however, in thus forewarning
you of my departure, is to inspire you with faith in my prescience,
when you shall have seen my declaration verified by its actually coming to pass.   30 I shall have but little opportunity after this of conversing privately with you; for the Satanic chief of this world's wicked
race will presently come upon me [in the person of some of his min-
ions, and thus separate me from you]: yet shall he not prevail eventually against me; 31 [his malice is to be allowed to succeed against
me only thus far, in order] that mankind may have a proof [in my
submission to my divinely-appointed fate,] how much I love my

JOHN XIV.

179*

the Father gave me commandment, even   JOHN XIV.
so I do.—Arise, let us go hence.·

¹ I am the *true vine*, and my Father is   John XV.
the husbandman : ² every branch in me
that beareth not fruit, he taketh away; and every
branch that beareth fruit, he purgeth it, that it
may bring forth more fruit : ³ now ye are clean
through 'the word which I have spoken unto you.
⁴ Abide in me, and I in you : as the branch cannot bear fruit of itself, except it abide in the vine,
no more can ye, except ye abide in me ; ⁵ I am the
vine, ye are the branches. He that abideth in me,
and I in him, the same bringeth forth much fruit ;
(for without me ye can do nothing :) ⁶ if a man
abide not in me, he is cast forth as a branch and is
withered ; and men gather them and cast them into
the fire, and they are burned. ⁷ If ye abide in me,
and my words abide in you, ye shall ask what ye
will, and it shall be done unto you : ⁸ herein is my
Father glorified, that ye bear much fruit ; so shall
ye be my disciples. ⁹ As the Father hath loved
me, so have I loved you : continue ye in my love :
¹⁰ if ye keep my commandments, ye shall abide in
my love ; even as I have kept my Father's commandments, and abide in his love. ¹¹ These things
have I spoken unto you, that my joy might remain
in you, and that your joy might be full. ¹² This is
my commandment, That ye love one another, as I
180

Father, and that I implicitly obey His instructions in   **JOHN XIV.**
my mission.
  "And now," concluded Jesus, "it is time for us to
rise from table, and prepare to leave the city."

¹ [The ceremonies of the repast being now entirely con-   **John XV.**
cluded, Jesus still lingered in the apartment to communicate to his disciples the following parting counsels and
encouragements: "In the great field of the gospel enterprise which
I have come to set on foot for you to carry out,] I occupy the position
of the grand central vine, [all others being mere offshoots of this genuine stock, or else worthless wildlings,] while my Father is the supreme Gardener of the vineyard [of grace. ² In the exercise of his
horticultural care,] He prunes off all such limbs attached to me the
living vine, as are found not to yield any fruit; whilst those that are
bearing limbs He rids of all encumbering shoots, so that they may yield
more fruit. ³ Thus *you* are already to a considerable extent divested
of these vitiating excrescences [in the shape of misguiding worldly notions respecting me], by means of the discriminative discourses which
I have all along been delivering to you. ⁴ [All that you have to do
therefore is, to] adhere still in your connection with me, in order to
preserve my vitalizing union with you; for just as no limb can bear
fruit of itself, dissevered from the main stem of the vine, so neither
can you effect anything of religious value, if you dissolve your connection with me; ⁵ I, then, am the trunk of the vine [of the spiritual
Church], while you my followers constitute its branches. Accordingly, whoever continues spiritually joined with me, and thus main-
tains the circulation of my influences through his soul, produces in
consequence an abundant yield of religious fruit; since it is by my
spiritual aid alone, that you are enabled to accomplish any sacred purpose: ⁶ on the other hand, whoever relinquishes his spiritual union
with me [in the heart-felt intercourse of divine love and confidence],
is at once lopped off from the body of the Vine, like a refuse branch,
doomed speedily to wither [in religious enjoyment], and eventually
to be consigned to the fate of such dry twigs, which are collected and
thrown into the fire [in this case of final perdition,—the ultimate sentence of this apostate nation], there to be irretrievably consumed.
⁷ Whereas, if you preserve your connection with me inviolate, and
habitually yield to my precepts their due influence over your hearts,
you are privileged, [as I before intimated,] with making any prayer to
which you shall be prompted [by the sentiments thus fostered], and it
will certainly be accomplished for you. ⁸ It is by your thus producing
abundant and valuable results, [especially in your Apostolical work,]
that my Father's honor is to be promoted on earth, and the same
course [of labor and prayer in union with me] will confirm and evince
your discipleship with respect to me. ⁹ Now the standard of intensity
according to which you are to preserve my affectionate interest in you,
is the unreserved love that the Father exercises toward me, to which
the love that I have displayed toward you corresponds; ¹⁰ and the
mode by which alone you will be enabled to retain this complacency
on my part respecting you, is by assiduously observing all my injunctions, just as *I* continually cherish my Father's infinite delight in me,
by steadily prosecuting His commands. ¹¹ My object therefore, [as you
will perceive,] in these communications to you, is to effect a perma-
nence of this my delighted satisfaction with your characters, and thus
lead you to a consummation of your bliss in me [by the conscious enjoyment of my entire favor here and in heaven]. ¹² Of these my injunctions one of the most important [especially under the tendencies

180*

have loved you : ^{13} greater love hath no   JOHN XV.
man than this, that a man lay down his
life for his friends ; ^{14} ye are my friends, if ye do
whatsoever I command you : ^{15} henceforth I call you
not *servants*, for the servant knoweth not what his
lord doeth; but I have called you *friends*, for all
things that I have heard of my Father, I have
made known unto you. ^{16} Ye have not chosen
me, but I have chosen you, and ordained you, that
ye should go and bring forth fruit, and that your
fruit should remain : that whatsoever ye shall ask
of the Father in my name, he may give it you.
^{17} These things I command you, that ye love one
another. ^{34} A new commandment I give   John XIII.
unto you, That ye love one another ; as
I have loved you, that ye also love one another :
^{35} by this shall all men know that ye are my disciples,
if ye have love one to another.

   ^{18} If the *world* hate you, ye know that   John XV.
it hated *me* before it hated you : ^{19} if ye
were of the world, the world would love his own;
but because ye are not of the world, but I have
chosen you out of the world, therefore the world
hateth you. ^{20} Remember the word that I said unto
you,* The servant is not greater than his lord :
if they have persecuted me, they will also persecute you; if they have kept my saying, they will
keep yours also : ^{21} but all these things will they
do unto you for my name's sake, because they
know not him that sent me. ^{22} If I had not come
and spoken unto them, they had not had sin; but
now they have no cloak for their sin : ^{23} he that

---

* See chap. xiii, 16, § 78.

to disunion that threaten you,] is, to exercise a tender   **JOHN XV.**
regard for each other, making my love as exhibited toward you its incentive and rule; 13 and [the depth of
this you may conceive by considering that] no one could evince a more
ardent love than by sacrificing his very life in his friends' behalf, [as
I am about to do for you.] 14 *You* are they that stand in the relation
of friends to me, provided you faithfully keep all my injunctions:
15 observe, I no longer designate you as mere servants, for the domestic is not of right admitted to a knowledge of his master's plans, [his
business being simply to execute them;] but I have addressed you familiarly as friends, inasmuch as I have confidentially acquainted you
with the entire series of purposes with which my Father has commissioned me in the privacy of His counsels. 16 Neither have you selected
me as the object of your intimacy; it is I who have chosen you to this
honorable companionship, and appointed you to your [Apostolical]
mission, in which you should bring about important results [in my
cause], and those too of a permanent character,—empowering you
with the privilege of making any request of the Father on my account
[i. e. in furtherance of my cause delegated to your charge], under the
guarantee that I would secure it for you. 17 [In view, therefore, of this
condescension in me toward you,] I again enjoin upon you to maintain
in turn a cordial love for each other, [as it will not only be appropriate
to your social relation to me, but also essential to your
success.] 34 This duty of mutual affection I prescribe to **John XIII.**
you with [an emphasis and authority that clothe the old
precept with] a new sacredness; and the model of disinterested fer-
vor according to which you are to love one another, is *my* devoted interest in your well-being. 35 By the exhibition of this tender regard
for each other, [so like myself,] the world of spectators will be won
to acknowledge that you are my genuine followers.
   18 "[Of this reciprocal love you will have the more **John XV.**
need," continued Jesus, "inasmuch as] the ungodly
world will nevertheless show you no kindness; but then you will have
the satisfaction of reflecting, that it has already vented its malice
against me in the first instance, [by persecuting me during life, and
putting me to an ignominious death. 19 This hostility you must therefore expect:] for were you identified with the religious community in
feeling and purpose, it would of course be friendly to you as a part of
itself; but [from this very enmity you may derive an assurance of being my disciples, for] it is precisely because you do not belong to the
unbelieving mass in your spiritual affinities, being selected by me out
of its ranks, that it bears you ill-will, [as having deserted it for the antagonist principles of my religion.] 20 Bear in mind, then, [for your encouragement under this opposition,] the aphorism that I have uttered
to you before this, that 'The servant cannot expect to fare better than
his master;' and therefore as the world [in the person of my countrymen and their sympathizers,] has persecuted me, it will doubtles treats
you in the same way; or had it entertained my teachings with docility,
it would be likely to heed your doctrines likewise. 21 But [so far from
yielding readily to your representations,] this depraved race will inflict this opprobrium upon you on account of your connection with me,
in whom they refuse to recognize the representative of Him who commissioned me. 22 Had I never thus appeared on earth and personally
addressed my claims to them, their inacquaintance with me might
have admitted some extenuation of its guilt; but now, after the full exposition of my character and doctrines before them, they have not the
slightest apology for their base rejection of me;—23 in their groundless

hateth me, hateth my Father also : [24] if JOHN XV.
I had not done among them the works
which none other man did, they had not had sin;
but now have they both seen and hated both me and
my Father. [25] But this cometh to pass, that the
word might be fulfilled that is written in their law,*
They hated me without a cause. [26] But when the
Comforter is come, whom I will send unto you from
the Father, even the Spirit of truth, which proceedeth
from the Father, he shall testify of me ; [27] and *ye*
also shall bear witness, because ye have been with
me from the beginning. [1] These things John XVI.
have I spoken unto you, that ye should
not be offended : [2] they shall put you out of the synagogues, yea, the time cometh, that whosoever killeth
you, will think that he doeth God service ; [3] and
these things will they do unto you, because they
have not known the Father nor me. [4] But these
things have I told you, that when the time shall
come, ye may remember that I told you of them :
and these things I said not unto you at the beginning,
because I was with you.

[5] But now I go my way to him that sent me, and
none of you asketh me, Whither goest thou ? [6] but
because I have said these things unto you, sorrow
hath filled your heart. [7] Nevertheless I tell you the
truth, It is expedient for you that I go away : for if
I go not away, the Comforter will not come unto you ;
but if I depart, I will send him unto you. [8] And
when he is come, he will reprove the world of sin
and of righteousness and of judgment; [9] of sin, because they believe not on me ; [10] of righteousness,
because I go to my Father, (and ye see me no more ;)
[11] of judgment, because the prince of this world is

---

* Psa. xxxv, 19 ; lxix, 4.

malignity toward me, they but show [as every one JOHN XV.
must do who fails to love me,] their real hatred to my
Father, [whose holiness and truth I reflect.] 24 Or,
had I not performed miracles in their presence unprecedented in
extent and authority, their crime of unbelief would have been more
excusable; but now, after they have been favored with a display of
divine power on my part, they have evinced an incorrigible aver-
sion to me, and thereby also to my Father, [whose character is visi-
bly portrayed in me.] 25 By this settled opposition on their part,
the language of former saints in their own Scriptures is illustrated
afresh in my case, that there are those—

'—— who hate me causelessly.'

26 [Despite this incredulity of theirs at present,] however, the Heaven-
originated Spirit who gives to divine truth its convincing power,
that Helper of whom I just now spoke as about to be dispatched to
you by me from my Father's presence, on His arrival [in full influence upon men's minds] will effectually impress upon them the evidences of my true character; 27 and you too, who have been my
companions from the outset of my public career, will then be enabled to testify convincingly [to the facts on which my
claims are grounded]. 1 I have therefore only ad- John XVI.
verted to these obstacles [arising from impenitent
prejudice against me], lest you should be discouraged [from adhering to my cause under pressure of the trials which will result there-
from to you]. 2 For not only will your adversaries expel you from
their religious assemblies, but the day is not far distant when your
murderous persecutors will be so inflamed with bigoted fury, as to
imagine that they are doing an act of piety toward God in causing
your very death, 3 being actuated by a perverse misconception of
my Father's character and therefore of me. 4 Observe now! I have
fairly forewarned you of these oppositions, so that when they actually occur, you may remember my prediction of them, [and thus
not only repose greater confidence in my knowledge, but also be
prepared to endure them cheerfully.]
"I have reserved these full intimations of future persecution
until this late period, because up to this time I have been in your
company, [and therefore had an opportunity of sustaining your
courage by personal counsels, and I did not wish needlessly to af-
flict you by such anticipations;] 5 but now I am on the point of departing to Him who sent me on my earthly mission, and [have
therefore freely opened my mind on all these subjects to you: yet]
the recital so far from eliciting from any of you the friendly inquiry,
'Whither are you going?' 6 has only had the effect of filling your
hearts with a selfish grief [of despondency at the prospect of the
exposure in which my departure will leave you]. 7 Yet, I candidly
assure you, this very departure of mine is of the greatest possible
advantage to you; for by this means alone will I be able to procure and send you that divine Helper. 8 His office, when His influences are thus exerted in full, will be to convince mankind [and
especially this impenitent people] of their heinous sin 9 in rejecting me, 10 of my own holy character as vindicated by the fact of
my withdrawal by ascension to my Father, out of your sight [yet
attested by you],—11 and of the signal doom of expulsion from his
spiritual power, which the Satanic tyrant of the mass of depraved

judged. ¹²I have yet many things to say
unto you, but ye cannot bear them now :
¹³ howbeit, when he, the Spirit of truth, is come, he
will guide you into all truth ; for. he shall not speak
of himself, but whatsoever he shall hear, that shall he
speak ; and he will show you things to come. ¹⁴ He
shall glorify me ; for he shall receive of mine, and
shall show it unto you : ¹⁵ all things that the Father
hath are mine ; therefore said I, that he shall take
of mine, and shall show it unto you. ¹⁶ A little
while, and ye shall not see me ; and again a little
while, and ye shall see me, (because I go to the
Father.) ¹⁷ Then said some of his disciples among
themselves, What is this that he saith unto us, A
little while, and ye shall not see me ; and again a
little while, and ye shall see me ; and, Because I go
to the Father ? ¹⁸ they said therefore, What is this
that he saith, A little while ? we cannot tell what
he saith. ¹⁹ Now Jesus knew that they were desirous to ask him, and said unto them, Do ye inquire
among yourselves of that I said, A little while, and
ye shall not see me ; and again a little while, and ye
shall see me ? ²⁰ Verily, verily I say unto you, that
ye shall weep and lament, but the world shall rejoice ; and ye shall be sorrowful, but your sorrow
shall be turned into joy : ²¹ a mother hath sorrow,
when her hour is come ; but as soon as the child is
born, she remembereth no more the anguish, for joy
that a man is born into the world : ²² and ye now
therefore have sorrow ; but I will see you again,
and your heart shall rejoice, and your joy no man
taketh from you. ²³ And in that day ye shall ask
me nothing ; verily, verily I say unto you, Whatsoever ye shall ask the Father in my name, he will
give it you : ²⁴ hitherto have ye asked nothing in my
name ; ask, and ye shall receive, that your joy may

men will then meet. ¹²There are many other doctrines [connected with the more profound designs of
the gospel], which I would like to communicate to
you; but your minds are not yet prepared for the appreciation of
these spiritual truths; ¹³when that truth-realizing Spirit shall be
dispensed, however, he will guide your minds [with inspired insight]
into the whole scheme of sacred truth, [thus qualifying you to expound its deepest mysteries with Apostolical authority;] for He will
reveal in His interior suggestions no self-devised system of dogmas,
but will disclose to you divinely-prescribed messages, imparting also
at times premonitions of future events [affecting your official work.]
¹⁴By this tuition He will enhance your regard for me, whose teachings He will second and rehearse in your minds; ¹⁵inasmuch as there
is a perfect community of attributes and sentiments between me and
the Father, and the Spirit as His Legate must therefore accord in all
communications with mine. ¹⁶[These considerations should recon-
cile you to my departure; for] although in a short time you will be
deprived of the pleasure of personally beholding me, yet in a short
additional time you will behold me again [in the spiritual disclosures
of the representative Spirit], a vision that is to be secured by my
withdrawal to the Father."

¹⁷At this point, [the minds of the disciples, who had but vaguely
traced their Master's meaning, became so completely puzzled with
these declarations so foreign to their habitual views concerning his
prospects, that] some of them could no longer refrain from whisper-
ing to each other, "What does he refer to by telling us, 'In a short
time you will cease to behold me, and after a short time again you
will behold me'? and then again by saying, 'It is to be secured by
my withdrawal to the Father'?" ¹⁸"Certainly we cannot tell," [re-
turned those appealed to,] "what he means by the 'short time' he
speaks of." ¹⁹Aware that they would have been glad [but for
their diffidence,] to put these questions to *him*, Jesus rejoined,
"Are you debating among yourselves the import of my declarations
concerning 'your soon beholding me no longer, and then shortly
beholding me again'? ²⁰[Well, events will ere long verify my
words; for] I distinctly warn you, that you will soon be made to
wail and lament in bitterest grief [at my violent death, which will
seem to extinguish all your hopes in me], while the persecuting
world will exult [in fancied triumph]; but your sorrow [at this dis-
appointing bereavement] will speedily give place to joy [at my
resurrection, and the succesful development of the gospel thereby
ushered in]. ²¹As a mother suffers excruciating anguish when
her pangs come on; but, [that brief crisis being past,] on the
birth of the babe, she forgets her pain in the maternal joy that a
new human being is brought into the world: ²²so you already
begin to feel the throes of grief [at the prospect of my loss];
but I will soon revisit you, and your bleeding hearts will then be
consoled with a joy [in my abiding inward presence,] of which no
earthly power will be able to deprive you. ²³In the succeeding
period [of full illumination], you will no longer have any unsolved
questions [as the problem with which you are now perplexed,] to
propound to me; nay further, I assure you that whatever *requests*
you make of the Father under my authority, He will grant you.
²⁴So far, you have scarcely availed yourselves at all of this privilege of petition as my delegated servants; you are henceforth to
pray in the full exercise of this grant, and you shall receive re-
sponses which will satisfy your hearts with full delight [at the ac-

be full. ²⁵ These things have I spoken   JOHN XVI.
unto you in proverbs ; but the time cometh
when I shall no more speak unto you in proverbs,
but. I shall show you plainly of the Father. ²⁶ At
that day ye shall ask in my name : and I say not
unto you, that I will pray the Father for-you ; ²⁷ for
the Father himself loveth you, because ye have loved
me, and have believed that I came out from God.
²⁸ I came forth from the Father, and am come into the
world ; again, I leave the world, and go to the Father.
²⁹ His disciples said unto him, Lo, now speakest thou
plainly, and speakest no proverb. ³⁰ Now are we
sure that thou knowest all things and needest not that
any man should ask thee ; by this we believe that
thou camest forth from God. ³¹ Jesus answered
them, Do ye *now* believe ? ³² Behold, the hour
cometh, yea, is now come, that ye shall be scattered
every man to his own, and shall leave me alone :
and yet I am not alone, because the Father is with
me. ³³ These things I have spoken unto you, that in
me ye might have peace ; in the world ye shall have
tribulation ; but be of good cheer, I have overcome
the world.

  ¹ These words spake Jesus, and lifted   **John XVII.**
up his eyes to heaven and said, Father,
the hour is come ; glorify thy Son, that thy Son also
may glorify thee : ² as thou hast given him power over
all flesh, that he should give eternal life to as many
as thou hast given him ; ³ and this is life eternal, that
they might know thee the only true God, and Jesus
Christ whom thou hast sent. ⁴ I have glorified thee
on the earth ; I have finished the work which thou
gavest me to do : ⁵ and now, O Father, glorify thou
me with thine own self, with the glory which I had
with thee before the world was. ⁶ I have manifested
thy name unto the men which thou gavest me out of
184

complishment of your most sanguine purposes in my behalf]. **25** I have been obliged to discourse to you on these topics in (to you) enigmatical language; but a period [of more vivid perception on your part] is approaching, when I will no longer [seem to] use an obscure figurative style, but communicate to your minds [by the suggestive Spirit] the needful insight into my Father's character and plans in plain terms. **26** You will then no longer be backward in offering petitions under my authority; and I do not merely say that I will present your cases [and recommend your prayers] before my Father, **27** for the Father Himself [far from needing such an inducement to favor,] most tenderly loves you, who have clung to me with the affectionate persuasion that I am God's Messenger. **28** I did indeed leave the society of the Father when I came on my mission to earth; and now therefore I am about to leave the world again and return to Him." **29** "Well," returned the disciples, "we are glad to hear you talk in such distinct terms, and no longer in those symbolical gloomy intimations. **30** We are now fully convinced [by your ready solution of our unexpressed cogitations] that in your universal knowledge you have no occasion for a query to be propounded, [in order to be able to answer it;] this is of itself sufficient to satisfy us that you are really a divine Messenger." **31** "Have you even yet full faith in this my character?" replied Jesus: **32** "[firm as you deem your confidence in me to be, mark my word!] the trying hour is just now close at hand, when you will all be scattered like a flock of sheep, each seeking his own safety, and leave me alone and unsupported;—yet even in such a desertion, I am not entirely alone, for my Father is ever present with me.—**33** My object in all the foregoing conversation with you has been, to render you tranquil and happy by a full reliance upon me under every adversity; persecution you must expect from the corrupt world, but be not disheartened, I [shall soon] have triumphantly foiled its wicked machinations, and you have but to prosecute the victory."

JOHN XVI.

1 These affecting counsels Jesus concluded by invoking with uplifted eyes the blessing of Heaven upon his followers in a prayer to this effect: "O Father, the destined hour [of my atonement] is at hand, in which thou wilt honor thy Son [with that sublime consummation of His earthly task], and thereby enable Him in turn to promote thy glory [by the praise that will accrue to thee from the results of this success]; **2** it is thus that thou conferrest upon Him the prerogative of rescuing a whole apostate race, by bestowing upon all whom thy gracious influences shall have attracted to Him, that boon of endless bliss **3** which flows from a hallowing acquaintance with the true character of thee as the one supreme God, and of me thy Legate as the Messiah, [especially in my sacrificial relation to thee.] **4** I have already honored thee on the *earth*, by bringing to a successful termination the great work [of illustrating the divine nature in human redemption,] which thou hadst assigned me; **5** now therefore, on thy part do thou exalt me, Father, to that celestial glory in thy society which I shared with thee before this world's existence. **6** I have clearly exhibited thy character [in my person and teachings] to that select portion of the human race whom thou hast inclined [by thy Spirit] to follow me; as they were originally thy genuine worshipers, so since thou hast intrusted them

John XVII.

AA   184*

the world; thine they were, and thou   JOHN XVII.
gavest them me, and they have kept thy
word : ⁷ now they have known that all things whatsoever thou hast given me are of thee; ⁸ for I have
given unto them the words which thou gavest me,
and they have received them, and have known surely
that I came out from thee, and they have believed
that thou didst send me. ⁹ I pray for them : I pray
not for the world, but for them which thou hast given
me ; for they are thine : ¹⁰ and all mine are thine, and
thine are mine; and I am glorified in them. ¹¹ And
now I am no more in the world, but these are in the
world, and I come to thee : holy Father, keep through
thine own name those whom thou hast given me, that
they may be one, as we are. ¹² While I was with
them in the world, I kept them in thy name ; those
that thou gavest me I have kept, and none of them is
lost, but the Son of perdition, (that the scripture might
be fulfilled :)* ¹³ and now come I to thee ; and these
things I speak in the world, that they might have my
joy fulfilled in themselves. ¹⁴ I have given them thy
word ; and the world hath hated them because they
are not of the world, even as I am not of the world :
¹⁵ (I pray not that thou shouldest take them out of the
world, but that thou shouldest keep them from the
evil :) ¹⁶ they are not of the world, even as I am not
of the world. ¹⁷ Sanctify them through thy truth,
(thy word is truth :) ¹⁸ as thou hast sent me into the
world, even so have I also sent them into the world ;
¹⁹ and for their sakes I sanctify myself, that they also
might be sanctified through the truth. ²⁰ Neither
pray I for these alone ; but for them also which shall
believe on me through their word : ²¹ that they all
may be one ; as thou, Father, art in me, and I in thee,

---

* Compare chap. xiii, 18; Acts i, 20; Matt. xxvi, 24.

to my discipleship, they have continued to pay a sacred regard to thy injunctions as communicated by $\quad$ JOHN XVII.
me : [7] in this manner they have come to realize that
all my doings and doctrines proceed originally from thee, [8] and at
length cordially admit my communications with the firm conviction that I am thy authorized Messenger.

[9] "And now I as their Teacher commit them in prayer to thy
paternal benediction; I do not now intercede for the world at
large, [nor for this one nation in general,] but for these thy own
followers passed by thee into my charge : [10] yes, [I the more confidently invoke thy interest in their behalf, because] whatever apper-
tains to thee or me is common with us both, and [I have the special
ground of identification in this case, that] my honor [in the successful propagation of my cause] has been made to depend upon their
representation of me. [11] But now I am about to quit this world, and
return to thee, leaving them behind me still amid its snares; I therefore pray thee, adorable Father, to preserve them faithful to those
principles into which thou hast commissioned me to indoctrinate
them, that they may continue firmly banded together in our common
cause [i. e. of me and thee in the gospel], with a unanimity parallel
to that which subsists between ourselves. [12] So long as I have remained in their company, I have sedulously preserved them thy faithful servants, without losing a single one of them from that fidelity,
except [Judas,] that fit subject of perdition,—and his apostasy was
an accomplishment of Scriptural prophecy, [so that such an exception was not unlooked for ;] [13] but now, being about to return to thee
and leave them, I make this prayer while yet lingering upon earth,
in order that [by its encouraging tone and cheering answer] the delight which I feel [in view of the speedy establishment of my cause,]
may be propagated in their hearts [to a degree now, but eventually]
with the fullness of satisfaction, [at the successful prosecution of their
mission.] [14, 16] I have imparted to them the communications of
truth with which thou hast charged me; but in consequence of
their adhesion to my doctrines, so unpalatable to the corrupt world,
it has already begun to hate them, especially as they have thus
learned to abandon its principles and practices, in imitation of my
contrariety to its character and policy. [15] Yet I do not request thee
to remove them as yet out of this scene of opposition, [where their
labors are so much needed,] but only pray thee to guard them from
its evil influences upon their hearts; [17] especially do thou qualify
them for their future work by spiritualizing their views and feelings
with a deeper insight into the genuine import of thy sacred communications, [particularly the gospel truths delivered through
me.] [18] For in pursuance of my own earthly mission from thee,
I have commissioned them with their Apostolical errand to mankind; [19] and it is with a view to this hallowed preparation on their
part by being thoroughly imbued with the spirit of divine truth,
that I have devoted myself to its elucidation before them [in my
discourses, temper, actions and sacrificial passion,] with most scrupulous sanctity of deportment.

[20] "Nor would I confine my petitions to these my Apostles alone;
I pray also for all who may believe in me through their preaching
[during their own ministry, and so on through the continuation of
their representations in all coming ages], [21] that my followers universally may be united in heart and effort as thoroughly and indis-
solubly, in their common identity with us in these respects, as thou
and I, Father, are with each other;—and thus will mankind be

185*

that they also may be one in us : that the   JOHN XVII.
world may believe that thou hast sent
me. ²² And the glory which thou gavest me, I have
given them : that they may be one, even as we are
one ; ²³ I in them, and thou in me, that they may be
made perfect in one ; and that the world may know
that thou hast sent me, and hast loved them as thou
hast loved me. ²⁴ Father, I will that they also whom
thou hast given me, be with me where I am ; that
they may behold my glory which thou hast given me :
for thou lovedst me before the foundation of the
world. ²⁵ O righteous Father, the world hath not
known thee ; but I have known thee, and these have
known that thou hast sent me : ²⁶ and I have declared
unto them thy name, and will declare it ; that the love
wherewith thou hast loved me, may be in them, and I
in them.

¹ When Jesus had spoken these words,   John XVIII.
[MATT. XXVI, 30] and when they had sung a hymn,
he went forth with his disciples, [LUKE XXII, 39] as he was
wont, to the Mount of Olives.

§ 127.—Christ's Agony and Arrest in Gethsem'ane.

(Foot of the Mount of Olives ; late in *Thursday* evening, *March* 17,
A. D. 29.)

³⁶ Then cometh Jesus with them   Matt. XXVI.
[JOHN XVIII, 1] over the brook Cedron, unto a
place [JOHN XVIII, 1] where was a garden called Gethsemane,
[JOHN XVIII, 1] into the which he entered and his disciples, and
saith unto his disciples, Sit ye here [LUKE XXII, 40] and
pray that ye enter not into temptation, while I go and
pray yonder. ³⁷ And he took with him Peter and the
two sons of Zebedee, and began to be sorrowful and
[MARK XIV, 33] sore amazed and very heavy. ³⁸ Then saith
he unto them, My soul is exceeding sorrowful, even

convinced of my divine mission, [by these its   JOHN XVII.
heaven-kindred fruits.] ²³ To enhance this conviction, and especially to evidence to an alien-
ated world the emphatic parity of thy love for my followers
with that which thou bearest for me, ²² I have extended this
their mutual union—so akin to ours, ²³ and secured by their
identification with thee through me the blending medium—
to its consummation [in their common participation of celestial
bliss], ²² by conferring upon them the same privilege of [fu-
ture] glory [in heaven], which thou hast allotted to me [in
the glorified state which I am so soon to enter] ; ²⁴ I therefore
desire of thee, Father, that I may [eventually] thus have the
perpetual company of those [my Apostles and subsequent be-
lievers] whom thou hast [and wilt have] inclined to my service, that they may behold and share my beatified glory [in thy
presence], which thou hast assigned me in token of thy eternal
love toward me. ²⁵ This profane world [and above all the Jews],
indeed, O Blessed Father, recognize not thy sacred character
and purposes, but I who am intimately acquainted with thee,
²⁶ have so disclosed thy nature and plans to these my disciples,
²⁵ that they are now convinced of my legation from thee : ²⁶ and
henceforth I shall continue to reveal thy counsels to my followers in general [by the significant incidents of my passion,
and the teachings of the Holy Spirit], by which means they
will be more closely united with me, and share thy love toward me [on earth and in heaven]."

¹ The little company now closed their evening's   John XVIII.
interview ᵃ with chanting a portion of the Scrip-
tures,| and then they all proceeded together out
of the city ᵃ toward the Mount of Olives,| ᵇ [on the road to
Bethany] where Jesus usually spent the night.|

§ 127.—Christ's Agony and Arrest in Gethsem'anè.

(Foot of the Mount of Olives; late in *Thursday* evening, *March* 17, A. D. 29.)

³⁶ ᶜ Crossing the brook Kedron, the party   Matt. XXVI.
reached the olive-yard| known by the name of
Gethsem'anè, at the entrance of which Jesus directed his disciples, " Sit down here a few minutes, ᵈ and occupy yourselves
with diligent prayer against the insidious influences of the trial
to which you will presently be exposed| [on my apprehension] ;
while I retire yonder for private devotion." ³⁷ He now took
Peter and Zebedee's two sons ᵉ James and John| apart with him
a short distance within, and told them, as the anticipation [of
the dreadful atonement he was about to undergo] rushed over
his thoughts with an ᵉ appalling| distinctness that made his
spirits sink within him, ³⁸ " My mind is just now so oppressed
with a deathlike anguish ᶠ at the prospect of the overwhelming

ᵃ Matt xxvi, 30.	ᵇ Luke xxii, 39.	ᶜ John xviii, 1.
ᵈ Luke xxii, 40.	ᵉ Mark xiv, 33.	ᶠ Luke xii, 50.

unto death : [Luke XII, 50] I have a baptism   MATT. XXVI.
to be baptized with; and how am I straitened
till it be accomplished! Tarry ye here and watch with
me. ³⁹ And he went a little farther [Luke XXII, 41] from
them about a stone's cast, and kneeled down and fell on his
face, and prayed saying, O my Father, if it be possible, let this cup pass from me; nevertheless not as *I*
will, but as *thou* wilt. ⁴⁰ And he cometh unto the
disciples, and findeth them asleep, and saith unto
Peter, What! could ye not watch with me one hour?
[Luke XXII, 46] Rise, ⁴¹ watch and pray, that ye enter not into
temptation : the spirit indeed is willing, but the flesh
is weak. ⁴² He went away again the second time, and
prayed saying, O my Father, if this cup may not pass
away from me, except I drink it, thy will be done.
⁴³ And he came and found them asleep again : for
their eyes were heavy ; [Mark XIV, 40] neither wist they
what to answer him. ⁴⁴ And he left them and went
away again, and prayed the third time, saying the
same words : [Luke XXII, 44] and being in an agony, he prayed
more earnestly ; and his sweat was as it were great drops of
blood falling down to the ground. [43] And there appeared an
angel unto him from heaven, strengthening him. ⁴⁵ Then
cometh he [Mark XIV, 41] the third time to his disciples, and
saith unto them, Sleep on now and take your rest?
[Mark XIV, 41] it is enough, behold, the hour is at hand, and
the Son of man is betrayed into the hands of sinners.
⁴⁶ Rise, let us be going : behold, he is at hand that doth
betray me. ⁴⁷ And while he yet spake, lo, Judas, one
of the twelve, [John XVIII, 2] who knew the place, (for Jesus
oft-times resorted thither with his disciples,) came [John XVIII, 3]
thither with lanterns and torches, and with him a great
multitude with swords and staves, [John XVIII, 3] having
received a band of men and officers from the chief-priests
[John XVIII, 3] and Pharisees and elders of the people;
[Luke XXII, 47] and he went before them. ⁴⁸ Now he that

187

ordeal through which I am soon to pass [in
achieving human redemption], that I can scarcely
command my feelings until the crisis be past.| I
wish you therefore to stay here and keep awake with me, while I
endeavor to gain relief in prayer." ³⁹ Then withdrawing ᵃ about a
stone's throw off,| he fell on his ᵃ knees,| and poured out his con-
flicting emotions in the following prayer, "O my Father! if Thy
ᵇ almighty| wisdom can accomplish its design [of man's pardon] in
any other mode, spare me the bitter draught of this [atoning] cup;
but if such a request be not consistent with Thy sacred purposes, I
bow to Thy will alone." ⁴⁰ On ᶜ rising from his prayer| and return-
ing to the three disciples, he found them fast asleep ᶜ from their ex-
haustion| [in passing through the sad scenes of the long evening],
and said pathetically to Peter, "What, ᵈ Simon,| ᵉ are you all asleep!|
Could you not then keep awake with me so short a time? ⁴¹ I am
aware that despite the readiness of your minds to do so, you are
overcome by physical weariness; but now you must ᵉ get up| and
engage in vigilant prayer, lest you be surprised by the coming
trial." ⁴² Then retiring a second time, he prayed ᶠ in the same
[deprecating but submissive] terms as before,| ⁴³ and returning
found the disciples once more slumbering; for their eye-lids were
so weighed down with drowsy fatigue, ᵍ that they had scarcely con-
sciousness left to reply| [in a coherent excuse to his reproof that
roused them from their second doze]. ⁴⁴ Thereupon quitting them
again, he repeated his supplication in the same language, ʰ but
with such agonized earnestness, that [in the violence of his mental
exercise,] the perspiration rolled from his brow to the ground, min-
gled with blood| [that exuded from the swollen veins]. ⁱ At this
moment of intense anxiety, an angelic form was seen to descend
from the skies, and support his fainting frame| [under the severe
paroxysm, imparting physical strength and consolatory communications. ⁴⁵ Reassured by this celestial visit,] he now returned ᵢ the
third time| to his three disciples, whose continued half-awake air
he reproved by saying, "Are you then sleeping here for the rest of
the night, [as if it were a comfortable lodging place?]—ᵢ Let this
napping suffice;| see! the eventful moment has arrived, and the
'Son of Man' is on the point of being betrayed into the power of
the profane [Romans]. ⁴⁶ Up! let us be going [to meet them]:
look! yonder comes my betrayer!"

⁴⁷ While Jesus was ᵏ in the very act of| speaking these words,
Judas (his disciple of that name, ˡ the traitor), aware that the spot
was a frequent place of resort for Jesus with his disciples,| suddenly
came up ᵐ guiding| a large tumultuous crowd of men armed with
swords and clubs, ⁿ consisting of the Temple guard and several officers of the San'hedrim whom he had procured, with torches and
lanterns| [for searching in the closer parts of the garden]. ⁴⁸ The
traitor had agreed upon a signal with them, that "the person whom

MATT. **XXVI.**

a Luke xxii, 41.   b Mark xiv, 36.   c Luke xxii, 45.   d Mark xiv, 37.
e Luke xxii, 46.   f Mark xiv, 39.   g Mark xiv, 40.   h Luke xxii, 44.
i Luke xxii, 43.   j Mark xiv, 41.   k Mark xiv, 43.   l John xviii, 2.
      m Luke xxii, 47.   n John xviii, 3.

187*

betrayed him, gave them a sign saying,   MATT. **XXVI.**
Whomsoever I shall *kiss*, that same is
he ; hold him fast, [MARK XIV, 44] and lead him away safely.
49 And forthwith he came to Jesus and said, Hail,
Master ; and kissed him.   50 And Jesus said unto him,
Friend, wherefore art thou come ?—[LUKE XXII, 48] Judas,
betrayest thou the Son of man with a kiss?
4 Jesus therefore, knowing all things that   **John XVIII.**
should come upon him, went forth and
said unto them, Whom seek ye ?   5 They answered
him, Jesus of Nazareth.   Jesus saith unto them, I am
he.   (And Judas also, which betrayed him, stood with
them.)   6 As soon then as he had said unto them, I
am he, they went backward and fell to the ground.
7 Then asked he them again, Whom seek ye ?   And
they said, Jesus of Nazareth.   8 Jesus answered, I
have told you that I am he ; if therefore ye seek me,
let these go their way :   9 (that the saying might be
fulfilled which he spake,* Of them which thou gavest
me, have I lost none.)   49 When they   **Luke XXII.**
which were about him saw what would
follow, they said unto him, Lord, shall we smite with
the sword ?   51 And behold, one of them   **Matt. XXVI.**
which were with Jesus, [JOHN XVIII, 10]
(Simon Peter, having a sword,) stretched out his hand and
drew his sword, and struck a servant of the high-priest
and smote off his [JOHN XVIII, 10] right ear.   [JOHN XVIII, 10]
(The servant's name was Malchus.) [LUKE XXII, 51] And Jesus
answered and said, Suffer ye thus far.   And he touched his
ear and healed him.   52 Then said Jesus unto him, Put
up again thy sword into his place : for all they that
take the sword, shall perish with the sword.   53 Thinkest thou that I cannot now pray to my Father, and he
shall presently give me more than twelve legions of

---

* See John xvii, 12, § 126.

he should salute with a *kiss*, was Jesus, and   MATT. **XXVI.**
they might then seize *a* and carry him off se-
curely;|" ⁴⁹ so on entering the inclosure, he
ran quickly up to his Master, greeting him with a familiar
salutation and a kiss. ⁵⁰ But Jesus replied with reproving
irony, "What is your errand with me, neighbor?—*b* Have you
the impudence, Judas, to betray the 'Son of
Man' with a kiss !!" ⁴ Aware of the approach-   **John XVIII.**
ing crisis, Jesus now went out to the entrance
of the garden, and meeting the crowd accosted them with the
question, "Of whom are you in search?" ⁵ "Jesus the Nazarene," answered they. With a commanding mien Jesus responded, "*I am the person;*" but the treacherous Judas merely
stood silent among the rest, [abashed by the lofty bearing of
his Master.] ⁶ At this majestic annunciation of himself, [an
almost preternatural thrill of trepidation seized the throng,
so that] the foremost fell backward in confusion upon the
ground. ⁷ Jésus then repeated his demand, "Of whom are
you in search?" "Jesus the Nazarene," replied they again,
[still unable to realize that so august a personage as stood
before them, could be one whom they came to apprehend.]
⁸ "I have already told you," returned Jesus, "that I am the
person; if you are in search of me, then, [here I am, but]
you have no occasion to detain these others about me."
⁹ (Jesus was influenced [in this anticipative reserve of his
followers by the same concern for their safety, to which he
referred in a spiritual sense] by his late declaration, "I have
not lost a single one from their fidelity, out of all those whom
Thou hast consigned to my care.")

⁴⁹ His attendant disciples, however, seeing   **Luke XXII.**
that matters were converging to an affray, be-
gan to urge him, "Master, shall we strike them
down with the sword?" ⁵¹ One of them in-   **Matt. XXVI.**
deed, *c* (Simon) Peter, who chanced to have a
sword by him,| went so far as to draw it, and aiming a blow
at one of the High-Priest's domestics, *c* Malchus by name,|
severed his *c* right| ear from his head. ⁵² But Jesus, *d* as he
cured the wounded ear with a touch,| reprovingly bade Peter,
d "Desist from further violence,| and return your weapon to
its sheath; remember that those who use the murderous
sword, are doomed to expiate their crime by a like violent
punishment. ⁵³ Do you not suppose that I could instantly
summon to my rescue, were I to request it of my Father,
more than a dozen battalions of angels, [in place of the aid

a Mark xiv, 44.   *b* Luke xxii, 48.   *c* John xviii, 10.   *d* Luke xxii, 51.

angels ? [54] but how then shall the scrip-   MATT. XXVI.
tures be fulfilled,* that thus it must be ?
[JOHN XVIII, 11]·the cup which my Father hath given me, shall I
not drink it?   [55] In that same hour said Jesus to the
multitudes, Are ye come out as against a *thief*, with
swords and staves for to take me ?   I sat daily with
you teaching in the temple, and ye laid no hold on me :
[LUKE XXII, 53] but this is your hour and the power of darkness.
[56] But all this was done, that the scriptures of the
prophets might be fulfilled.†   Then all the disciples
forsook him and fled.   [50] Then came [JOHN XVIII, 12] the
band and the captain and officers of the Jews, and laid hands·
on Jesus and took him, [JOHN XVIII, 12] and bound him
[LUKE XXII, 54] and led him away,   [51] And there   Mark XIV.
followed him a certain young man, having
a linen cloth cast about his naked body ; and the young
men laid hold on him :   [52] and he left the linen cloth,
and fled from them naked.

§ 128.—*Christ Brought before the Ex-High-Priest.*
(Jerusalem, Mansion of Hananiah ; midnight introducing *Friday,*
March 18, A. D. 29.)

[13] And they led him away to Annas   John XVIII.
first, (for he was father-in-law to Caiaphas, which was the high-priest that same year.
[14] Now Caiaphas was he which gave counsel to the
Jews, that it was expedient that one man should die
for the people.)‡   [15] And Simon Peter followed Jesus
[MATT. XXVI, 58] afar off, and so did another disciple : that
disciple was known unto the high-priest, and went in
with Jesus into the palace of the high-priest.   [16] But
Peter stood at the door without : then went out that

---

* See especially Isa, liii.
† See especially Gen. iii, 15 ; Isa. liii, 8 ; Dan ix, 26 ; Zech. xiii, 7.
‡ See John xi, 50, § 120.

of you twelve?] ⁵⁴ But how in that case,   MATT. XXVI.
would the predictions of Scripture [concern-
ing my passive submission to violence,] be
fulfilled? ᵃ Shall I refuse to quaff the cup [of sacrificial
passion] that my Father proffers me?¹'' ⁵⁵ Then turning to
the ᵇ assailant concourse of hierarchal retainers and Temple
guards,I he thus expostulated with them [on their tumul-
tuary proceedings], " What an array of swords and clubs you
present in coming to arrest me, as if I were some desperate
thief! and yet, while I sat teaching day after day in your presence in the Temple [this week and on former occasions], you
never offered to lay violent hands on me; [why then should
you seize upon this obscure occasion for your designs?]
⁵⁶ But, be it so : ᶜ this is your permitted hour, for executing
the diabolical schemes of iniquitous men against me;I and by
this very means will the Scriptural prophecies concerning me
receive their accomplishment [by my death]."   At this crisis,
his terrified disciples without exception abandoned him to his
fate, and fled for their lives. ⁵⁰ The ᵈ officersI therefore advancing to Jesus at once seized him, ᵈ pinioned
him,I ᵉ and led him off a prisoner.I   ⁵¹ [In the   Mark XIV.
skirmish,] they were also in the act of seizing
upon a young man, who chanced to be among his followers
with merely a night-mantle wrapped about his person, [and
seemed inclined to adhere to Jesus in the emergency;] ⁵² but
he dropped off the robe of which they had hold, and escaped
naked from their grasp.

§ 128.—Christ Brought before the Ex-High-Priest.

(Jerusalem, Mansion of Hananiah ; midnight introducing *Friday, March* 18, A. D. 29.)

¹³ Jesus was now hurried in the first place   John XVIII.
for judicial examination in the presence of
Hananiah, who was father-in-law [and deputy]
of Caiaphas, the regular High-Priest at that time. ¹⁴ (This
Caiaphas was the same who advised the San'hedrim to " put
one individual [Jesus] to death, for the security of the whole
nation.") ¹⁵ Peter meanwhile could not forbear following his
Master thither, ᶠ although he kept at a distance,I [for fear of
being involved in his fate.]   There was also another disciple,
[John] who followed on after Jesus ; and being acquainted
with the deputy High-Priest's household, he went in with his
Master [as far as the interior court of that functionary's
house]. ₁₆ As Peter however timidly continued outside [in
the street], this other disciple went out [into the front en-
trance], and by his familiarity obtained consent with a few

---

a John xviii, 11.   *b* Luke xxii, 52.   *c* Luke xxii, 53.
d John xviii, 12.   *e* Luke xxii, 54.   *f* Matt. xxvi, 58.

other disciple which was known unto the JOHN **XVIII.**
high-priest, and spake unto her that kept
the door, and brought in Peter. ¹⁸ And the servants
and officers stood [LUKE XXII, 55] together there, who had
made a fire of coals [LUKE XXII, 55] in the midst of the hall;
(for it was cold;) and they warmed themselves: and
Peter stood with them [MATT. XXVI, 58] to see the end, and
warmed himself. [MATT. XXVI, 69] Now Peter sat without in
the palace; and a damsel [MARK XIV, 66] (one of the maids of
the high-priest) [MATT. XXVI, 69] came unto him: [MARK XIV, 67]
and when she saw Peter warming himself [LUKE XXII, 56] as he sat
by the fire, she earnestly looked upon him; ¹⁷ then saith the
damsel that kept the door unto Peter, Art not thou also
one of this man's disciples? [MATT. XXVI, 70] But he denied
him before them all and saith, I am not: [MARK XIV, 68] I know
him not; neither understand I what thou sayest. And he
went out into the porch· and the cock crew. [LUKE XXII, 58]
And after a little while [MARK XIV, 69] a maid saw him again,
and began to say to them that stood by, This is one of them;
[MATT. XXVI, 71] and another maid saw him, and said unto them
that were there, This fellow was also with Jesus of Nazareth;
[LUKE XXII, 58] and another saw him, and said, Thou art also
of them. ²⁵ And Simon Peter stood and warmed himself: they said therefore unto him, Art not thou also
one of his disciples? [MATT. XXVI, 72] And again he denied
it [MATT. XXVI, 72] with an oath and said, I am not, [MATT XXVI, 72]
I do not know the man.

¹⁹ The high-priest then asked Jesus of his disciples
and of his doctrine. ²⁰ Jesus answered him, I spake
openly to the world; I ever taught in the synagogue
and in the temple, whither the Jews always resort;
and in secret have I said nothing: ²¹ why askest thou
me? ask them which heard me, what I have said unto
them; behold, they know what I said. ²² And when
he had thus spoken, one of the officers which stood
by, struck Jesus with the palm of his hand, saying,

words to the female door-keeper, to bring in   JOHN XVIII.
Peter. [18] By this time the domestics and officers had kindled a fire *a* in the middle of the
open court,| as the night air was chilly, round which they
were *a* seated| warming themselves; so Peter *b* on entering the
court, came| and stood near the fire among the group, to share
the warmth, *b* and at the same time watch the issue of his
Master's trial.| [17] Presently *c* one of the ex-pontiff's female
domestics,| the same who acted as porter, *d* came near| *e* where
Peter stood warming himself,| *f* and eyeing him sharply,| said
to him, "Ha! methinks you too are one of the disciples of
this *e* Nazarene Jesus?|" [Alarmed at being implicated in so
unexpected a manner,] Peter stoutly denied the woman's as-
sertion, declaring *g* before all the company,| "Not I, indeed!
h I don't know why you should charge me with such a connection." Peter now retreated [for fear of being detected,]
into the passage leading from the court to the street, and
at this moment, he heard the sound of a cock crowing for
midnight,| [but without thinking of his Master's warning,
so occupied was his mind with his own danger.] *i* Here in a
few minutes| *j* the same female servant seeing him repeated
her suggestion concerning him to those standing near|, *k* in
which another female now joined,| [25] *i* and presently one of
the men coincided| as Peter returned to the fire [to avoid
these queries], so that the remark became general, "I really
believe this fellow was one of the prisoner's company;" but
Peter protested to all their insinuations *l* by averring, with an
oath, "I tell you, I have no acquaintance with him what-
ever."|

[19] Meanwhile [the examination of Jesus was going on be-
fore] the deputy High-Priest, [in the course of which he] put
various questions to Jesus respecting the number and names
of his followers, and the doctrine which he taught them, [in
hopes of eliciting data by which to implicate him in a charge
of sedition.] [20] But Jesus simply replied to him, "I have
already publicly discoursed on these subjects; my constant
practice has been to deliver my doctrines in synagogues and
in the Temple, giving an opportunity to all who assemble there
to become acquainted with them, and I have never made a
secret of my views and teachings. [21] Why then should you
now ask me thus formally concerning these matters? inquire
of those who have heard my public expositions, as to what
my doctrines consist in; I have no doubt, any of your colleagues can answer all your questions." [22] At this pithy
reply, one of the officers standing near was so incensed as to
deal Jesus a blow, adding in a menacing tone, "Do you dare

a Luke xxii, 55.   *b* Matt. xxvi, 58.   *c* Mark xiv, 66.   *d* Matt. xxvi, 69.
e Mark xiv, 67.   *f* Luke xxii, 56.   *g* Matt. xxvi, 70.   *h* Mark xiv, 68.
i Luke xxii, 58.   *j* Mark xiv, 69.   *k* Matt. xxvi, 71.   *l* Matt. xxvi, 72.

Answerest thou the high-priest so? **John XVIII.**
23 Jesus answered him, If I have spoken
evil, bear witness of the evil ; but if well, why smitest
thou me ?

[LUKE XXII, 59] And about the space of one hour after, another confidently affirmed [MATT. XXVI, 73] to Peter [LUKE XXII, 59]
saying, Of a truth this fellow also was with him; for he
is a Galilean [MARK XIV, 70] and his speech agreeth thereto.
26 One of the servants of the high-priest (being his
kinsman whose ear Peter cut off) saith, Did not I see
thee in the garden with him? 27 Peter then denied
again, [MARK XIV, 71] and began to curse and to swear saying,
I know not this man of whom ye speak: and immediately
the cock crew [MARK XIV, 72] the second time.
61 And the Lord turned and looked upon **Luke XXII.**
Peter ; and Peter remembered the word
of the Lord, how he had said unto him, Before the
cock crow [MARK XIV, 72] twice, thou shalt deny me thrice :
62 and Peter, [MARK XIV, 72] when he thought thereon, went
out and wept bitterly.

24 Now Annas had sent him bound unto **John XVIII.**
Caiaphas the high-priest.

§ 129.—*Arraignment before the San'hedrim.*

(Jerusalem, Palace of Caiaphas; dawn of *Friday, March* 18, A. D. 29.)

57 And they that had laid hold on **Matt. XXVI.**
Jesus, led him away to Caiaphas the
high-priest ; where, [LUKE XXII, 66] as soon as it was day, the
scribes and the elders were assembled, [LUKE XXII, 66] and
led him into their council. 59 Now the chief-priests and
elders and all the council sought false witness against
Jesus, to put him to death ; 60 but found none : yea,
though many false witnesses came, yet found they
none. At the last came two false witnesses, [MARK XIV, 57]
and bare false witness against him saying, We heard him say,
I will destroy this temple that is made with hands, and within
191

to answer the [deputy] High-Priest so imper-   **John XVIII.**
tinently?"   ²³ Jesus calmly returned, "If I
have said anything false or injurious, you have
the privilege of testifying legally before the proper tribunal
of the wrong done, and thus causing my punishment; but if
I have answered correctly, what right have you thus to strike
me?"

²⁶ ᵃ It was now about an hour after Peter's last questioning, |
when another ᵇ of the bystanders confronted him | ᵃ with the
positive declaration, "Certainly this fellow must be one of
Jesus's followers; | ᶜ his Galilean pronunciation makes it evi-
dent." | "Yes," said one of the High-Priest's male servants,
a relative of Malchus whose ear Peter had cut off, "did I not
see you just now in the garden with him?"   ²⁷ [Finding himself pressed with the imputation,] Peter now endeavored to
repel it by repeating ᵈ with solemn imprecations and adjura-
tions, | "I certainly am not even acquainted with the person
of whom you are speaking."   That moment the
cock crowed ᵉ again; | ⁶¹ and as Peter caught his   **Luke XXII.**
Master's piercing glance of pitying rebuke, who
[overheard his faithless cowardice, and] just then turned
around [with a significance understood only by Peter,] the
recollection of Jesus's late warning to him, "Before the cock
crows ᶠ twice, | you will three times disown me," flashed across
his mind ᶠ with overwhelming force : | [stung with remorse,]
⁶² he rushed out [into the street], and there his heart-stricken
penitence found vent in a flood of scalding tears.

²⁴ [Unable to glean any satisfactory ground of   **John XVIII.**
crimination from Jesus,] Hananiah now ordered
him to be taken for trial, bound as he was, to Caiaphas the
regular High-Priest.

§ 129.—*Arraignment before the San'hedrim.*

(Jerusalem, Palace of Caiaphas; dawn of *Friday, March* 18, A. D. 29.)

⁵⁷ The officers who had Jesus in charge accord-   **Matt. XXVI.**
ingly conducted him to the residence of Caia-
phas, where ᵍ as soon as day dawned, | the full
San'hedrim was convened, ᵍ and Jesus was brought into their
midst for trial. | ⁵⁹ The members of the assembly were now
busily engaged in endeavoring to elicit from every witness
they could muster, some testimony, however false, which
might convict him of a capital offense [in exciting the people
to seditious innovations] : ⁶⁰ but all their efforts failed to produce any [that would answer a legal purpose], ʰ on account
of the contradiction in the statements of all the witnesses
they were able to adduce. | At last they bribed two witnesses

a Luke xxii, 59.   *b* Matt. xxvi, 73.   *c* Mark xiv, 70.
d Mark xiv, 71.   *e* Mark xiv, 72, (first part).   *f* Mark xiv, 72, (last part).
　　g Luke xxii, 66.   　　*h* Mark xiv, 56.

three days I will build another made without   MATT. **XXVI.**
hands ; ⁶¹ and the other said, This fellow
said, *I am able* to destroy the temple of God, and to build
it in three days ; [MARK XIV, 59] but neither so did their witness
agree together.   ⁶² And the high-priest arose [MARK XIV, 60]
in the midst, and said unto him, Answerest thou nothing ? what is it which these witness against thee ?
⁶³ But Jesus held his peace.   ⁶⁶ And they   Luke **XXII.**
asked him, saying, ⁶⁷ Art thou the Christ ?
tell us.   And he said unto them, If I tell you, ye will
not believe : ⁶⁸ and if I also ask you, ye will not answer me, nor let me go.   [MATT. XXVI, 64] Nevertheless I say
unto you, ⁶⁹ Hereafter shall [MATT. XXVI, 64] ye see the Son
of man sit on the right hand of the power of God,
[MATT. XXVI, 64] and coming in the clouds of heaven.   [63] And
the high-priest answered, and ⁷⁰ then said they all
[MATT. XXVI, 63] unto him, I adjure thee by the living God that
thou tell us, Art thou then [MATT. XXVI, 63] the Christ the
Son of God ?   And he said unto them, Ye say that I
am.   [MATT. XXVI, 65] Then the high-priest rent his clothes,
and they said, ⁷¹ What need we any further witness ?
for we ourselves have heard [MATT. XXVI, 65] his blasphemy
of his own mouth : [MATT. XXVI, 66] what think ye ?   They
[MARK XIV, 64] all [MATT. XXVI, 66] answered and said, He is guilty
of death.

⁶³ And the men that held Jesus, mocked him ;
[MARK XIV, 65] some began to spit [MATT. XXVI, 67] in his face, and
smote him ; ⁶⁴ and when they had blindfolded him, they
struck him on the face [MATT. XXVI, 67] with the palms of
their hands, and asked him saying, Prophesy [MATT. XXVI, 68]
unto us, thou Christ, who is it that smote thee ?   ⁶⁵ And
many other things blasphemously spake they against
him.

to come forward [61] and depose the following gar-   MATT. XXVI.
bled declarations, a "We have heard him say, 'I
will tear down this Temple of human architec-
ture, and in three days rear another without physical means;'" [1]
b but even in this evidence their testimony did not agree, [1] for one
merely said, "He affirmed, 'I *have power* to raze the Temple of
God, and rebuild it in three days.'" [62] Hereupon the High-Priest
rose up, [as if the crime were substantiated, but really to cover the
deficiency of testimony by an assuming air,] and publicly put this
brow-beating question to the accused, "What have you to answer
to these depositions against you?" [63] Jesus, however, replied not
a word to this pompous summons; [for the evidence
refuted itself.] [66] Some of the council then asked   Luke XXII.
him, [67] "Simply tell us whether you are the Mes-
siah, [as report states that you claim to be]?" Jesus replied, "Were
I to make the most candid profession, I well know that you have
no intention of crediting my claims: [68] nor, should I propound in-
terrogations to you on this subject in turn, [as I lately did,] would
you give me any satisfactory reply, [lest you should be forced to
concede to my arguments; nor even set me free, [after ever so
many proofs of my innocence of any civil offense, by my explanations.] [69] But ere long [events will occur (in the development of
my mission), in which] you will [have a convincing opportunity
to] behold [in its retributive effects upon your impenitent nation,]
c the '"Son of Man's" appearance on the clouds of the sky,' invested with divine power [to overwhelm all opposition to the progress of His cause.'" [70] d Determined still to push him to an avowal
that should definitely criminate him;] the High-Priest now addressed to him this solemn appeal, [1] which all present joined in insisting upon, d "I call upon you here, in the fear of the Almighty,
to confess to us, then, whether you are indeed the Messiah, the
actual 'Son of God'?" [At this repeated challenge, waving all
further reserve,] Jesus promptly returned, "You have said right,
e *I am* such. [1]" [71] f [As if shocked at this unequivocal assumption,]
the High-Priest tore his mantle [in a pretended transport of grief
at its profanity], [1] exclaiming, f "Blasphemy!! [1] What occasion have
we for further evidence? you have now all heard with your own
ears his horrid impiety from his very lips. g What is your pleasure
to be done with him?!" h "O!" cried they! g all eagerly in reply,
"he must be sentenced to immediate death. [1]"

[63] The men who held Jesus in custody, now indulged in the vilest
insults toward him for their own sport, i some spitting in his face, [1]
and giving him severe blows; [64] while i others! blindfolding him
j slapped [1] him on the face, and sneeringly asked him, to "tell them
by his prophetical knowledge, k if he were the Messiah, [1] who it
was that struck him?" [65] With these and many other abusive
terms and acts j the menials! continued to treat him for a considerable time.

a Mark xiv, 58.   b Mark xiv, 59.   c Matt. xxvi, 64, (last clause.)
d Matt. xxvi, 63.   e Mark xiv, 62.   f Matt. xxvi, 65.   g Mark xiv, 64.
h Matt. xxvi, 66.   i Matt. xxvi, 67.   j Mark xiv, 65.   k Matt. xxvi, 63.

§ 130.—*Accusation before Pilate.*

(Jerusalem, Proc'urator's [formerly Herod's] Palace; very early on *Friday* morning, *March* 18, A. D. 29.)

[Matt. XXVII, 1] When the morning was come,   **John XVIII.** all the chief-priests and elders of the people took counsel against Jesus to put him to death. [2] And when they had bound him, they [Luke XXIII, 1] arose, and 28 then led they Jesus from Caiaphas unto the hall of judgment, [Matt. xxv^II, 2] and delivered him to Pontius Pilate the governor; (and it was early :) and they themselves went not into the judgment-hall, lest they should be defiled; but that they might eat the passover. 29 Pilate then went out unto them, and said, What accusation bring ye against this man? 30 They answered and said unto him, If he were not a malefactor, we would not have delivered him up unto thee. 31 Then said Pilate unto them, Take ye him, and judge him according to your law. The Jews therefore said unto him, It is not lawful for us to put any man to death : 32 (that the saying of Jesus might be fulfilled,* which he spake signifying what death he should die.) [Luke XXIII, 2] And they began to accuse him saying, We found this fellow perverting the nation and forbidding to give tribute to Cesar, saying that he himself is *Christ;* a king. 33 Then Pilate entered into the judgment hall again, and called Jesus, and said unto him, Art *thou* the king of the Jews? 34 Jesus answered him, Sayest thou this thing of thyself, or did others tell it thee of me? 35 Pilate answered, Am *I* a Jew? Thine own nation and the chief-priests have delivered thee unto me : what hast thou done? 36 Jesus answered, My kingdom is not of this world : if my kingdom were of this world, then would my servants fight, that I should not be delivered to the Jews;

---

* See chap. xii, 32.

§ 130.—*Accusation before Pilate.*

(Jerusalem, Proc'urator's [formerly Herod's] Palace; very early on *Friday* morning, *March* 18, A. D. 29.)

[28] As *a* soòn as it was broad! day-light the *a* San'-   **John XVIII.**
hedrim,! *b* now swelled to its full attendance of mem-
bers, rose! *a* from their session,! *c* after passing a
formal resolution that Jesus should be capitally executed.! *d* In pursuance of this decree, they caused him to be more closely manacled,!
and then committed him to the custody of the officers, *d* to be consigned to the *Proc'urator* [i e. Roman provincial governor,] Pontius
Pilate,! [for civil punishment; numbers of the council attending the
party in person from the mansion of Caiaphas, in order to enforce the
prosecution.   On their arrival at that magistrate's quarters,] Jesus
was led into the *Preto'rium* [i. e. Roman hall of justice]; but the
Jewish senators did not themselves venture within the room, [but
remained in the open court in front of the Palace,] lest the ceremonial impurity contracted by entering a Gentile apartment, should
disqualify them for partaking of the religious festive offerings connected with the Passover exercises on that day: [29] Pilate therefore
[at their request,] came out to confer with them, and inquired "the
nature of the crime alleged by them against the prisoner?" [30] They
artfully replied, "If he had not been guilty of a breach of the [national
sacred] law, we would not have thus handed him over to you to be
punished as a convict." [31] "Well," returned Pilate, "in that case,
all you have to do, is simply to take him in your own hands, and
sentence him to whatever ecclesiastical penalty your law prescribes."
"But then," rejoined they, "we have no civil power to punish any
offender capitally, [and on this account we have referred the case
for your adjudication.]" [32] (This [reference of the matter to the
secular tribunal,] became the providential means of the accomplishment of Jesus's intimation respecting the *mode* of his appproaching
death; [for the Romans were accustomed to execute criminals by
crucifixion, but the Jewish law directed blasphemers to be stoned
to death].) *e* They then began to present accusations of flagrant
civil offenses against Jesus, [with which to move Pilate to an indignant decision in their favor,] alleging, "We have convicted this culprit of being an actual insurrectionist among the populace, having
caught him denouncing the payment of tribute to the Emperor, under pretensions of being lawful sovereign himself with the title of
'Messiah.'"! [33] Pilate hereupon went back into the court-room,
and asked Jesus *f* personally,! [with a scornful smile,] "Do *you* then
claim to be the 'King of Judea,' [whom this people has so much to
say about, in their dreams of national expectation?]" [34] Jesus
[directing his attention to the misconception couched under this
question,] asked him in reply, "Tell me whether you proposed this
inquiry for your own satisfaction, or at the suggestion of others
making such an insinuation concerning me?' [35] "Do you suppose
I am a Jew, [to care anything about such speculations?]" roughly
answered Pilate: "your own people [by their priestly senate] have
delivered you over for sentence to me; I am only asking you, What
is your crime? [i. e. Is their allegation as to your assumptions, true?]"
[36] "As to that, then," replied Jesus, "*my* kingdom is far from being
a temporal one over worldly subjects: were it such, my adherents

a Mark xv, 1.   *b* Luke xxiii, 1.   *c* Matt. xxvii, 1.
d Matt. xxvii, 2.   *e* Luke xxiii, 2.   *f* Matt. xxvii, 11.

but now is my kingdom not from hence.   JOHN XVIII.
³⁷ Pilate therefore said unto him, Art thou
a *king* then ?   Jesus answered, Thou sayest that I am
a king.   To, this end was I born, and for this cause
came I into the world, that I should bear witness unto
the truth : every one that is of the truth, heareth my
voice.   ³⁸ Pilate saith unto him, What is *truth ?*   And
when he had said this, he went out again unto the
Jews, and saith unto them, I find in him no fault
at all.

¹² And when he was accused of the   **Matt. XXVII.**
chief-priests and elders, he answered
nothing.   ¹³ Then saith Pilate unto him, [MARK XV, 4]
Answerest thou nothing? hearest thou not how many
things they witness against thee ?   ¹⁴ And he answered
him to never a word ; insomuch that the governor
marveled greatly.   ⁴ Then said Pilate to   **Luke XXIII.**
the chief-priests and to the people, I find
no fault in this man.   ⁵ And they were the more fierce,
saying, He stirreth up the people, teaching throughout
all Jewry, beginning from Galilee to this place.
⁶ When Pilate heard of *Galilee*, he asked whether the
man were a Galilean.   ⁷ And as soon as he knew that
he belonged unto Herod's jurisdiction, he sent him to
Herod, who himself was also at Jerusalem at that
time.

§ 131.—*The Trial Referred to Herod.*

(Jerusalem; early on *Friday* morning, *March* 18, A. D. 29.)

⁸ And when Herod saw Jesus, he was exceeding
glad : for he was desirous to see him of a long season,
because he had heard many things of him ; and he
hoped to have seen some miracle done by him.   ⁹ Then
he questioned with him in many words ; but he answered him nothing.   ¹⁰ And the chief-priests and
scribes stood and vehemently accused him.   ¹¹ And
194

of course, like those of other princes, would have **JOHN XVIII.** fought with the devotion of their lives to defend me from falling into the power of the hierarchy; but my dominion is not of earthly origin." [37] "But are you not then a *king* at all?" rejoined Pilate. "Yes," responded Jesus, "it is as you say; [I *am* a king in one sense: I cannot equivocate on this subject, for] the very object of my birth and mission on earth, is [not so much to rule (in this stage of my career), but simply] to substantiate [gospel] truth; and every sincere lover of [this religious] truth, listens to my representations, and thus becomes a member of my [spiritual] kingdom." [38] "What is this '*truth*,' of which you are talking?" asked Pilate; then [without waiting for an answer on a topic that seemed to him to have nothing to do with judicial proceedings,] he abruptly went out to the hierarchy and told them, "I can discover no ground for condemnation in the prisoner." [12] They, however, **Matt. XXVII.** urged their accusations *a* the more clamorously; but Jesus offered not a word of defense in reply [to these empty assertions]. [13] Pilate then earnestly asked him, "What plea have you to make in refutation of these charges, which you hear these persons testifying to against you?" [14] Jesus continued entirely silent, which heightened Pilate's wonder at his seeming indifference. [4] Pilate now [seeking to dis- **Luke XXIII.** miss the trial, by] repeating to the assembled prosecutors his "inability to fix upon any definite ground of conviction in the prisoner's case," [5] they still insisted upon their charges, alleging further, "He excites the seditious feelings of the lower classes by his inflammatory doctrines, which he publishes all over Palestine, from Galilee to Jerusalem itself."

[6] On hearing *Galilee* mentioned as the scene of Jesus's operations, Pilate inquired whether he were an inhabitant of that district; [7] and learning that he was, and therefore came under the jurisdiction of Herod An'tipas, glad thus to dispose of the affair, he ordered him to be taken for trial to that prince, who chanced at the time to be staying in the city for a short time.

§ 131.—*The Trial Referred to Herod.*

(Jerusalem; early on *Friday* morning, *March* 18, A. D. 29.)

[8] Herod An'tipas [into whose presence Jesus was accordingly next conducted,] was secretly overjoyed at the prospect of so favorable an interview; for he had been for some time exceedingly desirous of a convenient opportunity for seeing him, [as his curiosity had been excited] from the wonderful reports he had heard concerning him, and he thought he should now be able to induce him to effect some miracle in his sight. [9] But to the numerous and artfully-urged inquiries with which he plied him, the captive [well aware of his futile design,] maintained an imperturbable silence; [10] although the hierarchy surrounding him continued to press still more virulently their charges of sedition against him. [11] [Vexed at this unbending taciturnity,] Herod now gave the signal to his body-guard by heaping contemptuous invectives upon him, who immediately carried out the derision by investing him in a white robe, [as if a candidate for princely honors,] and in this mock

a Mark xv, 3.

Herod with his men of war set him at   LUKE **XXIII.**
naught and mocked him, and arrayed
him in a gorgeous robe, and sent him again to Pilate.
¹² And the same day Pilate and Herod were made
friends together; for before they were at enmity between themselves.

§ 132.—*Sentence extorted from Pilate.*

(Jerusalem, Proc'urator's [formerly Herod's] Palace; from about
sunrise to about 9 o'clock, *Friday* morning, *March* 18, A. D. 29.)

¹³ And Pilate, when he had called together the chief-
priests and the rulers and the people, ¹⁴ said unto them,
Ye have brought this man unto me, as one that per-
verteth the people; and behold, I, having examined
him before you, have found no fault in this man, touching those things whereof ye accuse him; ¹⁵ no, nor
yet Herod: for I sent you to him; and lo, nothing
worthy of death is done unto him.   ¹⁶ I will therefore
chastise him and release him.   ¹⁵ Now   **Matt. XXVII.**
at that feast the governor was wont to
release unto the people a prisoner, whom they would.
¹⁷ Therefore, when they were gathered together,
[MARK XV, 8] the multitude crying aloud began to desire him to
do as he had ever done unto them. But Pilate said unto
them, Whom will ye that I release unto you? Barabbas or Jesus, which is called Christ, [MARK XV, 9] the King
of the Jews?   ¹⁸ (For he knew that for envy [MARK XV, 10]
the chief-priests had delivered him.)
¹⁹ When he was set down on the judgment-seat, his
wife sent unto him saying, Have thou nothing to do
with that just man; for I have suffered many things
this day in a dream, because of him.—¹⁶ And they had
then a notable prisoner, called Barabbas, [JOHN XVIII, 40]
a robber, [LUKE XXIII, 19] who, for a certain sedition made in the
city and for murder, was cast into prison, [MARK XV, 7] bound

195

dignity escorted him back to Pilate. [12] [By LUKE **XXIII.**
this sportive deference for each other,] the
animosity which had before existed between
Pilate and Herod, [through jealousy of one another's con-
tiguous power,] was thereafter changed to a mutually-amica-
ble understanding.

§ 132.—*Sentence extorted from Pilate.*

(Jerusalem, Proc'urator's [formerly Herod's] Palace; from about sunrise to about
9 o'clock, *Friday* morning, *March* 18, A. D. 29.)

[13] Jesus being thus remanded to him, Pilate, now gathering
about him [in front of his palace] the prosecuting hierarchy,
with their supporters among the San'hedrim and crowd,
[14] thus expostulated with them: "You have brought this man
before me, charged with inciting the populace to insurrection; but upon investigation in your presence, I have found
no just ground of conviction for the offenses of which you accuse him; [15] and even Herod, to whom I referred you with
the trial, has evidently decided that he is guilty of no capital
crime. [16] I will therefore release him, with a
few lashes merely; [15] as it is *a* your custom **Matt. XXVII.**
to have some prisoner pardoned, at your re-
quest, by the Proc'urator on the holiday of the Passover."
[17] Pilate hoped in this way to elude the issue, *b* as the populace, who were flocking to the scene, *b* now began to clamor
[outside] for the granting of this annual privilege to them;
he therefore asked them, "Which of those now in custody do
you prefer to have me set free for you, Barabbas or Jesus the
c Jewish so-called 'Messiah *c* King?'" [18] Pilate knew that
it was out of pure jealousy that *d* the priesthood had delivered the latter into his hands; [19] and beside, while he was
seated on the tribunal, his wife sent him this warning, "I
entreat you to do no violence to that holy man; for I had a
dream about him last night, that has haunted me ever since."
[16] The other prisoner Barabbas was a notorious ringleader *e* of
a party of rebel *f* highwaymen *g* near the city, *e* who were
then in irons awaiting the penalty of the murders which they

a John xviii, 39.   *b* Mark xv, 8.   *c* Mark xv, 9.   *d* Mark xv, 10.
e Mark xv, 7.   *f* John xviii, 40, (last clause.)   *g* Luke xxiii, 19.

witH them that had made insurrection   MATT. XXVII.
with him.   ²⁰ But the chief-priests and
elders persuaded the multitude that they should ask
Barabbas, and destroy Jesus.   ²¹ The governor answered and said unto them, Whether of the twain will
ye that I release unto you ?   [JOHN XVIII, 40] Then again
they [LUKE XXIII, 18] all at once said, [JOHN XVIII, 40] Not this man;
[LUKE XXIII, 18] away with this man, and release unto us Barabbas.   ²² Pilate [LUKE XXIII, 20] therefore, willing to release
Jesus, saith unto them [LUKE XXIII, 20] again, What shall I
do then with Jesus, which is called Christ, [MARK XV, 12]
whom ye call the King of the Jews?   They all say unto
him [MARK XV, 13] again, Let him be *crucified.*   ²³ And
the governor said [LUKE XXIII, 22] unto them the third time,
Why, what evil hath he done ?   [LUKE XXIII, 22] I have
found no cause of death in him ; I will therefore chastise him,
and let him go.   But they cried out the more [MARK XV, 14]
exceedingly, saying [LUKE XXIII, 23] with loud voices, Let him
be crucified : [LUKE XXIII, 23] and the voices of them and of
the chief-priests prevailed.   ²⁴ When Pilate saw that he
could prevail nothing, but that rather a tumult was
made, he took water and washed his hands before the
multitude, saying, I am innocent of the blood of this
just person ; see *ye* to it.   ²⁵ Then answered all the
people and said, His blood be on us and on our children.
²⁶ Then [MARK XV, 15] Pilate, willing to content the people,
[LUKE XXIII, 24] gave sentence that it should be as they required:
and so released he Barabbas unto them : and when he
had scourged Jesus, he delivered him to be crucified.

²⁷ Then the soldiers of the governor took Jesus
[MARK XV, 16] away into the common hall [MARK XV, 16] called
Pretorium, and gathered unto him the whole band of
soldiers : ²⁸ and they stripped him, and put on him a
scarlet robe ; ²⁹ and when they had platted a crown of
thorns, they put it upon his head, and a reed in his
right hand ; and they bowed the knee before him, and

196

had committed in their insurrection.| ²⁰ The hierarchy therefore eagerly urged the populace to request the release of Barabbas, and

MATT. **XXVII.**

thus secure the death of Jesus. ²¹ [To anticipate the influence of these suggestions,] Pilate now hastened their decision by repeating his question, "Well, which of the two prisoners have you made up your minds to have me liberate for you?" But ^a the whole mob shouted together, "This is not the one we ask,| ^b away with him to execution;| but give us Barabbas free !" ²² Pilate, ^c in his anxiety to release Jesus,| still asked, [to induce them to reconsider,] "What, then, ^d do you wish| me to do with Jesus, whom you style your Messiah ^d and King?|" "Crucify him [as a usurper] !" shouted they all. ²³ "Why so ?" said Pilate, ^e making a third effort;| "what crime has he committed? ^e I can convict him of no capital offense: I will therefore dismiss him with a few stripes."| But they all cried out more vehemently than ever, "No, no; let him be crucified !" ^f and nothing could be heard but the clamor of the rabble instigated to persist in their demand by the members of the San'hedrim among them.|

²⁴ [Seeing that all his endeavors at persuasion were unavailing, and that their vociferations were only growing more riotous,] Pilate now ordered some water to be brought him, with which he washed off his hands in the presence of the assembly, [as a symbol of his protest against all participation in their procedure,] declaring, "I absolve myself from all share in the bloodshed of this innocent man; you are responsible for it." ²⁵ "Yes," shouted all the crowd, "we will bear all blame of his death, and accept the *blood-feud* for our descendants too." ²⁶ Pilate then ^g expressed his assent to their wishes| for the release of Barabbas, and the crucifixion of Jesus. Accordingly, as soon as the lashes, which he ordered to be given the prisoner, had been inflicted, ²⁷ the Proc'urator's body-guard hurrying Jesus away ^h within the *preto'rium*| [i. e. court-martial room], got together nearly their whole *cohort* [i. e. subdivision of Roman troops, numbering in this case about 600 men], for the purpose of making sport of him. ²⁸ Stripping off his outer garment, they dressed him in an officer's military cloak of rich scarlet [to serve as a royal robe], ²⁹ set a crown of hastily-twisted brier-shrubs on his head, and placed a reed-scepter in his hand ; and then kneeling in mock

a John xviii, 40 (first clause). b Luke xxiii, 18. c Luke xxiii, 20. d Mark xv, 12. e Luke xxiii, 22. f Luke xxiii, 23. g Luke xxiii, 24. h Mark xv, 16.

mocked him saying, Hail, King of the　MATT. **XXVII.**
Jews! [30] and they spit upon him, and
took the reed and smote him on the head, [JOHN XIX, 3] and
they smote him with their hands, [MARK XV, 19] and bowing
their knees worshiped him.

[4] Pilate therefore went forth again, and　**John XIX.**
saith unto them, Behold, I bring him forth
to you, that ye may know that I find no fault in him.
[5] Then came Jesus forth, wearing the crown of thorns
and the purple robe. And Pilate saith unto them,
Behold the man! [6] When the chief-priests therefore
and officers saw him, they cried out saying, Crucify
him, crucify him. Pilate saith unto them, Take *ye*
him and crucify him; for I find no fault in him.
[7] The Jews answered him, We have a law, and by
our law he ought to die, because he made himself the
Son of God. [8] When Pilate therefore heard that
saying, he was the more afraid; [9] and went again into
the judgment-hall, and saith unto Jesus, Whence art
thou? But Jesus gave him no answer. [10] Then
saith Pilate unto him, Speakest thou not unto *me?*
knowest thou not that I have power to crucify thee,
and have power to release thee? [11] Jesus answered,
Thou couldst have no power at all against me, except
it were given thee from above : therefore he that delivered me unto thee hath the greater sin. [12] And
from thenceforth Pilate sought to release him : but
the Jews cried out saying, If thou let this man go,
thou art not Cesar's friend; whosoever maketh himself a king, speaketh against Cesar. [13] When Pilate
therefore heard that saying, he brought Jesus forth,
and sat down in the judgment-seat, in a place that is
called the Pavement, but in the Hebrew, *Gabbatha :*
[14] and he saith unto the Jews, Behold your King!
[15] But they cried out, Away with him, away with him,
crucify him. Pilate saith unto them, Shall I crucify
197

homage before him, derided him with the salu-　MATT. XXVII.
tation, "Long live the 'Jewish King!'" [30] They
next spit in his face, and taking the reed struck
him on the head with it, *a* while others gave him blows with their
hands on various parts of his person; [b] and then varied their indignities by returning to their scornful prostrations before him. [l]

[4] The better judgment of Pilate by this time re-　John XIX.
turning, he now went out again [from the scene of
these barbarities, to the court where the hierarchy
continued feasting their eyes with the soldiers' mockery of their
victim], and thus expostulated with them, "Mark now, I am going
to bring the prisoner out again before you, as a distinct attestation
that I adjudge him guilty of no crime.—[5] See," continued he, as
Jesus was led out with the brier-crown and scarlet cloak still on,
"here comes the poor man; [he has suffered enough already!]"
[6] At the sight of him, the priests and their officials shouted the
more furiously, "Crucify him at once!" [Provoked at their inhu-
man obstinacy,] Pilate told them, "Then take him and crucify him
yourselves; I want no hand in the execution of one whom I cannot prove to be guilty." [7] The hierarchy now resorted to another
charge: "We have a statute," argued they, "which decrees the
penalty of death to such blasphemers as this, who has assumed the
title of *Son of God!*" [8] On hearing this name ascribed to him,
Pilate became the more alarmed, [9] and taking Jesus aside into the
preto'rium again, he inquired of him, "What is your parentage?"
But Jesus [knowing that all attempts to explain the subject to
Pilate's satisfaction would be as useless as before,] made him no
reply. [10] Irritated at his silence, Pilate exclaimed, "Will you not
answer *me?* Do you not know that I can crucify or release you at
my pleasure?" [11] "All your power," returned Jesus, "would be
of no avail whatever against me, but for the divine permission;
and on account of this [committal of my case to providential occur-
rences], the person [i. e. Judas] who willfully betrayed me into
your power [and thus constituted himself the first link in this chain
of events], is more guilty [of my death] than even you [who allow
yourself to be borne away by the course of circumstances thus
originated." [12] Struck with this noble bearing,] Pilate once more
tried to effect his release, but the hierarchy persisted in their demand, clamorously insinuating, "If you let this culprit escape, you
are no true friend of the Emperor, whose rights are invaded by
every such aspirant to royalty." [13] Swayed again by this impeach-
ment of his loyalty, Pilate now commanded Jesus to be brought
out into the open court [in front of the palace], and taking his seat
again upon the tribunal that stood on that part of it called the
Pavement [from the tesselated marble blocks with which it was
flagged] (in the vulgar Syro-Chaldee *gabbethaw'*, [i. e. *ridge* or *elevated place*,]), [14] he made this last appeal to the sympathy of the
crowd, "There stands your king!" [15] But they cried out with indignant rage, "Away with him to the cross!" "What!" exclaimed
Pilate, "shall I crucify your *King?*" "We acknowledge no other

a John xix, 3.　　　　　　　　*b* Mark xv, 19.

197*

your *King ?* The chief-priests answered, JOHN XIX.
We have no king but Cesar. ¹⁶ Then delivered he him therefore unto them to be crucified.—
¹⁴ (And it was the preparation of the passover, and
about the sixth hour.)

§ 133.—*The Suicide of Judas.*

(Jerusalem ; *Friday* morning, *March* 18, A. D. 29.)

³ Then Judas which had betrayed Matt. **XXVII.**
him, when he saw that he was con-
demned, repented himself, and brought again the thirty
pieces of silver to the chief-priests and elders ⁴ saying, I have sinned in that I have betrayed the innocent
blood. And they said, What is that to *us ?* see *thou*
to that. ⁵ And he cast down the pieces of silver in
the temple, and departed, and went and hanged himself: [Acts I, 18] and falling headlong, he burst asunder in the
midst, and all his bowels gushed out.

⁶ And the chief-priests took the silver pieces, and
said, It is not lawful* for to put them into the treasury, because it is the price of blood. ⁷ And they took
counsel, and bought with them the potter's field, to
bury strangers in. [Acts I, 19] And it was known unto all
the dwellers at Jerusalem ; ⁸ wherefore that field was
called [Acts I, 19] in their proper tongue, *Aceldama*, that is to
say, The field of blood, unto this day. ⁹ Then was
fulfilled that which was spoken by Jeremy the prophet
saying,† And they took the thirty pieces of silver, the
price of him that was valued, whom they of the children of Israel did value ; ¹⁰ and gave them for the
potter's field, as the Lord appointed me.

---

* Compare Deut. xxiii, 18.　　　　† Zech. xi, 12, 13.

sovereign than the Emperor," adroitly interposed the **JOHN XIX.**
priesthood in reply. ¹⁶ [Abandoning all further par-
ley,] Pilate then yielded to their demand, by a for-'
mal decree for the crucifixion of Jesus.—¹⁴ This sentence was pronounced about the *third hour* [i. e. 9 o'clock, A. M.] of that day in
the paschal week which, as it preceded the Sabbath, was specially
devoted to preparation for the coming solemnities.

§ 133.—*The Suicide of Judas.*

(Jerusalem; *Friday* morning, *March* 18, A. D. 29.)

³ The traitor Judas, on seeing his Master thus **Matt. XXVII.**
finally sentenced, was struck with remorse [at
the fatal consequences of his guilt], and hasten-
ing to the chief members of the San'hedrim, sought to return the
thirty *silverlings* which they had given him, ⁴ with the tardy confession, "I have done wrong in thus betraying an innocent person
to death! [Here, take back your bribe, and set him at liberty.]"
But they rejected his offer with the cool reply, "That is none of
our business; it was your own look-out." ⁵ [Failing to retrieve his
crime,] he franticly flung down the money at their feet in the entrance of the Temple edifice, and then hurrying away [to a secret
spot], hung himself in a fit of despair. *a* [The cord broke with his
weight, and] as he fell half-strangled to the earth, his abdo'men
burst with the force of the shock, and his bowels were shed out
upon the ground; [so that he died in frightful agony.]|
⁶ Meantime, the priesthood present, picking up the pieces of
money, were at a loss what to do with them: "for," said they, "it
would be a profanation to put them into the sacred treasury [de-
posited in the contribution chests standing in the Women's Court
of the Temple], since they are the reward offered to procure the
death of a person [i. e. Jesus]." ⁷ After a hasty consultation with
their colleagues, they concluded to appropriate the money to the
purchase of the old "Pottery Lot" near the city, as a burial-ground
for Jewish foreigners [and unknown persons who might die in their
pilgrimages at the capital]. ⁸ *b* The notoriety of this doubly tragic
origin of the cemetery [i. e. from the execution of Jesus, for which
the purchase-money had been designed as a bounty, and the suicide
of Judas, which left it at the public disposal,]| caused the plot of
ground to be thenceforward *b* currently known in the vulgar dialect
of the residents at Jerusalem by the expressive name of *hakal-
demaw'*, [Syro-Chaldee for]| *field-of-blood.* ⁹ This transaction bore
a singular correspondence with the occurrence related by the
prophet Zechariah, "They then weighed out for my pastoral wages
the sum of thirty *shekels* in silver; a compensation which showed
so paltry an estimation of my public services ¹⁰ that in accordance
with Jehovah's [inward] direction, I disdainfully took and threw
them down in the Temple as pay for the potter [who furnished the
sacred utensils of earthenware used there]."

a Acts i, 18.   *b* Acts i, 19.

§ 134.—*The Crucifixion of Christ, with the connected Incidents.*

(Jerusalem, eminence of Gol'gotha; from 9 A. M. to 3 P. M., *Friday, March* 18, A. D. 29.)

³¹ And after that they had mocked   MATT. XXVII.
him, they took the robe off from him,
and put his own raiment on him, and led him away to
crucify him : [JOHN XIX, 17] and he bearing his cross went forth.
³² And as they came out, they found a man of Cyrene,
Simon by name, [MARK XV, 21] who passed by coming out of
the country, the father of Alexander and Rufus; him they
compelled to bear his cross [LUKE XXIII, 26] after Jesus.
²⁷ And there followed him a great com-   Luke XXIII.
pany of people and of women, which also
bewailed and lamented him.   ²⁸ But Jesus turning
unto them, said, Daughters of Jerusalem, weep not for
me, but weep for yourselves and for your children:
²⁹ for behold, the days are coming in the which they
shall say, Blessed are the women that never bare and
which never gave suck; ³⁰ then shall they begin to
say to the mountains, Fall on us, and to the hills, Cover
us.* ³¹ For if they do these things in a green tree,
what shall be done in the dry ?
²² And they bring him unto the place   **Mark XV.**
[JOHN XIX, 17] called in the Hebrew *Golgotha*,
which is, being interpreted, The place of a skull:
²³ and they gave him to drink wine mingled with
myrrh ; but [MATT. XXVII, 34] when he had tasted thereof, he
received it not.   ²⁵ And it was the third hour, and
they crucified him [LUKE XXIII, 33] there.   ²⁷ And with him
they crucify two thieves, the one on his right hand,
and the other on his left: ²⁸ and the scripture was
fulfilled which saith,† And he was numbered with the

---

* Hosea x, 8; compare Rev. vi, 16.   † Isa. liii, 12.

§ 134.—*The Crucifixion of Christ, with the connected Incidents.*

(Jerusalem, eminence of Gol'gotha; from 9 A. M. to 3 P. M., *Friday, March 18,*
A. D. 29.)

³¹ The soldiers, having now satisfied themselves
with their malignant sport of Jesus, took off the **MATT. XXVII.**
scarlet cloak and put on him his own clothes
again, and so led him off to crucify him, *a* compelling him to carry
the cross on which he was to suffer, on his own shoulder.ᵢ ³² As
they were issuing from one of the city gates, [Jesus fainted under
the burden from the exhaustion of his previous inflictions, and] a
certain Jew from Cyre'nè, named Simon *b* (the father of Alexander
and Rufus [of subsequent Christian note]), just then coming along
on his way from the suburbs, l the soldiers *c* seized him l and pressed
him into their service to carry the cross *c* behind
Jesus l in his stead.—²⁷ The procession was fol- **Luke XXIII.**
lowed by crowds of the populace, especially fe-
males, who exhibited violent grief [by gestures and cries, for one
whom they affectionately regarded as suffering martyrdom]. ²⁸ But
Jesus turning round, thus mournfully checked their lamentations,
"Daughters of Jerusalem, weep not for me, but rather for yourselves and the impending fate of your children. ²⁹ Yes, mark my
warning, the period [of national retribution for your country's impenitent treatment of me] is approaching, when the wives that
shall have been unblessed with offspring, will be esteemed the
most fortunate [by being thus unembarrassed in flight with the
care of their infants, as well as free from the liability of seeing
them perish]. ³⁰ In that awful emergency [of your metropolis,]—

'The denizens will call in wild despair
For mountain piles to fall and shelter them,
A welcome tomb from all their weary woes.'

³¹ Think, 'if the green tree [of innocence] is thus cut off [as by
the inflictions heaped on me], what will be the issue [of retribu-
tion] upon the dry trunk [of impenitence, in the person of the
Jews]?'"
²² On their arrival at the usual spot for public exe- **Mark XV.**
cutions, which bore the appropriate designation, *a* in
the vernacular Syro-Chaldee, l of *gulgothaw'*, [a corruption from the Chaldee, *gulgaltaw'*, a skull,] i. e. *Skull-Place* [from
the number of bones of malefactors strewed about, whose carcasses were left to be devoured by dogs and vultures, ²³ the soldiers offered him [the customary stupefying draught of] *d* diluted
acid l wine with myrrh dissolved in it; but *d* on tasting the potion, l
he refused to drink it. ²⁵ They then fastened him to the cross and
reared it *e* on that spot, l it being now the *third hour* of the day [i. e.
about 9 o'clock, A. M.]; ²⁷ and at the same time with him they also
crucified two other persons, highwaymen, *f* whom they had brought
along for execution, l setting up one cross on the right hand of Jesus,
and the other on the left, *g* with him in the middle. l ²⁸ In this circumstance, the Scriptural prediction was signally illustrated,—

"E'en yields he to be reckoned with the vile,
In infamy by man, in doom by Heaven."

a John xix, 17.   *b* Mark xv, 21.   *c* Luke xxiii, 26.   *d* Matt. xxvii, 34.
e Luke xxiii, 33.   *f* Luke xxiii, 32.   *g* John xix, 18.

transgressors. ³⁴ Then said Jesus, Fa-　　**Luke XXIII.**
ther, forgive them; for they know not
what they do.

¹⁹ And Pilate wrote a title [MARK XV, 26] . **John XIX.**
of his accusation, and put it on the cross
[MATT. XXVII, 37] over his head. And the writing was, JESUS
OF NAZARETH, THE KING OF THE JEWS; ²⁰ and it was
written in Hebrew and Greek and Latin. This title
then read many of the Jews; (for the place where
Jesus was crucified was nigh to the city :) ²¹ then said
the chief-priests of the Jews to Pilate, Write not, The
King of the Jews; but that he *said*, I am King of the
Jews. ²² Pilate answered, What I have written, I
have written.

²³ Then the soldiers, when they had crucified Jesus,
took his garments and made four parts, to every soldier
a part; and also his coat: now the coat was without
seam, woven from the top throughout; ²⁴ they said
therefore among themselves, Let us not rend it, but
cast lots for it whose it shall be : that the scripture
might be fulfilled which saith,* They parted my
raiment among them, and for my vesture they did
cast lots; these things therefore the soldiers did.
³⁶ And sitting down, they watched him　　**Matt. XXVII.**
there.

³⁹ And they that passed by reviled him, wagging
their heads ⁴⁰ and saying, Thou that destroyest the
temple, and buildest it in three days,† save thyself;
if thou be the Son of God, come down from the cross.
[LUKE XXIII, 35] And the people stood beholding: ⁴¹ likewise
also the chief-priests mocking him, with the scribes
and elders, said, ⁴² He saved others; himself he cannot save: if he be [MARK XV, 32] Christ, the King of Israel,
let him now come down from the cross, and we will

---

* Psa. xxii, 18.　　　　　† See § 129, chap. xxvi, 61.

³⁴While the executioners were performing **Luke XXIII.**
their cruel office, Jesus meekly prayed, "Heavenly Father, forgive these men their barbarous
usage toward me ; they little know [in their blind but too willing performance of their orders,] whom they are
putting to death !" ¹⁹ ᵃ Over his head! they placed　**John XIX.**
an inscription bearing the indictment of the crime
for which he suffered, which Pilate had caused to be written
²⁰ in Greek and in Latin and in Syro-Chaldee [the first language
being that of foreigners and the polite generally, the second
that of the Roman residents and official transactions, and the
last that of the populace], ¹⁹ in the following terms : ᵃ "THIS
IS! THE NAZARENE JESUS, THE 'JEWISH KING.' " ²⁰ But as they
were putting it up, several of the hierarchy passing by read it,
as the place of crucifixion was a public one near the city, ²¹ and
[were so dissatisfied with its form, that] they hastened to Pilate
with the request, "Do not allow it to remain written without
qualification, 'the Jewish King ;' but [change it so as to state]
that 'he *claimed* to be King of the Jews.' " ²² " Never mind,"
answered Pilate, "I have written it as it suited me [in my
suspicion of its truth], and so it shall remain."—²³ As soon as
the soldiers had fixed the crosses in their position, they seized
on Jesus's garments, [of which they had entirely stripped
him, as their own booty,] and proceeded to share them among
themselves : the outer dress being a robe [i. e. a simple *sheet*
enveloping the entire person], they tore it into four pieces,
one for each soldier ; but on coming to the *tunic* [i. e. shirt,
the only under-garment worn by the lower classes], which
was seamless, being woven from the top all through, ²⁴ they
said, " It is a pity to tear this ; let us rather draw lots, who
shall have it whole." This partition of the clothes was another striking illustration of prophecy,—

> " My greedy foes divide my rifled robes,
> And gamble for my wardrobe with their lots."

³⁶ [Having thus fulfilled their task as execu- **Matt. XXVII.**
tioners,] the soldiers then sat down close by,
to guard the prisoners. ³⁹ [While Jesus was
thus suspended on the cross,] many of those who passed by
aimed gibes like this at him, with a scornful toss of their head,
⁴⁰ ᵇ "Aha !! you that offered to ' pull down the Temple and rebuild it in three days,' now give us a specimen of your power,
by extricating yourself from your present position. Get down
from the cross, if you are ' the Son of God' as you pretend."
⁴¹ "Yes," echoed the hierarchy ironically ᶜ to one another,!
ᵈ encouraging these scoffs among the crowd,! ⁴² " he used to be
so forward in helping other people, and now he cannot help
himself! If ᵈ this is really the Messianic! King of Israel, let
him just descend now from the cross, and then we shall be

ᵃ Matt. xxvii, 37.　　ᵇ Mark xv, 29.　　ᶜ Mark xv, 31.　　ᵈ Luke xxiii, 35.

believe him. ⁴³ He trusted in God; **MATT. XXVII.**
let him deliver him now if he will
have him: for he said, I am the Son of God.
³⁶ And the soldiers also mocked him, **Luke XXIII.**
coming to him and offering him vinegar,
³⁷ and saying, If thou be the King of the Jews, save
thyself. ³⁹ And one of the malefactors which were
hanged, railed on him saying, If thou be Christ, save
thyself and us. ⁴⁰ But the other answering, rebuked
him saying, Dost not thou fear God, seeing thou art in
the same condemnation? ⁴¹ and *we* indeed justly, for
we receive the due reward of our deeds; but this
man hath done nothing amiss. ⁴² And he said unto
Jesus, Lord, remember me when thou comest into thy
kingdom. ⁴³ And Jesus said unto him, Verily I say
unto thee, *To-day* shalt thou be with me in paradise.

  ²⁵ Now there stood by the cross of Jesus, **John XIX.**
his mother and his mother's sister (Mary
the wife of Cleophas, [MARK XV, 40] the mother of James the
less and of Joses) and Mary Magdalene; [LUKE XXIII, 49] and
all his acquaintance and the women that followed him from
Galilee, [MATT. XXVII, 55] ministering unto him, [56] (among which
was [MARK XV, 40] Salome, [MATT. XXVII, 56] the mother of Zebedee's children, [MARK XV, 41] and many other women which came
up with him unto Jerusalem,) [LUKE XXIII, 49] stood afar off, beholding these things. ²⁶ When Jesus therefore saw his
mother and the disciple standing by whom he loved, he
saith unto his mother, Woman, behold thy *son!*
²⁷ Then saith he to the disciple, Behold thy *mother!*
And from that hour that disciple took her unto his
own home.

  ⁴⁵ Now from the sixth hour there was **Matt. XXVII.**
darkness over all the land unto the ninth
hour, [LUKE XXIII, 45] and the sun was darkened. ⁴⁶ And
about the ninth hour Jesus cried with a loud voice
201

convinced. [43] He made his boast of the divine   MATT. XXVII.
intimacy and aid; let us see if the Almighty
will now show any such partiality for him by
rescuing him from his present predicament!"
[36] The soldiers too caught up the sneer, and   Luke XXIII.
running up to him with the insulting offer of
the drugged wine, [37] they bawled out to him, "Let us see you
rescue yourself, if you are this great 'Jewish King!'"   [39] Even
one of the malefactors hanging on the cross beside him, joined
in the scurrility, upbraidingly demanding of him, "If you are
the Messiah, why do you not deliver yourself and us from this
torture?"   [40] But the convict on the other side rebuked his
fellow-culprit with the considerate remark, "What! are you
too so lost to all sense [of shame and thoughts] of divine
retribution, as to indulge in these insults [in the very face of
death,] against one with whom you are suffering in common?
[41] We, indeed, are undergoing the just penalty of our crimes;
but this person has committed no offense."   [42] Then looking
toward Jesus, he fervently begged, "Master, remember me,
when you return [after your resurrection] to establish your
kingdom [by the resuscitation of saints and the renovation of
Judaism!"   [43] To this diffident appeal,] Jesus blandly replied,
"Yes, I assure you, that [without waiting for any future development of my mediation,] *this very day* you shall share
with me the immortal bliss of *Paradise.*"—
[25] There stood also near the cross of Jesus, his   John XIX.
mother Mary, [a] and at a distance, looking with
heart-stricken interest upon the scene, a number of females
who had attended Jesus from Galilee and ministered to his
temporal wants, among them his mother's sister [-in-law]
Mary (widow of Clopas [i. e. Alphe'us] [b] and mother of [the
Apostle] James II. and Joses), Salo'mè [([c] mother of Zebedee's
sons), [and Mary " of Mag'dala," [d] together with various male
acquaintances of Jesus. [[26] Observing the presence of his
mother and his favorite disciple [John], Jesus said to her
tenderly, "Mother, that person [nodding toward John,] is he
to whom you must henceforth look as your son!"   [27] And to
him he said, "Yonder is she whom I now confide to your
protection as your mother!"   Thereafter this disciple took
her to his own home, [and provided for her with filial attention.]
[45] The sufferer had now hung three hours   Matt. XXVII.
on the cross, when at the *sixth hour* [i. e. at
noon] an extraordinary darkness came over
the whole land [of Judea], which continued till the *ninth
hour* [i. e. 3 o'clock, P. M.], [e] and was so intense as to conceal
the mid-day sun itself. [[46] About this latter hour, Jesus in a
loud tone poured forth his agonized emotions [in the distressed

a Matt. xxvii, 55.   b Mark xv, 40.   c Matt. xxvii, 56.
d Luke xxiii, 49.   e Luke xxiii, 45.

saying, *Eli, Eli, lama sabachthani!* MATT. **XXVII.**
that is to say, My God, my God, why
hast thou forsaken me ?* ⁴⁷ Some of them that stood
there, when they heard that, said, This man calleth
for *Elias.* ⁴⁹ The rest said, Let be, let us see whether
Elias will come to save him. ²⁸ After this John XIX.
Jesus knowing that all things were now
accomplished, that the scripture might be fulfilled,†
saith, I thirst. ²⁹ Now there was set a vessel full of
vinegar : and [MATT. XXVII, 48] straightway one of them ran, and
they filled a sponge with vinegar, and put it upon hys-
sop, and put it to his mouth. ³⁰ When Jesus therefore had received the vinegar, he said, It is finished.
⁴⁶ And he said [MATT. XXVII, 50] again with a Luke XXIII.
loud voice, Father, into thy hands I com-
mend my spirit : and having said thus, he [JOHN XIX, 30]
bowed his head and gave up the ghost.
⁵¹ And behold, the vail of the temple **Matt. XXVII.**
was rent in twain from the top to the
bottom ; and the earth did quake, and the rocks rent;
⁵² and the graves were opened, and many bodies of
the saints which slept, arose, ⁵³ and came out of the
graves after his resurrection, and went into the holy
city and appeared unto many. ⁴⁷ Now Luke XXIII.
when the centurion [MARK XV, 39] which stood
over against him, [MATT. XXVII, 54] and they that were with him
watching Jesus, saw [MATT. XXVII, 54] the earthquake and what
was done, he glorified God saying, Certainly this was
a righteous man : ⁴⁸ and all the people that came together to that sight, beholding the things which were
done, smote their breasts and returned ; [MATT. XXVII, 54]
and they feared greatly, saying, Truly this was the Son of
God.

---

* Psa. xxii, 1.   † See Psa. lxix, 21.

exclamation of the Psalmist], *ᵃElohee' Elohee'*　MATT. XXVII.
lammawh' sebakthanee', [a Syro-Chaldee form
of the Hebrew, *Alee', Alee', lawmawh' azav-
taw'nee; My God, my God, why hast thou left me?*] i. e.—

　　"O why, my God, hast Thou abandoned me!"

⁴⁷ On hearing this, some of the bystanders [Jews] said [with a
taunting play upon his words], "This convict is calling out for
Elijah!"　⁴⁹ "Very well," cried the rest, "let him call; we shall
presently see whether Elijah is forthcoming, [as his forerunner,
from the grave,] to help him ᵇ down from his pres-
ent plight!"|　²⁸ The earthly mission of Jesus was　John XIX.
now almost completed; aware of this, he made a
last request, which called forth another marked illustration of
a Scriptural precedent, exclaiming, "I am thirsty!"　²⁹ ᶜIm-
mediately some one near [a Jew] hastily| dipped a sponge into
a vessel of *posca* [i. e. diluted acid wine, the common drink of
Roman soldiers on service,] which lay near, and sticking it on
the end of ᶜa stalk| of *hyssop* ᶜran| and thrust it to his lips ᶜto
moisten them.|　³⁰ After imbibing a few drops of the liquid,
Jesus for a moment recovered breath to exclaim,
"My work is done!"—⁴⁶ [and as he felt the con-　Luke XXIII.
vulsion returning, he rallied his last strength of
voice for the prayer,] "Father, I confide my soul into Thy care!"
These words were the last he uttered; the collapse ensued, ᵈhis
head sank upon his breast,| and he expired.

⁵¹ [At the moment of this solemn event, a　Matt. XXVII.
general shock was felt throughout nature:] the
inner vail of the Temple [in front of the Most
Holy Place] was torn in two from top to bottom; a terrific
earthquake split the rocks of the adjoining hills, ⁵² opening
fissures in the sepulchres which they contained; and several
corpses of holy persons interred there were not only restored
to life at the time, ⁵³ but issuing from their tombs even after
the resurrection of Jesus, and entering the city itself, were
there seen by their former acquaintances.

⁴⁷ The *centurion* [i. e. Roman captain of 100　Luke XXIII.
men] ᵉand his three assistants,| ƒ who stood|
ᵉon guard| ƒ opposite Jesus,| witnessing ᵉ the earthquake| and
other portents ƒ ensuing on his outcry and decease,| piously
ejaculated, "This must certainly have been an innocent man!"
⁴⁸ The very populace, too, that stood gazing on the scene,
ᵉ struck with deep awe at these preternatural phenomena,| re-
turned to the city, striking their breasts with sad remorse,
ᵉ and acknowledging, "This was indeed the [Messianic] 'Son
of God!'"|

---

a Mark xv, 34.　　　*b* Mark xv, 36.　　　*c* Matt. xxvii, 48.
d John xix, 30.　　　*e* Matt. xxvii, 54.　　　*f* Mark xv, 39.

§ 135.—*The Burial of Christ.*

(W. Suburbs of Jerusalem; a little before sunset of *Friday, March*
18, A. D. 29.)

³¹ The Jews therefore, because it was   **John XIX.**
the *preparation*, that the bodies should not
remain upon the cross on the sabbath-day, (for that
sabbath-day was a high-day,) besought Pilate that
their legs might be broken, and that they might be
taken away.   ³² Then came the soldiers, and brake the
legs of the first and of the other which was crucified
with him ; ³³ but when they came to Jesus, and saw
that he was dead already, they brake not his legs :
³⁴ but one of the soldiers with a spear pierced his
side, and forthwith came there out blood and water.
³⁵ (And he that saw it, bare record, and his record is
true : and he knoweth that he saith true, that ye might
believe.)   ³⁶ For these things were done, that the
scripture should be fulfilled,* A bone of him shall not
be broken ; ³⁷ and again another scripture saith,† They
shall look on him whom they pierced.

⁴² And now when the even was come,   **Mark XV.**
(because it was the *preparation*, that is, the
day before the sabbath,) ⁴³ Joseph, [Matt. XXVII, 57] a rich
man of Arimathea, [Luke XXIII, 51] a city of the Jews, an
honorable counselor, [Luke XXIII, 50] a good man and a just,
[51] (the same had not consented to the counsel and deed of
them, [John XIX, 38] being a disciple of Jesus, but secretly for
fear of the Jews,) which also waited for the kingdom
of God, came and went in boldly unto Pilate, and
craved [John XIX, 38] of Pilate that he might take away the
body of Jesus.   ⁴⁴ And Pilate marveled if he were
already dead ; and calling unto him the centurion,
he asked him whether he had been any while dead ;

* Exod. xii, 46; Num. ix, 12; compare 1 Cor. v, 7.
† Zech. xii, 10.

§ 135.—*The Burial of Christ.*

(W. Suburbs of Jerusalem; a little before sunset of *Friday, March* 18, A. D. 29.)

³¹ The hierarchy now began to be anxious lest the **John XIX.** bodies of the executed prisoners should be left hanging on the cross during the sabbath, which was drawing near [at sunset]; and [would disfigure by such a shocking spectacle the solemnity of that day,] which in this case was one of special sanctity, [as occurring during the Passover week:] they therefore went to Pilate with the request, that the criminals' legs might be broken [to hasten their death], and their corpses then removed. ³² Accordingly, the Proc'urator sent some soldiers, who proceeded to break the legs of the convicts on each side of Jesus [by striking them against the cross with a heavy mallet, just above the ancle; which soon put an end to their sufferings]. ³³ But on coming to Jesus, they perceived that he was already dead, and therefore abstained from breaking his limbs; ³⁴ but one of them [to make the matter sure], ran the point of his spear into the side of the corpse, and [on withdrawing it,] a jet of water mingled with clotted blood gushed from the incision. ³⁵ These facts were personally witnessed by the narrator [i. e. myself, John], whose statement is therefore unquestionably entitled to the full confidence of his readers; [so that there can be no doubt as to Christ's actual dissolution.] ³⁶ The omission to fracture the legs of Jesus, was a signal fulfillment of [the typical institution of the paschal lamb, in] the minute requirement, "Not a bone of it must be broken;" ³⁷ and the transfixion of his side was doubtless intimated in another prophetical declaration,—

"Then will they turn their eyes [in penitence]
   Toward [Me] whom they have pierced [with cruel scorn,
By their ungrateful murder of my Son]."

⁴² *a* Shortly afterward,| the evening drawing near, **Mark XV.** *b* which was to introduce the sabbath,| ⁴³ a certain *c* wealthy| and reputable member of the San'hedrim, by the name of Joseph, a [former] resident of *d* the Jewish| Ramah, ventured [at the risk of his colleagues' sneers,] to go to Pilate, with the request that he might be allowed *a* to remove| the body of Jesus for interment. (This individual *e* was a kind and pious man,| who, *d* so far from assenting to the vote and procedure of the rest of the San'hedrim respecting Jesus, was really an adherent of him|—being himself an earnest expectant of the ' Messiah's Reign' soon to be ushered in; *a* but he had never avowed his espousal of Jesus's claims, through dread of his associates' ridicule and persecution.|) ⁴⁴ Pilate was surprised to learn that Jesus had expired in so short a time, and called the *centurion* [who had superintended the execution], to inquire whether the prisoner had been dead long

a John xix, 38.   *b* Luke xxiii, 54.   *c* Matt. xxvii, 57.
      d Luke xxiii, 51.   *e* Luke xxiii, 50.

³⁸ and [MARK XV, 45] when he knew it of the cen-   **John XIX.**
turion, Pilate gave him leave. He came
therefore and [MARK XV, 46] bought fine linen, and took the
body of Jesus; ³⁹ and there came also Nicodemus
(which at the first came to Jesus by night)* and
brought a mixture of myrrh and aloes, about a hundred
pounds' weight: ⁴⁰ then took they the body of Jesus,
and wound it in linen clothes with the spices, as the
manner of the Jews is to bury. ⁴¹ Now in the place
where he was crucified, there was a garden; and in
the garden a new sepulchre, wherein was never man
yet laid: ⁴² there laid they Jesus therefore [MATT. XXVII, 60]
in his own new tomb, which he had hewn out in the rock;
and he rolled a great stone to the door of the sepulchre, and
departed, because of the Jews' preparation-day; for the
sepulchre was nigh at hand. ⁵⁵ And the   **Luke XXIII.**
women also, which came with him from
Galilee, [MARK XV, 47] Mary Magdalene and Mary the mother
of Joses, followed after, and [MATT. XXVII, 61] sitting over
against the sepulchre, beheld the sepulchre and how his
body was laid. ⁵⁶ And they returned, and prepared
spices and ointments; and rested the sabbath-day, according to the commandment.†

§ 136.—*The Sepulchre Guarded.*

(Jerusalem, vicinity of Gol'gotha; *Saturday, March 19,* A. D. 29.)

⁶² Now the next day that followed the   **Matt. XXVII.**
day of the preparation, the chief-priests
and Pharisees came together unto Pilate, ⁶³ saying, Sir,
we remember that that deceiver said,‡ while he was
yet alive, After three days I will rise again. ⁶⁴ Command therefore that the sepulchre be made sure until
the third day; lest his disciples come by night and

---

* See § 26.   † Exod. xx, 10.   ‡ See Matt. xii, 40; John ii, 19.

[enough to make it certain]; [45] ascertaining   MARK XV.
from him that such was the fact, he granted the
body to Joseph. [46] [a] As he was going to the scene
of the crucifixion| with a winding sheet which he
had purchased on the way, [39] he was joined by   John XIX.
Nicodemus (the same that paid the early visit to
Jesus by night), who was carrying a mixture of myrrh and
aloe-wood weighing perhaps a hundred *libræ* [i. e. about 72
lbs.], for the purpose of embalming the corpse. [38,][40] These
two therefore took the body of Jesus [b] down from the cross,|
and wrapped it in the [c] clean| sheet along with the aromatics,
in the usual Jewish method of preparation for burial. [41] In
the immediate vicinity of the place of crucifixion there was a
garden containing a new vault [d] hewn out of the face of a
rock, the property of Joseph himself,| in which no one had
yet been buried: [42] here therefore they laid the body, as the
sabbath was so nearly begun [that they had no time to make
arrangements for conveying it farther] ; [d] they then rolled a
large stone against the door of the sepulchre,
and left it thus secured.| [55] Two of the Gali-   Luke XXIII.
lean women, [e] Mary "of Mag'dala" and Mary
Joses's mother,| followed the body to the tomb, and [f] taking
their seat opposite it,| watched the process of burial, and
marked the spot: [56] they then returned in haste to the city,
to prepare additional spices and myrrh for embalming; but
the sabbath supervening [at sundown], they suspended their
operations, and religiously observed the day.

§ 136.—*The Sepulchre Guarded.*

(Jerusalem, vicinity of Gol'gotha; *Saturday, March* 19, A. D. 29.)

[62] Early on the following morning, a depu-   Matt. XXVII.
tation of the Pharisaical hierarchy waited on
Pilate [63] with this request, "Dear Sir, it has occurred to our
recollection, that that impostor [Jesus], while yet living, used
to predict, 'I will revive within three days after my death.'
[64] Will you therefore do us the favor to give orders, that the
tomb containing his body be rendered secure from all ingress,
till the expiration of the third day? for unless this precaution be taken, his disciples will be likely to come and clandes-
tinely take away the corpse, and then give out among the

a John xix, 38.   *b* Mark xv, 46.   *c* Matt. xxvii, 59.
d Matt. xxvii, 60.   *e* Mark xv, 47.   *f* Matt. xxvii, 61.

steal him away, and say unto the peo-   MATT. **XXVII.**
ple, He is risen from the dead : so the
last error shall be worse than the first.   [65] Pilate said
unto them, Ye have a watch ; go your way, make it
as sure as ye can.   [66] So they went and made the
sepulchre sure, sealing the stone and setting a watch.

§ 137.—*Further Preparation for Embalming the
Body.*

(Jerusalem ; evening of *Saturday, March* 19, A. D. 29.)

[1] And when the sabbath was past, Mary   **Mark XVI.**
Magdalene and Mary the mother of James,
and Salome, had bought sweet spices, that they might
come and anoint him.

CHAPTER VII.

CHRIST'S SUBSEQUENT STAY ON EARTH.

- (Time, *forty days.*)

§ 138.—*The Release from the Tomb.*

(Jerusalem, vault near Gol'gotha ; day-break of *Sunday, March* 20,
A. D. 29.)

[2] And behold, [MARK XVI, 9] when Jesus   **Matt. XXVIII.**
was risen early, the first day of the week,
there was a great earthquake : for the angel of the
Lord descended from heaven, and came and rolled
back the stone from the door, and sat upon it ; [3] his
countenance was like lightning, and his raiment white
as snow : [4] and for fear of him the keepers did shake,
and became as dead men.

205

people, that he has risen from death: that **MATT. XXVII.**
would make the deception more incurable
and dangerous than ever." [65] " Well," re-
turned Pilate, " the guard that I assigned you for his execution, is still at your disposal; take them with you, and make
whatever safeguards you think fit." [66] They then went and
secured the sepulchre by posting sentinels before it, at the
same time [preventing all clandestine movement of the stone
that blocked the entrance, by] sealing together the extremi-
ties of a cord connecting it with the door.

§ 137.—*Further Preparation for Embalming the Body.*

(Jerusalem; evening of *Saturday, March* 19, A. D. 29.)

[1] As soon as the sabbath closed [i. e. after sun- **Mark XVI.**
set], Mary " of Mag'dala," together with Mary,
James's mother, and Salo'mè, went out and purchased additional perfumery with which to anoint the body
of Jesus [next day].

CHAPTER VII.

CHRIST'S SUBSEQUENT STAY ON EARTH.

(Time, *forty days.*)

§ 138.—*The Release from the Tomb.*

(Jerusalem, vault near Gol'gotha; day-break of *Sunday, March* 20, A. D. 29.)

[2] [a] The morning of the first day of the week **Matt. XXVIII.**
had scarcely dawned, when suddenly the
ground about the sepulchre was agitated by
a violent earthquake, in the midst of which an angelic form
swiftly gliding down from the sky to the spot, with a touch
rolled aside the massive stone that barred the door of the
tomb, and then took his seat upon it. [a] At this instant, [the
corpse within shook off the sleep of death, and] Jesus issued
forth alive. [4] The sentinels on guard were petrified with
terror at the sight of the angel, as he sat there, [3] his whole
figure flashing with an unearthly glare like lightning, through
his dress that shone like dazzling snow; [4] and they fell senseless to the earth as if struck with death.

a Mark xvi, 9.

205*

§ 139.—*The Women, Visiting the Sepulchre, are Met on their Return by Christ.*

(Jerusalem, vicinity of Gol'gotha ; early dawn of *Sunday, March 20,* A. D. 29.)

² And very early in the morning, **Mark XVI.**
[MATT. XXVIII, 1] in the end of the sabbath, as it
began to dawn toward the first day of the week, [JOHN XX, 1]
when it was yet dark, [MATT. XXVIII, 1] Mary Magdalene and the
other Mary, [LUKE XXIV, 1] and certain others with them, came
unto the sepulchre at the rising of the sun, [MATT. XXVIII, 1]
to see the sepulchre, [LUKE XXIV, 1] bringing the spices which
they had prepared. ³ And they said among themselves,
Who shall roll us away the stone from the door of the
sepulchre ? ⁴ (and when they looked, they saw that
the stone was rolled away ;) for it was very great.
² Then Mary Magdalene runneth, and com-　**John XX.**
eth to Simon Peter and to the other disciple whom Jesus loved.

³ And the other women entered in, and　**Luke XXIV.**
found not the body of the Lord Jesus.
⁴ And it came to pass, as they were much perplexed
thereabout, behold, two men stood by them in [MARK XVI, 5]
long shining garments. ⁵ And as they were afraid,
and bowed down their faces to the earth, they said
unto them, [MATT. XXVIII, 5] Fear not ye : for I know that ye
seek Jesus, which was crucified. Why seek ye the living
among the dead ? ⁶ he is not here, but is risen,
[MATT. XXVIII, 6] as he said.❊ Come, see the place where the
Lord lay. Remember how he spake unto you when he
was yet in Galilee, ⁷ saying,* The Son of man must be
delivered into the hands of sinful men, and be crucified,
and the third day rise again. ⁸ And they remembered

❊ See § 72.

§ 139.—*The Women, Visiting the Sepulchre, are Met on their Return by Christ.*

(Jerusalem, vicinity of Gol'gotha; early dawn of *Sunday, March* 20, A. D. 29.)

² The *a* gray| light of the *b* dawn succeeding the **Mark XVI.** close of the sabbath| *c* was still struggling with the darkness of the night,| when guided by the faint rays shooting up from the yet unrisen sun of the first day of the week, the party of Galilean females [i. e. Mary "of Mag'dala," Mary widow of Clopas, Salo'mè, Joanna and others] set out for the sepulchre, *b* to see if all was safe there,| *a* and carrying with them the embalming materials which they had prepared over night.| ³ [As they approached the tomb, they bethought themselves of a difficulty,] " Whom shall we get," said they to one another, " to roll away for us the heavy stone that lies against the door of the vault?" ⁴ but on reaching the spot, they found [to their astonishment] that, huge as it was, it had been removed. ² [A **John XX.** horrible suspicion flashed across their minds, and in a transport of indignant grief,] Mary "of Mag'dala" instantly flew back to the city, to communicate her fears to Peter and Jesus's favorite disciple [John].

³ The rest of the women, [in order to satisfy **Luke XXIV.** themselves, entered the sepulchre, and] on penetrating to the inner chamber, found indeed to their dismay that the corpse was missing. ⁴ [Returning to the front apartment,] as they stood deliberating on the unaccountable disappearance, suddenly there appeared to them two *d* youthful figures seated at the right,| attired in *d* robes of | dazzling white. ⁵ Terrified at the startling vision, the females prostrated themselves in reverential awe to the ground; but the angels bade them, *e* " Be not alarmed. We are aware that the lately crucified| *f* Nazarene Jesus is the object of your search ;| but why are you looking in a tomb for one who is alive? ⁶ He is not here; *f* convince yourselves by inspecting yonder spot where he lay in burial.| No, he has revived; for you recollect what he told you while he was in Galilee, ⁷ ' The " Son of Man " is to be betrayed into the power of wicked men, and crucified; but on the third day he will revive.' " ⁸ Then as their auditors' memories recalled these

a Luke xxlv, 1.   *b* Matt. xxviii, 1.   *c* John xx, 1.
d Mark xvi, 5.   *e* Matt. xxviii, 5.   *f* Mark xvi, 6.

his words.   ⁷ And the angels said, Go   **Matt. XXVIII.**
[Mᴀʀᴋ XVI, ⁷] your way quickly and tell his
disciples [Mᴀʀᴋ XVI, ⁷] and Peter, that he is risen from the
dead, and behold, he goeth before you into Galilee ;
there shall ye see him, [Mᴀʀᴋ XVI, ⁷] as he said unto you :°
lo, I have told you.

⁸ And they departed quickly, [Mᴀʀᴋ XVI, 8] and fled from
the sepulchre with fear and great joy ; [Mᴀʀᴋ XVI, 8] (for
they trembled and were amazed : neither said they anything
to any man ; for they were afraid;) and did run to bring
his disciples word.   ⁹ And as they went to tell his
disciples, behold, Jesus met them, saying, All hail.
And they came, and held him by the feet, and worshiped him.   ¹⁰ Then said Jesus unto them, Be not
afraid : go tell my brethren, that they go into Galilee,
and there shall they see me.   ⁹ And they   **Luke XXIV.**
returned from the sepulchre, and told all
these things unto the eleven and to all the rest ; ¹⁰ (it
was Joanna and Mary the mother of James, and other
women that were with them, which told these things
unto the apostles :) ¹¹ and their words seemed to them
as idle tales, and they believed them not.

§ 140.—*The Report of the Watch.*

(Jerusalem ; gray of the morning, *Sunday, March* 20, A. D. 29).

¹¹ Now when they were going, be-   **Matt. XXVIII.**
hold, some of the watch came into the
city, and showed unto the chief-priests all the things
that were done.   ¹² And when they were assembled
with the elders, and had taken counsel, they gave large
money unto the soldiers, ¹³ saying, Say ye, His disciples came by night, and stole him away while we
slept : ¹⁴ and if this come to the governor's ears, we

° See Matt. xxvi, 32.

predictions of their Master, [7] the celestial messengers continued, " Now hasten and announce to his disciples [a] and to Peter especially,| that he has risen from death, and that he is going in advance of you into Galilee, [a] as he promised you ;| you will there have an interview with him: mark, we have given you explicit directions."

Matt. XXVIII.

[8] No sooner had the women received this information, than they hastened away from the sepulchre, to report it to the disciples, [b] not stopping to speak with any one on the way ;| so great was their [b] transport| of joy at the news, as well as [b] thrill| of fear [at its supernatural mode of communication]. [9] They had not proceeded far, when suddenly Jesus himself met them with the cheerful salutation, " Good morning !" At the sound of his familiar voice, they rushed forward, and [bending in adoration before him,] clasped his feet with mingled awe and delight.   [10] Jesus calmed their agitation by saying to them, " You need fear no alarm [as if an ominous specter were before you].   Go tell my beloved disciples to meet me in Galilee."—[9],[10] Continuing

Luke XXIV.

their return, the females reported the wonderful occurrences they had witnessed to the eleven Apostles and to all the other disciples whom they met ; [11] but their account seemed to them like the telling of a dream, so incredulous were they as to its possibility.

§ 140.—*The Report of the Watch.*

(Jerusalem ; gray of the morning, *Sunday, March* 20, A. D. 29.)

[11] Simultaneously with the return of the women, there might be seen entering the city some stragglers of the guard that had

Matt. XXVIII.

been stationed at the sepulchre, who came to report to the hierarchy the occurrences that had befallen them.   [12] [Seeing that their only way to prevent the public conviction that Jesus had really revived, was to hush up the matter,] the latter called a hasty meeting of the San'hedrim, in which they resolved to offer the soldiers a sum of money, [13] if they would give out [as an explanation of the affair,] that " while the sentinels were asleep, some of Jesus's disciples had come and stolen off the corpse ;" [14] and they promised the men, " Should this [report of your remissness] reach the Proc'urator's ear, we will see that you do not suffer by it, by pacifying

a Mark xvi, 7.   b Mark xvi, 8.

will persuade him, and secure you. MATT. XXVIII.
15 So they took the money, and did as
they were taught : and this saying is commonly reported among the Jews until this day.

§ 141.—*Peter and John Visit the Sepulchre.*

(Jerusalem, vicinity of Gol'gotha; twilight of *Sunday* morning,
March 20, A. D. 29.)

2 And Mary Magdalene saith unto Peter   **John XX.**
and John, They have taken away the Lord
out of the sepulchre, and we know not where they
have laid him. 3 Peter therefore went forth and that
other disciple, and came to the sepulchre : 4 so they
ran both together; and the other disciple did outrun
Peter, and came first to the sepulchre. 5 And he
stooping down and looking in, saw the linen clothes
lying ; yet went he not in. 6 Then cometh Simon
Peter following him, and went into the sepulchre ; and
[LUKE XXIV, 12] stooping down, he seeth the linen clothes lie,
7 and the napkin that was about his head, not lying
with the linen clothes, but wrapped together in a place
by itself. 8 Then went in also that other disciple
which came first to the sepulchre, and he saw and believed : 9(for as yet they knew not the scripture,* that
he must rise again from the dead.) 10 Then the disciples went away again unto their own home, [LUKE XXIV, 12]
wondering at that which was come to pass.

§ 142.—*Mary Magdalene, Returning to the Sepul-chre, Meets Christ there.*

(Jerusalem, vicinity of Gol'gotha ; broad daylight of *Sunday* morning, *March* 20, A. D. 29.)

11 But Mary stood without at the sepulchre, weeping : and as she wept, she stooped down and looked

---

○ Psa. xvi, 8–11.

him in some way." [15] The guard pocketed
the bribe, [glad to escape by] doing as they
were directed; and in this way originated
the fabrication which has passed current at Jerusalem ever
since, [to account for the undeniable disappearance of the
body from the tomb.]

MATT. XXVIII.

§ 141.—*Peter and John Visit the Sepulchre.*

(Jerusalem, vicinity of Gol'gotha; twilight of *Sunday* morning, *March* 20, A. D. 29.)

[2] Meanwhile Mary "of Mag'dala" [had reached
the house where Peter and John were lodging,
and] aroused them with her report, that "some
one had carried off their Master's body, and she could not
tell where it was!" [3] [Alarmed at this intelligence,] they
both started on a full run for the sepulchre; [4] but the other
disciple [John, being somewhat younger,] outran Peter, and
reached the spot in advance of him. [5] Stooping down at the
door and looking in, he saw the grave clothes lying [in the
inner chamber], but did not venture within.

John XX.

[6] Peter presently arrived, and going directly in [to the
front chamber], *a* as he stooped [at the entrance of the fur-
ther vault,| and looked in], he saw the shroud lying by itself
[where it had fallen from the corpse], [7] and the napkin which
had been bound over the head, wrapped up carefully in another place. [8] His companion then also entered, and seeing
[the orderly arrangement of the grave-clothes], was convinced [that his Master must have quietly withdrawn, instead
of being surreptitiously removed: [9] but the full truth as predicted (i. e. his having departed, by resurrection to life) did
not yet flash upon either of them], for they did not as yet
apprehend the import of the Scriptural intimations respecting his resuscitation.—[10] The two disciples then returned
home, *a* wondering at these strange occurrences.|

§ 142.—*Mary Magdalene, Returning to the Sepulchre, Meets Christ there.*

(Jerusalem, vicinity of Gol'gotha; broad daylight of *Sunday* morning, *March* 20,
A. D. 29.)

[11] By this time Mary [had arrived at the spot, and] stood
outside the sepulchre, weeping [at the body's seemingly hopeless removal]. Presently, stooping down and looking through

a Luke xxiv, 12.

into the sepulchre, [12] and seeth two angels   JOHN **XX.**
in white, sitting the one at the head and the
other at the feet, where the body of Jesus had lain.
[13] And they say unto her, Woman, why weepest thou?
She saith unto them, Because they have taken away
my Lord, and I know not where they have laid him.
[14] And when she had thus said, she turned herself
back, and saw Jesus standing, and knew not that it
was Jesus. [15] Jesus saith unto her, Woman, why
weepest thou? whom seekest thou? She, supposing
him to be the gardener, saith unto him, Sir, if thou
have borne him hence, tell me where thou hast laid
him, and I will take him away. [16] Jesus saith unto
her, *Mary!* She turned herself, and saith unto him,
Rabboni, (which is to say, Master.) [17] Jesus saith
unto her, Touch me not: for I am not yet ascended to
my Father: but go to my brethren and say unto them,
I ascend unto my Father and your Father, and to my
God and your God. [18] Mary Magdalene came and told
the disciples [MARK XVI, 10] that had been with him, as they
mourned and wept, that she had seen the Lord, and that
he had spoken these things unto her:
[11] and they, when they had heard that he   **Mark XVI.**
was alive and had been seen of her, be-
lieved not.

§ 143.—*Christ is Seen by Two Disciples on their Way
to Em'maüs, and by Peter.*

(Jerusalem and Em'maüs; afternoon of *Sunday, March 20,* A. D. 29.)

[13] And behold, two of them went that   **Luke XXIV.**
same day to a village called Emmaus,
which was from Jerusalem about threescore furlongs:
[14] and they talked together of all these things which
had happened. [15] And it came to pass, that, while they
communed together and reasoned, Jesus himself drew

her tears into the vault, [12] she perceived there two **JOHN XX.**
angelic forms in habiliments of brilliant white,
seated the one at the head and the other at the
foot of the spot which had been occupied by the corpse. [13] They
soothingly addressed her with the question, "Madam, what is
the cause of your tears?" "O!" sobbed she, "it is because
some one has carried away my Master's body, and I know not
what has become of it!" [14] With these words, [hearing a slight
rustling as of footsteps behind her,] she turned her head and
saw some one standing behind her, but did not at the moment
recognize him as being Jesus himself. [15] Jesus repeated the
same bland inquiry, "Madam, why are you weeping? whom are
you looking for?" She, still imagining that he must be the
keeper of the cemetery, replied [with a downcast look of sad-
ness], "O Sir! if he has been removed with your knowledge, I
beg you tell me where he has been placed; and I will cause him
to be removed to a decent interment." [16] Jesus then emphatically pronounced her name, "Mary!" [Thrilled with the familiar tones of his voice now recognized,] she turned full about toward him with the joyful cry, *Rabbonee'*, [(Syro-Chaldee for) *my
most honored Teacher*,] i. e. "Dearest Master!" [as she cast herself before him in a transport of devotion, and clasped his feet in
wild anticipation of his future triumph.] [17] Jesus checked [the
exuberant manifestation of her exultation, by bidding] her,
"Nay, do not now embrace me thus, [as if my 'Reign' were immediately to be ushered in;] for I have not yet ascended to my
Father, [in order to procure for you those privileges which I have
promised you, and therefore this is not my return of which I
spoke.] But go and tell my dear disciples that I am soon about
to ascend to our common Father and God."

[18] Receiving this charge, Mary went and told the disciples [as
she met them,] what she had seen and heard. [a] She found them
generally mourning and weeping for their double loss [in the
death of Jesus and the abstraction of his body],|
[11] but her announcement that he was alive and **Mark XVI.**
had even been seen by her, met with very little
credit among them.

§ 143.—*Christ is Seen by Two Disciples on their Way to Em'-
maüs, and by Peter.*

(Jerusalem and Em'maüs; afternoon of *Sunday, March* 20, A. D. 29.)

[13] In the afternoon of the same day, as two of **Luke XXIV.**
the disciples were walking to a village called
Em'maüs, distant some sixty *sta'dia* [i. e. about 6 miles] from
Jerusalem, [14] conversing with each other about the strange
events of the morning, [15] and discussing them with various
conjectures, suddenly Jesus himself approached and joined

a Mark xvi, 10.

near and went with them : ¹⁶ but their   LUKE **XXIV**.
eyes were holden, that they should not
know him ; [MARK XVI, 12] for he appeared in another form.
¹⁷ And he said unto them, What manner of communications are these that ye have one to another, as ye
walk, and are sad ?   ¹⁸ And the one of them, whose
name was Cleophas, answering said unto him, Art thou
only a stranger in Jerusalem, and hast not known the
things which are come to pass there in these days ?
¹⁹ And he said unto them, What things ? And they
said unto him, Concerning Jesus of Nazareth, which
was a prophet mighty in deed and word before God
and all the people : ²⁰ and how the chief-priests and
our rulers delivered him to be condemned to death, and
have crucified him.   ²¹ But we trusted that it had
been he which should have redeemed Israel : and, besides all this, to-day is the third day since these things
were done.   ²² Yea, and certain women also of our
company made us astonished, which were early at the
sepulchre ; ²³ and when they found not his body, they
came saying that they had also seen a vision of angels,
which said that he was alive : ²⁴ and certain of them
which were with us, went to the sepulchre, and found
it even so as the woman had said ; but him they saw
not.   ²⁵ Then he said unto them, O fools and slow of
heart to believe all that the prophets have spoken !
²⁶ Ought not Christ to have suffered these things, and
to enter into his glory ? ²⁷ And beginning at Moses
and all the prophets, he expounded unto them in all
the scriptures the things concerning himself.

²⁸ And they drew nigh unto the village whither they
went: and he made as though he would have gone
farther ; ²⁹ but they constrained him saying, Abide
with us ; for it is toward evening, and the day is far
spent.   And he went in to tarry with them.

³⁰ And it came to pass, as he sat at meat with them,

210

company with them; [16] [a] but his dress and ap-   LUKE **XXIV.**
pearance were so altered from what they had
last seen him wear,| that with a providential
obtuseness of vision they did not recognize him.   [17] "What is
this mournful topic of conversation," inquired he, "that interests you so much, as you walk along in such sorrowful
mood?"   [18] One of them, whose name was Cle'opas, replied,
"I presume you are the only one even of the temporary residents at Jerusalem, that is ignorant of what has transpired
there within a few days."   [19] "What events do you refer to?"
asked he.   "Why," said they, "we mean the tragical fate of
Jesus the Nazarene, an unquestioned prophet of distinguished
eloquence and miraculous power, who possessed the divine
sanction and great popular influence;   [20] and how our priesthood and civil authorities condemned and executed him by
crucifixion.   [21] Alas! we had hoped that he was the expected
Deliverer of the Jewish people; but [in extinction of our last
glimmering prospect,] it is now moreover the third day since
this event took place, [and no sign appears of a reversal of
its effects.   [22] It is true—but this only increases our perplexity,
that] a number of our female associates, who visited the sepulchre early this morning [23] without finding the body there, returned with a startling report of a vision of angels who informed them that he was alive; [24] and some of our own
number thereupon went to the sepulchre, and found things
just as the women had stated, but could not discover Jesus
himself."   [25] "Ah!" rejoined Jesus, "how stupid and tardy
you are in coming to a hearty conviction of the full import
of prophecy!   [26] Cannot you yet apprehend the necessity for
this the Messiah's passion, in order to accomplish the glorious
results of his mission?"   [27] Then running hastily over the
main points of prophecy and types, from the writings of
Moses down through the Prophets, he explained their allusion to himself.

[28] They had now entered the village which was their place
of destination, but Jesus was going on as if he had not arrived
at the end of his journey.   [29] They, however, [felt so much
interested in his conversation that they] urged him to "stay
over night with them, as it was now toward evening;" an invitation which he accepted, and entered the house with them.
[30] On their reclining together at supper, he took up the bread

[a] Mark xvi, 12.

he took bread and blessed it, and brake   LUKE **XXIV.**
and gave to them. ^{31} And their eyes
were opened, and they knew him : and he vanished
out of their sight. ^{32} And they said one to another,
Did not our heart burn within us while he talked with
us by the way, and while he opened to us the scriptures ?

^{33} And they rose up the same hour, and returned to
Jerusalem, and found the eleven gathered together and
them that were w$_i$t$_h$ them, ^{34} saying, The Lord is
risen indeed, and hath appeared to Simon. ^{35} And
they told [MARK XVI, 13] unto the residue what things were
done in the way, and how he was known of them in
breaking of bread : [MARK XVI, 13] neither believed they
them.

§ 144.—*Christ Appears among* (*Ten of*) *the Apostles.*

(Jerusalem ; evening of *Sunday, March* 20, A. D. 29.)

^{36} And as they thus spake, [JOHN XX, 19] the same day at
evening, being the first day of the week, when the doors were
shut where the disciples were assembled for fear of the Jews,
came Jesus himself [JOHN XX, 19] and stood in the midst of
[MARK XVI, 14] the eleven, as they sat at meat, and saith unto
them, Peace be unto you. ^{37} But they were terrified
and affrighted, and supposed that they had seen a spirit.
^{38} And he said unto them, Why are ye troubled ? and
why do thoughts arise in your hearts ?   [MARK XVI, 14] And
he upbraided them with their unbelief and hardness of heart,
because they believed not them which had seen him after he
was risen, saying, ^{39} Behold my hands and my feet, that
it is I myself : handle me, and see ; for a *spirit* hath
not flesh and bones, as ye see me have. ^{40} And when
he had thus spoken, he showed them his hands and
his feet [JOHN XX, 20] and his side.   Then were the disciples
glad when they saw the Lord. ^{41} And while they yet

211

after pronouncing the " blessing," and break-   Luke **XXIV.**
ing it, distributed it among them.   ³¹ This
familiar act instantly dissipated the illusion
which had obscured their eyesight as by a preternatural spell,
and they now recognized him; but [before they had recovered
from their astonishment,] he was gone [having suddenly risen
and abruptly quitted the house].   ³² " We might have known
it was he;" exclaimed they to one another: " for did not our
hearts glow [with the wonted inspiration of his instructions],
as he expatiated to us on the way hither in that delightful
exposition of Scripture?"
³³ They immediately resolved to return without delay to
Jerusalem, with the news; and on arriving there, found the
Apostles and others collected, ³⁴ and several of them earnestly
contending that " their Master must have revived, as he had
been seen by Peter."   ³⁵ These two disciples now related their
adventure ; ᵃ but their testimony as to Jesus's real appearance to them was received with great incredulity by many of
the company.|

§ 144.—*Christ Appears among (Ten of) the Apostles.*

(Jerusalem ; evening of *Sunday, March* 20, A. D. 29.)

³⁶ ᵇ On the evening of the same day,| ᶜ while the Apostles|
ᵇ were assembled; ᶜ to partake of a common repast, ᵇ with
closed doors for fear of interruption by the malicious hier-
archy,| as they were still discussing the question of their
Master's appearances, Jesus [having noiselessly opened the
door,] stood among them. announcing his approach by the
usual salutation of " Joy to you!"   ³⁷ But they were seized
with the utmost terror, conceiving that they beheld an ap-
parition.   ³⁸ He however expostulated with them, " Why are
you so agitated with alarm, and why do you indulge in such
foolish speculations [as you have just been doing in your conversation together, concerning me as a phantom]?"   ᶜ He
then proceeded still further to reprove their incredulity and
obduracy in disbelieving his resurrection after actually see-
ing him.| ³⁹ " Look at my hands and feet," said he, " and
convince yourselves that it is actually I; feel of me and look
at me: a *specter* has no flesh and bones like what you see on
me." ⁴⁰ He therefore presented for their inspection and touch,
his hands and feet ᵈ and side, [still retaining the scars of his
crucifixion.   ⁴¹ Reassured by these marks of identity,] the
disciples lost their fear in joy [at seeing him alive] ;| but as

ᵃ Mark xvi, 13.   ᵇ John xx, 19.   ᶜ Mark xvi, 14.   ᵈ John xx, 20.

believed not for joy, and wondered, he   LUKE XXIV.
said unto them, Have ye here any meat?
⁴² And they gave him a piece of a broiled fish, and of
a honey-comb : ⁴³ and he took it, and did eat before
them.

⁴⁴ And he said unto them, These are the words which
I spake unto you while I was yet with you,* that all
things must be fulfilled which were written in the law
of Moses and in the prophets and in the psalms concerning me.   ⁴⁵ Then opened he their understanding,
that they might understand the scriptures ; ⁴⁶ and said
unto them, Thus it is written, and thus it behooved
Christ to suffer and to rise from the dead the third
day : ⁴⁷ and that repentance and remission of sins
should be preached in his name among all nations, beginning at Jerusalem.   ⁴⁸ And ye are witnesses of
these things : ⁴⁹ and behold, I send the promise of my
Father† upon you ; but tarry ye in the city of Jerusalem, until ye be endued with power from on high.
²¹ Then said Jesus to them again, Peace be   John XX.
unto you : as my Father hath sent me, even
so send I you.   ¹⁵ And he said unto them,   Mark XVI.
Go ye into all the world and preach the
gospel to every creature : ¹⁶ he that believeth and is
baptized, shall be saved ; but he that believeth not,
shall be damned.   ¹⁷ And these signs shall follow them
that believe : In my name shall they cast out devils ;
they shall speak with new tongues ; ¹⁸ they shall take
up serpents [LUKE X, 19] and scorpions, and have power over
all the power of the enemy ; and if they drink any deadly
thing, it shall not hurt them ; they shall lay hands on
the sick, and they shall recover.   ²² And   John XX.
when he had said this, he breathed on them
and saith unto them, Receive ye the Holy Ghost:

---

* See on Luke xxiv, 7.   † See John xiv, 16, 26.

they could hardly yet realize so wonderful a fact, **LUKE XXIV.**
he asked them [in order to their full conviction],
"Have you any victuals here? [I will show you
that I can even eat.]" ^{42} They passed him part of a broiled fish
and a piece of honey-comb, ^{43} which he took and ate in their
sight.

^{44} He then thus addressed them: "This was what I meant in my
intimations to you while yet in your company, with reference to
[my death and revivification, which were to be] a fulfillment of the
various predictions contained in the several portions of Scripture
concerning me." ^{45} He now went on to specify and expound to
their comprehension the most important of these passages, ^{46} drawing the conclusion, "These events, you see, were predicted, and it
was requisite [for human redemption,] that the Messiah should
undergo these vicarious sufferings, and then revive on the third
day; ^{47} and [in the prosecution of this scheme,] repentance as a
prerequisite to the pardon of sins, is to be proclaimed under his
authority to all mankind, the offer being first tendered to the inhabitants of Jerusalem itself. ^{48} Now *you* my Apostles are my appointed vouchers for these fundamental facts, [i. e. my passion and
resurrection which form the basis of the Gospel,] which you have
personally witnessed; ^{49} and, observe! I will shortly bestow upon
you for this purpose the assisting influences [of the Spirit] promised
by my Father [through me].   Meanwhile, you are to remain quiet
at Jerusalem, until you are qualified for your work by
that celestial endowment of miraculous energy. ^{21} I **John XX.**
therefore again pronounce my blessing upon you, and
commission you to carry forward the same mission
which I have received from my Father. ^{15} Go forth **Mark XVI.**
then into the wide world, [when you shall have been
thus consecrated for your task,] and proclaim the good news [Gos-
pel] of salvation to the whole human race. ^{16} Whoever confides in
your communications, submitting to baptism in token of his faith,
will secure eternal salvation; but those that reject your proposals,
will be condemned to final perdition. ^{17} [By such miraculous evidences as the following shall you prove the authority of your Apos-
tolate,—and similar powers will you be enabled to impart to those
who accept your proclamations:] my followers [in the Apostolical
office, and others in a subordinate degree, whenever the progress
of my cause may require,] shall be empowered by virtue of my
authority, to expel demons, ^{18} to cure invalids by simple imposition of
their hands, ^{17} to speak fluently in foreign languages, ^{18} to handle *a* or
tread upon! venomous reptiles *a* and insects! with impunity, to drink
poison without injury, *a* and in fine to have such complete control over
the malignant influence of Satan [in his providentially allowed inflictions,] as to be secure against all physical harm in the execution of
their official duties."! ^{22} Thus saying, he closed his commission by breathing symbolically upon them, and bid- **John XX.**
ding them, "Receive the influence of the Holy Spirit

a Luke x, 19.

^{23} whosoever sins ye remit, they are re-   JOHN **XX.**
mitted unto them : and whosoever sins ye
retain, they are retained.

^{24} But Thomas (one of the twelve, called *Didymus*)
was not with them when Jesus came : $^{25.}$ the other
disciples therefore said unto him, We have seen the
Lord. But he said unto them, Except I shall see in
· his hands the print of the nails, and put my finger into
the print of the nails, and thrust my hand into his side,
I will not believe.

§ 145.—*Christ's Second Appearance among the*
(Eleven) Apostles.

(Jerusalem ; evening of *Sunday, March* 27, A. D. 29.)

^{26} And after eight days again his disciples were
within, and Thomas with them : then came Jesus, the
doors being shut, and stood in the midst, and said,
Peace be unto you. ^{27} Then saith he to Thomas,
Reach hither thy finger, and behold my hands ; and
reach hither thy hand, and thrust it into my side : and
be not faithless, but believing. ^{28} And Thomas answered and said unto him, My Lord and my God.
^{29} Jesus saith unto him, Thomas, because thou hast
seen me, thou hast believed ; blessed are they that
have *not* seen, and yet have believed.

§ 146.—*Christ's Third Appearance among (Seven of)*
the Apostles.

(Lake Gennesareth ; [*Wednesday,*] *March* [30?], A. D. 29.)

[MATT. XXVIII, 16] Then the eleven disciples went   **John XXI.**
away into Galilee. ^{1} After these things Jesus
showed himself again to the disciples at the sea of Tiberias ; and on this wise showed he himself : ^{2} There
were together Simon Peter and Thomas called Didy-
213

[now, in a degree, and ere long in its fullness].   **JOHN XX.**
²³ Whatever sins you entitle to remission [by your
Apostolical prescription of the conditions of par-
don], will be so forgiven [by God]; and those to which you
deny absolution, will remain uncanceled."

²⁴ Thomas (surnamed *Did'ymus* [i. e. the "Twin"], one of
the Apostles,) chanced to be absent at this interview with
Jesus; ²⁵ when therefore [on his coming in after their Master's
departure,] the others told him what they had just seen, he
obstinately declared, " I will never believe that he is alive
bodily, unless I can see with my own eyes the marks of the
nails [with which he was fastened to the cross,] in his hands,
and even put my finger in the prints, and my hand into the
gash in his side !"

§ 145.— *Christ's Second Appearance among the (Eleven) Apostles.*

(Jerusalem; evening of *Sunday, March* 27, A. D. 29.)

²⁶ Just one week after this meeting, the disciples, including
Thomas, were again similarly collected in the same room with
the doors shut; when Jesus came [in the same unobserved
manner,] and stood among them with the customary salutation, "Joy to you !" ²⁷ He then addressed Thomas [in the
very language which that disciple had used in proposing his
test], ".Come here and inspect my hands by the insertion of
your finger into the nail holes, and put your hand into the
wound in my side; satisfy yourself of my reality, and dismiss
these unworthy doubts." ²⁸ " O my divine Master !" exclaimed
the subdued Thomas, [as his eyes riveted conviction on his
heart.] ²⁹ " Ah ! Thomas," said Jesus chidingly, "*you* have
believed on seeing; happy those whose faith requires no such
ocular evidence ! [since believers in me will hereafter be compelled to receive the gospel truths on *testimony*.]"   ·

§ 146.— *Christ's Third Appearance among (Seven of) the
Apostles.*

(Lake Gennesareth; [*Wednesday*,] *March* [30 ?], A. D. 29.)

¹ Shortly afterward, *ᵃ* the eleven disciples hav-   **John XXI.**
ing gone to Galilee [in pursuance of their Mas-
ter's directions], as several of them were at the
Lake Gennesareth, Jesus appeared to them under the follow
ing circumstances. ² There chanced to be together (Simon)
Peter, Thomas (the "Twin"), Nathanael (of Cana in Galilee),

ᵃ Matt. xxviii, 16.

213*

mus, and Nathanael of Cana in Galilee, JOHN XXI.
and the sons of Zebedee, and two other
of his disciples. ³ Simon Peter saith unto them, I go
a-fishing. They say unto him, We also go with thee.
They went forth and entered into a ship immediately :
and that night they caught nothing. ⁴ But when the
morning was now come, Jesus stood on the shore ;
but the disciples knew not that it was Jesus. ⁵ Then
Jesus saith unto them, Children, have ye any meat ?
They answered him, No. ⁶ And he said unto them,
Cast the net on the *right* side of the ship, and ye shall
find. They cast therefore, and now they were not
able to draw it for the multitude of fishes. ⁷ Therefore that disciple whom Jesus loved saith unto Peter,
It is the Lord. Now when Simon Peter heard that it
was the Lord, he girt his fisher's coat unto him, (for
he was naked,) and did cast himself into the sea.
And the other disciples came in a little ship, (for they
were not far from land, but as it were two hundred
cubits,) dragging the net with fishes. ⁹ As soon then
as they were come to land, they saw a fire of coals
there, and fish laid thereon, and bread. ¹⁰ Jesus saith
unto them, Bring of the fish which ye have now caught.
¹¹ Simon Peter went up and drew the net to land full
of great fishes, a hundred and fifty and three ; and for
all there were so many, yet was not the net broken.
¹² Jesus saith unto them, Come and dine. (And none
of the disciples durst ask him, Who art thou ? knowing that it was the Lord.) ¹³ Jesus then cometh, and
taketh bread and giveth them, and fish likewise.
¹⁴ (This is now the third time that Jesus showed himself to his disciples, after that he was risen from the
dead.)

¹⁵ So when they had dined, Jesus saith to Simon
Peter, Simon son of Jonas, lovest thou me more than
these ? He saith unto him, Yea, Lord ; thou knowest
214

the two sons of Zebedee [John and James I.], JOHN XXI.
and two others of the Apostles; ³ so Peter proposed to the party to go a-fishing in the lake,
and the rest assented to accompany him. They started accordingly, taking a boat at once for that purpose; but after
fishing all night they caught nothing. ⁴ Day had just dawned
when Jesus stood upon the shore opposite them, but [being
at a distance and in the twilight,] they did not at first recognize him. ⁵ He then hailed them with the inquiry, "Well,
friends, have you caught any fish?" They answered in the
negative. ⁶ "Drop your seine on the right-hand side of the
boat," rejoined Jesus, "and you will have a good haul."
They did so, and now found themselves unable to drag up the
net into the boat, on account of the great weight of fish it
contained. ⁷ This unaccountable success suggested the truth
to the mind of Jesus's favorite disciple [John], who exclaimed
to Peter, "Why, it is our Master!" Fired with the thought,
Peter wound the flowing ends of his fisherman's frock around
him, (for it was the only garment he had on,) and [having
thus secured decency as well as freedom of motion,] then
plunged into the water to swim to his Master,—⁸ it being not
more than two hundred *ells* [i. e. about 350 feet] from land,
while the rest rowed ashore in the boat, dragging the loaded
net after them. ⁹ On landing, they found a fire of live embers
there, with a fish broiling over it, and some bread near by.
¹⁰ Jesus directed them to "bring some of the fish they had
just caught," [to cook.] ¹¹ Peter accordingly went and hauled
up on the shore the drag, which was found to contain one
hundred and fifty-three large fishes; and what was singular,
none of the meshes of the net were parted by the unusual
strain. ¹² Jesus then invited them to "come and take break-
fast," [as it was ready,]—all their queries meanwhile, as to
whence he had come, being overawed by their conviction of
the actual presence of their Master. ¹³ So he approached and
distributed the bread and cooked fish among them.—¹⁴ This
makes Jesus's *third* public exhibition of himself to his disciples generally, since his resurrection.

¹⁵ After they had breakfasted, Jesus put this question to
Peter, "Simon, [whose name I once changed from] 'son of
Jonah,' do you now love me more than these your fellow disciples do, [as you lately so confidently stated?]" With humbled tenderness Peter replied, "Yes, Master, [although I cannot go as far as that, yet] you know [by your divine penetra-

214*

that I love thee.   He saith unto him,   JOHN XXI.
Feed my lambs. ¹⁶ He saith to him
again the second time, Simon son of Jonas, lovest
thou me ?   He saith unto him, Yea, Lord ; thou knowest that I love thee. He saith unto him, Feed my
sheep. ¹⁷ He saith unto him the third time, Simon
son of Jonas, lovest thou me ?   Peter was grieved because he said unto him the third time, Lovest thou
me ? and he said unto him, Lord, thou knowest all
things ; thou knowest that I love thee. Jesus saith
unto him, Feed my sheep. ¹⁸ Verily, verily I say
unto thee, When thou wast young, thou girdedst thyself and walkedst whither thou wouldest ; but when
thou shalt be old, thou shall stretch forth thy hands,
and another shall gird thee, and carry thee whither thou
wouldest not. ¹⁹ (This spake he signifying by what
death he should glorify God.)   And when he had
spoken this, he saith unto him, Follow me. ²⁰ Then
Peter turning about seeth the disciple whom Jesus
loved, following ; (which also leaned on his breast at
supper and said, Lord, which is he that betrayeth
thee ?) ²¹ Peter seeing him, saith to Jesus, Lord, and
what shall this man do ? ²² Jesus saith unto him, If
I will that he tarry till I come, what is that to thee ?
follow thou me. ²³ Then went this saying abroad
among the brethren, that that disciple should not die :
yet Jesus said not unto him, He shall not die ; but, If
I will that he tarry till I come, what is that to thee ?

§ 147.—*Christ's Appointed Meeting with his Followers generally.*

(Mountain [near Capernaum ?] ; [*Thursday,*] *March* [31 ?], A. D. 29.)

[1 Cor. XV, 6] After that he was seen of   **Matt. XXVIII.**
above five hundred brethren at once,
¹⁶ who went out into a mountain where Jesus had
215

tion,] that [despite my sad defection,] I still   JOHN XXI.
love you sincerely!"   "I recommission you   ————————
then," rejoined Jesus, "to feed my flock [i. e.
the Church, with pure doctrine and wholesome discipline]."
16 The same question was again put, and answered in the
same manner, with a like charge in rejoinder.   17 Jesus put
the same question a third time, and Peter, whose yet sensi-
tive feelings were pained by the doubt implied in this repeated inquiry as to his affection, earnestly avowed, "O Master, your own omniscience testifies to the devotion of this
contrite heart!"   Again he received the same injunction, to
"take the faithful oversight of his Master's fold."—18 "Now
mark my prophetic assurance," continued Jesus to him, 19 referring to the manner in which he was to honor the truth of
God by his death [in martyrdom]; 18 "while you are in the
vigor of life, you now gird on your garments for yourself,
and go where you please; but when you grow old, you will
be compelled to extend your hands for others to bind, and
then carry you away [to the scene of your crucifixion] against
your will.—19 But I bid you, [as if by a fresh summons to my
service,] follow me as my faithful disciple."   20 Peter, [obey-
ing the call in a literal sense, rose and followed his retiring
Master; but] looking behind and seeing the favorite disciple
[John] also following, 21 he asked Jesus, "And what, Master,
is to be this man's fate?"   22 Jesus, however, evaded his
curiosity by replying, "Suppose it were my will that he
should survive till my appearance [in the threatened vengeance upon this nation], what would that have to do with
you? your concern is to remain faithful to my cause."—
23 From this intimation arose a report among the brethren
[i. e. Christians, subsequently], that this disciple [John] was
not to experience death; but Jesus's language did not imply
that he should be exempt absolutely from mortality, [but only
for a limited time.]

§ 147.—*Christ's Appointed Meeting with his Followers generally.*

(Mountain [near Capernaum?]; [*Thursday,*] *March* [31?], A. D. 29.)

16 The disciples soon proceeded to the moun-   **Matt. XXVIII.**
tain which Jesus had previously specified as   ————————
the place of rendezvous, *a* where they were
joined by his adherents [from the whole region about, who
had heard of the appointment,] to the number of over five

a 1 Cor. xv, 6.

215*

appointed them : [17] and when they   MATT. XXVIII.
saw him, they worshiped him; but
some doubted.   [18] And Jesus came, and spake unto
them saying, All power is given unto me in heaven
and in earth : [19] go ye therefore and teach all nations,
baptizing them in the name of the Father and of the
Son and of the Holy Ghost; [20] teaching them to observe all things whatsoever I have commanded you :
and lo, I am with you alway, even unto the end of the
world.   Amen.

§ 148.—*Christ's Subsequent Appearances and Ascen-sion.*

(Suburbs [East] of Jerusalem, and Eastern slope of the Mount of
Olives near Bethany; *Thursday, April* 28, A. D. 29).

[1 Cor. XV, 7] After that, he was seen of James;   **Acts I.**
then of all the apostles, [3] to whom also he
showed himself alive after his passion, by many in-
fallible proofs, being seen of them forty days, and
speaking of the things pertaining to the kingdom of
God ; [2] until the day in which he was taken up, after
that he through the Holy Ghost had given commandments unto the apostles whom he had chosen.
   [4] And being assembled together with them he commanded them that they should not depart from Jerusalem, but wait for the promise of the Father, which,
saith he, ye have heard of me :* [5] for John truly baptized with water ;† but ye shall be baptized with the
Holy Ghost not many days hence.   [6] When they
therefore were come together, they asked of him saying, Lord, wilt thou at this time restore again the
kingdom to Israel? [7] And he said unto them, It is
not for *you* to know the times or the seasons, which

° John xiv.   † Compare John i, 33, &c.

hundred persons.' ¹⁷To this entire assem-　MATT. XXVIII.
bly Jesus exhibited himself; and at the sight
of him, some [i. e. the Apostles] fell in adoration before him, but others [who now saw him for the first
time since his revivification,] hesitated to believe his reality.
¹⁸ But Jesus advancing familiarly among the circle of his Apos-
tles, thus commissioned them : "As I, in my Messianic character, am invested with supreme ecclesiastical prerogative over
the destinies of this world and the next, ¹⁹ I therefore now em-
power you to go and make converts to my religion of all mankind,—initiating them into my discipleship by administering
to them the rite of baptism, as a pledge of their espousal of the
truths implied in the divine Trinity [i. e. their profession of
the relations subsisting between them and each of the three
co-equal persons of the Godhead, as a characteristic faith],
²⁰ and indoctrinating them subsequently into the observance
of all those precepts which I have enjoined upon you [by my
personal inculcations, and will more maturely develop by the
Spirit's teachings] ; and, mark ! I will perpetually accompany
you [and your successors, by the Spirit's seconding influences],
in the prosecution of this your work, till the end of time.

§ 148.—Christ's Subsequent Appearances and Ascension.

(Suburbs [East] of Jerusalem, and Eastern slope of the Mount of Olives near Bethany; *Thursday, April 28, A. D. 29.*)

³ A period of forty days had now elapsed, during　Acts I.
which Jesus had palpably exhibited himself to the
Apostles at various times, since his revival from his
passion [a] (the last appearance being an incidental one to James
[II., his step-brother,] alone),' confirming his reality by numerous indubitable evidences, and giving them directions for their
future administration of his "Reign." ² The time had arrived,
when, having completed his inspired communications to them
in a personal capacity, he was to be removed from them by
ascension to the celestial world. ⁴ Having now met [a] the entire number of his Apostles for this purpose,' he directed them
"not to scatter away from Jerusalem, but continue there till
their reception of the promised endowment from the Father,
of which he had spoken to them ; ⁵ for John," said he, "used
to baptize merely with water, but you will be spiritually baptized with the influences of the Holy Spirit within a few days."
⁶ As the company were walking along together [up the hill of
Olives], they impatiently proposed this question to him, "Master, are you not then on this occasion about to reassert the inde-
pendence of the Jewish nation, [and establish its universal
sovereignty ?" ₇ To this misconceived notion,] Jesus replied,
"You are not interested in knowing the particular eras and

a 1 Cor. xv, 7.
EE　　　　　　　　　　216*

the Father hath put in his own power. ACTS I.
8 But ye shall receive power after that the
Holy Ghost is come upon you; and ye shall be witnesses unto me, both in Jerusalem and in all Judea
and in Samaria and unto the uttermost part of the
earth.

9 And when he had spoken these things, [LUKE XXIV, 50]
he led them out as far as to Bethany: and he lifted up his
hands and blessed them; [51] and it came to pass, while he
blessed them, he was parted from them, and while they beheld, he was taken up [MARK XVI, 19] into heaven, and sat
on the right hand of God, and a cloud received him out
of their sight. 10 And while they looked steadfastly
toward heaven as he went up, behold, two men stood
by them in white apparel; 11 which also said, Ye men
of Galilee, why stand ye gazing up into heaven? this
same Jesus which is taken up from you into heaven,
shall so come in like manner as ye have seen him go
into heaven: [LUKE XXIV, 52] and they worshiped him. 12 Then
returned they [LUKE XXIV, 52] with great joy unto Jerusalem
from the mount called Olivet, which is from Jerusalem
a sabbath-day's journey.

53 And they were continually in the　**Luke XXIV.**
temple, praising and blessing God.
Amen.—20 And they went forth and　**Mark XVI.**
preached everywhere, the Lord working
with them and confirming the word with signs following. Amen.

§ 149.—*Conclusion of the Biography of Christ.*

1 The former treatise* have I made, O　**Acts I.**
Theophilus, of all that Jesus *began* both to do
and teach.—24 This is the disciple which　**John XXI.**
testifieth of these things, and wrote these

---

* See Luke i, 1–4.

dates of political revolutions that are to occur, for   ACTS I.
these the Father reserves to His own providential
jurisdiction : [8] [your own appropriate sphere has
been assigned you in this great moral renovation of Judaism ;
to accomplish which,] you will shortly receive the plenary
influences of the Holy Spirit, qualifying you to become vouchers on my behalf not only in Jerusalem and Judea generally,
but also throughout Samaria and over the whole world."

[9] [a] Jesus had by this time led his disciples as far as the outskirts of the village of Bethany, where he closed his promise
by pronouncing with uplifted hands his divine benediction
upon them; and in this act,| [b] he was suddenly removed by
an invisible power from them,| and as they stood looking at
him, he rose from the earth [c] toward the sky,| and a cloud
enfolded him from their gaze, [c] as he took his destined posi-
tion of honor in the Almighty's presence ! | [10] As they stood
with their eyes riveted in speechless astonishment upon the
spot where he had disappeared, suddenly two airy forms stood
near them in dazzling attire, [11] and thus addressed them,
"Why, good sirs from Galilee, do you stand thus gazing up
into the sky? This very Jesus, who has just been borne away
from your midst up into heaven, will one day return [at the
general judgment] in precisely the same visible manner in
which you have beheld him ascend."—[12] [d] Comforted as well
as awed by this assurance, they fell on their knees in adoration of their beatified Master, and then with hearts filled
with sacred joy| returned across the Mount of Olives to Jeru-
salem (distant only about a *Sabbath-day's journey*, [i. e. about
⅔ of a mile, reckoned from the top of the hill to the eastern
city wall]).

[53] The Apostles [agreeably with their Master's   Luke XXIV.
instructions,] occupied themselves for some
time in religious exercises at the Temple ;
[20] after which they sallied forth on their mis-   Mark XVI.
sion, preaching the gospel in all directions, [as
detailed in the subsequent portion of this history,] meeting
with astonishing success through the divine aid which confirmed their promulgations with miraculous attestations.

§ 149.—*Conclusion of the Biography of Christ.*

[1] This first portion of the Gospel history comprises   Acts I.
only the introduction of the evangelical dispensation,
by the *personal* acts and teachings of Jesus himself; [24] the facts are narrated on the irrefragable   John XXI.
testimony of [myself John,] the disciple who was

a Luke xxiv, 50.   *b* Luke xxiv, 51.   *c* Mark xvi, 19.   *d* Luke xxiv, 52.

things : and we know that his testimony JOHN XXI.
is true.   25 And there are also many other-
things which Jesus did, the which, if they should be
written every one, I suppose that even the world itself
could not contain the books that should be written.
Amen.   30 And many other signs truly did John XX.
Jesus in the presence of his disciples, which
are not written in this book : 31 but these are written,
that ye might believe that Jesus is the Christ, the
Son of God ; and that believing ye might have life
through his name.

END OF THE GOSPELS.

218

actually conversant with them: [25] and besides those recounted here, there were innumerable other public incidents that occurred in the life of Jesus, which would require an indefinite number of volumes to record them all minutely. [30] Indeed, there were a great many striking miracles performed by him among his disciples privately, which have necessarily been passed over in this brief memoir; [31] but enough has been said—and this is the writer's object—to convince every reader that Jesus is really the Messiah, the predicted "Son of God," and through this faith to afford all the means of securing immortal bliss, by virtue of such connection with him.

JOHN XXI.

John XX.

END OF THE GOSPELS.

218*

Lightning Source UK Ltd.
Milton Keynes UK
UKHW02f0742160818
327336UK00010B/645/P